Supply Chain Management and Reverse Logistics

Springer
Berlin
Heidelberg
New York
Hongkong
London
Milan
Paris
Tokyo

Harald Dyckhoff · Richard Lackes
Joachim Reese (Editors)

Supply Chain Management and Reverse Logistics

With 115 Figures and 34 Tables

Springer

Professor Dr. Harald Dyckhoff
RWTH Aachen
Fakultät für Wirtschafts-
wissenschaft
Lehrstuhl für Unternehmens-
theorie
Templergraben 64
52056 Aachen
lut@lut.rwth-aachen.de

Professor Dr. Richard Lackes
Universität Dortmund
Wirtschafts- und
Sozialwissenschaftliche Fakultät
Lehrstuhl für Wirtschafts-
informatik
Vogelpothsweg 87
44221 Dortmund
wi-rila@wi.wiso.uni-dortmund.de

Professor Dr. Joachim Reese
Universität Lüneburg
Fachbereich Wirtschafts-
und Sozialwissenschaften
Lehrstuhl für Produktion
und Wirtschaftsinformatik
Scharnhorststraße 1
21335 Lüneburg
reese@uni-luenburg.de

ISBN 3-540-40491-0 Springer-Verlag Berlin Heidelberg New York

Cataloging-in-Publication Data applied for
A catalog record for this book is available from the Library of Congress.
Bibliographic information published by Die Deutsche Bibliothek
Die Deutsche Bibliothek lists this publication in the Deutsche Nationalbibliografie; detailed bibliographic data is available in the Internet at <http://dnb.ddb.de>.

Springer-Verlag Berlin Heidelberg New York
a member of BertelsmannSpringer Science+Business Media GmbH

http://www.springer.de

Printed in Germany

Hardcover-Design: Erich Kirchner, Heidelberg

SPIN 10942277 43/3130-5 4 3 2 1 0 – Printed on acid-free paper

Günter Fandel

Preface

The world of logistics has considerably changed in the last years. There has been a steady evolution due to globalization, modern information technology, and especially increasing ecological awareness. Many firms have meanwhile implemented large Supply Chain Management (SCM) systems - sometimes already developed to global logistic networks. This book reflects major trends of the recent decade in SCM and, additionally, presents ideas and visions for logistic networks of the 21st century from a strictly scientific point of view.

Though the book deals with quite a lot of different perspectives on the same problem, namely how to efficiently and effectively establish elements of a supply chain, it stresses one essential figure of SCM: closing the loop of a supply chain by integrating waste materials into logistic management decisions. Reverse logistics has gained central importance caused by sustainable developments in society and legislation in the past. The book is based on the premise that economic and political decision makers can no longer afford to ignore the ecological issues of logistics.

Many excellent researchers from several fields of logistics have contributed to this book. Most of them have been involved in the major developments of SCM methods and concepts during recent years. Therefore, we are very glad and grateful to have them gathered here together in this volume.

We are further indebted to many more persons without whom the book could not have been realized. Special thanks go to Karsten Hilgers, Jens Keilen, Marion Nölle, and Brigitte Stoevesandt for their strong technical support and operating activities when preparing the publication.

Last not least, many thanks to the Springer publishing company for the good cooperation in editing this book on behalf of the 60th anniversary of Günter Fandel.

Harald Dyckhoff

Richard Lackes

Joachim Reese

Contents

Part III:
Supply Chain Management and Advanced Planning

Günter Fandel – Scientist, University Manager and Business Consultant

On behalf of the 60th birthday of Günter Fandel this volume is published to honor his scientific work in the fields of production management, operations research and related topics. First and foremost, Günter Fandel has proved to be an outstanding representative of the theory of the firm and micro-economic production theory. His adaptations of activity analysis to production planning and control, data processing, dynamic lot sizing, services production, and university management have decisively contributed to the dissemination of activity analytic research in business administration. The German edition of his seminal work *Theory of Production and Cost* was originally published in 1987. The English translation appeared in 1991. The book is an excellent presentation – if not a climax - of production theory as a main topic of the theory of the firm. The many theoretical aspects of production economics are not only brought together, but a consistent framework for production theoretic research is also offered. Günter Fandel founded his concept on the general activity analysis approach of micro-economics and demonstrated how functional description and analysis of production processes can be coupled with the hypotheses of that approach. This is why the publication can be considered as a milestone in this discipline. Since 2001, Fandel is managing editor of *Zeitschrift für Betriebswirtschaft*, one of the oldest and among German speaking scientists most renowned economic journals due to its significant contributions to the theory of the firm.

The early origins of Günter Fandel's research activities are based on mathematics and operations research. He is a major contributor to multiple criteria decision making and a leading member of a group of international scientists in this field of research. Since the 1980s his algorithm for solving vector-optimization problems has been a challenge for contemporary researchers as well as for succeeding research generations. As president of the *German Society of Operations Research* and managing editor of the publishing journal *Operations Research Spektrum* he has essentially influenced the development of operations research not only in a national context.

Günter Fandel also is a well known and highly appreciated researcher in decision-based organization theory. He was one of the first to apply game and bargaining theory to problems of organizational decision making using Herbert Simon's concept of bounded rationality. An organization has not only been further explained as coalition of different and often conflicting interests, but Günter Fandel was ambitious to also find a way of solving those conflicts.

In the course of time, Günter Fandel has not remained a pure theoretical researcher, but he has always tried to adapt theory to practical problems. During the past years he has published a number of case studies in the automotive and other industries. For more than one decade, he has now been a partner of the Institute of

Automation, Information and Production Management at the Open University in Hagen which employs consultants in the field of information and production management and offers solutions for a variety of practical problems. The major publication resulting from Fandel's scientific work in this area is *PPS-Systeme* (first published in 1994), a large volume which analyses hundreds of existing production planning and control systems under several aspects and strictly following clear, transparent, and scientifically as well as practically required criteria. The book is widely spread in many German industries as an indispensable guide.

Honoring the scientific work of Günter Fandel would not be complete if one did not mention his intensive, long-lasting engagement in university management. Since 1976, he has been publishing models and policies for an efficient management design in the university sector. According to his quality standards, principles of economics should be far more applied in universities than could be surveyed in the last 25 years. Many of his arguments and models have carried wage at the authorities especially when Günter Fandel was elected *Rector of the Open University* in Hagen in 1993. The university reforms in Germany which have started in the last few years and are now to be continued in form of laws and legal devices are strongly supported by Günter Fandel's scientific and practical activities.

Since the last decade, Günter Fandel has turned his area of research more and more to modern concepts of production management. A considerable number of publications, e.g. in the field of just in time production and logistics, goes back to this very fruitful period. This is the reason why the editors of this book, all former assistants of Günter Fandel and now university professors themselves, have decided to publish this volume under the title *Supply Chain Management and Reverse Logistics,* to which many prominent researchers have contributed, and to dedicate it to their former teacher out of gratitude and acknowledgement of his large and inspiring work.

Günter Fandel's Publications in English

Rational Solution Principles and Information Requirements as Elements of a Theory of Multiple Criteria Decision Making. In: Thiriez, H., and Zionts, S. (Eds.): Multiple Criteria Decision Making, Berlin et al. 1976, pp. 215-230 (with J. Wilhelm).

A Multiple-Objective Programming Algorithm for the Distribution of Resources among Teaching and Research. In: Albach, H., and Bergendahl, G. (Eds.): Production Theory and its Applications, Berlin et al. 1977, pp. 146-174.

Two Algorithms for Solving Vector-Optimization Problems. In: Plenum Publishing Corporation, 1977, pp. 1721-1727 (with J. Wilhelm).

Public Investment Decision Making with Multiple Criteria; An Example of University Planning. In: Zionts, S. (Ed.): Multiple Criteria Problem Solving, Berlin et al. 1978, pp. 116-130.

Perspectives of the Development in Multiple Criteria Decision Making. In: Fandel, G., and Gal, T. (Eds.): Multiple Criteria Decision Making - Theory and Application -, Berlin et al. 1980, pp. IX-XVI.

Decision Concepts for Organizations. In: Morse, J.N. (Ed.): Organizations: Multiple Agents with Multiple Criteria, Berlin et al. 1981, pp. 91-109.

On the Applicability of the Nash-Solution and the Zeuthen-Theorem to Wage Bargaining Processes. In: Grauer, M., Lewandowski, A., and Wierzbicki, A.P. (Eds.): Multiobjective and Stochastic Optimization, Berlin et al. 1982, pp. 107-119.

Lines of Development in Multiple Criteria Decision Making. In: Systems Analysis-Modelling-Simulation 3, 1984, pp. 191-198.

On the Applicability of Group Decision Making Concepts to Wage Bargaining. In: Haimes, Y.Y., and Chankong, V. (Eds.): Decision Making with Multiple Objectives, Berlin et al. 1985, pp. 532-548.

MCDM on its Way to Maturity. In: Fandel, G., and Spronk, J. (Eds.): Multiple Criteria Decision Methods and Applications, Berlin et al. 1985, pp. 1-8 (with J. Spronk).

Decision Concepts for Organizations. In: Fandel, G., and Spronk, J. (Eds.): Multiple Criteria Decision Methods and Applications, Berlin et al. 1985, pp. 153-170.

On the Applicability of Game-Theoretic and Bargaining Methods to a Wage Bargaining Problem. In: Fandel, G., and Spronk, J. (Eds.): Multiple Criteria Decision Methods and Applications, Berlin et al. 1985, pp. 317-336.

Game and Bargaining Solutions for Group Decision Problems. In: Grauer, M., Thompson, M., and Wierzbicki, A.P. (Eds.): Plural Rationality and Interactive Decision Processes, Berlin et al. 1985, pp. 187-201.

On the Applicability of Group Decision Making Concepts to Wage Bargaining. In: Sydow, A., Thoma, M., and Vichnevetsky, R. (Eds.): Systems Analysis and Simulation I, 1985, pp. 62-68.

On the Applicability of Group Decision Making Concepts to Wage Bargaining. In: Systems Analysis-Modelling-Simulation 3, 1986, pp. 227-240.

A Queueing Theoretic Model for Planning Diagnosis Systems in Hospitals. In: Fandel, G., Grauer, M., Kurzhanski, A., and Wierzbicki, A.P. (Eds.): Large-Scale Modelling and Interactive Decision Analysis, Berlin et al. 1986, pp. 326-339 (with H. Hegemann).

MCDM in Hospital Planning. In: Sawaragi, Y., Inoue, K., and Nakayama, H. (Eds.): Toward Interactive and Intelligent Decision Support Systems 1, 1987, Berlin et al., pp. 260-269 (with H. Hegemann).

Surplus or Disposal Quantities in Optimal Program Planning in Joint Production. In: Grubbström, R.W., Hinterhuber, H.H., and Lundquist, J. (Eds.): Recent Developments in Production Economics, Amsterdam et al. 1987, pp. 143-158.

MCDM in Hospital Planning. In: Archiwum Automatyki i Telemechaniki 32/4, Warschau1987, pp. 355-365 (with H. Hegemann).

Surplus or Disposal Quantities in Optimal Program Planning in Joint Production. In: Engineering Costs and Production Economics 12, 1987, pp. 143-158.

Planning and Organization of Economic Units in the Field of Out-Patient Medical Care. In: Fandel, G. (Ed.): Management Problems in Health Care, Berlin et al. 1988, pp. 113-138 (with A. Prasiswa).

Special Problems of Resource Planning in Hospitals. In: Fandel, G. (Ed.): Management Problems in Health Care, Berlin et al. 1988, pp. 159-188.

Approaches to the Planning of the Optimal Supply of Beds in Hospitals. In: Fandel, G. (Ed.): Management Problems in Health Care, Berlin et al. 1988, pp. 189-234 (with E. Schmidt).

On Capacity Planning of Diagnosis Systems in Hospitals. In: Fandel, G. (Ed.): Management Problems in Health Care, Berlin et al. 1988, pp. 235-262 (with H. Hegemann).

Organization and Planning of Vehicle Utilization in a Chemical Firm. In: Fandel, G., Dyckhoff, H., and Reese, J. (Eds.): Essays on Production Theory and Planning, Berlin et al. 1988, pp. 16-28 (with J. Reese).

Rational Material Flow Planning with MRP and Kanban. In: Fandel, G., Dyckhoff, H., and Reese, J. (Eds.): Essays on Production Theory and Planning, Berlin et al. 1988, pp. 43-65 (with P. François).

Effects of Call-Forward Delivery Systems on Supplier's Serial per Unit Costs. In: Fandel, G., Dyckhoff, H., and Reese, J. (Eds.): Essays on Production Theory and Planning, Berlin et al. 1988, pp. 66-84 (with P. François and E. May).

Optimal Heat-Matched Cogeneration of Energy in a Firm Owned Power Station - A Case Study. In: Fandel, G., Dyckhoff, H., and Reese, J. (Eds.): Essays on Production Theory and Planning, Berlin et al. 1988, pp. 107-120 (with J. Reese).

Optimal Program Planning in Joint Production. In: Fandel, G., Dyckhoff, H., and Reese, J. (Eds.): Essays on Production Theory and Planning, Berlin et al. 1988, pp. 130-148.

Capacity Planning of Diagnosis Systems in Hospitals. In: Grubbström, R.W., and Hinterhuber, H.H. (Eds.): Production Economics: State-of-the-Art and Perspectives, Amsterdam et al. 1989, pp. 205-221 (with H. Hegemann).

Cost Minimization in a Firm's Power Station. In: Systems Analysis-Modelling-Simulation 11/12, 1989, pp. 805-817 (together with J. Reese).

Capacity Planning of Diagnosis Systems in Hospitals. In: Engineering Costs and Production Economics 17, 1989, pp. 205-221 (with H. Hegemann).

Group Decision Making: Methodology and Applications. In: Bana e Costa, C.A. (Ed): Readings in Multiple Criteria Decision Aid, Berlin et al. 1990, pp. 569-605.

A Theoretical Basis for the Rational Formation of Production Planning and Control (PPC) Systems. In: Fandel, G., and Zäpfel, G. (Eds.): Modern Production Concepts - Theory and Applications, Berlin et al. 1991, pp. 3-17.

Just-in-Time Logistics of a Supplier in the Car Manufacturing Industry. In: International Journal of Production Economics 24, 1991, pp. 55-64 (with J. Reese).

Just-in-Time Logistics of a Supplier in the Car Manufacturing Industry. In: Grubbström, R.W., and Hinterhuber, H.H. (Eds.): Production Economics: Issues and Challenges for the 90's, Amsterdam et al. 1991, pp. 327-336 (with J. Reese).

Hierarchical Planning for Just-in-Time Deliveries. In: Fandel, G., and Gehring, H. (Eds.): Operations Research, Berlin et al. 1991, pp. 387-400 (with J. Reese).

Theory of Production and Cost, Berlin et al. 1991

Analysis of Production Planning and Control (PPC) Systems as an Efficient Combination of Information Activities. In: Fandel, G., Gulledge, Th., and Jones, A. (Eds.): New Directions for Operations Research in Manufacturing, Berlin et al. 1992, pp. 40-59.

Information Production Functions in Dynamic Lot-Sizing. In: Fandel, G., Gulledge, Th., and Jones, A. (Eds.): Operations Research in Production Planning and Control, Berlin et al. 1993, pp. 473-496.

Activity Analysis of Production Planning and Control (PPC) Systems. In: Pappas, I.A., and Tatsiopoulos, I.P., (Eds.): Advances in Production Management Systems, Amsterdam et al. 1993, pp. 291-299.

Activity Analysis of Dynamic Lot-Sizing. In: Systems Analysis-Modelling Simulation 12, 1993, pp. 239-251 (with P. François).

Analysis of production planning and control (PPC) systems as an efficient combination of information activities. In: Operations Research-Spektrum. 15, 1994, pp. 217-224.

Performance of the Peer Review Procedure at University - Results of an Empirical Analysis on Teaching Activities at the FernUniversität. In: Fandel, G., Bartz, R., and Nickolmann, F. (Eds.): University Level Distance Education in Europe: Assessment and Perspectives, Weinheim 1996, pp. 161 - 177.

Lead-Time Scheduling and Capacity Balancing in PPC-Systems: Result of a Market Research. In: Artiba, A. (Ed.): Proceedings of the Workshop on Production Planning and Control, Mons 1996, pp. 193-209 (with P. François and K. Gubitz).

Successes, Prospects and Critical Aspects of Distance Teaching Degree Programmes in Economics at the FernUniversität Hagen. In: Innovation & Learning in Education 2, 1996, West Yorkshire/England.

Multiple Criteria Decision Making, Proceedings of the 12th International Conference, Berlin et al. 1997 (with T. Gal and Th. Hanne).

Separate Versus Joint Inventories when Customer Demands are Stochastic. In: Leopold-Wildburger, U., Feichtinger, G., Kistner, K.-P. (Eds.): Modelling and Decisions in Economics, Heidelberg 1999, pp. 239-253 (with M. Lorth).

Interdependencies between Network and Activity-Analytical Descriptions of Production Relationships in the Implementation of Large-Scale Projects. In: Albach, H., et al. (Eds.): Theory of the Firm, Berlin et al. 2000, pp. 336-351.

Managerial Disposition Efficiency and Performance Efficiency in Large-Scale Production Projects. In: Shi, Y., Zeleny, M. (Eds.): New Frontiers of Decision Making for the Information Technology Era, Singapore 2000, pp. 145-156.

Redistribution of Funds for Teaching and Research among Universities. In: Haimes, Y.Y., Steuer, R.E. (Eds.): Research and Practice in Multiple Criteria Decision Making, Berlin 2000, pp. 400-408 (with T. Gal).

Redistribution of Funds for Teaching and Research among Universities: The Case of North Rhine-Westphalia. In: European Journal of Operational Research 130, 2001, pp. 111-120 (with T. Gal).

Interdependencies between Network and Activity-Analytical Descriptions of Production Relationships in the Implementation of Large-Scale Projects. In: International Journal of Production Economics 70, 2001, pp. 227-235

Introduction

Abstract: *At the beginning of the new millennium industrial manufacturing is only slightly older than two centuries. In this, from a historical viewpoint, short period of time the production conditions have changed fundamentally. Especially in the last century, they altered faster and faster. How will it be in a hundred years? Forecasts concerning this are even more likely to fail than those made in 1900 for the year 2000. Nevertheless there are some grave developments which will be realized with high probability, at least if our current behavior does not change fundamentally. These developments will have to be taken into account when designing new concepts on how we will produce and consume in near future. Supply chain management seems to be such a concept worth further developing in order to be sustainable in this sense. The papers collected in this book may be considered as contributions to this aim.*

1. Natural conditions of production and consumption

One of the developments will be the increasing importance of the production factor *natural environment*. The need of the developing countries to catch up economically and the increasing population in many regions will sooner or later exceed the limits of the eco system 'space ship earth'. There is evidence for at least five global limits: human biomass appropriation, climate change, ozone shield rupture, land degradation, and biodiversity loss. Consequently, the technologically advanced countries will not be able to keep their environmental damage on the present level. In particular, one of the most important challenges for the next fifty years is to reduce the use of non-renewable carbon stocks such as mineral oil and natural gas, not only because the carbon reserves are running low but because of the climate change caused by carbon dioxide.

These limits cannot easily be adhered, perhaps even not at all. The first and second laws of thermodynamics give defined boundaries. In an isolated system energy neither increases nor decreases (conservation of energy) and there is an increasing amount of energy which can no longer be used (law of entropy). The whole of life is based on consuming high value energy (exergy) and transforming it into low quality energy. In fact, planet Earth is not an isolated system. High value energy is absorbed from the sunlight, while low-value energy is released into space as heat radiation from the Earth's surface. This results in an energy balance but not in an entropy balance. In the long term this entropy difference will act as a limit to energy (i.e. exergy) consumption und hence probably as a *limit to economic growth*, too. The current levels of exploitation of fossil fuels, oil, coal, and natural gas, mean that stocks which have taken hundreds of millions of years to form, will have been almost completely exhausted within a few centuries or even decades, such that future generations will not be able to use them (at least merely by burning them). Nuclear energy is currently the only source of non-renewable power which has a long-term perspective; however this comes with the associated catastrophic risk. Even if a harmless and lasting non-renewable energy technology was to eventually succeed (e.g. nuclear fusion), the surpassing of the current entropy limits will lead to a change in the energy balance in the Earth's atmosphere. This will almost certainly be the cause of a significant climate change.

As the Earth only exchanges negligible quantities of matter with space, industry and nature can be seen on a worldwide basis as a virtually closed system. Thus, a closed cycle within the bounds of the entropy limits cannot, when linked with nature, be excluded. Until now however, an open flow through economy has been practiced. Principally, nature plays two roles: On the one hand it is the source and on the other the sink for the matter used in economic activities. Problems result from the different time dimensions: Since the beginning of industrialization two centuries ago, the economic system has changed enormously in terms of size, quality, and dynamics. Evolutionary changes on Earth occur continuously over a much longer period of time. Many natural cycles last for thousands if not millions of years. An ecologically compatible economic system therefore demands harmonization between commercial activities and natural reactions. If industry does not adapt to nature, it can lead to adverse adaptation reactions in the environment, which may have catastrophic results. For example, the combustion of fossil fuels generates the unavoidable joint product of carbon dioxide (CO_2), which, amongst a number of other harmful gases, may have a dramatic impact on the Earth's climate.

The laws of nature make it virtually impossible to have entirely closed cycles in the economic system. Nevertheless, ecological systems exist from extensive closed material cycles, in which the material is almost completely recycled, solar energy is used and residual heat is given to their surroundings. The closure of the cycle comes about because, in principle, there are three groups of ways of living, all of which play their own roles, the producers, the consumers, and the reducers (or destructors). More simply the producers are the green plants which generate organic substances through photosynthesis, a reaction which requires sunlight. These are then consumed by animals and man as part of the food chain. The organic material which dies as a result of this production and consumption by plants and animals is broken down (reduced) into its basic substances by microorganisms that can then be used again by plants as the building blocks in a new cycle. Can this be a model for a sustainable economy?

2. Towards a circulatory economy embedded in nature

In more primitive times, man was simply a part of such closed ecological systems. Since industrialization, and even more with the impact of globalization, this is no longer the case. As a result of localized specialization and mass production resulting from the division of work and the existence of conurbations, the emissions from production and consumption continue to rise, with regard to place and time, in a concentrated manner. It becomes more and more difficult for nature to fight the resulting damage.

The basics of nature have for a long time played an unimportant role in the running of businesses. External effects have not been 'internalized' in the prices of the products, and therefore remain unconsidered in economic calculations. It is mainly this discrepancy which causes the underlying conflict between economy and ecology. Both terms stem from the Greek *oikos* for house(hold). The original meaning of ecology was the teaching of the housekeeping of nature. In order to be able to analyze and understand this, the mutual relationships and dependencies amongst organisms and their unknown environment have to be known. Ecology is therefore frequently described as the science of interactions between organisms and their environment.

The recognition of 'limits to growth' at the beginning of the 1970s led to an increased awareness of the need for protection of the natural world from overutilization of its resources and uncontrolled emissions of toxins and waste. Since then, many countries like Germany have introduced a large number of new laws to fight urgent environmental problems, to lead society to environmentally friendly behavior. Since most manufacturing companies are involved and have many and varied effects on the natural environment, these alterations to the laws for the environment had unquestioned effects on them. Other influences have, in part, gained importance for those firms close to consumers or in the public eye. The increased awareness among consumers has been the starting point for growing competition through the offering of environmentally friendly products and environmentally focused marketing. Moreover, some companies have been publicly confronted by 'green' groups, via the communication media, in order to put pressure on them to improve their practices. An additional influence, not to be underestimated, is given by a long term environmental vision from the head office, which is especially found in companies led by a single owner as 'entrepreneur'.

In spite of the progress since the 1970s, current waste disposal concepts of dumping into the ground at prescribed locations (concentration) or dispersing into the air or water (dilution) have reached their limits. It is no longer sufficient to organize the industrial production of goods and leave the decomposition of wastes to nature. It is becoming ever more necessary to consciously integrate a *reduction* phase into the economic system in order to close the material flows as far as possible by turning away from removal to recycling concepts.

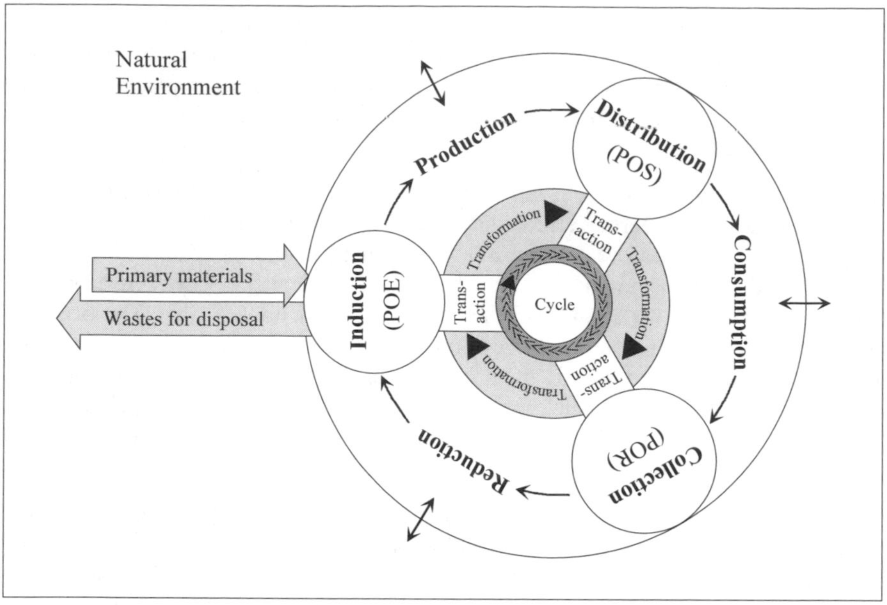

Fig. 1 A simple material cycle model

Figure 1 shows these ideas in terms of a simple model of a cycle. It represents the flow of material from the extraction of natural resources, to the manufacture, use and reuse of products and waste using the primary and secondary raw materials, until at last wastes are disposed of by returning them with minimized negative effects to the environment. Production, consumption and reduction can be seen as three basic categories of transformation processes of inputs into outputs. These are linked together to one or more material life cycles via three basic categories of economic transactions, namely representing the distribution of products (POS: point of sale), the collection or redistribution of old products as waste (POR: point of return) as well as the reintroduction of primary or secondary materials (POE: point of entry, re-entry or exit, respectively). The latter also represents the interface with nature: The economic system is not only fed by primary resources as input, it also gives back waste, which needs to be disposed of as output.

Such a sustainable economy requires the cooperation of all participants towards the realization of closed material cycles. In Germany a first step in this direction was taken in 1996 with the introduction of the Law for a Circulatory Economy (Kreislaufwirtschaftsgesetz). It makes everyone who is involved in the development, manufacture and distribution of a product responsible for the fulfillment of the aims of such an economy. This *product responsibility* means that the ecological product life cycle has to be designed in such manner that its manufacture and use minimize the existence of waste. It also demands an ecologically beneficial utilization and disposal of wastes which result at the end of the ecological product life cycle.

3. Closing supply chains to loop systems

Product responsibility requires *product-integrated environmental protection* as basic type of cycle-oriented corporate strategy: "We do as much as possible at our place as well as at other places!" Environmental protection therefore covers a cross section of tasks that affect both internal and external processes which the company can or does influence through its behavior. The realization of this strategy results in extensive planning and implementation efforts across all areas within the firm. Furthermore close cooperation with all participants along the product life cycle becomes a necessity. In the short term this strategy leads to very high costs and modification risks and in the long term to an increased level of complexity. The benefits of the higher ecological quality can only compensate for these consequences if it is combined with increased long term competitive advantage and economic success. If this is not the case it will undoubtedly lead to job losses and hence poor social acceptance.

In order to distinguish the manufacturer's product responsibility, the most important starting point is the definition of the product in terms of the development process. With the development of new products the company tries to ensure its survival in the marketplace. Ecological product innovations allow the organization to distinguish itself as a legitimate and responsible body as well as making its success against its competitors. This means that protection of environment has to be equivalent to the traditional targets of time, quality and cost. It is achieved through an offensive environmental policy in research and development (R&D) trying to realize an environmentally grounded circulatory economy. It cannot only be concerned with the main products; the creation of unwanted joint products during the entire life cycle also has to be taken into account.

The major problem with ecological product concepts is that they can only reach their targets if they are accepted by potential consumers. Thus the development of a 3-litre-car makes neither ecological nor economic sense if no one wants to buy it and its use will not remove other more harmful vehicles from the market. Offering environmentally friendly products has to find its market, otherwise the ecological innovator will find himself in conflict with economic restrictions. The awakening of new demands, finding a gap in the market and making the company's environmental activities clear to the customer are a significant part of environmentally focused marketing. Taking a broader view, marketing does not only deal with the entry into new product markets but can also build relationships to other markets, in particular for procurement and waste disposal. With respect to Figure 1 the subjects of environmental marketing are the transactions between different actors at the transformation interfaces of the material life cycle (points of sale, return, and re-entry).

Production and reduction management consider the circulation of material and the product life cycle with respect to the transformation processes involved. Apart from consumption and use by private households and government, companies regularly participate in the various phases of the product life cycles. In production the main purpose of the transformation is the manufacture of certain goods as output (called products). Reduction is the process of removal or disposal of certain bads being input of the transformation (called reducts). Recycling processes, where undesirable reducts are converted into desirable products, consist of simultaneous reduction and production (reproduction). A complete conversion of waste into new products without using other goods or creating new pollutants is impossible "no Cockaigne", in particular because of the law of entropy. Here a statement from the former US Vice-President Al Gore in his book *Earth in the Balance* (1992) is still valid: "Basically, the technology for disposing of waste hasn't caught up with the technology of producing it". It makes reduction management necessarily a main topic for the future.

While production and reduction usually mean qualitative changes of the objects of transformation, logistics is concerned with transformation (transfers) resulting in a space or time change of the main objects. An environmentally focused logistics management has to consider not only the usual *supply chain* but even more the remanufacturing and disposal chain, i.e. *reverse logistics* is concerned with the reverse supply chain. The traditional target of best possible delivery service is to be extended to the ecological quality of supply and disposal. A cycle-oriented strategy concentrates on all transfer processes taking place during the circulation of material for the products which the company is responsible for.

While R&D always considers the entire product life cycle and the circulation of material through the product design phase, marketing, production, reduction, and logistics management focus on specific aspects of the product life cycle. Together they will have to realize the chosen cycle-oriented strategy by an environmental friendly management of supply, recycling, and disposal chains or networks which may be called sustainable supply chain management or *closed-loop management (CLM)*.

4. Supply chain management and reverse logistics

The papers in this book contribute to the aim of developing a circulatory economy in various ways. A first group considers the extension of supply chains to closed-loop systems. A second group analyzes different aspects of the architecture and the coordination of supply chains and networks in reverse logistics. In this as well as in the last group, which deals with important topics of advanced planning, the emphasis is laid on aspects relevant for both ordinary supply chain management and closed-loop management.

From supply chains to closed loop systems

The six papers of the first part of the book all consider topics that are essential for closed-loop systems ranging from conceptual framework to specific models and algorithms. All contributions are mainly theoretical, most of them based on empirical facts, particularly from the automotive and the electronic industries.

In their paper on "The Expansion of Supply Chains to Closed-Loop Systems: A Conceptual Framework and the Automotive Industry's Point of View" *Dyckhoff*, *Souren* and *Keilen* discuss the theoretical and practical backgrounds of Closed-Loop Management. They present a double-layer closed loop model which extends the simple model shown in Figure 1. As an example the automotive cycle is used. Though 'reversing' the supply chain is possible to some extent, several problems appear that till today could not yet be solved. One of the main obstacles for transferring supply chain management knowledge to take-back processes is the degree of uncertainty regarding the composition and the amount of discarded products. In the contribution of *Schultmann*, *Zumkeller* and *Rentz* on "Integrating Spent Product's Material into Supply Chains: The Recycling of End-of-Life Vehicles as an Example" the automotive cycle is analyzed as well. Different design options for the reverse supply chain are presented by combining facility location planning with vehicle routing in an integrated approach. Introducing a problem-tailored algorithm including a Taboo Search heuristic results of several scenarios based on real case data are discussed.

As the two previous papers already include the automotive industry as an additional linking element, the extended similarities also apply to the next two resp. four contributions. These connections being product recovery and inventory management. In "Recovery Planning in Closed-Loop Supply Chains: An Activity Analysis based Approach" *Spengler*, *Stölting* and *Ploog* focus on the design and implementation of a decision support system for electronic scrap recovery companies in closed-loop systems which has been implemented in a major German electronic scrap recovery company and validated by real data. A typical problem is the high uncertainty in the amount, composition and quality of the delivered scrap. The study of *Inderfurth* on the "Product Recovery Behavior in a Closed-Loop Supply Chain" is also confronted with uncertainties. Here a manufacturer of original products is also engaged in remanufacturing used products taken back from its customers. It is investigated to which extent profit orientation in product recovery management will or will not stimulate an environmentally conscious behavior.

Fleischmann and *Minner* review mathematical models on "Inventory Management in Closed-Loop Supply Chains". They follow a standard structuring of traditional inventory theory and discuss applications to closed-loop settings for each case. Their analysis is centered around highlighting novel characteristics entailed by a closed-loop supply chain structure, in terms of both mathematics and business implications. In this context, *Richter* and *Dobos* examine a general model for "Production-inventory control in an EOQ-type reverse logistics system" which allows for repurchasing and recycling or disposing of used items. It includes other known EOQ recovery models as specific cases. As known from other models, mixed strategies of combined production and recycling are dominated by pure strategies.

Architecture and coordination of networks

The second part of the book contains five papers, two on the architecture of networks and three on their coordination. While the first two contributions still emphasize reverse logistics and environmental management, the following two and the last one are of a general nature. Hence the problems dealt with are of interest not only for closed-loop systems but for ordinary supply chains as well.

"Networks in Reverse Logistics" is the broad theme of *Steven*. She presents internal recycling, recycling cells and recycling networks as characteristic structures. Voluntary recycling networks are operated by the participants due to the economic profit generated, whereas compulsory recycling networks only exist as a result of legal force. In both cases one can usually find a conflict between economic and ecological goals. This conflict is also of importance for supply networks. *Tuma*, *Friedl*, and *Franke* model the process of "Environmental-Oriented Coordination of Supply Networks" between the enterprise and the factory level by a two-stage multi-agent system using goal programming and fuzzy Petri-nets. It is illustrated for a virtual network of the textile industry.

While supply networks are systems of enterprises as interconnected subsystems consisting of production and storage units, transportation networks emphasize the connection between these units and subsystems as pickup or delivery points. *Zäpfel* and *Wasner* suggest and analyze a typology of alternative "Architectures of transportation networks and their effects on economic efficiency". The impact on the economic efficiency is also analyzed by *Hofmann* and *Asseburg* in their paper. They describe the "Cash Flow- and Inventory-oriented Coordination of the Supply Chain" focusing on a three-tiered supply chain consisting of a component manufacturer, a carrier, and a buyer performing a final assembly operation, thereby differentiating between a simultaneous and a successive coordination of the chain. Efficiency differences between the coordination concepts are determined based on numerical examples and sensitivity analyses. "The Bullwhip Effect and its Suppression in Supply Chain Management" are a further main coordination problem. *Takahashi* and *Myreshka* give an overview of this effect, its causes and respective solution methods.

Supply chain management and advanced planning

In the last part six papers deal with topics which will help advance the planning systems in supply chain management based on the expertise of the authors. The topics range from model aggregation by shadow prices, customer orientation, order picking, advanced purchasing, optimal maintenance to hybrid flow shop scheduling.

Schneeweiß and *Kleindienst* develop two procedures for the "Aggregation of Mixed Integer Production Models by Shadow Prices in Supply Chain Management". Based on an extensive numerical investigation they compare these new aggregation devices with traditional approaches and even simpler aggregation procedures in practice. The paper by *Fleischmann* and *Meyr* identifies tasks for "Customer Orientation in Advanced Planning Systems" and shows their varying importance for different lines of business by means of the decoupling point concept. Mathematical optimization models are presented which may be helpful for both understanding the planning functions and improving the quality of customer related software modules like 'Order Promising' and 'Demand Fulfillment'. Customer orientation also requires a good performance of the warehouse functions. In "Order Picking: A Survey of Planning Problems and Methods" *Wäscher* addresses item location, order batching, and picker routing as central issues.

Tempelmeier and *Reith-Ahlemeier* consider the problem of simultaneous supplier selection and purchase order sizing for several items under dynamic demand conditions and under consideration of limited capacity. A new model formulation for this problem of "Advanced Purchasing and Order Optimization" is presented and a simple but easily extendible heuristic procedure is developed and tested. *Reese* considers an element of the supply chain within a JIT setting which is „technically" unreliable, e.g. due to a reduced machine productivity over time, and which therefore has to be maintained in order to fulfill the organizational issues of reliability. A special preventive policy of "Optimal Maintenance in the Supply Chain" is developed where the maintenance activities must not interfere with production and are shifted towards the end of each production period. The last contribution to this book considers "Hybrid Flow Shop Scheduling with Batching Requirements". *Voß* and *Witt* solve a real-world scheduling problem in the steel industry in which the resources form a hybrid flow shop consisting of 16 production stages with problem instances of about 30,000 jobs. *Lackes* discusses the relevance of different information conveyed in the supply chain. It is shown why the quality of information is a critical and limiting success factor of supply chain management. A specialised supply chain oriented production planning and control system is presented.

PART I

From Supply Chains to Closed Loop Systems

The Expansion of Supply Chains to Closed Loop Systems: A Conceptual Framework and the Automotive Industry's Point of View

Harald Dyckhoff, Rainer Souren, Jens Keilen

Institute for Corporate Environmental Management and Industrial Controlling
Faculty of Economics and Management
University of Aachen
Templergraben 64
D-52056 Aachen, Germany

Abstract: *An environmental orientated supply chain management (SCM) should not be limited to SCM processes, but instead include the analysis of recycling processes as well, for example reverse logistic aspects. Consequently, SCM must be expanded to closed loop management (CLM). In this paper, we discuss the theoretical and practical backgrounds of CLM, presenting a "double-layer closed loop model" and analyzing the example of the automotive cycle.*

Keywords: *closed loop systems, end of life vehicles, automotive cycle, recycling collaboration*

1. Introduction

In the last decade, supply chain management (SCM) has become a vital topic in management science and industry. Methods for collaborative planning and guidelines for cooperation between corresponding partners -from supplier's suppliers to customer's customers- have been developed and upgraded in short time frames. Furthermore, due to changes in stakeholders' ecological attitudes and legal environmental regulations, every firm has had to enlarge its management system to include environmental aspects. In particular product responsibility, as it is, for example, prescribed under § 22 of the German Closed Substance Cycle and Waste Management Act (Kreislaufwirtschafts- und Abfallgesetz), changes the competence of waste management from a state-run task to an enterprise-wide assignment. Management now has to deal with the entire product lifespan "from cradle to grave" or, more correctly, "from cradle to cradle". An environmental enhancement of SCM cannot merely be limited to the forward flow of materials and products. The "way back" is more important than ever and SCM has to evolve to closed loop management (CLM)[1], for example, by integrating concepts of reverse logistics.

This paper deals with the expansion of supply chains to closed loop systems. In doing so, it broadly discusses strategic problems and solutions concerning the implementation of the closed loop systems for (disused) cars. Before dealing with this practice-orientated subect, a "double-layer closed loop model", which can function as an orientation framework, is developed in chapter 2. In chapter 3, the legal specifications leading to the necessity of developing an automotive cycle are presented. Furthermore, the participants, as well as their functions and interactions, are described in detail. The development and implementation of such a cycle are accompanied by several difficulties. In chapter 4, these problems, together with corresponding recycling gaps and upcoming solutions, are presented. Finally, chapter 5 summarizes important findings from the example of the automotive loop, leading to refinements of the conceptual closed loop model.

2. "Double-layer closed loop model" as an orientation framework

This chapter presents a conceptual framework which can be used for orientation purposes in describing closed loop systems. First, a "double-layer closed loop

---

1 In the literature the term management of closed-loop supply chains can also be found, see for example Guide/Van Wassenhove 2002, in particular p. 56.

model", consisting of a transformation and a transaction level, is presented. Its purpose is not to serve as a general pattern for all possible loops, but to provide a grid for further practical analysis. (Necessary variations of this model, which occur when analyzing the automotive closed loop system, are described in chapter 5). Later on, the main tasks in CLM are described, structured by the aspects of the closed loop model. In particular, links to SCM and new assignments deriving from recycling tasks are presented.

2.1. Model description

Firms act within complex economic systems which can be characterized as (vertically and horizontally linked) transformation and transaction networks. Due to the networks' high complexity, management processes often merely focus on fractions of the whole system which can then be analyzed more clearly. SCM is confined to one branch or chain of the network which comprises a part of the product life cycle (and several preliminary products). The main tasks of SCM can be defined as the coordination of production, transport and storage processes, as well as the collaboration between the producing and distributing actors.

Just like SCM, life cycle assessment[2] and material flow management of closed loop systems[3] also deal with transformations and transactions along the path of one object. Traced objects can be single materials as well as entire products or product waste, for example, (disused) cars, electrical devices/waste or packaging.[4] For this reason, the environmental enhancement of SCM to CLM can be based on ecological management research in the field of circular flow systems. *Figure 1* illustrates a simple "double-layer closed loop model" which points out the necessary enhancements for changing transformation processes and transaction relationships of a flow through system into a closed loop system.[5] In this section, the model is presented, whereby the link between the model and SCM is also described in order to allow a clearer overview of the new processes and actors in CLM.

---

[2] See ISO-standards 14040 et sqq. and, for example, Frankl/Rubik 2000.

[3] See, for example, analysis of the packaging cycle in Souren 2002.

[4] For further practical examples of closed loop supply chains also see Guide/Van Wassenhove 2002.

[5] By separating the cycle into both a transformation and a transaction layer, the „double-layer closed loop model“ is able to provide a well-structured framework for practical systems. But it is important to realize that both layers do not exist uncoupled and – when describing real cyclic systems – that connections have to be analyzed.

The lower layer visualizes the material flow in circular or closed loop systems[6] and differentiates between six transformation phases.[7] In the *production phase,* a product is manufactured in material transformation processes which combine different raw materials from the natural environment as well as preliminary products from economic or other closed loop systems. Due to the fact that most products are not used at the production site itself, the products are dispensed in the *distribution* phase. Afterwards, the product is used during *consumption.* In contrast to production, consumption processes lower the product's value and former product or product parts are now classified as waste.

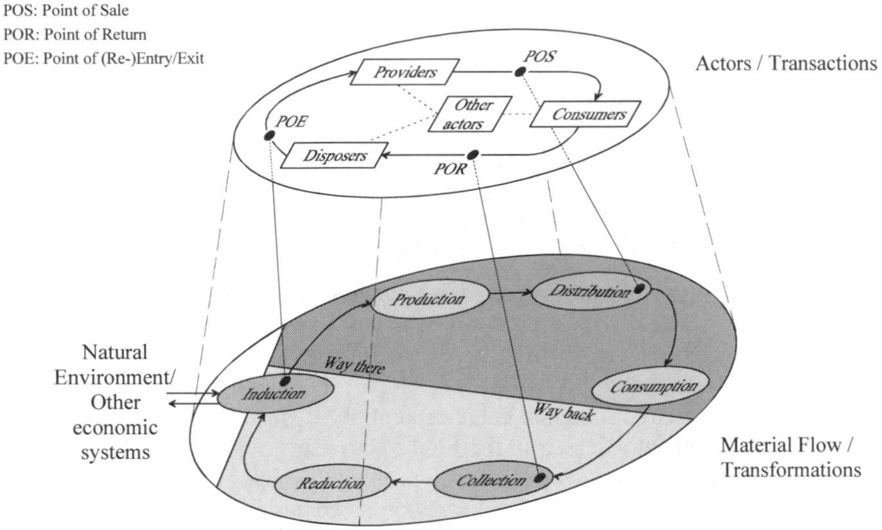

Fig. 1. A basic "double-layer closed loop model"

Although, strictly speaking, neither a starting nor an ending point exists in closed loops, these three phases can be defined as the "way there" and you can find similarities to flow through systems. Supply chains are situated in the production and

[6] Even now, for thermodynamic reasons alone, all circular material flow systems must be characterized as open systems. As seen in figure 1, the circular system exchanges materials with other systems, particularly in the induction phase. Nevertheless, we use the term "closed loop" in this paper, not only for the conceptual model and the new management tasks, but also for the material flow systems described.

[7] Cf. the following: Kirchgeorg 1999, pp. 78 et sqq.. and Dyckhoff 2000, p. 11. Kirchgeorg, in particular, differentiates between a functional view on transformations and an institutional view on transactions, but in some cases he attains other results, especially when localizing the transaction points.

distribution phases, while consumption processes are not principally an SCM topic.[8]

The main differences between flow through systems and closed loop systems lie in the three phases of the "way back". During *collection,* the waste is gathered and transported to the sites, where it is converted. This material conversion into secondary raw materials or less hazardous substances is the most important topic of the *reduction* phase. As in production, but in contrast to consumption, reduction processes increase the value of the cycle object. Finally, in the *induction* phase, the secondary raw materials are transported back to the production plants and the circular system then matches a closed loop. Furthermore, induction also includes the discharge of materials to other economic systems or to the natural environment, on the one hand, and the entry of primary materials into the circular system, on the other.[9]

In SCM, the "way back" is not very important. If any recycling processes are considered, for example, in newer releases of the SCOR-Model,[10] they only affect the return processes for reasons of warranty or maintenance. However, these processes merely describe a small portion of the recycling processes in real life. A widespread management of circular systems will, therefore, only be possible if SCM is enhanced to CLM by looking at different types of collection, reduction and induction processes, and especially by integrating corresponding processes of reverse logistics.

Splitting up the transformation layer into six phases helps to identify the purpose of these phases. They can be distinguished according to their main transformation types. While production, consumption, and reduction are mainly characterized as material transformation phases, distribution, collection and induction emphasize spatiotemporal transformations ("transfers", i.e., logistic processes).[11]

The spatiotemporal phases are primarily necessary because different actors realize the material transformations at different places and times. This brings us to the upper level of the double-layer closed loop model, where the actors and their

---

[8] This does not mean that consumers are not important for SCM. Consumer orientation is, in fact, a vital character of SCM, see Sürie/Wagner 2002, p. 33, but in supply chains, consumers usually do not act as active subjects in the material flow.

[9] As shown in figure 1, the exchanges with other systems are, strictly speaking, not an item in the closed loop.

[10] See the Supply Chain Council's "Supply-Chain Operations Reference (SCOR)-model" version 5, including the new return process, for details: http://www.supply-chain.org/slides/SCOR5.0OverviewBooklet.pdf

[11] Characterizing the phases throughout the main transformation processes does not mean that there are no other transformation types in all the phases. For example, the production phase is usually split up into several production steps, making several transactions and transports necessary.

transactions are modeled in a rather simplified manner.[12] In contrast to company-internal cycles, complex product or product waste cycles are distinguished by the variety of participating actors. For reasons of simplification, they are divided into four main groups. *Providers* (such as producers, wholesalers, retailers or logistical service firms), *consumers* (public or private) and *disposers* participate directly in the material flow. In addition, actors exist who only indirectly influence the circular material flow. In particular, the state is one actor who restricts the circular systems through legislation. Other actors are focal enterprises which coordinate the material flow. For example, in Germany the DSD (Duale System Deutschland AG) inspects and coordinates the recycling flow in one-way packaging waste cycles.

While involved in the material flow, actors of the three groups function differently, so a definite correlation between actors and transformations is seldom possible (some cycles do not even possess special disposers)[13]. For example, consumers do not only consume the products, but also participate in their distribution (taking the product back home from the retail store) and their collection (filling the waste into different waste containers). The specific responsibility assignment may differ from case to case.

This also applies to the localization of transaction points. At least the crossover between the different actor groups can be linked to one of the transformation phases. In this case, the *point of sale* (POS) is localized in the distribution phase and is identified as the transaction point where control over the product migrates from the providers (for example, a retailer) to the consumer.[14] This transaction is usually embedded in spatiotemporal transformation processes undertaken by the provider, on the one hand, and the consumer on the other hand. Therefore, the POS does not specify the end of the distribution phase, but is localized somewhere in the middle of this phase.

Analogically, the *point of return* (POR) can be identified as the transaction point between the consumer and the disposer. It lies in the middle of the collection phase because not only disposers but also consumers take part in collection processes. Its localization depends on the turnover point of the object control and can be sited at different locations. For example, the POR of waste paper could be sited at a public container park or in the waste storage room of an apartment building. The *point of (re-)entry or exit* (POE), which is embedded in the induction phase, is the transaction point, where the secondary materials are transmitted from dispos-

---

[12] See, similarly, Kirchgeorg 1999, pp. 98 et sqq.

[13] A number of practical multi-usage packaging systems do have special disposers which also deal with the recycling of the empty containers.

[14] The point of sale is often interpreted as a specific transaction place, such as a retail store. But sometimes its localization is very difficult, for example, in mail order trading or trading via the Internet.

ers to providers (for example, producers of preliminary products), or the waste is submitted to the natural (closed) system.

Similarly to the lower level, SCM merely deals with a section of the upper level. Its focus lies on the cooperation between different producers, wholesalers, retailers and logistical service firms, which all fall into the provider category. Consumers' needs play a very important role, but consumers do not directly participate in the material flow of supply chains. Therefore, the POR and the POE are not an SCM topic. If the POS could even be considered a part of the supply chain, then it must be the final point (or, from the planning point of view, the starting point).

2.2. Management tasks in closed loop systems

CLM has to handle a huge variety of tasks which exceeds the breadth of SCM assignments by far. If you want to structure these tasks, the double-layer closed loop model can be useful in two ways. Firstly in this section, an assignment division according to the different layers is presented, in which a task of SCM as well as an analogical task dealing with the "way back" are mentioned as examples. After that, new assignments are presented which deal with the problem of closing the loop in the different return phases.

Tasks which are attributed to the lower layer, apply to the functional (i.e., without reference to an actor) analysis as well as to the configuration of the material flow and the different transformations.[15] The coordination of transportation and storage quantities at the different stages of the supply chain, for example, to prevent the bullwhip-effect,[16] is one example of this kind of task. A similar task on the "way back" deals with the question in which quantities (and in which order) waste should be collected and converted. Another task, dealing with both the "way there" and the "way back", is the linkage of delivery and pick up,[17] for example, for multi-usage beverage containers. Instruments dealing with these tasks can be operations research algorithms and material flow analysis tools which support the modeling of the circular system.

Tasks linked to the upper layer of the double-layer closed loop model deal with institutional transaction analysis, based particularly on neo-institutional and marketing science considerations. In particular questions as to how the transactions are developed and what brings the actors to participate in the transaction process are

---

[15] It should be pointed out that actors can be relevant for process modeling. But, in principle, the problem can be solved independently of the institutional arrangement.

[16] For a description of the bullwhip-effect, see, for example, Lee/Padmanabhan/Whang 1997.

[17] For OR-Models dealing with pick up and delivery problems, see Dethloff 2001 or Fleischmann 2000, pp. 63 et sqq.

of particular importance. One typical task is the negotiation and contracting with regard to the preliminary product supply or the waste collection. Another topic on the management list is the incentive design for encouraging cyclic disposing behavior in consumers.

Management tasks, which deal with both the transformation and the transaction layer, are institutional analysis of the transformation processes, particularly the question as to which actor should provide which transformation process. In SCM, for example, the question is whether a production firm should distribute its products on its own or put wholesalers, retailers or service firms in charge (make-or-buy-decision). Analogical tasks result on the "way back" if, for example, the recycling of multi-usage beverage containers could be realized by the producers or by a pooling system which is run by several producers and often operated by a service firm. Such decisions on the institutional arrangements of closed loop systems can be based particularly on transaction cost theoretical analysis of vertical integration or outsourcing measures.

Besides CLM tasks, which can be inherited from SCM or at least deal with analogical items, many new tasks exist because closing the loop itself is a difficult job to do. In every phase of the "way back", functional- or institutional-based gaps occur.[18] As shown in this and the following chapters, there are several legal guidelines which try to bridge these gaps and which have to be taken into consideration by CLM. On the other hand, different measures of entrepreneurial CLM can also help to close the gaps.

One main problem of the collection phase consists in the fact that, for many products, a collection system for recycling waste does not yet exist. Legal regulations, such as the German Packaging- or End-of-Life-Vehicle-Ordinances, enforce the implementation of these systems and have to be considered by the firm. However, such regulations do not always affect the consumers (as in the packaging recycling system). Due to the fact that proper waste recycling incurs more expense, there must be incentives for the consumers to take part in closing the loop. These incentives could be initiated by the state (for example, collection of separated waste free of charge) or firms (for example, collection premiums for disused products).

A reduction gap may occur if material transformation processes are not developed or very cost-intensive. Particularly low waste quality, disassembly problems and waste inhomogenity often cause the above-mentioned problems. CLM solutions for these problems are, on the one hand, cooperations with waste management firms, who have the expertise of waste transformation processes. More important, on the other hand, are measures that come out of the producer's developing process and have an impact on future reduction processes (for example, material labeling or disassembly orientated construction). For these measures, a cooperation of producers and waste management firms is recommendable.

---

[18] See here and in the following Kirchgeorg 1999, pp. 226 et sqq..

Finally, an induction gap can occur if the generated secondary raw materials lose the competition against primary raw materials. In this case, due to small price differences and (apparently) high quality deviations, secondary raw materials are not reused in production. As in the collection phase, there are legal regulations in induction, such as recycling quotas, which push the secondary raw materials back into the closed loop and have to be considered by management while establishing closed loop systems. However, firms can also try to close the loop through their own measures. In particular, firms that get back the recycled product waste in a direct way can implement an integrated production and recycling planning system (PRPS-system)[19]. Even more important for closing the induction gap are incentives for those actors who pull the recycled materials out of the induction phase. The producers of preliminary products are positioned among these actors, but mainly consumers must be stimulated to buy recycled products (for example, if retreated, but high-quality tires are sold on a lower price level).

3. The automotive cycle

Having presented a basic overview of the theoretical and conceptional background of supply chains and closed loop systems and having combined them in a model, we now take a closer look at an authentic system – the German automotive cycle[20] – keeping the structure of the framework in mind. The new set of regulations in combination with physical restrictions and the status quo of technical developments confront the members of the preliminary automotive industry's supply chain with several challenges. Chances, as well as risks, arise. Additional participants need to be included in the chain in order to close the loop and meet new requirements. This chapter primarily describes the architecture of this closed loop system as well as the processes and collaborations.

First, the actors of the automotive cycle system are presented in accordance with our model's group classification. Besides the actors who directly participate in the material flow, the most important legal regulations of the state (as an indirectly participating actor) are described. After that, we then explain the actors' functions, obligations and interactions by successively following the actual material flow through different established loops. In doing so, we mainly focus on the "way back", i.e., the flow of the final product (car) and disused vehicles and the material flow of their components.[21]

---

[19] See Rautenstrauch 1997.

[20] For a detailed description (status 2000), see Wallau 2001. We owe further insights to enlightening dialogs with members of the "Ford Forschungszentrum Aachen (FFA)".

[21] For more detailed information on the design and production of automobiles as well as the development of the automotive industry, see Fandel/Dyckhoff/Reese 1994, pp. 72 et sqq..

3.1. The actors in the automotive cycle

Car producers' main management tasks exist in selling the products and optimizing the supply chain from suppliers to end-consumers. The car having been sold, the only transactions between providers and consumers used to result from maintenance and repairs. Thus, the automotive industry already possesses a reverse logistic system for damaged parts retrieved during repairs. But this return system merely represents a very small part of a closed loop system which has to be implemented in order to recycle car waste, particularly the vast masses from end-of-life-vehicles (ELVs).

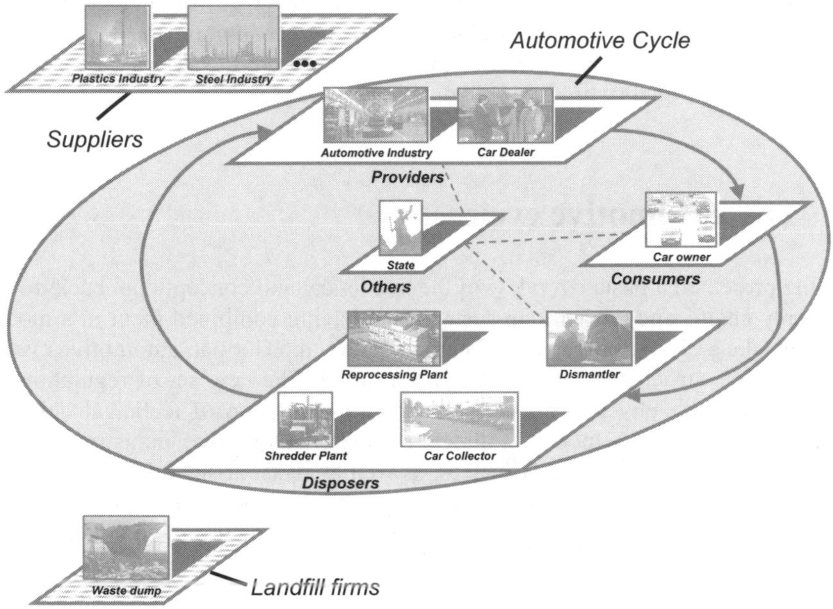

Fig. 2. The participants of the automotive cycle

It is obvious that the automotive manufacturers are not capable of closing the loop on their own. In order to guarantee an environmentally acceptable reprocessing and disposal of ELVs, they are dependent on the cooperation of several other participants as well as on the last owner of the car. This results in the necessity of having to deal with "new actors joining the play". More precisely, *figure 2* illustrates the required actors in the new cycles and presents a possible integration into the different groups specified in our model (see chapter 2).

The *providers* mainly consist of the automotive industry itself and the car dealers. The second group of participants is identified as the *consumers*. The *disposers*, including the car collectors, dismantlers, shredder plants and reprocessing plants, represent the third party. The waste dumps and the suppliers of the automotive industry are shown additionally in the figure for the sake of completeness.[22]

Having named the participants considered in the material flow and before taking a closer look at their functions, responsibilities and interactions (see section 3.2.), we now describe the role of the state as a legislator. The basis of all newer actions and legislative developments on behalf of environmental awareness in Germany lies in the "Closed Substance Cycle and Waste Management Act". Using this law and especially the requirements regarding product responsibility (§ 22) as an incentive, 14 industrial associations led by the Association of the Automobile Industry (VDA) joined in the "Voluntary Pledge by Industry for Environmentally Compatible ELV Waste Management" (Freiwillige Selbstverpflichtung (FSV)) on 21 February 1996.[23] This voluntary pledge lacked legal support, of course. The consequent "next step" was the adoption of the "Ordinance on the Disposal of End of Life Vehicles and the Adjustment of Provisions under Road Traffic Law" (Altautoverordnung, AltautoV) and its entry into force on 1 April 1998 in conjunction with the voluntary pledge. But the development did not stay on a national level. On 21 June 2002, the "Law Governing the Disposal of End of Life Vehicles (ELV Act – AltfahrzeugG)" was issued to transpose the Directive 2000/53/EC of the European Parliament and the Council of 18 September 2000 on ELVs into German law.[24] The renamed and modified ordinance, now called "German Ordinance on the Transfer, Collection and Environmentally Sound Disposal of End of Life Vehicles (ELV-Ordinance – AltfahrzeugV)" came into force on 1 July 2002.

The main topic in this ordinance is product responsibility which states that the car producers are required to take back all old vehicles of their particular make.[25] On the other side, the legislators also anchored (unlike other cycle ordinances) regulations which directly affect the consumer's part in ELV collection. Consumers have to return the ELVs to certified collecting facilities[26] in order to receive a so-called "certificate of destruction". Only with this verification form can they deregister the car at the motor vehicle administration office and be subsequently relieved of taxes.

Beyond these regulations, the last owners are not obligated to fulfill any further requirements, but can return their vehicles free of charge by 2007 at the latest. The

[22] If you are asking yourself why they are not directly included in the cycle viewed, we would at this point like to refer you to section 3.2., where the material flow is described.

[23] For the detailed development of the voluntary pledge, together with the first steps of the ELV-Ordinance, see Wallau 2001, pp. 74 et sqq.

[24] For a more detailed description of the European development on ELV directives, see Wallau 2001, pp. 103 et sqq.

[25] The ELVs to be taken into consideration are specified to have a total weight of less than 3.5 t and may contain non-original spare parts.

[26] See ELV-Ordinance (AltfahrzeugV) 2002, Annex, § 2.

free of charge acceptance of the ELV was one of the most discussed issues. In the 2002 version of the ELV-Ordinance, the resolution now foresees the manufacturers/importers bearing all costs related to the retrieval and sound disposal of ELVs.

Additionally, the automotive industry is obligated to provide an area-wide network of certified collecting points, enabling the last owner to access a collecting point within a reasonable distance. Collecting points can be located at car dealers, especially established collecting centers or certified dismantlers, as long as they fulfill the requirements in the Annex, §2 of the ELV-Ordinance (2002). According to the bill, the different car manufacturers are allowed to collaboratively use the collecting points, yet each manufacturer is responsible for the disposal of the cars of his particular make. The changes in EU-Regulations and in the ELV-Ordinance foresee the obligation of the automotive industry to retrieve and recycle or dispose of every single car of their brand produced after January 2002, as well as all vehicles over fifteen years of age.

The method of recycling the ELVs in reduction and induction processes is also regulated by law. By January 2006 (January 2015), 85% (95%) of the ELVs' empty weight will have to be re-used or reprocessed, while 80% (85%) will have to be re-used or reprocessed materially (§5 ELV-Ordinance). Furthermore, a minimum level, to which the disassembly process of components needs to be realized, is defined in the ELV-Ordinance. It mainly consists of removing the battery and other hazardous substances (in particular: oil, gasoline and other fluids).[27]

The regulations described do not only apply to Germany, where the car industry finds an excellently developed infrastructure regarding the distribution of already existing collecting points, dismantlers and shredder plants. The regulations are relevant for most of Europe – with some minor modifications. This includes the necessity of a large range of developments and investments. Different solutions will have to be found for different countries.

3.2. The transactions and material flows of the collaborative automotive cycle

A definite solution for the automotive closed loop system has not been implemented yet, but the vital actors, transactions and transformations can already be identified. In this paragraph, the transactions between the participants of the automotive cycle are presented. While focusing on the transactions, we also describe those transport processes which the transactions are usually embedded in, and the most important material converting processes which are necessary for closing the loop. In contrast to the description of the conceptual background discussed in chapter 2, where an effort was made to clearly distinguish between the participants

[27] The exact requirements and listings can be found in the ELV-Ordinance (AltfahrzeugV) 2002, Annex, §3.2.2.1.

and their obligations, it now seems more plausible to combine these two layers into a horizontally integrated description (see *figure 3*). In this model, the actor level serves as an orientation framework. The following description points out the different flows which are numbered from 1 to 8, sometimes divided up into additional sub-flows (a, b, c).

The automotive manufacturers produce vehicles and sell them via car dealers to the consumers. One possible scenario at this point would be -as shown in *figure* 3 – that the consumers sell their used cars directly to other consumers (1). Since these actions take place inside of one and the same actor category, these proceedings can be defined as an inner cycle of a single actor group and usually cannot be identified within this black-box model. A second variation describes the consumers returning their used vehicles to the car dealer as a trade-in and the car dealer reselling the used cars (2). We would like to define these two loops as the "reusable-vehicle" cycle. Both scenarios were mentioned at this point for the sake of completeness, yet are not further discussed due to lacking effects on the automotive industry.

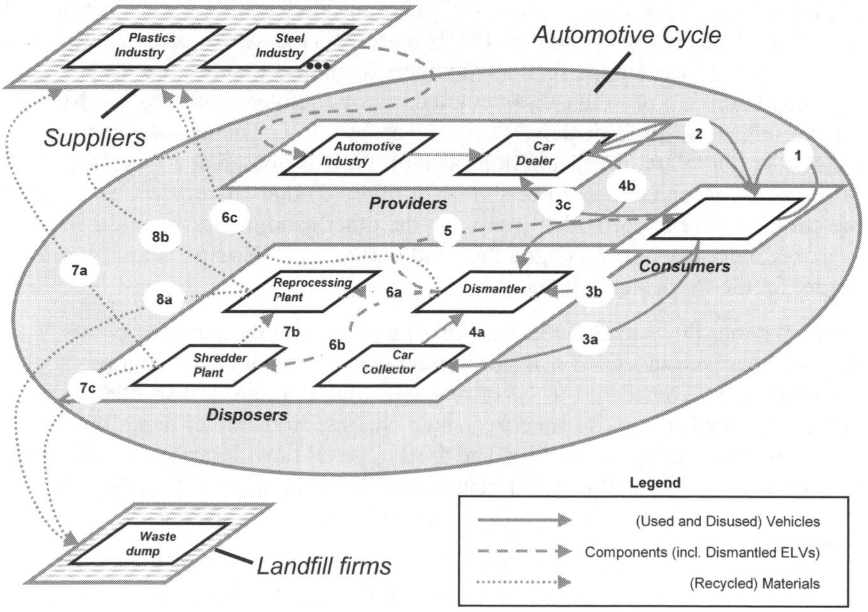

Fig. 3. Material flow in the automotive cycle

Relatively new cars involved in accidents, and therefore having to be disposed of, are not taken into consideration either. They do not create any problems in terms of expenses for the manufacturers, since newer, damaged cars represent a potentially high source of value. Consequently, all of the junk dealers try to get their hands on these vehicles.

Cars usually possess a long lifespan, making it difficult to predict the condition in which the ELVs are going to be returned. At the end of a car's lifecycle, the last owner is obligated to deliver it to either a certified car collector (3a) or dismantler (3b) that act as *disposers*. In addition, car dealers can also be certified collectors. However, they are prohibited from disassembling the vehicles, as are other collectors;[28] their primary function as a collector is to merely gather the disused cars (3c). At this point, the clear distinction between providers and disposers can be considered obsolete. The car dealers function in two different roles: they introduce the new vehicles and reintroduce used cars onto the market (provider-functions) at the POS and take part in the collecting process (disposer-function) at the POR when receiving the ELVs from the consumers.

The next participant in the cycle is the dismantler. He receives ELVs from consumers (3b), collectors (4a) or car dealers (4b) and then disassembles the vehicles. A squeezer follows on from the dismantling process. The dismantler squeezes the ELVs to make higher storage quantities possible and to enhance the transportable batch size.

Figure 3 shows three different kinds of material flows exiting the dismantler. The first arrow leads to the consumers (5). It represents the "spare-parts-cycle". Spare parts, such as, for example, fenders, bumpers or starters that turn out to be in reusable condition and are then disassembled, can be reintegrated into used-vehicle-repairs, either by junk dealers, garages[29] or by the consumers themselves. The dismantler, therefore, often functions as a provider of reused spare parts. It is also principally conceivable (but not shown in *figure 3*) that spare parts be reused by the car dealers of the provider group. On the other hand, the dismantled ELVs are probably older than ten years and the condition of their spare parts are often insufficient for the car dealers' demands.

Other material flows lead to the reprocessing plants and the shredder plants. Those disassembled substances that need pretreatment (for example, batteries or glass) before they are considered to be in reusable condition, are transported to the reprocessing plants (6a). The squeezed scrap chassis, on the other hand, must be delivered to the shredder plant (6b). The third material flow describes special parts – not consisting of a variety of different materials – that may be directly sold to the steel or plastic industry (6c).

Following the flow of the ELVs leads us to the next stage of the cycle – the shredder plants. Here, the ELVs are thrown into the shredder where they are torn apart and afterwards divided into three main fractions. These fractions are: ferrous

---

[28] These restrictions are valid in Germany. In other countries, the law can deviate.

[29] Junk dealers and garages not selling cars, but merely being responsible for spare parts and repairs, could also be considered as participants in the chain or loop, but are not specifically included in *figure 2* or *figure 3*.

scrap, non-ferrous scrap and shredder light fraction[30]. Depending on the configuration of the output substances, the shredder plants achieve different profits when they are sold to, for example, the steel industry or the reprocessing plants. The shredder plants again possess three outlets which are more or less consistent with the three produced fractions. The ferrous scrap is sold to the steel industry (7a) at the daily stock exchange rate and then melted down for reuse. The non-ferrous scrap goes on to reprocessing plants (7b) and the valuable materials, such as copper and aluminum, are extracted, for example, via the eddy current method. Depending on the composition of the material mixture and, of course, the quantity of valuable non-ferrous metals, the shredder plants receive their remuneration. The shredder light fraction, for which there is no further use, has to be disposed of and is brought to the waste dumps (7c). This fraction of materials is accompanied by high costs and it poses an additional threat to the environment, since most of it is merely collected or incinerated.

As described before, the reprocessing plants separate the reusable materials – received from the shredders – from those which have to go to the waste dumps (8a). In addition, they also reprocess other materials from the dismantlers and make them usable for production. This is where the cycle is closed and the reprocessed materials flow into the production of new products (8b).

The suppliers of the automotive industry were not specifically included in the cycle itself, since it is not possible to definitely determine exactly which new products are produced from the input of the recycled materials. Consequently, different materials are, in fact, recycled but leave the automotive cycle which, therefore, is only partially closed.

The automotive closed loop, as described in this chapter, is not yet a stable institution, but is confronted with different obstacles and gaps where the loop is disrupted (for general remarks see section 2.2.). In the next chapter, we will present these occurring problems.

4. Gaps, difficulties and management tasks in closing the automotive loop system

The creation and implementation of a closed loop system can involve several kinds of obstacles. This chapter points out the accruing difficulties – be they of technical nature, interpersonal or a question of jurisdiction. In order to make the linkage of the difficulties to our model more clear, we divide them into two sections. First, problems and possible solutions, which arise at the point of return, are presented. They are of special interest because the reflux will end before it begins,

[30] Shredder light fraction may consist of foams from car seats, different plastics and, due to technical barriers, some ferrous particles.

if the consumer cannot be persuaded to take part in the correct cycle system. After that, the rest of the way back is analyzed, particularly to show the transformation, transaction, and collaboration problems between the automotive industry and the different disposers which compromise the fulfillment of the recycling quotas.

4.1. Problems relating to consumer behavior at the point of return

According to the regulations, all old vehicles should be collected and properly disposed of or recycled. Primarily, in order to prevent a collection gap in closing the loop, non-cyclic consumer behavior must be thwarted by either imperative rules or incentives. Therefore, the "retrieving method" as an incentive to "steer" owner behavior was implemented in the ELV-Ordinance. To simply leave the car standing by the side of the road has now ceased to be a realistic alternative, since the car can only be deregistered with the appropriate destruction verification.

Beside the governmental measure of the ELV-Ordinance, the automotive industry also has to facilitate an easier and area-wide collection of the ELVs. They have to provide the last owner with a network of collecting possibilities and are also to bear all costs for vehicle recycling procedures (including transportation costs). The last owner is obligated to deliver his car to a certified collector within a 50-kilometer radius.[31] If he cannot find one close enough, the automotive company has to pick up the vehicle and pay for the transport itself. For this reason, an area-wide network of collecting points has to be established to save transport costs. Yet spreading the network over increasingly more participants is only reasonable until higher transaction (in particular monitoring) costs surpass the transportation cost savings. To lower the implementation and transaction costs referring to establishing a network of collectors, it also seems sensible to cooperate with different manufacturers and to make use of joint collecting points. This, furthermore, shows that the decision on an optimal (vertical and horizontal) collection network is a vital topic of CLM which has to analyze very complex reverse logistical scenarios in order to meet regulations and to minimize expenses.

Although the above-mentioned legal and company measures assist in closing the collection gap, it is still open in other directions. A lot of vehicles possess some kind of residual or market value in foreign countries and can be exported. Estimates on the number of cars annually leaving Germany this way range up to 1.5 million.[32] This trend eases the car manufacturers' problems and expenses due to

[31] In the earlier ELV-Ordinance, the formulation was "reasonable" distance. In the ELV-Ordinance 2002, it is now specified as a 50-kilometer perimeter in §3 (3).

[32] The foreign trade statistics for the year 2001 state 740103 exported used vehicles. Experts even estimate the number to be double, see Röpke 2002. The differentiation between used vehicles and ELVs is not consistent. Further difficulties involved with obtaining concrete figures and the estimates can be found in Wallau 2001, pp. 114ff.

the exported cars not being included in calculations of the recycling quotas. However, even if it can be argued that the exported cars are still in the automotive cycle loop, this of course represents one of the loopholes in the new regulations targeted at protecting the environment. In the countries mentioned, the recycling regulations are not valid and at the end of their lifespan, the ELVs are not properly handled. So, if defining the automotive cycle as a regional or nationwide system, you can speak of a grave collection gap which will have to be closed by legal regulations in the future.

4.2. Problems in collaboration between the automotive industry and different disposers on the way back

Not only the above-mentioned collection gap, but also the reduction gap, exists in the automotive cycle. Among other reasons, it results from the fact that cars are very complex products consisting of a large variety of components and materials.[33] Consequently, the separation of these substances and the regaining of reusable materials are difficult. The status quo of the shredder technology today, which is not yet capable of prorating the consistence of the input to the output substance, poses another serious problem. The complexity of subdividing the material mixture and regaining pure basic materials also occurs in the reprocessing plants. Since the materials are partially mixed, several reusable components have to be disposed of and so leave the cycle.

These material losses can only be prevented by law or economic incentives to force further technological developments. The fact that non-recyclable waste, consisting of wood, plastics, foams (from car seats), etc. has to be reduced to a minimum of 5% of the empty weight of the vehicles by January 2015, is without a doubt a severe regulation which may cause problems in the relationship between the disposers and the responsible car manufacturer. Hopefully, this volatile situation might be defused if the shredder and reprocessing plants – by paying increasingly more for the waste dumps to take their residues – are forced to ensure better separation before 2015.

The automotive industry's contribution to solving the separation problem should be a rethinking and redesigning of their new vehicles, with focus on decreasing the range of material mixtures (which is difficult to clearly subdivide during reprocessing) and hazardous materials. The manufacturers would also be forced to consider the future disassembly process during the early development phases. They are already obligated to provide the dismantlers with disassembly handbooks for their vehicles. This will make it easier and faster to dismantle future vehicles.

The problem is that these procedures will have an effect on new vehicles being manufactured today. Consequently, car manufacturers can "harvest the seeds they

---

[33] See Wallau 2001, p. 437.

have sown today" in approximately 10 to 15 years from now. Most of these ideas had not been taken into consideration for those vehicles which have to be handled today. A solution has to be found for the present and for up to about fifteen years into the future.

Closing this time gap is impossible, so, for the time being, two main measures are being evaluated to mitigate the problem. One solution would be to drive forward the development of shredder technology. In that case, the dismantlers would merely disassemble the parts of the ELVs specified by the regulations and the shredders could meet the recycling criteria. The other scenario, which seems more probable, would be that the dismantlers enhance the amount of components they disassemble. In other words, in order to meet the quotas, additional parts of the vehicle would have to be stripped one by one and then individually reprocessed up to the amount necessary to meet the requirements. This solution is, of course, associated with higher expenses due to an increment of transport for the additionally dismantled components and the longer disassembly times. The question as to the profitability of further disassembling additional parts, beyond those legally specified, is one of the issues discussed today. One example is the extraction of those parts that may contain a high density of aluminum. They are sold directly to the reprocessing plants instead of merely a lump sum being paid for each vehicle delivered to the shredder plant.

With the ecologically favorable cannibalization of the ELV, a further potential conflict in the described situation occurs, because the decision in favor of a specific responsibility assignment may not only result in different material flows but also in different values in the transaction processes. Since these actions already influence the necessary disassembly-time, different materials could additionally be disassembled and sold to make a profit. Consequently, the shredders will receive scrap chassis with a lower value, due to missing components consisting of the more profitable substances. They might try to negotiate a lower price or even demand compensation.

Independently of the development of collaborations between manufacturers, dismantlers and shredders, one point should be clear: The automotive industry is not capable of managing, nor is it intended to manage the entire recycling process on its own. Yet, with its center role and the correspondingly strong influence on the other participants in the already existing chain, it is called upon to run intercompany dismantling and reprocessing planning systems,[34] to drive forward development in recycling technologies and to also audit the material flow.

In doing so, the automotive industry is obligated to build a monitoring system for reasons of verifying compliance with the quotas. The main problem in implementing such a system – and a vital CLM topic – lies in the intercompany structure of

[34] For dismantling planning approaches – which only take intracompany aspects into account – see, for example, Gupta/Taleb 1994, Spengler et al. 1997, pp. 311 et sqq., or the literature review in Moore/Güngär/Gupta 2001.

the observed system. It causes a lot of coordination between the different actors. Therefore, this monitoring system's only chance of success lies in the collaboration of all parties involved. The cooperation, of course, will have to be based on contracts. The car manufacturers are analyzing the annual amount of ELVs to be expected for different regions in order to guarantee certain volumes for the dismantlers. This can improve their basis of negotiation and it enables the manufacturers to bind the dismantlers to them.

Finally, the monitoring system is exposed to another problem which is connected with the calculation of the recycling quotas. Shredder plants today do not merely process ELVs but instead try to enrich the output by including additional ferrous parts (iron girders, steel plates and different kinds of ferrous materials). At this point, several product cycles collide and it is no longer possible to trace the automotive cycle separately. The difficulty of verifying the fulfillment of recycling quotas without the possibility of determining which output quantities belong to which input is obvious.

The induction phase is not only diffused by mixed inputs but also because the reprocessed material can find its way into the car manufacturing process as well as into other new products. In other words, a material mix of different products comes out of the shredder and leaves the automotive cycle without knowing if it will return or not. If one is very precise, the automotive cycle, therefore, cannot be defined as an entirely closed loop. Nevertheless, it should be pointed out that this gap is not such a big problem for the automotive industry because the quotas do not differentiate between recycling for the same or for a different purpose. Therefore, from a higher viewpoint, the cycle system could still be recognized as a closed loop.

5. Conclusions on the practical closed loop system

The conceptual "double-layer closed loop model" serves as an orientation framework, which could be used to describe and analyze circular systems from different viewpoints. In this sense, the model was helpful in analyzing the automotive cycle system, too. However, the description of that practical loop made clear that a one-to-one usage of this model does not fit and further refinements have to be made when analyzing practical systems.

One of these refinements deals with the multitude of different material flows while recycling product waste. The single rope, which links consumption, collection, reduction and induction phases in the purely conceptual model, is in reality a network of different ropes, which each symbolizes a specific cycle (see again *figure 3*). This results from the fact that different components and materials (in size, type and quality) come out of one product waste category and therefore have to be dealt with in separate ways in order to realize an economically and ecologically reasonable recycling. In some cases, this even leads to variations in the process or transformation layer's architecture. For example, if used cars are bought and sold directly from car dealers, the reduction and induction phase can hardly be identified.[35]

Closely connected to this point is the fact that one actor in concrete circular systems can be integrated into different actor groups. For example, as mentioned in chapter 4, the car dealers' function mainly consists of distributing new and used vehicles, but they sometimes also collect ELVs and therefore can be seen as "part-time" disposers. On the other hand, dismantlers are mainly disposers, although they sell spare-parts, too. In addition to this overlapping of actor categorization, the main transaction points (POS, POR, POE) cannot be localized that easily. In particular, if consumers submit the ELV to car dealers, the transaction point should, furthermore, be identified as the POR, even if a consumer negotiates with a (primary) provider. If the car dealer then sells the used car to another consumer, the loop is closed without crossing over a POE.

Laterally reversed to the fact that a closed loop system often consists not only of one but also of several cycles, the closed loop system can also be seen as a subsystem of a bigger circular system. This becomes obvious when regarding the fact that the material flows of the shredded vehicles are mixed with other product waste and attain in material conversion processes which significantly alter their shape. Due to the fact that the recycled materials enter different production processes, an exact tracing is no longer possible. This may not be a problem as long as the usage in other (circular) systems does not lead to a dramatic down-cycling effect or even to an ultimate gap of the whole economic system.

When resuming the theoretical and practical analysis in this paper, it can be pointed out that the "double-layer closed loop model" serves as an orientation framework when analyzing complex circular systems. Especially the material flows, processes, actors, responsibility assignments, gaps and problems in closing the loop could be analyzed in well-organized proceedings. This makes it possible to recognize similarities and necessary extensions between SCM and CLM. The practical analysis, on the other hand, made clear that the conceptual framework always has to be adjusted for practical research, particularly in stipulating the system borders of the analyzed system and the subsystems, such as actors, transformation phases and transaction points.

---

[35] However, modifications might be needed to serve the retention of the conceptual framework, but these will definitely not lead to practical, understandable analysis.

References

Dethloff, J. (2001): Vehicle routing and reverse logistics: the vehicle routing problem with simultaneous delivery and pick-up. In: OR Spektrum 23, pp. 79-96.

Dyckhoff, H. (2000): Umweltmanagement – Zehn Lektionen in umweltorientierter Unternehmensführung. Springer, Berlin et al.

Fandel, G., Dyckhoff, H., Reese, J. (1994): Industrielle Produktionsentwicklung – Eine empirisch-deskriptive Analyse ausgewählter Branchen, 2nd edn. Springer, Berlin et al.

Fleischmann, M. (2000): Quantitative Models for Reverse Logistics. Doct. Thesis, Rotterdam.

Frankl, P., Rubik, F. (2000): Life Cycle Assessment in Industry and Business – Adoption Patterns, Applications and Implications. Springer, Berlin et al.

Guide, V.D.R., Wassenhove, van L.N. (2002): Closed-loop Supply Chains. In: Klose, A., Speranza, M.G., Wassenhove, van L.N. (eds.) Quantitive Approaches to Distribution Logistics and Supply Chain Management. Springer, Berlin et al., pp. 47-60.

Gupta, S.M., Taleb K.N. (1994): Scheduling disassembly. In: International Journal of Production Research 32, pp. 1857-1866.

Kirchgeorg, M. (1999): Marktstrategisches Kreislaufmanagement – Ziele, Strategien und Strukturkonzepte. Gabler, Wiesbaden.

Lee, H.L., Padmanabhan, V., Whang, S. (1997): Information Distortion in a Supply Chain: The Bullwhip Effect. In: Management Science 43, pp. 546-558.

Moore, K.E., Güngär, A., Gupta, S.M. (2001): Petri net approach to disassembly process planning for products with complex AND/OR precedence relationships. In: European Journal of Operations Research 135, pp. 428-449.

Rautenstrauch, C. (1997): Fachkonzept für ein integriertes Produktions-, Recyclingplanungs- und –steuerungssystem (PRPS-System). Springer, Berlin et al.

Röpke, T. (2002): Wie aus Schrott Geld wird. In: Die Zeit 36, p. 29.

Souren, R. (2002): Konsumgüterverpackungen in der Kreislaufwirtschaft: Stoffströme – Transformationsprozesse – Transaktionsbeziehungen. Deutscher Universitäts-Verlag (DUV), Wiesbaden.

Spengler, T., Püchert, H., Penkuhn ,T., Rentz O. (1997): Environmental integrated production and recycling management. In: European Journal of Operations Research 97, pp. 308-326.

Sürie, C., Wagner, M. (2002): Supply Chain Analysis. In Stadtler H., Kilger C. (eds.) Supply Chain Management and Advanced Planning – Concepts, Models, Software and Case Studies, 2nd edn. Springer, Berlin et al.

Wallau, F. (2001): Kreislaufwirtschaftssystem Altauto – Eine empirische Analyse der Akteure und Märkte der Altautoverordnung in Deutschland. Deutscher Universitäts-Verlag (DUV), Wiesbaden.

Integrating Spent Products' Material into Supply Chains: The Recycling of End-Of-Life Vehicles as an Example

Frank Schultmann, Moritz Zumkeller, Otto Rentz

Institute for Industrial Production (IIP)
University of Karlsruhe
Hertzstrasse 16
D-76187 Karlsruhe, Germany

Abstract: *Economic, ecological and legal forces are emphasizing the need to recycle spent products in an enhanced way, i.e. reprocessing material in production processes. Hence, increasing reverse material flows are to be coordinated in the next few years. However, this coordination task, also known as 'reverse' supply chain management, has not yet been discussed as extensively as supply chain management objectives. Though 'reversing' the supply chain is possible to some extent, the main obstacle for transferring supply chain management knowledge to take-back processes is the degree of uncertainty regarding the composition and the amount of discarded products. Especially in the design stage of a reverse supply chain, continuous adaptations in these fields have to be taken into account.*

In this contribution, the peculiarities of establishing a reverse supply chain are presented, based on an example considering the end-of-life vehicle (ELV) treatment. Different design options for the reverse supply chain are put up by combining facility location planning with vehicle routing in an integrated approach. Introducing a problem-tailored algorithm that uses a Tabu Search heuristic, results of several reverse supply chain scenarios are discussed which are based on real case data, depicting measures from German ELV stakeholders.

Results show that the area-wide collection of spent materials bears many cost-relevant decision variables, crucially affecting the total expenses necessary. The examples investigated provide an impression of the different options possible for strategic network planning in terms of reverse logistics.

Keywords: *reverse supply chain, take-back obligations, end-of-life vehicles, facility location planning, vehicle routing planning*

1. Introduction

Despite representing a relatively young field of research, a wide variety of establishing reverse supply chains has already been proposed for numerous different applications in practice. In this contribution, we present a heuristic approach for the strategic planning of a *Product Recovery Network* (PRN). This expression is used according to the properties introduced in Fleischmann (2001, pp. 37 et sqq.): Spent products of a defined product group are to be collected area-wide in order to add value or regain valuables, including resale preparation. Activities considered comprise processing and logistics. Subsequently, we refer to *Strategic Network Planning* (SNP) as a procedure for establishing a PRN, focusing on long-term effects.

This approach is tailored to the task of recycling plastics from end-of-life vehicles (ELV) in Germany, which will become necessary due to enhanced legal requirements (see chapter 3). As plastics material recycling for automotive residuals is still in its infancy, a Germany-wide recovery network does not exist yet. Providing an overview over the application's peculiarities without getting lost in details, the following categories help to position the case investigated within the fields of reverse logistics and point out the central issues of the application.

The *motivation* for tackling reuse issues can be distinguished between economic, ecological and legislative targets (Schultmann et al., 2002b, pp. 1277 et sqq.). For the current example, motivation is mainly induced by the need to meet legal requirements as mentioned. Thus, the take-back obligations cause spent products to trigger the reprocessing sequence rather than any demand for secondary materials, according to a "supply push" (Fleischmann et al., 2000, p. 658) in supply chain management. Determining the *recovered item type* as consumer product points out that material composition, item age and condition are widely unknown in advance, in contrary to other types like package material or spare parts. These aspects limit the *form of reuse* (Thierry et al., 1995, p. 120) to material recycling; repair or refurbishing of components cannot be taken into account. Pursuing this kind of reuse, a multi-stage recycling process is necessary, performed by specialist actors. Thus, the *degree of interaction* between forward and reverse channel is fairly low: Apart from integrating the secondary material into the genuine supply chain of automotive components' manufacturing, forward and reverse channel are run independently. The sketched network design thus indicates the primary aim to generate secondary material suitable for replacing raw material in production processes. Consequently, a predefined reintegration goal is to be achieved by utilizing sophisticated recycling techniques while optimizing the economic side of the total Product Recovery Network.

Technical specifications of reprocessing are not subject to change, since the secondary material quality standards to be achieved are predefined. Hence, economic optimization potential can mainly be seized in the field of reverse logistics, especially for shipping disassembled plastic components from the dismantlers to the recycling sites, representing an extremely converging flow of material. While the locations of the dismantlers are known, recycling facilities are still to be established, thus facility location planning for these sites is necessary. To determine economically preferable locations, vehicle routing tasks need to be tackled also, as transportation issues in the example investigated allow adaptations with the aim of minimizing cost: Contrary to just-in-time concepts,[1] hardly any constraints in terms of delivery deadlines impede the design of shipping tasks. Furthermore, neither stock expenses nor material value are decisive for the total cost, but transportation cost represent a major portion of the total cost for this recycling step.

With this framework set, the modeling approach seeks to generate viable PRN solutions, taking into account facility location aspects as well as vehicle routing planning (Fleischmann, 2001, pp. 56 et sqq., Klose, 2001, pp. 293 et sqq.). With regard to long product lifetime and uncertainties in material amount, the approach needs to be robust for basic parameter changes. In this way, different network design options can be realized and become comparable in terms of economics.

We proceed as follows: As the theoretical foundation necessary for designing the PRN is similar to Supply Chain Management concerns, chapter 2 deals with corresponding basics and application-specific adaptations. Afterwards, relevant peculiarities concerning ELV treatment are laid down in chapter 3. With these foundations determined, the approach for strategic network planning is introduced in chapter 4, followed by the presentation of some application results in chapter 5. At last, conclusions are drawn and an outlook for further paths to be explored is given in chapter 6.

2. Supply chain management and end-of-life aspects

The Supply Chain Management (SCM) concept as an approach for the coordination of production processes across company borders has been extensively discussed in literature. However, most SCM contributions comprise mainly procurement, production, and sales aspects, whereas conceptual extensions beyond the point of sale are few. Focusing on the coordination of production and recycling processes, this chapter contains a brief overview of key SCM issues, concentrating on the long- and mid-term planning of logistics. Subsequently, applying these SCM methods to a Product Recovery Network will reveal options as well as impediments for the additional coordination of recycling processes. With regard to the example introduced in chapter 1, strategic planning issues are addressed in detail.

---

[1] For a characterization of just-in-time concepts see Fandel, 1999, pp. 461 et sqq..

2.1. Supply chain management framework

Although numerous publications in SCM theory have been emerging since the end of the 1980s, no commonly accepted definition of the term 'supply chain management' can be given, mainly because this topic has been addressed by different economic fields. For example, SCM standpoints can be found within transaction costing theory, organizational behavior, or game theory (Pfohl, 1999, p. 175). A classification of SCM theories can be obtained in Bechtel and Jayaram (1997, p. 17). Concentrating on the logistics perspective, SCM addresses the coordination of transfer processes between the stakeholders of product manufacturing. These transfer processes comprise material, products, money, and information (Pfohl, 1994, pp. 216 et sqq., Pfohl, 1996, pp. 314 et sqq.). For example, SCM tries to avoid rapid changes in stock levels at supply chain members which occur when individual order policies remain uncoordinated. This phenomenon is known as the bullwhip effect and may cause material shortages within a supply chain (Lee et al., 1997 pp. 93 et sqq.). Without running short of material at any point of the supply chain, competitive advantages can be realized for all stakeholders from the first supplier to the customer (Stölzle, 1999, p. 8).

The background of the genuine SCM framework can be characterized by the term *linear economy* (see figure 1): Emphasis is on utilizing natural resources for the production of goods, while end-of-life options are mainly incineration or disposal. Without take-back obligations for spent products, there is hardly any necessity for the manufacturer to coordinate the process chain beyond the point of sale.[2] With new legal restrictions emerging, however, more and more manufacturers will have to face take-back obligations soon.[3] Consequently, this effect will change the SCM framework, which can then be characterized as closed loop[4] economy: This change comprises two significant adaptations:

- Instead of single-stage disposal options for end-of-life-products like incineration or landfilling, multi-stage, enhanced reprocessing techniques are necessary to transfer spent products' components into secondary material that meets the quality requirements for reuse in technical applications. An additional supply chain in reverse direction, a *Reverse Supply Chain*, becomes necessary.
- When this secondary material is integrated into the genuine production process in order to avoid downcycling, feedback effects to the supply chain with regard to adaptations in time and quantity will occur. Apart from establishing the reverse supply chain, coordinating both chains becomes necessary.

---

[2] Exemptions mainly occur due to warranty or service reasons.

[3] Examples for take-back systems are given in Schultmann et al., 2002b, p. 1278.

[4] With respect to thermodynamic and processing restrictions, the term *closed loop* comprises an inevitable rise of total entropy as well as material losses during recovery activities.

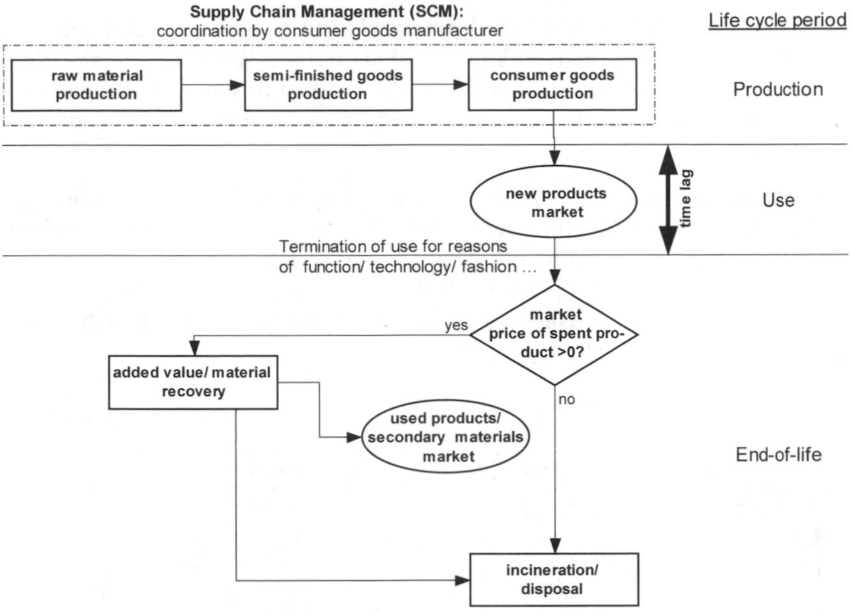

Fig. 1. Linear economy (status quo)

2.2. Including recycling processes: enhanced framework

Compared to the linear economy alternative, producers will face additional tasks like recovery and secondary material processing (see figure 2). Thus, additionally coordinating a *reverse supply chain* for the after-use phase of the product requires *Reverse Supply Chain Management* (RSCM). Since the amount of spent products collected in future is stochastic to a certain extent, the coordination of a supply chain and a reverse supply chain requires decisions under uncertainty. The longer the time between production and recovery, i.e. the average product life time, the higher is the degree of uncertainty. Thus, forecasting methods are necessary for planning recovery scenarios (Inderfurth and Jensen, 1999; Kelle and Silver, 1989, p. 349, Toktay, 2002). With the help of these scenarios, an evaluation of the cost and the technical feasibility of different reverse supply chain options is carried out.

Apart from different possibilities in reprocessing techniques, one major reason for the necessity of mid-term planning adaptations is the significant rise of recyclables which will be collected after having established a product-specific take-back system. Especially for long-life and complex products like cars, the following aspects are accountable for this effect:

- Combining consumer-oriented and recycling-oriented product design became necessary in the last few years for new products and components. Thus, *Design*

For Recycling (DFR) issues have been considered increasingly (Birkhofer and Schott, 1996, Grüner and Birkhofer, 2000, p. 120; Warnecke et al., 1996, pp. 123 et sqq.). Projecting this trend to the end-of-life-situation, the possibilities of recovery will improve. Accordingly, a rise in the amount of material available can be predicted.

- Along with the aim of recycling-oriented product design, the selection and composition of materials for new products has already been altered in order to enable recycling procedures. For example, the variety of plastics used in cars has been reduced and compounds are avoided as far as possible while the total amount per car is still rising for weight reducing reasons (Kohlhepp, 1999, pp. 64 et sqq., Kurth, 1995b, p. 201).

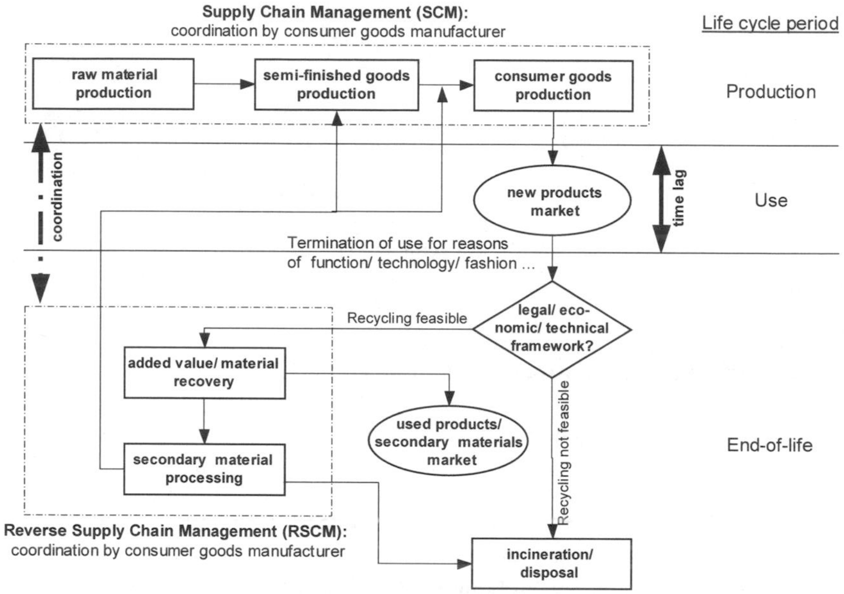

Fig. 2. Closed loop economy (future situation)

Considering the average time gap between production and recovery, the future tendency of quantity development can be determined. With this framework, planning variables are determined by the facility location, the capacity, and the mid-term extension options for sites in which reprocessing will be performed. As recovery of plastics from spent vehicles requires area-covering backhauling, vehicle routing tasks have to be addressed simultaneously. The interdependencies between these tasks require a combined approach as shown in chapter 4. Before presenting this approach, the end-of-life vehicle treatment in Germany is addressed in the following chapter.

3. End-of-life vehicle treatment in Germany

3.1. Current practice

Since legal restrictions for the recycling of ELV have not been regulating the way of recycling crucially so far, the current ELV-treatment is realized according to value regaining criteria mainly. Representing an example of end-of-life processing in a linear economy (see figure 1), ELV treatment focuses on added value- resp. material recovery (see figure 3).

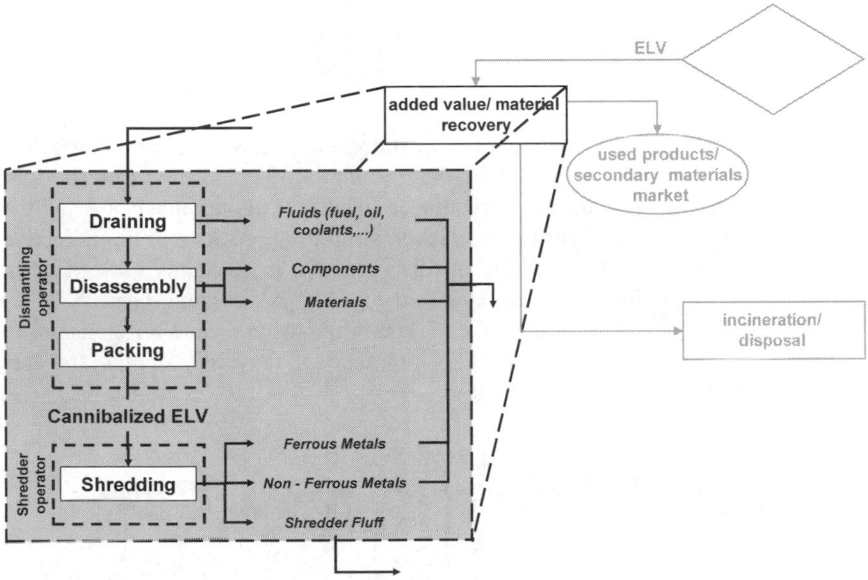

Fig. 3. Current practice for ELV treatment in Germany (simplified)

In particular, this product-specific recycling process can be described as following (Kurth, 1995a, pp. 26 et sqq., Püchert, 1994, , pp. 59 et sqq., Wallau, 2001, pp. 151 et sqq.):

- Before starting any recovery process, all vehicles need to be drained in order to remove all fluids like oil, fuel, coolants etc. Apart from avoiding the danger of spilling harmful substances during further dismantling activities, draining protects the latter shredder output from being contaminated and thus from losing sale value resp. from rising deposition cost.

- Vehicle parts expected to have significant resale value are disassembled first. Most promising ELVs for this step are accident cars and medium-aged ELV of common models, serving as source for spare parts; whereas other ELV can often not be disassembled economically.

- After components' recovery, economic dismantling is continued with valuable materials' recovery: Components which cannot be resold but consist of materials worth recycling are disassembled (i.e. copper and PVC from wiring harnesses (Diegmann, 2000), or platinum from catalytic converters).
- The cannibalized ELV is sent for shredding in order to regain the metal fractions. After metal separation, a mixture consisting of plastics, glass, dust and other components in varying composition, the so-called shredder fluff, remains unrecycled. Lacking any possibility of regaining valuables from the fluff economically, this fraction is usually landfilled.

3.2. Future situation

Initial efforts to legally enhance vehicle recycling efficiency in Germany resulted in the ELV Ordinance of 1997 (Altautoverordnung, 1997), representing the first national restriction to demand the surveillance of weight quotas for measuring the recycling success of ELV. On European level, similar targets lead to the Directive 2000/53 EC. The national adaptation of this Directive in Germany took place in 2002 when the *Law Governing the Disposal of ELV* (Altfahrzeug-Gesetz, 2002) came into effect. All major aspects like recycling quotas and time horizons are in compliance with the EC Directive. A comparison of recycling quotas and due dates is depicted in figure 4.

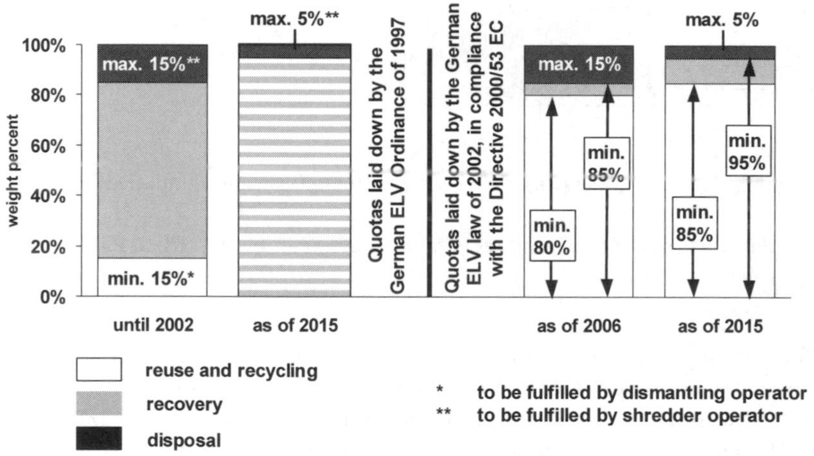

Fig. 4. Quotas according to German ELV legal framework

As automotive manufacturers strive for weight reduction of cars, plastics are replacing metal applications in new cars to an increasing extent (see figure 5). With a declining metal fraction in ELVs and rising weight quotas for reuse, recycling and recovery, it becomes inevitable to tackle the challenge of recycling materials which are currently landfilled with the shredder fluff. Among these materials, best options for recycling are expected for thermoplastics, since the possibility of melting and reshaping while preserving material properties allows subsequent use (Wallau, 2001, p. 247). Furthermore, only few different types of thermoplastics are used in cars, thus collecting significant quantities is viable with reasonable effort.

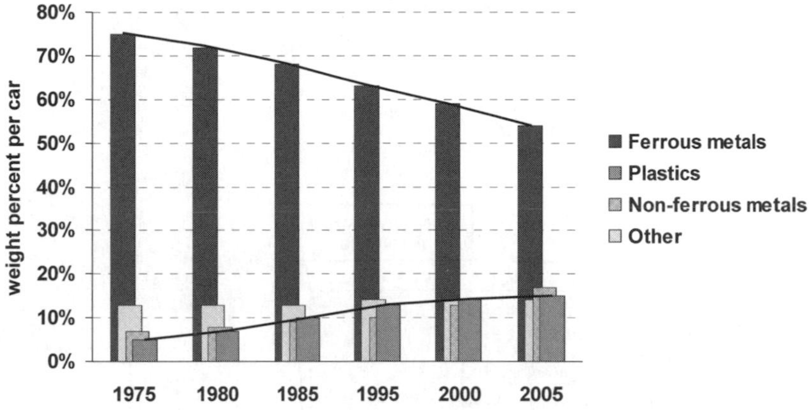

Fig. 5. Development of material composition for vehicles in use source: Hackenberg and Grubel, 2001, p. 3

3.3. Reverse supply chain for recycling thermoplastics

Contrary to metal reprocessing, which has been established decades ago, feasible options to regain other ELV materials are still under development. Establishing a closed loop economy (see figure 2) for ELV recycling comprises secondary material processing for thermoplastics. To recycle this material, a multi-stage process chain consisting of the steps depicted in figure 6 needs to be performed.

Contrary to existing processes for recycling thermoplastics from ELV (Wallau, 2001), this procedure is designed for regaining secondary material with properties comparable to the corresponding virgin material. Hence, one precondition is the separate collection of the different thermoplastic types, as mixed plastic fractions are not suitable for material recycling in genuine applications. Since integrating spent products' material into the supply chain is the most promising possibility to fulfill legal requirements and ensure sufficient demand for the secondary material, an elaborate recycling process as sketched is under development. The behavior of the recycling processes and the reactions between the chemical components can appropriately be modeled and simulated with flowsheeting programs as shown for metallurgical processes in Schultmann et al. (2002a, pp. 460 et sqq.) and in

Schultmann et al. (2002b, pp. 1284 et sqq.). For the economic evaluation of this process chain, a managerial accounting approach has been established, which takes into account life cycle aspects and activity-based costing principles (Schultmann et al., 2002c, pp. 10 et sqq.). This approach comprises upscaling aspects and has been applied to the reprocessing steps depicted in figure 6. This alternative avoids downcycling and ensures closing the material loop, taking advantage of the growing market of plastics for automotive applications.

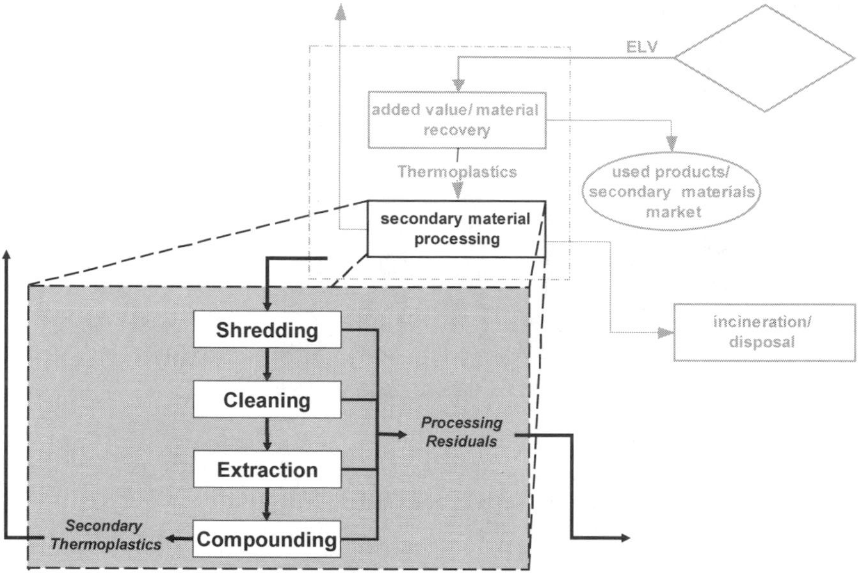

Fig. 6. Process chain for thermoplastics recycling from ELV (simplified)

Currently, this process chain only exists in laboratory scale, or is reduced to small-sized, local applications. To support future ELV treatment instead, a Germany-wide reverse supply chain is to be established, taking into consideration the future development of ELV treatment in Germany. In particular, major adaptations of a reverse supply chain once put up are necessary due to the steadily rising amount of thermoplastics to be collected in the long run. Considering the average vehicle lifetime of over 10 years, the effects of rising thermoplastics fraction in cars and the need to fulfill enhanced legal quotas will cause the amount of recyclable thermoplastics from ELV to rise at least until the year 2015.

Disassembling thermoplastic components from ELV, the dismantlers represent the first reprocessing stage. Thus, the adaptations described are to be taken into account by modeling the changing material amount at the reverse supply chain's source. While the subsequent recycling steps are to be carried out in specialized companies, the collection and backhaul of thermoplastics to one or few central locations is highly dependant on the dismantlers' structure and the amount collectable per dismantler. The expected changes described exert a crucial influence on

Strategic Network Planning (SNP). Consequently, any concept for establishing a reverse supply chain has to be adaptable to altered frameworks as named above. In the following section, a concept tailored to these requirements is introduced.

4. Strategic network planning for recycling thermoplastics

4.1. Reverse supply chain specifications

To integrate secondary thermoplastics from ELV in the genuine production process, the reverse supply chain, consisting of the reprocessing steps named, is to be put up in order to prepare the material for further use. With approximately 1,200 dismantlers existing in Germany presently, the material source for thermoplastics from ELV can be considered as area-wide. As investments for reprocessing sites are considerably high, material treatment at one or few locations only is necessary to keep the cost per material unit reasonable. Since the amount of thermoplastics will continue to rise within the next years (see chapter 3), adaptations in the reverse supply chain have to be considered in advance. Basically, the following possibilities for extending reprocessing capacity are feasible:

- Establishing one central reprocessing site, providing options for extensions to adapt to the future situation (*centralized treatment*), or
- planning one or more initial plants with fixed capacity and taking into account the additional implementation of further plants of the same size when the appropriate amount of material is due (*decentralized treatment*).

Both types are to be examined in order to determine which one is economically advantageous. Hence, expenses for the construction and operation of reprocessing sites have to be considered as well as those for reverse logistics. With regard to the latter aspect, the backhaul of material is expected to be performed on the road only, as area-wide coverage is not possible by rail or other carriers and transshipment would cause rather additional cost than transport economies of scale. Consequently, the investigation focuses on transportation by truck.

Since the reprocessing facilities do not exist yet, planning this network consists of two interdependent steps:

- On the one hand, the geographic determination of the reprocessing sites is necessary. Considering aspects of micro- and macroeconomics as well as entrepreneurial factors, *Facility Location Planning* (FLP) contains numerous approaches for this problem (Domschke and Drexl, 1996, pp. 60-110, Klose, 2001, pp. 9 et sqq.). Since FLP deals with *strategic planning* horizons, expected future effects like the development of the material amount available exert significant influence on decision making in this field.

- On the other hand, the material collection at any point of time requires *short-term planning*. For this kind of problem, *Vehicle Routing Planning* (VRP) provides methodologies (Domschke and Drexl, 1997, pp. 204-267). Despite of operational planning dimensions, VRP issues have to be taken into account for strategic network planning, since tour schedule characteristics are highly dependent on facility locations. In terms of economic evaluation, transportation cost represent a crucial share of the total reprocessing cost, thus VRP becomes part of Strategic Network Planning for the investigated application.

Finding long-term, cost-minimal combinations of facility locations for recycling sites and tour plans for the collection and further treatment of thermoplastics from ELV requires the integrated consideration of both problems named above. As simultaneous approaches are highly complex and are thus applicable for small-sized problems mainly, a sequential procedure is performed in the following: At first, facility location(s) for the centralized resp. the decentralized approach are determined. Subsequently, tour plans considering these facility locations are calculated.

4.2. Model formulation

The objective function for the VRP seeks to minimize the total length of all tours necessary. Apart from general limitations, i.e. ensuring the service for every dismantler or guaranteeing the construction of tours that start and end at the reprocessing site, restrictions occur mainly due to capacity limitations of the trucks used: The total amount of material collectable per tour limits the number of dismantlers that can be served in one tour. Additionally, exceeding a length limit per tour results in overnight tours. These tours are to be avoided, because the expenses for driving staff will then rise significantly. To cope with both effects, limits and penalty values need to be assigned for the number of customers served and for the total tour distance.

Formally speaking, we refer to a symmetric capacitated vehicle routing problem (CVRP) with one depot (i.e. the reprocessing site) and a defined maximum tour distance. We assume the number of trucks available to be sufficient, thus the number of tours not to be restricted. Objective is to generate a tour schedule with minimal cost, with those related to the tour distance in an initial approximation (see objective function (1)). Introducing $n+1$ nodes, consisting of n dismantlers and one depot (Index 0), and M tours, the model can be formulated as following (with variations taken from Domschke and Drexl, 1997, pp. 215 et sqq.):

With

D maximum distance per tour [km]
Q maximum capacity per tour [kg resp. m^3]
c_d variable cost per distance unit [€/km]
d_{ij} distance between nodes i and j [km]
b_j load collectible at dismantler j [kg resp. m^3]

$$y_{jk} = \begin{cases} 1 & \text{if dismantler } j \text{ is served in tour } k \\ 0 & \text{else} \end{cases}$$

$$x_{ij} = \begin{cases} 1 & \text{if node } j \text{ is the successor of node } i \\ 0 & \text{else} \end{cases}$$

Minimize:

$$F(x,y) = \sum_{k=1}^{M} c_d \cdot \sum_{i=0}^{n} \sum_{j=0}^{n} d_{ij} \cdot x_{ij} \cdot y_{jk} \tag{1}$$

Subject to:

$$\sum_{i=0}^{n} \sum_{j=0}^{n} d_{ij} \cdot x_{ij} \cdot y_{jk} \le D \qquad \text{for } k = 1,\ldots,M \tag{2}$$

$$\sum_{j=1}^{n} b_j \cdot y_{jk} \le Q \qquad \text{for } k = 1,\ldots,M \tag{3}$$

$$\sum_{k=1}^{M} \sum_{i=0}^{n} x_{ij} \cdot y_{jk} = 1 \qquad \text{for } j = 1,\ldots,n \tag{4}$$

$$\sum_{j=1}^{n} x_{0j} \cdot y_{jk} = 1 \qquad \text{for } k = 1,\ldots,M \tag{5}$$

$$\sum_{i=1}^{n} x_{i0} \cdot y_{ik} = 1 \qquad \text{for } k = 1,\ldots,M \tag{6}$$

The restrictions (2) and (3) ensure that maximum tour distance and maximum capacity are not exceeded, whereas constraints (4) imply that every dismantler is served and belongs to exactly one tour. Constraints (5) and (6) require every tour to start and end at the depot, thus no invalid tour can be constructed.

An example for heuristic approaches to solve the problem is suggested in Domschke and Drexl (1997, p. 216). However, the procedure stated there requires a predefined customer (i.e. dismantler) combination per tour; optimization potential is thus limited to different combinations of each dismantler set per tour.

4.3. A tabu search approach

In spite of the problem relaxation already realized by applying a step-by-step procedure, the problem size is still too large for accessing it with exact optimization techniques with reasonable effort. Hence, heuristics are applied in order to obtain good, not necessarily optimal results using time-saving algorithms. For this purpose, intelligent search methods have been established, which represent search structures for picking promising problem solutions including refinement. To enhance efficiency in searching performance, heuristics themselves are often controlled by so-called metaheuristics, representing the memory of the algorithm. Examples for these metaheuristics are *Simulated Annealing*, *Genetic Algorithms*, or *Tabu Search*. Especially *Tabu Search (TS)* has been proving to cope sufficiently with VRP problems (Fiechter, 1994; Gendreau et al., 1994). Furthermore, FLP is in most cases interrelated with VRP (Berman et al., 1995, p. 427), like the problem treated here. Thus, TS is chosen to tackle the task introduced above.

The TS concept has been mainly developed by Glover, who also introduced the expressions *Tabu Search* and *metaheuristics* (Glover, 1986). An overview of TS is provided in Glover, 1989, and Glover, 1990, whereas basic applications of TS are laid down in Voss, 1993. Despite of representing a relatively young strategy, TS has been successfully used in various business cases, such as container loading (Bortfeldt and Gehring, 1997), delivery problems (Rochat and Semet, 1994), or flight network design (Büdenbender et al., 2000).

Before going into details for the special application of strategic network planning, a brief overview of TS peculiarities is presented. Relying on a viable problem solution, the so-called starting solution, TS seeks to improve the objective function by altering the starting solution in details to be defined in advance. This detail alteration, consisting of a so-called move, is realized when representing the best improvement of all moves possible. The entity of all moves is determined by the definition of a solution's neighborhood, i.e. all alterations allowed to be performed in one single move.

So far, TS shows all properties of common greedy algorithms for optimization. Differences show up when no further improvement of the objective function is possible by any move: Instead of terminating, TS proceeds by exerting the move that represents the minimal change for the worse in the objective function. In order to avoid cycling by alternatively exerting the last improvement move possible and the complementary move for the least deterioration, TS 'remembers' the moves made by storing them in a Tabu list. These moves are temporarily forbidden. In designing the duration of the Tabu state and the conditions for Tabu setting, problem-tailored avoidance of cycling is possible.

Furthermore, invalid solutions (i.e. those violating one or more constraints set) can be accepted temporarily in order to diversify the search to previously unexplored fields of possible solutions. Guiding the search towards the return to admissible solutions is realized by applying penalty terms to the calculation of the objective function, which cause significant deterioration to the objective value if one or more constraints are not met. However, results of these solutions are comparable to valid ones and can thus be part of the search process.

With these features, TS algorithms can overcome local optima and continue searching for better solutions. However, the finding of the global optimum – if there is one – cannot be guaranteed. Consequently, a termination criterion needs to be defined to truncate the search process, for example the total number of moves to be made.

As described, the set of facility locations to be investigated is determined prior to VRP calculation and serves as an input for the TS application. The algorithm design allows the subsequent input of different facility location sets, varying in region and total number. For each of these sets, a tour schedule is generated by using a TS metaheuristic. By specifying the same framework of constraints and penalties, the different facility location / vehicle routing combinations become comparable in terms of total cost.

An additional variation is made regarding the point of time in future for calculation: As a significant rise of material is expected within the next years, two 'snapshots' are calculated per scenario; one for 2005 and one for 2015. Since the rise in capacity needed requires the extension of reprocessing facilities or the construction of additional sites, the investigation of different dates is necessary to comprehensively compare the scenarios.

To seize the potential of altering dismantler combinations per tour and to enable broad search diversification, the Tabu Search approach implemented is designed to alter significantly from the tour composition of the starting solution during the search process. Therefore, the algorithm yields to capacity and tour distance restrictions to a certain extent when the objective function is calculated, as penalty terms are provided if the corresponding restrictions are violated.

With the additional parameters

pD penalty cost for exceeding the maximum distance per tour [€/km]
p_Q penalty cost for exceeding the maximum capacity per tour [€/kg]

the objective function (1) is altered as follows:

$$F(x,y)=\sum_{k=1}^{M}\left\{\begin{array}{c} c_d\cdot\sum_{i=0}^{n}\sum_{j=0}^{n}d_{ij}\cdot x_{ij}\cdot y_{jk} \\ +\,p_D\cdot\max\left[0,\left(\sum_{i=0}^{n}\sum_{j=0}^{n}d_{ij}\cdot x_{ij}\cdot y_{jk}\right)-D\right] \\ +\,p_Q\cdot\max\left[0,\left(\sum_{j=1}^{n}b_j\cdot y_{jk}\right)-Q\right]\end{array}\right\} \quad (7)$$

Replacing objective function (1) with (7) and omitting restrictions (2) and (3) results in the cost minimization model underlying the Tabu Search approach. After the initial tour schedule is generated, the TS procedure starts to search enhanced solutions by taking into account the following move types:[5]

- swapping the position of two dismantlers within an existing tour,
- swapping the position of two dismantlers located in two different existing tours,
- swapping connections of two dismantlers to their successors within an existing tour, and
- swapping connections of two dismantlers to their successors located in two different existing tours.

Before exerting a move, every of these move types is evaluated according to the objective function, testing the dismantlers' structure for promising candidates in advance. The pool of neighborhood solutions is further determined by the entity of successors per candidate. After testing all combinations allowed, the move representing the best improvement resp. the least deterioration of the objective function is performed. The new tour schedule then serves as an origin for the next iteration. After exerting a given number of iterations, the algorithm is terminated and the best solution found within the iterations is provided.

While the search procedure is almost standard, the problem characteristics differ widely with the scenarios chosen. For example, the number and the geographic position of reprocessing facilities influence the candidate and the neighborhood choice, and the maximum tour distance necessary to serve all dismantlers, to name the most important parameters only. In order to provide a reasonable computing time for every scenario calculated, the algorithm construction needs to be easily adaptable for such changes. Hence, the following parameters are eligible for every application:

- number of iterations to be performed,
- candidate and neighborhood choice,
- maximum distance per tour allowed and corresponding penalty,
- maximum dismantler number per tour allowed and corresponding penalty,
- Tabu list length, and
- criteria for Tabu setting.

Beyond these structural adaptations, the fundamental framework is determined in advance by choosing the collecting frequency: As differences in material amount per dismantler occur, the repetitiveness of collecting must take place according to the amounts due and to vehicle capacity restrictions. To ensure steady material supply for the reprocessing site(s) and to keep the frequency of servicing as low as possible to minimize the total tour distance, a service concept based on collection on demand with respect to maximum capacity utilization is generated.[6]

---

[5] The move type systematic is adapted from a procedure introduced by Scholl and Weber, 2000, who carried out similar research for a distribution task.

[6] For details of the service concept see Schultmann et al., 2002d.

5. Results

In order to obtain results which are relevant for the ELV situation depicted in chapter 3, real data from the fields of automotive recycling has been gathered. Concentrating on one of the main fractions of thermoplastics from ELV, high density polyethylene (HD-PE), the following information serves as general data framework for all scenarios investigated:

- Geographic location of 1,200 dismantlers in Germany via ZIP code
- Forecasted material amount available for 2005 (6,000 tons per year) and for 2015 (14,000 tons per year), subdivided into regional fractions on German state level.
- Predefined rotational collection sequence of four weeks for every facility location in order to guarantee steady material supply without the need of extensive material stocks.
- Load capacity per truck according to the material hauled (7.2 tons), including the corresponding freight rate of 1.10 €/km.
- The maximum distance per tour is uniformly set to 600 km, for reasons of scenario comparability.

Consequently, differences between the scenarios encompass the number and the location of the facilities as well as the tour size, mainly specified by the number of dismantlers to be served per tour. In the following, two exemplary scenarios referred to as *centralized treatment* and *decentralized treatment* are investigated. For both scenarios, the choice of the facility location(s) has been realized with regard to the following aspects:

- The region attached to one facility cannot be split into fragments, thus a coherent area has to be covered, and
- the material amount collectible per area has to be approximately equal to guarantee comparable capacity utilization of the processing facilities.

Combined with the input data named above, applying these restrictions results in the facility locations stated below:

scenario	facility location	region served
centralized treatment	North of Fulda	Germany
decentralized treatment	North of Dortmund	northwestern Germany
	North of Magdeburg	northeastern Germany
	West of Nuremberg	southeastern Germany
	South of Mannheim	southwestern Germany

Table 1. Facility locations and corresponding regions used for the scenarios

Further peculiarities regarding the procedure of facility location choice by using the constraints above are discussed in Schultmann et al. (2002d).

5.1. Centralized treatment

Although central reprocessing, i.e. one single facility for treating the entire material amount collectible in Germany does not seem favorable at the first glance, this scenario is chosen in order to obtain a basis to which decentralized options can be compared to. Rising material amounts will thus mainly result in site capacity extensions rather than in crucial rerouting, since a uniformly rising amount collectible per dismantler will basically entail in higher frequency of collection.

To cover all dismantlers in Germany by using only one central reprocessing site results in extremely long tours, which cannot always be realized within one day, even with a centrally located depot. Since exceeding the maximum tour distance (see above) cannot be avoided for most of the tours, a collection strategy of serving many dismantlers per tour seems feasible. In contrary, truck capacity restrictions have to be obeyed carefully as early termination of collecting within a tour would affect the collection schedule for numerous dismantlers, since tour sizes are large. To apply these specifications to the Tabu Search algorithm, the values below were assigned to the corresponding parameters.

- maximum number of dismantlers served per tour 10
- distance penalty p_D 1.10 €/km
- load penalty p_Q 0.42 €/kg

Choosing p_D equal to the regular freight rate c_d causes variable distance cost to double for every kilometer beyond the maximum tour distance. In contrary to the load penalty value, which has proved to prohibit overloads, tour distance extensions beyond the limit set are inevitable because of the area size to be covered. Accordingly, the share of total cost which is induced by distance penalties exceeds 25%, even for good solutions found. Figure 7 contains exemplary tour schedules for one rotational collection sequence of the Tabu Search result for central treatment.

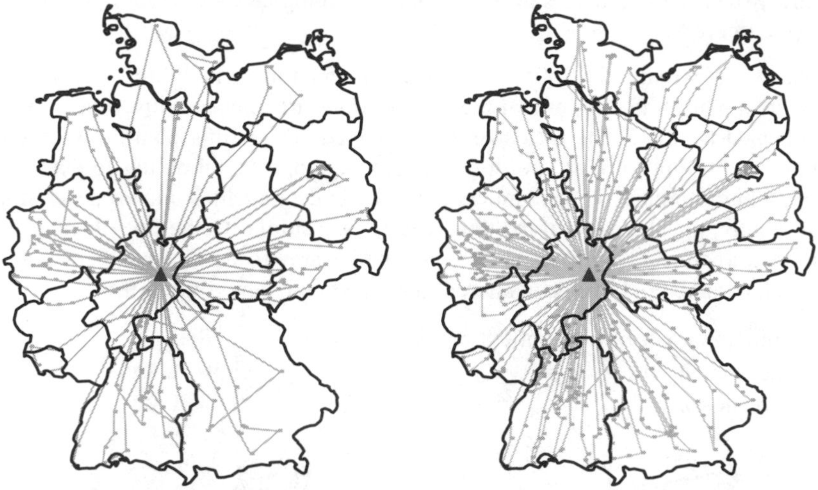

Fig. 7. Centralized treatment: tour schedules for 2005 (left) and 2015 (right)

Comparing both tour schedules, it is obvious that the total annual distance will more than double by 2015, since the material amount is expected to rise accordingly, while all other constraints remain unchanged. The total distance and cost information is summarized in table 2. Since the average length per tour does not change crucially between 2005 and 2015, the decreasing cost per ton are mainly induced by the shortage of the average distance between two consecutive dismantlers.

	annual distance	annual transportation cost		% distance-related cost	% penalty cost
2005	590,444 km	971,345 €	161.89 €/ton	67%	33%
2015	1,228,500 km	1,880,843 €	134.35 €/ton	72%	28%

Table 2. Central treatment: results

5.2. Decentralized treatment

Favoring a regional segmentation instead, one must consider the sequential implementation of the different processing sites: Due to economic reasons, the gross reprocessing capacity available must roughly match the material amount collectible at any time. Hence, decentralized facility location will at first result in a subset of one or few sites, supplemented by additional ones at a later point of time. Appropriate tour schedules have to be put up accordingly. Our example shows the option of subsequently establishing four sites in total, subdivided into two steps:

Initially, two sites operate as starting set in 2005, completed by two further ones in 2015 (see figure 8).

Starting with two sites in 2005, thc framework for tour scheduling is similar to central treatment. Since the initial facility locations are chosen with respect to the sites planned for 2015, the area size to be covered per facility is still too large to keep the length limit of 600 km for every tour. Again, scheduling has to deal with serving a high number of dismantlers per tour, collecting little material per stop. Consequently, the structure of the tour schedules is similar to the one obtained for centralized treatment. With respect to the smaller area to be covered per facility, the search parameters have been altered to match to the new routing task.

- maximum number of dismantlers served per tour 8
- distance penalty p_D 3.30 €/km
- load penalty p_Q 0.03 €/kg

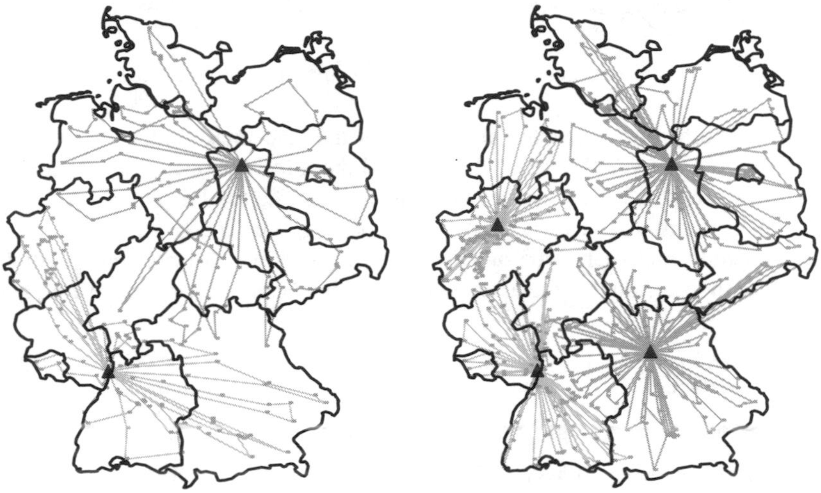

Fig. 8. Decentralized treatment: tour schedules for 2005 (left) and 2015 (right)

With four sites in total, the situation for 2015 will change significantly, since the coverage is then suitable to avoid exceeding the length limit for most of the tours. Furthermore, as the amount of material collectible will have more than doubled compared to 2005, only few dismantlers need to be served per tour and the utilization of vehicle capacity will rise. Consequently, the parameters used for calculation have to be adapted as follows:

- maximum number of dismantlers served per tour 4
- distance penalty p_D 5.50 €/km
- load penalty p_Q 0.42 €/kg

In this way, tour schedules can be generated which violate the restrictions set for few exemptions only. In this way, penalty values for overnight tours or capacity violations hardly emerge. Hence, the 2015 annual transportation cost[7] are significantly lower than those of 2005, in spite of higher values for the total distance and the amount of material available (see table 3). However, expenses for erecting two additional facilities have to be taken into account as well.[8] For this task, the analysis of this scenario provides the material collection-related figures necessary for comparison.

	annual distance	annual transportation cost		% distance-related cost	% penalty cost
2005 (2 sites)	524,225 km	741,423 €	123.99 €/ton	78%	22%
2015 (4 sites)	583,167 km	641,484 €	46.11 €/ton	99%	1%

Table 3. Decentralized treatment: results

6. Conclusions

Representing a small choice of all options possible, the results shown underline the vast variety of influence factors for the problem investigated. In this contribution, we pointed out that flexible algorithms are necessary to compare different scenarios of establishing a reverse supply chain for collecting secondary material. The model proposed provides an overview of the degrees of freedom which have to be taken into account for comprehensively planning secondary material integration with long-term perspective, as currently forced by take-back obligations. With easy possibilities for adaptation, the algorithm presented can be utilized with reasonable amendment effort for similar applications, starting from other fractions of ELV up to tasks for reprocessing other discarded products, like electric and electronic equipment, for example. Applying Tabu Search for spent material collection has proved to be a viable modeling option, since large-sized problems like these can be tackled with reasonable effort, providing satisfying solutions. Especially for long-term planning, the accuracy of the facility location / tour schedule combinations is sound enough to provide comprehensive decision support.

The information obtained by investigating the collection of secondary material represents one among several components for evaluating reverse supply chains. Economically speaking, collecting cost are expressive for the entire reverse supply chain only when the corresponding reprocessing cost are taken into account also.

---

[7] Calculated in prices of 2005.

[8] A model formulation can be found in Schultmann et al., 2002b.

Hence, the model proposed needs to be combined with evaluation tools for assessing the cost of processing activities as well (Schultmann et al., 2001, pp. 20 et sqq.). The activity based costing related approach introduced in Schultmann et al. (2002c) seems suitable to supplement the evaluation. In order to determine the economic effects of activities for enhanced recycling in advance, the different options for establishing take-back systems as shown need to be modeled for all elements of the reverse supply chain. Realizing this enhancement for evaluation will be subject to further research.

References

Altautoverordnung (1997): Verordnung über die Entsorgung von Altautos und die Anpassung straßenverkehrsrechtlicher Vorschriften. BGBL. I: pp.1666-1678.

Altfahrzeug-Gesetz (2002): Gesetz über die Entsorgung von Altfahrzeugen. BGBL. I: pp. 2129-2211.

Bechtel, C., Jayaram, J. (1997): Supply Chain Management: A Strategic Perspective. In: The International Journal of Logistics Management 8: pp. 15-34.

Berman, O., Jaillet, P., Simchi-Levi, D. (1995): Location-Routing Problems with Uncertainty. In: Drezner Z (Ed): Facility Location. A survey of applications and methods. Springer Verlag, New York, pp. 427-452.

Birkhofer, H., Schott, H. (1996): Die Entwicklung umweltgerechter Produkte – eine Herausforderung für die Konstruktionswissenschaft. In: Konstruktion 48: pp. 386-396.

Bortfeldt, A., Gehring, H. (1997): Ein Tabu Search-Verfahren für Containerbeladeprobleme mit schwach heterogenem Kistenvorrat. In: OR Spektrum 20: pp. 237-250.

Büdenbender, K., Grünert, T., Sebastian, H-J. (2000): A Hybrid Tabu Search/Branch-and-Bound Algorithm for the Direct Flight Network Design Problem. In: Transportation Science 34: pp. 364-380.

Diegmann, W. et al (2000): Profitable Recycling of Automotive Wiring Harnesses. SAE World Congress Detroit, March 6-9, 2000.

Directive 2000/53 EC of the European Parliament and of the Council of 18 September 2000 on end-of-life vehicles. Official Journal of the European Communities L 269: pp. 34-42.

Domschke, W., Drexl, A. (1996): Logistik: Band 3: Standorte. 4th Ed., Oldenbourg Verlag, München; Wien.

Domschke, W., Drexl, A. (1997): Logistik: Band 2: Rundreisen und Touren. 4th Ed., Oldenbourg Verlag, München; Wien.

Fandel, G. (1999): Just-in-time-Anlieferungskonzepte. In: Weber J, Baumgarten H (Eds): Handbuch Logistik. Schäffer-Poeschel Verlag, Stuttgart: pp. 460-468.

Fiechter, C. (1994): A parallel tabu search algorithm for large traveling salesman problems. In: Discrete Applied Mathematics 51: pp. 243-267.

Fleischmann, M. (2001): Quantitative Models for Reverse Logistics. Springer Verlag, Berlin et al.

Fleischmann, M. et al. (2000): A characterisation of logistics networks for product recovery. In: Omega 28: pp. 653-666.

Gendreau, M., Hertz, A., Laporte, G. (1994): A Tabu Search Heuristic for the Vehicle Routing Problem. In: Management Science 40: pp. 1276-1290.

Glover, F. (1986): Future Paths for Integer Programming and Links to Artificial Intelligence. In: Computers and Operations Research 13: pp. 533-549.

Glover, F. (1989): Tabu Search – Part I. In: ORSA 1: pp. 190-206.

Glover, F. (1990): Tabu Search – Part II. In: ORSA 2: pp. 4-32.

Grüner, C., Birkhofer, H. (2000): Umweltgerechte Produktentwicklung. In: Zeitschrift für wirtschaftlichen Fabrikbetrieb 95: pp. 230-233.

Hackenberg, U., Grubel, H. (2001): Kunststofftechnik im Automobilbau – quo vadis? In: VDI-Gesellschaft Kunststofftechnik (Ed): Kunststoffe im Automobilbau. Tagung Mannheim 4./5. April 2001. VDI-Verlag, Düsseldorf: pp. 3-19.

Inderfurth, K., Jensen, T. (1999): Analysis of MRP Policies with Recovery Options. In: Leopold-Wildburger, U., Feichtinger, G., Kistner, K-P. (Eds): Modelling and decisions in economics. Physica-Verlag, Heidelberg: pp. 189-238.

Kelle, P., Silver. E, (1989): Purchasing Policy of New Containers Considering the Random Returns of Previously Issued Containers. In: IIE Transactions 21: pp. 349-354.

Klose, A. (2001): Standortplanung in distributiven Systemen: Modelle, Methoden, Anwendungen. Physica-Verlag, Heidelberg.

Kohlhepp, K. (1999): Technische Kunststoffe im Automobilbau. In: Kunststoffe 89: pp. 64-71.

Kurth, H. (1995a): Automobilverwertung und -beseitigung. Status – Möglichkeiten – Perspektiven; Tagungsbericht zum 1. Kreislaufwirtschafts-Symposium vom 12. bis 14.09.1995 in Giessen. IUP, Herborn.

Kurth, H. (1995b): Integriertes Konzept zur wirtschaftlichen Demontage und Verwertung von Altfahrzeugen. Teil 2. Kraftfahrzeugrecyclingwirtschaft: Stoff- und Teilekreisläufe. IUP, Herborn-Seelbach.

Lee, H., Padmanabhan, V., Whang, S. (1997): The Bullwhip Effect in Supply Chains. In: Sloan Management Review 38: pp. 93-102.

Pfohl, H-C. (1994): Implementierung der Logistikkonzeption in und zwischen Unternehmen. Springer Verlag, Berlin et al.

Pfohl, H-C. (1996): Logistiksysteme: betriebswirtschaftliche Grundlagen. 5th Ed., Springer Verlag, Berlin et al.

Pfohl, H-C. (1999): Konzept des Supply Chain Managements und das Berufsbild des Logistikmanagers. In: Pfohl, H-C. (Ed): Logistikforschung. Entwicklungszüge und Gestaltungsansätze. Erich Schmidt Verlag, Berlin: pp. 173-228.

Püchert, H. (1994) Autorecycling: Demontage und Verwertung; wirtschaftliche Aspekte; Logistik und Organisation. Economica Verlag, Bonn.

Rochat, Y., Semet, F. (1994): A Tabu Search Approach for Delivering Pet Food and Flour in Switzerland. In: Journal of the Operational Research Society 45: pp. 1233-1246.

Scholl, A., Weber, M. (2000): Distributions-Logistik: Entscheidungsunterstützung bei der periodischen Belieferung von Regionalvertretungen. In: Zeitschrift für Betriebswirtschaft 70: pp. 1109-1132.

Schultmann, F., Engels, B., Rentz, O. (2002a): Cleaner Technology by Using Flowsheet-Simulation for Decision Support in Process Industries. In: Pillmann, W., Tochtermann, K. (Eds.): Environmental Communication in the Information Society. Proceedings of the 16th International Conference Informatics for Environmental Protection. Vienna, 25-27 September 2002, Metropolis Verlag, Marburg: pp. 459-466.

Schultmann, F., Engels, B., Rentz, O. (2002b): Reverse Supply Chain Management for Spent Batteries. In: Christiansen, K., Boer, H. (Eds): Operations Management and the New Economy. Proceedings of the 9th International Conference, European Operations Management Assiociation (EurOMA). Copenhagen, 2-4 June 2002. Vol 2: pp. 1277-1291.

Schultmann F, Jochum R, Rentz O (2001): A Methodological Approach for the Economic Assessment of Best Available Techniques- Demonstrated for a Case Study from the Steel Industry. In: International Journal of Life Cycle Assessment 6: pp. 19-27.

Schultmann, F., Zumkeller, M., Rentz, O. (2002c): Betriebswirtschaftliche Bewertung von Produkt- und Stoffkreisläufen auf Basis von Lebenszykluskonzepten und Prozesskostenrechnung. In: Fichtner, W., Geldermann, J. (Eds): Einsatz von OR-Verfahren zur techno-ökonomischen Analyse von Produktionssystemen. Lang Verlag, Frankfurt/Main et al.: pp. 5-19.

Schultmann, F., Zumkeller, M., Rentz, O. (2002d): Kombinierte Touren- und Standortplanung in der Kreislaufwirtschaft, dargestellt am Beispiel der Altautoverwertung. In: Schenk, M., Ziems, D., Inderfurth, K. (Eds.): Logistikplanung und –management. Begleitband zur 8. Magdeburger Logistiktagung „Logistik aus technischer und ökonomischer Sicht". Magdeburg, 14-15 November 2002: pp. 172-187.

Stölzle, W. (1999): Industrial Relationships. Oldenbourg Verlag, München.

Thierry, M. et al. (1995): Strategic Issues in Product Recovery Management. In: California Management Review 37: pp. 114-135.

Toktay, B. (2002) Forecasting Product Returns. In: Guide, Jr.D, Corbett, C., Dekker, R., Wassenhove, van N. (Eds): Business Perspectives in Closed loop Supply Chains. Forthcoming 2002.

Voß, S. (1993): Tabu Search: Applications and Prospects. In: Du, Z., Pardalos, P,: Network optimization problems: algorithms, applications, and complexity. Utopia Press, Singapur: pp. 333-353.

Wallau F (2001): Kreislaufwirtschaftssystem Altauto. Eine empirische Analyse der Akteure und Märkte der Altautoverwertung in Deutschland. Dt. Univ.-Verlag, Wiesbaden.

Warnecke, G., Düll, M., Sigl, M. (1996): Effektive Gestaltung des Produktentwicklungsprozesses unter besonderer Berücksichtigung des Recyclings. In: Feser, H-D., Flieger, W., von Hauff, M. (Eds): Integrierter Umweltschutz. Transfer Verlag, Regensburg: pp. 123-139.

Recovery Planning in Closed Loop Supply Chains: An Activity Analysis Based Approach

Thomas Spengler, Wiebke Stölting, Martin Ploog

Department of Production Management
Braunschweig University of Technology
Katharinenstr. 3
D-38106 Braunschweig, Germany

Abstract: *Due to the latest developments in European environmental legislation, supply chains in most major industrial branches have to be closed and producers will be responsible for collecting, sorting and recovery of discarded products at the end of their service life. Therefore, a close cooperation with recovery companies and their integration in producers supply chains, e.g. as suppliers of spare parts and secondary raw materials, will be necessary. A cost-efficient management of material flows between suppliers, producers, customers and recovery companies requires an integrated information management as well as advanced planning systems between all members of the supply chain. The paper focuses on the design and implementation of a decision support system for electronic scrap recovery companies in closed loop supply chains. This requires an efficient provision of relevant information, so that at the beginning of this paper a concept for the inter-organizational information management is presented. Then, based on detailed empirical analysis of disassembly and bulk recycling processes, an activity analysis based material flow model will be developed and the required capacity of the disassembly and recycling processes will be determined. Due to high uncertainties in the amount, composition and quality of the delivered electronic scrap, the long term capacity planning has to be supplemented by a detailed short term planning at regular intervals. The decision support system has been implemented in a major German electronic scrap recovery company and validated by real data.*

Keywords: *closed loop supply chains, activity analysis, recovery planning, information management, electronic scrap*

1. Introduction

Producers of electrical and electronic equipment (EEE) increasingly face requirements to implement systems to manage the take-back and recovery of their products at the end of the use phase. This is caused by new laws and regulations which assign an extended product responsibility to the producers. Not only coping with these challenges efficiently, they should also take advantage of additional potentials that will arise from closing loops in supply chains. Instruments to plan and control the emerging processes will have to be developed and provided with relevant information. Cooperation between producers and recovery companies has to be coordinated and supported by adequate instruments. Based on the presentation of the legal framework and resulting planning problems of closed loop supply chains in the EEE-industry, an inter-organizational information management concept will be formulated. Furthermore, an activity analysis based modelling approach of material flows in closed loop supply chains is developed and applied to a practical EEE-scrap recycling planning problem.

2. Closed Loop supply chains in the EEE-industry

2.1. Background

Due to a constant increase in sales of electrical and electronic equipment (EEE), it can be assumed that the quantity of waste electrical and electronic equipment (WEEE) will rise likewise. Because most households are saturated with this kind of equipment, it can be anticipated that these will be replaced within time due to the limited product life. As a result of sales and average life span considerations for the products, at this time a potential of 2 million tons of WEEE per year is predicted for Germany (BVSE 1999).

In addition to the rising quantity of WEEE, the hazardous substances contained in the discarded products contribute to the problematic situation. Negative effects on the environment can be caused by heavy metals, PCB or halogenated flame retardants. Furthermore, a great share of valuable materials and some reusable components can be found within the WEEE. Since nowadays discarded products are usually disposed, this valuable potential is lost without use.

In order to cope with this unsatisfying situation, two proposals for directives have been formulated on the European level, which later on will be put into national legislation. These are the Directive of the European Parliament and of the Council on WEEE (WEEE-Directive) and the Directive of the European Parliament and of the Council on the restriction of the use of certain hazardous substances (RoHS-Directive) in EEE (European Commission 2000). Therein the producer's responsibility for the end of life of their products is stated. This includes the financial responsibility for the treatment, recovery and final disposal of the WEEE. Furthermore, fixed recycling quotas are determined for the product categories. Article 10 regulates that the treatment and recovery facilities have to be provided with information "to identify the different electrical and electronic equipment components and materials, and the location of dangerous substances and preparations" (European Commission 2000, Article 10). The goal of the RoHS-Directive is to decrease the content of hazardous substances like lead, mercury, cadmium, hexavalent chromium or bromine compounds in the EEE. Furthermore, there is a working paper on European level that will be transferred into another proposal for a Directive which is supposed to follow these first ones. It will focus on the design and production of EEE and contains the obligation of the suppliers to provide the manufacturers with information on their components (EEE-Directive).

Since manufacturers are responsible for their products throughout the entire life-cycle, the traditional supply chain has to be extended by the after-use phase. Thus, disassembly and recycling companies have to be included into the considerations. It can be expected that the actors of this extended supply chain will cooperate in order to efficiently meet the stated requirements and furthermore take advantages of synergy effects. This trend can be supported by developing concepts for integrated planning instruments and approaches for the planning and control of the substance flows within the supply chain. This way ecological aspects can be considered, but additionally economical potentials can be realized. On a strategic level, the company has to make the decision which recovery option shall be pursued for each of their products. Generally the following strategies can be taken into consideration[1]:

- **materials recycling** of metals or plastics in order to gain raw materials,
- **reuse** of parts and components as spare parts or for the production of new devices,
- **refurbishing** of entire discarded products to use them as second-hand devices.

The simplified structure of an extended supply chain is shown in Fig. 1.

[1] For a definition of different product recovery options confer (Thierry et al. 1995).

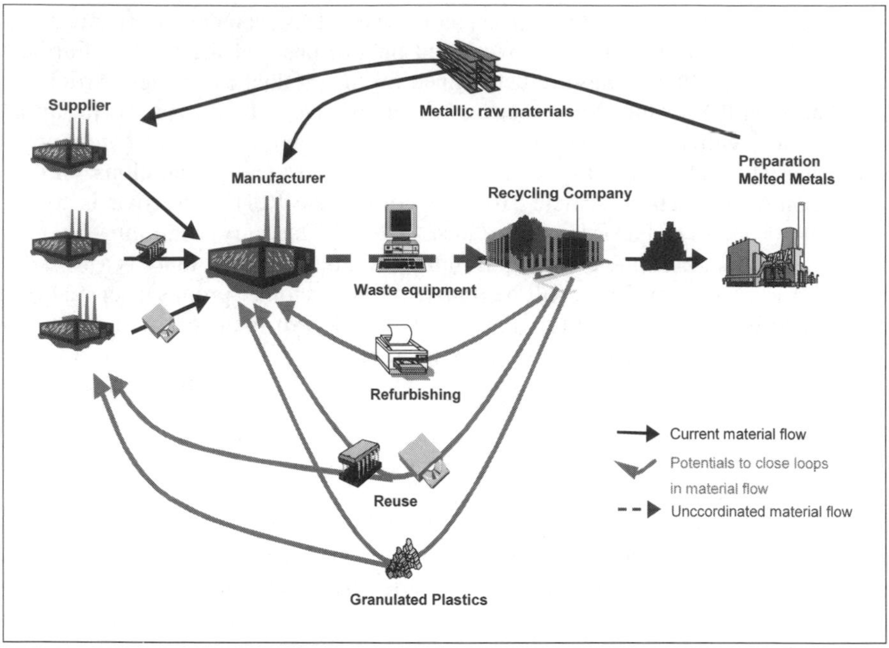

Fig. 1. Extended supply chain and evolving potentials (Hesselbach et al. 2001b)

2.2. Planning problems

The extension of the producer's responsibility into the after-use phase comes along with the necessity to develop instruments to cope with the arising planning problems. Whereas a traditional supply chain ends at the customer, in a closed loop supply chain a number of additional aspects have to be considered. The most relevant are (Krikke et al. 2002):

- Uncertainty in reference to volumes, quality, composition and timing of the collected discarded products leads to an increased system complexity.
- An imbalance of supply of discarded products on the one hand and the requirements of the producers as demand on the other hand can often be determined.
- The additional market opportunities that can arise from these processes are unexplored until now.

The instruments to support planning and control of closed loop supply chains should assist decision making both on strategic as well as on operational level and thereby consider the listed aspects. On the strategic planning level, instruments that enable decision makers at the producer to model and evaluate different scenarios with varying technical, socio-economic and legal conditions are needed. Methods to forecast volumes and conditions of discarded products as well as the timing of the upcoming WEEE have to be developed. Form and content of the co-operation agreements between producers and recovery companies have to be determined. On the operational planning level, a coordination and reconciliation of the production planning and control of the producer with the recovery planning and control of the recovery company has to be considered. As discussed in the following sections, this can be supported by conceiving operational planning instruments which allow the recovery company to determine cost-efficient recovery programs for a range of discarded products.

3. Inter-organizational information management

3.1. Information needs

Due to the current legal proposals on the European level for the handling and treatment of EEE, the manufacturers are facing an extensive obligation to provide product related information. Particularly this concerns the forthcoming WEEE-Directive and the EEE working paper. The current proposal of the WEEE-Directive stipulates the requirement that information about components, valuable and hazardous materials and their collocation within the devices has to be submitted. Furthermore, the publishing of handbooks for maintenance, reuse, upgrading and refitting is discussed. The EEE working paper states that suppliers have to provide information about the material composition, the resource consumption and - if available - about the results of environmental evaluations. In order to anticipate the effort related to the provision of this information it seems necessary to develop concepts to determine how to fulfil the mentioned requirements.

Information needs can not only be derived from the legal demands. Further demands on the provision of information evolve from the chosen strategies for the recovery of scrap products. The selection of the strategy out of the ones mentioned above has a significant influence on the type and the level of detail of the needed information.

For materials recycling, primarily information about kind and quantity of the hazardous and valuable substances that can be found within the discarded products is needed as well as a description about where they are located within the devices. Furthermore, an adequate labelling particularly of the plastic parts as well as indications for disassembly can support a strict separation into the single materials.

In order to realize reuse-strategies for single parts and components, information about potentially reusable components and about accessibility and connecting techniques are needed. Information from the use-phase of the products which can give hints about the conditions of the considered parts is also useful. Beyond this, information about supply and demand as well as about functionality and quality is needed for an effective disassembly and recycling planning.

The most extensive information is needed for refurbishing processes of entire units. Besides offering the above mentioned data about contents and structure of the products, it is necessary to provide information about the function and control of the devices and, where applicable, about the utilized software.

The resumed information requirements show that the needed data usually do not originate in the recovery companies but still are used by them (Schneider 1999). The information is spread among the other actors of the extended supply chain, which are the suppliers and manufacturers. Thus, it can be derived that the first step for a successful information concept is that the needed data is to be collected at the producer, then it has to be merged and aggregated adequately. The second step will then be to provide and transfer the information with the aid of inter-organizational information structures and systems in order to support the planning processes at the recovery company.

3.2. The recycling passport concept

Single EEE manufacturers already came up with first approaches to fulfil the stated information duties. An outstanding position is taken by the recycling passport concept of the Agfa-Gevaert AG (Dietrich 1999). This is a document of four or five pages which gives basic information about the content of the Agfa devices. It contains a general view of the device, a table that lists all relevant material groups and their corresponding weights and disassembly indications for hazardous substances.

First, the needed information has to be collected. For the materials recycling strategy this is primarily information about the kind and quantity of the hazardous and valuable substances and its collocation within the device. In addition, it is necessary to include information about potentially reusable parts and their accessibility within the device to enable a component reuse. Since the needed data currently can not be provided by producer's IT-systems at defined locations and in an appropriate format, it is necessary to attain the required information by disassembling the device and to identify and weigh the content components and materials. The gained data then have to be fed manually into the recycling passport of the device. Thereby it is crucial to assign the materials to the following predetermined categories:

- Material / components, which must be removed and treated separately, for example lithium-batteries. As a basis for this category the material lists from the EICTA[2] and from the WEEE-Directive could be used.
- Material / components, which can disturb certain recycling processes, for example circuit boards due to the contained flame-retardant because if these are treated in an incineration facility dioxin may emerge.
- Material / components through which benefits can normally be achieved, for example metal fractions like steel or copper which can be sold to smelting plants.

An overview of the recycling passport data of a reference device is shown in Fig. 9 in subsection 5.3 of this paper.

This concept is well suited as a first approach for an information exchange to support the materials recycling strategy. Recovery companies can base their decisions on which discarded products to disassemble and recycle on this information and perform their planning of the recovery program. How this can be realized with the support of the recycling passport information will be demonstrated in section 5 of this paper. Furthermore, it seems reasonable to enhance this concept under consideration of the information needs derived from the different recovery strategies.

3.3. Information provision via communication platform

In this subsection, a concept for the provision of product related data will be developed under consideration of the stated information needs. First, a focus is set on the intra-organizational collection, consolidation and aggregation of the information. Then, possibilities for the inter-organizational provision of this information will be pointed out bearing in mind and advancing the recycling passport concept (Spengler et al. 2002).

In order to integrate all the required information for closing loops in extended supply chains, the development of a communication platform is advisable. It will connect the product manufacturing phase with the after-use phase and enables all the involved partners to have access to the needed information. On this platform all relevant product and process data for both the upstream as well as the downstream information flow from the recovery company to the producer will be provided. The concept of such a communication platform is shown in Fig. 2.

[2] This list from the European Information, Communications and Consumer Electronics Technology Industry Association (EICTA) includes all the fundamental information on the hazardous materials used in this industrial sector.

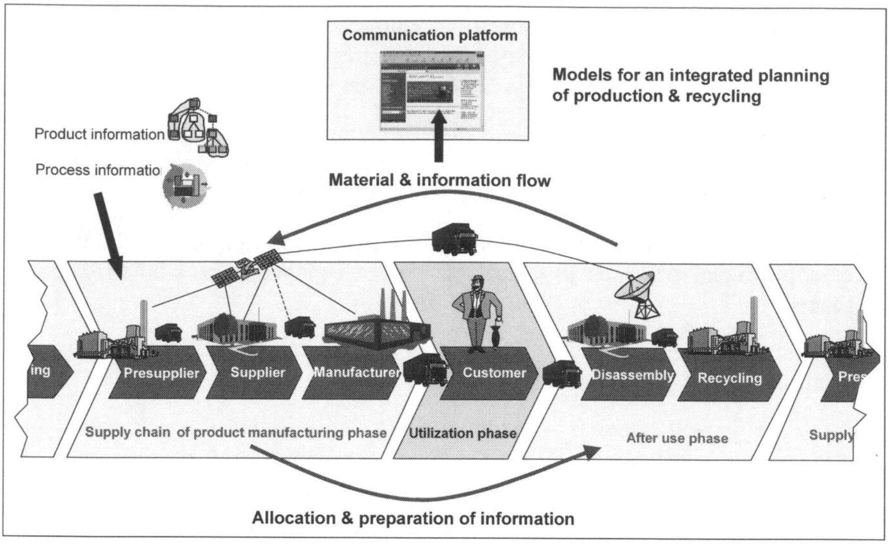

Fig. 2. Information flow between product manufacturing and after-use phase (Hesselbach et al. 2001a)

The collection of information has to be realized on two levels:

- First, the inter-organizational level between suppliers and manufacturers as stated in the EEE-working paper and
- second, the intra-organizational level, where information out of the manufacturers own information systems has to be gathered.

Of significant importance within this task is the utilization of consistent categories and terminologies. On the inter-organizational level this can be achieved by calling upon the suppliers to use defined internet forms where they have to insert their data according to predetermined material codes. These codes will then be assigned to the recycling passport categories in a standardized way. On the intra-organizational level the materials and components have to be matched to these material codes within the product development phase. This way, the product data can be directly extracted from the CAD-data bases and assigned to the recycling passport categories. The collected information must be inserted into a recycling data base. It is reasonable to set up this data base at the manufacturer within the product data management system that he is already utilizing. It is assumed that by implementing such a standardized proceeding a majority of the required product related information can be registered and assigned properly. The remaining materials and components will have to be assigned manually to the categories since here knowledge and experience of the employees play an important role.

The inter-organizational provision of the information from the manufacturers to the recovery companies will be realized on the communication platform on two different levels. First, the generated recycling passports will be made available in the internet. Thereby it is important to use a format that can not be changed or modified and to permit search-processes to find the recycling passport of a specific device. This level allows the manufacturers to meet the legally required information duties. The second level of information provision goes further and tends to support decision and planning processes within the cooperation between manufacturers and recovery companies. This permits the realization of high grade recovery processes like reuse and refurbishing strategies. Thus, it is necessary that a high level of security can be guaranteed since now detailed information will be provided. With support of the internet technology the recovery companies will be enabled to access relevant information by the use of retrieval functions. The recovery company's browser connects to a web-server and a request form can be filled in. The web-server will then access the recycling data base of the manufacturer by using predefined logics. The requested information will be extracted from this data base and provided to the recovery company by the internet. The structure of this concept is shown in the following Fig. 3.

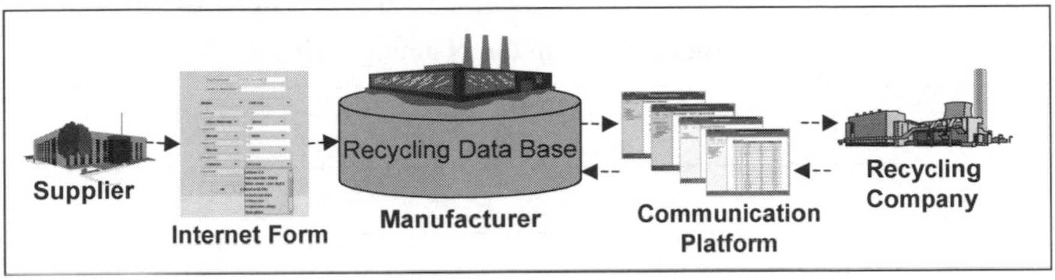

Fig. 3. Approach for an information flow concept (Spengler and Stölting 2003)

In the following section an activity analysis based approach for recovery planning in closed loop supply chains is developed and a basic optimization model is formulated. This model will be applied to a typical electronic scrap recovery planning problem in section 5.

4. Activity analysis based modelling of supply chains

4.1. Basic ideas

In the last years, the activity analysis based on (Koopmans 1951) and (Debreu 1959) has been widely used for the formulation of joint production processes (Fandel 1990, Dyckhoff 1994, Oenning 1997, Spengler 1998, Rüdiger 2000, Souren 2002). Compared to traditional approaches, the linear activity analysis permits a very simple formulation of material flows in multi-stage joint production systems. Closed loop supply chains can be modelled as multi-stage production systems, where every stage represents either a single enterprise or a business unit of a certain company. The level of aggregation depends on the necessary details of information concerning the material flows between the relevant technical unit operations of the considered enterprises or business units. For the sake of simplicity, in a first approach, each company or business unit r $(r=1,...,R)$ of the supply chain will be modelled by an activity vector $v^r \in IR^I$, where the index i $(i=1,...,I)$ describes all material flows which have to be considered in the actual planning period τ (see Fig. 4).

$$v^r = \begin{pmatrix} v_1^r \\ \vdots \\ v_i^r \\ \vdots \\ v_I^r \end{pmatrix} \in IR^I \tag{4.1}$$

Negative $v_i^r < 0$ describe input materials and positive $v_i^r > 0$ describe output materials of the enterprise or business unit r in the planning period τ.

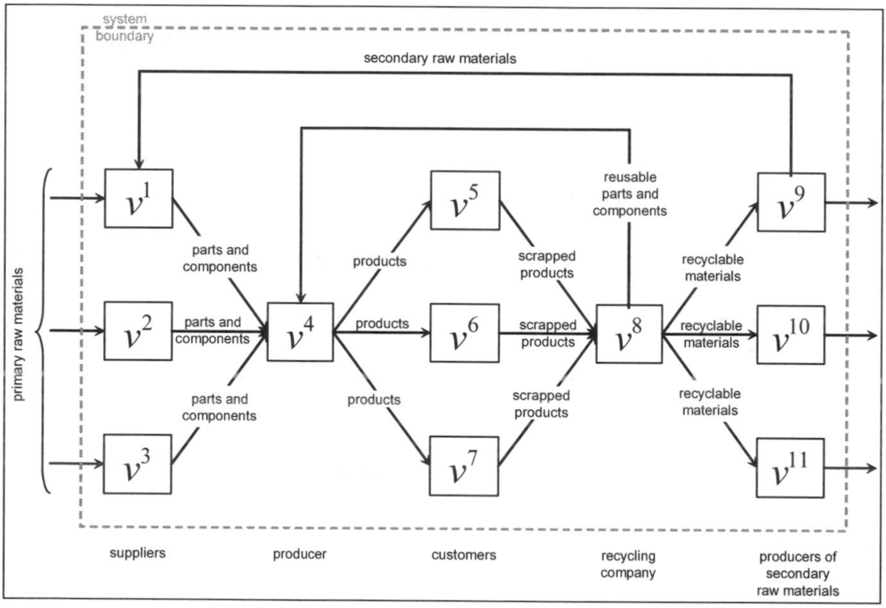

Fig. 4. Structure of an activity analysis based model of closed loop supply chains

The activity vectors v^r depend on the production schedules of the enterprises or business units r and can be controlled by strategic, tactical and operative production management policies, depending on the considered planning period. The overall planning of supply chains requires detailed information on the production processes of all partners belonging to the supply chain. In other terms, the possible ranges of the activity vectors v^r and all feasible production management policies have to be known by all members of the supply chain. In market economies, generally companies are not willing to share such detailed information, therefore a centralized overall planning approach seems not to be very realistic. The economically efficient coordination of individual production management policies still remains an unsolved problem in practice, although a lot of promising research has been carried out during the last years (Stadtler and Kilger 2000, Simchi-Levi et al. 2000, Shapiro 2001). In the following subsection, we will focus on the planning problems of recovery companies $(r = 8)$ in closed loop supply chains.

4.2. Modelling of disassembly processes

As a starting point of the disassembly and recycling planning process, recycling passports have to be downloaded from the internet, for all scrapped products to be recycled in the planning period. Due to long-term contracts between producers and suppliers in closed loop supply chains, the previously mentioned second level of information provision is relevant. Therefore, the recovery company has access to all recycling relevant product data on the one hand, and operative planning data of the producers and suppliers, such as demand for reusable parts and components or expected amounts of scrapped products, on the other hand. The recovery process of EEE-scrap usually consists of a disassembly and a bulk recycling step. The disassembly process serves to remove harmful substances and reusable parts; the bulk recycling process serves to gain ferrous and non-ferrous metals through size-reduction of the partially disassembled products and mechanical separation steps.

For each product, the technically and organizationally feasible disassembly activities can be modelled by so called disassembly activity vectors

$$v_j = \begin{pmatrix} v_{1j} \\ \vdots \\ v_{ij} \\ \vdots \\ v_{Ij} \end{pmatrix} \in IR^I, \tag{4.2}$$

where the index j $(j=1,\dots,J)$ describes a certain disassembly activity and the index i $(i=1,\dots I)$ a certain scrap type (product, component, part or material) which occurs in at least one of the scrapped products. The total available amount y_i of a scrap type i at the end of the planning period depends on the accepted amount $y_i^A \geq 0$ of that scrap type in the beginning of the planning period and the number of executions of those disassembly activities v_j, where the component v_{ij} does not disappear. A positive component $v_{ij} > 0$ counts the amount of the scrap type i which is gained by one execution of the disassembly activity v_j. A negative component $v_{ij} < 0$ counts the amount of scrap type i which is disassembled by one execution of v_j. The number of executions $x_j \in IN_0$ of a certain disassembly activity v_j in the considered planning period determines the activity vector v^r, which describes the input/output material flows of the recovery company r:

$$v^r = \begin{pmatrix} v_1^r \\ \vdots \\ v_I^r \end{pmatrix} = \begin{pmatrix} y_1^A \\ \vdots \\ y_I^A \end{pmatrix} + \sum_{j=1}^{J} x_j \cdot \begin{pmatrix} v_{1j} \\ \vdots \\ v_{Ij} \end{pmatrix} = y^A + \sum_{j=1}^{J} x_j \cdot v_j \tag{4.3}$$

Equation (4.3) describes a linear activity analysis based model of the disassembly process of a recovery company (Spengler et al. 1997). If the recovery company r additionally runs a bulk recycling process, the computation of the activity vector v^r has to be extended in order to take into account the various steps of the bulk recycling process. In that case, a detailed technical analysis of the recycling process, the material flows and the relevant decision variables becomes necessary (see section 5).

4.3. Recovery planning in closed Loop supply chains

In order to make optimal decisions concerning the determination of the recovery schedule in the considered planning period, a variety of necessary information has to be gathered by the recovery company (see section 3). The most relevant planning data can be classified as follows (see Fig. 5):

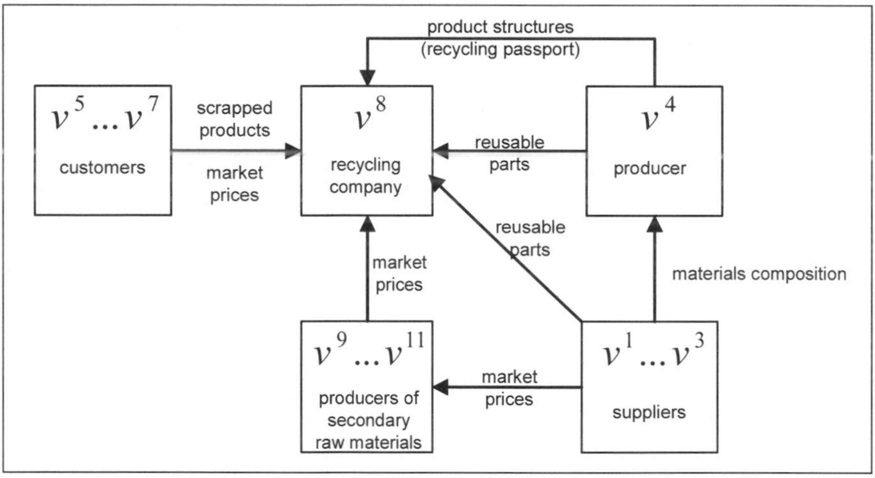

Fig. 5. Necessary planning data for recovery companies

- **Product Structures:** disassembly activities, hazardous substances, reusable parts and components, materials composition, …
- **Scrapped Products:** types and amounts of scrapped products in the considered planning period
- **Reusable Parts and Components:** demand for reusable parts and components in the considered planning period
- **Market Prices:** market prices for scrapped products, reusable parts and components, secondary raw materials
- **Internal Processing Data:** disassembly costs and capacities, recycling costs and capacities

In a given planning period, the activity vector v^r of the recovery company r can be determined by an optimal solution of the following planning problems:

- Which discarded products should be recycled (recovery schedule)?
- Which level of disassembly should be chosen for the scheduled products?
- Which scrap types should be treated in the internal bulk recycling facilities or marketed externally?
- Which reusable parts and components should be delivered to producers or suppliers belonging to the supply chain?
- Which reusable parts and components should be marketed externally?

Based on a detailed analysis of the available disassembly and bulk recycling processes, as well as on the internal and external constraints, the recovery company r will be able to describe the set of all feasible activity vectors v^r by the intersection of the sets T and R. The set T encloses all technically feasible activity vectors v^r and the set R all activity vectors v^r which meet the relevant capacity and market constraints inside and outside the supply chain. The economic success of a certain activity vector $v^r \in T \cap R$ can be measured by the calculation of all relevant yields $e(v^r)$ and costs $c(v^r)$ resulting from the solutions of the above formulated recovery planning problems in the considered planning period. This leads to the following optimization problem

$$\begin{aligned} Max \quad & e(v^r) - c(v^r) \\ s.t. \quad & v^r \in T \cap R \end{aligned} , \tag{4.4}$$

which generally can be formulated as a mixed-integer linear programming model (MILP). In the next section, a practical recovery planning problem concerning a major German electronic scrap recycler and a typical range of discarded electronic products will be presented from a case study point of view. The available disassembly and bulk recycling process steps will be modelled by linear activity analysis. Therefore, the optimization problem (4.4) can be formulated as a MILP and solved by standard OR software packages.

5. Case study: electronic scrap recovery

5.1. Case description

The development of cost-efficient recovery concepts for discarded products can be supported by the application of operations research models. This case study refers to the tasks supply, disassembly and bulk recycling of a major electronic scrap recovery company that recovers industrial and consumer electronics. In the company, the recovery process is divided into disassembly in order to remove harmful substances or reusable parts and into bulk recycling in order to gain ferrous and non-ferrous metals through size-reduction and separation steps.

Since the recovery of EEE scrap depends on two markets that may contribute to success, the recovery company can derive benefit from being integrated into the producer's supply chain. On the one hand, deviations in the supply of scrap may be avoided by long-term cooperation with the producers of equipment. On the other hand, the delivery of reusable parts for spare parts management and equivalent-to-new-parts for the use in production processes leads to output proceeds, especially concerning investment goods.

The material flow throughout the recovery company can be seen in Fig. 6. The delivery of scrap from the input storage to the recovery works is assessed with a given transfer price, since the storage is a separated profit centre that may acquire and sell scrap. Thus the recovery works manager faces the "acquisition" decision which products from the storage have to be taken and recovered as seen at (*). The first recovery step "disassembly" is composed of manual or partly-automated processes. Planning the disassembly step, the recovery works manager has to determine the disassembly level at point (**) in Fig.6. The second step "bulk recycling" is designed to gain precious fractions such as ferrous and non-ferrous metals from mixed EEE scrap using a sequence of unit operations like crushing and separation steps. When planning the bulk recycling step, the recovery works manager has to decide which scrap types are to be recycled internally or are to be marketed externally as seen at point (***) in Fig. 6. Since the long-term capacity of each unit is calculated on the basis of an expected specific input composition, variations from this composition can lead to bottlenecks in the subsequent units if the components that should be separated in the preceding units of the facility, e.g. ferrous metals, are underrepresented in the feed. Thus, a recycling company can benefit from the blended composition of the bulk recycling input adjusted by the feed of different scrap types.

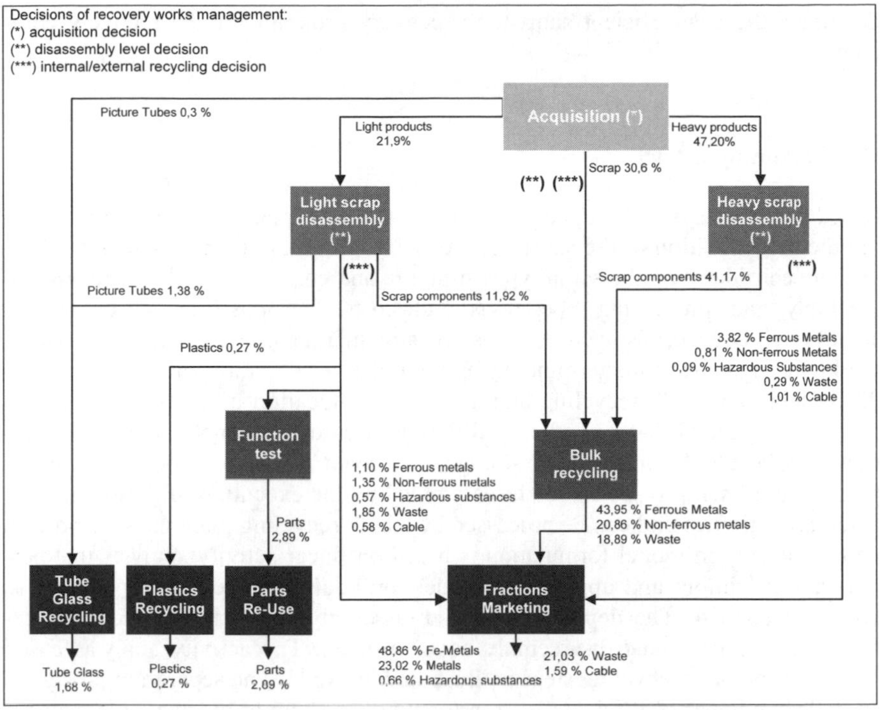

Fig. 6. Material flows in recovery centre

The three planning problems "choice of scrap types to recover" (*), "disassembly operations" (**) and "internal/external treatment" (***) have to be solved daily by the same person, i.e. the recovery works manager. They show a complex interaction and are dependent on the daily situation. Thus, the application of an integrated short term planning model is advisable. Relevant publications that deal with recycling planning (Lund et al. 1994, Sodhi et al. 1999, Stuart and Lu 2000a,b) can not directly be applied to this complex planning problem due to the following aspects:

- The company has to actively acquire scrap. Thus, it is advisable to additionally apply methods used in the operations management for the determination of master production schedules.
- The consideration of the impact of input composition in combination with the basic engineering foundations of the processes in every single separation unit seems to be advisable due to the capacity constraints of these units.
- The interactions of subsequent recovery processes have to be considered.

Therefore, a new mixed-integer linear programming method for integrated disassembly and bulk recycling planning problems has been developed. It is applied to determine the cost-efficient short term recovery program for the recovery company.

5.2. Planning model

Based on the analysis of recovery operations, the daily planning problem concerning the determination of the short term recovery program becomes apparent: Taking into consideration the scrap types structure and composition, the different disassembly and processing operations and costs, the possible reuse options, achievable proceeds as well as capacity and market constraints, the recovery works manager has to determine an optimal choice of scrap types to recover in disassembly and bulk recycling and an optimal allocation of disassembly operations. It is assumed that a number of different discarded products, parts and materials i are available in the input storage at a given negative or positive transfer price. These I scrap types can be disassembled by the execution of J different disassembly activities and can be processed by a bulk recycling plant using K process units. The chosen model formulation is based on linear activity analysis that permits a very simple and appropriate model formulation of recovery planning as seen in section 4. The depiction of the disassembly sector in the model corresponds to the presented disassembly equation (4.3). The activity analysis based model for the bulk recycling steps is illustrated in Fig. 7. The separation process is modelled by linear coefficients u_{kl} representing the share of the available material l in the input of the unit k that is directed into the material fraction l of this unit, e.g. a share of 0,75 from the available ferrous metals (l=3) is removed in the magnet 1 (k=2) (see Fig. 7). Since the units are arranged in sequence, the input masses of the following units can be calculated by the mass balance equations for each unit and material fraction.

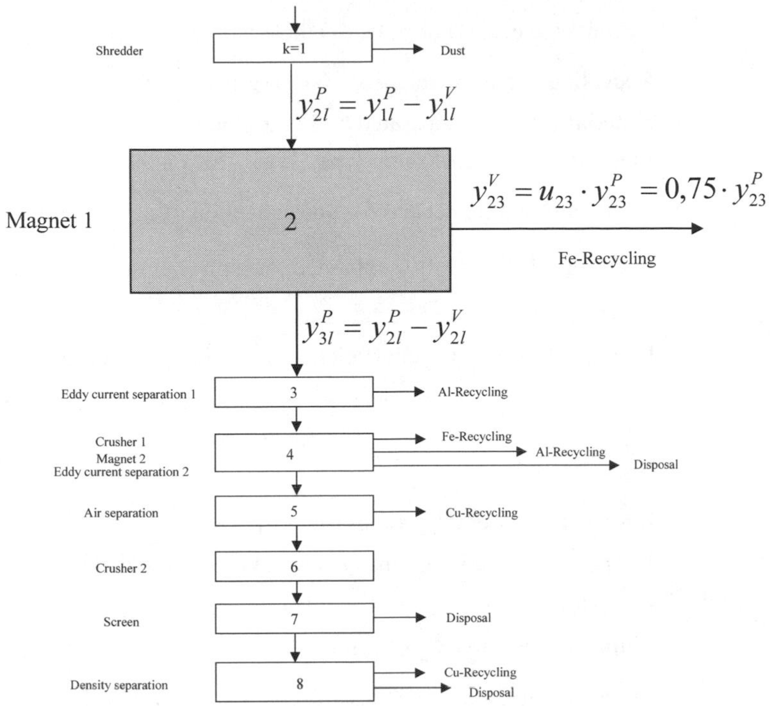

Fig. 7. Model of bulk recycling – separation depiction of unit magnet (k=2) to remove ferrous metals (l=3)

The following notation is used:

Indices

i:	Index of scrap type ($i \in \{1,...,I\}$): products, parts, materials
j:	Index of disassembly activity $j \in \{1,...,J\}$
k:	Index of unit operation $k \in \{1,...,K\}$
l:	Index of material $l \in \{1,...,L\}$

Parameters and Coefficients

a_{il}	Composition factor that assigns scrap type i composition to material component l [kg/kg] $(0 \le a_{il} \le 1)$
c_k^P	Bulk recycling cost factor for unit k [€/kg]
c^Z	Disassembly labour cost factor [€/h]
e_i^{Ex}	Cost (-) or price (+) factor for scrap type i to external recycling [€/kg]

e_i^A	Acceptance cost (-) or price (+) factor for scrap type i [€/kg]
e_{kl}^V	Recycling material sale cost (-) or price (+) factor of isolated material fraction l separated by separation unit k [€/kg]
m_i	Mass of one piece of scrap type i [kg] $(m_i > 0)$
t_j^Z	Disassembly time needed for one execution of activity j [h/act]
u_{kl}	Fraction of material l extracted at unit operation k [kg/kg] $(0 \le u_{kl} \le 1)$
v_{ij}	Disassembly activity coefficient for the input (-) or output (+) masses of scrap type i caused by one execution of activity j [kg/act]

Limits

$T^{\max}$	Limit for disassembly labour time [h]
$y_i^{A,\max}$	Limit for the maximum mass of scrap type i that can be obtained from storage [kg]
$y_i^{Ex,\max}$	Limit for sale capacity of scrap type i to external recycling [kg]
$y_k^{P,\max}$	Limit for equipment capacity of separation unit k [kg]
$y_{kl}^{V,\max}$	Limit for sale capacity of isolated material fraction l separated by separation unit k [kg]

Variables

x_j	Integer decision variable for the number of executions of disassembly activity j [act]
y_i^A	Decision variable for the mass of scrap type i that is taken from storage to be processed [kg]
y_i^D	Variable for the mass of scrap type i after disassembly [kg]
y_i^{Ex}	Variable for the mass of scrap type i to external recycling [kg]
y_i^{In}	Decision variable for the mass of scrap type i to internal recycling [kg]
y_{kl}^P	Variable for the mass of material component l in the mixture that is treated in separation unit k [kg]
y_{kl}^V	Variable for the mass of isolated material fraction l separated by separation unit k [kg]

Based on these notations the decision problem can be formulated as a mixed-integer linear programming (MILP) model:

$$\underset{\substack{y_1^A,\ldots,y_I^A;\\ x_1,\ldots,x_J;\\ y_1^{In};\ldots;y_I^{In}}}{MAX} \sum_{i=1}^{I}(y_i^A \cdot e_i^A + y_i^{Ex} \cdot e_i^{Ex}) + \sum_{k=1}^{K}\sum_{l=1}^{L} y_{kl}^V \cdot e_{kl}^V \tag{5.1}$$

$$-\sum_{j=1}^{J} x_j \cdot t_j^Z \cdot c^Z - \sum_{k=1}^{K} c_k^P \cdot \left(\sum_{l=1}^{L} y_{kl}^P\right)$$

subject to:

$$y_i^D = y_i^A + \sum_{j=1}^{J} x_j \cdot v_{ij} \qquad i = 1,\ldots,I \tag{5.2}$$

$$y_i^D = y_i^{Ex} + y_i^{In} \qquad i = 1,\ldots,I \tag{5.3}$$

$$y_i^{In} \begin{cases} = 0 & \text{if i contains hazardous substances} \\ \geq 0 & \text{else} \end{cases} \qquad i = 1,\ldots,I \tag{5.4}$$

$$y_{kl}^P = \begin{cases} \sum_{i=1}^{I} a_{il} \cdot y_i^{In} & \text{if } k = 1 \\ y_{(k-1)l}^P - y_{(k-1)l}^V & \text{if } k = 2,\ldots,K \end{cases} \qquad l = 1,\ldots,L \tag{5.5}$$

$$y_{kl}^V = u_{kl} \cdot y_{kl}^P \qquad k = 1,\ldots,K \; l = 1,\ldots,L \tag{5.6}$$

$$y_i^A \leq y_i^{A,\max} \qquad i = 1,\ldots,I \tag{5.7}$$

$$y_i^{Ex} \leq y_i^{Ex,Max} \qquad i = 1,\ldots,I \tag{5.8}$$

$$y_{kl}^V \leq y_{kl}^{V,\max} \qquad k = 1,\ldots,K \; l = 1,\ldots,L \tag{5.9}$$

$$\sum_{l=1}^{L} y_{kl}^P \leq y_k^{P,\max} \qquad k = 1,\ldots,K \tag{5.10}$$

$$\sum_{j=1}^{J} x_j \cdot t_j^Z \leq T^{\max} \tag{5.11}$$

$$\frac{y_i^A}{m_i}; \frac{y_i^{Ex}}{m_i} \in IN_0 \qquad i = 1,\ldots,I \tag{5.12}$$

$$x_j \in IN_0 \qquad j = 1,\ldots,J \tag{5.13}$$

The objective function (5.1) maximizes the total achievable marginal income subject to mass balance equations and capacity constraints for disassembly and bulk recycling. It results from acceptance revenues/costs, disassembly output revenues/costs, bulk recycling output revenues/costs, variable disassembly costs and variable unit costs. The three short term decision questions are depicted by these decision variables (see Fig. 8):

- the "mass of scrap type *i* that is taken from storage to be processed" y_i^A,
- the "number of executions of disassembly activity *j*" x_j and
- the "mass of scrap type *i* to internal recycling" y_i^{In}.

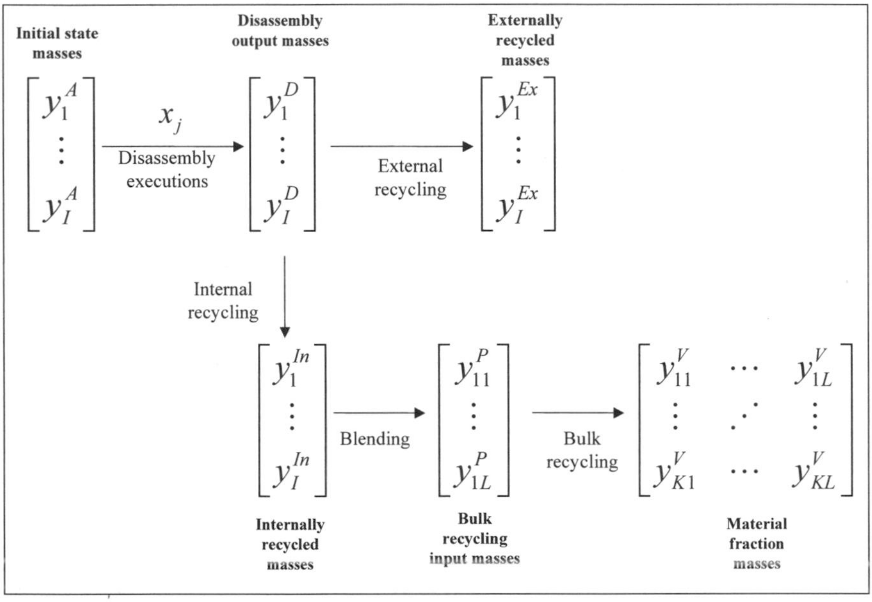

Fig. 8. Model of material flows

Disassembly operations are modelled with the number of executions of the disassembly of this activity x_j and linear input-output coefficients v_{ij} that represent the input-output-relationships of the disassembly activities shown in Table 1 in the appendix (5.2). The obtained disassembly output y_i^D has to be directed either to external or to internal treatment (5.3). The mandatory removal of hazardous substances before the treatment in bulk recycling is forced by the setting $y_i^{In} = 0$ initiating external treatment for scrap types *i* that contain hazardous substances (5.4). It is assumed that disassembly output to internal treatment y_i^{In} is completely processed in the bulk recycling units. At the moment of destruction in the first unit shredder, the composition coefficients a_{il} assign the scrap types *i* to a material component l. The input masses of the other units can be calculated by the mass balance equations for each unit (5.5). The separation units are described by linear coefficients u_{kl} (5.6). The values of u_{kl} have been determined by empirical data. Based on this, the values of the other variables are determined by the constraints. Capacity restrictions represent input supply capacity (5.7) as well as output sales capacity (5.8) (5.9). Capacity constraints in bulk recycling must be depicted by limits for every unit, since bottlenecks can appear in every unit due to variations in feed composition (5.10). The disassembly capacity restriction refers to the maximum of labour time of the available workers (5.11). Disassembly activities as well as the number of discarded products and parts are modelled as integer variables (5.12) (5.13), since the dismantling of a discarded product can not be split. A detailed description of the model can be found in (Spengler et al. 2003).

5.3. Planning data

As discussed in subsection 4.3, the external information needed by the recovery company consists of market and product structure data. Collaborating in a closed loop supply chain, manufacturing companies are sending market data like scrapped product offers, reusable part demands and market prices to the recovery company. A practical scheme for the transmission may be the communication platform that has been presented in subsection 3.3. The offers, demands and prices from different customers have to be aggregated in the recovery company. Recycling-relevant product information can be delivered by means of the "recycling passport" (see subsection 3.2). It allows to derive a range of possible disassembly operations as well as an inventory of material composition. Thus the product parameters v_{ij} and a_{il} in the optimization model can be determined. The concept to gain planning data from the recycling passport is illustrated on the basis of a reference product. For that purpose a reference "personal computer" has been selected for which the required information will be collected and integrated into the prototype data base. The reference device has a size of about 400x180x600 mm^3 and a total weight of 10kg. It has been determined that materials recycling in combination with component reuse would be the appropriate recovery strategy. Concerning the given recycling passport in Fig. 9, a possible structure of mandatory and optional recovery operations can be seen in Fig. 10. A "personal computer" chosen from the discarded products range must be opened and the harmful part "battery" has to be removed. The option to recover spare parts can be exercised if there is a market or a supply chain demand for these parts. Residues can be treated in bulk recycling in order to recover metals or can be marketed externally.

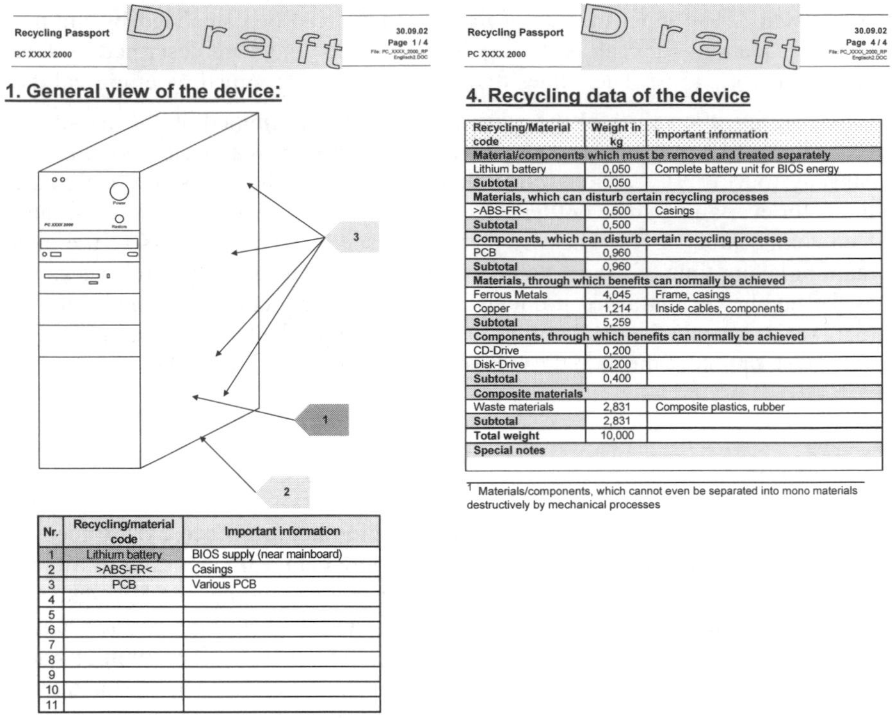

Recycling Passport PC XXXX 2000 — Draft — 30.09.02 Page 1/4

1. General view of the device:

Nr.	Recycling/material code	Important information
1	Lithium battery	BIOS supply (near mainboard)
2	>ABS-FR<	Casings
3	PCB	Various PCB
4		
5		
6		
7		
8		
9		
10		
11		

Recycling Passport PC XXXX 2000 — Draft — 30.09.02 Page 4/4

4. Recycling data of the device

Recycling/Material code	Weight in kg	Important information
Material/components which must be removed and treated separately		
Lithium battery	0,050	Complete battery unit for BIOS energy
Subtotal	0,050	
Materials, which can disturb certain recycling processes		
>ABS-FR<	0,500	Casings
Subtotal	0,500	
Components, which can disturb certain recycling processes		
PCB	0,960	
Subtotal	0,960	
Materials, through which benefits can normally be achieved		
Ferrous Metals	4,045	Frame, casings
Copper	1,214	Inside cables, components
Subtotal	5,259	
Components, through which benefits can normally be achieved		
CD-Drive	0,200	
Disk-Drive	0,200	
Subtotal	0,400	
Composite materials[1]		
Waste materials	2,831	Composite plastics, rubber
Subtotal	2,831	
Total weight	10,000	
Special notes		

[1] Materials/components, which cannot even be separated into mono materials destructively by mechanical processes

Fig. 9. Recycling passport for personal computer (based on: Dietrich 1999)

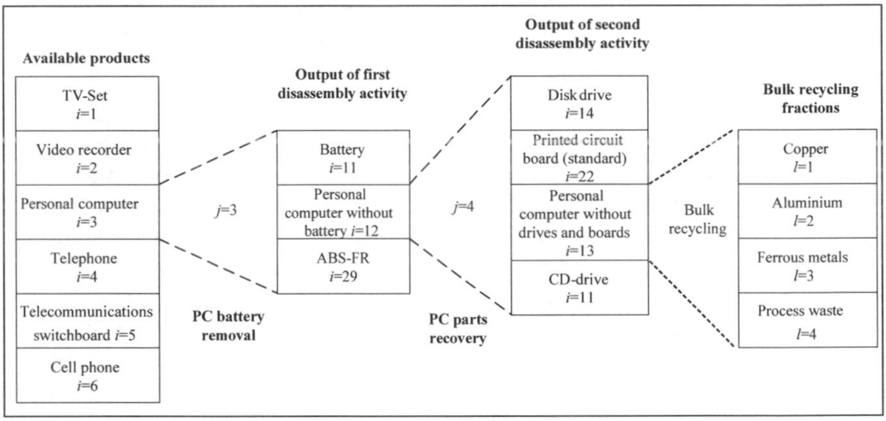

Fig. 10. Processing operations

Using the recycling passport data as shown in Fig. 9, the activity analysis based model of the disassembly step can be determined. The input of the first mandatory disassembly activity is the "personal computer" with a mass of 10 kg. The output consists of a "battery" of 0,05 kg (taken directly from recycling passport), "ABS-FR" from casings of 0,5 kg (taken directly from recycling passport) and a "personal computer without battery" of 9,45 kg (the difference between input and other output parts). This last item is input of the second disassembly activity that results in a "disk-drive" of 0,2 kg, "PCB" of 0,96 kg and a CD-drive of 0,2 kg. These masses can be taken directly from the passport. The mass of the "personal computer without drives and boards" is determined by the difference between input and other output parts. Thus the disassembly activities are defined by:

$$v_1 = \begin{pmatrix} -10 \\ 9{,}45 \\ 0 \\ 0{,}05 \\ 0{,}5 \\ 0 \\ 0 \\ 0 \end{pmatrix} \quad v_2 = \begin{pmatrix} 0 \\ -9{,}45 \\ 8{,}09 \\ 0 \\ 0 \\ 0{,}2 \\ 0{,}96 \\ 0{,}2 \end{pmatrix} \tag{5.14}$$

where the components v_{ij} define the impact on the activity vector v^r [kg] of the recovery company r per execution of disassembly activity v_j (see 4.2):

$$\begin{pmatrix} \text{Personal Computer} \\ \text{Personal Computer without battery} \\ \text{Personal Computer without drives and boards} \\ \text{Battery} \\ \text{ABS}-\text{FR} \\ \text{Disk}-\text{drive} \\ \text{PCB} \\ \text{CD}-\text{Drive} \end{pmatrix}$$

The input of the first mandatory disassembly activity is the "personal computer". The "personal computer without drives and boards" consists of the "ferrous metals" (4,045 kg), "copper" (1,214 kg) and "waste materials (2,831 kg)" as seen in the recycling passport. Thus the composition factors a_{il} for this scrap type can be calculated using recycling passport data as well:

$$a_i = \begin{pmatrix} 1{,}214/(1{,}214+0+4{,}045+2{,}831) \\ 0/(1{,}214+0+4{,}045+2{,}831) \\ 4{,}045/(1{,}214+0+4{,}045+2{,}831) \\ 2{,}831/(1{,}214+0+4{,}045+2{,}831) \end{pmatrix} = \begin{pmatrix} 0{,}15 \\ 0 \\ 0{,}5 \\ 0{,}35 \end{pmatrix} \tag{5.15}$$

where the components a_{il} define the shares of: $\begin{pmatrix} \text{Cu} \\ \text{Al} \\ \text{Fe} \\ \text{Waste} \end{pmatrix}$

The composition of the other parts (e.g. "disk-drives") can be taken from a standard components data base. Using these part compositions, one is enabled to calculate the composition of the assembled scrap types (e.g. "personal computer"). This composition is needed to depict the shredding of these scrap types without disassembly.

5.4. Results and discussion

The optimization and data model that has been presented in the previous subsections has been verified in example calculations with given planning data concerning a range of 6 typical discarded products as visualized in Table 1, 2 and 3 in the Appendix section. A 3).

The mixed-integer linear optimization model consists of 70 Integer Variables, 226 Non-Integer Variables and 328 Constraints. It has been solved by the application of the standard optimization software LINGO that uses Branch-and-Bound Techniques and that provides a quick solution for the given problem complexity. The optimal short term recovery program that is determined consists of a calculated choice of recovered scrap in disassembly and bulk recycling as well as of an optimal allocation of disassembly operations.

All available "TV-sets" (i=1) are taken and disassembly (j=1) is enforced. The subsequent parts like "picture tubes" (i=10), "housing parts" (i=16) and "cheap circuit boards" (i=21) are marketed externally. A share of the obtained "mixed entertainment electronic parts" (i=15) is treated internally, another share of them is treated externally due to the capacity restrictions in the bulk recycling units. "Video recorders" (i=2), which are all accepted, are sent to bulk recycling directly. Only a fraction of available "personal computers" (i=3) is taken. This quantity is limited by the market restriction for "CD-drives" (i=11). Mandatory disassembly (j=3) is done and the "battery" (i=7) is sent to a recycling specialist. The resulting parts from the operation spare part recovery (j=4) – "disk-drives" (i=14), "CD-drives" (i=11) and "standard circuit boards" (i=22) – are marketed externally. The entire amount of "telephones" (i=4) are also accepted and sent immediately to bulk recycling (j=5). "Telecommunication switchboards" (i=5) are all taken and disassembled (j=6,7) to recover "precious circuit boards" (i=20) for sale. The "accumulators" (i=9) of taken "cell phones" (i=6) need to be removed (j=9) and treated by specialists. Further disassembly (j=10) of cell phones is not recommended. The objective function represents a value of about 3,000 € per daily planning period. The main contribution to the objective value results from acceptance fee revenues.

The presented optimization model provides practicable decision support since the solution outperforms intuitive concepts that have been used so far. Concerning the total achievable marginal income, a benefit of at least 10% compared to intuitive strategies that have been applied in the considered recovery company has been reached in all market situations. The integer constraints in the present model formulation are not essential, since there are only minor changes of the objective function value in the mixed-integer linear program and the related LP-relaxation.

6. Perspective

In order to take advantage of the potentials arising in closed loop supply chains, the development and implementation of adequate information management and planning instruments are essential factors of success. Upcoming European legislation that extends the product responsibility into the after-use phase, supports the integration of recovery companies into the producer's supply chain. It can be expected that there will be a rising number of collaborative partnerships between producers and recovery companies in order to efficiently meet the stated requirements. Here the presented concept can contribute to an effective management of these closed loop supply chains.

The presented approach for a communication platform will have to be completed in order to coordinate producers or suppliers demand planning and the recovery program planning of the recycling company. Thus the development of interfaces to the information systems of producers and recovery companies is a necessary step ahead. It has to be examined if the use of standard software like Enterprise Resource Planning (ERP) or Advanced Planning Systems (APS) could be a practical and suitable solution.

Acknowledgement

This article is based on the work realized within the project "Substance Flow Oriented Closed loop Supply Chain Management in the Electrical and Electronic Equipment Industry" (StreaM) which is kindly sponsored by the German Ministry of Education and Research under the label 01RU0036. The authors thank the sponsor for his support in the name of all participants.

References

BVSE (1999): Elektronikschrottrecycling: Fakten, Zahlen und Verfahren.

Debreu, G. (1959): Theory of Value, New Haven.

Dietrich, K.H. (1999): Recyclinggerechte Produktgestaltung im Unternehmen Agfa-Gevaert AG. In: VDI-Berichte 1479, Düsseldorf, pp. 19-26.

Dyckhoff, H. (1994): Betriebliche Produktion: Theoretische Grundlagen einer umweltorientierten Produktionswirtschaft, 2.Auflage, Springer, Berlin.

European Commission (2000): "Proposal for a Directive of the European Parliament and of the Council on waste electrical and electronic equipment" and "Proposal for a Directive of the European Parliament and of the Council on the restriction of the use of certain hazardous substances in electrical and electronic equipment". COM(2002) 347 final, Brussels, June 13th 2000.

Fandel, G. (1990): Aktivitätsanalytische Fundierung der Produktionstheorie. Diskussionsbeitrag des Fachbereichs Wirtschaftswissenschaft der Fernuniversität Hagen, Hagen.

Hesselbach, J., Herrmann, C., Ohlendorf, M., Graf, R. (2001a): Approach of Substance Flow Oriented Closed Loop Supply Chain Management in the Electrical and Electronic Equipment Industry. In: Proceedings of EcoDesign '01 (IEEE), Tokyo, pp. 725-728.

Hesselbach, J., Spengler, T., Graf, R., Ploog, M. (2001b): Materialkreisläufe schließen. In: VDI-Umwelt, 4/5: pp. 37-39.

Koopmans, T. (1951): Efficient Allocation of Resources. In: Econometrica 19, pp. 455-465.

Krikke, H., Pappis, C.P., Tsoulfas, G.T., Bloemhof-Ruwaard, J.M. (2002): Extended Design Principles for Closed Loop Supply Chains: Optimising Economic, Logistic and Environmental Performance. In: Klose, A, Speranza, M.G., Wassenhove, van L.N. (eds.) Quantitative Approaches to Distribution Logistics and Supply Chain Management, Springer Verlag, Berlin et al., pp. 61-74.

Lund, J.R., Tchobanoglous, G., Anex, R.P., Lawyer, R.A., (1994): Linear Programming for Analysis of Material Recycling Facilities. In: Journal of Environmental Engineering, 5, pp. 1082-1094.

Oenning, A. (1997): Theorie betrieblicher Kuppelproduktion. Physica-Verlag, Heidelberg.

Rüdiger, C. (2000): Betriebliches Stoffstrommanagement. Deutscher Universitäts Verlag, Wiesbaden.

Schneider, B. (1999): Recycling-Informationssysteme: Integration von Produktion und Recycling. Diss., Münster.

Shapiro J.F. (2001): Modeling the Supply Chain. Duxbury, Pacific Grove

Simchi-Levi, D., Kaminsky, P., Simchi-Levi, E. (2000): Designing and Managing the Supply Chain. McGraw-Hill, Boston et al.

Sodhi, M. S., Young, J., Knight, W.A. (1999): Modelling material separation processes in bulk recycling. In: International Journal of Production Research, 37, pp. 2239-2252.

Souren, R. (2002): Konsumgüterverpackungen in der Kreislaufwirtschaft. Deutscher Universitäts Verlag, Wiesbaden.

Spengler, T. (1998): Industrielles Stoffstrommanagement, Betriebswirtschaftliche Planung und Steuerung von Stoff- und Energieströmen in Produktionsunternehmen, Erich-Schmidt-Verlag, Berlin.

Spengler, T., Stölting, W. (2003): Recycling Oriented Information Management in Closed Loop Supply Chains in the Electrical and Electronic Equipment Industry. In: Seuring S., Müller M., Goldbach M., Schneidewind U. (eds.) Strategy and Organization in Supply Chains, Physica Verlag, Heidelberg, to be published in Spring 2003.

Spengler, T., Ploog, M., Schröter, M. (2003): Integrated Planning of Acquisition, Disassembly and Bulk Recycling: A Case Study On Electronic Scrap Recovery . To appear in: OR Spectrum, Vol. 25, 3/2003.

Spengler, T., Schröter, M., Stölting, W. (2002): Bereitstellung recyclingrelevanter Produktdaten im Rahmen eines stoffstrombasierten Supply Chain Managements. In: Dangelmaier W., Emmrich A., Kaschula D. (eds.) Modelle im E-Business (Models in E-Business), ALB-HNI-Verlagsschriftenreihe, Bd. 8, Paderborn, pp. 301-315.

Spengler, T., Püchert, H., Penkuhn, T., Rentz O. (1997): Environmental Integrated Production and Recycling Management. In: European Journal of Operational Research, 97, pp. 308-326.

Stadtler, H., Kilger, C. (2000): Supply Chain Management and Advanced Planning. Springer, Berlin.

Stuart, J. A., Lu, Q. (2000a): A Model for Discrete Processing Decisions for Bulk Recycling Of Electronics Equipment. In: IEEE Transactions on Electronics Packaging Manufacturing, 4, pp. 314-320.

Stuart, J. A., Lu, Q. (2000b): A Refine-or-Sell Decision Model for a Station with Continuous Reprocessing Options in an Electronics Recycling Center. In: IEEE Transactions on Electronics Packaging Manufacturing, 4, pp. 321-327.

Thierry, M., Salomon, M., Nunen, van J., Wassenhove, van L. (1995): Strategic Issues in Product Recovery Management. In: California Management Review, Vol. 37, 2/1995, pp. 114-135.

Appendix: Selected Planning Data

	Operation	TV dismantling	Video dismantling	PC battery removal	PC parts gaining	Telephone dismantling	Switchboard opening	board removal	Switchboard parts removal	Cell Phone Accu removal	Board removal
	j=	1	2	3	4	5	6	7	8	9	10
	Scrap Type	kg	kg	kg	kg	kg	kg	kg	kg	kg	kg
i=1	TV-set	-25	0	0	0	0	0	0	0	0	0
2	Video recorder	0	-4	0	0	0	0	0	0	0	0
3	Personal Computer	0	0	-10	0	0	0	0	0	0	0
4	Telephone	0	0	0	0	-1,5	0	0	0	0	0
5	Telecommunication switchboard	0	0	0	0	0	-100	0	0	0	0
6	Cell phone	0	0	0	0	0	0	0	0	-0,2	0
7	Battery	0	0	0,05	0	0	0	0	0	0	0
8	Coverings	0	0	0	0	0	5	0	0	0	0
9	Accumulator	0	0	0	0	0	0	0	0	0,1	0
10	Picture tube	13,75	0	0	0	0	0	0	0	0	0
11	CD-Drive	0	0	0	0,2	0	0	0	0	0	0
12	Personal Computer without battery	0	0	9,45	-9,45	0	0	0	0	0	0
13	Personal Computer without drives and boa	0	0	0	8,09	0	0	0	0	0	0
14	Disk-drive	0	0	0	0,2	0	0	0	0	0	0
15	Mixed entertainment electronics parts	6,25	3,2	0	0	0	0	0	0	0	0
16	Housing parts	3,75	0,4	0	0	0	0	0	0	0	0
17	Telephone back	0	0	0	0	0,6	0	0	0	0	0
18	Cell phone body	0	0	0	0	0	0	0	0	0,1	-0,1
19	Cell phone waste	0	0	0	0	0	0	0	0	0	0,05
20	Printed circuit board (precious)	0	0	0	0	0	0	4,75	0	0	0
21	Printed circuit board (cheap)	1,25	0,4	0	0	0	0	0	0	0	0
22	Printed circuit board (standard)	0	0	0	0,96	0	0	0	0	0	0,05
23	Switch board parts	0	0	0	0	0	0	0	9,025	0	0
24	Telephone front	0	0	0	0	0,45	0	0	0	0	0
25	Telecommunication switchboard (without b	0	0	0	0	0	0	90,25	-90,3	0	0
26	Telecommunication switchboard (open)	0	0	0	0	0	95	-95	0	0	0
27	Telecommunication switchboard (frame)	0	0	0	0	0	0	0	81,23	0	0
28	Telephone receiver	0	0	0	0	0,45	0	0	0	0	0
29	ABS-FR	0	0	0,5	0	0	0	0	0	0	0
30	Waste	0	0	0	0	0	0	0	0	0	0
	Cost Factor [€/execution]	2,5	0,75	0,75	0,5	0,15	0,25	1,25	1,25	0,125	0,375

Table 1. Disassembly data

	Index	Acceptance price	Available mass	Mass per device	Material composition			
	i	[€/kg]	[kg/day]	[kg/item]	Cu	Al	Fe	Waste
TV-set	1	0,625	3000	25	3%	0%	13%	85%
Video	2	0,3	2000	4	9%	0%	40%	51%
PC	3	0,1	2000	10	15%	0%	47%	38%
Telephone	4	0,25	600	1,5	9%	0%	8%	84%
Switchboard	5	0	2000	100	11%	10%	62%	17%
Cell phone	6	1	500	0,2	5%	0%	0%	95%

Table 2. Product data

			External recycling price	External recycling restriction
i	**Parts from disassembly**		[€/kg]	[kg/day]
11	CD-Drive	Part	5	6
14	Disk-drive	Part	1	5
20	Printed circuit board (precious)	Part	1	none
22	Printed circuit board (standard)	Part	0,5	none
l	**Materials from bulk recycling**		[€/kg]	[kg/day]
1	Copper (from density separation)	Fraction	1,5	none
2	Aluminium (from eddy current separation)	Fraction	1	none
3	Ferrous-metals (from magnet 1)	Fraction	0,05	none
4	Process waste (from shredding dust separation)	Fraction	-0,15	none

Table 3. Output data

Product Recovery Behaviour in a Closed Loop Supply Chain

Karl Inderfurth

Department of Production and Logistics
Faculty of Economics and Management
Otto-von-Guericke-University Magdeburg
P.O. Box 41 20
D-39016 Magdeburg, Germany

Abstract: *Product recovery is an emerging business area which is attractive from both an economic and an environmental point of view. It is investigated to which extent profit orientation in product recovery management will or will not stimulate an environmentally conscious behaviour. This study refers to a product recovery system where a manufacturer of original products is also engaged in remanufacturing used products taken back from its customers. For this type of a closed loop supply chain, which additionally is characterized by uncertainty of demands and product returns, the optimal recovery and production policy is evaluated. By a numerical analysis, it is shown how cost-efficient decision-making affects the product recovery behaviour. In a sensitivity analysis, it is evaluated how various problem determinants influence the preference for product recovery under conditions of uncertainty. Exploiting the respective insights, it is discussed which measures can be taken to harmonize economical and environmental-driven behaviour in product recovery management.*

Keywords: *closed loop systems, product recovery behaviour, remanufacturing processes*

1. Introduction

Due to both economic incentives and legal pressure, more and more companies are going to be engaged in the product recovery business which concerns all activities associated with regaining materials and value added out of used products. A very important field of product recovery is remanufacturing which refers to those activities that bring used products or their major modules back to such a condition that recovered items are just as good as new. This is widely found for high-valued industrial products like copiers, computers, vehicle engines, or medical equipment. Over the past years remanufacturing developed into a fast growing business which is even passing traditional industries of the 'old economy' (Guide, 2000, pp. 467-483). In many industries, original equipment manufactures (OEMs) are also active in the remanufacturing business because of their specific know-how in products and markets. In this case, OEMs not only act as suppliers in a forward logistics chain, but they also organize reverse logistics operations concerning collection and recovery of used products. By bringing remanufactured goods back to customer markets, these OEMs directly establish links between forward and reverse logistics activities, thus building up and operating closed loop supply chains (CLSC).

From a company's point of view, it is mainly the profitability of the remanufacturing business, which is the driver of its engagement in this sector (Guide, 2000, pp. 467-483). This also holds for countries where environmental-oriented legislation forces companies to pay attention to an extended product responsibility and take care of reintegrating their products into the supply chain after customer usage. Respective governmental actions may affect relevant prices (e.g. for waste disposal) or determine management restrictions (e.g. fixed recycling quotas). However, to which extend product recovery is carried out by companies will eventually be determined by the profits they can expect from these activities. Fortunately, as we see from the progress of the remanufacturing business, economic and environmental interests can – at least partly – coincide. However, in order to gain insight into how far environmental-friendly behaviour is triggered by economic incentives, it has to be investigated up to which level product recovery can be a profitable way of dealing with used products. In this way, it can become more clear to which extent environmentally conscious manufacturing and product recovery is not only a matter of a company's attitude towards supporting the environment but also a consequence of its intention to make profits (Gungor and Gupta, 1999, pp. 811-853).

Following common economic reasoning, profitability will mainly depend on costs for production and product recovery processes and on market prices for respective process inputs and outputs. However, simple cost and price comparisons are not sufficient for explaining the product recovery behaviour in total. This is because such a view disregards uncertainty, which has a major influence on product recovery decisions. From practical experience it is known that uncertainty is a highly important factor companies face in product recovery management (Thierry, 1997, and Guide, 2000, pp. 467-483). In addition to demand uncertainty from forward logistics, managers of closed loop supply chains have to deal with even more considerable uncertainties referring to timing, quantity and quality of returned products. Thus, product recovery management has to cope with a highly uncertain environment, which has to be taken into account in decision-making.

In this contribution, an analysis will be given in which way specifically this uncertainty will affect the product recovery behaviour. This investigation will address the impact of source and level of uncertainty itself as well as the impact of other input parameters, which are known with certainty but may influence the effect of uncertain inputs. The analysis will be presented for a closed loop system of an OEM who is collecting and remanufacturing (part of) its used products. In such a system product recovery management faces the challenging problem of coordinating production, remanufacturing and disposal decisions, which aim to fulfil customer demands for serviceable products in a most economical way. Apparently, solving this decision problem under major uncertainties concerning demands for new products and returns of used ones is an extremely complicated task. In this context, it is by no means obvious how different sources and levels of uncertainty affect the recovery behaviour, i.e. specifically the tendency to remanufacture used products for re-use purposes instead of disposing them.

In order to analyse the respective effects, a model-based approach is chosen. To this end, a basic model of a hybrid production and remanufacturing system will be introduced which includes uncertainty by describing demands and returns as stochastic processes. By deriving the optimal policy in a stationary multi-period setting, it becomes visible how remanufacturing is coordinated with production and disposal decisions in a stochastic environment. However, through complexity of interdependencies, it is not possible to give analytical insights into how optimal product recovery activities depend on different problem parameters. Therefore, a numerical study is carried out which reveals how product recovery behaviour is affected by stochastic and non-stochastic model inputs under qualitative and quantitative aspects.

2. A stochastic CLSC decision model

The model to be formulated will be used to provide some insight into the structure of an optimal coordination of production, remanufacturing and disposal decisions in a stochastic multi-period setting. In a second step, knowledge of the policy structure will be used to investigate the influence of different model parameters on the level of product recovery activities.

We address a typical CLSC situation where an OEM is engaged in remanufacturing used products, which are returned by the customers. Both demands for serviceable products and returns of used products are considered to be stochastic. Product returns consist of items, which after coming back from customers and after being inspected turn out to be in such a condition that they can be remanufactured to serviceable items again. Thus besides production of original items, remanufacturing provides a second source of creating serviceable products which are assumed to be made to stock in order to satisfy stochastic customer demands. It has to be noted that both production and remanufacturing of items will take certain processing times, and that these lead-times may be different for the two processes. Since the inflow of returns is not under management control in such a CLSC, a disposal option for treating returned items is reasonable in order to avoid (excessive) stocks of remanufacturables in case of mismatch of return and demand quantities. It has to be noted that disposal of a product does not necessarily mean that the respective item will be landfilled or incinerated. The disposal option can also reflect a lower-value recovery option like materials recycling. The general structure of the CLSC as considered in this paper is illustrated in Fig. 1.

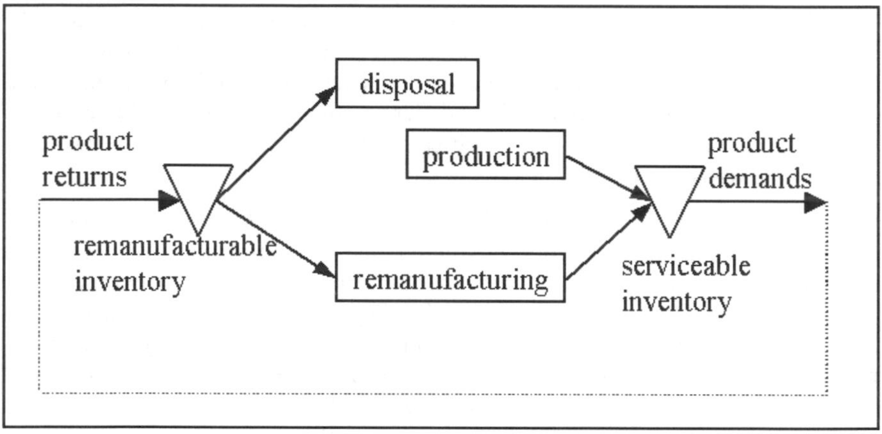

Fig. 1. CLSC structure with remanufacturing

The managerial objective is to run the CLSC system in a most economical way, i.e. such that the total relevant costs are minimized. Costs arise from production, remanufacturing and disposal activities as well as from inventory holding and from shortages in demand fulfilment. Disposal costs may be negative (i.e. they represent revenues) if the disposal option reflects material recycling. It is obvious that the CLSC decisions, i.e. production, remanufacturing and disposal, are interrelated. An additional interaction within the CLSC policy has to be taken into account if we consider the decision problem over multiple periods, since in this case CLSC decisions in consecutive periods are depending on each other. It is exactly this challenging decision making situation that will be chosen as basis for the subsequent analysis of product recovery behaviour. To some extent this complex planning problem resembles the task of program planning in joint production where mainly linear programming as recommended supporting decision making

(Fandel, 1988, pp. 130-148). However, these approaches do not appropriately address the impact of uncertainties, which is essential in the product recovery system under consideration.

A growing body of research is emerging in the field of stochastic dynamic CLSC decision problems, the above-described problem belongs to (e.g. Fleischmann et al., 1997, pp. 1-17 and van der Laan et al., 1999, pp. 733-747). Since our purpose is to give a detailed insight into the dependency of optimal recovery decisions on various problem parameters, we will restrict the model under consideration in such a way that the optimal policy has a fairly simple structure, which provides a reasonable basis for a more comprehensive decision analysis. In this context, the main assumption will be that (1) production and remanufacturing lead-times are deterministic and that (2) only proportional costs are considered. Under these conditions it can be shown that the optimal policy in many cases can be characterized by a quite simple structure (Inderfurth, 1997, pp. 111-122).

For describing the model and its solution properties we use the following notation where all variables refer to the beginning of a period.

Decision and state variables:

p : number of originally produced items

r : number of remanufactured items

d : number of disposed items

x_R : on-hand inventory of remanufacturables

x_S : inventory position of serviceables (including on-hand items plus all in-production/remanufacturing-process items minus backorders)

Stochastic variables:

$\tilde{D}$: demand for serviceables per period (independently distributed)

$\tilde{R}$: returns of remanufacturables per period (independently distributed)

Problem data:

μ_D and σ_D : expectation and standard deviation of $\tilde{D}$

μ_R and σ_R : expectation and standard deviation of $\tilde{R}$

c_P : production cost per unit

c_R : remanufacturing cost per unit

c_D : disposal cost per unit

h_R : holding cost of remanufacturables per unit and period

h_S : holding cost of serviceables per unit and period

v : shortage cost of backorders per unit and period

λ_R : remanufacturing lead-time in periods

λ_P : production lead-time in periods

Formulating the multi-period CLSP problem of minimizing total expected costs as a stochastic dynamic decision problem in case of equal lead-times (i.e. $\lambda_R = \lambda_p$) results in a problem description as follows. In each period decisions *p, r* and *d* have to be made which must depend on period-specific state variables x_R and x_S specifying the relevant information at the beginning of a period. For cost minimization the following recursive relationships (Bellman's functional equations) will hold which link the minimum expected costs $f(x_R, x_S)$ of decision processes starting in arbitrary consecutive periods *t* and *t*+1 (Inderfurth, 1997, pp. 111-122):

$$\begin{aligned} f_t(x_R, x_S) = \min_{\substack{p,r,d \\ r+d \le x_R}} \Big\{ & c_P \cdot p + c_R \cdot r + c_D \cdot d + \mathop{\mathrm{E}}_{R}\left[h_R \cdot \left(x_R - r - d + \tilde{R}\right)\right] \\ & + \mathop{\mathrm{E}}_{D^{\lambda+1}}\left[h_S \cdot \left(x_S + p + r - \tilde{D}^{\lambda+1}\right)^+\right] \\ & + \mathop{\mathrm{E}}_{D^{\lambda+1}}\left[v \cdot \left(\tilde{D}^{\lambda+1} - x_S - p - r\right)^+\right] \\ & + \mathop{\mathrm{E}}_{R,D}\left[f_{t+1}\left(x_R - r - d + \tilde{R}, x_S + p + r - \tilde{D}\right)\right] \Big\} \end{aligned} \tag{0.1}$$

Here we use as notation E[.] for the expectation and $(y)^+ = \max\{y, 0\}$. $\tilde{D}^{\lambda+1}$ stands for a sum of $\lambda+1$ stochastic demand variables $\tilde{D}$ where λ represents the (equal) lead-time.

Exploiting the above recursive functions it can be shown that the optimal policy in each period is a quite simple one with three policy parameters *S, M* and *U* (with $S \le M \le U$) which can be interpreted as produce-up-to level *S*, remanufacture-up-to level *M* and a dispose-down-to level *U*. Using these parameters, the complete policy which gives the optimal combination of production, product recovery and disposal decisions in each period, can be described as follows (Inderfurth, 1996):

$$\begin{aligned} p &= \max\{S - (x_R + x_S); 0\} \\ r &= \min\{x_R, \max\{M - x_S; 0\}\} \\ d &= \max\{x_R - \max\{U - x_S; 0\}; 0\} \end{aligned} \tag{0.2}$$

This so-called (*S,M,U*)-policy describes the optimal reaction on the two relevant inventory levels in each period which themselves change over time according to CLSC decisions and stochastic demands and returns. In case that no inventory for remanufacturables exists, all returned items must immediately either be remanufactured or disposed of. In this case, the above policy simplifies insofar as the policy parameters *M* and *U* coincide and the recoverable stock level x_R has to be replaced by the last periods' returns (Inderfurth, 1997, pp. 111-122). In general, the parameters of the (*S,M,U*) policy will depend on all problem data and on the respective time period. Unfortunately, parameters *S, M* and *U* cannot be determined analytically. In case of time-invariant problem data and unlimited planning horizon, the policy parameters will remain constant from period to period. Under this condition only three (stationary) parameters in all have to be computed to describe the optimal decision rule for the multi-period problem.

3. Determinants of product recovery behaviour

Applying the optimal (*S, M, U*) policy will result in certain average production, remanufacturing and disposal quantities per period. The level of remanufacturing is specifically affected by the size of the remanufacturing parameters *M*. However, it also depends on the development of the inventory variables x_R and x_S over time, which itself is determined by the realization of the stochastic return and demand process as well as by the sequence of former production, remanufacturing and disposal decisions. Thus, product recovery is influenced by the uncertainty from return and demand side as well as by all cost and lead-time data going into the computation of the policy parameters *S, M* and *U*.

In the present investigation, product recovery behaviour will be measured by the (expected) fraction of returns, which is not disposed of but used again by remanufacturing. Depending on how far the disposal option is applied this so-called *recovery fraction* (*RF*) will be more or less smaller than one. From an environmental point of view *RF* should have a value of 100%, meaning that all used products which have been collected and are in a recoverable condition will be remanufactured. From an economical sight, remanufacturing only makes sense if there exists a cost advantage over production and if this advantage, in case of a temporary excess of returns over demands, is not compensated by inventory holding costs. Since returns and demands are assumed to be uncertain, the occurrence of excess returns is stochastic and the respective probability will have a major influence on the product recovery behaviour. However, since the optimal policy also is affected by all other problem data in a very complex way, it is not clear what their specific impact on the recovery fraction will be. The subsequent investigation aims to provide a comprehensive insight into this interdependency.

In order to structure the analysis, we introduce a classification with five types of determinants of product recovery behaviour. These types refer to different characteristics like return level, uncertainty, costs, lead-times and supply chain structure, as is pictured in Figure 2.

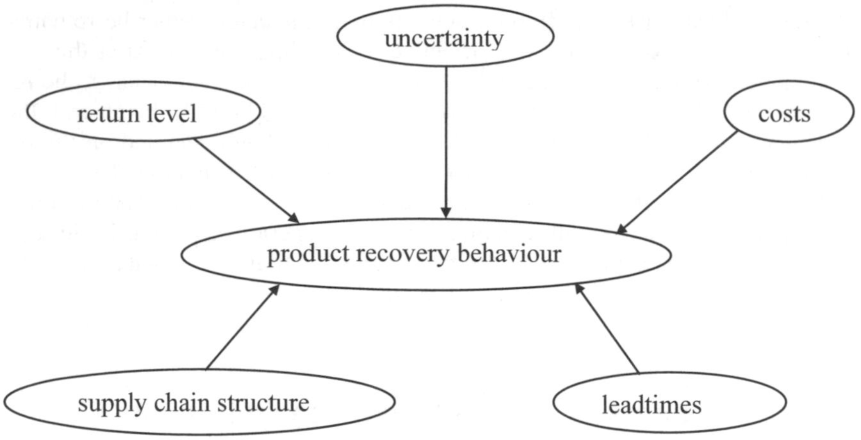

Fig. 2. Types of determinants of product recovery behaviour

Each category from this classification consists of one or more determinants. The first one concerns the relative magnitude of returns, which can be expected to have a major impact on the recovery behaviour. This impact factor can be expressed by the relation of expected returns to expected demands. Using the above table of notation, this so-called *return ratio* (*RR*) is defined as

$$RR = \mu_R / \mu_D .$$

In the group of uncertainty determinants we differ between *return uncertainties*, expressed by the coefficient of variation of returns (CV_R)

$$CV_R = \sigma_R / \mu_R ,$$

and *demand uncertainty*, analogously expressed by

$$CV_D = \sigma_D / \mu_D .$$

Cost characteristics are reflected by two relevant impact factors. Direct costs of activities (c_R, c_P and c_D) are put together to a normalized level of remanufacturing costs called *remanufacturing cost ratio* (*CR*) which is defined by

$$CR = c_R / \left(c_P + c_D \right).$$

This cost parameter measures cost superiority of remanufacturing. Since the alternative to recovery of a returned item is its disposal and the production of a new one, remanufacturing is always advantageous if the cost ratio *CR* is smaller than one, i.e. $c_R < c_P + c_D$. Furthermore, with decreasing *CR* the relative cost advantage of remanufacturing over production is rising. A second cost-related determinant describes the impact of holding cost parameters. The level of holding costs determines the time span for which returned items economically should be kept in stock in case of excess returns, before disposal is the more profitable option. In general, returned products should be stocked either as remanufacturables or as serviceable (after remanufacturing) respectively, depending on which holding cost parameter h_R or h_S is the lower one. Since the cost advantage of remanufacturing one item is $c_P + c_D - c_R$, the critical *holding time HT*, which limits profitability of stock keeping, is

$$HT = (c_P + c_D - c_R) / \min\{h_R, h_S\}$$

Thus, *HT* will be used as second cost factor in order to describe the relevant holding cost impact.

Concerning lead-time aspects, two determinants will be distinguished. The first one is the *lead-time length LL* that will be studied for the standard case when both production and remanufacturing lead-times are equal $(\lambda_P = \lambda_R)$. The second one is the *lead-time deviation* $(LD = \lambda_P - \lambda_R)$. Since the attractiveness of product recovery may not only depend on cost parameters, but also on the time advantage of remanufacturing compared to production, we will analyse the impact of an equal lead-time situation in contrast to an environment where remanufacturing has a lead-time superiority, i.e. $\lambda_R < \lambda_P$ or $LD > 0$, respectively. As final determinant we will consider the *supply chain structure* with respect to the existence of stockholding points *SP*. We will distinguish a supply chain design with two stocking points (i.e. one for serviceable and one for remanufacturables) and a structure where no inventory is provided for returned products (what is equivalent to a situation with extremely high recoverable holding cost, i.e. $h_R \to \infty$). The relevant determinants of product recovery behaviour considered in this study are summarized in Table 1.

Category	**Determinant**	**Definition**
return level	return ratio *RR*	$RR = \mu_R / \mu_D$
uncertainty	return uncertainty CV_R demand uncertainty CV_D	$CV_R = \sigma_R / \mu_R$ $CV_D = \sigma_D / \mu_D$
costs	remanufacturing cost ratio *CR* holding time *HT*	$CR = c_R / (c_P + c_D)$ $HT = (c_P + c_D - c_R) / \min\{h_R, h_S\}$
lead-times	lead-time length *LL* lead-time deviation *LD*	$LL = \lambda_P = \lambda_R$ $LD = \lambda_P - \lambda_R$
supply chain structure	stocking points *SP*	$SP \in \{1, 2\}$

Table 1. Determinants of product recovery behaviour

Since product recovery behaviour is measured by the recovery fraction *RF*, it will be the objective of the subsequent investigation to reveal the dependence of *RF* on the various determinants $(RR, CV_R, CV_D, CR, HT, LL, LD, SP)$.

4. Analysis of product recovery behaviour

4.1. Study design

As mentioned above, a numerical study is necessary to provide insight into product recovery behaviour. To this end, the recursive functions in equ. (0.1) have to be exploited to gain solutions to the optimal remanufacturing policy and thus to be able to determine the recovery fraction which is caused by this policy. For numerical computations a proper discretization of the problem is needed. Even if such a discretization is rather coarse the computational effort is considerable, because the problem in equ. (0.1) is a two-dimensional stochastic dynamic optimisation problem with three decision variables. However, problem solving is facilitated by the knowledge of the (*S, M, U*) structure of the optimal policy. In case of a single stocking point (*SP*=1) the computational burden is even further reduced, since under this condition the problem reduces to an one-dimensional one (only variable x_S is necessary to describe the state of the system) and the optimal policy is more simple since parameters *M* and *U* coincide. In case of lead-time deviation ($LD > 0$) the optimal policy can be extremely complex and the numerical analysis can become intractable due to high-dimensionality of the state space (Inderfurth, 1996). The only exception holds for $LD = 1$ where still a simple policy structure can be shown to be optimal (Inderfurth, 1997, pp. 111-122). Thus in the following study only this situation will be investigated in comparison to the equal-lead-time case $LD = 0$.

In order to concentrate on revealing the main aspects of the recovery behaviour issue without going into excessive computations, some additional limitations are set. We will focus on the stationary product recovery behaviour by assuming an unlimited planning horizon and identically distributed demands and returns through time. Thus we face a stationary optimal policy with three parameters *S*, *M* an *U* being identical for each period. We assume that demands and returns are normally distributed so that they can be specified by their respective means and variances alone. Correlation between demands and returns are not taken into consideration since for the majority of products in the remanufacturing business their useful life with the customer exceeds the planning horizon of the recovery management problems under consideration. Furthermore, under stationary conditions we will not face permanent excess returns. Thus we assume that the mean returns will not be larger than the mean demand per period. Given the above conditions, in all cases of the study numerical optimisation has been carried out by applying the policy improvement technique (e.g. Hillier and Lieberman, 2001, pp. 1064-1073) to the Markovian decision model resulting from the discretization of the stochastic dynamic optimisation problem.

Within the above frame, a wide range of constellations of product recovery determinants will be investigated. The respective parameter spaces are presented in Table 2.

Determinant	Parameter values
return ratio	$0 \le RR \le 1$
return uncertainty	$0 \le CV_R \le 1$
demand uncertainty	$0 \le CV_D \le 1$
reman. cost ratio	$0 \le CR \le 1$
holding time	$0 \le HT \le 5$
lead-time length	$0 \le LL \le 5$
lead-time deviation	$LD \in \{0,1\}$
stocking points	$SP \in \{1,2\}$

Table 2. Parameter values of product recovery determinants

The impact of the various determinants in Table 2 will be investigated separately starting with a base case scenario, which describes a situation where remanufacturing is of moderate profitability and where high return uncertainty is combined with moderate demand uncertainty. The return ratio is fixed in such a way that product recovery can play a major role in satisfying demands for serviceable. For ease of computation the base case reflects the single-stocking point situation, i.e. stock keeping of recoverable is not allowed, or equivalently: $h_R \to \infty$. A complete overview of the base case data and respective values of determinants is given in Table 3.

Base case data	Base case determinants
$\mu_D = 10, \quad \mu_R = 7$	$RR = 0.7$
$\sigma_D = 4, \quad \sigma_R = 7$	$CV_D = 0.4, \quad CV_R = 1.0$
$c_R = 8, \quad c_P = 9, \quad c_D = 1$	$CR = 0.8$
$h_S = 1, \quad h_R \to \infty$	$HT = 2$
$v = 9$	$SP = 1$
$\lambda_R = 2, \quad \lambda_P = 2$	$LD = 0$

Table 3. Base case data and determinants

Given these base case situation, optimisation leads to policy parameters $S = 39$ and $M = U = 48$. The respective policy is connected with a recovery behaviour resulting in an economically optimal recovery fraction of $RF = 0.9$. This shows that, due to profitability reasons, in the long run it does not make sense to recover more than 90 % of all returns if uncertainty is as described in the base case scenario.

4.2. Product recovery behaviour

Before we report the results of the numerical study in order to describe how uncertainty affects recovery behaviour, we first will take a look at the expected outcome if uncertainty would not play any role at all. Under these circumstances (i.e. if $CV_R = CV_D = 0$) it is obvious that product recovery will never be economical if the remanufacturing cost ratio is larger than one (i.e. if $CR > 1$). On the other hand, in case of $CR < 1$ it is profitable to remanufacture *all* returned items as long as no excess returns exist which have to wait more than *HT* periods before they can be used to fulfil customer demands. If the returns are lower than demands in each period (i.e. $RR < 1$), excess returns will not occur, and thus there will be no reason to dispose of any returned product. In this situation, the recovery fraction *RF* will always reach the maximum level of 100%, without regard to the values of the other determinants *HT, LL, LD* and *SP*. Applied to the base case, this means that due to the parameter constellation $RR < 1$ and $CR < 1$ the recovery fraction would amount to RF=1.0 if returns and demands would be deterministic. This makes it clear that the level of uncertainty assumed in the base case scenario is responsible for a 10% loss of recovery volume.

Under uncertainty, all product recovery determinants will affect the amount of reduction in recovery volume in specific ways. In order to reveal these effects, we present a sensitivity analysis in which for each determinant the respective parameter values are changed separately according to the value sets described in Table 2 (holding all other parameters constant). We start with the determinant which is basically responsible for the general product volume which can be used for remanufacturing, i.e. the return ration *RR*. Figure 3 gives an impression of how the return ratio influences the recovery fraction.

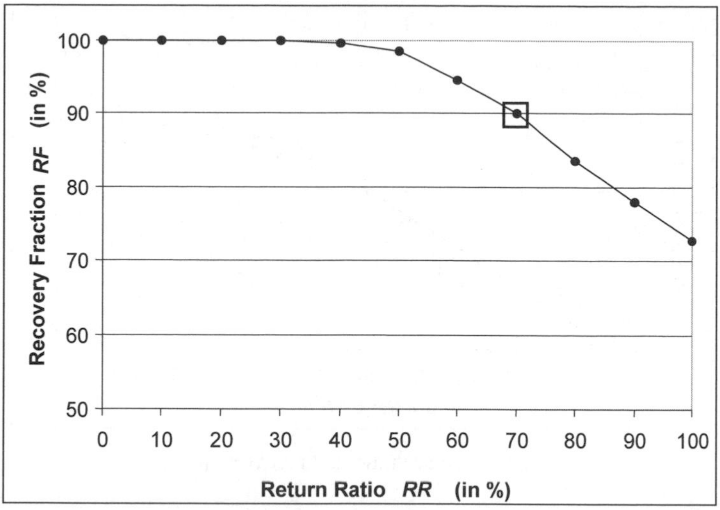

Fig. 3. Return ratio and recovery fraction

It can be seen that for small return ratios (of less than 40%) more or less all returned products would be used for remanufacturing. If the return ratio is increased, the recovery fraction falls below 100% and continues to decrease, first with increasing margins, and for *RR* > 0.6 almost proportional to the return ratio. For *RR* = 0.7 the recovery fraction reaches 90% (this point in Figure 3 is set in a box to show that it represents the base case), and in the extreme case of equality of expected demands and returns (i.e. if *RR* = 1.0) the recovery fraction goes down to 73%. This means that despite of the fact that in the long run all returns can be used for meeting the serviceable' demand, less than 3 out of 4 returned products will really be recovered while the rest will be disposed of. This effect, which is very undesirable from an environmental point of view, is due to the occurrence of temporary excess returns caused by the variability in demand and returns. Amount and duration of excess returns is (for given demand and return variability) growing with increasing return ratio so that (given the 2 periods holding time *HT* in the base case) disposing of returns becomes more and more effective despite of a remanufacturing cost advantage of 20%. The considerable deterioration of product recovery behaviour associated with high return ratios is also visible from Figure 4, which displays how the recovery quota, i.e. the ratio of products recovered and products sold to customers, is developing with increasing return ratio. It becomes obvious that the more recoverable are collected the larger the gap between the maximum (=straight line) and realized (=line with dots) recovery percentage of products in the market will be. This underlines the environmental misbehaviour, which is generated by the way economical-oriented decision making responds to uncertainty.

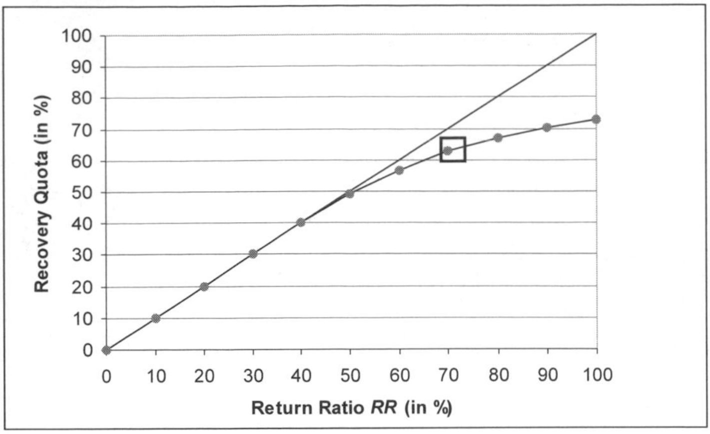

Fig. 4. Return ratio and recovery quota

The next category of determinants that will be investigated is the risk itself, represented by the coefficient of variation regarding returns and demands. In Figure 5 it is shown in which way return uncertainty influences the recovery behaviour.

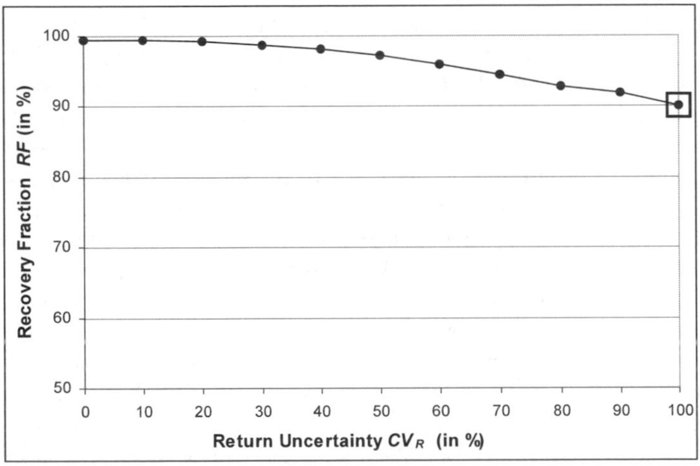

Fig. 5. Return uncertainty and recovery fraction

For the base case scenario a very high level of uncertainty has been chosen by assuming that $CV_R = 1$ meaning that the standard deviation of returns is equal to their expected value. In Figure 5, we find this level as an upper limit and see how the recovery fraction develops when the risk in return variability goes from zero to this limit. It can be seen that the recovery fraction is monotonically decreasing as return uncertainty increases. This outcome is quite logical since increasing uncertainty generates increasing risk of excess returns, which causes increasing disposal activities. What may be surprising is that the decrease of recovery fraction seems to be quite limited and is developing in a nearly linear dependence on return uncertainty. Thus, also in case of extraordinarily high levels of uncertainty regarding returns, the product recovery behaviour is only affected in a moderate degree. However, note that even under deterministic returns the recovery fraction will not reach 100%, but a somewhat smaller level. This is due to the influence of demand variability, which can lead to situations of excess returns even if returns themselves are stable. In detail, the impact of demand uncertainty is shown in Figure 6.

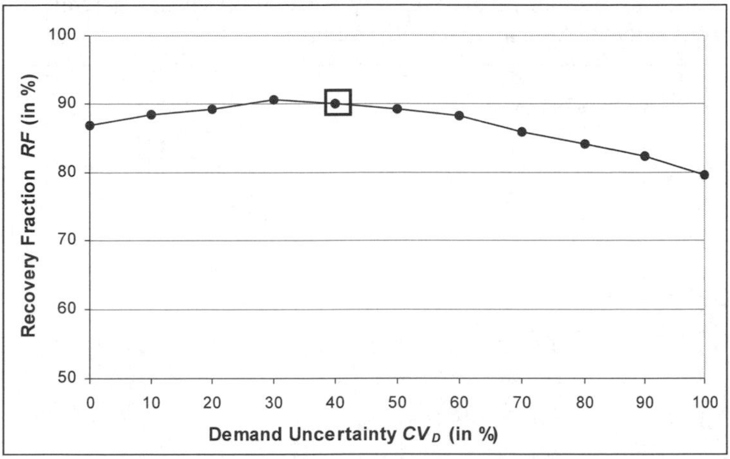

Fig. 6. Demand uncertainty and recovery fraction

The investigation of demand uncertainty leads to a result, which at first glance contradicts intuition, because the recovery fraction is not decreasing monotonically with increasing demand variability. What we see from Figure 6 is that the recovery fraction moves downwards from 90% to 80% as CV_D rises from 0.3 to 1.0. This is not unexpected since higher demand variability is associated with an increase of below-average demands resulting in higher excessive returns. However, if we look at the CV_D region between 0.0 and 0.3 we face a (moderate) rise in the recovery fraction with growing demand uncertainty. This somewhat surprising effect can be explained by the fact that increasing demand variability generates both underage and overage demand values. Above-average demands can compensate the influence of extremely high return realizations with respect to magnitude and time, so that an increase of demand risk can yield a decrease of excess net returns. For low levels of demand uncertainty, this effect seems to be the superior one, while for high levels the excess returns amplification effect seems to dominate. Thus it turns out that demand uncertainty has an impact on the product recovery behaviour, which is considerably different from that of return uncertainty. However, in general, it can be stated that the level of uncertainty only has an influence, which is less significant than it could be expected beforehand. Specifically there is some evidence from the study that the recovery fraction is reacting more sensitive on the return level parameter than on the two risk parameters.

With respect to the cost-oriented determinants, we first consider the remanufacturing cost ratio, which displays how many percent of production (and disposal) cost has to be spent for recovering an used product. We know that under certainty we face an all-or-nothing situation (given *RR* < 1), i.e. if the ratio is less than one all returned items are remanufactured, if it is larger than one all recoverable are disposed of, and in case of a ratio equal to one the decision is ambiguous. If uncertainty exists, the reaction of the recovery fraction on changing remanufacturing cost ratios is smoother as can be seen from Figure 7.

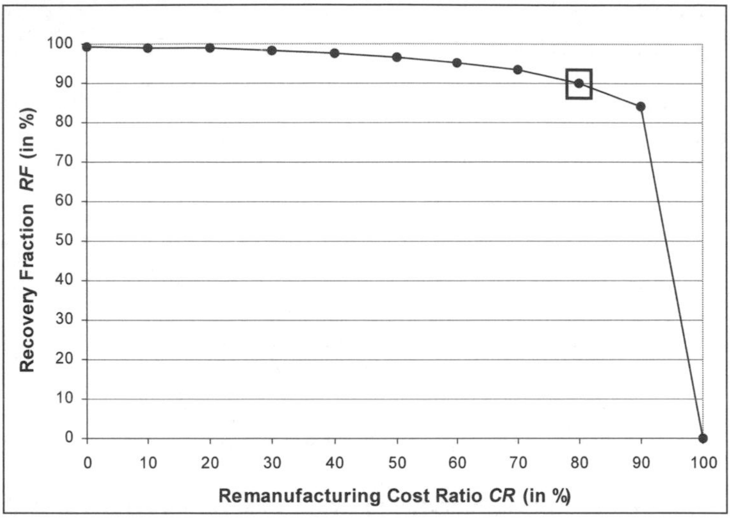

Fig. 7. Remanufacturing cost ratio and recovery fraction

It is evident that the recovery fraction is decreasing as remanufacturing is losing relative profitability with increasing cost ratio C*R*. It is also observable that the recovery fraction is decreasing at an increasing rate. Thus, if the cost ratio approaches 100%, the tendency towards recovery can go down considerably. A similar situation is faced when we consider the relevant holding cost effects, which are measured by the critical holding time. Figure 8 displays the recovery fraction against holding time *HT* which here refers to the holding cost parameter for serviceable (due to *SP* = 1).

A zero holding time is equivalent to a situation with a remanufacturing cost rate equal to one which indicates that product recovery is not profitable. For that reason the respective recovery fraction is zero. Given that remanufacturing is profitable, an increasing holding time *HT* is a consequence of a relative decrease of holding costs. With decreasing holding costs it becomes more economical to recover returned items even if excess returns occur. Therefore, the recovery fraction is monotonically increasing in the number of critical holding time periods. Summarizing, we find that cost-based determinants can have a major impact on the product recovery behaviour.

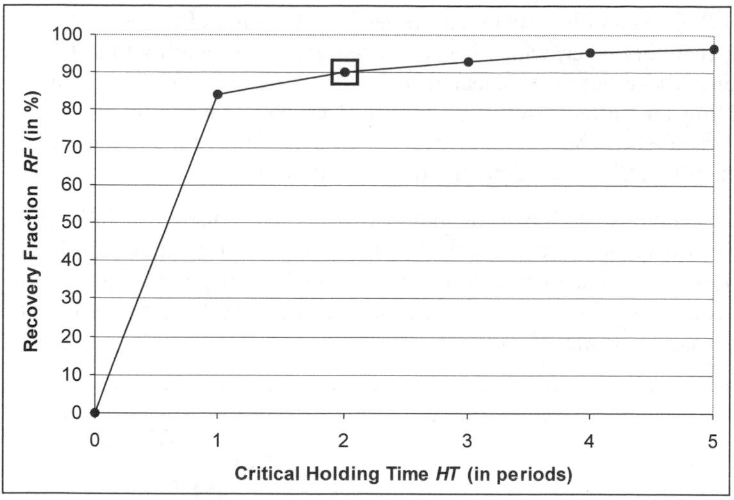

Fig. 8. Critical holding time and recovery fraction

Different from the certainty situation, lead-time aspects can have an influence on the degree of recovery activities if returns and demands are stochastic. Figure 9 portrays what happens if the number of lead-time periods for production and remanufacturing is steadily growing.

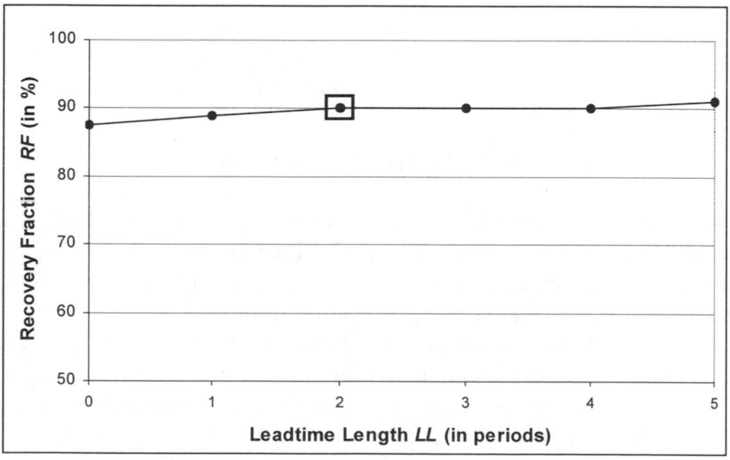

Fig. 9. Lead-time length and recovery fraction

It can be seen that the recovery fraction is slightly increasing with rising lead-time length *LL*. This effect is caused by the fact that with increasing lead-times the expected holding costs per period are becoming larger since these costs are affected by the cumulated demands over all lead-time periods as is shown in the cost function in (1). Thus an increase in lead-times has the same effect as an increase in the holding cost parameter, which leads to a rising critical holding time *HT*. Therefore increasing lead-times are connected with a growing recovery fraction as seen from the holding cost effect. However, Figure 9 reveals that the overall sensitivity of product recovery behaviour with respect to a change in the common production and remanufacturing lead-time duration is only minor.

In order to investigate how a deviation in both lead-times may influence product recovery, we compare the results for an equal lead-time situation (i.e., $LD = 0$) with those for a situation where the remanufacturing lead-time is one period shorter (i.e., $LD = 1$). The dependence of the recovery fraction on the return ratio for both cases is displayed in Figure 10.

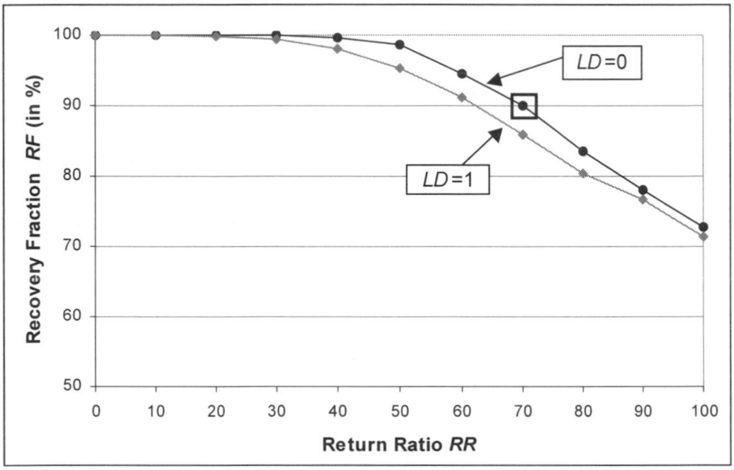

Fig. 10. Lead-time deviation and recovery fraction

In Figure 10 the curve for $LD = 0$ is the base case curve with equal lead-times which is identical with the curve in Figure 3. Since the curve for $LD = 1$ is located below the base case curve, it turns out that the lead-time difference results in a lower recovery fraction. This finding is counter-intuitive, because the normal expectation is that a lead-time advantage of recovery over production (associated with a one-period remanufacturing lead-time reduction in case of moving from $LD = 0$ to $LD = 1$) would lead to a growing use of the remanufacturing option. An explanation for this odd system behaviour is found when we take a precise look at the interaction between production and remanufacturing decisions in case of the above lead-time difference. Remanufacturing (with $\lambda_R = 1$) can be used for short-term adjustments of the serviceable inventory in case of unexpected high demand, while production (with $\lambda_P = 2$) offers only a longer-term option to adjust the inventory level. Because the production-based procurement decision with respect to a certain future period has to be made one period ahead of the recovery-based decision, it has to take into account that due to possibly insufficient return flows an additional supply risk emerges which has to be protected by a higher level of production orders. Thus it finally is the return uncertainty, which is responsible for the lack in using the short-term remanufacturing option since this option is not sufficiently reliable from the long-term production perspective. Additionally, a close look at Figure 10 reveals that the recovery fraction reduction effect is increasing first, but decreasing when the return ratio exceeds a certain level and approaches 100%. This can be explained by the fact that with growing high-level return ratios the procurement option in form of production is steadily loosing importance since more and more demand is regularly satisfied by remanufacturing. Thus also the influence of production as a means of risk protection is diminishing.

Finally, we will consider the effects of stocking point availability in the supply chain structure. Figure 11 shows how the recovery fraction curve develops in the base case scenario without a remanufacturable inventory (i.e., $SP = 1$) in comparison to a situation where stocking points for both serviceable *and* recoverable exist (i.e., $SP = 2$).

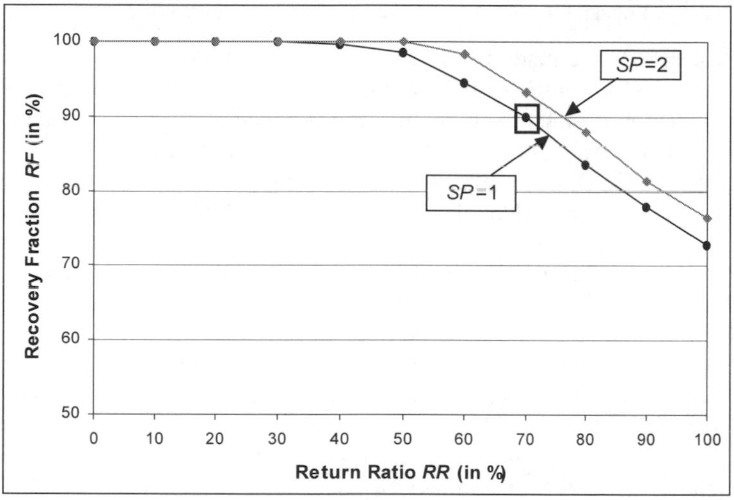

Fig. 11. Stocking point structure and recovery fraction

Stocking returns in a remanufacturable inventory provides an additional option in product recovery management, which can replace disposal or immediate remanufacturing of returned products. From Figure 11, it can be seen that the effect of this option is beneficial from an environmental point of view since the recovery fraction is significantly higher in case of an additional stocking opportunity, at least for medium and high return ratios where excess returns play a role. However, this effect has largely to be attributed to a holding cost impact, which is associated with inventory holding of remanufacturables. Since returned products will have a value, which is not as high as that of serviceable, the respective holding cost parameter will also be lower. In our case it is assumed that the recoverable holding cost is just half of the serviceable cost value (i.e., $h_R = 0.5$ and $h_S = 1$). Thus the critical holding time *HT* is increasing from 2 to 4 periods in this case. This effect more or less explains the recovery fraction deviation between the curves in Figure 11 what can be verified for the base case scenario with $RR = 0.7$ by comparing the recovery fraction in Figure 8 for $HT = 2$ and $HT = 4$.

5. Managerial and environmental insights

From a managerial point of view, product recovery management in an OEM environment is a challenging task, because it has to balance production, recovery and disposal decisions under often-considerable uncertainty of demand and return processes. For the hybrid production/remanufacturing system described in section 2, the decision rule in equ. (0.2) shows how balanced decisions look like when they are designed to solve this management problem in the most cost-effective way. Thereby, uncertainty is taken into consideration in two different ways.

First, all decisions are made in reaction to the respective levels of the inventory states (i.e. x_R and x_S) in the system which in case of x_S also include in-process inventories. Hereby it should be noted that the production quantity only depends on the total system stock (i.e. $x_R + x_S$). Second, the policy parameters *S*, *M*, and *U* which play the role of target inventory levels, also reflect a response to uncertainty insofar as to a certain extent they contain safety stocks. These stocks can be viewed as safety minimum stocks in case of *S* and *M* and as a safety maximum stock in case of *U*. This reveals that the optimal decision rule in the hybrid system is a policy with multiple safety stocks for serviceable products. In the base case example in section 4.1, the optimal serviceable inventory position in case of *certainty* would amount to 30 units, calculated from the well-known demand-demand formula, saying that the target inventory level is equal to the demand per period (=10) times demand plus one (=3). Since the optimal policy parameter values turn out to be $S = 39$ and $M = 48$, we realize that the safety stocks are 9 units for production and 18 units for remanufacturing decisions, respectively. Besides the respective probability information on returns and demands, these safety stocks take into account all cost parameters of the problem.

The cost minimization objective thus results in a policy, which according to the differences in the policy parameters creates a weaker or stronger tendency towards using all returning goods for recovery purposes. This tendency is exactly the interesting topic from an environmental point of view. The main finding in our computational study is that under uncertainty it cannot be taken for granted that a simple cost superiority of remanufacturing over production will guarantee a 100% recovery fraction even if all returns can be used to satisfy product demands.

Going into details and looking for reasons why economical-oriented decision making does not always coincide with an environmental benign recovery behaviour we find that it is mainly the influence of the return level which causes deviations from an all-recovery attitude. The bad news in this context is that specifically a growing effort to take back and redistribute used products in order to make them available for remanufacturing and thus to increase the return ratio is associated with a decreasing recovery rate. Figure 4 gives an impressive picture of this effect.

What we can learn from the investigation is that it is possible to weaken this effect. This can be done by reducing the uncertainty through diminishing the variability of returns as well as of demands, for instance by using better forecasting systems or by actively controlling the return uncertainty in form of offering lease contracts and initiating buy-back campaigns (Thierry et al., 1995, pp. 114-135). Another means to considerably increase the recovery fraction is to influence cost parameters in such a way that remanufacturing becomes more profitable. This can be done by investing in product recovery technology or by improving the efficiency of remanufacturing processes what may reduce the unit remanufacturing cost directly. Additionally, as we have seen also measures to reduce inventory-holding costs will lead to increasing recovery rates. Providing an opportunity for stock keeping of returned products can be very helpful in this context. The study reveals that using the cost-based measures will be specifically effective when the cost advantage of recovery as expressed by the remanufacturing cost ratio is only minor. In this case, investing in steps to improve the remanufacturing cost situation can be much more successful in stimulating an environmentally advantageous product recovery behaviour than taking actions to reduce uncertainty will do.

6. Conclusions

A main issue in product recovery management, which has to be carefully considered in decision-making, is the existence of a significant level of uncertainty. It is shown that uncertainty in returns and demands can be a considerable obstacle to follow a consequently environmental-benign recovery strategy within a CLSC environment. This effect would certainly be even stronger if additional sources of uncertainty would have had to be taken into account. Major uncertainties in this context can be associated with the recovery processes themselves. So it is often found that the duration of these processes as well as the process yields can vary in a quite unpredictable way (Guide, 2000, pp. 467-483). This is mainly due to a poor knowledge of the quality of returned products as well as to the low level of automation in remanufacturing processes. Better testing and quality information systems may help to overcome some of these problems.

Additionally, it can be expected that an increasing level of returns which will result from environmental-oriented governmental regulations like take-back obligations will create further incentives to invest in better remanufacturing technologies. This may decrease both operating costs and uncertainty, and thereby lead to a higher recovery fraction. With rising return volumes also other means of environmentally conscious manufacturing and product recovery like life cycle analysis and design for disassembly (Gungor and Gupta, 1999, pp. 811-853) become economically worth-wile. These activities again create potential for reducing remanufacturing costs and for better control of remanufacturing processes. In this way, governmental actions which force companies to take care of their products, also after their useful life-time, can be expected to stimulate firms to organize their reverse logistics systems in such a manner that they may favour an environmentally beneficial product recovery behaviour just in following their economic objectives.

Acknowledgement

The research presented in this paper is part of the research on re-use in the context of the EU supported TMR project REVerse LOGistics (ERB 4061 PL 97-0650) in which apart from Otto-von-Guericke University Magdeburg also Eindhoven University of Technology (NL), Aristoteles University of Thessaloniki (GR), Erasmus University Rotterdam (NL), INSEAD (F) and University of Piraeus (GR) take part.

References

Fandel, G. (1988). Optimal planning in joint production. In: Essays on Production Theory and Planning, Fandel, G., Dyckhoff, H., Reese, J. (eds.), Springer, Berlin, pp. 130-148.

Fleischmann, M., Bloemhof-Ruwaard, J.M., Laan, van der E., Nunen, van J.A.E.E., Wassenhove, van L.N. (1997). Quantitative models for reverse logistics: a review. In: European Journal of Operational Research, 103: pp. 1-17.

Guide Jr., V.D.R. (2000). Production planning and control for remanufacturing: industry practice and research needs. In: Journal of Operations Management, 18: pp. 467-483.

Gungor, A., Gupta, S.M. (1999). Issues in environmentally conscious manufacturing and product recovery: a survey. In: Computers and Industrial Engineering, 36: pp. 811-853.

Hillier, F.S, Lieberman, G.J. (2001). Introduction to Operations Research. 7th ed., McGraw-Hill, New York.

Inderfurth, K. (1996). Modelling period review control for a stochastic product recovery problem with remanufacturing and procurement lead-times. In: Preprint 2/1996, Faculty of Economics and Management, University of Magdeburg, Germany.

Inderfurth, K. (1997). Simple optimal replenishment and disposal policies for a product recovery system with lead-times. In: OR Spektrum, 19: pp. 111-122.

Laan, van der E., Salomon, M., Dekker, R., Wassenhove, van L.N. (1999). Inventory control in hybrid systems with remanufacturing. In: Management Science 45: pp. 733-747.

Thierry, M.C. (1997). An analysis of the impact of product recovery management on manufacturing companies. PhD-Thesis, Erasmus University Rotterdam, The Netherlands.

Thierry, M.C., Salomon, M., Nunen, van J.A.E.E., Wassenhove, van L.N. (1995). Strategic issues in product recovery management. In: California Management Review 37: pp. 114-135.

Inventory Management in Closed Loop Supply Chains

Moritz Fleischmann and Stefan Minner

Rotterdam School of Management / Faculteit Bedrijfskunde
Erasmus University Rotterdam
PO Box 1738
NL-3000 DR Rotterdam, Netherlands

Faculty of Economics and Management
Otto-von-Guericke-University Magdeburg
PO Box 4120
D-39016 Magdeburg, Germany

Abstract: *Inventory management is playing a key role in setting up efficient closed loop supply chains. Companies are recognizing product returns as a critical supply source, which they need to integrate into their material management. Uncertainty and a limited span of control add to the complexity of managing this particular source. In this chapter we review inventory management issues related to closed loop supply chains. We start by discussing different roles of inventories in this context and by proposing an overall framework. Subsequently, we review literature on corresponding mathematical inventory control models. To this end, we follow a standard structuring of traditional inventory theory and discuss applications to closed loop settings for each case. Our analysis is centered around highlighting novel characteristics entailed by a closed loop supply chain structure, in terms of both mathematics and business implications.*

Keywords: *reverse logistics, closed loop supply chains, inventory control*

1. Introduction

The traditional view of a supply chain, reflected in numerous textbooks, software packages, and company presentations refers to a linear structure, conveying goods from suppliers to manufacturers, wholesalers, retailers, and finally to the consumer. Yet recent developments have led to refining this picture. Today's companies are co-operating as complex, general networks rather than as linear 'chains'.

In particular, these networks involve several types of goods flows 'upstream' the traditional supply chain, such as returns of overstocks, service parts, and reusable packaging. The management of these upstream flows has been denoted by 'reverse logistics'. Their integration into an overall supply chain concept is emphasized in literature by the term 'closed loop supply chains' (Guide and Van Wassenhove, 2003; REVLOG, 2002).

A particularly important class of such 'reverse' goods flows concerns returns of used products at the end of their normal lifecycle. Waste reduction and resource conservation have been a motivation for an ever-increasing number of countries, in particular in Europe and Eastern Asia, to hold manufacturers responsible for their products throughout the entire lifecycle, including take-back and recovery after use. Electronic scrap recycling in the Netherlands (VROM, 2002), packaging recycling in Germany (Duales System, 2002), and scrap car recycling in Japan (JAMA, 2002) are but a few of the manifold examples.

At the same time, companies have been discovering used products as a valuable resource. A scale of recovery options, including refurbishing, remanufacturing, and recycling may allow for recovering significant shares of the original value added and/or material value, thereby opening the route to extended profits (Thierry et al., 1995). For example, automotive remanufacturing, copier remanufacturing, and recycling of nylon carpet fibers have proven viable business opportunities. In this light, it comes as no surprise that original equipment manufacturers (OEM) face competition by specialized newcomers in acquiring potentially attractive cores. Toner cartridges, cellular phones, and retreadable truck tires are among the most prominent examples.

Successfully exploiting the value potential of recoverable resources requires a conscious adaptation of inventory management. Overly simplistic approaches may result in excessive inventories of non-reusable junk, or in poor service due to growing uncertainty, both of which counterweigh the value recovered. In particular, companies need to integrate the emerging inbound flows of secondary resources into their supply decisions. The following business examples illustrate some of the added complexity in this area.

- *Dismantling spare parts from end-of-life electronics:*

  IBM is taking back used equipment from expiring lease contracts and trade-in programs. Recovery options include refurbishing of a complete machine and dismantling of valuable parts for use as spare parts in the service business. The latter option proves an attractive alternative in view of ever-shortening product lifecycles. Setting up dismantling as a regular source of spare parts requires a decision rule as to which dismantling opportunity to make use of, considering current stock levels, expected future demand, and available supply alternatives. Furthermore, one needs to decide about the location of inventory buffers between the individual processing steps of the dismantling channel. In addition, the dismantling input needs to be coordinated with the alternative parts supply sources, such as procurement of new parts or repair of defective replacement parts. Coordination is complicated by the fact that machine returns are difficult to forecast (Fleischmann, Van Nunen and Gräve2003).

- *Managing a reusable packaging pool:*

  Heineken is selling the majority of its beer products in reusable packaging such as refillable bottles, crates, and kegs. Packaging is kept in a closed cycle by means of a deposit system. The size of the packaging pool is adjusted annually by means of an investment decision. In order to determine the total packaging requirements one needs to estimate cycle times, in combination with the regular demand forecast. Seasonality is a major issue here. Estimating cycle time behavior faces the difficulty that issuing dates and return dates are not known on an individual product level and that stocks of empty packaging are not visible along the entire supply chain. Therefore, estimates have to rely on aggregate data solely. In a pilot project Heineken addressed this drawback by equipping crates with microchips that allow for logging a detailed product history (Wilens, 2002).

- *Internal recycling in pharmaceutics manufacturing:*

  One of the core manufacturing activities of a pharmaceutics company, such as Schering, concerns the production of active ingredients. Typically, the same production equipment is used for many different products. Cleaning requirements cause significant changeover times between batches of different ingredients. Therefore, challenging lot-sizing and scheduling problems arise. Recycling options complicate these decisions even further. The manufacturing processes require different solvents as major input resources. During processing, impure solvents are retained and stored. Subsequently, they can be partly recovered through distillation and then serve as a substitute for new pure solvents. The distillation process calls for additional lot-sizing and scheduling decisions. Moreover, demand for and returns of a given solvent are directly linked to the manufacturing of associated main products. Therefore, the overall production planning problem involves two complex and interacting lot-scheduling problems (Teunter et al., 2000a).

In this contribution we systematically address inventory management issues in closed loop supply chains such as in the above examples. To structure our presentation we introduce a general framework in the next section. Specifically, we highlight different functions of inventory in a closed loop supply chain. Moreover, we discuss inventory management issues that are specific of closed loop chains and contrast them with more conventional settings. The core of our contribution concerns a review of quantitative inventory control models for closed loop chains. To this end, we follow a standard textbook structuring of inventory models. Specifically, we distinguish between deterministic and stochastic models. We further subdivide the first class, which we address in Section 3, into stationary versus dynamic models. Within the second class, considered in Section 4, we distinguish between single-period and multi-period models and further subdivide the latter into single-echelon, two-echelon, and multi-echelon models. For each class we review results from literature, where we focus on pointing out differences with corresponding traditional inventory models. Section 5 wraps up our contribution by summarizing the main results and pointing out directions for further research.

2. Framework

To structure the presentation we capture the topic of our analysis in an overall framework. Figure 1 depicts our concept of a closed loop supply chain. Specifically, we consider a general supply chain facing external demand from a certain market. In addition, the chain is receiving an inbound flow of product returns. Returns may (partly) be recovered in order to satisfy future demand. We are interested in the management of the different inventories within the supply chain in such a setting.

We use this framework for anchoring the individual models that we are reviewing throughout this chapter. Each model is characterized by a combination of several factors, namely

- the assumed *supply chain structure*, which may range from a single stock point to a complex multi-echelon network, and the corresponding *transformation processes*;
- the associated *performance evaluation* (cost structure and service measures);
- the *demand process*;
- the *return process* and, in particular, its relation with the demand process; both processes may be independent or show some correlation, e.g. through a time-lag; this factor is tightly linked to the type of return flow considered (commercial returns, end-of-life returns, packaging returns,...);

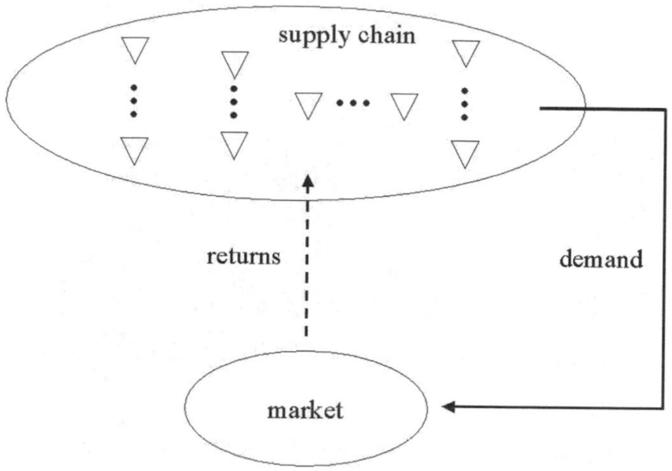

Fig. 1. An inventory framework for closed loop supply chains

- the *re-entry point* of returns in the supply chain; returns may occur at the end-item level or further upstream in the chain; this factor is closely related with the assumed form of recovery (direct reuse, remanufacturing, recycling…).

While the first three of these factors apply for any inventory model, the last two factors refer to the essence of a closed loop chain.

In order to understand inventory decisions in closed loop supply chains it is helpful to consider the different functions that inventory is fulfilling. Cycle stock, safety stock, and seasonal stock are important categories that are commonly distinguished in traditional inventory models. In closed loop chains we observe another important motive for keeping inventories. As discussed, product returns may represent a valuable resource that allows for production cost savings or additional revenues. In general, however, returns do not occur at the moment that they are needed. Hence, one has to trade off the profit contribution of a returned product against the costs for stocking it until the moment of use. We denote this type of inventory as 'opportunity stock'. It is worth noting that its role is similar to situations with price variations, e.g. the inventory built up by 'forward buying' in response to an occasional discount from a supplier (see e.g. Moinzadeh, 1997). Figure 2 illustrates the break-up of the above inventory types in a closed loop chain.

In the above framework one observes a number of issues that complicate inventory control decisions in a closed loop supply chain, namely:

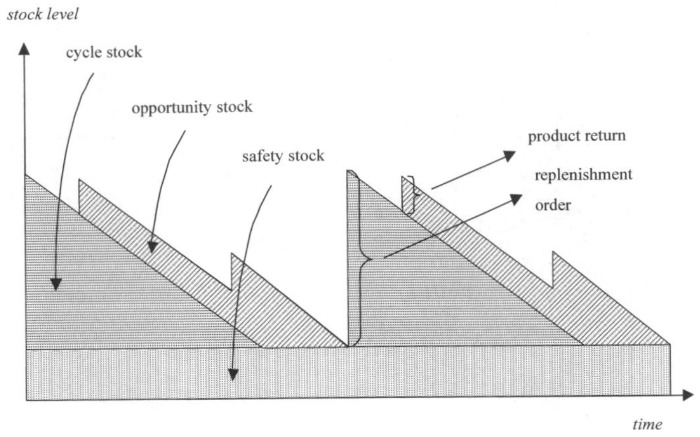

Fig. 2. Inventory functions in a closed loop supply chain

- *Supply uncertainty and lack of control*:

  In a conventional supply chain, demand is typically seen as the main uncertain factor, whereas supply can be controlled. Product returns however are often initiated by the sender rather than by the receiving party. Moreover, companies often lack sufficient data for a reliable forecast of their returns. Therefore, uncertainty with respect to timing, quantity, and quality of product returns is commonly cited as a major difficulty in reverse logistics in general, and in inventory management in particular.

- *Multi-sourcing*:

  As illustrated in the examples in the previous section, product returns often serve as a substitute for some regular supply. Therefore, inventory management requires a coordination of multiple alternative sources. While multi-sourcing as such is not new, this context involves a particular trade-off. Traditional two-supplier inventory models address the trade-off between procurement costs and lead time advantages. Typically, the models include a slow yet cheap supplier and a faster but also more expensive one. Yet, in a closed loop supply chain the option of recovering returns may be both cheaper and faster than regular supply. Rather than a lead time reduction it is the restricted availability of the recovery channel that calls for an alternative supply source.

- *Capacity constraints:*

  Continuing the previous thought, we observe that closed loop chains involve an inherent capacity restriction. At any time, the quantity that can be provided by the recovery channel is bounded by the number of returned items on hand. Since it is well known that capacity restrictions are a complicating factor of importance in traditional inventory models, one can expect similar difficulties in a closed loop setting.

– *Loss of monotonicity*:

  Given an exogenous return process, stock levels between replenishments may no longer be monotonously decreasing (see Figure 2). This complicates the mathematical analysis of these inventory systems, since common recursion procedures for evaluating Markov chains are no longer (directly) applicable.

In our review we discuss how different modeling approaches deal with these difficulties. At this point we already mention two common managerial approaches. The most simplistic way to deal with product returns is to ignore them until they have actually arrived. This means that one determines replenishment policies and control parameters for a situation without returns and simply updates stock levels upon return arrivals. In the sequel we refer to this policy as 'reactive'. Obviously, this approach risks excessive stock levels in case of high return volumes.

As an alternative one may want to cancel out returns against some of the demand. We denote this policy by 'netting'. Since this approach implicitly assumes each return to coincide with a demand, which may not be the case in reality, it tends to overestimate the resulting service level. This effect can be reduced by offsetting expected returns against replenishment orders rather than against demand. In Sections 3 and 4 we comment on the performance of these managerial approaches in different settings.

We conclude this conceptual introduction by briefly addressing the issue of performance evaluation in closed loop supply chains. As in any supply chain setting, companies need to strike a balance between cost and service. Customer service may be measured in terms of service levels or shortage costs, as usual. Likewise, one faces the usual fixed and variable costs associated with transformation processes. Variable costs include, for example, procurement costs for new material, return acquisition costs, manufacturing costs, and reprocessing costs. Moreover, it is worth noting that there may be positive or negative disposal costs, depending on the salvage value of used items. Finally, we have inventory holding costs, which usually comprise out-of-pocket costs and opportunity costs for capital tied up in inventories.

It is the latter category that becomes a slightly more delicate issue in a closed loop setting. Specifically, defining these cost rates is complicated by the multi-sourcing issue discussed above. That is, finished goods inventory may stem from different sources, notably 'virgin' manufacturing and remanufacturing of returns, that caused different expenditures in the past. In accounting practice, the valuation of stocks with different acquisition prices requires additional assumptions on inventory depletion, such as FIFO, LIFO, or weighted averages (see e.g. Horngren et al., 2000). As a basis for decision making, however, one is not interested in past expenditures but in consequences on future cash flows. In this light, simplistic holding cost rates may cause suboptimal decisions. For example, using a single holding cost rate for finished goods inventory overestimates the cost consequences of remanufacturing a returned item compared to manufacturing a new item (assuming that manufacturing is more expensive than remanufacturing) and therefore underestimates the benefits of recovery. Teunter et al. (2000b) point out that an appropriate choice of the holding cost rates in an average cost approach may not always be obvious. An exact assessment that incorporates all associated payments requires a more complicated discounted cash flow analysis. Yet by a proper definition and choice of holding cost rates, an average cost approach yields an approximation of such a discounted cash flow approach in many cases (see also Fleischmann 2001a).

In the sequel we review quantitative models that support inventory control decisions in the closed loop setting presented above. Specifically, the models address replenishment rules, control parameter choices, performance evaluation, and more generally, the question of how to make the best use of the available information. We exclude two special classes from our discussion, namely models for repairable spare parts systems and models for internal rework. While these classes fall within the closed loop supply chain setting delineated above, they have both been addressed in much detail in literature, such that we content ourselves by referring to previous reviews. Repair systems are characterized by the fact that each item return triggers an immediate demand for a replacement item, i.e. return and demand processes are perfectly correlated. Repair systems have been analyzed extensively since the 1960s (see e.g. Sherbrooke, 1992). Rework concerns the case of production defectives that need to be reprocessed to meet quality standards. We refer to Flapper et al. (2002) for a review of this issue.

3. Deterministic models

In deterministic models all elements of the framework in Figure 1 are assumed to be known with certainty. In particular, demand and return are known a priori for the entire planning horizon. Inventories primarily take the role of cycle stock and possibly seasonal stock here. The models provide insight as to how to resolve the associated multi-sourcing and capacity issues of closed loop systems. In the following, we start by discussing the most simple case of constant parameters and then address additional complexities under time-varying data.

3.1. Constant demand and returns

In an environment with constant deterministic data, inventories mainly result from transaction motives, i.e. significant setup costs that lead to batching of processes. In basic inventory models with a single supply source and a single inventory, the trade-off to be made is between setup costs for placing an order/releasing a batch and holding costs over the resulting inventory cycle. In a closed loop environment one faces several trade-offs simultaneously. First, we have the selection of the supply mode, one of them being capacitated. Second, for each source we have the above trade-off between setup and holding costs. Third, the trade-off for a single mode with respect to serviceable inventory has to be further balanced with the associated consequences on upstream stocks, in particular on recoverable inventory.

The most basic case concerns a single stock point to which returns arrive at a constant rate. This corresponds with the setting of the standard *EOQ*-model, extended with a stream of negative demand. It is easy to see that the optimal replenishment lot size in this case is obtained from the *EOQ*-formula applied to the net demand rate, i.e. demand minus returns per unit of time (assuming that demand exceeds returns). That is, in this basic case the aforementioned 'netting' approach is indeed optimal.

The situation becomes more complex if a fixed cost is associated with the recovery of returned items. In this case, it is beneficial to collect returns in a distinct stock until a sufficient recovery batch has accumulated. Several authors have proposed variations of the *EOQ*-model for this setting, assuming different policy structures. Schrady (1967) considers the case that a single manufacturing batch, used for compensating return deficits, is followed by several remanufacturing batches of identical size. The cost structure comprises setup costs K_p for each manufacturing batch, K_r for each remanufacturing batch, and unit holding costs h_s and h_r per unit of time for serviceable and recoverable inventories, respectively. The resulting optimal batch sizes are

$$EOQ_p = \sqrt{\frac{2K_p(d-r)}{h_s\left(1-\frac{r}{d}\right)+h_r\,\frac{r}{d}}},\quad EOQ_r = \sqrt{\frac{2K_r d}{h_s + h_r}}\,. \tag{1}$$

Taking a closer look at these expressions proves helpful for understanding the underlying trade-offs. The production batch EOQ_p relies on the net demand rate, as in the above basic model, yet the relevant holding cost rate is a weighted average of serviceable and recoverable stocks. The remanufacturing quantity EOQ_r depends on the gross demand rate, and the corresponding effective holding cost rate is the sum of the serviceable and recoverable holding costs. The rationale behind this term is that remanufacturing an additional unit not only increases serviceable inventory but also lets other recoverables wait longer.

Teunter (2001) investigates the opposite case where several manufacturing batches are followed by a single remanufacturing batch. The optimal batch sizes in this case are

$$EOQ_p = \sqrt{\frac{2dK_p}{h_s}},\quad EOQ_r = \sqrt{\frac{2rK_r}{h_s\,\frac{r}{d}+h_r}} \tag{2}$$

i.e. the production batch size coincides with the original *EOQ*, whereas the recovery batch is based on the return rate and an adjusted holding cost rate. Further, Teunter presents generalizations that include a disposal option and use different holding cost rates for manufactured and remanufactured items (compare discussion in Section 2). Another lot-sizing model with slightly different assumptions but similar insights is discussed by Nahmias and Rivera (1979). Similarly, Richter (1996) addresses the case of multiple consecutive manufacturing and remanufacturing batches. He shows that the optimal solution to a relaxed problem, where the number of setups may be non-integer, uses multiple setups for at most one of the sources. We refer to the contribution of Richter and Dobos in this volume for a more detailed discussion of this model.

All of the above approaches are heuristic in the sense that they consider a limited class of policies. In particular, they all assume that consecutive batches from the same source have equal sizes. Minner (2001b) shows that, under an average cost criterion, identical manufacturing batches are indeed optimal. However, in an optimal policy at least the final of several remanufacturing batches in a cycle will be smaller than its predecessors. This is intuitive since returns accumulating during the last batch sub-cycle remain longer in the recoverable inventory (namely during the entire next manufacturing time) such that there is a cost incentive to reduce the final recovery batch. In general, an optimal remanufacturing batch sequence consists of some identical batches, followed by batches that always deplete the recoverable inventory and therefore decrease geometrically with a factor of r/d.

Buscher and Lindner (2002) analyze a more general lot-sizing problem than the approaches discussed so far. First, manufacturing and remanufacturing rates are both finite and the start of each process requires a setup time. Second, both processes share a common capacitated facility. Third, finished items (either from manufacturing or remanufacturing) do not enter serviceable inventory instantaneously but are transferred in transportation batches. The authors use a common cycle approach, i.e. each manufacturing batch is followed by a single remanufacturing batch, to analyze this generalization of the above lot-sizing models to a lot-scheduling model (recall also the pharmaceutics case in Section 1).

3.2. Time-varying demand and returns

In the case of time-varying demand and returns inventory control involves additional trade-offs. Specifically, it may be beneficial to keep current excessive returns in inventory for future recovery. This refers to the concept of opportunity stocks discussed in Section 2. Minner and Kleber (2001) analyze this issue in a continuous-time optimal control model. In this setting, recoverable inventories have a time dependent value (shadow price), reflecting the timing of return arrivals and usage. This value provides a basis for coordinating inventory management with marketing/product acquisition decisions that may influence product returns, such as advertising or buy-back offers, which are current practice, e.g. for toner cartridges (Minner and Kiesmüller 2002).

Alternatively to continuous time optimal control models, several authors have proposed discrete time models with dynamic demand and returns. From an inventory management perspective, the use of discrete time buckets (days, weeks, months) in combination with forecasting in a rolling horizon planning framework is standard practice in Material Requirements Planning (MRP). Extensions of MRP-schemes including customer (external) and process (internal) returns have been proposed by Inderfurth and Jensen (1999).

The associated lot-sizing problems lead to variants of the classical dynamic lot-sizing model (Wagner and Whitin, 1958). As in the static case discussed in the previous subsection, it makes sense to distinguish whether returns enter serviceable stock immediately or are collected separately. Note that accumulating returns prior to recovery is motivated by lot-sizing and postponement considerations here. In other words, recoverable inventory can be interpreted as a mixture of cycle stock and opportunity stock.

Beltran and Krass (2002) consider the case of commercial returns that directly enter serviceable inventory. This is equivalent with a relaxation of the original Wagner-Whitin-model that allows demand to be positive or negative. Moreover, decisions include procurement and disposal, both of which have associated fixed plus concave costs. The authors show that the well-known zero-inventory-property of the original model generalizes here in the sense that in an optimal policy there is a least one period of zero inventory between any two actions (procurement or disposal). This property can be exploited in a dynamic programming algorithm for computing the optimal manufacturing and disposal policy.

As in the static case, the introduction of a distinct recoverable stock complicates the model significantly. Specifically, Golany et al. (2001) show that the computational complexity of the dynamic recovery lot-sizing problem is NP-complete, in general. This does not seem surprising since the problem resembles two other NP-complete inventory problems, namely the capacitated multi-item lot-sizing model where the items share a manufacturing facility (Florian et al., 1980) and the multi-level-lot-sizing problem (Arkin et al., 1989). It is worth noting that in the special case of zero setup costs and purely linear manufacturing, remanufacturing, and disposal costs, the problem reduces to a standard transportation problem, where the manufacturing opportunities and returns of each period represent the sources and customer demand of each period represents the destinations (Golany et al., 2001).

Furthermore, the original zero-inventory-property does no longer hold for serviceable inventory here. The reason essentially is that return quantities do not necessarily match with demand of entire subsequent periods. For lot-sizing reasons it may still be appropriate to recover all available returns at a given time. In that case, the next manufacturing batch may be required while there is some serviceable inventory left, yet not enough to cover the next period's demand entirely. The interaction between both channels' lot-sizing decisions has more counter-intuitive effects. In particular, the optimal manufacturing quantity is not necessarily decreasing in the serviceable stock on-hand, even in the case of stationary data (see Fleischmann, 2001b, Chapter 8).

Richter and Sombrutzki (2000) identify special cases where the zero-inventory-property remains valid, namely if (i) remanufacturing is the only source, or (ii) there is a large initial stock of recoverables, and no units are returned during the planning horizon.

Heuristics for setting the lot sizes in a product recovery context can be adapted from the well-known single-stage dynamic lot-sizing heuristics (Wojanowski, 1999). In particular, if the setup cost for one of the replenishment modes is negligible, a netting approach can be expected to be reasonable. If the remanufacturing setup cost is negligible it seems appropriate to remanufacture for demand (using current returns or recoverable inventories from previously returned units) and to combine the remaining net demands into batches by means of traditional techniques (Wagner-Whitin-algorithm, Silver-Meal-heuristic etc.). Similarly, if the manufacturing setup cost is negligible, first build remanufacturing lot sizes (using one of the above mentioned techniques) and then manufacture for the remaining demands. If setup costs for both sources are significant a netting approach cannot be expected to provide good results, in general, such that one needs to consider the lot-sizing effects of both channels in more detail. One possibility is to use the netting approach as a starting point for a savings heuristic. Starting with a solution that remanufactures for demand and manufactures for remaining net requirements (i.e. using lot-for-lot replenishments for both modes), one computes the savings from combining two consecutive manufacturing or remanufacturing batches into a single one and chooses the option with the maximum savings. Note that this method still does not make use of the problem specific structure that the zero inventory-property does no longer hold.

4. Stochastic models

If demand and returns are uncertain, inventory assumes the role of a safety buffer, in addition to the functions addressed in the previous section. In particular, as discussed in the framework in Section 2, uncertain product returns, while reducing expected net demand, may increase its variability and therefore the need for safety stock. This section reviews analyses that address safety stock aspects in closed loop chains by modeling demand and returns as stochastic processes.

4.1. Single-period models

We start by considering a single-period model. As in a traditional supply chain context, the single-period analysis has a value of its own right by reflecting trade-offs concerning perishable products and products with a single selling period and as a building block for various multi-period models.

An extensive body of supply chain literature addresses the impact of end-of-period product returns in a manufacturer-retailer relation (see e.g. Chopra and Meindl, 2001, Chapter 9). It is well known that a return option, e.g. in the form of a buy-back contract, may be beneficial for both parties as it increases the expected sales volume to the final costumer. In what follows we take a slightly different perspective by considering returns received during the selling season by the ordering party, i.e. the retailer in the above setting.

To be specific, consider the setting of the classical newsvendor model, i.e. a single replenishment decision for a single stock point facing stochastic demand and bearing linear costs for any overage or underage (see e.g. Silver et al., 1998, Chapter 10). In addition to the traditional setting, assume that product returns are received during the selling season, which may be added to the stock, possibly after some reprocessing. In the first place, this flow may reflect commercial returns, i.e. recently ordered, unused products returned for refunding. Commercial returns are an important factor, e.g. in catalogue and Internet sales, where they may easily exceed 30% of the gross sales volume (see, e.g., Beltran and Krass, 2002). More general interpretations of the return flow arise from sub-problems of a multi-period analysis.

The impact of the return flow on the complexity of the model depends on the relation between sales and returns and on the cost structure of the return channel. If returns and related recovery costs are independent of the order quantity, then the standard marginal analysis goes through by replacing the demand distribution by the distribution of net demand. In this way one obtains the usual newsboy expression for the optimal order quantity. Negative orders are truncated to zero.

The above condition of independence holds in particular if demand and returns are independent stochastic variables, as assumed in many of the multi-period models (see below). For commercial returns this condition may be less appropriate. Typically, one would expect returns to be dependent on sales, and thus on the order quantity. For high service levels a reasonable approximation may be obtained by treating returns as a function of demand rather than sales, which again fulfills the above condition.

Explicitly modeling dependent returns and sales requires a slightly more extensive analysis. Vlachos and Dekker (2000) model returns as a fixed fraction of demand and assume that a fixed fraction of the total return volume is reusable, whereas the remainder arrives after the end of the sales period and has to be salvaged. The authors derive newsboy-like expressions for the optimal order quantity in this model under several alternative cost structures. In order to estimate the reusable fraction of returns a more detailed model of the demand and return process during the sales period is required.

4.2. Multi-period, single-echelon models

Analogous with traditional supply chains, many closed loop chains involve repeated replenishments during the sales horizon, rather than a single up front decision. Moreover, inventory may be carried over from one period to another (see the examples in Section 1). Therefore, many authors have developed stochastic multi-period models. The most basic setting restricts the 'supply chain' in the setting of Figure 1 to a single stock point. This implies, in particular, that product returns are not stocked separately but enter the serviceable stock right away. This holds if returns are reusable 'as is', such as some reusable packaging, or, more generally, if returns are recovered lot-for-lot upon arrival.

Such a multi-period, single-stock setting corresponds with conventional single-item stochastic inventory control models, where an (s,S) order policy is known to be optimal under fairly general conditions, provided that any unmet demand is backordered (see e.g. Zheng and Federgruen, 1991). Product returns, however, may complicate the situation considerably. In particular, actions may affect the inventory level at multiple points in time. Therefore, the problem cannot, in general, be modeled as a single-dimensional Markov chain any more. Consequently, additional assumptions are required in order to guarantee a simple structure of the optimal control policy.

Fleischmann and Kuik (2002) show that an (s,S) order policy remains average cost optimal under the following conditions: (i) demand and returns are independent, (ii) the lead time of a potential recovery process does not exceed the regular replenishment lead time, (iii) returns may not be disposed. In this case, the model can be transformed into an equivalent (s,S)-model without returns by decomposing the overall system into a conventional (s,S)-system and an autonomous random walk which have independent long-run distributions. Conventional methods can then be used for computing the optimal control parameter values (see, e.g. Zheng and Federgruen, 1991). For the special case of an $(S-1,S)$-policy Mahadevan et al. (2002) propose several simple approximations for the optimal order-up-to level, analogous with the usual normal demand approximations (see, e.g. Silver et al., 1998, Chapter 7).

Muckstadt and Isaac (1981) use the above policy, in the special form of an (R,Q)-policy, as a heuristic in a slightly more general model where the recovery process is reflected in a multi-server queue. Van der Laan et al. (1996) propose a normal demand approximation for determining the corresponding control parameter values.

The above optimality results rely crucially on the assumption that returns may not be disposed. Based on numerical experiments, Teunter and Vlachos (2002) and Fleischmann, van Nunen and Gräve (2003) argue that inventory costs rarely outweigh procurement cost savings for returns that still have a market value and hence that disposal may not be a relevant option in these cases.

Things may be different though at the end of a product lifecycle where return volumes may be excessive. Inderfurth (1997) provides an optimal two-parameter policy for this case, which can be characterized as 'order-up-to L, dispose down-to U'. If procurement and recovery are both instantaneous and the inventory is reviewed continuously, the policy reduces to setting an optimal disposal level (Heyman, 1977). The increased flexibility in terms of the action space has its price in the form of more restrictive lead time conditions: Inderfurth shows that for the disposal case one only obtains a simple optimal policy if the procurement lead time equals the recovery lead time or exceeds it by exactly one period. In all other cases the underlying Markov chain becomes fairly intractable due to its increasing dimensionality.

All of the above results require demand and returns to be stochastically independent. In the case of dependent returns the situation becomes more involved since more detailed information needs to be taken into account, including individual sales occurrences. Essentially, optimality results have only been established for the case of an exponentially distributed time lag between demand and return of an item. In this case all items outstanding can be aggregated, due to the memorylessness of the exponential distribution. Whisler (1967) shows that the above (L, U)-policy is optimal in this case for Poisson distributed demand if procurement and recovery are instantaneous. For the case without disposal, Buchanan and Abad (1998) prove optimality of a procurement policy that depends on two state variables, namely on-hand inventory and the number of items in the market. For other dependencies between demand and returns, such as fixed or generally distributed time lags, several authors have proposed alternative heuristic replenishment policies (see e.g. Kelle and Silver, 1989, Cohen et al., 1980, Yuan and Cheung, 1998, Kiesmüller and van der Laan, 2001).

The significant complexity reduction resulting from independent demand and returns calls for assessing the appropriateness of this assumption. By their very nature, returns do depend on some previous sales transaction. Yet this transaction is not necessarily related with the demand process of the inventory system considered, since returns may enter an alternative supply chain. For an illustration, recall the example of IBM in Section 1, where machine returns serve as a source of spare parts. Even in the case of a 'closed loop' chain in a strict sense, independence between demand and returns may not be unrealistic in the short run, though. In many cases, order cycles range between a few weeks to a few months. If the average market sojourn time of an item is much longer, then the impact of correlation within the planning horizon is low. Instead, information on past demand can then be useful for updating the return rate throughout the product lifecycle. Things are different in the case of short return cycles, as e.g. for reusable packaging. In general, taking dependencies into account is more important in case of high demand variations (e.g. due to seasonal peaks). Toktay et al. (2000) address the value of different levels of product return information in this case. They conclude that aggregate sales and return data are often sufficient for return forecasting purposes.

4.3. Multi-period, two-echelon models

As discussed for deterministic models in Section 3, it may be beneficial to accumulate returned items in a distinct stock, rather than to recover them on a lot-for-lot basis upon arrival. This extends the setting of the previous sub-section to a two-level inventory system. In Section 3 we have identified lot-sizing and postponement arguments for such a two-level approach. In a stochastic environment we observe an additional trade-off concerning the location of safety buffers. Keeping items in the upstream recoverable inventory is desirable from a holding cost perspective since value adding operations are postponed. Placing the buffer in serviceable inventory is supported by customer service arguments since serviceable items are immediately available for satisfying customer demand.

Different lead times for the alternative supply processes complicate this trade-off further. Technically speaking, the presence of two supply modes with different lead times affects the relation between net stock and inventory position. (Stated differently, it is no longer clear how to define an appropriate inventory position.) To be specific, decisions on the faster supply mode affect the net stock during an order lead time of the slower mode. Therefore, the inventory level upon arrival of an order is more difficult to compute. Consequently, one cannot hope for the optimal inventory policy to have a simple structure, in general. This is similar to other dual sourcing inventory models where the optimal policy is described by a complex, multi-state stochastic dynamic program (Whittemore and Saunders, 1977).

For the special case of zero lead times and zero setup costs Simpson (1978) shows optimality of an (L,M,U)-policy, which extends the (L,U)-policy discussed for the single-echelon case above. Specifically, the policy can be described as 'remanufacture while the serviceable stock is below M and then adjust the echelon stock (i.e. the sum of serviceable and recoverable inventory) by means of manufacturing and disposal according to an (L,U)-policy'. Note that manufacturing and remanufacturing decisions are based on different control statistics in this case, namely echelon stock and serviceable stock, respectively. Inderfurth (1997) shows that, by defining an appropriate inventory position, this result also holds if the lead times of both processes are positive but identical.

Given the complex form of the optimal policy in the general case, several authors have studied the performance of certain structured policy classes that depend on a few parameters only. Within such a class, control parameter values can then be optimized. In this vein, van der Laan (1997) and van der Laan et al. (1999) propose several alternative push and pull strategies for incorporating remanufacturing into inventory control. In their push approach, recoverable inventory is controlled purely based on lot-sizing considerations. Returns are recovered as soon as a sufficient batch size has accumulated. A pull approach also takes into account the postponement versus safety stock trade-off by releasing a recovery batch only if the inventory position, defined as net serviceable stock plus all outstanding (manufacturing and remanufacturing) orders, drops below a certain trigger level. The manufacturing process is controlled by an (s,Q)-rule based on this same inventory position in both cases. The long-run expected costs in these systems can be computed via a two-dimensional Markov chain. The authors note that the inventory position used here has some drawbacks when the lead times of both channels differ considerably. Therefore, Inderfurth and van der Laan (2001) propose a modified inventory position for this case, which only takes into account orders that are within a certain time window.

Alternatively, one may use a different control statistic (i.e. inventory position) for each of the sources, in analogy with the aforementioned (L,M,U)-rule. To this end, it seems reasonable to define the relevant inventory position for the faster mode to include all orders that will arrive before the order yet to be placed. In contrast, the process with the longer lead time should take all outstanding orders into account. Kiesmüller and Minner (2002) and Teunter et al. (2001) analyze such a policy in a periodic review and a continuous review setting, respectively. The authors concur that this inventory control strategy outperforms other heuristics in numerical experiments.

Another issue concerns the computation of appropriate control parameter values. For a periodic review, order-up-to type of policy based on the above inventory positions, Kiesmüller and Minner (2002) present an approach that uses the basic concepts of the single-period newsvendor model by estimating the cost consequences of overages and underages. Since this approach highlights some of the inherent dynamics of recoverable inventory systems, we present it in some more detail. With respect to the remanufacturing decision, an overage in serviceable inventory, i.e. remanufacturing one unit too many, causes additional holding costs of h_s in serviceables but avoids recoverable holding costs of h_r. Therefore, it is reasonable to consider overage costs of $c_o=h_s-h_r$. In case of an underage, a shortage penalty h_b applies and recoverable holding costs h_r could have been avoided. This leads to an underage cost of $c_u=h_b+h_r$. Given these values, the remanufacture-up-to-level can be determined from the corresponding critical fractile of demand during a (remanufacturing) lead time plus review period. For the manufacturing decision the cost of an underage is simply the shortage penalty, $c_u=h_b$. The choice of an appropriate overage cost depends on the relation between the two lead times. If manufacturing is the faster source (or both are equal) the direct cost of an overage is h_s. In addition, one needs to take into account second order effects that arise since future remanufacturing orders may have to be postponed. If remanufacturing is the faster mode the argument becomes slightly more subtle. In that case, the manufacturing mode only needs to buffer for net requirements during its lead time plus review horizon. Moreover, an additional unit does not necessarily increase serviceable stock since it may possibly be deducted from one of the next remanufacturing orders. However, this entails additional holding costs h_r for recoverables, and future remanufacturing orders may be postponed.

4.4. Multi-period, multi-echelon models

The models discussed so far limit the analysis of multiple stock points to a distinction between recoverable and serviceable stock. More general approaches explicitly address multiple manufacturing and/or distribution stages. This places the results obtained for single-/two stage recovery systems in the context of general multi-echelon inventory systems. Contributions in this area are still few and far between. Recently, some analyses have been presented that build upon the seminal work of Clark and Scarf (1960).

On top of the lot-sizing and safety stock trade-offs outlined for the basic recovery models, additional complexities arise in a multi-echelon setting due to multi-level lot-sizing and multi-echelon safety stock placement problems. Additional safety stock issues in a multi-echelon environment concern the trade-off between keeping buffers upstream or downstream (allocation and associated buffer sizes). The trade-off is between cheaper inventory holding costs at upstream stages (less capital tied up in raw and semi-finished materials) and higher reaction flexibility at downstream stages (lower lead time until process completion, shorter cumulative lead time). The additional complexity introduced by a closed loop supply chain structure heavily depends on the re-entry point of product returns, which may be downstream in the case of commercial returns or further upstream in the case of remanufacturing or recycling. The main problem is that the echelon stock concept can no longer be applied if downstream inventory can be influenced during the lead time of an upstream process. This is the case, e.g. if downstream returns are disposed in one of the following periods.

DeCroix (2001) analyzes a series manufacturing system with a recovery option serving as an alternative source to one of the stages. This model extends the (L,M,U)-model discussed in Section 4.3 to a series system. In particular, returns can be stocked or disposed of, as in the two-stage case. The author shows that only a few special cases yield simple optimal policies. In particular, the lead time of the recovery process needs to be equal to the regular supply lead time at that stage. In addition, disposal is only feasible for returns to the most upstream stage. In this case, one obtains an optimal policy analogous with the two-stage system, yet using the echelon inventory position as the relevant information. If the recovery option is located at a more downstream stage, a simple, base-stock like policy is optimal only for the case without disposal. Otherwise, the echelon stock concept breaks down, as explained above. It is worth noting that these conclusions parallel Clark and Scarf's result, who argued that a setup cost complicates the analysis considerably except for the most upstream stage. DeCroix et al. (2002) present a method for optimizing the control parameter values in the case of lot-for-lot recovery. As an alternative, one may combine the newsvendor ideas discussed for the two-echelon model with the multi-echelon approach of van Houtum and Zijm (1991). Finally, DeCroix and Zipkin (2002) discuss conditions, under which an assembly system with product returns can be transformed into an equivalent series system, analogous with Rosling's result for traditional assembly systems (Rosling, 1989).

In the most general case, multi-echelon systems may involve three types of product returns simultaneously, namely commercial returns of final products, external returns of intermediate products (for material or parts recovery) and internal returns due to by-products and reworkable defectives. Minner (2001a) shows how these types of returns impact general network safety stock sizing and allocation procedures, under the assumption that all returns are directly processed, such as to enter the network on a lot-for-lot basis. One important finding is that safety stocks at intermediate stages should be set such that effective lead times of competing manufacturing and remanufacturing processes become compatible.

5. Conclusions and outlook

In this chapter we have addressed inventory management issues in closed loop supply chains. Several examples illustrate that sound inventory management plays a key role in the realization of efficient closed loop chains. Product returns may be an attractive resource that offers opportunities for cutting procurement and production costs and for extending revenues. Yet, in order to strike these opportunities companies need to integrate product return flows into their inventory management, such as to avoid excessive stocks of non-reusable scrap and to protect against increasing uncertainty.

In addition to traditional functions such as cycle stock, safety stock, and seasonal stock, inventories fulfill an important role as opportunity stock in a closed loop setting. Product returns, in general, do not occur exactly when they are needed from a resource perspective. Therefore, one needs to trade off inventory build-up against future cost savings or additional sales.

Closed loop supply chains pose several extra challenges to inventory control. First, multiple alternative sources need to be balanced since product returns may serve as a substitute for some regular input resources. In contrast with other multi-sourcing settings the trade-off ruling the source selection is not one between cost and speed but one between cost and uncertain availability. Second, companies tend to have less control over their product returns than over their regular supply orders. Therefore, closed loop chains tend to involve higher degrees of uncertainty, which may call for additional safety stocks. Third, the limited availability of product returns – at the moment that they are needed – poses an additional capacity constraint on inventory control decisions in closed loop chains.

In our discussion we have reviewed inventory control models that have been proposed for addressing these challenges. Literature provides variants of many standard inventory control models, both deterministic and stochastic, adapted to a closed loop supply chain context.

Despite this substantial body of literature, insight into inventory management issues in closed loop supply chains is far from complete. In particular, evidence from real-life case studies is still limited. To date, most contributions take a mathematical perspective predominantly and rely on extending standard inventory control models with some product return process. Additional efforts for rooting these models in business practice seem desirable for further establishing this field. From a mathematical perspective, much effort has been put into establishing optimal policy structures for different closed loop settings. To our opinion, the limits in that direction have largely been reached, except possibly for some additional multi-echelon models. Therefore, we think that future research effort would be most valuable if it focused on deriving well-grounded heuristics for more general settings and easy, spreadsheet-like approximations for setting appropriate control parameter values.

In addition, almost all contributions in this field to date take a single actor perspective. Given the recent lessons learned from supply chain management, it certainly seems advisable to address the interactions between multiple actors in closed loop supply chains more explicitly. In the same vein, the time seems right for addressing the interfaces of inventory management with other business functions in closed loop supply chains. To this end, the interaction of inventory management with production planning and scheduling on the one hand and with distribution management on the other hand deserves closer attention. This broader scope would also help integrate product returns into advanced planning systems.

Finally, as closed loop supply chains are beginning to mature, one may expect the conditions around product returns to change. To date most companies perceive their product return flow as an exogenous factor. This is reflected in the modeling approaches discussed above, which typically capture the return stream as an autonomous process. Yet, as recoverable resources are gaining importance, companies should be seeking control over their product returns rather than to accept them as a given. Financial incentives may be implemented to actively influence the timing, quantity, and quality of returns. Recent advances in information technology, allowing for, e.g. remote monitoring and sensing can be expected to play a key role in this transition. Such an active return flow management may eventually call for different modeling approaches than those available to date.

References

Arkin, E., Joneja, D., Roundy, R. (1989): Computational complexity of uncapacitated multi-echelon production planning problems. In: Operations Research Letters 8, pp. 61-66.

Beltran, J.L., Krass, D. (2002): Dynamic lot sizing with returning items and disposals. In: IIE Transactions 34, pp. 437-448.

Buchanan, D.J., Abad, P.L. (1998): Optimal policy for a periodic review inventory system. In: IIE Transactions 30, pp. 1049-1055.

Buscher, U., Lindner, G. (2002): An optimal lot and batch size policy for a single item produced and remanufactured on one machine in the presence of limitations on the manufacturing and handling capacity. Working Paper, Faculty of Economics and Management, Otto-von-Guericke-University Magdeburg.

Chopra, S., Meindl, P. (2001): Supply Chain Management: Strategy, Planning and Operation. Prentice Hall, New Jersey.

Cohen M.A., Nahmias S., Pierskalla W.P. (1980): A dynamic inventory system with recycling. In: Naval Research Logistics Quarterly 27, pp. 289-296.

Clark, A.J., Scarf, H. (1960): Optimal policies for multi-echelon stochastic inventory systems. In: Management Science 6, pp. 475-490.

DeCroix, G.A. (2001): Optimal policy for a multi-echelon inventory system with remanufacturing. Working Paper, The Fuqua School of Business, Duke University.

DeCroix, G.A., Zipkin, P.H. (2002): Inventory management for an assembly system with product or component returns. Working Paper, The Fuqua School of Business, Duke University.

DeCroix, G.A., Song, J., Zipkin, P.H. (2002): A series system with returns: Stationary analysis. Working Paper, The Fuqua School of Business, Duke University.

Duales System (2002): Der grüne Punkt. Retrieved on August 6, 2002 from http://www.gruener-punkt.de/en/home.php3

Flapper, S.D.P., Franso,o J.C., Broekmeulen R.A.C.M., Inderfurth, K. (2002): Production planning and control of rework in the process industries: A review. In: Production Planning and Control 13, pp. 26-34.

Fleischmann, B. (2001a): On the use and misuse of holding cost models. In: Kischka, P., Leopold-Wildburger, U., Möhring, R.H., Radermacher, F.-J. (Eds.), Models, Methods and Decision Support for Management. Physica, Heidelberg, pp. 147-164.

Fleischmann, M. (2001b): Quantitative Models for Reverse Logistics. Springer, Berlin.

Fleischmann, M., Nunen, van J.A.E.E., Gräve, B. (2003): Integrating closed loop supply chains and spare parts management at IBM. In: Interfaces, forthcoming.

Fleischmann, M., Kuik, R. (2002): On optimal inventory control with independent stochastic item returns. In: European Journal of Operational Research, forthcoming.

Florian, M., Lenstra, J.K., Rinnooy, Kan A.H.G. (1980): Deterministic production planning: Algorithms and complexity. In: Management Science 26, pp. 669-679.

Golany ,B., Yang, J., Yu, G. (2001): Economic lot-sizing with remanufacturing options. In: IIE Transactions 33, pp. 995-1003.

Guide, Jr V.D.R., Wassenhove, van L.N. (2003): Business Perspectives on Closed loop Supply Chains. Carnegie Bosch Foundation, Pittsburgh, Pennsylvania, forthcoming.

Heyman, D.P. (1977): Optimal disposal policies for a single-item inventory system with returns. In: Naval Research Logistics Quarterly 24, pp. 385-405.

Horngren, C.T., Datar, S.M., Foster, G. (2000): Cost Accounting, 11th ed. Prentice-Hall, New Jersey.

Houtum, van G.J., Zijm, W.H.M. (1991): Computational procedures for stochastic multi-echelon production systems. In: International Journal of Production Economics 23, pp. 223-237.

Inderfurth, K. (1997): Simple optimal replenishment and disposal policies for a product recovery system with leadtimes. In :OR Spektrum 19, pp. 111-122.

Inderfurth, K., Jensen, T. (1999): Analysis of MRP policies with recovery options. In: Leopold-Wildburger U., Feichtinger G., Kistner K.P. (Eds.) Modelling and Decisions in Economics. Physica, Heidelberg, pp. 189-228.

Inderfurth, K., Laan, van der E.A. (2001): Lead time effects and policy improvement for stochastic inventory control with remanufacturing. In: International Journal of Production Economics 71, pp. 381-390.

JAMA (2002): Bill on Resource Recycling for Used Cars Gains Diet Passage, JAMA Press Room, retrieved on August 6, 2002 from http://jamaserv.jama.or.jp/e_press/index.html

Kelle, P., Silver, E.A. (1989): Purchasing policy of new containers considering the returns of previously returned containers. In: IIE Transactions 21, pp. 349-354.

Kiesmüller, G.P., Minner, S. (2002): Simple expressions for finding recovery system inventory control parameter values. Journal of the Operational Research Society, forthcoming.

Kiesmüller, G.P., Laan, van der E.A. (2001): An inventory model with dependent product demands and returns. In: International Journal of Production Economics 72, pp. 73-87.

Laan, van der E.A. (1997): The Effects of Remanufacturing on Inventory Control. PhD Thesis, Rotterdam School of Management, Erasmus University Rotterdam.

Laan, van der E.A., Dekker, R., Salomon M. (1996): Production planning and inventory control with remanufacturing and disposal: A numerical comparison between alternative control strategies. In: International Journal of Production Economics 45, pp. 489-498.

Laan, van der E.A., Salomon, M., Dekker, R., Wassenhove, van L.N. (1999): Inventory control in hybrid systems with remanufacturing. In: Management Science 45, pp. 733-747.

Mahadevan, B., Pyke, D.F., Fleischmann M. (2002): Periodic review, push inventory policies for remanufacturing. In: European Journal of Operational Research, forthcoming.

Minner, S. (2001a). Strategic safety stocks in reverse logistics supply chains. In: International Journal of Production Economics 71, pp. 417-428.

Minner, S. (2001b). Economic production and remanufacturing lot-sizing under constant demands and returns. In: Fleischmann B., Lasch R., Derigs U., Domschke W., Rieder U. (Eds.), Operations Research Proceedings 2000. Springer, Berlin Heidelberg New York, pp. 328-332.

Minner, S., Kiesmüller, G.P. (2002): Dynamic product acquisition in closed loop supply chains. Working Paper 9/2002, Faculty of Economics and Management, Otto-von-Guericke-University Magdeburg.

Minner, S., Kleber, R. (2001): Optimal control of production and remanufacturing in a simple recovery model with linear cost functions. In: OR Spektrum 23, pp. 3-24.

Moinzadeh, K. (1997): Replenishment and stocking policies for inventory systems with random deal offerings. In: Management Science 43, pp. 334-342.

Muckstadt, J.A., Isaac, M.H. (1981): An analysis of single-item inventory systems with returns. In: Naval Research Logistics Quarterly 28, pp. 237-254.

Nahmias, S., Rivera, H. (1979): A deterministic model for a repairable inventory system with a finite repair rate. In: International Journal of Production Research 17, pp. 215-221.

REVLOG (2002): Revlog – The European Working Group on Reverse Logistics. Retrieved on September 26, 2002 from http://www.fbk.eur.nl/OZ/REVLOG.

Richter, K. (1996): The EOQ repair and waste disposal model with variable setup numbers. In :European Journal of Operational Research 96, pp. 313-324.

Richter, K., Sombrutzki, M. (2000): Remanufacturing planning for the reverse Wagner/Whitin models. In: European Journal of Operational Research 121, pp. 304-315.

Rosling, K. (1989): Optimal inventory policies for assembly systems under random demands. In: Operations Research 37, pp. 565-579.

Sherbrooke, C.C. (1992): Optimal Inventory Modeling of Systems: Multi-Echelon Techniques. Wiley, New York.

Silver, E.A., Pyke D.F., Peterson R. (1998): Inventory Management and Production Planning and Scheduling, 3rd edition. Wiley, New York.

Schrady, D. (1967): A deterministic inventory model for reparable items. In: Naval Research Logistics Quarterly 14, pp. 391-398.

Simpson, V.P. (1978): Optimum solution structure for a repairable inventory problem. In: Operations Research 26, pp. 270-281.

Teunter, R. (2001): Economic ordering quantities for recoverable item inventory systems. In: Naval Research Logistics 48, pp. 484-495.

Teunter, R., Inderfurth, K., Minner, S., Kleber, R. (2000a): Reverse logistics in a pharmaceutical company: A case study. Working Paper 15/2000, Faculty of Economics and Management, Otto-von-Guericke-University Magdeburg.

Teunter, R., Laan, van der E.A., Inderfurth, K. (2000b): How to set the holding cost rates in average cost inventory models with reverse logistics? In: Omega 28, pp. 409-415.

Teunter, R., Laan, van der E.A., Vlachos D. (2001): Inventory strategies with fast remanufacturing. Working Paper EI 2001-40, Econometric Institute, Erasmus University Rotterdam.

Teunter, R.H., Vlachos, D. (2002): On the necessity of a disposal option for returned items that can be remanufactured. In: International Journal of Production Economics 75, pp. 257-266.

Thierry, M.C., Salomon, M., Nunen, van J., Wassenhove, van L. (1995): Strategic issues in product recovery management. In: California Management Review 37, pp. 114-135.

Toktay, L.B., Wein, L.M., Zenios, S.A. (2000): Inventory management of remanufacturable products. In: Management Science 46, pp. 1412-1426.

Vlachos, D., Dekker, R. (2000): Return handling options and order quantities for single period products. Working Paper EI2000-29/A, Econometric Institute, Erasmus University Rotterdam.

VROM (2002): Waste of Electric and Electronic Equipment Decree, The Netherlands Ministry of Housing, Spatial Planning and the Environment. Retrieved on August 6, 2002 from http://www2.minvrom.nl/pagina.html?id=5003

Wagner H.M., Whitin T.M. (1958): Dynamic version of the economic lot size model. Management Science 5, pp. 89-96.

Whisler, W.D. (1967): A stochastic inventory model for rented equipment. In: Management Science 13, pp. 640-647.

Whittemore, A.S., Saunders, S.C. (1977): Optimal inventory under stochastic demand with two supply options. In: SIAM Journal of Applied Mathematics 32, pp. 293-305.

Wilens, C. (2002): Managing Returnable Packaging. Masters Thesis, Rotterdam School of Management, Erasmus University Rotterdam.

Wojanowski, R. (1999): Zur Güte von dynamischen Losgrößenheuristiken in einem deterministischen Produktions-Lagerhaltungsmodell mit Recycling. Masters Thesis, Faculty of Economics and Management, Otto-von-Guericke-University Magdeburg.

Yuan, X.M., Cheung, K.L. (1998): Modeling returns of merchandise in an inventory system. In :OR Spektrum 20, pp. 147-154.

Zheng, Y.S., Federgruen, A. (1991): Finding optimal (s,S) policies is about as simple as evaluating a single policy. In: Operations Research 39, pp. 654-665.

Production-Inventory Control in an EOQ-Type Reverse Logistics System

Knut Richter, Imre Dobos

Department of Industrial Production
Faculty of Economics and Management
European University Viadrina, Frankfurt (Oder)
Grosse Scharrnstr. 59
D-15230 Frankfurt (Oder), Germany

Department of Business Economics
Budapest University of Economics and Public Administration
H-1053 Budapest, Veres Pálné and 36, Hungary

Abstract: *In this paper a general reverse logistics system to satisfy a steady demand for one product by production and recycling is studied. The model incorporates the two extreme policies of production (the pure production model) and of recycling (the pure recycling model) only. This general model, which has been introduced recently by the authors and is therefore called RD-model, examines the possibility of repurchasing and recycling or disposing used items. Since the total cost of the model contains both EOQ-related (setup cost and holding cost) and non-EOQ-related costs (waste disposal, recycling, production and repurchasing costs), first the optimal lot sizes for the EOQ-related cost function are presented. Then, the transformation of the RD-model into a special fractional optimization program follows. The optimization program for the RD-model, let us call it RD-program, includes other known EOQ recovery models as special cases and, in this sense, it can be regarded as a meta-program for all of them. An analysis of the material flow in various models will be provided, and a classification of the models is suggested. Moreover, cost-minimal repurchasing rates and use rates of used items are determined. The analysis shows – as it is known for other models – that the mixed strategies of combining production and recycling are dominated by the pure strategies (either production or recycling), i. e. – if technologically feasible – either pure production or recycling is optimal.*

Keywords: *EOQ model, production recycling, waste disposal, cost minimization*

1. Introduction

In this paper a EOQ type model is developed and analyzed, in which a producer serves customers with stationary demand, occurring at the rate of $D > 0$ per time unit. This demand is served by producing (or procuring) new items as well as by recycling some part $0 \leq \delta \leq 1$ of the used products coming back to the producer at a constant return rate $d = \alpha D$, $0 \leq \alpha \leq 1$. It is assumed that the producer is in the situation to buy back all used product to recycle and/or to dispose of them. The parameters δ and α are called *marginal use rate* and *marginal repurchase (buyback, return) rate*, respectively. The remaining part of the non-serviceable products $(1-\delta)d$ will be disposed off. $(1-\delta)$ is called *marginal disposal rate.*

First, an analysis of the situation is provided. The inventory stocks for *serviceable* products from the *production and recycling processes* (PRP) and for the *non-serviceable* items are determined. On the basis of these results the lot sizes and cycle times for the PRP can be found which minimize the total setup and holding costs per time unit. This results in the explicit determination of an EOQ-related cost function $C_I(\alpha,\delta)$ which expresses these minimal costs as function of the marginal use and repurchasing rates.

Secondly, if linear waste disposal, production, recycling and repurchasing costs are introduced and their sum is denoted by a non-EOQ-related costs function $C_N(\alpha,\delta)$, the problem appears at which δ and α the total setup, holding and linear costs $C_I(\alpha,\delta)+C_N(\alpha,\delta)$ is minimal. In this formulation the producer makes decision about how large portion of the used items should be repurchased and recycled.

A deterministic EOQ-type reverse logistic model was first analyzed by Schrady (1967, pp. 391-398). He has examined a model with more than one recycling/repair cycles and one production/procurement cycle, and he has calculated the corresponding optimal lot sizes. Nahmias and Rivera (1979, pp. 215-21) have generalized this model for the case of finite recycling/repair rates. Mabini, Pintelon and Gelders (Mabini et al., 1998, pp. 173-192) discussed an extension of the basic model of Schrady to a multi-item case. Dobos (2001) offered a generalization for the case of more than one production/procurement cycle. However, these authors have not investigated the optimal use and return rates. In these models all returned items are reusable.

Some times ago Richter (pp. 313-324, 1996, pp. 443-447, 1997, pp. 123-129), Richter and Dobos (1999, pp. 463-467) and Dobos and Richter (1999, pp. 69-78, 2000, pp. 173-194) have studied a waste disposal model, where the return rate is a decision variable. This model is based on the ideas of Kelle and Silver (1989, pp. 349-354) for repaired containers, which did not – however – come from the EOQ-environment. They have determined the optimal number of remanufacturing and production batches depending on the return rate. In (Richter, 1997, pp. 123-129), Richter has examined the optimal inventory holding policy, when the waste disposal (return) rate is a decision variable. The result of this paper is that the optimal policy has an extremal property: either to reuse all items without disposal or to dispose off all items and produce new products.

Teunter (2001, pp. 484-495) has offered a model, where not all items are remanufactured, i.e. the decision maker decides about the reuse of items returning at a known return rate. The authors of this paper have analyzed Teunter's model in an earlier work (Dobos and Richter, 1999), and they have shown that the manufacturing and remanufacturing batch size depends on the reuse rate.

Recently, another production/recycling model, a certain precursor of the model studied here, was investigated by Dobos and Richter (2001). It is assumed that there is only one recycling lot and one production lot and the cost minimal marginal use and return rates have to be determined. Two types of models have been analyzed: a model with minimal EOQ type costs and another with minimizing the relevant EOQ and non-EOQ related costs. A generalization of this model for the case of more than one production and/or recycling batches, we call it now RD-model, has been examined in the paper (Dobos and Richter, 2002, pp. 47-60) first time. The result of these papers is that it is optimal either to produce or to recycle all items repurchased. This result supports the extremal optimal policy proposed in (Richter, 1997, pp. 123-129).

This paper is organized as follows. The next section introduces the parameters and decision variables of the new model and it explains the behavior of the production and recycling processes. In section 3 the EOQ cost function $\widetilde{C}_A(m,n,\alpha,\delta)$ for variable recycling/production batch numbers and repurchasing/use rates will be constructed. In the following section 4 we determine the formulae for the cost minimal cycle time and batch numbers for production and recycling, depending on the repurchasing and use rates in a new compact way. These efforts result in the function $C_I(\alpha,\delta)$ which minimizes the cost function from the previous section subject to m and n. Section 5 provides an analytical examination of the above mentioned one-product reverse logistics models by transforming them into fractional optimization programs. It will be pointed out that these models are special versions of the appropriate program for the RD-model. The analysis of the material flows showing the features which are common for all models, or unique to some of them, is provided in the section 6. In section 7 the optimal policies for the total (EOQ and non-EOQ related) cost models will be investigated. The analysis shows – as it is known for other models – that the mixed strategies (combining production and recycling) are dominated by the pure strategies (either production or recycling), i. e. – if technologically feasible – either pure production or recycling is optimal. In the last section we summarize the results obtained and show some directions for generalization.

2. Parameters and functioning of the system

First the parameters and variables of the RD-model are introduced.

Lot-size related parameters of the RD-model:

- D per time unit demand rate,
- $P=\frac{1}{\beta}D$ per time unit production rate ($\beta < 1$),
- $d=\alpha D$ per time unit repurchasing rate ($0 \leq \alpha \leq 1$),
- $R=\frac{1}{\gamma}D$ per time unit recycling rate ($\gamma < 1$),
- S_R setup costs of recycling,
- S_P setup costs of production,
- h_s per unit per time unit holding cost of serviceable items,
- h_n per unit per time unit holding cost of non-serviceable items.

Lot-size independent cost parameters of the RD-model (per unit):

- C_w waste disposal cost for $(1-\delta)\cdot\alpha d\cdot T$,
- C_P linear production cost for $(1-\delta\alpha)d\cdot T$,
- C_R linear recycling cost for $\delta\cdot\alpha d\cdot T$,
- C_B repurchasing cost for $\alpha\cdot d\cdot T$.

Decision variables of the RD-model:

- δ marginal use rate,
- α marginal repurchasing rate,
- m number of recycling lots, positive integer,
- T_R time interval of recycling,
- x_R recycling lot size, $x_R = D \cdot T_R$
- n number of production lots, positive integer,
- T_P time interval of production,
- x_P recycling lot size, $x_P = D \cdot T_P$
- T length of production and recycling cycles.

Now the modeled situation can be described:

The material flow is shown in Fig. 1 with the introduced parameters and decision variables. The inventory status is illustrated in Fig. 2. Both figures allow to explain the model:

It can be easily seen that for a given length T of the PRP cycle the steady demand D is satisfied first by recycling nonserviceables at the recycling rate R and after that by producing (procuring) new items at the rate of P. For fixed repurchasing and use rates α and δ, respectively, $\delta \cdot \alpha D \cdot T$ units will be repurchased and recycled, and therefore $(1-\delta\alpha)D \cdot T$ units must be produced or procured. If recycling and production lots are accomplished by the numbers m and n, respectively, the recycling lot size equals $x_R = \delta \cdot \alpha D \cdot T/m$ and the production lot size equals $x_P = (1-\delta\alpha)D \cdot T/n$. The $D \cdot T$ units, which have been recycled or produced pass the serviceable stock and serve then the customer.

The producer buys back $\alpha D \cdot T$ units, which pass the nonserviceable stock, but he disposes of $(1-\delta) \cdot \alpha D \cdot T$ units.

Let T_R be the length of each of the *m recycling cycle intervals*. During these intervals the demand is satisfied by recycled non-serviceable products from the serviceable store. The non-serviceable products arrive at the rate $d < D = \alpha d$. Due to the given recycling rate $R > D = \gamma R$ the process of recycling lasts for some $\gamma \cdot T_R$ time units. When the recycling process is stopped the demand can be served by the accumulated stock of recycled products. (compare Fig. 2).

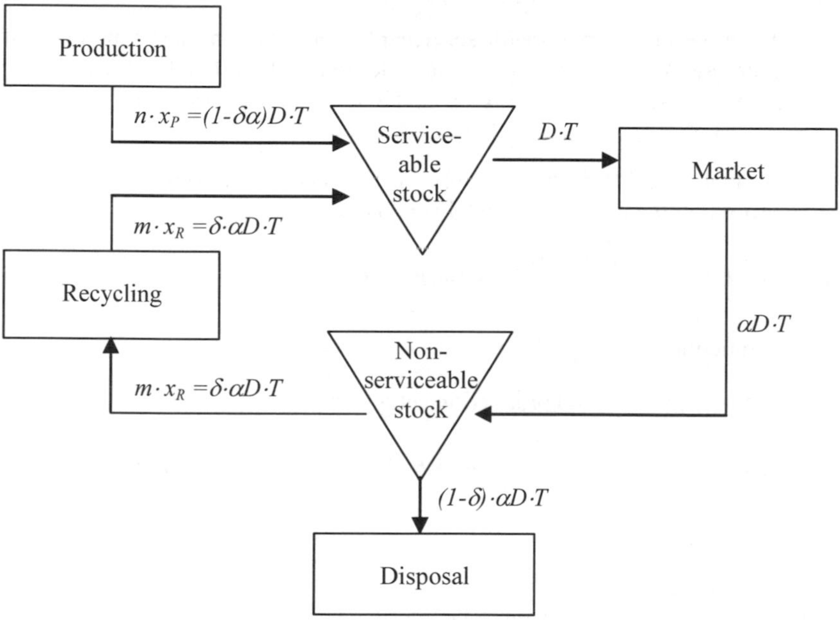

Fig. 1. The PRP cycle material flow in the RD-model

After completing the recycling process, at $m \cdot T_R$, the producer has to start the production (or procurement) process n times at the rate P, $D = \beta P < P$, satisfying the demand for each of the production cycle intervals of the length T_P. $T = m \cdot T_R + n \cdot T_P$ gives the length of the production and recycling cycle.

The process of storing and disposing of non-serviceable goods can be organized in the following way: the $(1-\delta)\alpha DT$ units which have to be disposed during some interval T are disposed during the time disposal interval $T_D = (1-\delta)T$ just when they arrive. Hence some stock of non-serviceable items is set up during the collection interval $T_{RC} = T - T_D = \delta T$.

At the end of the production cycle the inventory stock of non-serviceable products attains its peak $I_n = [(1-\alpha)m+\alpha(1-\gamma)]\cdot DT_R$ which is the initial inventory level at the beginning of the production and recycling cycle. At the end of a recycling period the inventory stock of serviceable recycled products attains its peak $I_R = (1-\gamma)\cdot DT_R$. The peak of the inventory stock of newly produced items is $I_P = (1-\beta)\cdot DT_P$.

3. The inventory holding costs and the optimal PRP cycle time for the RD-model

Let h_s denote the inventory cost for serviceable items per unit and time unit, and let h_n denote the same cost for non-serviceable items. If the length of the PRP cycle T is given, the sum of average setup cost and inventory cost – let it be denoted by $C_A(T,m,n,\alpha,\delta)$ – is as shown in Lemma 1.

Lemma 1 (Dobos and Richter, 2002, pp. 47-60): The sum of setup cost and average inventory holding cost of the model is equal to

$$C_A(T,m,n,\alpha,\delta) = \frac{S_T(m,n)}{T} + \frac{1}{2} TD \cdot V(m,n,\alpha,\delta) \tag{1}$$

where the function $S_T(m,n) = S_R \cdot m + S_P \cdot n$ (2)

covers the total recycling and production setup cost and

$$V(m,n,\alpha,\delta) = (h_s + h_n)(1-\gamma)\alpha^2\delta^2 \cdot \frac{1}{m} + h_s(1-\beta)(1-\alpha\delta)^2 \cdot \frac{1}{n} + h_n\alpha(1-\alpha)\delta^2 \tag{3}$$

provides the holding cost per demand and time units as function of m, n, α and, δ.

We can note that if $n=0$, $m=1$ and $\alpha=1$, $\delta=1$ ($m=0$, $n=1$ and $\alpha=0$), i. e. if there is no production and everything must be repurchased and used (no recycling and nothing will be repurchased), then

$$V(1,0,1,1) = (h_s + h_n)(1-\gamma) \text{ and } V(0,1,0,0) = h_s(1-\beta) \tag{4}$$

provide the corresponding inventory cost for ordinary lot sizing models with one production (or recycling) activity.

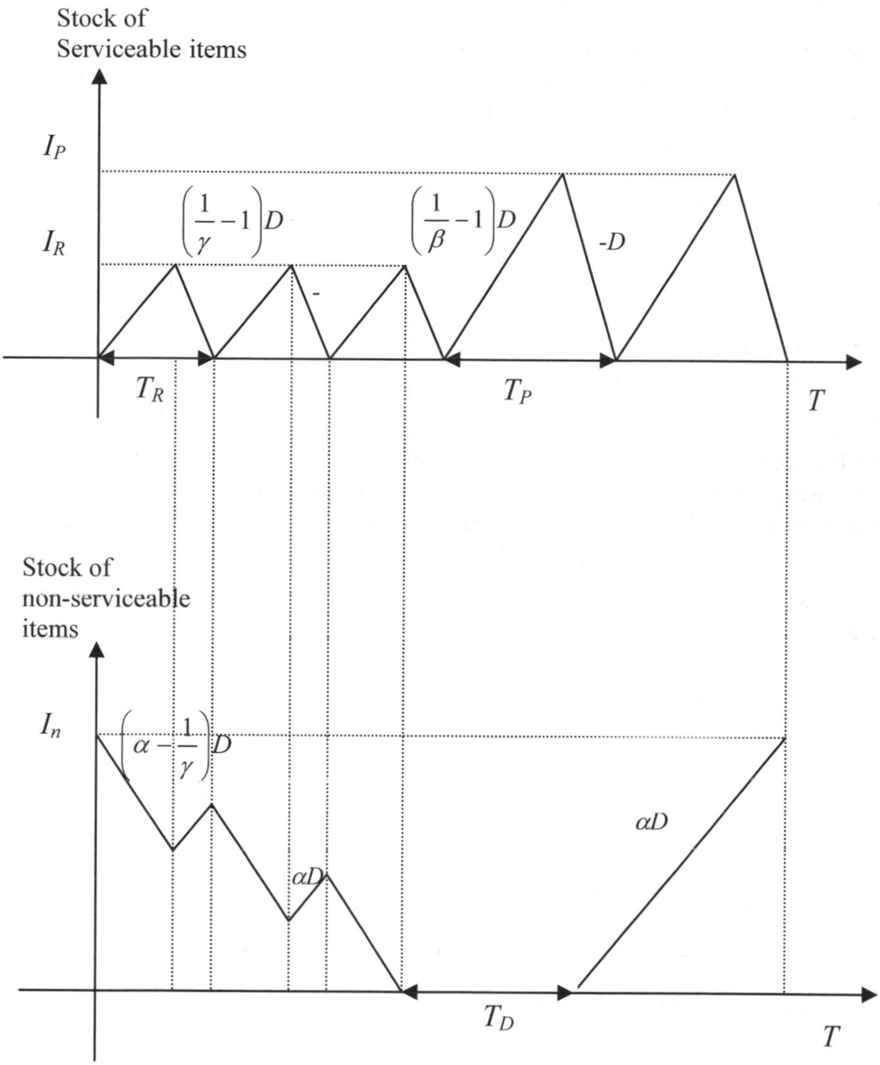

Fig. 2. Inventory status in the model (m = 3, n = 2)

Interestingly, the activities of serving the demand of one product unit for one time unit require the a inventory cost of € $V(m,n,\alpha,\delta)$ independently from the length T of the PRP cycle. An simple proof of this lemma is given in (Dobos and Richter, 2002, pp. 47-60).

Let the formula (3) be presented as

$V(m,n,\alpha,\delta) = H_R(\alpha,\delta)\cdot\frac{1}{m} + H_P(\alpha,\delta)\cdot\frac{1}{n} + H_n(\alpha,\delta)$, where the factors express three different types of inventory holding cost occurring in our system: those induced by collecting and recycling used items, those induced by the production of new items, and those induced by collecting those items which were used for the first time. Later we need the relationships

$$M(\alpha,\delta) = \frac{H_R(\alpha,\delta)}{H_R(\alpha,\delta)+H_n(\alpha,\delta)} \text{ and } N(\alpha,\delta) = \frac{H_P(\alpha,\delta)}{H_P(\alpha,\delta)+H_n(\alpha,\delta)}, \tag{5}$$

which show the rate of the recycling (production) induced inventory cost compared with the sum of the recycling (production) induced inventory cost and the collection induced inventory cost. We call these values recycling (production) induced inventory cost rates.

Example 1: Let $S_P = 1{,}960$, $S_R = 440$, m = 1 and, n = 2, then $S_T(m,n) = 4{,}360/T$. Furthermore, let D = 1,000, $h_s = 850$, $h_n = 80$, $\beta = 2/3$, $\gamma = 2/3$, $\alpha = 0.73$ and $\delta = 2/3$. Then $V(m,n,\alpha,\delta) = 117.78$ holds, i. e. the inventory cost of € 117.78 is needed to satisfy the demand of one unit. The recycling (production) induced inventory cost rates are equal to $M(\alpha,\beta) = 0.913$ and $N(\alpha,\delta) = 0.956$.

The cost minimal PRP cycle time T^o can be determined by solving the following problem:

$$C_A(T,m,n,\alpha,\delta) = \frac{S_T(m,n)}{T} + \frac{1}{2}T\cdot D\cdot V(m,n,\alpha,\delta) \to \min \tag{6}$$

Because of the convexity of the cost function $S_T(m,n)$ the cost minimal cycle time is

$$T^o(m,n,\alpha,\delta) = \sqrt{\frac{2S_T(m,n)}{D\cdot V(m,n,\alpha,\delta)}} \tag{7}$$

and the minimal total setup and inventory cost per time unit is

$$\widetilde{C}_A(m,n,\alpha,\delta) = \sqrt{2D\cdot S_T(m,n)\cdot V(m,n,\alpha,\delta)}\,. \tag{8}$$

More results are given in Table 1.

As it could be guessed from formula (4), these results contain the formulae for pure strategies, i.e. for the cases of no recycling ($\alpha=\delta=0$) and no production ($\alpha=\delta=1$). The optimal costs and lot sizes can be written for these cases, as

$$\begin{array}{ll} \widetilde{C}_P = \widetilde{C}_A(0,1,0,0) = \sqrt{2DS_P\cdot h_s(1-\beta)}, & \widetilde{x}_P = \sqrt{2DS_P/h_s(1-\beta)} \\ \widetilde{C}_R = \widetilde{C}_A(1,0,1,1) = \sqrt{2DS_R\cdot (h_s+h_n)(1-\gamma)}, & \widetilde{x}_R = \sqrt{2DS_R/(h_s+h_n)(1-\gamma)} \end{array}, \tag{13}$$

where parameter $\widetilde{C}_P$ ($\widetilde{C}_R$) denote the minimal cost for the pure strategy production (recycling), and $\widetilde{x}_P$ ($\widetilde{x}_R$) denote the appropriate lot sizes.

optimal recycling and production cycle times	optimal lot sizes
$T_R^o(m,n,\alpha,\delta)=\frac{\alpha\delta}{m}\sqrt{\frac{2S_T(m,n)}{D\cdot V(m,n,\alpha,\delta)}}$ (9)	$x_R^o(m,n,\alpha,\delta)=\frac{\alpha\delta}{m}\sqrt{\frac{2DS_T(m,n)}{V(m,n,\alpha,\delta)}}$ (11)
$T_P^o(m,n,\alpha,\delta)=\frac{1-\alpha\delta}{n}\sqrt{\frac{2S_T(m,n)}{D\cdot V(m,n,\alpha,\delta)}}$ (10)	$x_P^o(m,n,\alpha,\delta)=\frac{1-\alpha\delta}{n}\sqrt{\frac{2DS_T(m,n)}{V(m,n,\alpha,\delta)}}$ (12)

Table 1. Optimal recycling and production cycle times and optimal lot sizes for given m, n, α and, δ in the RD-model

Example 2: Let the data of example 1 be used to determine the cost minimal PRP cycle time and the other parameters and let the time unit be equal one year, i. e. $D = 1{,}000$, is the demand for one year and, $h_s = 850$ and $h_n = 80$ give the appropriate per unit inventory cost for one year. The cost curve is now given by $C_A(T,1,2,\alpha,\delta)=\frac{4360}{T}+58.88\cdot T$. The optimal length of the production cycle and recycling cycle is $T^o(1,2,\alpha,\delta)=0.272$ of one year or, 99 days. The minimal cost per time unit is $\widetilde{C}_A(1,2,\alpha,\delta)=\sqrt{2\cdot D\cdot 4{,}360\cdot 117.76}=32{,}044.84$. Compared with these cost the minimum costs for the pure strategies are $\widetilde{C}_P=33{,}326.67$ and $\widetilde{C}_R=16{,}516.66$, respectively. The lot sizes are given by $\widetilde{x}_P=117.62$ and $\widetilde{x}_R=$ 53.28. One should keep in mind that the pure production strategy is such a "cheap", since so far no disposal cost has been regarded.

4. The optimal number of lots for production and recycling

Now we will minimize the cost function (8) in order to determine the optimal number of lots m^o and n^o:

$$\widetilde{C}_A(m,n,\alpha,\delta)\rightarrow \min \qquad m,\, n\geq 1. \tag{14}$$

Now, the integrality conditions of the variables m and n will be ignored and the optimal continuous solutions $m^o(\alpha,\delta)$ and $n^o(\alpha,\delta)$ and the appropriate minimal cost $C_I(\alpha,\delta)$ will be found.

After some transformations the cost function (6) can be written in the following the form:

$$\widetilde{C}_A(m,n,\alpha,\delta)=\sqrt{2D\cdot\left[A(\alpha,\delta)\cdot\frac{m}{n}+B(\alpha,\delta)\cdot\frac{n}{m}+C(\alpha,\delta)\cdot m+D(\alpha,\delta)\cdot n+E(\alpha,\delta)\right]}\rightarrow\min \quad (15)$$

where

$$A(\alpha,\delta)=S_R\cdot H_P(\alpha,\delta),\quad B(\alpha,\delta)=S_P\cdot H_R(\alpha,\delta),$$
$$C(\alpha,\delta)=S_R\cdot H_n(\alpha,\delta),\quad D(\alpha,\delta)=S_P\cdot H_n(\alpha,\delta),\quad E(\alpha,\delta)=S_R\cdot H_R(\alpha,\delta)+S_P\cdot H_P(\alpha,\delta).$$

To solve this problem, which is called *RD-program*, we can use the results known already for the following general fractional program, called *GF-program* (see (Dobos and Richter, 1999, pp. 69-78, 20, pp. 173-194, (Richter, 1996, pp. 313-324, 1999. pp. 443-447, 1997, pp. 123-129, (Richter and Dobos, 1999, pp. 463-467)):

$$S(m,n)=A\frac{m}{n}+B\frac{n}{m}+Cm+Dn+E\rightarrow\min,\qquad m\geq 1,\ n\geq 1. \quad (16)$$

The RD-program, and by this way the RD-model, is obviously a special case of the GF-program. Every method which solves the GF-program, solves also the RD-program and the RD-model. The solution to the GF-program is rather simply (Dobos and Richter, 2000, pp. 173-194) and considers three different cases (note that the problem (16) is symmetric with respect to the variables *m* and *n*):

(i) If $A\leq 0 \wedge B\leq 0$ then $m=n=1$ is optimal.

(ii) If $A+C>0 \wedge B+D>0$ and $B\ (A)\leq 0 \wedge A\ (B)>0$ then $n=1\ (m=1)$ holds.

(iii) If $A>0,\ B>0$ and $D=C=0$ then $\sqrt{A}m=\sqrt{B}n$ holds.

Applying the results from (Dobos and Richter, 2000, pp. 173-194) for the analysis of the function (15), the optimal continuous solution (m^o,n^o) can be always found in one of three regions *I, J* or *K* from $\{(\alpha,\delta):0<\alpha,\delta\leq 1\}$. It is remarkable that $m^o=1$ always for given $(\alpha,\delta)\in I\cup J$ and $n^o=1$ for given $(\alpha,\delta)\in J\cup K$. The properties proved in (Dobos and Richter, 2002, pp. 47-60) will be presented in a more compact way:

Lemma 2: There are three cases of optimal continuous solutions $\left(m^o(\alpha,\delta),n^o(\alpha,\delta)\right)$ and minimum cost expressions $C_I(\alpha,\delta)$ for the RD-program (14): Let $m^+(\alpha,\delta)=\frac{\alpha\delta}{1-\alpha\delta}\cdot\frac{\widetilde{x}_P}{\widetilde{x}_R}\cdot\sqrt{N(\alpha,\delta)}$ and $n^+(\alpha,\delta)=\frac{1-\alpha\delta}{\alpha\delta}\cdot\frac{\widetilde{x}_R}{\widetilde{x}_P}\cdot\sqrt{M(\alpha,\delta)}$ (17)

(i) If $m^+(\alpha,\delta)\leq 1,\ n^+(\alpha,\delta)\geq 1 \Leftrightarrow (\alpha,\delta)\in I$. Then

$$\left(m^o(\alpha,\delta),n^o(\alpha,\delta)\right)=\left(1,\,n^+(\alpha,\delta)\right) \text{ and } C_I(\alpha,\delta)=(1-\alpha\delta)\cdot\widetilde{C}_P+\alpha\delta\cdot\widetilde{C}_R/\sqrt{M(\alpha,\delta)}$$

(ii) if $m^+(\alpha,\delta)\leq 1,\;\; n^+(\alpha,\delta)\leq 1 \Leftrightarrow (\alpha,\delta)\in J$, then

$$\left(m^o(\alpha,\delta),n^o(\alpha,\delta)\right)=(1,\,1) \text{ and } C_I(\alpha,\delta)=\sqrt{2D(S_R+S_P)\cdot V(1,1,\alpha,\delta)}$$

(iii) If $m^+(\alpha,\delta)\geq 1,\;\; n^+(\alpha,\delta)\leq 1 \Leftrightarrow (\alpha,\delta)\in K$, then

$$\left(m^o(\alpha,\delta),n^o(\alpha,\delta)\right)=\left(m^+(\alpha,\delta),\,1\right) \text{ and } C_I(\alpha,\delta)=\alpha\delta\cdot\widetilde{C}_R+(1-\alpha\delta)\cdot\widetilde{C}_P/\sqrt{N(\alpha,\delta)}.$$

Interpretation: The optimal batch numbers depend on three factors: on the fraction of returned goods, on the relationship between the pure lot sizes and on the inventory cost rates. For instance, if we regard the case (iii), it is understandable, that the batch number for the recycling lots increases, if the fraction of returned goods increases, if the pure recycling lot size decreases and if the rate of the production induced inventory cost increases. We also see that the minimum cost expressions appear as the convex combinations of the pure strategy minimum cost values, where always one of them is corrected by an inventory cost rate.

Note once more that the expressions for the optimal lot (batch) numbers found are not necessarily integer! Nevertheless we shall see in the next sections that this (immediately practically not very useful) result will help us to prove that the mixed strategies are dominated by pure ones.

Example 3: Let as in the former examples $D = 1{,}000$, $h_s = 850$, $h_n = 80$, $\beta = 2/3$, $\gamma = 2/3$, $S_P = 1{,}960$, $S_R = 440$, $\alpha = 0.73$ and $\delta = 2/3$. The optimal batch numbers are $m^+(\alpha,\delta) = 2$ and $n^+(\alpha,\delta) = 0.456$. Hence the optimal batch numbers are given by $(m^\circ,n^\circ) = (2,1)$, and one optimal PRP cycle consists of two recycling and one production batch. The minimal cost is $C_I(\alpha,\delta) = 25{,}930.69$, which is much lower than the value found in example 2 for $m=1$ and $n=2$.

5. Other deterministic one-product reverse logistics models and the GF-program

In this section we analyze and compare three earlier published reverse logistics models: the models of Schrady, Richter and Teunter. We call them *S-model, R-model* and *T-model,* respectively. We show that they all can be transformed into a special case of the GF-program, and therefore be solved by the proposed method. All of these models follow a predetermined inventory holding policy. (See Fleischmann et al., 1997, pp. 1-17).

In order to be able to compare the RD-model with these contributions, we have summarized the system parameters and decision variables of these papers in Table 2. The notations of parameters and decision variables follow those of the original publications. In Fig. 3. the material flows of these reverse logistics systems are considered together. It presents the different management concepts for disposing items and the warehouse structure in the examined situations. By the help of Fig. 4., i.e. the inventory status in time, the inventory holding costs and the cost functions can be calculated. On the basis of the time dependent inventory level function we can construct the average inventory cost functions for these contributions presented below. The interested reader can produce the formulae with some elementary operations.

5.1. The S-model: A purchasing model with repair

Schrady (1967, pp. 391-398) has analyzed a repair system of the U.S. Naval Supply Systems Command. A manufacturer uses repairable items. The items can fail and in that case they can be returned to the overhaul and repair department, but not all repairable items return to the department. The disposal activity is completed by the user. All returned products are stored and repaired, and then employed by the user as new ones. The losses are replaced through the procurement of new products. The repaired and procured items are stocked in a common store. The repairable items are stored at the overhaul and repair department. The basic model of Schrady covers only the case of one procurement batch. The results of Schrady were generalized by Dobos (2002) for the case of more than one procurement batches. We present the model in this extended form.

The average costs of this extended Schrady model is:

$$C_A^{Schrady}(Q_P,Q_R,m,n,T,r)=\frac{nA_R+nh_1\frac{Q_R^2}{2d}}{T}+\frac{mA_P+mh_1\frac{Q_P^2}{2d}}{T}+\frac{h_2\frac{Q_R^2}{2d}\left\{n^2\left(\frac{1}{r}-1\right)+n\right\}}{T} \tag{18}$$

under the conditions $nQ_R+mQ_P=dT,\quad nQ_R=(1-r)dT$.

After substituting and minimizing the lot sizes, we obtain the following simple average cost function:

$$\tilde{C}_A^{Schrady}(m,n,r)=\sqrt{2d\left(A(r)\frac{n}{m}+B(r)\frac{m}{n}+C(r)n+D(r)m+E(r)\right)} \tag{19}$$

where

$$A(r)=A_Rh_1(1-r)^2,\quad B(r)=A_P(h_1+h_2)r^2,\quad C(r)=A_Rh_2(1-r)r,$$
$$D(r)=A_Ph_2(1-r)r,\quad E(r)=A_R(h_1+h_2)r^2+A_Ph_1(1-r)^2$$

The model in this form is a subcase of the GF-program (16) and it can be solved in the same way as the RD-model.

	Generalized model of Schrady ((Dobos, 2002), (Schrady, 1967, pp. 391-398)])	*Model of Richter* ((1996, pp. 313-324))	*Model of Teunter* ((Dobos and Richter, 1999), (Teunter, 2001, pp. 484-495))
		Parameters	
Demand rate	d	d	λ
Return/recovery rate	r	β	r
Remanufacturing/repair cost	-	k	c_r
Manufacturing/procurement cost	-	b	c_m
Disposal cost	-	e	c_d
Setup cost for remanufacturing/repair	A_R	r	K_r
Setup cost for manufacturing/ procurement	A_P	s	K_m
Holding cost for remanufactured/repaired item	h_1	h	h_r
Holding cost for manufactured/procured item	h_1	h	h_m
Holding cost for disposing item	h_2	u	h_n
		Decision variables	
Batch (lot) size for remanufacturing/repair	Q_R	$\frac{\beta x}{m}$	Q_r
Number of batches for remanufacturing/repair	n	m	R
Batch (lot) size for manufacturing/procurement	Q_P	$\frac{\alpha x}{n}$	Q_m
Number of batches for manufacturing/procurement	m	n	M
Reuse/repair/recovery rate	r	$\beta = 1-\alpha$	$u \leq r$
Lot size	$dT = nQ_P + mQ_R$	$x = dT$	$\lambda T = RQ_r + MQ_m$
Cycle time	T	T	T

Table 2. Notations of the models

5.2. The R-model: A waste disposal model

This model describes the production of new and the repair of used products in a first shop and the employment of the products in a second shop. The used products can either be stored at the second shop and then be repurchased at the end of the collection interval $[0,T]$ to the first shop for repair, or be disposed somewhere outside. In the first shop lot sizes or newly manufactured products and of repairable products have to be determined in order to meet the constant demand rate of the second shop. Some of the used products are collected at the second shop according to a not necessarily unique repair rate. The share of the used products not provided for repair is called waste disposal rate. The setup number for manufacturing is n and for repair m. The average cost function for this model can be written as

$$C_A^{Richter}(x,m,n,\alpha)=\frac{mr+h\frac{\beta^2x^2}{2dm}}{T}+\frac{ns+h\frac{\alpha^2x^2}{2dn}}{T}+\frac{u\frac{\beta Tx}{2}}{T}+\frac{u\frac{\beta^2x^2(m-1)}{2d}}{T} \tag{20}$$

under the condition $x=dT$.

After substitution and minimizing for x, we have the next average cost function:

$$\tilde{C}_A^{Richter}(m,n,\alpha)=\sqrt{2d\left(A(\alpha)\frac{m}{n}+B(\alpha)\frac{n}{m}+C(\alpha)m+D(\alpha)n+E(\alpha)\right)} \tag{21}$$

where

$$A(\alpha)=rh\alpha^2,\qquad B(\alpha)=s(h-u)\beta^2,\qquad C(\alpha)=ru(\beta+\beta^2)$$
$$D(\alpha)=su(\beta+\beta^2),\qquad E(\alpha)=sh\alpha^2+r(h-u)\beta^2$$

This model form was extensively analyzed by the authors of this paper (see (Dobos and Richter, 1999) – (Dobos and Richter, 2002, pp. 47-60), (Richter, 1996, pp. 313-324) – (Richter and Dobos, 1999, pp. 463-467))

5.3. The T-model: A remanufacturing model with continuous disposal

Teunter (2001, pp. 484-495) has investigated a situation where the items which return from market can be remanufactured or disposed of. The returned items can be stored and then be remanufactured. Some part of the returned items are disposed after the last remanufacturing batch. The remanufactured items are seen as new ones and stored with the manufactured products. It is assumed that the holding cost of remanufactured products is smaller than the manufactured products because remanufacturing is supposed to be easier and hence cheaper. Teunter argues that in an optimal continuous solution either the manufacturing or the remanufacturing batch number is equal to one. However, the authors of this paper have shown that under certain conditions both batch numbers can be strictly greater than one (Dobos and Richter, 1999, pp. 69-78). In addition to the manufacturing and remanufacturing batch sizes, this model seeks the cost minimal disposal rate for the sum of EOQ and non-EOQ cost, when linear manufacturing, remanufacturing and disposal costs are introduced. We will here analyze only the setup and inventory holding costs. The performance of this model is shown in Figures 3. and 4. The average cost function is as follows:

$$C_A^{Teunter}(Q_m,Q_r,M,R,T,u)=\frac{RK_r+Rh_r\frac{Q_r^2}{2\lambda}}{T}+\frac{MK_m+Mh_m\frac{Q_m^2}{2\lambda}}{T}+\frac{h_n\frac{Q_r^2}{2\lambda}\left\{R^2\left(\frac{1}{r}-1\right)+R\right\}}{T} \quad (22)$$

under the conditions $MQ_m+RQ_r=\lambda T,\quad RQ_r=u\lambda T$.

After substituting the batch sizes in the average cost function and minimizing the cycle time, we can analyze the next average cost function:

$$\tilde{C}_A^{Teunter}(M,R,u)=\sqrt{2\lambda\left(A(u)\frac{R}{M}+B(u)\frac{M}{R}+C(u)R+D(u)M+E(u)\right)} \quad (23)$$

where

$$A(u)=K_rh_m(1-u)^2,B(u)=K_m(h_r+h_n)u^2,C(u)=K_rh_n\left(\frac{1}{r}-1\right)u^2,$$

$$D(u)=K_mh_n\left(\frac{1}{r}-1\right)u^2,E(u)=K_r(h_r+h_n)u^2+K_mh_m(1-u)^2$$

It can be seen that Teunter's model can be also analyzed by using the results of the GF-program (16), and it can be solved by formulae similar to those in Lemma 2.

In this part of the paper we have presented other reverse logistics models, and it is shown that different reverse logistics models lead to a common GF-program which can be treated as meta-model for all these models. This meta-model is probably the most appropriate tool for analyzing and solving this kind of problems.

6. Some characteristics of material flow logistics in the production/recycling model

All of the regarded models rely on the assumption that the repaired/remanufactured products have the same quality as the newly manufactured items, i.e. the models apply the as-new-as-good principle. To our knowledge there is no EOQ-type reverse logistics model with consideration of downgraded remanufactured items.

Except the R-model, the S-model, the T-model, and the RD-model analyze a situation with two stocking points for inventories of serviceable and nonserviceable products. The model of Richter examines a situation with three stocking points. The repairable items in this case are e.g. containers in which spare parts are transported to a manufacturing point from a warehouse. These containers are to be remanufactured in the firm and then brought back for further transport. So the material flow of this model differs from other models. This model will be not compared to other ones because of the assumption we made in connection with the stocking points.

Generalized model of Schrady (Dobos, 2002), (Schrady, 1967, pp. 391-398))	*Model of Richter (1996, pp. 313-324)*	*Model of Teunter ((Dobos and Richter, 1999), (Teunter, 2002, pp .67-73))*

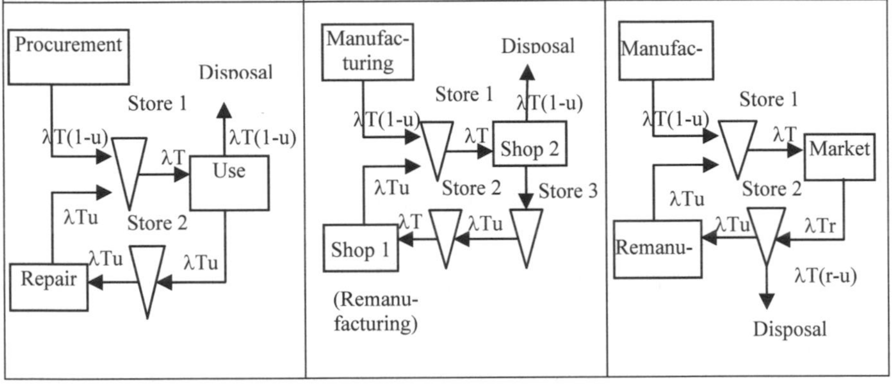

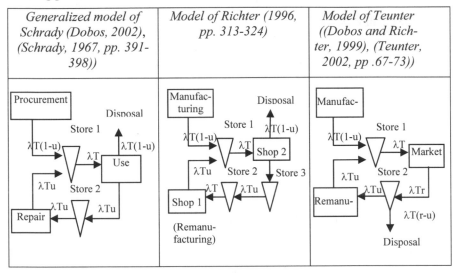

Fig. 3. Material flows in the reverse logistics models using the notations of Teunter

Let us continue the comparison of the three models: the S-model, the T-model, and the RD-model. The extended model of Schrady (Dobos, 2002) investigates a purchasing situation. The failing items are procured if not all used items turn back to the repairing point. There is no disposal at the non-ready-to-issue stocking points in this model. The analyzed situation can be extended to the case when the new items are not procured but manufactured in the firm. Such a problem leads to the classical make-or-buy decision for spare parts or products. We can point out that this model can lead to a situation proposed by Teunter and by Dobos and Richter (2002, pp. 47-60). If in the T-model and RD-model all returned items are reused, i.e. there is no disposal, then these two models contain the S-model. We can say that the last models are a generalization of the S-model.

The cost structure of the three compared models is the same: this concerns the setup costs for manufacturing and remanufacturing, as well as the holding costs for serviceable and nonserviceable items. The difference is that in Teunter's model it is assumed that the holding costs for remanufactured new items are lower than those of manufactured one. The argumentation is that the holding costs are measured as a percent (interest rate) of manufacturing/remanufacturing cost of an item, but the cost of manufacturing is higher then that of remanufacturing. If the remanufactured and manufactured products are stored in a common inventory stock then probably it is difficult to distinguish the items.

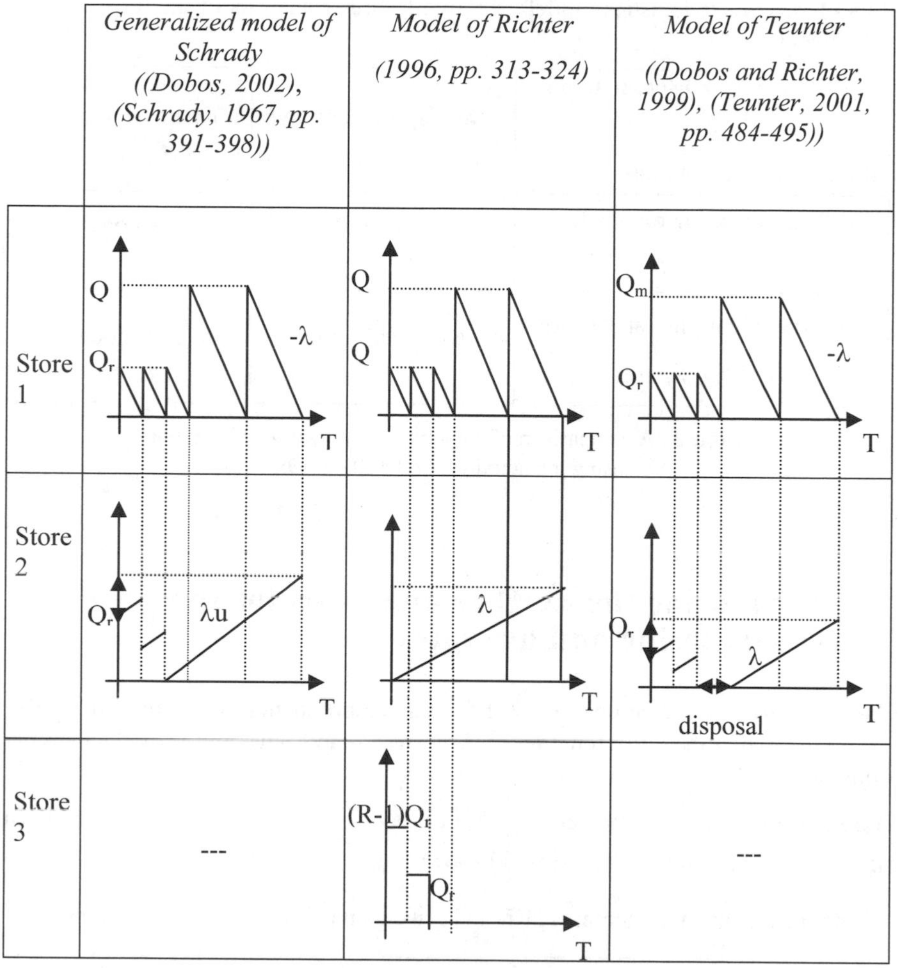

Fig. 4. Inventory status in reverse logistics models in a cycle using the notations of Teunter (R = 3, M = 2)

It is obvious that the most general model among the three ones is RD-model, presented in this paper apart from the assumption of the difference of holding costs of remanufactured and manufactured items. Through the finite rates this model takes into account that the production/manufacturing and recycling/remanufacturing processes need time. If these rates tend to infinity, we first obtain the T-model, and if in addition to this property we suppose total reuse without disposal, the S-model as a special case of the RD-model. (In the model of Schrady all returned items are reused without disposal.) An overview of these models depicted in Table 3. with the parameters of the RD-model. It can be seen that the RD-model includes the two other models. In case of an appropriate substitution we can have the results for other models with two stocking points. After this short review of EOQ type reverse logistics models we give a further analysis of the most general RD-model.

Disposal activity / Re-/Manufacturing rates	No disposal activity ($\delta = 1$)	Disposal activity ($0 \le \delta \le 1$)
Re-/Manufacturing rates infinite ($\beta = \gamma = 0$)	S-model	T-model
Re-/Manufacturing rates finite ($\beta \ge 0, \gamma \ge 0$)	No contribution	RD-model

Table 3. A comparison of the models with two stocking point using the notations of the RD-model

7. Minimizing the EOQ related costs for the repurchasing and use rates

Let us return to the examination of the extended production/recycling model. Before minimizing the costs function $C_I(\alpha,\delta)$ over α and δ we will provide a simple lemma.

Lemma 3 (Dobos and Richter, 2001): Let values a, b, c and d be positive. Then the following equality holds $\sqrt{(a+b)(c+d)} \ge \sqrt{ac} + \sqrt{bd}$. (24)

Using the results of the lemmas 2(ii) and 3 we gain the following inequalities

$$C_I(\alpha,\delta) \ge \sqrt{2DS_P \cdot h_s(1-\beta)(1-\alpha\delta)^2} + \sqrt{2DS_R \cdot \left[h_s(1-\gamma)\alpha^2\delta^2 + h_n\alpha(1-\alpha)\delta^2\right]} \ge$$
$$\ge (1-\alpha\delta)\cdot \tilde{C}_P + \alpha\delta \cdot \tilde{C}_R \quad (25)$$

Due to $M(\alpha,\delta)$, $N(\alpha,\delta) \le 1$ the last inequality (25) holds obviously also for the cases (i) and (iii).

The right hand side of the expression (25) shows a convex linear combination of the minimal cost for the case of production and no recycling and of the recycling case with no production. The weights are given by the products of the marginal use and repurchasing rates $\alpha\delta$ which are non-negative and not greater than one.

This minimum cost expression $C_I(\alpha,\delta)$ is always greater than the smallest of the minimal costs of the both pure strategies:

$$(1-\alpha\delta)\cdot\widetilde{C}_P+\alpha\delta\cdot\widetilde{C}_R\geq\min\{\widetilde{C}_P;\widetilde{C}_R\} \tag{26}$$

By this last inequality a proof is given for the finding the optimal repurchasing and use rates:

$$C_I(\alpha,\delta)\rightarrow\min,\quad \delta\in[0,1],\quad \alpha\in[0,1] \tag{27}$$

Theorem 1: The optimal production/recycling strategy in the EOQ-model (27) is a pure strategy: either to produce to meet the demand ($\alpha^o=\delta^o=0$) or to buy back and to recycle all used product without production ($\alpha^o=\delta^o=1$).

Example 4. Let D=1,000, $\beta=\gamma=2/3$, S_P =1960, S_R =440, h_s = 850 and h_n = 80. Then the $\widetilde{C}_R$ = 16,516.66 and $\widetilde{C}_P$ = 33,326.67. It is economical to recycle with the repurchasing of all used items.

Example 5. Let $D=1,000$, $\beta=2/5$ $\gamma=2/3$, $S_P=360$, $S_R=440$, $h_s=85$ and $h_n=80$. Then the costs of production is $\widetilde{C}_P=6,059.7$ and that of recycling $\widetilde{C}_R=6,957.01$. It is more effective to produce new items and not to recycle at all.

The results provided by the Theorem 1 are somewhat theoretical, since no waste disposal cost are regarded, for example. Therefore now we minimize the sum of the EOQ related and non-EOQ related costs. The cost function is given by

$$C_T(\alpha,\delta)=C_I(\alpha,\delta)+C_N(\alpha,\delta) \tag{28}$$

where the function

$$C_N(\alpha,\delta)=C_W\cdot(1-\delta)\alpha D+C_R\cdot\delta\alpha D+C_P\cdot(1-\delta\alpha)D+C_B\cdot\alpha D \tag{29}$$

is the sum of the linear waste disposal, recycling, production and repurchasing costs.

Now, the problem to be solved has the form

$$C_T(\delta,\alpha)\rightarrow\min,\quad \delta\in[0,1],\quad \alpha\in[0,1] \tag{30}$$

Due to relation (26), the cost $C_I(\alpha,\delta)$ is not greater than the convex linear combination of the cost for the pure production and recycling strategies. The non-EOQ related costs can be approximated in the following way

$$C_N(\alpha,\delta)\geq(1-\delta\alpha)\cdot D\cdot C_P+\delta\alpha\cdot D\cdot(C_B+C_R). \tag{31}$$

This inequality holds immediately, if we reduce the lot-size independent costs by the waste disposal costs $C_W\cdot(1-\delta)\alpha D$ and by the buy back costs for not recycled items $C_B\cdot(1-\delta)\alpha D$.

Using these two approximations we can give a lower bound of the total cost function

$$C_T(\alpha,\delta) \geq (1-\alpha\delta)\cdot\left(\widetilde{C}_P + D\cdot C_P\right) + \alpha\delta\cdot\left[\widetilde{C}_R + D\cdot\left(C_B + C_R\right)\right]. \tag{32}$$

The right-hand expression in (32) is again a convex linear combination of the pure strategies, so

$$(1-\alpha\delta)\cdot\left(\widetilde{C}_P + D\cdot C_P\right) + \alpha\delta\cdot\left[\widetilde{C}_R + D\cdot\left(C_B + C_R\right)\right] \geq \min\left\{\widetilde{C}_P + D\cdot C_P;\ \widetilde{C}_R + D\cdot\left(C_B + C_R\right)\right\}.$$

This result proves the next statement.

Theorem 2: The optimal production/recycling strategy for the total (EOQ and non-EOQ related) cost model is either to buy back all sold and used items ($\alpha^o = \delta^o = 1$) or to produce new items without buying back and recycling ($\alpha^o = \delta^o = 0$).

In the case of linear waste disposal, production, recycling and repurchasing costs and free choice of repurchasing and recycling rates between *0* and *1* one of the pure strategies to buy back and recycle, or to produce, is optimal. The optimal pure strategy can be found by comparing the values $\sqrt{2DS_P\cdot h_s(1-\beta)} + D\cdot C_P$ and $\sqrt{2DS_R\cdot(h_s+h_n)(1-\gamma)} + D\cdot(C_B + C_R)$.

8. Conclusions and further research

In this paper we have investigated a production/recycling model. We have shown that the GF-program will solve all the formulated reverspe logistics models. By minimizing the setup and inventory holding costs of the extended model, it was shown that one of the pure strategies (to produce or to recycle all products) is optimal. This extremal property was first proved by Richter (1997, pp. 123-129) for a waste disposal model with remanufacturing and then by Dobos and Richter (2001, 2002, pp. 47-60) in a production and recycling model.

Probably these pure strategies are technologically not feasible and some used products will not return or, even more than the sold ones might come back, and some of them will not be recyclable. This kind of generalization of this basic model could be the introduction of an upper bound on the repurchasing rate which is strongly smaller than one. In such a case a mixed strategy would be economical compared to the pure strategy of "production".

Another way to generalize this model is to consider the quality of the repurchased products. In the proposed model we have assumed that all returned items are serviceable. One can raise the question: Who should control the quality of the returned items? If the suppliers examine the quality of the reusable products, then the repurchasing rate is strongly smaller than one. If the user makes it, then not all returned items are recyclable, i.e. the use rate is smaller than one. Which one of the control systems are more beneficial in this case?

References

Dobos, I. (2002): The generalization of Schrady´s model: a model with repair, Working Paper Nr. 7, Department of Business Economics, Budapest University of Economics and Public Administration.

Dobos, I., Richter, K. (1999): The number of batch sizes in a remanufacturing model, Discusion paper 132, Viadrina European University of Frankfurt (Oder), Faculty of Economics and Business Administration.

Dobos, I., Richter, K. (1999): Comparison of Deterministic One-Product Reverse Logistics Models, in: Hill, R., Smith, D. (Eds.): Inventory Modelling: A Selection of Research Papers Presented at the Fourth ISIR Summer School (1999), Exeter 1999, pp. 69-78.

Dobos, I., Richter, K. (2000): The integer EOQ repair and waste disposal model – further analysis. Central European Journal of Operations Research 8, pp. 173-194.

Dobos, I., Richter, K. (2001): A production/recycling model with stationary demand and return rates, Central European Journal of Operations Research, to appear.

Dobos, I., Richter, K. (2002): An extended production/recycling model with stationary demand and return rates, Proceedings of the 12th International Working Seminar on Production Economics, Vol. 1, 47-60, Igls/Innsbruck.

Fleischmann, M., Bloemhof-Ruwaard, J.M., Dekker, R., Laan, van der E. Nunen, van J.A.E.E., Wassenhove, van der L.N. (1997): Quantitative models for reverse logistics: a review. European Journal of Operational Research 103, pp. 1-17.

Kelle, P., Silver, E.A. (1989): Purchasing policy of new containers considering the random returns of previously issued containers, IIE Transactions 21(4): pp. 349-354.

Mabini, M.C., Pintelon, L.M., Gelders, L.F. (1998): EOQ type formulation for controlling repairable inventories. International Journal of Production Economics 54, pp. 173-192.

Nahmias, N., Rivera, H: (1979): A deterministic model for repairable item inventory system with a finite repair rate. International Journal of Production Research 17(3), pp. 215-221.

Richter, K. (1996): The EOQ repair and waste disposal model with variable setup numbers, European Journal of Operational Research 96, pp. 313-324.

Richter, K. (1996): The extended EOQ repair and waste disposal model, International Journal of Production Economics 45, pp. 443-447.

Richter, K. (1997): Pure and mixed strategies for the EOQ repair and waste disposal problem, OR Spektrum 19, pp. 123-129.

Richter, K., Dobos, I. (1999): Analysis of the EOQ repair and waste disposal model with integer setup numbers, International Journal of Production Economics 59, pp. 463-467.

Schrady, D.A. (1967): A deterministic inventory model for repairable items. Naval Research Logistic Quarterly 14, pp. 391-398.

Teunter, R.H. (2001): Economic Ordering Quantities for Recoverable Item Inventory Systems, Naval Research Logistics, Vol. 48, 484-495 (first published: Preprint No. 31, 1998, Faculty of Economics and Management, Otto-von-Guericke University of Magdeburg, Germany).

Teunter, R., Laan, E. van der (2002): On the non-optimality of the average cost approach for inventory models with remanufacturing, Int. Journal of Production Economics Vol. 79, pp. 67-73.

PART II

Architecture and Coordination of Networks

Networks in Reverse Logistics

Marion Steven

Department of Production Economics
Faculty of Economic Management
Ruhr University Bochum
Universitaetsstr. 150
D-44801 Bochum, Germany

Abstract: *Reverse logistics deals with the organization of the various processes which are necessary for returning waste materials and used goods to their producers resp. into the economic cycle. In the first section of this paper, the impact of reverse logistics on the improvement of the economic and ecological performance of an economy is discussed. Compared to the traditional flow economy, such a closed-loop economy implies savings of raw materials and energy on the input side and of landfill capacity on the output side of the production process, so that the economic and ecological efficiency of the enterprises and of the economy as a whole can be improved. This generates on one hand advances towards a sustainable development, on the other hand considerable cost reductions to some or even all of the enterprises involved.*

The second section deals with the evolution of reverse logistics. A typology of its different appearances and relevant dimensions is given and the models and methods employed are discussed. Network structures used to organize reverse logistics are dealt with in the third section. Starting with a classification of recycling processes, internal recycling, recycling cells and recycling networks are presented as the characteristic recycling structures. Recycling networks can be classified into two subsections: Voluntary recycling networks are operated by the participants because of the economic profit generated, whereas compulsory recycling networks only exist due to legal force. The paper closes with an outline of the future perspectives of networks in reverse logistics.

Keywords: *recycling, waste reduction, network structures, sustainable development*

1. Necessity of reverse logistics

1.1. Definition

In literature, a great variety of definitions of reverse logistics can be found. In this paper the following wide definition will be used:

Reverse logistics comprises all activities involved in managing, processing, reducing and disposing of hazardous or non-hazardous waste from production, packaging and use of products, including the processes of reverse distribution.

Reverse logistics is sometimes also called "logistics backward" because its flow of goods is just opposite to the flow in the conventional supply chain. Whereas the forward flow of goods runs from the supplier over the manufacturer and the retailer to the consumer, reverse logistics deals with all the flows of goods and information that are necessary to collect used products, packaging materials, production scrap and other residues (in the following the general term "waste" will be employed) and bring them to places where they can be reused, remanufactured, recycled or disposed of properly, see fig. 1.

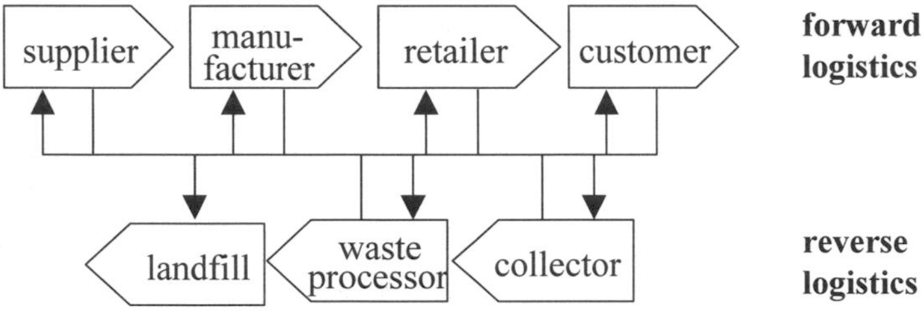

Fig. 1. Flow of goods in forward and reverse logistics

As the arrows in fig. 1 indicate, relations between the actors in the forward supply chain and the reverse logistics chain are manifold. Waste arises from all activities in the forward supply chain, but also from collection and waste processing. Recycled materials can be used as secondary materials by suppliers and manufacturers or substitute new products for the retailers and customers. Waste deposit in landfills is the last measure which has to be taken if no secondary use of a material is possible.

Reverse logistics comprises different processes, some of which are also relevant in supply and distribution logistics, whereas others are specific for backwards logistics (see Stölzle 1993, Vogel 1993, Bruns 1997, Fleischmann 2001):

- Collection comprises all activities of gathering waste from its various places of origin which are typically widely distributed in an area.

- Sorting serves to split the waste volume into separate fractions which will undergo different measures of treatment.
- Transportation and transshipment are necessary to span the physical distance between consecutive processes of reverse logistics.
- Warehousing takes place before transportation, transshipment or processing activities. It is mainly necessary in order to receive lot sizes that fully utilize transportation or processing facilities. As waste has little or no value, capital lockup in stock does not have the same importance as in traditional warehousing.
- Processing activities result in the transformation of waste into reusable products or into a condition in which it is harmless to the environment.

1.2. Activities of reverse logistics

The German commercial and industrial waste avoidance and management act (Kreislaufwirtschafts- und Abfallgesetz, KrW-/AbfG) which came into force in 1996 defines a hierarchy of waste related activities. The highest priority is given to waste avoidance which can be achieved by measures such as avoidance of redundant packaging or extension of a product's lifespan. If waste avoidance is not possible, activities concerning the treatment of residues and used products are ranked as illustrated in fig. 2: Reuse has priority to remanufacturing, remanufacturing has priority to recycling, and recycling has priority to disposal, either with energy recovery or in landfill.

Fig. 2. Hierarchy of waste treatment activities (Fig. based on Carter/Ellram 1998, p. 92)

These activities can be characterized as follows (see Rogers/Tibben-Lemke 1998, Gotzel et al. 1999, Haasis 1999):

- Reuse means that a product is used again for the same or a different purpose without major additional treatment. This activity is situated at the top of the hierarchy because the product as a whole is kept in the economic cycle. Reuse thus generates the highest increase of system efficiency. A well known example for reuse is the deposit return system for glass bottles.
- The activity on the next level of the hierarchy is remanufacturing. This means that a product or its components can be used again after overhauling or repair processes. Often the remanufactured products are of a poorer quality than new ones. An example for remanufacturing is the use of a replacement engine in a car.
- Even more additional treatment is required for the recycling of products. The products are disassembled into components some of which can be reused directly whereas others can only be taken as raw materials and used for the production of the same or inferior products. An example for the latter are flower pots or park benches that are made from recycled plastics collected in the German DSD system.
- The activity on the lowest level of the hierarchy is disposal because the products vanish from the economic system and their material is passed into the environment. Disposal with energy recovery still makes use of the caloric value of the products and reduces their volume so that less landfill capacity is needed. Disposal in landfill makes no use at all of the material or energy embodied in the products.

In order to carry out these activities, the reverse logistics processes discussed in section 1.1 are needed. Reverse logistics provides the links between a used product or material and its recovery.

1.3. Effects of reverse logistics

The necessity and the effects of reverse logistics can be derived from the general problems of environmental economics (see e.g. Wagner 1997):

On one hand we observe a continuous growth of world population and an increase in goods demanded by the customers. This implies increasing requirements on natural resources at the input side of the economic system and a growing amount of waste to be disposed of at the output side.

On the other hand, we face the fact that natural resources from which input materials are taken are not infinite and in some cases already close to depletion. On the output side we are confronted with limitations of landfill capacities as well as the ability of natural systems to absorb the residues of economic activities (see fig. 3).

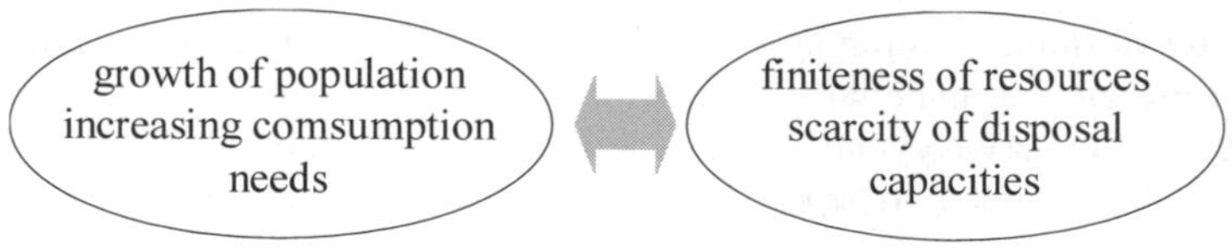

Fig. 3. Environmental problems

This contradiction of needs and supplies of natural resources and capacities can be relaxed if the traditional flow economy is at least partially transformed into a closed-loop economy. That means that, wherever possible, economic processes have to imitate cyclic structures that can be found in natural ecosystems. It is characteristic for such a cyclic economy that waste, used products and other residues are not disposed of directly, but that they are returned into the same or other economic processes in order to substitute input materials that are normally extracted from natural resources.

In such a closed-loop economy, the various processes of reverse logistics are used. Compared to the traditional flow economy, a closed-loop economy can create several positive effects for the enterprises and for the environment (see e.g. Steven 1994):

- On the input side of production, raw materials are saved because they are partially substituted by residues of other economic processes which are used as secondary resources.
- Further on, in many cases input of energy can be reduced because these secondary resources maintain a high level of value added.
- On the output side, less emissions are brought into the environment and less landfill capacity is needed because less waste is getting out of the economic system.
- Landfill costs are increasing steadily and thus encourage enterprises to reduce their amounts of waste to be disposed.

Thus by reverse logistics the economic efficiency which is expressed in cost reductions as well as the ecological efficiency of the production system are increased. Reverse logistics can support the transformation of the economy towards the ideal of sustainability which has been required by the UNCED conference in Rio de Janeiro 1992.

On the other hand, reverse logistics faces the following limitations:

- From the economic point of view, recycling is only profitable if the costs of the additional reverse logistics processes are not higher than the savings obtained from the reduction of materials and energy on the input side and of waste on the output side.

- A technical limitation to recycling is the fact that in most cases a complete re-use of products or material is impossible. Often the quality of a material deteriorates with every recycling process unless primary material is added. This effect which occurs e.g. in paper recycling is called down cycling.
- From the ecological point of view, the negative environmental impacts that can be avoided by recycling have to be more important than those resulting from the reverse logistics processes needed to perform the recycling. Although it is difficult to measure these impacts, recent studies indicate that material recycling of small plastic objects in the German DSD system has no positive overall effect.
- Finally, recycled products often come across mental obstacles in the opinion of their potential users. They suppose recycled products to have a lower quality than products made from primary resources and are not willing to buy them, at least not at the same price.

2. Evolution of reverse logistics

2.1. Development

Reuse and recycling of materials can look back at a very long history: Already in the Old and Middle Ages it was usual to collect and melt metallic parts due to the high economic value incorporated in the material. Also, many industries started quite early to feed back scrap and spoilage into their production processes or to use undesired complementary products as input for other processes.

In the 1980s and 1990s, many European countries enforced their environmental legislation in various fields, especially concerning waste treatment, packaging and product returns. Germany always was and still is one of the pioneers in issuing progressive laws for the implementation of a closed-loop economy.

Already in 1986, the waste management act (Abfallgesetz) which emphasized the importance of waste reduction came into force. In 1996, it has been replaced by the commercial and industrial waste avoidance and management act. This act extends the producers' responsibility to the whole lifespan of their products including the obligation to take them back after use and to care for treatment and disposal processes which are innocuous to the environment. Additionally, special take-back ordinances have been issued concerning packaging materials (Verpackungsverordnung, 1991), used cars (Altautoverordnung, 1998), used batteries (Batterieverordnung, 1998), electronic scrap (Elektronikschrottverordnung, 1991) and information processing devices (Informationstechnik-Geräte-Verordnung, 1996).

In order to comply to these regulations, reverse logistics activities have to be carried out throughout the economy. This development evoked the rise of specialized reverse logistics service providers which offer to the enterprises the various processes discussed in section 1.1. The co-operation of the participants in the reverse logistics chain can be organized in different ways which will be discussed in section 3.

2.2. Dimensions of reverse logistics

In order to give an overview of the large field of activities covered by reverse logistics, the following morphology based on a classification given by Fleischmann et al. (1997) can be used, see fig. 4.

kind of goods	used products	packaging material	warranty returns	production scrap	excess products
time horizon	static	short term	medium term	long term	
motivation	cost savings	regulations	image improvement		
kind of process	reuse	remanufacturing	recycling	disposal	

Fig. 4. Dimensions of reverse logistics

- According to the kind of goods which are the object of reverse logistics activities, used products, packaging material, warranty returns, production scrap and excess products can be distinguished.
- Due to the representation in a model, the time horizon can either be static or cover a short, medium or long term horizon. This coincides with the planning horizon of the actors involved in reverse logistics processes.
- The motivation for an enterprise to implement processes of reverse logistics can be cost savings or other economic advantages, governmental regulations, or the expectation to improve its image in the public opinion.
- The different alternatives of waste treatment in reverse logistics – reuse, remanufacturing, recycling, and disposal – have already been explained in section 1.2.

2.3. Models of reverse logistics

Due to the manifold fields of interest in reverse logistics, different approaches can be identified in literature. As the space in this paper is limited, a comprehensive review of relevant literature cannot be given here. Instead, for each topic some characteristic publications are presented that give insight into the respective problems:

- A very important field of reverse logistics are models dealing with the processes employed on the different levels, especially waste processing and recycling (see e.g. Kleinaltenkamp 1985, Spengler 1994, Bruns 1997).
- When the packaging ordinance came into force in Germany, the reduction of packaging and the possibilities to organize the German packaging take-back system DSD were broadly discussed. Another topic brought up by legislation is product return which is related to the release of the German commercial and industrial waste avoidance and management act (see e.g. Püchert et al. 1996, Gotzel et al. 1998, Haasis 1999, Souren 2002).
- For an optimal solution of many reverse logistics problems, quantitative and OR models have to be formulated. The modelling of reverse logistics processes by the means of OR methods is a complex and pretentious problem. Although OR provides a lot of standard methods that can be used in reverse logistics with no or only slight adaptations, the discussion of OR applications in reverse logistics (see e.g. Fleischmann et al. 1997, Fleischmann 2001, Spengler/Schröter 2001, Fichtner/Geldermann 2002) is still at its beginning and thus involves a great potential.
- Another important topic is the implementation of reverse logistics and its effect on the performance of a closed-loop economy (see e.g. Wagner/Matten 1995, Kaluza 1998).
- The following section of this paper will focus on redistribution and recycling networks that are fundamental for the performance of reverse logistics (see e.g. Strebel/Schwarz 1995, Kaluza/Blecker 1996, Wildemann 1996).

3. Network structures in reverse logistics

3.1. Features of recycling processes

Recycling processes as described in section 1.2 are the core construct of reverse logistics systems. They can be characterized by the following features which are illustrated in fig. 5:

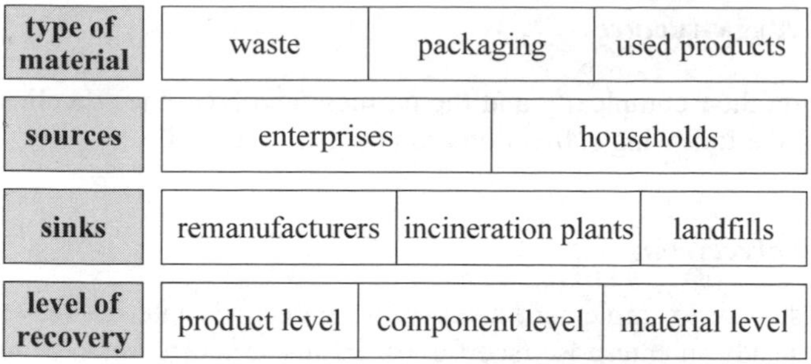

Fig. 5. Classification of recycling processes

- According to the type of material to be recycled, waste, packaging and used products can be distinguished. The treatment of waste and packaging is performed in reverse logistics systems with a short planning horizon because these materials occur in large quantities with a rather regular pattern. Used products however normally come back to the producers after a long period of use in irregular quantities, so their taking back and recycling have to be organized over a long planning horizon.
- Materials handled in reverse logistics can stem from different sources: On one hand, enterprises which act on the various stages of the supply chain (procurement, production, distribution) pass their specific residues to the recycling and disposal system. Due to special waste regulations, these residues are mostly well sorted and specified. Thus they can be separated into different fractions to each of which appropriate recycling or processing methods can be applied. On the other hand, the waste that households and customers give into public collection systems is often a mix of materials such as glass, plastics, paper, and organic substances. In the last years, appeals to the customers' environmental consciousness and local regulations concerning waste separation have already improved this situation.
- Corresponding to the sources of material flows, their sinks have to be examined as well. If a material is partly or totally designated to be returned into the economic system, it will go to an adequate remanufacturing or reprocessing plant. All other materials will take their way to disposal activities. These materials can either be incinerated in order to use their caloric value and reduce their volume or directly brought to landfill. So incineration plants and landfills are very important sinks of material flows in reverse logistics.
- The recycling process itself can be characterized by the extent to which recovery is possible: In a remanufacturing process the value added embodied in the waste materials is maintained on the product level. A process on the component level in which only selected parts or subassemblies of the products are recovered is called cannibalisation. Recycling in the term's most narrow meaning performs recovery on the material level, so that neither form nor functionality of the original products are maintained (see Gotzel et al. 1999).

3.2. Recycling structures

Depending on their complexity and the partners involved, the recycling structures discussed in the following subsections can be distinguished.

3.2.1. Internal recycling

The simplest way to implement a recycling process is internal recycling which takes place inside an enterprise (see fig. 6). In this structure, scrap or residues of a production process are reused as input either in the same process or in other processes. Examples for a use in the same process which is illustrated in fig. 6(a) are the melting of broken pieces and spoilage in the glass industry or the reuse of regenerated thinners in the varnish industry. Use in a different process takes place e.g. if waste heat from production processes is used for heating offices, see fig. 6(b).

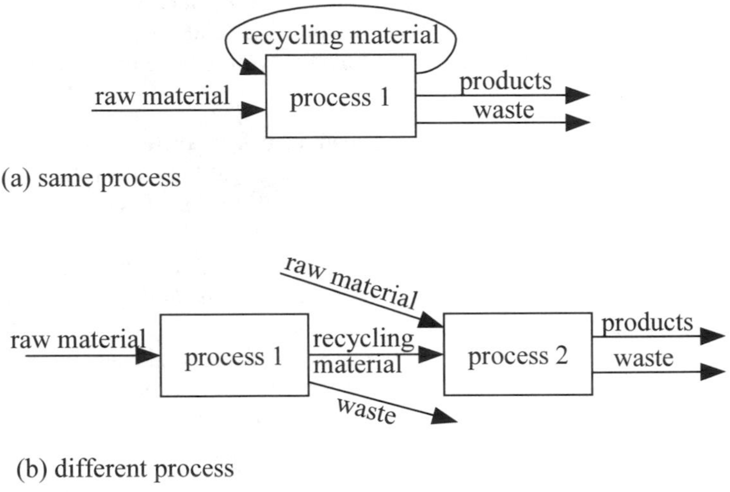

Fig. 6. Internal recycling

Internal recycling is established in many industries. Compared to the alternatives of external recycling presented hereafter, it requires little organizational effort and normally leads to a considerable cost reduction for the enterprise applying it.

3.2.2. Recycling cells

A recycling cell is the elementary external recycling structure. In a recycling cell, a residue is exchanged between two enterprises which are legally and economically independent, the residue submitter and the residue accepter. As the material exchanged is classified as waste by the submitting enterprise and as raw material by the accepting enterprise, this type of co-operation transforms a waste material with a negative economic value into a secondary raw material with positive value (see Schwarz 1996).

The structure of a recycling cell which is illustrated in fig. 7 resembles the internal recycling into a different process (see fig. 6(b)). As an example for a recycling cell we can examine the relation between a sawing mill and a producer of furniture: The sawing mill needs logs as raw material and produces besides boards as its main product sawing dust and other waste materials. The sawing dust can either be deposited or delivered to the producer of furniture who uses it as input for the production of chip boards. So the co-operation in the recycling cell saves deposit costs to the sawing mill, reduces procurement costs for the producer of furniture and, last but not least, releases the environment from supplying resp. absorbing the quantity of material exchanged.

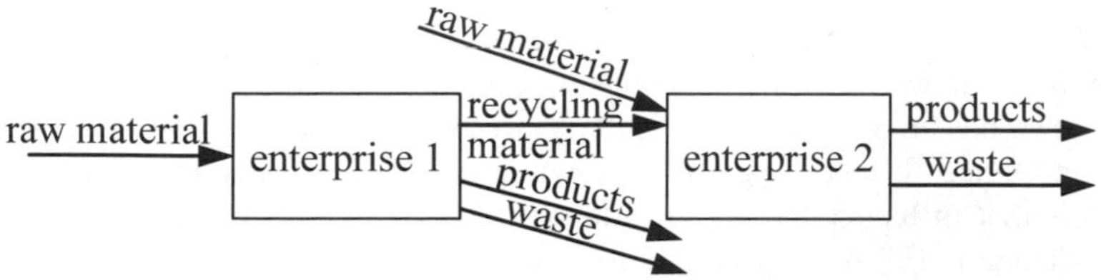

Fig. 7. Recycling cell

The co-operation in a recycling cell is mainly determined by repeated market relations. In some cases the recurrent exchange of the recycling material is regulated by medium or even long term contracts in which e.g. the quantity and the quality of the material and its price level are fixed. In the ideal case, each partner faces a substantial cost reduction, so that the transactions in the recycling cell cause a win-win-situation. A numeric example for this situation is given by Kaluza/Dullnig (2002, p. 238). If one partner experiences a rise of cost which is overcompensated by the cost reduction of the other partner, a compensating payment can be agreed on. So the co-operation in a recycling cell is profitable as long as the sum of the cost reductions of the partners is higher than the additional costs occurring for transport of the material etc.

Although it produces positive economic and ecological effects, a recycling co-operation is often difficult to implement because the respective markets are intransparent or very volatile. One important problem is to coordinate supply and demand, that is to find a partner offering resp. needing exactly the material that an enterprise is looking for resp. emitting. This lack of information can be overcome by the help of second-hand dealers, reprocessing enterprises or special exchange agencies. The second problem is the volatility of markets for secondary material which can seriously endanger the co-operation in a recycling cell. It can be solved by long-term contracts that consider the interests of both partners adequately.

3.2.3. Recycling networks

Often an enterprise is engaged not only in a single recycling cell, but sustains comparable relations with many other enterprises, sometimes submitting and sometimes accepting residues of industrial processes. Especially in industrialized areas, multiple possibilities to exchange residues under economically profitable conditions can be found. By using them, the ecological advantages outlined in section 1.3 are generated, so that a further step towards a closed-loop economy and towards sustainability is taken.

The use of multilateral recycling relations can undergo a development towards a recycling network as time goes by. This development taking place in reverse logistics resembles the formation of supply chains in forward logistics. In order to establish a closed-loop economy, the forward and the reverse logistics chains have to be linked as it has already been discussed in section 1.

Recycling networks can appear in many forms which vary from a loose co-operation arranged by single contracts to a hierarchical organization which sometimes even has an own corporate identity. In the last case the network is of strategic importance for the long-term existence of the participating enterprises. Parameters that influence the organization of a recycling network are discussed e.g. in Wildemann (1996). An example for a part of a bigger recycling network in the steel industry is presented in fig. 8 (see Strebel/Schwarz 1997). The steel mill is accentuated because it has the function of a hub firm for this network around which the other enterprises and their activities are arranged (see Sydow 1992).

The recycling network shown in fig. 8 is part of a bigger recycling network in the German industrial region Ruhrgebiet that was discovered in an empirical study by Schwarz et al. (1996). The recycling network Ruhrgebiet comprises 17 enterprises mostly operating in steel-related industries. 33 material flows of 19 different types of material could be identified, some of which have already been established before the discussion on environmental protection began. The co-operations taking place in this network lead to a reuse of altogether 6,33 mio. t of material per year. The main fractions are 2,36 mio. t of blast furnace slag and sand, 2 mio. t of scrap and 0,91 mio. t of steel slag. Additional to the direct savings these material flows create on the input and output side of the respective production processes, there are considerable reductions in the use of energy and water as well as in emissions from the production processes. E.g., the production of one ton of iron from iron ore requires an energy supply of 4.270 kWh whereas production from scrap needs only 1.666 kWh/t.

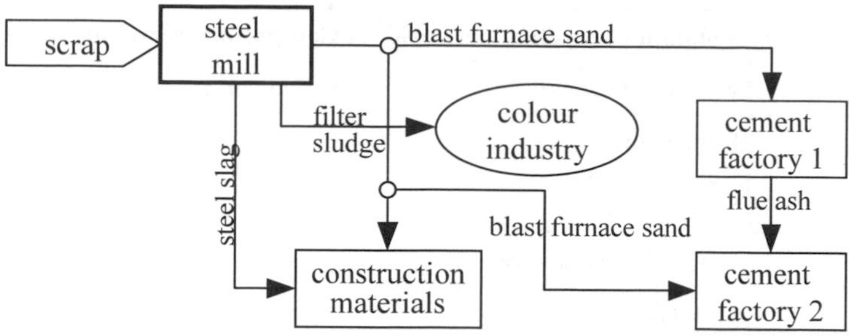

Fig. 8. Recycling network in the steel industry

Other examples for recycling networks that are discussed in literature are the industrial symbiosis Kalundborg in Denmark (see Elkington et al. 1991) and the recycling network Steiermark in Austria (see Posch et al. 1998).

In the ideal case, all recycling opportunities are realized in a recycling network that are advantageous from an ecological point of view and that produce an economic advantage for the participants. Reverse logistics serves as a link between the different stages resp. processes in such a recycling network. It helps to span the gap between use and recovery of a material, or, from another point of view, between the source and the sink of a material flow. Obviously, the importance of the logistical processes rises as the size of the network increases.

3.3. Types of recycling networks

Literature on recycling networks primarily focuses on the type described in section 3.2.3. It is typically characterized by a mix of different industries that maintain mainly vertical recycling relations. As this network type is established by voluntary contracts between the participating enterprises, it will be called voluntary recycling network. Kaluza/Blecker (1996, p. 392) even restrict recycling networks to vertical or diagonal relations and consider horizontal relations as inadequate for a recycling network.

But taking a closer look, recycling relations can also be found between enterprises on the same level of production or even in the same industry and a hub firm that organizes the occurring reverse flows of material, e.g. the German DSD system for plastics material recovery or public waste disposal activities. As these relations also show a network structure, but come into existence by legal force or public regulation, they will be called compulsory recycling networks.

In the following, the main differences between voluntary and compulsory recycling networks will be discussed. Fig. 9 gives a comprehensive overview of the characteristics of voluntary and compulsory recycling networks.

	Voluntary recycling network	Compulsory recycling network
Direction	vertical / diagonal	horizontal
Examples	Kalundborg Ruhrgebiet Steiermark	German DSD system public waste disposal
Incentive	economic advantages	governmental regulation
Objective	cost reduction synergies	legal compliance e.g. recycling quota economies of scale
Participants	producers suppliers service providers	producers service providers disposal agencies
Principles	confidence negotiation of contracts	force instructions fixed charges
Creation	organic growth	construction
Organization	market	hierarchy
Efficiency	economic ecological	ecological (?)

Fig. 9. Characteristics of recycling network types

- The main incentive for the use of voluntary recycling relations are economic advantages for the participating enterprises. Compulsory recycling relations however have to be established due to the relevant regulations even if they evoke an overall cost increase.
- This difference is also reflected in the objectives of the network types. Whereas voluntary recycling networks aim at synergetic effects and cost reductions that generate a win-win-situation for all partners, the main objective of compulsory recycling networks is legal compliance concerning e.g. recycling quota. Beyond that, economies of scale are achieved by the centralization of certain activities at specialized service providers.
- Participants of voluntary recycling networks are on one hand suppliers and producers that exchange reverse flows of material, on the other hand specialized service providers that support the different processes of reverse logistics. In compulsory recycling networks, producers that emit a certain type of material and service providers are coordinated by a disposal agency or a comparable institution.
- The main principle of the relations in a voluntary recycling network is confidence into the partners, contracts are negotiated on an equal basis. As compul-

sory recycling networks are brought into existence by initiative of legislation, members are often forced to participate. The relations are dominated by instructions, and charges are mostly fixed.

- Voluntary recycling networks typically undergo a continuous development over time that can be characterized as organic growth. Compulsory recycling networks are constructed soon after the respective piece of legislation has come into force, so that their growth is performing much more quickly.
- With regard to the organization, two opposite principles are applied. Whereas in voluntary recycling networks market relations are dominating, compulsory recycling networks are determined by hierarchical structures.
- An important measure to evaluate recycling networks is their efficiency. As has been pointed out before, voluntary recycling networks typically show an increase in economic as well as in ecological efficiency, whereas compulsory recycling networks lead to cost increases and thus to a loss of economic efficiency. Even their ecological efficiency is sometimes doubtful.

4. Perspectives

Actually, intense research activities in various fields of reverse logistics can be observed. Further research will not only help to improve the different processes and reduce the costs of reverse logistics, but will also contribute to an increase in economic and ecological efficiency and thus improve the level of environmental protection. As the comparison in section 3.3 has shown, voluntary recycling networks are better qualified for an efficient performance of reverse logistics activities. So there is a challenge to transform compulsory recycling networks in order to resemble voluntary recycling networks and thus increase their economic and ecological performance.

References

Ayres, R.U., Ferrer, G., Leynseele, T. van (1997): Eco-efficiency, asset recovery and remanufacturing. In: European Management Journal 15, pp. 557-574

Barry, J., Girard, G., Perras, C. (1993): Logistics shifts into reverse. In: Journal of European Business 5, Sept./Oct. 1993, pp. 34-38.

Beuermann, G., Halfmann, M. (1998): Zwischenbetriebliche Entsorgungskooperationen aus transaktionskostentheoretischer Sicht. In: UWF 6, 1998, Heft 1, pp. 72-77.

Bruns, K. (1997): Analyse und Beurteilung von Entsorgungslogistiksystemen – Ökonomische, ökologische und gesellschaftliche Aspekte. Gabler, Wiesbaden.

Bruns, K., Steven, M. (1998): Strukturen von Entsorgungslogistiksystemen. In: Zeitschrift für Angewandte Umweltforschung 10, pp. 457-471.

Carter, C.R., Ellram, L.M. (1998): Reverse logistics: A review of the literature and framework for future investigation. In: Journal of business logistics 19, No. 1, pp. 85-102.

Elkington, J., Knight, P., Hailes, J. (1991): The green business guide. Victor Gollancz, London.

Fichtner, W., Geldermann, J. (Hrsg.) (2002): Einsatz von OR-Verfahren zur techno-ökonomischen Analyse von Produktionssystemen, Peter Lang, Frankfurt a. M.

Fleischmann, M. (2001): Quantitative models for reverse logistics. Springer, Berlin et al.

Fleischmann, M., Bloemhof-Ruwaard, J.M., Dekker, R., Laan, van der E., Nunen, van J. A.E.E., Wassenhove, van L. N. (1997): Quantitative models for reverse logistics: A review. In: EJOR 103, pp. 1-17.

Haasis, H.-D. (1999): Produktkreislauflogistik. In: Pfohl, C. (Hrsg.), Logistikforschung – Entwicklungszüge und Gestaltungsansätze, Schmidt, Berlin, pp. 253-277.

Harrington, L. (1994): The art of reverse logistics. In: Inbound logistics 14, pp. 29-36.

Kaluza, B. (1998): Kreislaufwirtschaft und Umweltmanagement, Schmidt, Berlin.

Kaluza, B., Blecker, T. (1996): Management interindustrieller Entsorgungsnetzwerke. In: Bellmann, K., Hippe, A. (Hrsg.), Management von Unternehmensnetzwerken, Gabler, Wiesbaden, pp. 379-417.

Kaluza, B., Dullnig, H. (2002): Ansätze eines Logistik-Controlling in Verwertungs- und Entsorgungsnetzwerken (VEN). In: Seicht, G. (Hrsg.), Jahrbuch für Controlling und Rechnungswesen 2002, Orac, Wien, pp. 219-245.

Kleinaltenkamp, M. (1985): Recycling-Strategien. Erich Schmidt, Berlin.

Posch, A., Schwarz, E., Steiner, G., Strebel, H., Vorbach, S. (1998): Das Verwertungsnetz Obersteiermark und sein Potential. In: Strebel, H., Schwarz, E. (Hrsg.): Kreislauforientierte Unternehmenskooperationen: Stoffstrommanagement durch kreislauforientierte Verwertungsnetze. Oldenbourg, München / Wien.

Püchert, H., Spengler, T., Rentz, O. (1996): Strategische Planung von Kreislaufwirtschafts- und Redistributionssystemen – am Fallbeispiel des Altautorecycling. In: Zeitschrift für Planung 7, pp. 27-44.

Rautenstrauch, C. (1997): Fachkonzept für ein integriertes Produktions-, Recyclingplanungs- und Steuerungssystem (PRPS-System). Springer, Berlin et al.

Rogers, D.S., Tibben-Lembke, R.S. (1998): Going Backwards: Reverse Logistics Trends and Practices. Working Paper, University of Nevada, Reno.

Schwarz, E.J. (1996): Industrielle Verwertungsnetze – Ein Beitrag zur Integration ökologischer Aspekte in die Produktionswirtschaft. In: Bellmann, K., Hippe, A. (Hrsg.), Management von Unternehmensnetzwerken, Gabler, Wiesbaden, pp. 349-377.

Schwarz, E.J., Bruns, K., Lopatka, M. (1996): Regionale Zusammenarbeit in der Abfallwirtschaft: Die Verwertung von Produktionsrückständen am Fallbeispiel „Ruhrgebiet". In: Handbuch Umwelt und Energie, Gruppe 4, pp. 297-321.

Souren, R. (2002): Konsumgüterverpackungen in der Kreislaufwirtschaft. DUV, Wiesbaden.

Spengler, T. (1994): Industrielle Demontage- und Recyclingkonzepte, Schmidt, Berlin.

Spengler, T., Schröter, M. (2001): Einsatz von Operations Research im produktbezogenen Umweltschutz – Stand und Perspektiven. In: Betriebswirtschaftliche Forschung und Praxis 53, pp. 227-244.

Steven, M. (1994): Produktion und Umweltschutz. Gabler, Wiesbaden.

Steven, M., Bruns, K. (1998): Entsorgungslogistik. In: Das Wirtschaftsstudium 27, pp. 695-700 u. 802-806.

Stölzle, W. (1993): Umweltschutz und Entsorgungslogistik – Theoretische Grundlagen mit ersten empirischen Ergebnissen zur innerbetrieblichen Entsorgungslogistik. Schmidt, Berlin.

Stölzle, W. (1996): Grundzüge des Outsourcing von Entsorgungsleistungen. In: ZfB Ergänzungsheft 2/96, Betriebliches Umweltmanagement 1996, Gabler, Wiesbaden, pp. 121-145.

Stölzle, W. (2001): Umweltverträgliche Logistik. In: Schulz, W. F. (Hrsg.), Lexikon Nachhaltiges Wirtschaften, Oldenbourg, München / Wien, pp. 216-221.

Strebel, H., Schwarz, E. (1997): Rückstandsverwertung in industriellen Netzwerken. In: Weber, J. (Hrsg.), Umweltmanagement, Schaeffer Poeschel, Stuttgart, pp. 321-333.

Strebel, H., Schwarz, E. (Hrsg.) (1998): Kreislauforientierte Unternehmenskooperationen: Stoffstrommanagement durch kreislauforientierte Verwertungsnetze. Oldenbourg, München / Wien.

Strebel, H., Schwarz, E.J., Schwarz, M.M. (1996): Externes Recycling im Produktionsbetrieb. Manz, Wien.

Sydow, J. (1992): Strategische Netzwerke – Evolution und Organisation. Gabler, Wiesbaden.

Sydow, J. (2002): Zum Management von Logistiknetzwerken. In: Logistik Management 4, pp. 9-15.

Vogel, A. (1993): Controlling in der gewerblichen Entsorgungslogistik. Lang, Frankfurt a. M. et al.

Wagner, G.R. (1997): Betriebswirtschaftliche Umweltökonomie. Lucius & Lucius, Stuttgart.

Wagner, G.R., Matten, D. (1995): Betriebswirtschaftliche Konsequenzen des Kreislaufwirtschaftsgesetzes. In: Zeitschrift für Angewandte Umweltforschung 8, Heft 1, pp. 45-57.

Williamson, O.E. (1975): Markets and Hierarchies: Analysis and antitrust implications. The Free Press, London.

Environmental-Oriented Coordination of Supply Networks

Axel Tuma, Jürgen Friedl, Stephan Franke

Department of Economics
University of Augsburg
Universitaetsstraße 16
D-86159 Augsburg, Germany

Abstract: *Following current thought concerning modern production concepts, an increasing trend to network organizations (supply networks) can be identified. On a macro level such networks consist of more or less independent subsystems (enterprises). The subsystems represent networks of interconnected production and storage units. The enterprises as well as the production und storage units are linked by energy and material flows. Using this model, environmental impacts can be identified at any stage of the production process.*

On the macro level (enterprise level) energy and material flows are mainly determined by the total amount and the allocation of the workload between individual enterprises. In this context production coordination mechanisms are needed to coordinate the flows in question taking into account economical (e.g. maximization of marginal income) and ecological (e.g. minimization of emissions) goals. Furthermore the specific preference of the individual enterprises, concerning the weighting of economical and ecological aspects, must be considered. For this reason mixed policies focusing simultaneously on economical aims (reactive approach) and ecological aims (proactive approach) are implemented. On the micro level (factory level) control mechanisms are needed to implement the reference values (production program) given by the enterprise level.

Due to the structure of supply networks (more or less independent enterprises on the enterprise level with frequent and specific transactions on the factory level) the coordination process of a whole enterprise is modelled by a cascade controller implemented by a two-stage multi-agent system. The multi-criteria objective function of the enterprise agents is modelled via goal programming which captures the mixed policies above mentioned. The multi-agent system of the controller on the factory level is implemented by a Fuzzy-Petri Net.

The coordination mechanisms are illustrated with the help of a virtual supply network of the textile industry.

Keywords: *supply chain management, virtual enterprise, environmental production control, agent-oriented simulation, goal programming, fuzzy-petri net*

1. Analysis of supply networks under consideration of environmental aspects

A framework for an analysis of relations between individual elements of network organizations is given by Williamson's theory of transactions costs (Coase, 1937 and Williamson, 1985). In this context, transaction costs are defined as costs for the acquisition of information, selection of potential partners, negotiation, agreement, settlement and controlling of distributed business processes (Picot, 1991). They also include costs of a subsequent adjustment of processes in order to adapt to changing business conditions. According to Williamson, transaction costs depend on the specificity, uncertainty and frequency of transactions. With decreasing specificity, uncertainty and frequency, the transactions should be organized outdoors (enterprise level). In the case of increasing specificity, uncertainty und frequency of the transactions (factory level) an indoor production should be preferred. The key factor of these parameters is the specificity.

Conclusions concerning enterprise level: Typical for enterprise level are less specific transactions. This means that specific capital in kind, common investments and a common production site play a less important role in comparison to the factory level. According to this concept, the subsystems (enterprises) interact with changing partners. Nevertheless the companies at the enterprise level produce a common product. Especially under quality and environmental aspects there must be a high level of trust (Wildemann, 1996). This means, for example, that an enterprise which interacts directly with the customer must be sure that their suppliers did not use any hazardous substances in order to fulfil the customers' (and other stakeholders') requirements. Taking into account the above mentioned characteristics, the coordination at the enterprise level is a distributed process of more or less independent companies.

An adequate model of the enterprise level has to address the distributed coordination structure. Additionally multi-criteria objectives of different stakeholders of these specific individual enterprises with regard to the different weights of economical and ecological goals (e.g. marginal income versus reduction of CO_2-emissions) must be considered. In this context, a multi-agent approach seems to be well suited (Corsten and Gössinger, 2000).

Conclusions concerning factory level: Transactions at factory level are characterized by specific capital in kind, common investments (e.g. pipeline between a "dye-house" and a "neutralization facility") and specificity of site (e.g. "blast furnace" and "rolling mill" of a steel company). Furthermore the frequency of the transactions at this level is relatively high. This means that the production units at the factory level form a common enterprise with strongly interconnected material and energy flows.

An adequate modelling of the factory level includes all production and storage units as well as all relevant input- and output-streams. In this context a specific multi-agent approach with a reduced selection of negotiation partners (determined by the relatively fixed production structure) seems to be recommendable.

Figure 1 represents an interconnected supply network from the textile industry. At the enterprise level, the companies (different spinning mills, weaving mills and dye-houses) are able to interact with changing cooperation partners in order to produce a common product for the customers. To guarantee strict quality and ecological standards, all potential negotiation partners form a common enterprise pool. In case of insufficient performance, individual enterprises can be excluded. At the factory level, the different subsystems are highly interconnected production systems with fixed interactions (e.g. pipeline between "boiler-house" and "neutralization facility"). The production of these subsystems is located at a special production site (e.g. "combined heat and power generation unit" and "spinning mill").

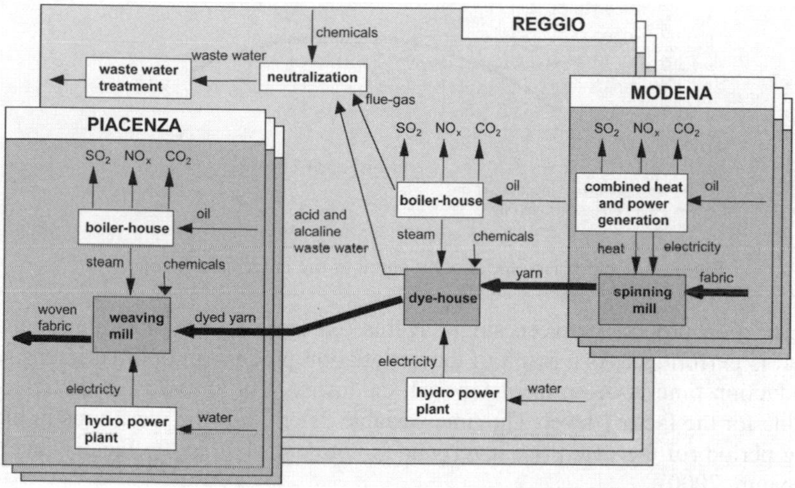

Fig. 1. Exemplary supply network of the textile industry

2. Concept of the coordination mechanism

The basic requirement in designing appropriate coordination mechanisms for both levels, the enterprise level as well as the factory level, is the identification of the relevant planning and controlling tasks. One of the key tasks at the enterprise level is the allocation of workload between different partners (e.g. different spinning mills), taking into consideration economical and ecological goals. The aim at the factory level is the controlling of production units and inventory/buffer units on the one hand and the energy and material flows on the other hand in order to fulfil the guidelines from the enterprise level. In order to realize these tasks a two-stage cascade controller is implemented (Fig. 3). Due to the structure of the supply network (network of more or less independent companies at the enterprise level with interconnected production and storage units at the factory level) each controller is modelled as a multi-agent system, taking into account the different specificity of transactions (Zelewski, 1998).

Modelling approach of the controller (enterprise level): For each enterprise a single agent with economical and ecological objectives is designed. In this context, its tasks, possible actions, communication structure as well as its knowledge of the production process and the planning capabilities must be specified (see chapter 3.1). The agent's view of the enterprise is modelled according to the Gutenberg production function (Gutenberg, 1969 and Fandel, 1991). Based on intensity and production time, unit costs with regard to marginal income and emissions are calculated (Fig. 2).

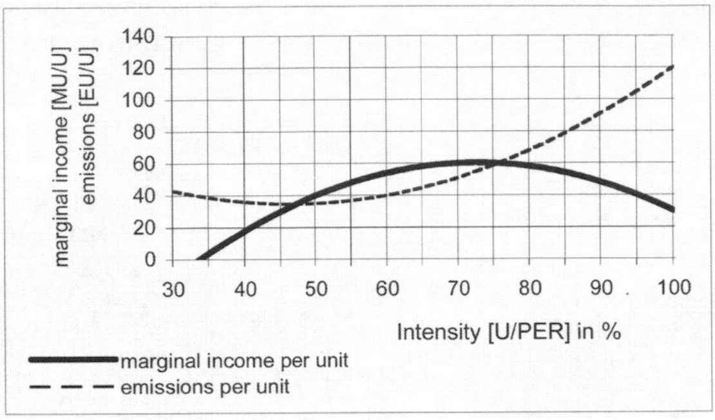

Fig. 2. Enterprise model of an agent at the enterprise level

In a negotiation process between single agents (enterprises) an allocation of the workload is performed. As a result of the negotiation process an optimal intensity and production time is determined for each enterprise. The intensity is the reference value for the factory level. The time variable determines the work time in the planning period (of the enterprise level) and is not controlled at the factory level[1] (Kreikebaum, 2000).

Modelling approach of the controller (factory level): The agents at the factory level are designed by analogy to the enterprise level (see chapter 4.1). The agent's view of a production unit and a storage unit respectively is modelled according to a Fuzzy-Petri Net methodology. This approach addresses the relatively fixed production structure as well as technical, economical and ecological restrictions (see chapter 4.2). In a negotiation process between single agents (production and storage units), intensities (output values) for the production units are calculated taking into account the resulting stocks of the storage units.

After dealing with the controller architectures, the information flows have to be described: Output of the enterprise agent is the desired intensity. It will be disaggregated. The so-calculated intensities serve as reference values for the controller

[1] Due to the length of the control period (varying from a minute to daily basis) an adjustment of the time variable can only be done on the enterprise level.

at the factory level. On the basis of these values and the actual (measured) intensities the controller calculates the new input variables for the production system. Furthermore the actual (measured) intensities are integrated over time and transmitted to the enterprise level. If a significant difference between desired and actual[2] marginal income with regard to the emissions occurs, a new negotiating process at the enterprise level will be initiated. Otherwise the enterprise agent tries to solve the problem indoor (e.g. adjustment of work time). In the case of a sustainable breakdown of production equipment, the model at the enterprise level (production function, cost function, emission function) will be adapted.

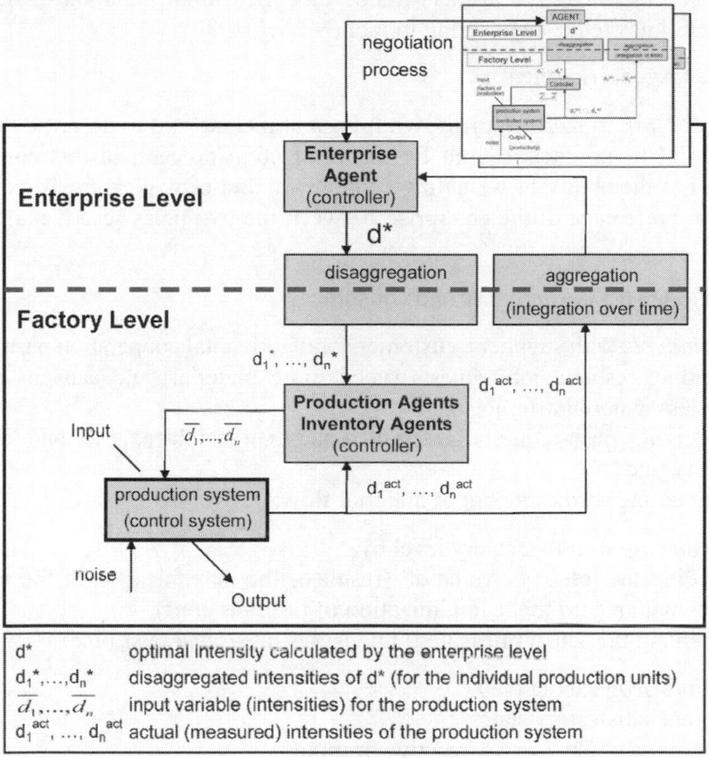

Fig. 3. Concept of the coordination mechanisms

[2] The actual marginal income with regard to the emissions is calculated as a function of the aggregated intensities.

3. Coordination mechanism at the enterprise level

3.1. Configuration of the enterprise agents

The task of the enterprise agents is the determination of the workload in order to increase the marginal income with regard to decreasing the emissions. According to these requirements the enterprise agents have to be defined, their knowledge and behaviour have to be characterized and their communication mechanisms have to be described. The agents will be modelled in an imitation of the CommonKADS knowledge engineering model (Müller, 1997).

Enterprise Agents (E-Agent):

- have the *task* to increase their own marginal income and to decrease the emissions and by-products caused by the production process; in this context the agent has the ability of weighting economical and ecological goals (representing the preference of the enterprise between the two poles reactive and proactive);
- perform the *actions*: produce and consume;
- *communicate* with suppliers, customers and horizontal cooperation partners by
  a) sending resource/job-requests (need more material) and capacity-requests (need less material/offer jobs),
  b) receiving push-requests and pull-requests, i.e. job-requests and capacity-requests, and
  c) negotiating on the amount of material flow;
- *communicate* with the factory level by
  a) sending the reference value d* (result of the maximization of the marginal income with regard to the minimization of the emissions),
  b) receiving the actual (measured) intensities integrated over time;
- have *knowledge* about their
  a) current satisfactory state,
  b) enterprise policy (active, reactive or mixed),
  c) production model, and
  d) producing/consuming relationships and needs;
- *plan* in order to forecast their local situation and plan the communication. The planning process includes the reasoning capabilities of the agents.

Each enterprise agent acts essentially on the basis of its state of satisfaction, which reflects the fulfilment of its task. If an enterprise agent is not satisfied, it communicates its needs to the potential negotiation partners in order to increase or decrease its workload. The agent's ability to negotiate enables each agent to partially accept the requests and postpone the necessary activities in order to fit into the currently calculated plans. In the following the satisfaction calculation will be discussed in detail. Negotiation principles are discussed in Müller (1996).

3.2. Calculation of the satisfaction level of the enterprise agents

The basic idea constructing the individual enterprise agent's satisfaction level is the evaluation of the workload taking into account economical and ecological criteria. In this context the enterprise agent will be modelled according to the Gutenberg production function as mentioned before (Fig. 2). In order to find an evaluation value for the possible workloads, the multi-criteria character of the problem has to be addressed. In principle this can be done via different methods like scoring-models, goal programming and aspiration level approaches.

In the following a goal programming approach will be explained in detail (Fig. 4).

$$
\begin{aligned}
&Max\ MI(d)\cdot X\\
&Min\ EM(d)\cdot X\\
&(1)\quad MI(d)\cdot X \geq MI_{\min}\\
&(2)\quad EM(d)\cdot X \leq EM_{\max}\\
&(3)\quad d_{\min} \leq d \leq d_{\max}\\
&(4)\quad d\cdot t_{\min} \leq X \leq d\cdot t_{\max}
\end{aligned}
$$

GOAL PROGRAMMING

$$
\begin{aligned}
&Max\ a_1 + k\cdot a_2\\
&(1)\quad MI(d)\cdot X - a_1 = MI_{\min}\\
&(2)\quad EM(d)\cdot X + a_2 = EM_{\max}\\
&(3)\quad d_{\min} \leq d \leq d_{\max}\\
&(4)\quad d\cdot t_{\min} \leq X \leq d\cdot t_{\max}\\
&(5)\quad a_1, a_2 \geq 0
\end{aligned}
$$

d = intensity [U/PER]	k = key parameter [MU/EU]
MI = marginal income function [MU/U]	EM = emission function [EU/U]
EM_{max} = legal emission standard [EU]	X = (fixed) production quantity [U]
MI_{min} = enterprise specific minimal marginal income [MU]	
d_{min}/d_{max} = enterprise specific minimal/maximal intensity [U/PER]	
t_{min}/t_{max} = enterprise specific minimal/maximal flexible time per period [PER]	

Fig. 4. Goal programming approach

In a first step for each individual enterprise, the key parameter k of the evaluation process, reflecting the preference of the enterprise, has to be selected. For k=0 the evaluation process will only focus on the economical point of view. The ecological aspects will not be considered. In contrast, for $k \rightarrow \infty$ the economical evaluation part will be neglected. According to Hansmann (1998) the model for k=0 represents a reactive approach of the production unit (for $k \rightarrow \infty$ a proactive approach). In order to reflect the behaviour between the two poles, proactive and reactive, adequate levels of the parameter k have to be specified. In this context a so-called minimal emission level (EMU_{min}) and the maximal marginal income is calculated. The point of the maximal marginal income denotes also the so-called maximal emission level (EMU_{max}) considering the intensity and time constraints (Fig. 5.).

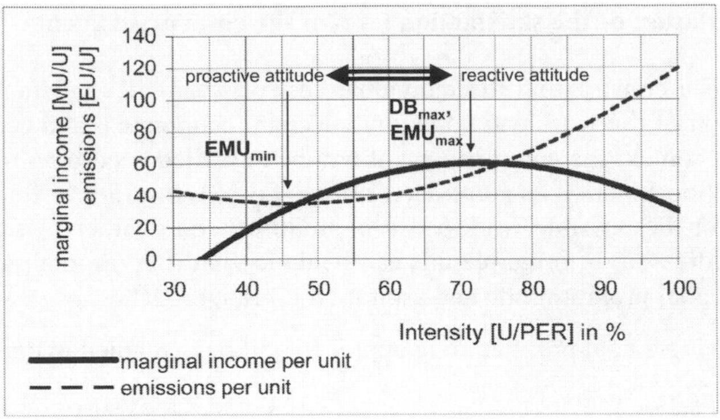

Fig. 5. Marginal income and emissions per units

In the next step the difference between EMU_{max} and EMU_{min} is divided in n equidistant intervals. For each of the intervals i=1,…,n the corresponding value k_i (related to the maximal value of the interval) is calculated according to the following equation:

$$EM(d_{k_i}^{\ *}) = EMU_{min} + (EMU_{max} - EMU_{min}) * \frac{i}{n} \quad i = 1,\dots,n \tag{3.1}$$

where d_{ki}* represents the optimal solution of the goal program of figure 4. Under the assumption that $EM(d)=a_1 \cdot d^2+b_1 \cdot d+c_1$ and $MI(d)= a_2 \cdot d^2+b_2 \cdot d+c_2$, k_i can be calculated (independently of X) by equation 3.2.

$$k_i = -\frac{EM^{-1}[EM_{min} + (EM_{max} - EM_{min}) \cdot \frac{i}{n}] \cdot 2a_1 + b_1}{EM^{-1}[EM_{min} + (EM_{max} - EM_{min}) \cdot \frac{i}{n}] \cdot 2a_2 + b_2} \tag{3.2}$$

Fig. 6 shows an evaluation function for the workload of a production unit for parameter k_8=0,1 and k_4=0,5 (n=10).

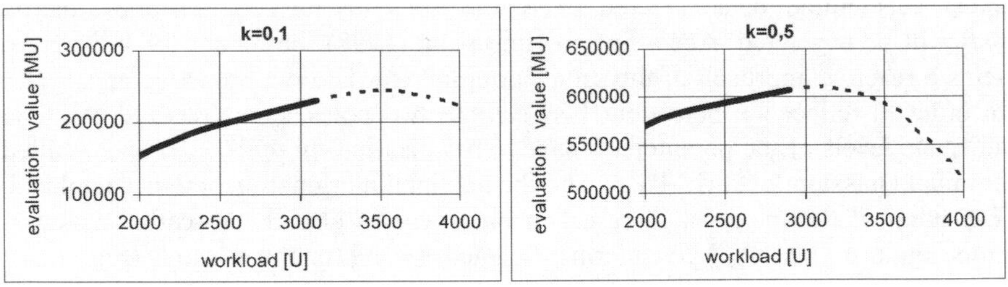

Fig. 6. Evaluation values for different key parameters[3]

[3] Within the dashed part the emission per unit due to the equation 3.2 can not be guaranteed.

3.3. Exemplary negotiation process

To illustrate the negotiation process a short example consisting of a horizontal co-operation of two spinning mills (E-Agent 1 and E-Agent 2) as they typically occur in the Emilia district, is sketched out (Buzacott, 1999). Fig. 7a-b shows the evaluation functions of the two enterprise agents (with identical key parameter k)[4] including the actual state of the workload (underlined in Fig. 7a-b). Assuming that the workload of EA1 is below a given satisfaction level α of e.g. 85% (of the difference between maximal and minimal evaluation value), a negotiation process will be initiated by this enterprise agent. This means a job-request will be sent from EA1 to EA2. In the following the evaluation function of EA2 will be calculated as a function of potential workloads of EA1 (Fig. 7c). To determine the new allocation of workload between EA1 and EA2, the sum of the evaluation functions of Fig. 7c is calculated (Fig. 7d).

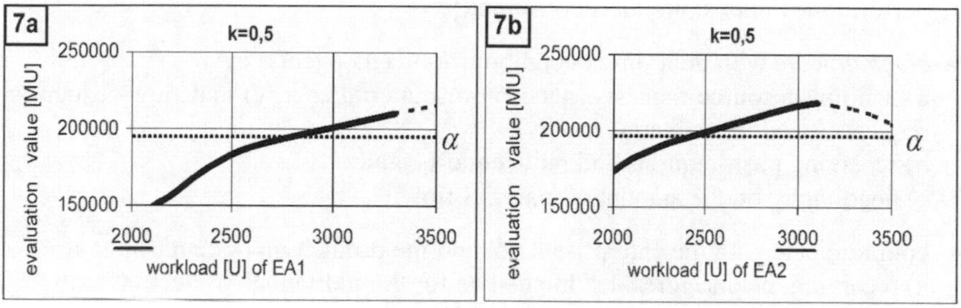

Fig. 7a-b. Evaluation values and satisfaction level

The result (workload of EA1) of the negotiating process is determined by the maximal value of the aggregation function in Fig. 7d. According to this the workload of EA2 can be computed.

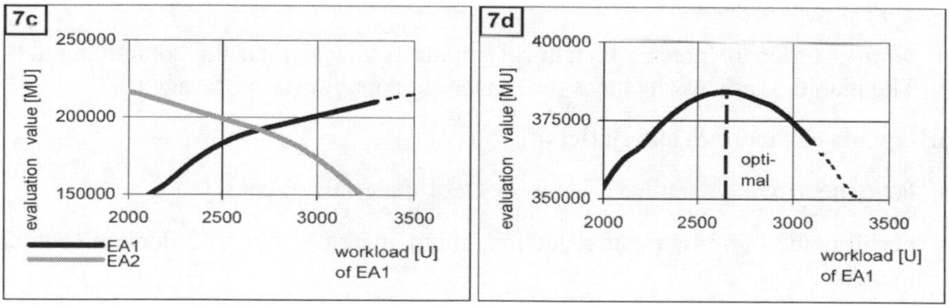

Fig. 7c-d. Negotiation process

4 A negotiation process requires identical parameters k for each company of the enterprise level. That means that all companies involved in a negotiation process have the same preference concerning the weighting of economical and ecological aspects.

4. Coordination mechanism at the factory level

4.1. Configuration of the factory agents

The task of the factory agents is the realization of the guidelines given by the enterprise agent (Fig. 3). The agents at this level represent a single production unit, inventory or buffer system at a time. Their communication structure is restricted to the relatively fixed structure of the dedicated subsystems. In a similar way to our approach at the enterprise level, the agents at the factory level are described in CommonKADS.

PU-agents (Production Units):

- have the *task* to realize the reference values given by the enterprise agent;
- perform the *actions*: produce, consume;
- *communicate* with their direct neighbourhood (IB-agents) by
  a) sending resource-requests (need more material/energy) and flow-reduction-requests (need less material/energy),
  b) receiving push-requests and pull-requests, and
  c) negotiating on the amount of material flow;
- communicate with the enterprise level and the production system by
  a) receiving the disaggregated intensities for the individual production units,
  b) sending the input variables for the production system, and
  c) receiving the actual (measured) intensities from the production system;
- have *knowledge* about their
  a) current satisfactory state,
  b) intensity, and
  c) producing/consuming relationships and needs;
- *plan* in order to forecast their local situation and to plan the communication. The planning process includes the reasoning capabilities of the agents.

IB-agents (Inventories and Buffers):

- have the *task* to guarantee a stable stock of materials or energy;
- perform the *actions*: input reduction, input increase, output reduction, output increase;
- *communicate* with their direct neighbourhood (PU-agents) by
  a) sending push-requests (offering material) and pull-requests (asking for material),
  b) receiving resource-requests and flow-reduction-requests, and
  c) negotiating on the amount of material flow;
- have *knowledge* about their
  a) current satisfactory state,

b) capacity,
c) stock, and
d) commitments (how much has to be delivered how long to whom);

- *plan* in order to forecast their local situation and to plan the communication. The planning process includes the agents' capability to reason.

The main feature of the described multi-agent system with its inventory/buffer and production agents is the restricted communication structure between neighbouring units. Therefore a Petri Net model consisting of transitions, places, tokens and arcs with its fixed network structure seems to be well suited for the modelling of the actions and the communication structure (Dyckhoff, 1994 and Spengler, 2000).

Figure 8 shows a Petri Net model of a subsystem sketched out in figure 1. The individual units can be interpreted as follows:

- *Transitions* (symbolized by rectangles) represent PU-agents (e.g. boiler-house, dye-house), sources of input-streams (e.g. raw-materials) and sinks of emission streams and final products.
- *Places* (symbolized by circles) represent IB-agents.
- *Tokens* characterize the state of the IB-agents (e.g. the level of the waste water reservoir).
- *Arcs* connect transitions and places in a Petri Net and determine the structure of the production system, and thus the communication structure of the multi-agent system. Two types of arcs can be discriminated: input and output arcs.

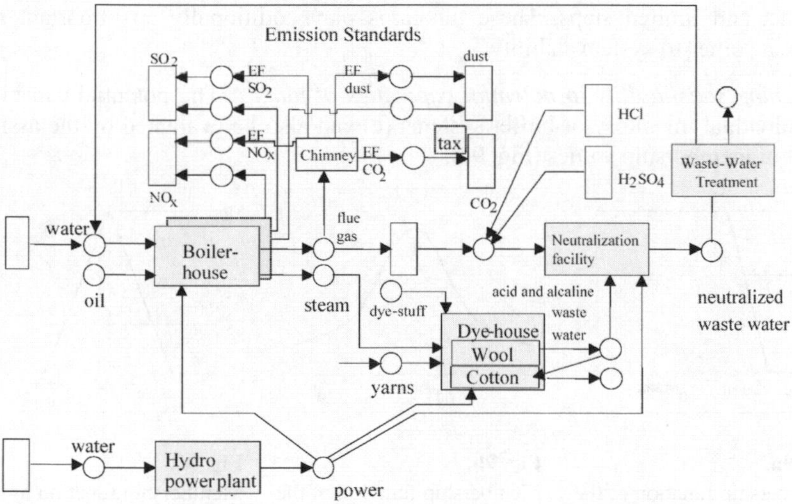

Fig. 8. Petri net model of the factory level

From the point of view of production theory such models can be interpreted as combined production functions. Therefore the balancing of all relevant material and energy flows is possible.

To give the so modelled agents the ability to plan and fulfil their tasks, the Petri Net approach has to be extended. Especially individual goal functions have to be defined for each agent. This can be done methodically by a Fuzzy-Petri Net approach (Tuma and Müller, 2000).

4.2. Calculation of the satisfaction level of the factory agents

To integrate the fuzzy controlling knowledge, intensities of PU-agents (transitions) and capacities of IB-agents (places) are modelled by Fuzzy Sets. The membership functions of these Fuzzy Sets are based on the reference values of the enterprise agents.

Assigning satisfiability (membership value) to potential intensities of transitions: Potential intensities (d) of individual production units can be evaluated by the assignment of the degree of satisfiability represented by the corresponding membership values (Fig. 9a). By a certain analogy to “valves” the intensity of a transition is a variable parameter. The same model can be applied to sources and sinks of input and output streams.

Evaluating potential variations of the intensities of transitions: By this, the variation of the intensities (Δ d) is evaluated by a membership function (Fig. 9b). The reason for this is that intensities of real processes usually can be manipulated in distinct and limited steps. These functions play additionally an important role when it comes to system stability.

Assigning satisfiability to potential capacities of places: The potential capacities of individual inventory or buffer systems (c) can also be evaluated by the assignment of membership values (Fig. 9c).

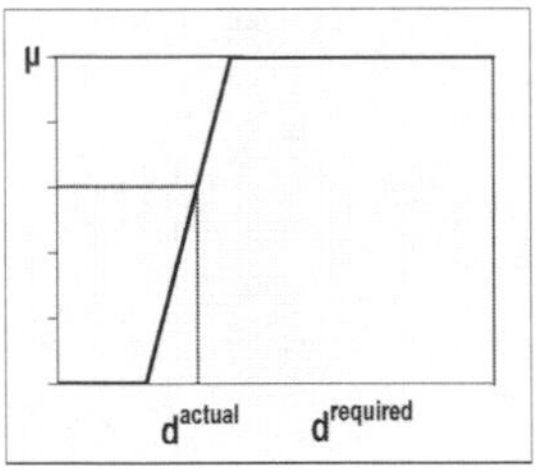

Fig. 9a.
Membership function of the intensity

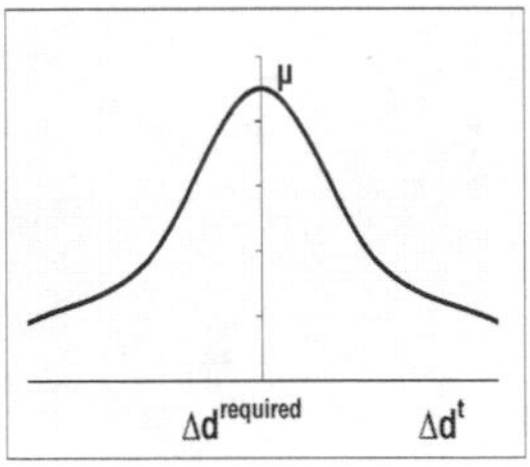

Fig. 9b.
Membership function of the variation of the intensity

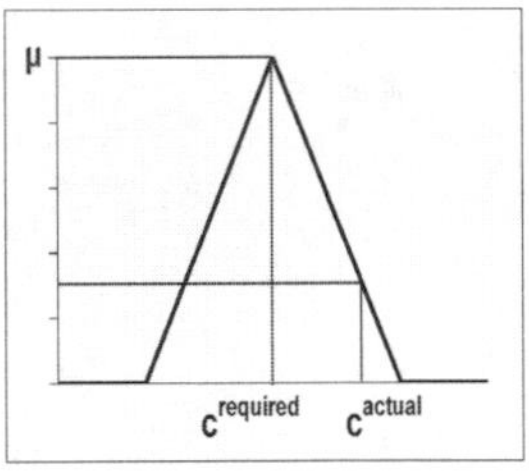

Fig. 9c.
Membership function of the capacity

4.3. Exemplary negotiation process

The goal of the coordinating process is to detect the best compromise between all units at the factory level (maximization of the membership values of all components as far as possible). This means especially the detection of intensities. In calculating such values the negotiation process roughly works as follows:

To improve the membership value of a place, the intensity of at least one of the transitions has to be changed. A broadcast of the change request to all connected transitions will result in finding the best suited transition to satisfy the request. I.e. the transition with the highest degree of satisfaction (defined as a function of the difference between required and actual amount of material/energy) will be selected.

If a transition is selected, the negotiation process between the selected transition and all preceding und succeeding places is initiated. The goal is to find a compromise. This results in a maximization of the minimal membership value of all negotiating partners.

To illustrate the problem solving mechanism at the factory level, a subsystem of figure 1, consisting of a cogeneration unit, an (emergency) power storage, a spinning mill and a yarn storage, is investigated (Fig. 10). The subsystem is linked to an external power plant as well as to the dye-house (partner of the production network). The input-output-relations are modelled by production functions.

According to the negotiation process at the enterprise level, a demand of 80 units (per control period of the factory level) has to be supplied to the dye-house (this corresponds to the calculated intensity of the spinning mill of 80%).

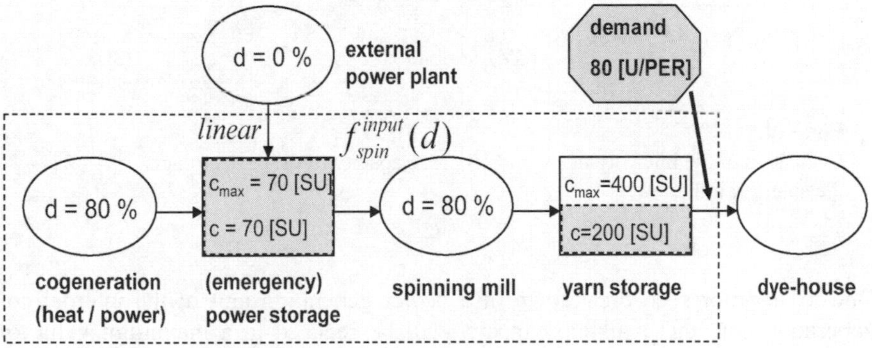

Fig. 10. Subsystem of a production network
(desired state of the enterprise level)

For reasons of simplification we will assume that in an initial state all internal productive units (cogeneration unit, spinning mill) work at the desired intensity (d^{cogen}_{ref} = 80%, d^{spin}_{ref} = 80%) corresponding to the reference value of the enterprise level. Due to the policy to avoid external power supply, as far as possible, the desired intensity of the external power plant is $d^{ext}_{opt} = 0\%$. This means that the considered subsystem does not use any energy produced by the external power plant. According to the defined satisfiability functions, all production units are evaluated with a maximal membership value (Fig. 11a, 11b, 11d)[5]. The power storage is not used (filled to 100%, i.e. 70 storage units [SU]) (Fig. 11c), the yarn storage is filled to 50% (Fig. 11e). This means optimal fill-up levels and implies also maximal membership values.

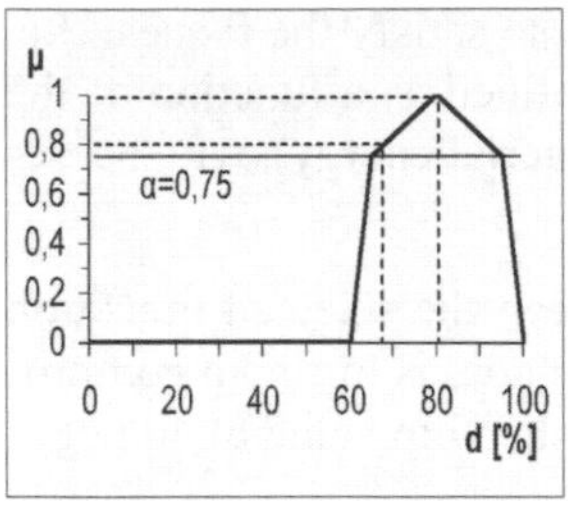

Fig. 11a.
Evaluation of the intensity of the cogeneration unit

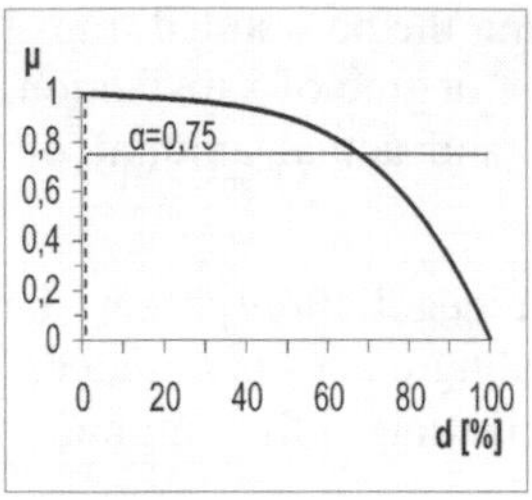

Fig. 11b.
Evaluation of the intensity of the external power plant

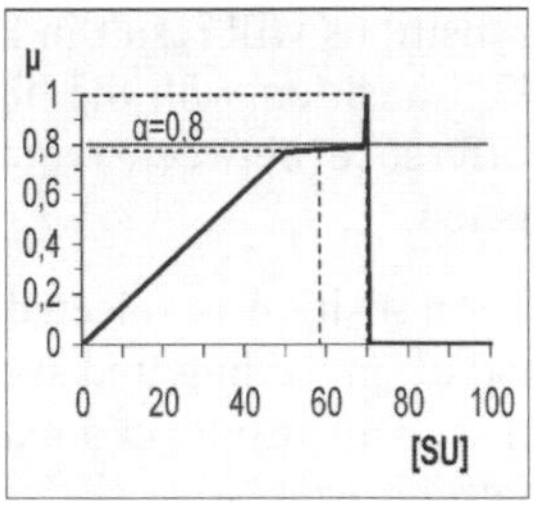

Fig. 11c.
Capacity of the power storage

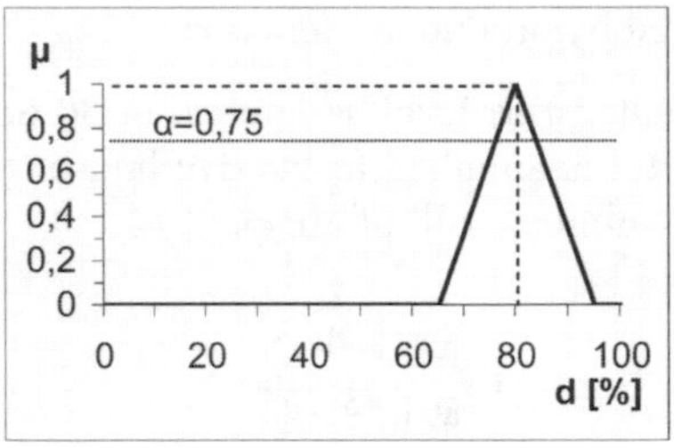

Fig. 11d.
Evaluation of the intensity of the spinning mill

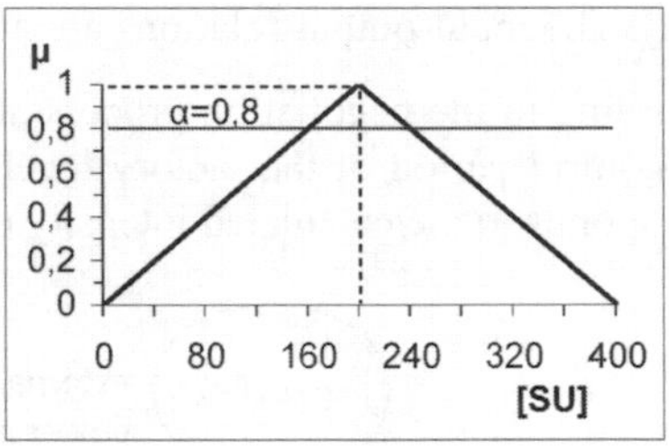

Fig. 11e.
Capacity of the yarn storage.

Due to an unforeseen breakdown of a power generation unit of the internal cogeneration unit, the available capacity will be reduced to a maximum value of 68% ($d^{cogen}_{max} = 68\%$; $\mu=0.8$) (Fig. 12). For this reason the energy demand of the spinning mill can not be fulfilled by the cogeneration unit totally. For reasons of simplification we assume that the 12% decrease of the intensity of the cogenera-

[5] The shape of the membership functions is defined by adequate experts. The maximal value of the membership function of the production units considers the reference values from the enterprise level.

tion unit results in a decrease of the power storage stock of 12 [SU] (μ=0.78)[6]. This leads to a crossing of the predefined α–niveau line (0.8) of the power storage and initiates the negotiation process. Due to the fact that the "power storage" is modelled as a place, an improvement of its satisfiability level requires a change of the intensity of one of the associated transitions (cogeneration unit, external power plant or spinning mill).

To harmonize the difference between the needed and the actual supplied energy in principle three options are possible:

- taking the difference from emergency power storage
- using an external power plant
- reduction of the intensity of the spinning mill

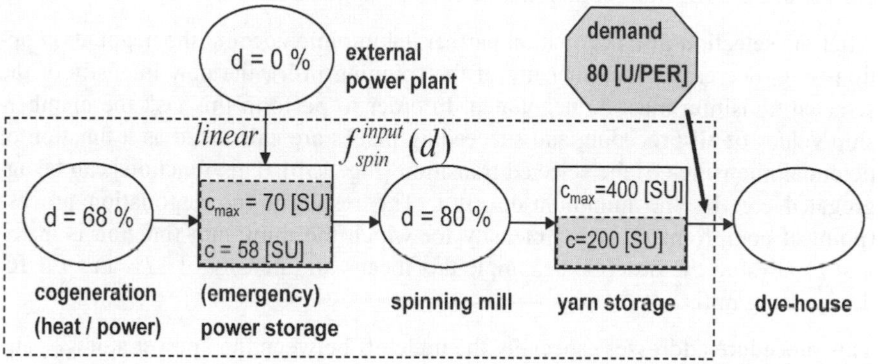

Fig. 12. Subsystem of a production network (partial breakdown of cogeneration unit)

The selection of the transition (selection of an option, i.e. of a negotiation partner) is implemented according to figure 13a. For each place a linguistic variable "selection of a transition" is defined. This variable consists of several terms representing possible options for all associated transitions. E. g. the term $t_p^{increase}$ represents the option "increasing the intensity of one of the preceding transitions" (cogeneration unit or external power plant)[7]. The term $t_s^{decrease}$ represents the option "decreasing the intensity of the succeeding transition" (spinning mill). The term t represents the option "no reaction". This option should keep the system in a stable condition, if the difference between desired and real production figures is

[6] Thereby we suppose that the given intensity of the spinning mill (d^{spin}_{opt}) causes a consumption of 80 SU downstream (partly from the cogeneration unit, partly from the power storage).

[7] In principle internal transitions are preferred in contrast to external transitions. In the case of more internal or external transitions, additional terms have to be defined.

below a certain threshold. The terms are implemented by Fuzzy Sets. The terms regarding the membership functions of the linguistic variable are defined by adequate experts taking into account economic, ecological and technical aspects. The input variable indicates the difference between the actual (measured) and the required fill-up level of the considered place (e. g. the power storage). This difference is evaluated with a membership value (satisfiability value). The term (option) with the highest assigned value is selected and determines the negotiation partner, i.e. the required option (increasing or decreasing the intensity of a transition). Analysing the considered application example, a membership value of $\mu = 0.8$ for the option "decreasing the intensity of the spinning mill" and a membership value of $\mu = 0.2$ for the option "increasing the intensity of one of the preceding production units" can be calculated (Fig. 13a). This means that the selected negotiation partner is the transition "spinning mill".

After the selection of a negotiation partner, taking into account the negotiation option (e. g. decreasing the intensity of the spinning mill), the new intensity of the selected transition must be negotiated. In order to perform this task the membership values of all preceding and succeeding places are calculated as a function of potential intensities of the selected transition (Fig. 13b). This functions can be aggregated e.g. by the minimum-operator. The result of the negotiation process (point of compromise) is the intensity for which the minimum-function is maximal. Analysing the described example this means an intensity of 77% in t + 1 for the spinning mill.

This procedure addresses especially the trade off between the "power storage" and the "spinning mill" and results in increasing the satisfiability level of the "power storage" by a modest reduction of the intensity of the spinning mill. Concerning the "yarn storage" the described situation leads ceteris paribus to a reduction of its membership value.

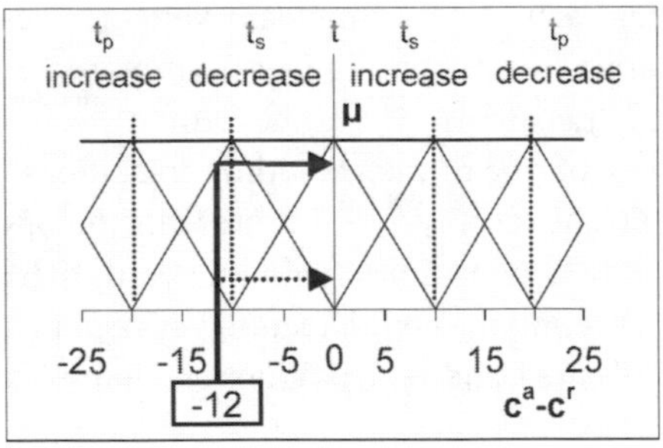

Fig. 13a.
Selection of the transition and its required behaviour

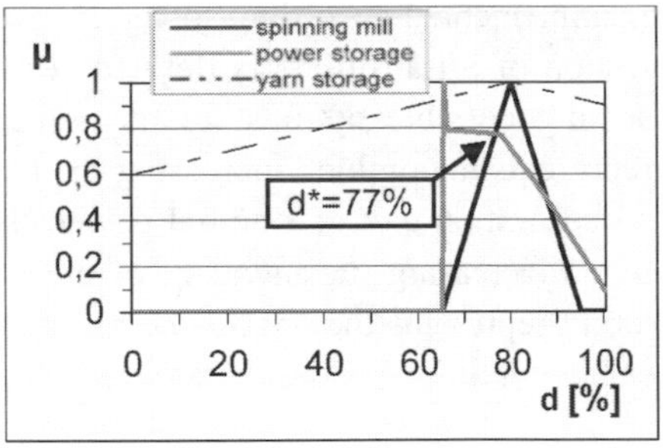

Fig. 13b.
Negotiation and calculation of d* for the spinning mill

An adjustment of the intensity of the spinning mill to 77% implies the following production figures for the other units.

state t+1	Production Intensity	Production Input	Production Output	Fill-Up Level	Membership Value (μ)
Cogeneration	68%	227 [IU]	68 [OU]		0,80
External Power	0%	0 [IU]	0 [OU]		1,00
Power Storage				48 [SU]	0,74
Spinning Mill	77%	78 [IU]	77 [OU]		0,77
Yarn Storage				197 [SU]	0,99
[OU] = output units, [IU] = input units, [SU] = storage units					

Table 1. State of the production system in t+1

The difference between output[8] and input figures describes the non-linear character of the production function of the cogeneration unit and the spinning mill.

In the following step, one unit ("power storage") with a membership value (satisfiability value) below the α-niveau can be identified. An evaluation of the unit "power storage" (Fig. 14a) shows a preference for the option "increase the intensity of the external power plant" (preceding unit)[9]. An analysis of the negotiation process, which means an investigation of the membership value of the unit "power storage" as a function of potential intensities of the transition "external power plant", results in a compromise of a 32 % intensity for the "external power plant" in t+2 (Fig. 14b).

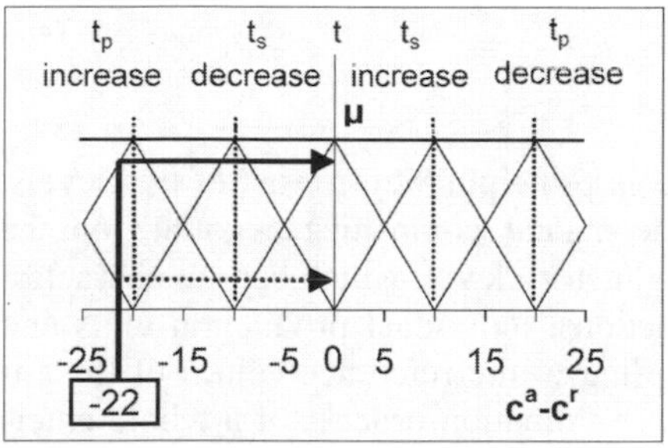

Fig. 14a.
Selection of the transition and its required behaviour

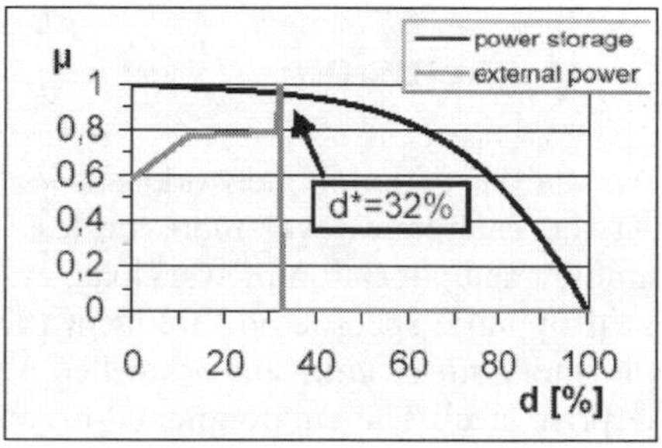

Fig. 14b.
Negotiation and calculation of d* for the external power plant

---

[8] The output is normalized according to the intensity.

[9] Due to the fact that the cogeneration unit operates at its maximal intensity of 68%, it can not be selected in the negotiation process. According to this the term $t_p^{increase}$ denotes the external power plant.

Based on this the following production figures can be calculated:

state t+2	Production Intensity	Input	Output	Fill-Up Level	Membership Value (μ)
Cogeneration	68%	227 [IU]	68 [OU]		0,80
External Power	32%	-	32 [OU]		0,96
Power Storage				70 [SU]	1,00
Spinning Mill	77%	78 [IU]	77 [OU]		0,77
Yarn Storage				194 [SU]	0,97
[OU] = output units, [IU] = input units, [SU] = storage units					

Table 2. State of the production system in t+2

In principle the described algorithm tries to follow the given intensities at the enterprise level. The breakdown of one of the energy generation units of the cogeneration facility results in a slightly decreased intensity of the spinning mill. For some periods the missing production can be compensated by the yarn storage (safety stock). The moderate reduction of the intensity of the spinning mill causes an iterative use of external power which leads to higher production costs and emissions (emission efficiency of the cogeneration unit is higher in comparison to the external power plant). This means that the measured values (feedback values) for the enterprise agent differ from its desired values (Fig. 3). In the following this initiates a new negotiation process with other spinning mills at the enterprise level.

5. Conclusion

An analysis of supply networks shows that in principle they consist of two levels. At the enterprise level more or less independent companies negotiate on the amount and allocation of workload. At the factory level, which can be characterized by more specific and frequent transactions, individual production units and inventory/buffer units are controlled according to the reference values of the enterprise level. The environmental-oriented coordination process of a whole enterprise can be modelled by a cascade controller, implemented by a two-stage multi-agent approach.

In order to model the multi-criteria objective functions (economical and ecological) of the enterprise agents, goal programming can be applied. Thereby the different behaviour between the poles, proactive and reactive, can be modelled by a parameter k. This parameter describes the enterprise strategy and must be identical for all enterprises at the enterprise level. It is one of the key elements of a common culture (precondition for an enterprise pool) and represents a common language which is obligatory for a common negotiation process.

The implementation of the multi-agent system at the factory level as a Fuzzy-Petri Net addresses the specific communication structure (specific transactions) with regard to the relatively fixed input and output relations. The Petri Net allows not only a balancing of energy and material flows, but due to the integration of individual goal functions, it furthermore allows a controlling of the energy and material flows according to the guidelines at the enterprise level.

Further research work has to focus on different cooperation relations in supply networks as well as on the evaluation of different strategies for the simultaneous addressing of economical and ecological goals. One of the key problems of the approach discussed is the conflict between stability and convergence. In this context the potential learning capabilities of the single agents should be investigated.

References

Buzacott, J.A. (1999): The Structure of Manufacturing Systems: Insights on the Impact of Variability. In: International Journal of Flexible Manufacturing Systems 11, pp. 127-146.

Coase, R.H. (1937): The nature of the firm, Economica (New Ser.), vol. 4, pp. 386-405.

Corsten, H.; Gössinger, R. (2000): Opportunistische Koordinierung bei Werkstattfertigung - Ein multiagentensystemgestützter Lösungsansatz. In: v. U. Götze, B. Mikus und J. Bloech (eds.): Management und Zeit, pp. 493-540.

Dyckhoff, H. (1994): Betriebliche Produktion – Theoretische Grundlagen einer umweltorientierten Produktionswirtschaft, 2. edn., Springer, §§ 11.1, p. 14.

Fandel, G. (1991): Theory of Production Costs, Springer, pp. 250-261.

Gutenberg, E. (1969): Grundlagen der Betriebswirtschaftslehre, vol. 1, Die Produktion, 16. edn., Springer-Verlag , pp. 314-325.

Hansmann, K.W. (1998): Umweltorientierte Betriebswirtschaftslehre, Gabler, pp. 10-12.

Kreikebaum, H. (2000): The Impact of Gutenberg's Theory of Organisation upon Modern Organisational Conceptions. In: Albach et al. (eds.): Theory of the Firm, Springer, pp. 88-103.

Müller, H.J. (1996): Negotiation Principles. In: O`Hare, G.M.P. and Jennings, N.R. (eds.): Foundations of Distributed Artificial Intelligence, Wiley Intersience Pub , pp. 211-230.

Müller, H.J. (1997): Towards Agent Systems Engineering, Data & Knowledge Engineering, vol. 23, pp. 217-245.

Picot, A. (1991): Ein neuer Ansatz zur Gestaltung der Fertigungstiefe, In: Zeitschrift für betriebswirtschaftliche Forschung, vol. 4 , pp. 336-357.

Spengler, Th. (2000): Industrielles Stoffstrommanagement – Modellierung von Stoff- und Energieströmen in Produktions- und Recyclingnetzwerken. In: Inderfurth, K. (ed.): Proceedings zum Symposium Operations Research, Springer, pp. 524-535.

Tuma, A., Müller, H.-J. (2000): Using Fuzzy-Directed Agents for Ecological Production Control. In: Nguyen, Zadeh (eds.): Intelligent Automation and Soft Computing, vol. 6, no. 3, pp. 233-242.

Wildemann, H. (1996): Management von Produktions- und Zuliefernetzwerken. In: Wildemann, H. (ed.): Produktions- und Zuliefernetzwerke, TCW-Verlag, pp. 13-42.

Williamson, O.E. (1985): The Economic Institutions of Captitalism. In: The Free Press, pp. 68-84.

Zelewski, St. (1998): Multi-Agenten-Systeme – ein innovativer Ansatz zur Realisierung dezentraler PPS-Systeme. In: Wildemann, H. (ed.): Innovationen in der Produktionswirtschaft – Produkte, Prozesse, Planung und Steuerung, TCW-Verlag, pp. 133-166.

Architectures of Transportation Networks and their Effects on Economic Efficiency

Günther Zäpfel, Michael Wasner

Institute of Industry and Production Management
University of Linz
Altenbergerstraße 69
A-4040 Linz, Austria

Abstract: *The aim of transportation networks is to ensure delivery of a given quantity of traffic from pickup points to delivery points within a defined regional, national or transnational area and within a specified delivery time (for example, within 24 hours in a country). Therefore, the elements of a transportation system are pickup points and delivery points. Pickup points are the customers from whom goods are collected. Delivery points are customers to whom goods are delivered. Consolidation points represent on the one hand the terminals (depots), which perform bundling services locally for their customers, and on the other hand the hubs, which bundle quantity streams out of sending depots in order to transport them to the receiving depots. Bundling can also be achieved if several sending depots combine their delivery quantities within the scope of one transport. For example, if three depots are involved, this is called triangle traffic. The connections can be characterised by various features, for instance, the means of transport.*

An architecture of a transportation system is a specific and mutually compatible selection of the elements and relations of a transportation system. Combining the possible elements and relations of a transportation system gives rise to alternative architectures. The paper suggests a typology of architectures of transportation systems and traces the impact of these alternative architectures on the economic efficiency of the network.

Keywords: *transportation networks, economic efficiency, hub-and-spoke systems, typology of transportation systems*

1. Introduction

Transportation networks serve the purpose of assuring service between pickup and delivery zones within a defined area for a given volume of transport goods and considering a required delivery time restriction (e.g., within 24 hours in a nation). The defined area can be regional, national or transnational.

A *transportation network* is defined generally as a material flow system characterised by elements such as pickup points, delivery points and consolidation points as well as relationships between these elements. We clarify this definition using the hub-and-spoke system as an example of a transportation network. A hub-and-spoke system is characterised by a spatial and temporal organisation of the logistical flows within a geographic area; this organisation assures that the individual spokes (depots) form a comprehensive system with defined service areas and that these spokes are interconnected by at least one central hub. The individual depots collect piece goods from demand points in their service area (i.e., the customers) and deliver piece goods for other spokes. Both these activities are termed *pickup and deliveries*. The service area is also characterised by its number of pickup and delivery routes. The size of the service area directly influences the dimensioning of the spokes and the volume of transport goods in a spoke. Material flow between the spokes is co-ordinated by bundling all shipments from one depot to a corresponding target depot via the central hub. The consolidation (bundling) of transport volumes takes place through the hub. Local pickup and delivery transports in the respective service areas and transports between collection depots and the hub or between the hub and receiving depots through line haul shipments form the transportation network. All line haul shipments are termed line haul or trunk haulage (Fig. 1).

The elements of a transportation system are demand points (pickup points and delivery points as well as consolidation points). Pickup points are the customers from whom piece goods are collected for delivery. Delivery points are customers to whom the piece goods are delivered. Consolidation points are the depots themselves, which handle the local pickup and delivery service for their customers, as well as the hubs, which bundle goods from the collection depots in order to transport them to the receiving depots. Consolidation can also be achieved by multiple collection depots bundling their delivery traffic in a transport; for three depots, this constitutes a triangular transport.

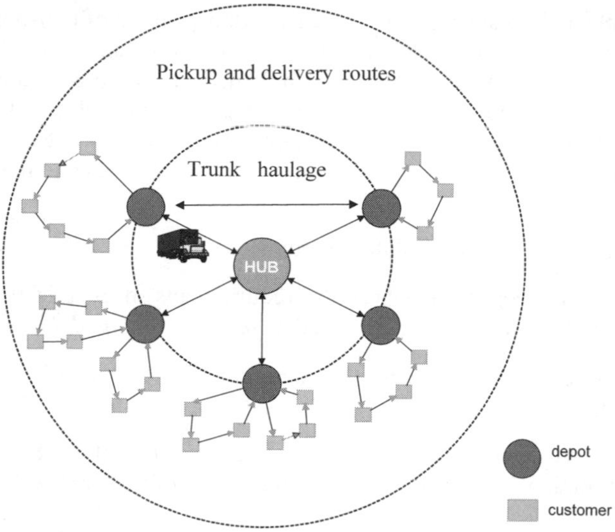

Fig. 1. Example of a transportation network

The arrows in Fig. 1 represent the interconnection of these elements (pickup, delivery and consolidation points); arrows symbolise transport flow and set the pickup, delivery and consolidation points in relationship to one another. These interconnections are described by various characteristics such as the transport vehicles employed for their transport flows.

The *architecture of a transport system* is the specific and mutually compatible definition of the elements and relationships of a transportation system; a specific combination of the possible elements and relationships of a transportation system yields the architecture of the transportation network. In this paper we consider alternative designs of transportation networks and propose a typology of architectures for the transportation systems; we also derive statements concerning the effects of these alternative architectures on the economic efficiency of the systems. Before we tackle this problem, we present more precisely the terms *transportation network*, *typologies of architectures* of a transportation network, and *economic efficiency* of a network.

2. Systematic alternative architectures for transportation networks

In general, a connected network $TR = (DP, R)\ with\ R \subseteq DPxDP$, where DP = set of demand points within a certain (regional, national or transnational) area and R = transport relationships between them, is called a transportation network.

A demand point can be a source from which a certain volume of transport goods is sent, or it can be a target to which goods finally flow, or it can be both source and target. Furthermore, a demand point can simultaneously serve as a consolidation point where goods are bundled in order to transport them collectively by some means of transportation to other demand points. There can also be consolidation points that serve only to bundle goods but that do not represent (real) demand points.

We distinguish two types of consolidation points:

- *Depot:* a consolidation point where the requirements of at least two demand points are bundled. Depots are designated as *first-order consolidation points*.
- *Hub*: a consolidation point where the requirements of at least two first-order consolidation points are bundled.

Hubs can also serve as consolidation points of higher order (third, fourth, ...). An nth order consolidation point bundles at least the traffic of two consolidation points of order n-1.

With respect to traffic, a first-order consolidation point determines the pickup and deliveries in that the demand points need to be serviced; i.e., the transport goods are picked up and delivered to customers, where spatial planning takes the form of routes. Trunk haulage consists of all transports in the realm of the spatial planning (in the form of long-distance transports) that are carried out between consolidation points of order ≥ 1. Exception: If no consolidation points are planned, then the line haul shipments are the direct traffic between the demand points; in this case there are no local transports.

More general, a consolidation point can also be characterised by a certain path of a transportation network. A path of a transportation network $p(v_i, v_k) = (v_i, v_{i+1})$, (v_{i+1}, v_{i+2}), …, (v_{k-1}, v_k) is the direct succession of transport relationships whereby v_i is equal the source demand point and v_k is identical the target demand point. Let $\tilde{p}(v_i, v_k)$ be the *shortest* path between v_i and v_k then the set of the intermediate successive demand points $W_{ik} = \{\tilde{v}_{i+1}, \tilde{v}_{i+2}, .., \tilde{v}_{k-1}\}$ are *consolidation points*. The number of elements is given by $|W_{ik}|$. If only paths exist in a transportation network where $|W_{ik}|$=0, $\forall i, k$, then there exist no consolidation points and only direct transports between the demand points arise. If at least there is one path with $|W_{ik}|$ =1 in a transportation network there follows that at least one depot has been erected. In the case where the transportation network has at least one path with $|W_{ik}|$ >2 one hub or more are existent.

Alternative architectures of transportation networks can be derived using these characteristics of paths within a transportation network. In general, a transportation network is categorised *by the highest occurring order of its consolidation points* (Fig. 2).

Transportation networks $TR = (DP, R)$ whereby $R = DPxDP$ are called *transportation networks of order 0* if the longest path $W := \max_{\substack{i,k \in DP \\ i \neq k}} |W_{ik}| = 0$.

Transportation networks $TR = (DP, R)$ whereby $R \subseteq DPxDP$ are named *transportation networks of order 1 if* the longest path $W := \max_{\substack{i,k \in DP \\ i \neq k}} |W_{ik}| = 1$ or 2.

Transportation networks $TR = (DP, R)$ whereby $R \subseteq DPxDP$ are designated as *transportation networks of order 2* if the longest path $W := \max_{\substack{i,k \in DP \\ i \neq k}} |W_{ik}| = 3$ or 4.

Generalised, transportation networks $TR = (DP, R)$ whereby $R \subseteq DPxDP$ are called *transportation networks of order n* if the longest path $W := \max_{\substack{i,k \in DP \\ i \neq k}} |W_{ik}| = 2n - 1$ or $2n$, where $n \geq 1$.

Remark: If $W = 2n - 1$ then there exists exactly one consolidation point of order n. If $W = 2n$ then we have more than one consolidation point of order n. A transportation network of order n consolidates respectively bundles at least the volume of transport goods of **two** consolidation points of order n-1.

Therefore, we can define an architecture of a transportation network as follows:

Definition: The architecture of a transport network is of order n if at least one consolidation point of order n and none of higher order occurs that is the maximum number of consolidation points is n.

Architectures **(Types)**	**Characteristics of alternative architectures of transportation networks**
Type 1: Transportation networks of order 0	No consolidation points (depots, hubs), that means there is no bundling of traffic volume Local transport: no pickup and deliveries Long distance transport (line haul shipments): only direct transports between all demand points
Type 1: Transportation networks of order 1	Consolidation points via depots (first order consolidation points) Local transport: demand point-to-depot traffic (collection routes) and depot-to-demand point traffic (delivery routes) per depot. Variants: separate or shared pickup and delivery Line haul shipments: depot-to-depot transports (if at least two depots exist)
Type 2: Transportation networks of order 2	Consolidation points via depots and hubs (second order consolidation points) that bundle only the traffic between depots. Local transports: demand point-to-depot traffic (collection routes) and depot-to-demand point traffic (delivery routes) per depot. Variants: separate or shared pickup and delivery Line haul shipments: depot-to-depot transports, depot-to-hub transports, hub-to-hub transports (for more than one hub), hub-to-depot transports
Type 3: Transportation networks of order 3	Consolidation points via depots and hubs that bundle the traffic volume of depots where additionally exists at least one hub (third order consolidation point) that also bundles the traffic volume between at least two second order consolidation point-hubs Local transports and line haul shipments: all variants can exist as by type 2
Type n >3: Transportation networks of order n	Consolidation points via depots and hubs that bundle the traffic volume of depots where additionally exists at least one hub (consolidation point of order n) that bundles the traffic volume between at least two hubs ((n-1)-order consolidation points) Local transports and line haul shipments: all variants can exist as by type 2

Fig. 2. Architectures of transportation networks

Familiar types or architectures of transportation networks are:

- Transportation networks without consolidation points: Here we have only *direct transports* between the demand points (compare Fig. 3 a).
- Transportation networks that contain only first-order consolidation points: Here only direct transports between the depots area possible (compare Fig. 3 b). These first two transportation networks are also called *raster transportation systems.*_
  A simple example of a first-order transportation network is realised in the area carrier concept. A transport firm picks up the respective jobs from the suppliers on a route and takes these to its depot. From there it conducts a consolidated delivery to the target customer (e.g., automobile producer).
- Transportation networks that contain exactly one consolidation point of order 1 represent *a pure hub-and-spoke system* if no direct transports between demand points occur (compare Fig. 3 c).
- Transportation networks with consolidation points of order n (n≥3): These are designated as multiple-stage transportation networks and occurs in transnational networks (Fig. 3 e)

Fig. 3 illustrates some familiar architectures of transportation networks.

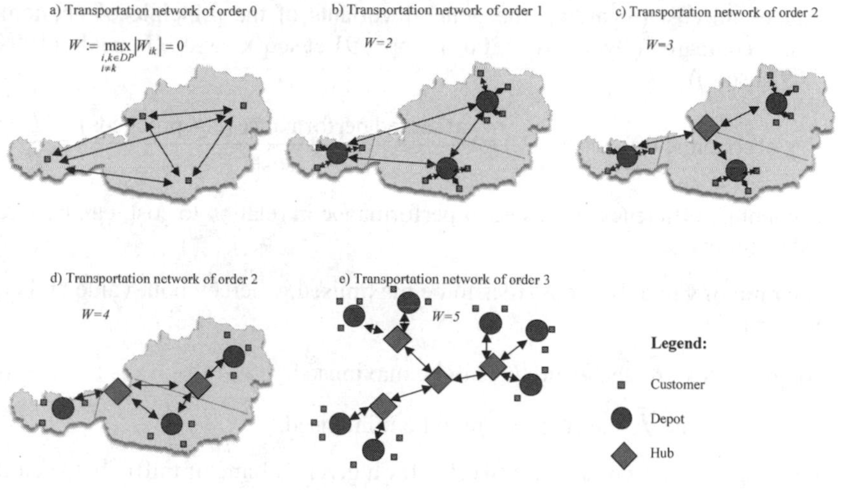

Fig. 3. Transportation networks of various order

In the design of a transportation network, decisions need to be made for a given volume of traffic between the demand points:

- Design of pickup and deliveries, i.e.:
  - the number and locations of depots and service areas (number of demand points assigned to a depot)

  - the routes that are necessary between the demand points of the service area of each depot
  - Number and capacity of the transport vehicles for the pickup and delivery routes
- Design of trunk haulage, i.e.:
  - Number and location of hubs (consolidation points of order 2 or more)
  - Number of line haul shipments or the number of transports between consolidation points of various orders
  - Number and capacity of the transport vehicles for the line haul shipments

To determine the optimal transportation network the aim of economic efficiency of a transportation network is especially important.

3. Economic efficiency of transportation networks

Eonomic efficiency in a narrow sense is the relationship between assessed performance and cost (regarding the general variants of the principle of economic success, compare (Dyckhoff (2000), pp. 191 et sqq.), and (Fandel (1994), pp. 209 et sqq.)):

$$\text{economic efficiency (W)} = \frac{\text{assessed performance (e.g. proceeds)}}{\text{cost}} = \frac{L}{K}$$

The economic efficiency, as assessed performance in relation to cost, can be interpreted as follows:

1. The ratio of value L to cost K is to be maximised, whereby both value and cost are variable.
2. For given cost $\overline{K}$ the value L is to be maximised.
3. For given value $\overline{L}$ the costs K are to be minimised.

In the design of transportation networks, for a given volume of traffic between the demand points, above all the costs need to be influenced, assuming that the prices for transport goods are already given. Thus for this area of application, the economic efficiency principle in formulation 3 above and, if the proceeds are affected, in formulation 1 above bear particular relevance.

If the volume of traffic is given and the tariffs for piece goods are unambiguously set (e.g., for a parcel service provider the prices differentiated according to volume and distance), then proceeds can be estimated. Then economic efficiency is given in formulation 3 above. A transportation network works economically if the following applies: assessed performance (e.g. proceeds) in relation to cost are greater than one.

If the proceeds from a specific transportation network cannot be directly estimated, then a special form of economic efficiency can be employed: logistical economic efficiency. For certain logistical performances, the costs are to be minimised. The logistical performance of a company becomes visible by the customer service level which can be expressed as follows (compare, e.g., Pfohl 2000, pp. 30-41; Schulte 1999, pp. 6-11):

- delivery time
- delivery reliability
- delivery quality.
- delivery flexibility

In the design of the architecture of a transportation network, delivery time and delivery reliability play a profound role in assuring competitive success. Thus for piece goods, we assume 24-hour service for national and 48-hour service for transnational service providers. Assuring delivery quality (error-free delivery) and delivery flexibility are also important prerequisites for the competitiveness of a logistic service provider.

Thus the design of transportation networks often assumes that for a given volume of traffic in a delivery area the costs need to be kept as low as possible, whereby a delivery time, as prescribed by competitive constraints, for all demand points in the delivery area must not be exceeded. Thus logistical economic efficiency in formulation 3 above becomes particularly relevant. Cost leadership attained on the basis of a certain architecture of a transportation network enables a competitive edge in the transport branch due to greater price flexibility (for a particular delivery service).

In the following we consider how to optimise the design of a transportation network and how architectures of transportation networks relate to economic efficiency.

4. Economic effects shown in examples

This section presents four small examples and illustrates effects on their economic efficiency. In this section we assume the definition of the term economic efficiency in formulation 3 above, so that it suffices to study the effects of various architectures on the costs. Economic efficiency plays a decisive role in the operative handling of transport jobs in transportation networks. However, the prerequisites for economic handling are already defined in the design of the architecture of the transportation network. Thus in determining the architecture of a transportation network, special attention needs to be paid to its economic efficiency. As significant cost structures, in the design of a transportation network the transport costs as well as the operating costs for all consolidation points are predefined. In the realm of economic efficiency studies we therefore distinguish among the following types of costs:

- Transport costs generally depend primarily on the number of required transport vehicles (truck, rail, ship, etc.) and the distances that these transport vehicles need to cover between pickup points and delivery points in a prescribed area for a given architecture.
- Operating costs encompass primarily the costs of the consolidation points and consist of the costs of depots and hubs. Operating costs consist primarily of the costs of facilities and personnel. Here the behaviour of operating costs can be linear or stepwise fixed in relation to the number of transport jobs. Stepwise fixed cost behaviour results primarily when exceeding a certain amount of the traffic volume at a consolidation point (depot, hub) which necessitates additional investment in capacity.

In these examples, transport costs are assumed as 1 monetary unit/km/truck, the maximum load capacity of a truck as 1000 parcels. The first three examples are based on Austria as the delivery area and assume total traffic of 6000 parcels per day.

- Example 1: Network structure of order 0

  The number of customers (senders) is very low at 3. Each of the 3 customers has a transport volume of exactly 1 truck (1000 packets) for each of the other 2

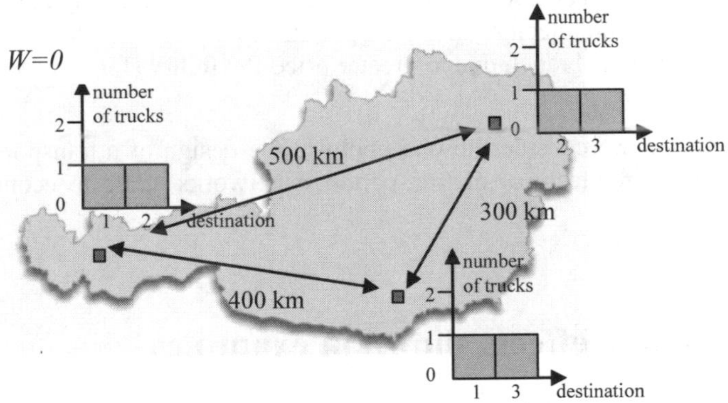

Fig. 4. For the optimal network (order 0), transport costs are 2400 monetary units

customers, which yields a total parcel volume of 6000 per day (Fig. 4). Establishing a depot, i.e., a first-order consolidation point, does not make sense because full trucks always run between two senders. The transport costs for a pure raster system are 2×(500+400+300) = 2400 monetary units.

Establishing a consolidation point in the form of a depot or hub cannot be optimal because in this case, due to the pairing of volumes of traffic between the demand points and the resulting full loads for the transport vehicles, transport costs cannot be reduced by consolidation points, yet additional operating costs would be incurred (see statement at the end of this section).

- Example 2: Network structure of order 1

The total number of customers is 30, whereby groups of 10 customers are situated in close proximity to one another (Fig. 5). Establishing a depot now makes sense because the volume of traffic of the 10 customers in a cluster to the 10 customers in another cluster is exactly 1000 parcels, which is exactly one truckload.

If the customers are situated in a circle around the depot with a radius of 20 km, then pickup or delivery requires 2×20km×π (circumference of the route) plus twice the radius (2×20km), which makes a total of approximately 165 km pro depot. Transport costs for 3 depots then are 2×(500+400+300) + 3×165 = 2895 monetary units.

If there is no consolidation in a depot, i.e., each pickup vehicle takes its volume of traffic (which is low in relationship to the capacity of the transport vehicles) directly to the target customer, the resulting total costs are exactly ten times as high as in Example 1 (10 customers per depot, cluster), thus 24,000 monctary units. The advantage of consolidation points (depots) in Example 2 results because the volume of traffic for the pickup vehicle is much lower than in Example 1 in relation to maximum vehicle capacity.

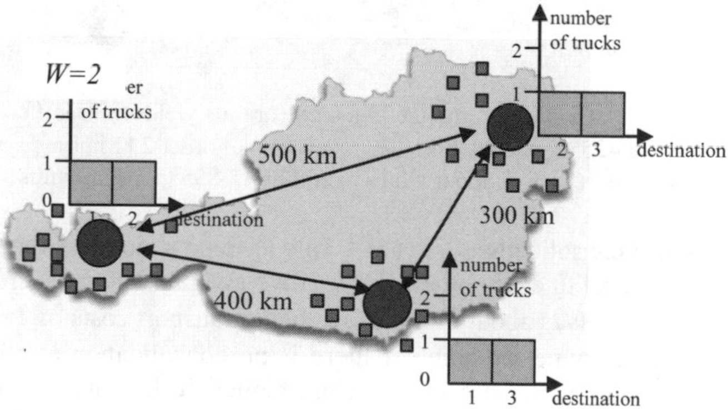

Fig. 5. Changed constraints produce transport costs of 2895 monetary units for a network of order 1 (3 depots), while transport costs without consolidation amount to 24,000 monetary units

If we compare the two alternatives, transport costs for an architecture of a transportation network without consolidation points prove much greater than for the alternative solution with three depots. As long as the operating costs for the depots are less than 24,000 – 2,895 monetary units, a transportation network with consolidation points is the better solution. However, this does not tell us how many and which consolidation points need to be established for an optimal solution.

- Example 3: Network structure of order 2 with one hub

The total number of customers is 35, whereby 5 customers are situated in close proximity in clusters (subregion of the of the total service area) (Fig. 6). Establishing a hub now makes sense because the volume of traffic of each of the 5 customers of a cluster to 5 customers of another cluster is exactly 1000/6. The transport volume from and to a hub thus amounts to 6×1000/6 = 1000, which is exactly one truckload.

If we assume as in Example 2 that the customers area arranged in a circle around a depot (r=20km), then the transport costs for establishing 7 depots and one hub are 2×(400+300+150+150+200+ 200+150) + 7×165 = 4255 monetary units.

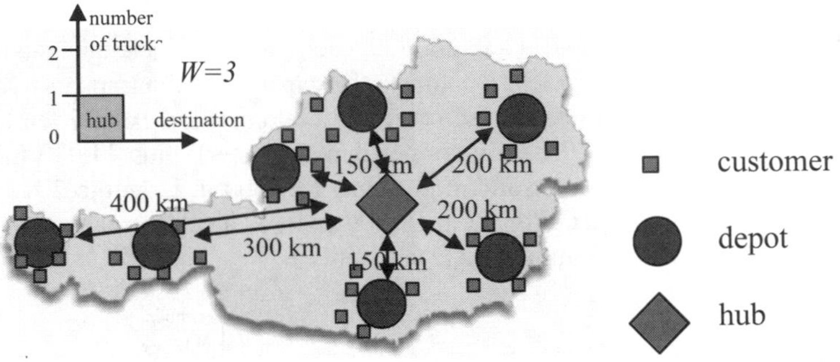

Fig. 6. An additional change in the constraints yields transport costs of 4255 monetary units for a network of order 2 (1 hub). Transport costs without a hub would be 15.855 monetary units

If we establish consolidation of order 1 only (7 depots, no hub), then each depot must be connected to every other depot. If we assume that the average distance between two depots is about 300 km, we have transport costs of 7×7×300km + 7×165 = 15,855 monetary units. If there is no consolidation at all (no depots and no hubs), the transport costs are even higher. In Example 3 the advantage in relation to transport costs of a consolidation point of order 2 is due to the fact that the volume of traffic for the pickup vehicle, similar to Example 2, is very low in relation to the maximum transport capacity and also that the customers, in contrast to Example 2, are more spread out.

To determine the optimal solution in relation to economic efficiency, we need to incorporate the operating costs into our analysis. If the operating costs for a consolidation point of order 2 (hub) are less than 15,855 – 4,255 monetary units, then a pure raster solution cannot be optimal. However, to determine the optimal solution we also need to observe that the number of hubs and depots mutually affect the costs and further combinations with varying numbers of depots and hubs need to be considered to determine the optimal solution.

- Example 4: Network structure of order 2 with 2 hubs

Here we assume a larger number of customers, whereby we now have 6 clusters. Groups of 3 such clusters are relatively close (Fig. 7). Here is a situation for a service area such as the United States, which can be characterized by large cities (depots) on the east and west coasts. Any two cities on the east coast (west coast) are in closer proximity to another than one city on the east coast and one on the west coast.

The volume of traffic between two arbitrary depots is given as 1000/9, so that between a depot and a hub we always have 5×1000/9 = 555 parcel shipments, which requires a truck. Between the two hubs the volume of traffic is 3×3×1000/9 = 1000 parcel shipments, which likewise corresponds to a truck (plane).

If the customers are again situated in a circle around a depot with a radius of 20 km, then the transport costs with two hubs are 2× (400+400+400+400+400+400) + 2×3000 + 6×165 = 11,790 monetary units.

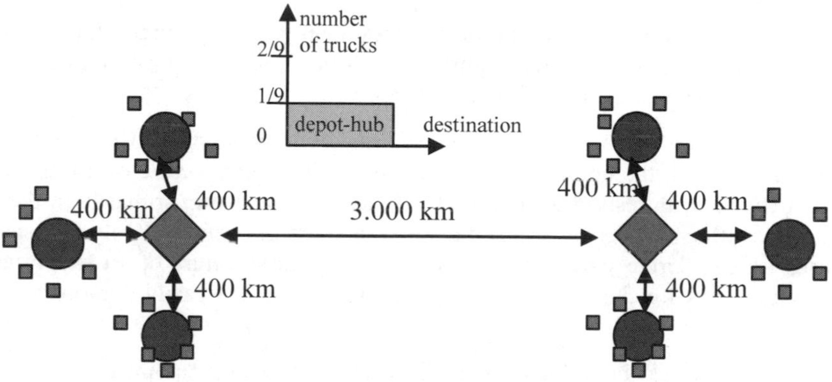

Fig. 7. Network of order 2 with 2 hubs. Transport costs with two hubs (see sketch) are 11,790 monetary units, and for one hub 18,990 GE, and with no hub 24,510 monetary units

If we establish only one (central) hub as in the previous example, then the average distance between depot and hub is over 1500 km. Since a transport vehicle is necessary from each depot to the hub, total costs are 2×6×1500 + 6×165 = 18,990 GE. With no hub, the average distance between two depots is more than 1960 km (=(3×3000+2×400)/5), which yields total transport costs of 2×6×1960 + 6×165 = 24,510 monetary units.

To determine the optimal network architecture in this case, the operating costs for the consolidation points must be considered additionally along with the effects of various combinations of the consolidation points.

These examples show that an optimal architecture of the transportation network with respect to both transport and operating costs is determined by quite a number of factors. Cost factors of an optimal network architecture include:

1. The location and number of the demand points for a given service area (customer structure)
2. The degree of pairing of the volume of traffic to be transferred between the demand points, i.e., to what extent the volume of traffic between two given demand points is balanced
3. The capacity of the transport vehicles (truck, rail, ship, etc.)
4. The number, location and capacity of the depots (consolidation points of order 1)
5. The service area of each depot, i.e., the demand points assigned to a depot
6. The number of routes as well as the route planning in each service area
7. The number, location and capacity of the hubs (consolidation points of order 2 or higher)
8. The types of transports in the transportation network, e.g., direct transports between demand points, direct transports between depots, depot-to-hub and hub-to-depot transports, hub-to-hub transports.

The multiplicity of cost factors generally makes it impossible to derive general statements about the optimal network or the optimal architecture of a transportation network with respect to economic efficiency. This is due primarily to the fact that the influences between cost factors and costs are mutual. Only for special cases we can derive statements about the optimal architecture of a transportation network. Thus for the special case of Example 1 we can easily demonstrate the following:

> As long as the volume of traffic from each demand point to every other demand point in a given service area is completely balanced pair wise and amounts to exactly a whole multiple of a fully loaded transport vehicle, only a network structure of order 0 can be optimal with respect to economic efficiency.

In general, however, we cannot derive valid statements about the optimal network: From the viewpoint of economic efficiency, a network of order 0 can be just as optimal as one of order 1, 2 or higher. However, we can derive statements about tendencies: The more customers who send parcels respectively piece goods in the service area that are small in relationship to the load capacity of the transport vehicles, the more consolidation points (at least of order 1) make sense (Examples 2, 3 and 4). The less the volume of traffic in relation to the maximum transport capacity, the more economical the consolidation points become (Examples 2, 3 and 4). The greater the distances to be covered, the more consolidation points of order 2 and higher are employed (Example 4).

Designing an optimal architecture of the transportation network frequently requires considering all of the above cost factors. In order to solve the decision problem of the optimal network structure, it is generally necessary to incorporate the interdependencies among these factors into our analysis. Especially suitable for this purpose are optimisation models that frequently employ the first three factors above as input data and as their result determine factors 4 to 8, i.e., the optimal consolidation points and thus the architecture of the transportation network. The complexity of these optimisation models and which significant optimisation models exist for planning transportation networks are treated in the following section.

5. Optimisation models for determining the optimal architecture of a transportation network

The economic efficiency depends on the resulting costs of the line haul shipments and pickup and deliveries and thus on their collective optimisation. The following figure shows the fundamental approach for determining the optimal transportation network structure:

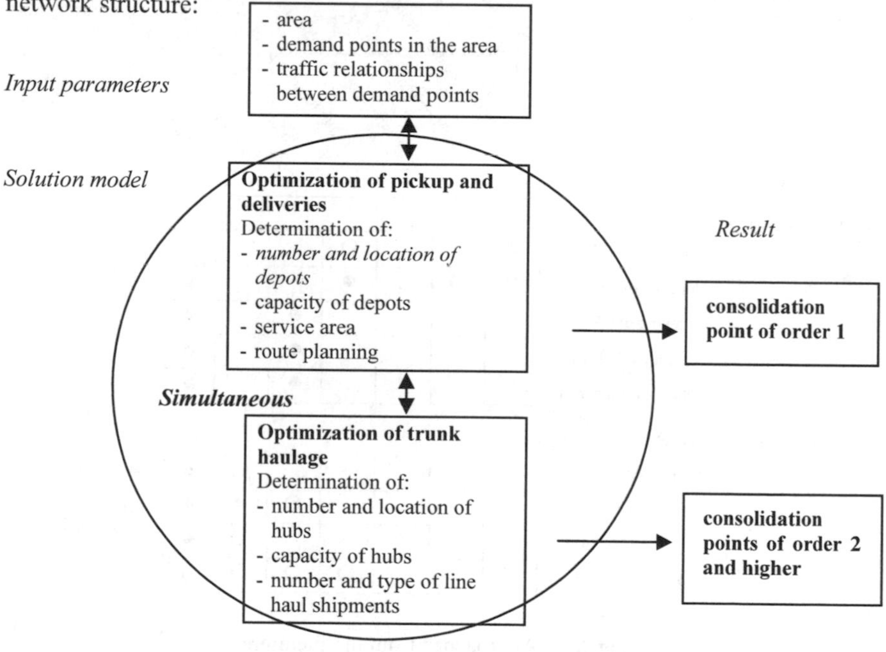

Fig. 8. Fundamental structure of a solution model for network structure design

The input parameters always derive from the service area, the demand points in the respective area, and the volume relationships between the demand points. Based on these parameters, an optimal network structure is to be determined; i.e., pickup and deliveries and line haul shipments are to be optimised. For pickup and deliveries, the number of depots, their locations, and capacity dimensions need to be decided, the service area needs to be determined, and corresponding route planning needs to be conducted. The line haul shipments are determined by the number and locations of the consolidation points of second and higher order as well as their capacities, number and type (direct transports, hub-to-hub transports, etc.). As Fig. 8 shows, there are mutual dependencies between the optimisation of the trunk haulage and pickup and deliveries, so that these need to be considered simultaneously in the realm of optimal network design. The result is then the optimised transportation network.

All the models for strategic network and operative process design discussed in the literature share some similarities with the problem considered in this work, yet direct application proves impossible. The following table groups important approaches from the literature according to the degree of fulfilment of the above requirements.

	warehouse location problem	location problem in R^2	Steiner-Weber problem	p-hub location problem	location routing problem	vehicle routing problem	Wasner's (2001) approach
DEFINITION of ...							
number and location of CP 3.0 and higher							
number of CP 2.0	●			○			●
location of CP 2.O	●	○	○	●			●
numer of CP 1.0					●		●
location of CP 1.O					●		●
depot coverage area					●		●
under CONSIDERATION of ...							
operational organisation						○	●
vehicle routing					○	●	●
infrastructure						○	●
diverse fix costs	○			○	○	○	●

● fulfilled

○ partly fulfilled

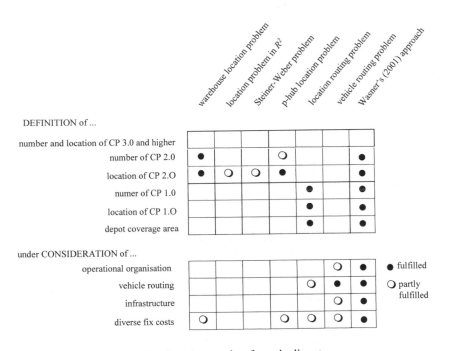

Fig. 9. Approaches from the literature

This shows that the literature[55] has dealt with optimisation of sub-problems, yet there has been no simultaneous consideration of the individual decision problems. This is due to the high complexity of the overall modelling and optimisation, and also due to the fact that involving operative costs in strategic decisions does not suggest itself. However, a comprehensive view requires the consideration of all sub-problems because there are a number of mutual influences: The number and locations of the depots influence the optimal network and so the number of hubs and their locations; on the other hand, the number of depots or depot locations significantly influences pickups and deliveries because the number of customers to be serviced on a route depends significantly on the travel times from and to depots. These travel times depend on the process organisation and the infrastructure. The assignment of customers to depots (determination of depot service areas) depends on the pickup and delivery design and the quantity of transhipments at a depot, which in turn influences line haul transports and thus the optimal number of hubs and their locations.

One of the most comprehensive approaches is presented in (Wasner (2001)). The author develops a model that simultaneously treats line haul shipments and pickup and deliveries and delivers an optimal network structure with consolidation points up to order 2. The mathematical formulation of this model and the solution concept can be found in (Wasner (2001)) and (Wasner/Zäpfel (2002)).

We can conclude that there is still a research gap above all for the optimal design of transportation networks of order $n \geq 3$, which concern primarily the design of transnational transportation networks.

6. Conclusions

The results of our study show that the economic efficiency of logistics service providers depends on the optimal architecture of their transportation networks. Economic efficiency can be measured in terms of a trade-off analysis between customer service (e.g., maximum number of days allowed for delivery to customers from the sourcing locations) and resulting supply chain costs. In pursuing this goal of economic efficiency, we need to determine a trade-off curve, or an efficient boundary. An efficient boundary is characterised by a trade-off curve that is not dominated in the sense „that no achievable strategy exists that is at least as

[55] For an overview of approaches to solving depot location problems, see Wlcek (1998). Location determination in R^2 and the Steiner-Weber approach are presented in Domschke/Drexl (1996). p-hub location problems were first introduced by O`Kelly (1986). An overview of variants and solution approaches to the problem are found in Wlcek (1998) and in Mayer (2001). The location routing problem is explored in Laporte/Norbert/Taillefer (1988) and in Chan/Carter/ Burnes (2001). For route planning refer to Laporte (1992) or Golden/Assad (1988), and Fleischmann et. al. (1998) also treat basic location literature.

good as is it is with respect to customer service and cost, and strictly better on one criteria" (Shapiro 2001, p. 9).

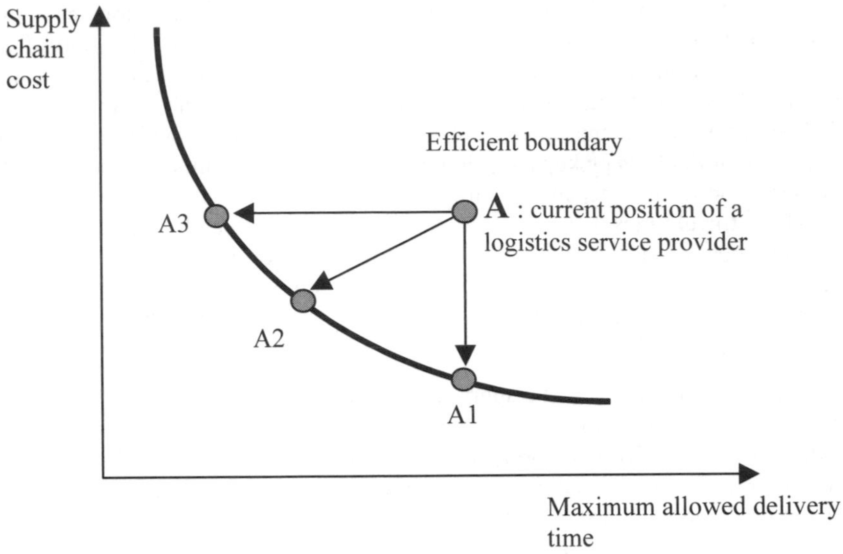

Fig. 10. Efficient boundary of transportation networks

The logistics service provider in Fig. 10 is currently in an inefficient position A. In principle, the service provider can move in the following directions:

Point A1: lower costs while maintaining the same customer service policy

Points on the curve between A1 and A3: improve customer service and reduce cost in relation to point A; e.g., choose point A2

Point A3: improve customer service to a maximum extent without increasing the current cost (in comparison to point A)

The points of the efficient boundary can be generated by iteratively solving an optimisation model for determining the optimal architecture of a transportation network for different maximum allowed delivery times. Section 5 clearly shows that many models in the literature solve this problem, but there is also a research gap regarding transportation networks of 3rd order and higher.

References

Chan, Y., Carter, W. B., Burnes, M. D. (2001): A multiple-depot, multiple-vehicle, location-routing problem with stochastically processed demands. In: Computers & Operations Research, Vol. 28, p. 803-826.

Domschke, W., Drexl, A. (1996): Logistik: Standorte, 4th edition, R. Oldenbourg, München.

Dyckhoff, H. (2000): Grundzüge der Produktionswirtschaft, 3rd edition, Springer, Berlin-Heidelberg.

Fandel, G. (1994): Produktion I: Produktions- und Kostentheorie, 4th edition, Springer, Berlin-Heidelberg.

Fleischmann, B., van Nunen, J. A. E. E, Speranza, M. G., Stähly, P. (Eds.) (1998): Advances in Distribution Logistics, Lecture Notes in Economics and Mathematical Systems, Springer, Berlin.

Golden, B. L., Assad, A. A. (Eds.) (1988): Vehicle Routing: Methods and Studies, North Holland, Amsterdam.

Laporte, G. (1992): The vehicle routing problem: An overview of exact and approximate algorithms. In: European Journal of Operational Research, Vol. 59, pp. 345-358.

Laporte, G., Norbert, Y., Taillefer, P. (1988): Solving a family of multi-depot vehicle routing and location routing problems. In: Transportation Science, Vol. 22/3, pp. 161-172.

Mayer, G. (2001): Strategische Logistikplanung von Hub&Spoke-Systemen, Gabler Edition Wissenschaft: Produktion and Logistik, Deutscher Universitäts-Verlag, Wiesbaden.

O'Kelly, M. E. (1986): The location of interacting hub facilities. In: Transportation Science, Vol. 29, pp. 92-106.

Pfohl, H.Chr. (2000): Logistiksysteme. Betriebswirtschaftliche Grundlagen, 6th edition, Springer, Berlin-Heidelberg.

Schulte, Chr. (1999): Logistik, München.

Shapiro J.F. (2001): Modeling the Supply Chain, Duxbury.

Wasner, M. (2001): Standortmodellierung und -optimierung im flächendeckenden Sammelgutverkehr, Dissertation, Johannes Kepler Universität Linz.

Wasner, M., Zäpfel, G. (2002): Optimal Design of Transportation Networks: Development and practical application of a generalised location model for third party logistics providers, submitted to International Journal of Production Economics.

Wlcek, H. (1998): Gestaltung der Güterverkehrsnetze von Sammelgutspeditionen, Gesellschaft für Verkehrsbetriebswirtschaft and Logistik (GVB) e.V., Nürnberg.

Cash Flow- and Inventory-Oriented Coordination of the Supply Chain

Christian Hofmann, Holger Asseburg

Department of Controlling
University of Hanover
Königsworther Platz 1
D-30167 Hanover, Germany

Abstract: *In this paper we describe a cash flow-oriented and an inventory-oriented approach to model the supply chain and characterize the determination of the inventory holding cost based on the capital tied up in inventory. Our study focuses on a three-tiered supply chain consisting of a component manufacturer, a carrier, and a buyer performing a final assembly operation. We differentiate between a simultaneous and a successive coordination of the supply chain. Based on numerical examples we determine efficiency differences of the coordination concepts. Sensitivity analyzes additionally show the parameters' influence on the efficiency differences.*

Keywords: *integrated vendor-buyer model, coordination of inventory, supply chain modelling*

1. Introduction

The discussion on advanced planning systems for supply chains focuses on the integration of planning problems at different levels and locations, and on the development of procedures that yield acceptable feasible solutions.[1] From a modelling point of view, however, it is not obvious whether to integrate models that are inventory-oriented or whether to use cash flow-oriented models of the supply chain. We address models as *inventory-oriented* if they value the average inventory level with holding costs. While *cash flow-oriented* models also consider the inventory levels within the supply chain, their criterion discounted cash flow reflects the cash payments of the members of the supply chain and, hence, the time value of money. Clearly, the former approach focuses on the material flow within the supply chain, thus considering an important aspect of optimally designed supply chains. However, the latter approach additionally highlights the fundamental economic consequences of the decisions for the supply chain.

Generally, long-term objectives and decisions fundamentally generate the framework for short-term planning.[2] Moreover, short-term planning must also be evaluated based on its impact on long-term objectives: "each decision taken by an efficiently functioning firm must always be evaluated in terms of long-term profitability."[3] While the criterion discounted cash flow considers the time value of money and, hence, reflects long-term objectives, the criterion average costs of inventory-oriented models may result in suboptimal decisions. To compare both modelling approaches, we therefore determine the decisions based on an inventory-oriented model of the supply chain and evaluate their economic consequences by calculating the resulting discounted cash flow.[4]

We illustrate the general question of the optimality of inventory-oriented models by considering the lot size decisions in a three-tiered supply chain consisting of a component manufacturer (vendor), a transport company (carrier), and a buyer performing final assembly operations. Our model reproduces the processing of a single product in serial production processes. Hence, two production lot size decisions and one transportation lot size decision must be made.

Cash flow-based stationary lot size models have been studied by Grubbström (1980) and Küpper (1991) for single-stage production processes, and Grubbström/Thorstenson (1986) and Hofmann (1995, 2000) for multi-stage production proc-

[1] See, e.g., *Stadtler/Kilger* (2002).

[2] See, e.g., *Küpper* (1985).

[3] *Grubbström* (1980).

[4] See also *Demski/Feltham* (1976), p. 55.

esses. However, inventory-oriented multi-stage lot size models seem to be more prevalent in the literature. In a series of papers, Goyal and Szendrovits analyze lot size models with multi-level production and transport processes.[5] Furthermore, Fandel/François/May (1988) and Stadtler (1992) consider the relation between transport and production processes based on inventory-oriented models. More recently, Hill (1997) and Viswanathan (1998) analyze different strategies for integrated vendor-buyer inventory models.[6]

While it is well established that inventory-oriented models yield a satisfying approximation of cash flow-oriented models for single-stage production processes[7], their approximation quality is less clear for multi-stage production processes that are prevalent in supply chains. Here, due to time-consuming production and transportation processes the time value of money is supposed to be especially important for determining optimal lot sizes.

The article proceeds as follows: In section 2 we describe the supply chain under study. Next, we develop a cash flow-oriented model in section 3 and the corresponding inventory-oriented model in section 4, and determine the optimal lot size decisions under both successive and simultaneous planning. Additionally, we numerically compare the efficiency differences of the two planning approaches. Section 5 integrates both analyzes by comparing the efficiency differences of both modelling approaches. Finally, section 6 summarizes our findings.

2. Characterization of the supply chain

The three-tiered supply chain consists of a vendor, a carrier, and a buyer. The vendor v obtains material from preliminary resource markets, processes it, and stores the intermediate product in a warehouse (component store). Subsequently the carrier t transports the component to the buyer b, where it is stored in a stock receipt store, until its usage in the buyer's final assembly operation. Ultimately, the demand is satisfied from the buyer's warehouse (finished product store).

We assume finite production rates p_b, p_v for the vendor and the buyer. The transportation process is assumed to be discontinuous and instantaneous. To prevent stock-outs, the constant demand rate d is less than both production rates:

[5] See Szendrovits (1976, 1978a, 1978b), Goyal (1977a, 1977b, 1978a, 1978b, 1988), Goyal/Szendrovits (1986), and Drezner/Szendrovits/Wesolowsky (1984). See also Banerjee (1986).

[6] Goyal/Gupta (1989), Bhatnangar/Chandra/Goyal (1993), and Thomas/Griffin (1996) provide overviews of the literature on integrated vendor-buyer models.

[7] See, e.g., Hadley (1964). See also Helber (1994) w.r.t. the efficiency of inventory-oriented models in a dynamic setting.

$d < \min(p_v, p_b)$. Vendor, carrier, and buyer must determine their lot sizes (q_v, q_t, q_b). All lot size decisions are supposed to lead to cyclic processes. The lot size ratios for the carrier $(n_t \equiv q_b/q_t)$ and the vendor $(n_v \equiv q_v/q_t)$ follow from the lot sizes of two adjacent processes. To simplify the complexity of the multi-stage production process, we restrict the solution space to integer lot size ratios: $n_i \in N$, $i \in \{v,t\}$. As a consequence, one production lot of the buyer is divided into one or several transport lots and one production lot of the vendor combines one or several transport lots. Szendrovits (1983) shows that for two-stage production processes optimal integer lot size ratios exist.[8]

Subsequently, we distinguish between a simultaneous and a successive planning approach. The former determines optimal lot sizes based on the total value of the criterion used, i.e., total discounted cash flow or total average costs. The latter, however, sequentially determines the production lot size q_b, the transportation lot size q_t, and the production lot size q_v based on the respective local criteria, e.g. the discounted cash flow of the buyer. Hence, interdependencies of the decisions are not considered, resulting in suboptimal decisions.

3. Cash flow-oriented model of the supply chain

3.1. Analytical derivation of optimal lot sizes

The decision-relevant payments of the buyer consist of the payoffs F_b for each setup, cp_b^{ME} for each processed unit, and of the sales returns e_b^{ME} for each unit (see figure 1). Due to the constant production rate p_b and demand rate d it is possible to express both quantities in terms per time unit cp_b and ce_b, i.e., $cp_b = cp_b^{ME} \cdot p_b$ and $ce_b = e_b^{ME} \cdot d$. We assume that any internal transfer payments between the supply chain members are subject to long-term contracts, and, hence, do not depend on the lot size decisions. Therefore, we can eliminate them from the analysis.

[8] Alternatively, Kumar/Vrat (1978) reduce complexity by assuming a unique lot size on all stages, while Crowston/Wagner/Williams (1973) assume an infinite production rate.

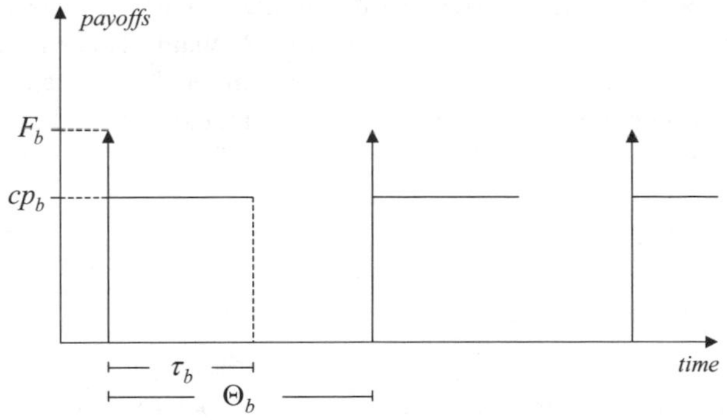

Fig. 1. Temporal distribution of the buyer's payoffs

The buyer's production time τ_b for one lot follows from the quotient of the lot size and the production rate: $\tau_b = q_b / p_b$, while the production cycle period reflects the demand rate: $\Theta_b = q_b / d$. To determine the net present value we assume a complete capital market. The net present value for a single production cycle, related to its beginning, follows from the difference between the sales returns discounted by the continuous interest rate i, the quantity-independent payoffs per setup F_b, and the discounted payoffs for the lot processing (eq. 1). For the sales returns the limit of integration is the cycle period Θ_b, while for the processing payoffs the cycle period τ_b is employed.

$$\begin{aligned} C_b^{\Theta_b} &= \int_0^{\Theta_b} ce_b \cdot e^{-i \cdot t} dt - F_b - \int_0^{\tau_b} cp_b \cdot e^{-i \cdot t} dt \\ &= \frac{ce_b}{i} \cdot \left(1 - e^{-i \cdot \Theta_b}\right) - F_b - \frac{cp_b}{i} \cdot \left(1 - e^{-i \cdot q_b / p_b}\right) \end{aligned} \tag{1}$$

Using stationary lot size models with an infinite planning horizon, the production cycle repeats infinitely. Equivalent to determining the net present value of infinite identical investment chains, the function of the net present value of one cycle can be transferred into the respective function C_b of the infinite chain[9]:

$$C_b = \frac{1}{1 - e^{-i \cdot \Theta_b}} \cdot \left\{ \frac{ce_b}{i} \cdot \left(1 - e^{-i \cdot \Theta_b}\right) - F_b - \frac{cp_b}{i} \cdot \left(1 - e^{-i \cdot q_b / p_b}\right) \right\}. \tag{2}$$

---

[9] The transformation is based on the fact that the net present value of the infinite chain is identical at the beginning of each cycle. Thus, it is the sum of the net present value of one cycle and the net present value of the infinite chain discounted for the length of the cycle period. See, e.g., Grubbström (1967).

Equation (3) shows the net present value of the payoffs for the carrier with a transportation cycle of $\Theta_t = q_t/d$ for an infinite chain. The lot size dependent cash flows consist of the fixed transportation payment F_t per transport operation and some handling payments ch_t per unit. We suppose that both payments occur at the transport date.

$$C_t = \frac{1}{1-e^{-i\cdot\Theta_t}} \cdot \{-F_t - ch_t \cdot q_t\} \tag{3}$$

Due to the cyclic lot-splitting transport process, i.e. $q_t \leq q_b$, multiple deliveries might be necessary before starting the buyer's production process. Figure 2 depicts the cumulated inventory levels in the buyer's stock receipt store.

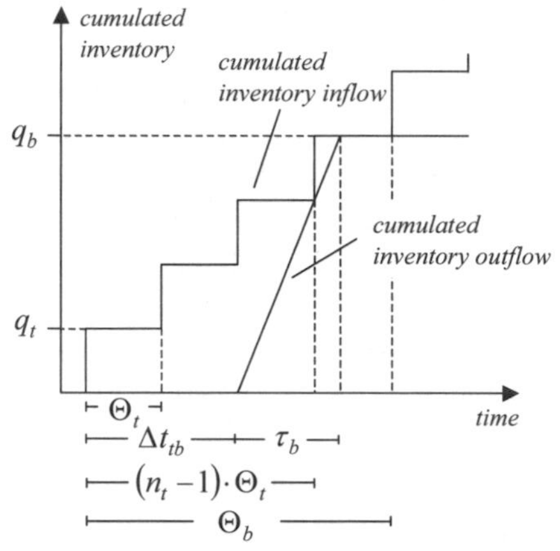

Fig. 2. Cumulated inventory levels in the buyer's stock receipt store for a cyclic lot-splitting transport process

The time-displacement Δt_{tb} between the first transport and the start of the buyer's production process follows from the cumulated inventory inflow and outflow at the time of the final transport operation. Previous to the delivery of the final transport lot, the $(n_t - 1)$ lots already delivered are just used in the buyer's production process:

$$(n_t - 1)\cdot q_t = [(n_t - 1)\cdot\Theta_t - \Delta t_{tb}]\cdot p_b$$

$$\Delta t_{tb} = \Theta_b \cdot \left(1 - \frac{1}{n_t}\right)\cdot\left(1 - \frac{d}{p_b}\right). \tag{4}$$

Finally, the vendor's net present value per cycle follows from the payoffs F_v for each setup, the input of materials cm_v, and the discounted payoffs arising during the processing time $\tau_v = q_v/p_v$:

$$C_v^{\Theta_v} = -F_v - cm_v \cdot q_v - \int_0^{\tau_v} cp_v \cdot e^{-i \cdot t} dt \ . \tag{5}$$

Transferring (5) into the infinite chain gives with $\Theta_v = q_v / d$:

$$C_v = \frac{1}{1 - e^{-i \cdot \Theta_v}} \cdot \left\{ -F_v - cm_v \cdot q_v - \frac{cp_v}{i} \cdot \left(1 - e^{-i \cdot q_v / p_v}\right) \right\} . \tag{6}$$

Because of the vendor's finite production rate, the production process starts $\Delta t_{vt} = q_t / p_v$ time units ahead of the first transportation process, i.e., the first transport lot is just produced at the transport date.

The models of the single-stage processes can be combined to a multi-stage model by considering the lot size ratios n_t and n_v. Hence, we obtain

$$\begin{aligned} C_v &= \frac{1}{1 - e^{-i \cdot n_v \cdot q_b / (d \cdot n_t)}} \cdot \left\{ -F_v - cm_v \cdot n_v \cdot \frac{q_b}{n_t} - \frac{cp_v}{i} \cdot \left(1 - e^{-i \cdot n_v \cdot q_b / (p_v \cdot n_t)}\right) \right\} \\ C_t &= \frac{1}{1 - e^{-i \cdot q_t / (d \cdot n_t)}} \cdot \left\{ -F_t - ch_t \cdot \frac{q_b}{n_t} \right\} \\ C_b &= \frac{1}{1 - e^{-i \cdot q_b / d}} \cdot \left\{ \frac{ce_b}{i} \cdot \left(1 - e^{-i \cdot q_b / d}\right) - F_b - \frac{cp_b}{i} \cdot \left(1 - e^{-i \cdot q_b / p_b}\right) \right\} . \end{aligned} \tag{7}$$

We determine the optima of the choice variables by means of differential calculus. For the *successive planning approach* (SU), the lot size q_b as well as the lot size ratios n_v and n_t can be found by sequential optimization. The first order condition of the optimal lot size of the buyer is given by

$$\begin{aligned} \frac{dC_b}{dq_b} &= \frac{e^{-i \cdot q_b / d}}{\left(1 - e^{-i \cdot q_b / d}\right)^2} \cdot \\ & \left\{ \frac{i}{d} \cdot F_b - \left[-\frac{1}{d} + \left(\frac{1}{d} - \frac{1}{p_b} \right) \cdot e^{-i \cdot q_b / p_b} + \frac{1}{p_b} \cdot e^{i \cdot q_b \cdot (1/d - 1/p_b)} \right] \cdot cp_b \right\} = 0 . \end{aligned} \tag{8}$$

Because of the exponential functions within the braces, equation (8) cannot be solved analytically for the optimal lot size $q_b^{CF,SU}$. For this kind of necessary conditions we can only provide approximate and numerical solutions. An approximation of the exponential functions can be realized by the Taylor expansion.[10] Approximating the exponential functions with three terms of the Taylor expansion in equation (8) and simplifying gives:

---

[10] See, e.g., Trippi/Lewin (1974).

$$F_b - \frac{1}{2} \cdot \frac{cp_b}{p_b} \cdot i \cdot q_b^2 \cdot \left(\frac{1}{d} - \frac{1}{p_b} \right) = 0 \ . \tag{9}$$

Now, it is straightforward to solve equation (9) for the optimal lot size $q_b^{CF,SU}$ of the cash flow-oriented model (CF). Equivalently, we determine the successive lot size ratios $n_t^{CF,SU}$ and $n_v^{CF,SU}$. Finally, the transport lot size $q_t^{CF,SU}$ and the lot size of the vendor $q_v^{CF,SU}$ result from inserting the lot size ratios into the equations (figure 3).

$$q_b^{CF,SU} = \sqrt{\frac{2 \cdot F_b \cdot d}{i \cdot \frac{cp_b}{p_b} \cdot \left(1 - \frac{d}{p_b}\right)}} \qquad q_t^{CF,SU} = \sqrt{\frac{2 \cdot F_t \cdot d}{i \cdot ch_t}}$$

$$q_v^{CF,SU} = \sqrt{\frac{2 \cdot F_v \cdot d}{i \cdot \left(cm_v + \frac{cp_v}{p_v} \cdot \left(1 - \frac{d}{p_v}\right)\right)}}$$

Fig. 3. Analytical approximation of the successive optima of the cash flow-oriented model of the supply chain.

The *simultaneous planning* (SI) of the choice variables is based on the total discounted cash flow of the complete supply chain. Hence, the simultaneous optimization considers the existing interdependencies between the vendor, the carrier, and the buyer. Therefore, the net present value functions of the three organizational units (eqs. (7)) have to be added (eq. (10)). Here, any time-displacements of the production and transport processes must be considered. Hence, we discount C_t and C_b for the time Δt_{vt}, reflecting the vendor's necessary production time to produce the first transport lot. In addition we discount C_b by Δt_{tb}, i.e., the time-displacement between the start of the transportation processes and the start of the buyer's production. Due to the discounting, the criterion C_G reflects an additional trade-off between q_b and n_t. The successive planning approach does not consider this additional trade-off.

$$C_G(q_b, n_t, n_v) = C_v + C_t \cdot e^{-i \cdot q_b/(p_v \cdot n_t)} + C_b \cdot e^{-i \cdot \left(q_b/(p_v \cdot n_t) + q_b/d \cdot (1-1/n_t) \cdot (1-d/p_b)\right)} \tag{10}$$

The necessary conditions for the existence of optima related to the three choice variables are obtained by partial differential calculus. Since even the approximation with the Taylor expansion approach results in complicated mathematical expressions, we restrict our study to a numerical analysis.

3.2. Numerical comparison: successive versus simultaneous coordination of the cash flow-oriented model

Consider a three-tiered supply chain with a demand rate $d = 250$, a buyer's production rate $p_b = 400$, a vendor's production rate $p_v = 400$, sales revenues $ce_b = 2000$, a setup payoff of the buyer $F_b = 120$, production payments per time unit $cp_b = 600$, a fixed payoff of a transport process $F_t = 10$, transport payments per quantity unit $ch_t = 1$, a setup payoff of the vendor $F_v = 100$, production payments per time unit of the vendor $cp_v = 400$, and material input payments of the vendor $cm_v = 1$. The interest rate is $i = 0{,}1$.

Figure 4 illustrates the differences ΔC_G^{CF} of the total discounted cash flow between the simultaneous and the successive planning approach for varying demand rates d.

$$\Delta C_G^{CF} \equiv C_G\left(q_b^{CF,SI}, n_t^{CF,SI}, n_v^{CF,SI}\right) - C_G\left(q_b^{CF,SU}, n_t^{CF,SU}, n_v^{CF,SU}\right) \tag{11}$$

As the figure shows, the differences decrease for an increasing demand rate. This general result holds true when we compare the relaxed solutions (continuous dotted line) and when we include the integer constraints of the lot ratios (discontinuous line). The discontinuities occur when the lot ratio $n_t^{CF,SU}$ increases by one. Furthermore, the individual discounted cash flows decrease for both the simultaneous and the successive planning approach. While q_b increases for an increasing demand rate for all planning approaches, q_t and q_v increase with d only for a given lot ratio.

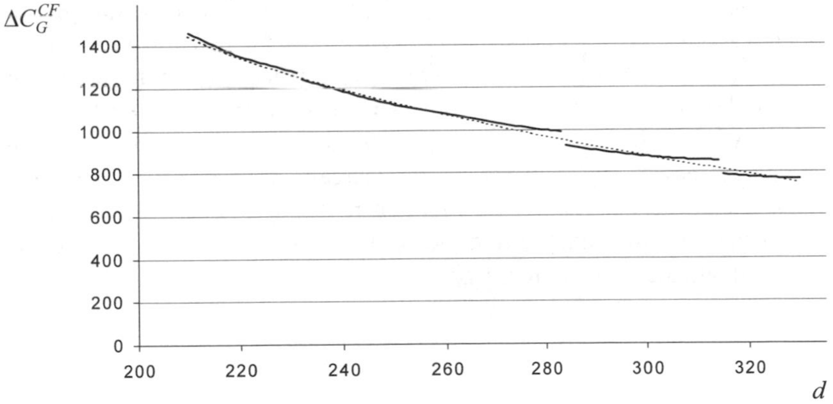

Fig. 4. Differences in total discounted cash flows between the simultaneous and the successive coordination of the cash flow-oriented model for varying demand rates

The differences depicted in figure 4 follow from the different production lot sizes q_b of the two approaches. Basically, $q_b^{CF,SI} < q_b^{CF,SU}$ for all demand rates, and the larger production lot size of the successive planning approach leads to $C_b^{CF,SU} > C_b^{CF,SI}$. However, when *aggregating* the individual discounted cash flows, a larger production lot size leads to an increased time-displacement Δt_{tb}, i.e., a longer discounting period for C_b.[11] While the simultaneous approach considers this aspect of aggregation when choosing q_b, the successive approach chooses q_b such that C_b is maximized. Hence, the first approach results in a smaller production lot size which leads to a lower discounted cash flow of the buyer but a higher total net present value. The key to the decreasing differences ΔC_G^{CF} is the variation of the time-displacement. In general, Δt_{tb} approaches zero when the demand rate equals the available capacity. As a consequence, we observe decreasing differences $\Delta t_{tb}^{CF,SU} - \Delta t_{tb}^{CF,SI}$ for increasing demand rates, thus mitigating the discounting effect neglected in the successive planning approach.

Consequently, the advantages of the simultaneous planning approach decrease for an increasing demand rate. This implies that under conditions of a *high capacity utilization* the simultaneous planning approach yields relatively smaller absolute benefits to the total supply chain as under conditions of a rather low capacity utilization.

Figure 5 shows the differences ΔC_G^{CF} for varying fixed setup payments F_b. Generally, we observe larger differences for higher setup payments. Again, the differences follow from the impact of F_b on q_b. The successive planning approach does not consider the relevance of q_b via Δt_{tb} for the total discounted cash flow, and, hence, $q_b^{CF,SU}$ increases monotonically for increasing F_b. While we also observe an increasing $q_b^{CF,SI}$ for increasing F_b, the rise is dampened due to an appropriate variation of $q_t^{CF,SI}$. As a consequence, $q_b^{CF,SU}$ increases to a larger extent than $q_b^{CF,SI}$, the neglected *discounting effect* becomes more severe, and, hence, the discounted cash flow differences increase. Here, the discontinuous decrease of ΔC_G^{CF} follows from the integer constraints for the lot size ratios, which result in a decrease of $q_t^{CF,SU}$ when $n_t^{CF,SU}$ increases by one. For a smaller transportation lot, the delay q_t/p_v of the first transport process decreases thus mitigating the neglected discounting effect. However, figure 5 illustrates that the variation of q_b dominates the difference ΔC_G^{CF}.

[11] See equation (10). Hence, we observe $\Delta t_{tb}^{CF,SI} < \Delta t_{tb}^{CF,SU}$.

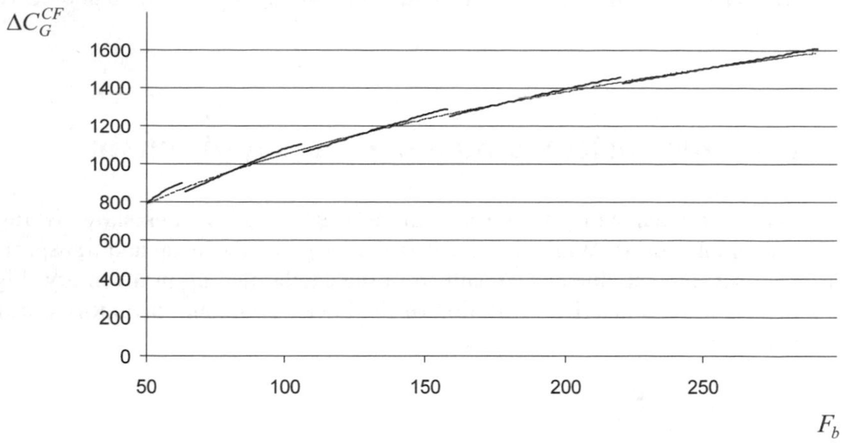

Fig. 5. Differences in total discounted cash flows between the simultaneous and the successive coordination of the cash flow-oriented model for varying fixed setup payments

Figure 5 suggests that a simultaneous planning approach becomes more beneficial to the total supply chain for high fixed setup payments F_b, while for low fixed setup payoffs a successive planning approach results in a relatively small loss to the total supply chain. Hence, under the conditions of *JIT-production*[12] with flexible manufacturing systems, i.e., relatively low setup payments, a successive planning approach can be used, while for costly setup processes a simultaneous planning approach seems to be appropriate.

Although not reported here, we observe that ΔC_G^{CF} decreases with the fixed transportation payments F_t. The key to this result is the fact that the transport lot increases with F_t, hence decreasing Δt_{tb}. In the limit, the transport lot equals the production lot size and no time-displacement is necessary.[13] This result suggests that the simultaneous planning approach is especially relevant for relatively low fixed transportation payments. Further numerical variations show that the setup payments of the vendor have a negligible impact on ΔC_G^{CF}. This result follows from the low sensitivity of q_b and q_t for varying values of F_v. Hence, F_v has nearly no impact on the discounting effect. Interestingly, this result suggests that investments in flexible production systems on behalf of the vendor are hardly of

[12] See, e.g., Fandel/François (1989).

[13] Furthermore, $\partial q_b^{CF,SU} / \partial F_t = 0$, i.e., in the successive approach increasing fixed transport payments have no impact on the buyer's optimal production lot size.

relevance for the benefits of a simultaneous planning approach over a successive planning approach.

4. Inventory-oriented model of the supply chain

In inventory-oriented stationary lot size models the cost functions show average fixed and variable costs. While the fixed costs depend on the setup and transportation processes, the variable costs result from the capital tied up in inventory. Figure 6 depicts the characteristic variation of the buyer's outgoing inventory during two production cycles.

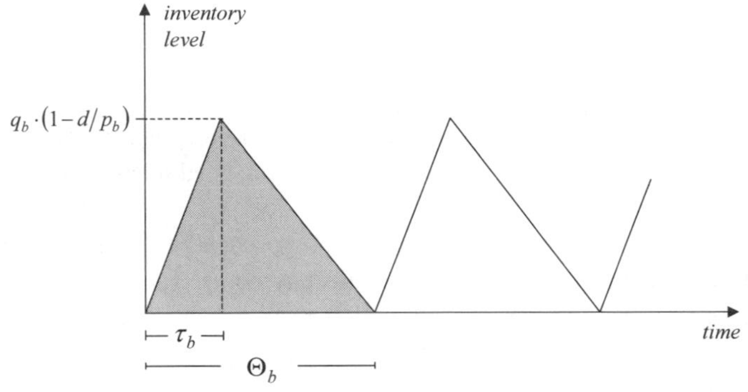

Fig. 6. Inventory variation in the buyer's finished product store

The maximum amount of the inventory level stock in the buyer's finished product store is determined by the lot size q_b, diminished by the goods sold during the processing time. Equation (12) shows the cost function of the buyer, where T is the planning period. The cost function follows from multiplying the setup cost U_b per lot with the number of setups per planning period, and from multiplying the average inventory level with a holding cost coefficient for the outgoing stock l_{os} per unit and time unit.

$$K_b = \frac{T}{\Theta_b} \cdot \left\{ U_b + \frac{1}{2} \cdot l_{os} \cdot q_b \cdot \left(1 - \frac{d}{p_b}\right) \cdot \Theta_b \right\} \tag{12}$$

The carrier's cost function follows from the fixed transport cost U_t per transport operation, the number $n_t \cdot T/\Theta_b$ of transport operations during the planning period T, the holding cost coefficient of the stock receipt store l_{rs} per unit and time unit, and the average inventory level. Due to the lot-splitting transport process it can be necessary to build-up inventory by one or several transport processes before the production process starts (see fig. 2). Based on the time-displacement Δt_{tb}, the average inventory q_b^{rs} in the stock receipt store of the buyer is

$$\begin{aligned} q_b^{rs} &= \left\{ q_t \cdot \Theta_t \cdot \sum_{i=1}^{n_t} i - \frac{1}{2} \cdot \frac{q_b^2}{p_b} - \left(\Theta_b - \frac{q_b}{p_b} - \Delta t_{tb} \right) \cdot q_b \right\} / \Theta_b \\ &= \frac{1}{2} \cdot q_b^2 \cdot \left[-\frac{1}{n_t} \cdot \left(\frac{1}{d} - \frac{2}{p_b} \right) + \left(\frac{1}{d} - \frac{1}{p_b} \right) \right] / \Theta_b \; . \end{aligned} \tag{13}$$

The first term in braces indicates the cumulated inventory inflow, while the second term represents the cumulated inventory outflow for the processing period. The last term shows the cumulated inventory outflow for the time between the end of the production process and the next transport. The average inventory level follows when we divide the integrals by the duration Θ_b of the buyer's production cycle. Finally, the carrier's cost function K_t follows from the sum of the fixed transport cost and the inventory holding cost:[14]

$$K_t = \frac{T}{\Theta_b} \cdot \left\{ U_t \cdot n_t + \frac{1}{2} \cdot l_{rs} \cdot q_b^2 \cdot \left[-\frac{1}{n_t} \cdot \left(\frac{1}{d} - \frac{2}{p_b} \right) + \left(\frac{1}{d} - \frac{1}{p_b} \right) \right] \right\} . \tag{14}$$

The decision relevant costs of the vendor depend on the fixed setup cost U_v per lot, the number of lots, the holding cost coefficient l_v per unit and time unit, and the average inventory level. While the inventory build up takes place with a finite production rate, the inventory depletion is instantaneous at certain points in time. Hence, the inventory level of the vendor's component store depends on the carrier's transportation lot size. Equation (15) shows the average inventory level q_v^{os} in the component store of the vendor during a production cycle.[15] The first two terms in braces are the cumulated inventory inflow, the third is cumulated inventory depletion. Finally, the last term shows the delay of the first stock depletion process for the time period q_t / p_v which is necessary for manufacturing the first transport lot. We obtain q_v^{os} by dividing these integrals by the time length $\Theta_v \equiv q_v / d$ of one production cycle.

---

[14] In general, a ratio $p_b < 2 \cdot d$ is necessary for the existence of an optimal transportation lot size. Otherwise, only positive marginal costs exist for varying the lot size ratios n_t.

[15] See Fandel/François/May (1988), p. 81.

$$q_v^{os} = \left\{ \frac{1}{2} \cdot \frac{q_v^2}{p_v} + q_v \cdot \left(\Theta_v - \frac{q_v}{p_v} \right) - q_t \cdot \Theta_t \cdot \sum_{i=0}^{n_v - 1} i - q_v \cdot \left(\Theta_t - \frac{q_t}{p_v} \right) \right\} / \Theta_v$$
$$= \frac{1}{2} \cdot n_v \cdot q_t \cdot \left[(n_v - 1) \cdot \Theta_t - (n_v - 2) \cdot \frac{q_t}{p_v} \right] / \Theta_v \quad (15)$$

With T/Θ_v representing the number of setup processes in the planning period, we obtain the vendor's cost function as

$$K_v = \frac{T}{\Theta_v} \cdot \left\{ U_v + \frac{1}{2} \cdot l_v \cdot n_v \cdot q_t \cdot \left[(n_v - 1) \cdot \Theta_t - (n_v - 2) \cdot \frac{q_t}{p_v} \right] \right\} . \quad (16)$$

The optima of the *simultaneous planning* approach can be found by minimizing the sum of the three cost functions (12), (14), and (16). In case of *successive coordination*, we first determine the optimal lot size of the buyer $q_b^{I,SU}$ of the inventory-oriented model (I). Subsequently the optimal lot size ratios ($n_v^{I,SU}$, $n_t^{I,SU}$) are derived, considering ($n_t^{I,SU}$, $q_b^{I,SU}$) as constant. Based on the lot size ratios, figure 7 shows the optimal lot sizes of the inventory-oriented model.

$q_v^{I,SI} = \sqrt{\dfrac{2 \cdot U_v \cdot d}{l_v \cdot \left(1 - \dfrac{d}{p_v}\right)}}$	$q_v^{I,SU} = \sqrt{\dfrac{2 \cdot U_v \cdot d}{l_v \cdot \left(1 - \dfrac{d}{p_v}\right)}}$
$q_t^{I,SI} = \sqrt{\dfrac{2 \cdot U_t \cdot d}{l_{rs} \cdot \left(2 \cdot \dfrac{d}{p_b} - 1\right) - l_v \cdot \left(1 - 2 \cdot \dfrac{d}{p_v}\right)}}$	$q_t^{I,SU} = \sqrt{\dfrac{2 \cdot U_t \cdot d}{l_{rs} \cdot \left(2 \cdot \dfrac{d}{p_b} - 1\right)}}$
$q_b^{I,SI} = \sqrt{\dfrac{2 \cdot U_b \cdot d}{(l_{os} + l_{rs}) \cdot \left(1 - \dfrac{d}{p_b}\right)}}$	$q_b^{I,SU} = \sqrt{\dfrac{2 \cdot U_b \cdot d}{l_{os} \cdot \left(1 - \dfrac{d}{p_b}\right)}}$

Fig. 7. Simultaneous and successive lot size optima of the inventory-oriented model of the supply chain

An analytical comparison of the aggregated cost functions $K = K_b + K_t + K_v$ shows that the simultaneous planning approach yields lower total costs than the successive planning approach. However, the cost differences ΔK only approximate the real economic differences of the two approaches. To identify the 'real' consequences, we have to determine the discounted cash flows of the total supply chain based on the decisions that follow from the inventory-oriented model.

Moreover, we have to establish the relations between the cost parameters (U_b, U_t, U_v, l_{os}, l_{rs}, and l_v) and the cash flows (F_b, F_t, F_v, cm_v, cp_v, ch_T, and cp_b) used in both approaches. Based on these relations, we can identify the economic differences of the inventory-oriented models and their approximation quality regarding the cash flow-oriented models.

5. Numerical comparison of the cash flow- and the inventory-oriented approach

5.1. The relation between cost parameters and cash flows

In general, we can equate cash payments and costs for the setup and transportation processes: $F_i = U_i$, $i \in \{v,t,b\}$. To determine the holding cost coefficients we have to compare the average inventory levels and the average tied up capital. Thereby we neglect any inventory costs that are independent of the inventory level. As an example, figure 8 shows the finished product inventory level, the cash flows depending on the processing of a lot, and the tied up capital as the difference between cash outflows and cash inflows.

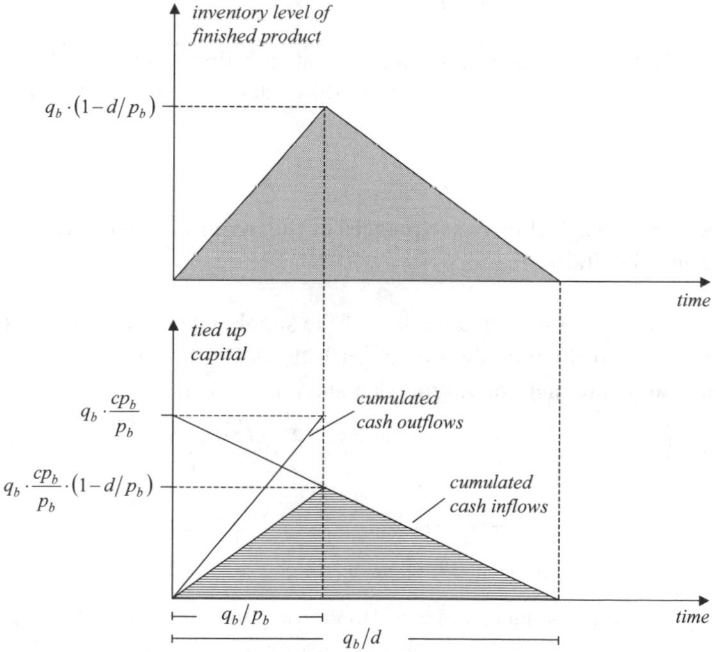

Fig. 8. Inventory level and tied up capital for the buyer's outgoing stock

Equivalent to equation (12), the inventory holding costs are

$$K_b^h = \frac{1}{2} \cdot l_{os} \cdot \frac{q_b^2}{d} \cdot \left(1 - \frac{d}{p_b}\right). \tag{17}$$

The overall cash outflow $q_b \cdot cp_b / p_b$ occurs continuously over the processing time q_b / p_b. On the other hand, the cash inflow from sales occurs continuously over the whole production cycle, resulting in a tied up capital of zero at the end of the cycle. Hence, at the end of the buyer's lot processing period the maximal tied up capital is $q_b \cdot cp_b / p_b \cdot (1 - d/p_b)$. Multiplying the integral over the tied up capital with the interest rate i gives the interest costs for the buyer's outgoing stock:

$$K_b^i = \frac{1}{2} \cdot i \cdot \frac{cp_b}{p_b} \cdot \frac{q_b^2}{d} \cdot \left(1 - \frac{d}{p_b}\right). \tag{18}$$

Comparing (17) and (18) yields the holding coefficient $l_{os} = i \cdot cp_b / p_b$. Thus, l_{os} is equal to the interest on the payments per processed production unit. An analogous derivation leads to the carrier's and the vendor's holding coefficients:[16]

$$l_{rs} = i \cdot ch_t \quad \text{and} \quad l_v = i \cdot \left(\frac{cm_v}{1 - d/p_v} + \frac{cp_v}{p_v} \right). \tag{19}$$

Based on the relation of the cost parameters and cash flows, we are able to analyze efficiency differences between the cash flow- and the inventory-oriented approaches.

5.2. Discounted cash flow consequences of the inventory-oriented model of the supply chain

Based on the inventory-oriented models of the supply chain, we first consider the differences ΔC_G^I of the total discounted cash flows for the simultaneous and successive planning approach for varying demand rates [17], with

$$\Delta C_G^I \equiv C_G\left(q_b^{I,SI}, n_t^{I,SI}, n_v^{I,SI}\right) - C_G\left(q_b^{I,SU}, n_t^{I,SU}, n_v^{I,SU}\right). \tag{20}$$

[16] For the derivation see Hofmann (1995), pp. 98-105.

[17] The analysis is based on numerical calculations using the parameter values documented at the beginning of section 3.2. In addition, we set $U_b = F_b = 120$, $U_t = F_t = 10$, and $U_v = F_v = 100$, and determine the holding cost coefficients according to the results of the previous section.

As for the cash flow-oriented approach, ΔC_G^I decreases for an increasing demand rate. Moreover, the magnitude of the differences is slightly smaller especially for low demand rates. Unlike the cash flow-oriented approach, however, the decreasing differences in case of the inventory-oriented approach follow from the tendency of the transportation lot size to decrease with the demand rate. The analysis of the closed form solutions confirms that observation, i.e., we obtain $\partial q_t^{I,SU} / \partial d < 0$ and $\partial q_t^{I,SI} / \partial d < 0$ within the relevant range of parameter values.[18] Moreover, $q_b^{I,SI}$ increases at a faster rate than $q_b^{I,SU}$, resulting in smaller differences of the production lot sizes q_b for higher demand rates.[19]

As a consequence of the decreasing transport lot, the impact of the discounting effect over Δt_{vt} time periods is mitigated, and, hence, the differences of the total discounted cash flows decrease. In addition and equivalent to the cash flow-oriented model, Δt_{tb} diminishes when demand rate approaches the systems capacity. Hence, the cash flow-oriented model and the inventory-oriented model yield identical general results regarding the benefits of a simultaneous planning approach.

Equivalent to the cash flow-oriented model, figure 9 illustrates that ΔC_G^I increases for increasing fixed setup costs U_b. Again, $q_b^{I,SU}$ increases substantially more than $q_b^{I,SI}$, thus intensifying the discounting effect for high setup costs.[20] Moreover, the results for varying vendor's setup costs and carrier's transport costs are similar to the results when considering the cash flow-oriented model of the supply chain.

Therefore, the two modelling approaches yield comparable results regarding the advantages of a *simultaneous planning*. This planning approach seems to be beneficial especially for rather low demand rates, and high fixed setup costs in the buyer's production process. Moreover, the differences of the discounted cash flows seem to be rather insensitive to variations of the vendor's setup costs. Hence, the general results regarding the advantages of the simultaneous planning approach coincide for both models.

---

18 For a given lot ratio n_t, however, q_t increases with the demand rate.

19 Mixed results follow w.r.t. the impact of d on Δt_{tb}, i.e., for both planning approaches a concave relation follows.

20 Moreover, the discontinuities follow when the lot ratio n_t increases by one.

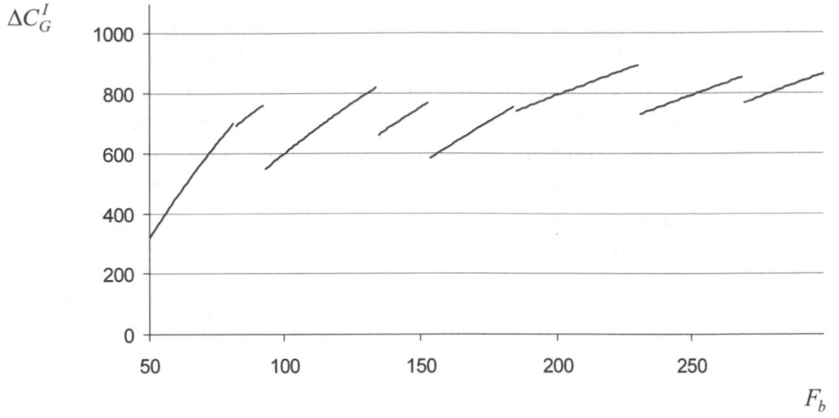

Fig. 9. Differences in total discounted cash flow between the simultaneous and the successive coordination of the inventory-oriented model for varying buyer's setup costs

5.3. Numerical comparison of the cash flow- and the inventory-oriented model of the supply chain

Finally, we analyze the differences in the net present value for the cash flow-oriented model and the inventory-oriented model of the supply chain. We restrict our analysis to the simultaneous planning approach. Generally, the inventory-oriented model of the supply chain approximates the cash flow-oriented model. Hence, the latter always results in a higher total net present value for the supply chain. Subsequently, we consider the impact of various model parameters on the magnitude of the differences.

Figure 10 illustrates the impact of the demand rate on the differences in total discounted cash flows ΔC_G^{SI} of the two modelling approaches, with

$$\Delta C_G^{SI} \equiv C_G\left(q_b^{CF,SI}, n_t^{CF,SI}, n_v^{CF,SI}\right) - C_G\left(q_b^{I,SI}, n_t^{I,SI}, n_v^{I,SI}\right). \tag{21}$$

The figure shows decreasing differences for increasing demand rates. The decrease is due to the general result that both discounting periods, i.e., Δt_{vt} and Δt_{tb} decrease for an increasing demand rate. This tendency mitigates the discounting effect neglected in the inventory-oriented model. Therefore, the inventory-oriented model of the supply chain yields an *acceptable approximation* of the cash flow-oriented model for relatively high demand rates.

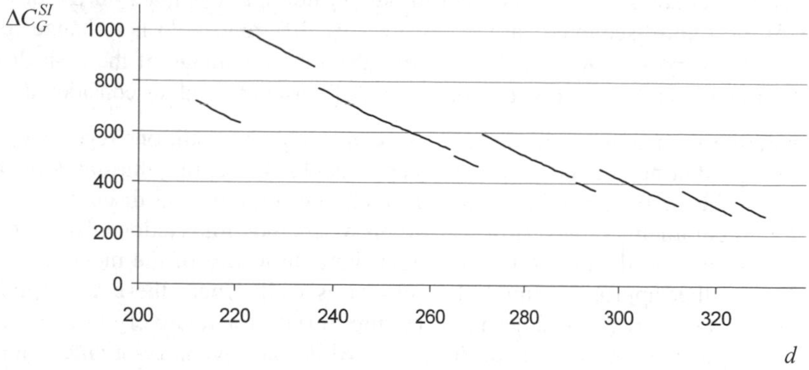

Fig. 10. Differences in total discounted cash flows between the cash flow- and the inventory-oriented model for a simultaneous coordination and for varying demand rates

Next, figure 11 shows ΔC_G^{SI} for varying fixed setup costs F_b. The figure shows discontinuously increasing differences. Generally, the discontinuities occur when $n_t^{I,SI}$ increases by one, resulting in a smaller transport lot and a substantially larger lot size $q_b^{I,SI}$. Although the first effect reduces the discounting period Δt_{vt}, it is clear from figure 11 that the resulting increase in Δt_{tb} dominates and leads to a substantial increase of ΔC_G^{SI}.[21] Therefore, the cash flow-oriented model of the supply chain seems to be beneficial especially for larger fixed setup costs of the buyer.

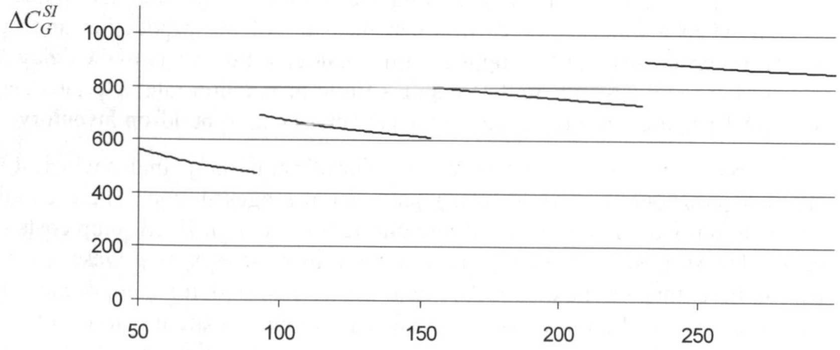

Fig. 11. Differences in total discounted cash flows between the cash flow- and the inventory-oriented model for a simultaneous coordination and for varying buyer's fixed setup costs

[21] For given lot ratios, however, the differences decrease for increasing F_b. Then, $q_b^{CF,SI}$ increases to a larger extent then $q_b^{I,SI}$, thus mitigating the neglected discounting effect.

Finally, the vendor's setup costs seem to have a negligible impact on the differences of the total discounted cash flows, i.e., the differences do not change substantially for varying values of F_v. I.e., the absolute advantage of the cash flow-oriented model is unchanged within the ranges of parameter values considered.[22]

Summarizing the results derived above, we can establish conditions regarding the use of the modelling and the coordination approaches. Generally, the *simultaneous solution* to the *cash flow-oriented model* yields the highest total discounted cash flow for all parameter values. However, when we include transaction costs that increase with the coordination effort and with the complexity of the modelling approach, the other approaches might be optimal as well. Under these assumptions the cash flow-oriented model seems to be appropriate for relatively low demand rates and high fixed setup costs of thc buyer, while the inventory-oriented model yields a relatively small difference in total net present value for relatively high demand rates and relatively low fixed setup costs. Moreover, the successive (simultaneous) planning approach seems to be relevant especially for a dominant role of the demand rate (fixed setup costs).

6. Conclusion

The objective of this paper has been to illustrate how different modelling and coordination approaches of the supply chain influence the quality of the supply chain's lot size decisions. Basically, the fundamental difference of inventory-oriented and cash flow-oriented models is that the latter models consider any discounting that is necessary when aggregating the individual calculus. Discounting is essential when a time lag exists between the start of the production and the transportation processes. For the supply chain considered this refers to the delay of the transportation process due to the vendor's finite production rate, and the delay of the buyer's production process due to the carrier's need to build-up inventory.

Based on several numerical comparisons we identify conditions under which it is important to consider the time-displacements for the aggregation. These conditions refer to a relatively low demand rate and relatively high fixed setup costs of the buyer. Then, substantial time-displacements follow. Interpreting these results, the use of inventory-oriented models seems to be justified for a high capacity utilization and when the buyer uses a flexible production system. Moreover, the results suggest that the conditions for the modelling and the coordination approaches coincide, i.e., it is beneficial to simultaneously plan the lot sizes based on a cash flow-oriented model of the supply chain.

---

[22] Moreover, no clear result follows regarding the impact of the fixed transport costs on ΔC_G^{SI}.

Future research questions refer to the robustness of the above conditions for other structures of the supply chain, and to the allocation of the gains of a simultaneous coordination approach to the vendor, the carrier, and the buyer. Then, the analysis may provide insights into the consequences of information asymmetries and divergent preferences, i.e., the design of accounting systems based on arguments from information economics.

References

Bhatnangar, R., Chandra, P., Goyal, S.K. (1993) Models for Multi-Plant Coordination. In: European Journal of Operational Research 67(2): pp. 141-160.

Banerjee, A. (1986) A Joint Economic-Lot-Size Model for Purchaser and Vendor. In: Decision Sciences 17(3): pp. 292-311.

Crowston, W.B., Wagner, M.H., Williams, J.F. (1973) Economic Lot Size Determination in Multi-Stage Assembly Systems. In: Management Science 19(5): pp. 517-527.

Demski, J.S., Feltham, G.A. (1976) Cost Determination: A Conceptual Approach. Iowa State University Press, Ames/Iowa.

Drezner, Z., Szendrovits, A.Z., Wesolowsky, G.O. (1984) Multi-Stage Production with Variable Lot Sizes and Transportation of Partial Lots. In: European Journal of Operational Research 17(1): pp. 227-237.

Fandel, G., François, P., May, E. (1988) Effects of Call-Forward Delivery Systems on Suppliers' Serial per Unit Costs. In: Fandel G, Dyckhoff H, Reese J (eds) Production Theory and Planning. Physica, Heidelberg, pp. 66-84.

Fandel, G., François, P. (1989) Just-in-Time-Produktion und -Beschaffung – Funktionsweise, Einsatzvoraussetzungen und Grenzen. In: Zeitschrift für Betriebswirtschaft 59(5): pp. 531-544.

Goyal, S.K. (1977a) An Integrated Inventory Model for a Single Product System. In: Operational Research Quarterly 28(3): pp. 539-545.

Goyal, S.K. (1977b) Determination of Optimum Production Quantity for a Two-Stage Production System. In: Operational Research Quarterly 28(4): pp. 865-870.

Goyal, S.K. (1978a) An Alternative Approach for Determining Economic Production Quantity in a Two-Stage Production System – A Rejoinder. In: Journal of the Operations Research Sociaty 30(2): pp. 177-179.

Goyal, S.K. (1978b) Economic Batch Quantity in a Multi-Stage Production System. In: International Journal of Production Research 16(4): pp. 267-273.

Goyal, S.K. (1988) A Joint Economic Lot Size Model for Purchaser and Vendor: A Comment. In: Decision Sciences 19: pp. 236-241.

Goyal, S.K., Szendrovits, A.Z. (1986) A Constant Lot Size Model with Equal and Unequal Sized Batch Shipments between Production Stages. In: Engineering Costs and Production Economics 10(3): pp. 203-210.

Goyal, S.K., Gupta, Y.P. (1989) Integrated Inventory Models: The Buyer-Vendor Coordination. In: European Journal of Operational Research 41(1): pp. 261-269.

Grubbström, R.W. (1967) On the Application of Laplace Transform to Certain Economic Problems. In: Management Science 13(7): pp. 558-567.

Grubbström, R.W. (1980) A Principle for Determining the Correct Capital Costs of Work-In-Progress and Inventory. In: International Journal of Production Research 18(2): pp. 259-271.

Grubbström, R.W., Thorstenson, A. (1986) Evaluation of Capital Costs in a Multi-Level Inventory System by Means of the Annuity Stream Principle. In: European Journal of Operational Research 24(1): pp. 136-145.

Hadley, G. (1964) A Comparison of Order Quantities Computed Using the Average Annual Cost and Discounted Cost. In: Management Science 10(3): pp. 472-476.

Helber, S. (1994) Kapazitätsorientierte Losgrößenplanung in PPS-Systemen. M&P, Stuttgart.

Hill, R.M. (1997) The Single-Vendor Single-Buyer Integrated Production-Inventory Model with a Generalised Policy. In: European Journal of Operational Research 97(3): pp. 493-499.

Hofmann, C. (1995) Interdependente Losgrößenplanung in Logistiksystemen. M&P, Stuttgart.

Hofmann, C. (2000) Supplier's Pricing Policy in a Just-in-Time Environment. In: Computers and Operations Research 27(24): pp. 1357-1373.

Küpper, U. (1985) Investitionstheoretische Fundierung der Kostenrechung. In: Zeitschrift für betriebswirtschaftliche Forschung 37(1): pp. 26-46.

Küpper, U. (1991) Multi-Period Production Planning and Managerial Accounting. In: Fandel, G., Zäpfel, G. (eds) Production Concepts-Theory and Applications, Springer, Berlin et al., pp. 46-62.

Kumar, U., Vrat, P. (1978) Optimum Batch Size for Multi-Stage Production-Inventory System. In: Operations Research 15(2&3): pp. 78-94.

Stadtler, H. (1992) Losgrößenentscheidungen bei zyklischem Lieferabruf. In: Zeitschrift für Betriebswirtschaft 62(12): pp. 1361-1380.

Stadtler, H., Kilger, C. (eds) (2002) Supply Chain Management and Advanced Planning, 2nd eds. Springer, Berlin et al.

Szendrovits, A.Z. (1976) On the Optimality of Sub-Batch Sizes for a Multi-Stage EPQ Model – A Rejoinder. In: Management Science 23(3): pp. 334-338.

Szendrovits, A.Z. (1978a) A Comment on "Optimal and System Myopic Policies for Multi-Echelon Production/Inventory Assembly Systems". In: Management Science 24(8): pp. 863-864.

Szendrovits, A.Z. (1978b) A Comment on Determination of Optimum Production Quantity for a Two-Stage Production System. In: Journal of the Operations Research Sociaty 29(10): pp. 1017-1020.

Szendrovits, A.Z. (1983) Non-Integer Optimal Lot Size Ratios in Two-Stage Production/ Inventory Systems. In: International Journal of Production Research 21(3): pp. 323-336.

Thomas, D.J., Griffin, P.M. (1996) Coordinated Supply Chain Management. In: European Journal of Operational Research 94(1): pp. 1-15.

Trippi, R.R., Lewin, D.E. (1974) A Present Value Formulation of the Classical EOQ Problem. In: Decision Sciences 5(1): pp. 30-35.

Viswanathan, S. (1998) Optimal Strategy for the Integrated Vendor-Buyer Inventory-Model. In: European Journal of Operational Research 105(1): pp. 38-42.

The Bullwhip Effect and its Suppression in Supply Chain Management

Katsuhiko Takahashi and Myreshka

Department of Artificial Complex Systems Engineering
Graduate School of Engineering
Hiroshima University, 4-1, Kagamiyama 1 chome
Higashi-Hiroshima 739-8527, Japan

Abstract: *In order to achieve an efficient supply chain, it is necessary to harmonize production with distribution. There is a lot of research into both production and distribution and also into the integration of production and distribution. However, there has been little published in the area of the integration of production and inventory distribution. In order to integrate production, inventory, and distribution, deterministic models have been developed.*

As the configuration of the supply chain becomes more complicated and a lot of stochastic elements have to be included in the supply chain, it becomes difficult to formulate the problems in supply chain management using a deterministic mathematical programming model, and it is necessary to adopt the approach to the problem. For this purpose, a stochastic model of supply chain management is constructed, and the ordering systems for determining the times and quantities in order release for each stage in the supply chain system are formulated.

In their stochastic model for supply chain management, Lee et al. (1997) show that the distortion of information causes a bullwhip effect, where the fluctuations of inventory amplify as ones going upstream in the supply chain process. The amplification of the fluctuations in multi-stage production systems is also pointed out by Kimura and Terada (1981) and Takahashi et al. (1994).

In this paper, the bullwhip effect is demonstrated and its causes are discussed. Furthermore, the methods developed in the previous literature for suppressing the bullwhip effects are presented.

Keywords: *order policies, demand uncertainties, inventory management, bullwhip effect*

1. Introduction

In order to achieve an efficient supply chain, it is necessary to harmonize production with distribution. Further, harmonizing production and distribution also requires integrating inventory. There are many researches dedicated to both production and distribution, and also to the integration of production and distribution. However, there have been only some few publications concerning the overall integration of production, distribution and inventory. In order to integrate production, distribution and inventory, deterministic models have been developed in the literature, some mathematical programming models have been constructed, and the objective functions were optimized using a deterministic approach.

As the configuration of the supply chain becomes more complicated and a lot of stochastic elements have to be considered in the supply chain, the difficulties to formulate optimization problems in supply chain management are increasing, thus new approaches are required. For this purpose, the construction of a stochastic model of supply chain management is necessary, and the formulation of an ordering system for determining the time and quantity in order release for each stage in the supply chain is needed.

Among the publications on the stochastic model for supply chain management, Lee et al. (1997) show that the distortion of information causes a phenomenon known as a bullwhip (or whiplash) effect. The bullwhip effect refers to the phenomenon where the fluctuations of inventory amplify as one goes upstream the supply chain. This effect is not only known in supply chain management, but also exists in multistage production processes, known there as demand amplification. Several researches were dedicated to find the cure for this phenomenon in both the supply chain and the multistage production area.

The basic phenomenon of the bullwhip effect and demand amplification is not new and has been known to management scientists for some time. The first empirical evidence of the existence of the bullwhip effect was given by Forrester (1961), and many other researchers continued his work in defining and searching for the sources and their counter-measures in minimizing the negative effect of the bullwhip phenomenon in the supply chain area (Caplin, 1985; Lee et al., 1997; Baganha and Cohen, 1998; Dejonckheere et al., 2002). This amplification of the fluctuation phenomenon in multistage production systems has also been pointed out by Kimura and Terada (1981) and Takahashi et al. (1994a).

In this paper, the existence of the bullwhip effect is shown by reviewing the literature both in the supply chain and in the multistage production system. Further, the sources of the bullwhip effect and the respective counter-measures for each source are explained.

After this introduction, the existing literature on the bullwhip effect and the demand amplification are briefly reviewed. Next, the sources of the bullwhip effect are presented and evaluated in sect. 3. According to the above-mentioned sources, sect. 4 presents the possible counter-measures for each source. Finally, sect. 5 presents the conclusions of this study.

2. Review of literature

The basic phenomenon of the bullwhip effect in the supply chain and also in a multistage production system is not new. It has been known to management scientists for some time. Forrester (1961) presented the first empirical evidence of the existence of the bullwhip effect from a system dynamics viewpoint.

In supply chain management, Sterman (1989) created a game to confirm the existence of the bullwhip effect which is known nowadays as the MIT beer distribution game. The game simulates a supply chain consisting of four players who make independent decisions without consulting other members. The decision of each player solely relies on orders from the neighboring players. This experiment showed that the variances of orders amplify as one moves up in the supply chain, confirming the existence of the bullwhip effect. Here, the effect is caused by the irrational behavior of the decision makers (players) or by the misperceptions of feedbacks. Seeing this effect, individual education is proposed to diminish the bullwhip effect. However, Lee et al. (1997) argued that even rational behavior of the decision maker causes the bullwhip effect, as it is an outcome of the strategic interactions among the supply chain members. Another critic to the beer distribution game is that it did not take the capacity issues into consideration. Nevertheless, this research is a valuable contribution to easily understand the bullwhip phenomenon.

Continuing the original arguments of the beer distribution game, Jacobs (2000) proposed to play the game using the internet. Holweg and Bicheno (2002) created a powerful tool that can be used by academics and practitioners to better understand their own supply chain network and to deploy, discuss and validate changes to the real world supply network. Further, Kimbrough et al. (2002) evaluated the possibility to use an artificial agent (computers) to manage the supply chain, by letting the computer play the beer distribution game.

As the existence of the bullwhip effect in the supply chain is proven, the sources of this phenomenon need to be identified and the counter-measures to diminish this effect need to be uncovered. Various studies have been dedicated to this area. Caplin (1985) proposed a stationary model to measure the impact of batch ordering on the bullwhip effect and found that the variances of orders linearly increase with the size of orders. Kahn (1987) proved that the bullwhip effect is also reduced when the retailer follows an optimal inventory and either when demand in each period is positively serially correlated or when the backlogging of excess demand is permitted. This study explicitly considers the dynamic aspects of production/inventory requirements.

Lee et al. (1997) identified demand signal processing, the rationing game, order batching and price variations as the general four sources of the bullwhip effect and also proposed counter-measures for each source. They provided a mathematical model of the supply chain that captured the essential aspects of the institutional structure and the decision behavior of agents in the supply chain.

Related to the order batching and demand-signaling sources given by Lee et al. (1997), Baganha and Cohen (1998) proposed an analytical multi-echelon model that combined the relevant features of the different systems in the supply chain. They proved that inventory could sometimes have a stabilizing effect based on the interaction of cost, technology and market attributes, so that the bullwhip effect was not always present throughout the supply chain. Further measures to suppress the bullwhip effect caused by order batching were also reported by other researchers (Cachon, 1999; Riddals and Bennet, 2001). Additionally, methods to analyze and/or to quantify the bullwhip effect were developed by Dejonckheere et al. (2002) and Chen et al. (2000a, b).

On the other hand, the bullwhip effect in the multistage production system, formerly known as demand amplification, was also evaluated over time. Many techniques have been developed to diminish this effect. In general, production control systems for a multistage production process can be classified into push type systems and pull type systems. The former systems, such as a Material Requirements Planning (MRP) system, calculate production orders on the basis of demand forecasts, and the latter systems, such as a 'Kanban' system, calculate production orders on the basis of the actual demand. The two types of production ordering systems were analyzed from various viewpoints and compared with each other.

Kimura and Terada (1981) introduce the above mentioned pull systems as new systems that can prevent the transmission of amplified fluctuations, i.e. the bullwhip phenomenon, of the demand or production volume of a succeeding process to the preceding process. Such a system was implemented in the Toyota Motor Co., Ltd. to minimize the bullwhip effect by using a sort of tag, called Kanban. It worked better in reducing the bullwhip effect, as the amplification did not further fluctuate in the upper stream.

The differences between the push and pull systems do not only affect the economic performances of a production system but also its flexibility (Takahashi et al., 1994a). Looking at the flexibility of a push-type production ordering system, Tabe et al. (1980) and Bertrand (1986) studied a proportional control mechanism of feedback information. Takahashi et al. (1987) extended this research towards the different feedback information processes. In the pull type system, Kimura and Terada (1981) studied the influence of the order unit, Hiraki et al. (1989) studied the influence of transportation lead-time, while Takahashi et al. (1994a) clarified the flexibility of production control systems by considering demand fluctuations and downstream fluctuations due to machine breakdowns and the production ordering system's response to those changes.

In order to improve the performance of production ordering systems, not only pure push-type or pure pull-type production ordering systems, but also systems that integrate both types of those ordering systems have proved to be effective. Since the 1980s, methods to integrate these two types of ordering systems have been a very active research area (Larsen and Alting, 1993). In these integrated systems, two types of integration have been introduced. One is the "vertical integration", and the other is the "horizontal integration". The former type of integration implies that the system consists of two levels, the upper level consisting of a push type production ordering system and the lower consisting of a pull type ordering system (Gupta and Brennan, 1993). The latter type of integration implies that at some stages a push type ordering system is established while at the other stages there exists a pull type ordering system.

Much research work has been done on the analysis and comparison of horizontal integration. An optimal integration of push and pull type control strategy based on the optimization results of a Markov decision process (MDP) has been proposed (Hodgson and Wang, 1991a,b) using a push type ordering system at all initial stages of each production line branch and a pull type ordering system at all other stages. However, the incapability of the MDP model that cannot be used to analyze more complicated systems, leads to unconvincing quantified results. To overcome this weakness, Wang and Xu (1997) proposed a simulation method to analyze control strategies of a large manufacturing system and recommended a hybrid push/pull strategy as the best control strategy for a mass production manufacturing system.

The effectiveness in integrating push/pull type systems in production ordering systems to suppress the amplification of demand and/or inventory has also been clarified by Takahashi et al. (1994b) and Takahashi and Soshiroda (1996).

3. The sources of the bullwhip effect

Lee et al. (1997) described four sources of the bullwhip effect from a managerial perspective, i.e. demand signal processing, the rationing game, order batching, and price variations:

- Demand signal processing:
  This source refers to the situation where demand is non-stationary and one uses past demand information in updating the forecast. Using a forecast based on fluctuating demand will transmit the forecast error to the supply side. Therefore, the bullwhip effect occurs due to an amplification from the actual demand. This amplification will increase as one goes upstream in the supply chain.
- The rationing game:
  The rationing game refers to a situation where a retailer places a higher demand than required in order to secure more units from a manufacturer with a produc-

tion capacity constraint. Generally, under this shortage situation, where the capacity of the manufacturer is limited, the manufacturer would ration the supply of the product. Consider a supply chain consisting of three layers – a manufacturer, multiple wholesalers, and multiple retailers. If the manufactured products tend to be in short supply, the wholesalers will play the rationing game to get a large share of the supply. Seeing the possibility of the wholesaler not getting enough from the manufacturer, retailers also play the same game. Thus, the demand and its variance are amplified as one moves up the supply chain.

- Order batching:
  Order batching refers to a policy used by a retailer to accumulate the demand for several periods and release the order at the beginning of the accumulated period. Subsequently, this policy amplifies demand fluctuation. That means, as batching at the retail level increases the variance of demand to wholesalers, batching at the wholesale level may also increase the variance of the demand to the distributor or the manufacturer.

- Price variations:
  Price variations refer to a change in the price for a product, causing the retailer to order a higher quantity of a particular product when the price is lower.

From a different viewpoint, the sources of the bullwhip effect can also be classified based on the position in the supply chain where they occur. Table 1 shows such a classification which also includes the sources stated by Lee et al. (1997). In the next subsections, an explanation concerning each source based on this classification is provided.

Demand	Ordering Process	Supply
Demand fluctuation	Order cost	Capacity
Demand uncertainty	Order lot (Batch)	Lead-time
Penalty cost fluctuation	Order cycle	Price fluctuation
	Ordering method	Delivery cycle

Table 1. The sources of the bullwhip effect

3.1. Sources on the demand side

The sources on the demand side might be classified into three factors, i.e. demand fluctuation, demand uncertainty, and penalty cost fluctuation. Demand fluctuation is a condition where demand is not constant (non stationary) over time. Bullwhip occurs when any fluctuation on the demand side is carried over to the supply side, causing an amplified demand on the supply side. This amplification will increase as one goes upstream the supply chain.

Fig. 1 shows changes in the inventory level when the order quantity is constant. With a constant demand, an inventory will be consumed in a constant rate during the period between the release of an order and the delivery of the goods (Fig. 1(a)). On the other hand, with fluctuating demand, the decrease of an inventory varies (Fig. 1(b)). This might cause run out of inventory or, in contrast, excess inventory at the end of the period. To avoid running out of inventory, two methods are usually conducted – increasing the reorder point or adjusting the release time of an order. Increasing the reorder point does not necessarily lead to a change of the order quantity itself. In such a case, changes in demand do not amplify changes in order quantity. However, adjusting the release time will either accelerate or delay the ordering period. As a result, any demand fluctuation amplifies changes in the order quantity.

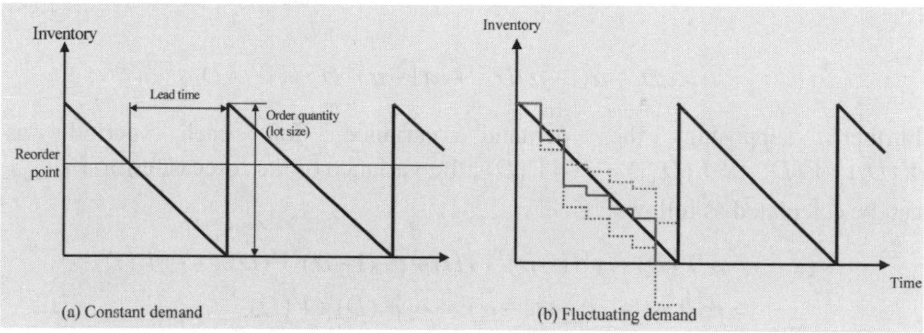

Fig. 1. Changes in the inventory level

The second source on the demand side is demand uncertainty. Demand uncertainty illustrates the condition when future demand is unknown. This source corresponds to the demand signal processing described by Lee et al. (1997). If the future trend is known or if a future order is fixed, it would be easy to suppress the amplification. Moreover, as no forecast is required with a zero procurement lead-time, no problem will occur even with uncertain future demand. Nevertheless, in the case when procurement lead-time exists and demand is not only fluctuating but also uncertain, forecasting future demand to provide the necessary order quantity is required. However, an error in forecasting future demand is unavoidable and this error becomes the factor that amplifies the fluctuations in procurement quantity.

Let us consider a simple case where the demand of each period is illustrated by an independent and identically distributed stochastic variable D_t, and the demand $\hat{D}_{t+i:t}$ for period t+i is forecasted by a single exponential smoothing equation as follows:

$$\hat{D}_{t+i:t} = \alpha D_t + (1-\alpha)\hat{D}_{t-1+i:t-1}$$

Here, α is the smoothing factor, usually $0<\alpha<1$. Brown (1959), who proposed to apply this forecasting method for inventory control, recommended to use a small value, such as $\alpha=0.1$.

The forecast error, i.e. the difference between a forecast and the actual demand $e_{t+i:t} = \hat{D}_{t+i:t} - D_{t+i}$, can be calculated as follows:

$$\begin{aligned} e_{t+i:t} &= \hat{D}_{t+i:t} - D_{t+i} \\ &= \alpha D_t + (1-\alpha)\hat{D}_{t-1+i:t-1} - D_{t+i} \\ &= \alpha D_t + (1-\alpha)\left\{\alpha D_{t-1} + (1-\alpha)\hat{D}_{t-2+i:t-2}\right\} - D_{t+i} \\ &= \alpha D_t + \alpha(1-\alpha)D_{t-1} + (1-\alpha)^2 \hat{D}_{t-2+i:t-2} - D_{t+i} \\ &\vdots \\ &= \alpha D_t + \alpha(1-\alpha)D_{t-1} + \alpha(1-\alpha)^2 D_{t-2} + \cdots - D_{t+i} \end{aligned}$$

Further, supposing the demand variance for each period as $V(D_t) = V(D_{t+1}) = V(D_{t+2}) = \cdots = V(D)$, the variance of the forecast error $V(e_{t+i:t})$ can be calculated as follows:

$$\begin{aligned} V(e_{t+i:t}) &= \alpha^2 V(D) + \alpha^2(1-\alpha)^2 V(D) + \alpha^4(1-\alpha)^4 V(D) + \cdots + V(D) \\ &= \alpha^2\left\{1 + (1-\alpha)^2 + (1-\alpha)^4 + \cdots\right\}V(D) + V(D) \\ &= \alpha^2 \frac{1}{1-(1-\alpha)^2} V(D) + V(D) \\ &= \frac{\alpha^2}{1-(1-2\alpha+\alpha^2)} V(D) + V(D) \\ &= \frac{\alpha^2}{2\alpha-\alpha^2} V(D) + V(D) \\ &= \left(\frac{\alpha}{2-\alpha} + \frac{2-\alpha}{2-\alpha}\right) V(D) \\ &= \frac{2}{2-\alpha} V(D) \end{aligned}$$

From this equation, it is clear that for $0<\alpha<1$, the variance of error is greater than that of demand. It is easy to understand that when procurement is based on a demand forecast, the demand fluctuation will be amplified, yielding to the occurrence of the bullwhip phenomenon.

The situation explained above happens when we consider demand as an independent and identically distributed stochastic variable. Lee et al. (1997) introduced this phenomenon when demand is serially correlated. In this case, it is possible to suppress the demand fluctuation by using appropriate forecasting methods. However, even with those methods, generally the fluctuation is still amplified due to the other sources, as e.g. lead-time and batching.

The third factor on the demand side is the penalty cost fluctuation. The penalties for running out of inventory vary over time. For example, sales people tend to rush and close deals toward the end of an accounting period to meet their sales target. This means that the demand for a product increases at the end of an accounting period or at the end of an accounting year. At this point of time, running out of inventory has to be avoided as far as possible, and it can be observed that the penalty cost will be much higher than usual. It is clear that the increasing of penalty cost will result in reduced inventory cost. Further, to suppress the increasing penalty cost, one usually increases the inventory level to avoid running out of inventory. When the penalty cost varies over time, usually the inventory level is adjusted, yielding to a further adjustment in procurement. Thus, the fluctuation in penalty cost will be transmitted to the supply side.

3.2. Sources on the ordering process side

Except from the sources on the demand side, further sources of the bullwhip effect exist in the ordering process. There are four sources that can be derived from the ordering process, i.e. order cost, order lot (batch), order cycle, and ordering method.

Order cost is defined as the cost required to place an order. There are two types of order cost; order cost that is proportional to the change of the order quantity, and the cost that is not affected by the quantity of an order. The former type of cost will be explained in subsection 3.3. In this subsection, we deal with the latter type of order cost as a factor that causes the bullwhip effect from the ordering process side.

Increasing the order quantity will increase the average inventory level and the inventory holding cost. As the result of the tradeoff relationship between the order cost and the inventory cost, an economic order quantity (EOQ) that minimizes the total cost of order and inventory cost in a convex function is utilized. The relationships between the above factors are shown in Fig. 2. Further, it is also shown that the EOQ increases with every increase of the order cost. Thus, to minimize the total cost, one tends to order more quantity at one order when the order cost is high.

With no consideration of order cost, thus only considering inventory cost, it is preferable to use a just-in-time procurement system. The policy of this system is to order the required quantity for one period only, which yields to zero inventory cost. However, considering order cost, it is preferable to accumulate the order quantities for several periods to minimize total cost. The accumulation is considered as one order lot. The consequences for the quantity fluctuations are explained below.

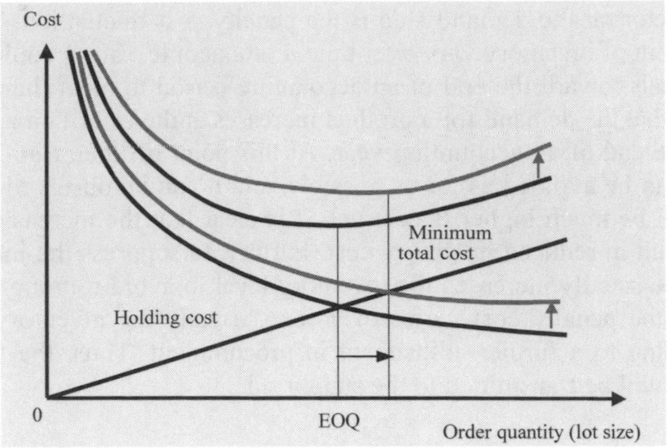

Fig. 2. Relationship between order quantity and cost

The second factor on the ordering process side is the order lot. Generally, the order quantity that takes a discrete value is called a lot, whereas the one which takes a continuous value is called a batch. This refers to a condition where a particular product should be ordered in a certain multiplied unit, e.g. dozen, or has a minimum and maximum value. Similar to the previous explanation concerning the order cost, the fluctuation caused by accumulating the order quantity into lots will cause the bullwhip effect, as it will cause deviations from the actual demand and these deviations will be transmitted to the supply side. Further, these transmitted quantities might be further amplified in the upper stream, causing the bullwhip effect. This factor is indicated in Lee et al. (1997) as the order batching factor, though the authors did not further classify this factor as explained here.

The third factor, the order cycle, is defined as a constant interval between two orders. Under the reorder point method in inventory control, an order is released as soon as the inventory falls below a certain reorder point. Thus, the interval between two orders varies when the demand fluctuates. No problem will be encountered if we are dealing with a product/part that is made-to-stock, i.e. the supply side has sufficient inventory to fulfill the order placed by the ordering process side. In this case, letting the interval variable is possible. However, when dealing with a unique or particular product/part that requires a special production preparation (made-to-order product), variable intervals between orders will lead to unreliable delivery dates. To avoid a late delivery, an order is usually based on a particular order cycle, such as once a week, once a day, or like procurement of fresh meat in convenience stores, several times a day.

Any constant order cycle requires the ordering process to order a certain amount of quantity to fulfill the demand until the next order. With uncertain and fluctuating demand, the timing and quantity of an order are determined based on a demand forecast. As mentioned previously, using a forecast method to decide at the order quantity will amplify the demand fluctuation. When no order cycle is determined, i.e. the interval between these orders is variable, the difference between the actual demand and the demand forecast can be adjusted. This will allow for controlling the transmission of demand fluctuations to order fluctuations. That is to say, when a constant order cycle is utilized, fluctuations in demand are immediately transmitted to order fluctuations, thus provoking the bullwhip effect.

The last factor on the ordering process side is the ordering method utilized in the inventory control system. There are many ordering methods utilized in an organization nowadays. Perpetual systems (S-s methods), periodic ordering systems, push ordering systems, such as Material Requirements Planning (MRP) systems, and pull ordering systems, such as Kanban in JIT production systems, can be named as the general ordering systems utilized in nowadays environment. Tersine (1985) classified the inventory systems based on the nature of demand, as shown in Fig. 3.

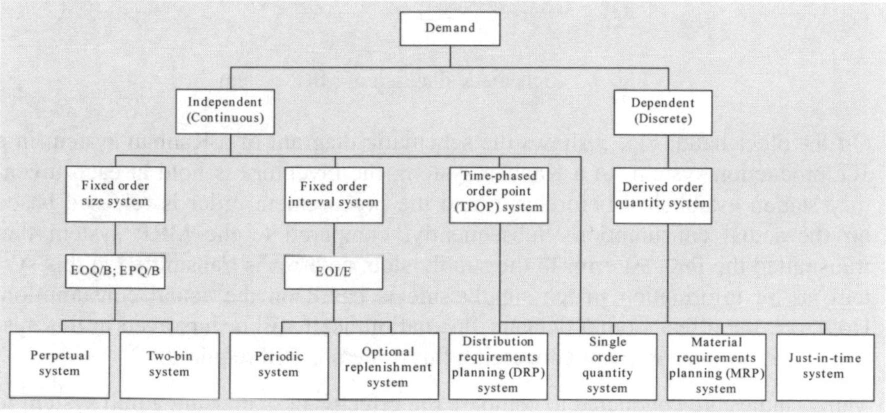

Fig. 3. Demand-based inventory systems (Tersine 1985)

A perpetual control system keeps continuous records of the quantities used in production and prepares an order for a fixed order quantity when the stock is equal or less than the reorder point. The other fixed order size system, the two-bin system, does not keep any records of the units consumed. Here, the inventory is divided in two separate bins, one equals to the reorder point quantity and one contains the remaining units. An order is released when the amount in the second bin is consumed. On the other hand, in a fixed order interval system (periodic system), the inventory is reviewed at specified time intervals, thus it is treated discretely and dependently. A hybrid system that integrates both the perpetual and the periodic system is illustrated by the optional replenishment system (see Tersine, 1985, for a detailed explanation).

Fig. 4 shows the schematic diagram of the MRP system. In the MRP system, an order quantity is calculated based on net requirements for a future demand and a determinate lead-time. Then, the period of order release is calculated by subtracting the lead-time from the point of expected delivery. A forecast method is required when the demand fluctuates and is uncertain. This forecast will affect the production plan, as it will contain a forecast error. The planned order release forecasted for the product will be used as demand in part and/or material planning, so that any fluctuation in demand will immediately be transmitted to the supply side. As the DRP is based on the MRP concept, it has the same characteristics as the MRP system. Other ordering systems that utilize demand forecasts in their methodology are push type ordering systems, and all of the push type ordering systems show the similar characteristics as the MRP system.

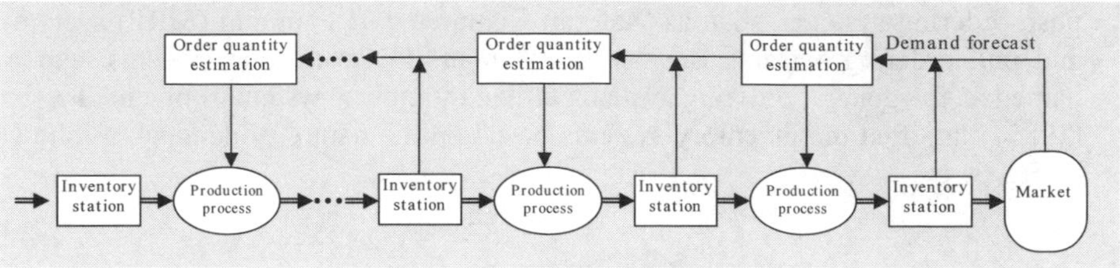

Fig. 4. Schematic diagram of MRP system

On the other hand, Fig. 5 shows the schematic diagram of a Kanban system in a JIT production system. In a Kanban system, the inventory is hold at each inventory station established beforehand, and the procurement order is released based on the actual consumption. Subsequently, compared to the MRP system that transmitted the forecast error to the supply side, no error is transmitted in this system, as all information to the supply side is based on the actual consumption. However, the effect from a demand fluctuation itself still occurs even in this system. Thus, an improvement concerning this system is still required.

Many studies are conducted to compare the effectiveness in using a pull system to avoid demand amplifications (Krawjesky et al., 1987; Rees et al., 1989; Sarker and Fitzsimmons, 1989; Takahashi et al., 1994a). Also, several studies are conducted to integrate both systems to achieve a better performance and avoid the bullwhip effect (Hodgson and Wang, 1991a, b; Takahashi et al., 1991, 1994b; Gupta and Brennan, 1993; Takahashi and Soshiroda, 1996; Wang and Xu, 1997).

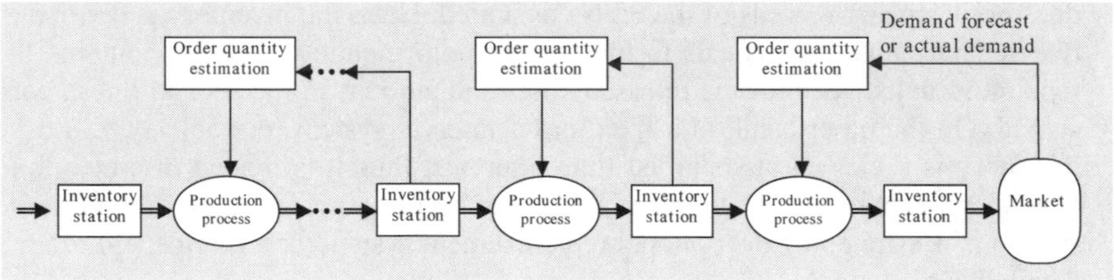

Fig. 5. Schematic diagram of Kanban system

3.3. Sources on the supply side

Apart from the demand and ordering process side, several factors that cause the bullwhip effect also exist at the supply side. They are capacity, lead-time, price fluctuation, and delivery cycle.

Capacity is the upper bound ability to fulfill an order. Suppose procurement is obtained from a supplier who has several vendors. In this case, a problem will occur when the total demand from all vendors exceeds the capacity of the supplier. This type of problem is also explained in the shortage game in Lee et al. (1997). As each vendor tends to avoid shortage in the procurement quantity, he tends to place an order with more quantity than required and to adjust the difference by ordering less quantity. As a result, the fluctuation in procurement in future exceeds the actual demand fluctuation. Generally, from the supplier's point of view, it is necessary to suppress every procurement fluctuation, as it is seen as a constraint. However, when vendors play the shortage game, the total procurement fluctuation cannot be avoided. The problems concerning a single supplier that fulfill the procurement for multi vendors have been evaluated in previous literature as inventory control problems of single depot and multi retailers (Chen, 1999).

The second source, lead-time, indicates the time required by the suppliers from receiving an order to supplying a particular product. Fig. 6(a) shows the effect of lead-time to the inventory level in the case of a constant demand. It can be clearly seen that an increasing reorder point does not amplify the fluctuation of both procurement amount and its fluctuation, even when the lead-time is long. For fluctuating and uncertain demand, determining the order quantity and the reorder point is shown in Fig. 6(b). Making a necessary adjustment based on order quantity fluctuations will lead to a longer lead-time. This will amplify the demand fluctuation during the new adjusted lead-time and, as a result, longer lead-time ends in fluctuations in order quantity that amplify demand fluctuations on the supply side, yielding the occurrence of the bullwhip phenomenon. The above-mentioned problem caused by lead-time is particularly essential for a supplier who has a comparatively long lead-time, for example, for a global supply chain that uses sea transportation to deliver the products. Among several studies available in the literature, Hiraki et al. (1989) evaluate the effectiveness of a low inventory ordering system for a global (international) supply chain.

The next factor at the supply side, price fluctuation, is defined as fluctuation of the price required to supply a particular product. Lee et al. (1997) also deal with problems in price variation in their paper. Though it might be difficult to consider a price variation other than the one that is caused by speculation in material cost, using a price differing from the usual price in a campaign sale is included in this problem.

Additionally, price variations have a strong relationship with inventory cost. For example, high price products that require special care to hold in inventory, have high order cost or have high return profits, usually related to high inventory cost.

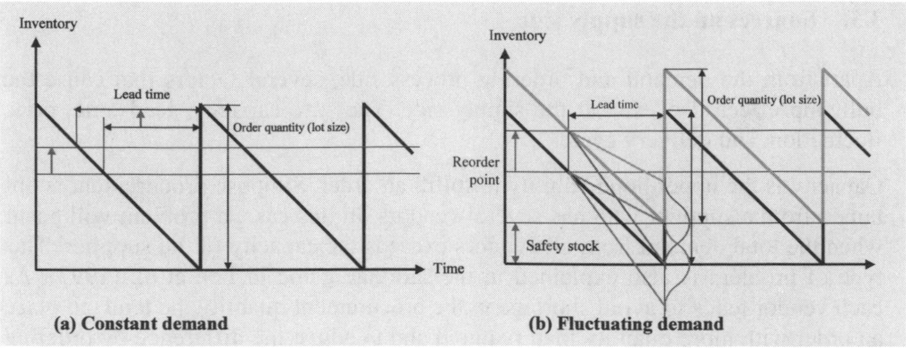

Fig. 6. Relationship between lead-time and change in inventory

Fig. 7 shows the relationship between a change in inventory cost and EOQ. As shown in Fig. 7, the inventory cost increases corresponding to the increase in price, the cost in placing an order will be comparatively reduced, causing the reduction in EOQ.

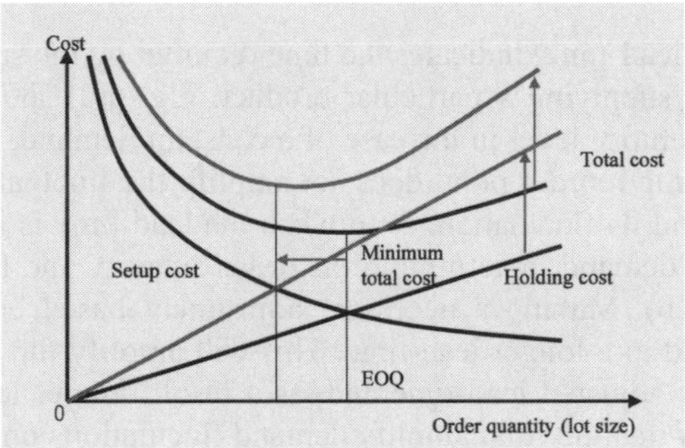

Fig. 7. Relationship between the change in inventory cost and EOQ

In contrast, a lower price might cause the EOQ to increase. Moreover, price fluctuations cause fluctuations in the order quantity as the EOQ to minimize total cost is affected by price fluctuations. Thus, demand fluctuations will be transmitted to the supply side in an amplified form.

The last factor at the supply side is the delivery cycle. The delivery cycle refers to a particular interval required by the supplier for two consecutive deliveries. As mentioned previously, the existence of an order cycle causes the bullwhip effect from the ordering process side. Similar to the order cycle, using a constant delivery cycle requires a consideration to supply a certain amount of quantity to fulfill the demand until the next delivery. Further, with fluctuating and uncertain demand, the timing and quantity of an order is based on a demand forecast. As also mentioned before, using a demand forecast to decide at the delivery quantity will amplify the fluctuation in demand. When no delivery cycle is determined, i.e. the interval between consecutive deliveries is variable, the differences between the actual demand and the demand forecast can be adjusted, even when the order and delivery quantities are based on demand forecasts.

4. Suppressing the bullwhip effect

In this section, several counter-measures for each source explained previously are discussed. Table 2 shows several methods that can be applied.

Sources		Method for suppressing the bullwhip effect
Demand	Demand fluctuation	Inventory as buffer
	Demand uncertainty	Information sharing (access sell-thru data)* Single control of replenishment* Lead-time reduction* Forecasting method Without forecasting in calculating order
	Penalty cost fluctuation	Special sales contract
Ordering process	Order cost	Accumulate assorted order
	Order cycle	Online CAO
	Lot (batch)	Computer Assisted Ordering (CAO) for reducing the transaction cost* Discount on assorted truckload, consolidation by 3rd party logistics* Regular delivery appointment*
	Ordering method	Ordering method that suppress fluctuations, small and constant order quantity, not using extreme value of forecast
Supply	Supply capacity	Allocate based on past sales* Shared capacity and supply information* Flexibility limited over time; capacity reservation* (free return) Multiple sources
	Lead-time	Setting additional delivery point Vendor Managed Inventory (VMI)
	Price fluctuation	Every Day Low Price strategy* Special purchase contract* Multiple sources
	Delivery cycle	Discount on assorted truckload, consolidation by 3rd party logistics* Regular delivery appointment*

*: Methods that are also mentioned in Lee et al. (1997)

Table 2. Methods for suppressing the bullwhip effect for each source

4.1. Counter-measures for sources on the demand side

First, managing the inventory as a buffer between the demand and supply side can be seen as a counter-measure for demand fluctuations, as it will absorb the fluctuation of demand, thus suppressing the fluctuation of the order quantity. Settling an inventory station between demand and supply diminishes the need for the supply side to deal with the fluctuation in demand. Dealing effectively with the demand fluctuation might lead to a significant reduction in inventory. However, if the buffer cannot completely absorb the demand fluctuation, it could become the cause for a bullwhip effect and lead to a significant loss on the supply side. From the tradeoff relationship between the loss caused by the bullwhip effect and the loss caused by holding an inventory, it is required to set an optimal order quantity and inventory level. Some studies are conducted to deal with this kind of fluctuation for a serial production type (Kimura and Terada, 1981). While some studies are also available for more complicated supply chains, they are still not conducted thoroughly and more studies are required.

To deal with demand uncertainty, Lee et al. (1997) give several counter-measures, such as information sharing (access sell-thru data), single control of replenishment and lead-time reduction. In addition, appropriate forecasting methods and calculating order quantities without forecasting can also be given as suitable counter-measures. With information sharing, all members in the supply chain have access to actual sales data at any time. Gavirneri and Tayur (1999), Iyer (1999), and Kerke et al (1999) analyze the influence and effectiveness of this kind of access. Further, as mentioned previously, using forecasting values to determine an order quantity and/or a lot with uncertain demand will transmit an amplified demand fluctuation to the supplier. However, it is still possible for the suppliers to avoid amplifying demand fluctuations if they have the same access to the sales data used as a base by the vendors.

Taking into consideration the next counter-measure, single control of replenishment, not only all members of the supply chain have access to the demand data in conducting information sharing, but also have one specific place to control all procurement activities. When the bullwhip effect occurs as a result of demand uncertainty, the procurement control method can be utilized to obtain the overall supply chain.

The third possible counter-measure refers to controlling or avoiding the bullwhip effect by reducing production and/or procurement lead-time. As known, forecasting future demand is required because of the existence of a positive lead-time. A long lead-time is increasing the forecasting error of fluctuation, enforcing the bullwhip effect. Thus, reducing the lead-time might reduce the amplification caused by demand uncertainty, leading to the possibility to suppress the bullwhip effect.

The fourth counter-measure for demand uncertainty refers to the method used by the members of the supply chain to forecast future demand. Choosing a suitable forecasting method that minimizes the forecast error can lead to sufficient control in suppressing the bullwhip effect. Further, taking the influence of the bullwhip effect into consideration in setting the required parameters in the utilized forecasting method can also suppress the bullwhip effect.

Determining the required order quantity without any forecasting can be regarded as another possible counter-measure to suppress the bullwhip effect. Among several possible methods in calculating orders without using demand forecast data, Kimura and Terada (1981) introduce the pull-type ordering system which uses actual consumption data to release the required order quantities. The effectiveness in using this kind of system to suppress the bullwhip effect has been studied by some researchers (Krajewsky et al., 1987; Rees et al., 1989; Sarker and Fitzsimmons, 1989; Takahashi et al., 1994a). However, even with this kind of system, the influence from actual demand fluctuations cannot be completely avoided. To deal with these particular fluctuations, it is required to keep sufficient inventory in each production point. Nevertheless, it is better to discontinue utilizing the forecasted amount as order quantity and switch to the above-mentioned pull-type ordering system to suppress the bullwhip effect. Subsequently, some literature evaluated the possibilities in integrating both the pull-type ordering system for some parts of the production process and letting the remaining parts to use the forecasted data in releasing an order, i.e. the push type ordering system (Hodgson and Wang, 1991a, b; Takahashi et al. 1991, 1994b; Gupta and Brennan, 1993; Takahashi and Soshiroda, 1996; Wang and Xu, 1997).

Lastly, special sales contracts can be suggested as a counter-measure for penalty cost fluctuation. As soon as penalty cost fluctuates, one tends to increase the inventory level when the forecasted cost in a particular period increases. Therefore, applying a sales contract to reduce the penalty cost by turning the order in that particular period to another period, for example by offering a lower price if an order is not placed at the end of the year, can be implemented.

4.2. Counter-measures for sources on the ordering process side

In this subsection, some possible counter-measures to deal with the sources on the ordering process side are discussed.

First of all, accumulating several products into one order can be seen as a counter-measure in decreasing the required order cost. By utilizing the computer's assistance, it is possible to hold the release of an order until several products are required. Subsequently, the cost per item will decrease, yielding to a reduction on order size and order interval. In the end, the accumulation might be able to suppress the amplification of the demand fluctuation. Further, more benefit can be expected if it is possible to gather a variety of products not only in one order, but also in one delivery.

For the second source, the order cycle, utilizing online computer assisted ordering (CAO) can be chosen as a counter-measure. The main factor that causes the necessity to have an order cycle or that lengthens that cycle, is the effort required by the supply side in conducting procurement activities and in processing a received order. By utilizing the online system, the above-mentioned efforts for both vendor and supplier are reduced as the procurement procedure is conducted by the computer. The reduction of the effort yields to a shorter order cycle. Subsequently, a suppression of the amplified fluctuation can be expected.

As an alternative for the above-mentioned CAO, Lee et al. (1997) suggested the use of discount on the assorted truckload, regular delivery appointment, etc., as counter-measures for the lot (batch) sources of the bullwhip effect. As mentioned, CAO allows sufficient control in accumulating the orders by lessening the effort needed to deal with large order units. Another advantage on the delivery side is the possibility to use assorted truckloads (different kind of products in one delivery) and regular delivery appointments. Hence, it can be expected that accumulating orders can be avoided.

Selecting an appropriate ordering method can be also regarded as a counter-measure for suppressing the bullwhip, for example, selecting small and constant size orders or methods that do not utilize an extreme forecast value even when orders fluctuate. The effectiveness in applying a pull-type ordering system or an integrated system can again become a reasonable counter-measure for this source of the bullwhip effect.

4.3. Counter-measures for sources on the supply side

When there is a capacity constraint on the supplier side and several vendors struggle to obtain a bigger portion, allocating supply to the vendors based on past sales will diminish the vendors' incentives to amplify order quantities beyond the actual demand. Similarly, applying the concepts of shared capacity and supply information will allow a good vendor to take other vendors' conditions under consideration and realize moderate procurement activities. Increasing the flexibility of the vendors will suppress their engagement in gaming and can be conducted in the form of a contract that increases the vendor's flexibility, e.g. with an unrestricted choice of order quantity, free return and generous order cancellation policies. Additionally, disposing of the multiple sources is another way to minimize the supply constraint of a single supplier.

As counter-measures for the second source on the supply side, i.e. lead-time, setting a delivery point and a vendor-managed inventory (VMI) can be suggested. To counter the amplification caused by lead-time, it is necessary to find an appropriate method to reduce the length of the lead-time. Establishing a delivery point and an inventory between the supplier and the vendor will absorb the fluctuation of demand and thus can suppress the bullwhip effect. It is also possible to build the supplier's inventory at the vendor's site as a VMI to reduce the required lead-time. Utilizing the VMI allows the vendor to take the required quantity according to the actual consumption, without considering the supplier's lead-time. Thus, the lead-time is reduced, and it becomes possible to suppress the bullwhip effect. However, it is still necessary for the supplier to hold a sufficient inventory in his own site and also at the VMI, as the lead-time to procure a particular product remains the same.

For the third source, i.e. price fluctuation, Lee et al. (1997) suggested an Every Day Low Price (EDLP) strategy and special purchase contracts as counter-measures. Apart from that, multiple sources can also be taken into consideration. With the EDLP strategy, the supplier is obligated to have a stabilized price over a finite time horizon to avoid amplified orders during the low price period. However, if the cost associated to stabilize the price is higher than the gains obtained from having a stabilized price, there is no need to apply this kind of policy. Similarly, making a special purchase contract with the vendor, where the vendor agrees to buy a large quantity of products at a discount price, but the products are delivered in multiple charges is a way of suppressing the supplier's price fluctuation. Further, procuring from multiple sources can impose price competition between suppliers in order to suppress price fluctuation.

Lastly, to handle the delivery cycle as source of the bullwhip effect, it is effective to use the counter-measures suggested for the lot factor source in the ordering process, i.e. discounts on assorted truckloads and regular delivery appointments. Moreover, a consolidation by third party logistics management is also considered effective to suppress the bullwhip effect. It is possible to reduce the delivery cycle if the third party logistics management is used, supported by having a contract on assorted and regular delivery.

5. Conclusions

In this paper, we classified the sources of the bullwhip effect, based on the position where they occur. Three different positions of the sources are the demand side, the ordering process side and the supply side. Subsequently, the counter-measures available to suppress the bullwhip effect are also discussed for each source. A bullwhip effect occurs when there is a gap between order and demand. This gap is the consequence of the policy taken by supply chain members, such as accumulating orders and using forecasts. It can be claimed that the bullwhip effect can be suppressed by avoiding or reducing the gap mentioned above by utilizing one or, if possible, several of these methods according to the organizational needs.

References

Baganha, MP., Cohen, MA. (1998): The stabilizing effect of inventory in supply chains. In: Operations Research 46: pp. S72-S83.

Bertrand, JWM. (1986): Balancing production level variations and inventory variations in complex production systems. In: International Journal of Production Research 24: pp. 1059-1074.

Brown, R.G. (1959): Statistical Forecasting for Inventory Control. Mc-Graw-Hill, New York.

Cachon, GP. (1999): Managing supply chain demand variability with scheduled ordering policies. In: Management Science 45: pp. 843-856.

Caplin, AS. (1985): The variability of aggregate demand with (S, s) inventory policies. In: Econometrica 53: pp. 1396-1409.

Chen, F. (1999): (R,NQ) policies in serial inventory systems. In: Quantitative models for supply chain management. pp. 71-109.

Chen, F., Ryan, JK., Simchi-Levy, S. (2000a): The impact of exponential smoothing forecasts on the bullwhip effect. In: Naval Research Logistics 47: pp. 269-286.

Chen F, Drezner Z, Ryan JK, Simchi-Levy S (2000b): Quantifying the bullwhip effect: The impact of forecasting, lead time and information. In: Management Science 46: pp. 436-443.

Dejonckheere, J., Disney, SM., Lambrecht, MR., Towil, DR. (2002): Transfer function analysis of forecasting induced bullwhip in supply chains. In: International Journal of Production Economics 78: pp. 133-145.

Forrester, J. (1961) Industrial dynamics. MIT Press, and John Wiley & Sons, Inc., New York.

Gavirneri, S., Tayur, SR. (1999):. Value of information sharing and comparison with delayed differentiation. In: Quantitative models for supply chain management. pp. 441-466.

Gupta, SM., Brennan, L. (1993): A knowledge based system for combined just-in-time and material requirement planning. In: Computers and Electrical Engineering 19: pp. 157-174.

Hiraki, S., Ichimura, T., Ishii, K., Naganuma, T., Ando, Y., Takahashi, K., Muramatsu, R. (1989): Low-inventory ordering systems for the international cooperative knockdown production systems. In International Journal of Production Research 27: pp. 831-846.

Hodgson, TJ., Wang, D. (1991a): Optimal hybrid push/pull control strategies for a parallel multistages system: Part 1. In: International Journal of Production Research 29: pp. 1279-1287.

Hodgson, TJ., Wang, D. (1991b): Optimal hybrid push/pull control strategies for a parallel multistages system: Part 2. In: International Journal of Production Research 29: pp. 1453-1460.

Holweg, M., Bicheno, J. (2002): Supply chain simulation – A tool for education, enhancement and endeavour. In: International Journal of Production Economics 78: pp. 163-175.

Iyer AV (1999): Modeling the impact of information on inventories. In: Quantitative models for supply chain management. pp. 337-357.

Jacobs, FR. (2000): Playing the beer distribution game over the internet. In: Production and Operations Management 9: pp. 31-39.

Kahn, JA. (1987): Inventories and the volatility of production. In: American Economic Review 77: pp. 667-679.

Kerke, S., Mukhopadhyay, T., Srinivasan, K. (1999): Modeling impacts of electronic data interchange technology. In: Quantitative models for supply chain management. pp. 359-379.

Kimbrough, SO., Wu, DJ., Zhong, F. (2002): Computers play the beer game: Can artificial agents manage supply chains? In: Decision Support Systems 33: pp. 323-333.

Kimura, O., Terada, H. (1981): Design and analysis of pull system: A method of multistages production control. In: International Journal of Production Research 19: pp. 241-253.

Krajewsky, LJ., King, BE., Ritzman, LP., Wong DS (1987): Kanban, MRP, and shaping the manufacturing environment. In: Management Science 33: pp. 39-57.

Larsen, NE., Alting, L. (1993): Criteria for selecting a production control philosophy. In: Production Planning and Control 4: pp. 54-68.

Lee, HL., Padmanabhan, V., Whang, S. (1997): Information distortion in a supply chain: The bullwhip effect. In: Management Science 43: pp. 546-558.

Riddalls, CE., Bennet, S. (2001): The optimal control of batched production and its effect on demand amplification. In: International Journal of Production Economics 72: pp. 159-168.

Rees, LP., Huang, PY., Taylor III., BW, (1989): A comparative analysis of an MRP lot-for-lot system and a Kanban system for amultistagess production operation. In: International Journal of Production Research 27: pp. 1427-1443.

Sarker, BR., Fitzsimmons, JA. (1989): The performance of push and pull systems: A simulation and comparative study, In: International Journal of Production Research 27: pp. 1715-1731.

Sterman, JD. (1989): Modeling managerial behavior: Misperceptions of feedback in a dynamic decision making experiment. In: Management Science 35: pp. 321-339.

Tabe, T., Muramatsu, R., Tanaka, Y. (1980): Analysis of production ordering quantities and inventory variations in a multistages production ordering system. In: International Journal of Production Research 18: pp. 245-257.

Takahashi, K., Soshiroda, M. (1996): Comparing integration strategies in production ordering system. In: International Journal of Production Research 44: pp. 83-89.

Takahashi, K., Muramatsu, R., Ishii, K. (1987): Feedback method of production ordering system inmultistagess production and inventory systems. In: International Journal of Production Research 25: pp. 925-941.

Takahashi, K., Hiraki, S., Soshiroda, M. (1991): Estimating inventory variance with the batch means method. In: International Journal of Production Research 25: pp. 23-33.

Takahashi, K., Hiraki, S., Soshiroda, M. (1994a): Flexibility of production ordering system. In: International Journal of Production Research 32: pp. 1739-1752.

Takahashi, K., Hiraki, S., Soshiroda, M. (1994b): Pull-push integration in production ordering system. In: International Journal of Production Economics 33: pp. 155-161.

Tersine (1985): Production/Operation Management: Concepts Structure, & Analysis. 2nd ed., North-Holland.

Wang, D. and Xu, CG. (1997): Hybrid push/pull control strategy simulation and its application. In: Production Planning and Control 8: pp. 142-151.

PART III

Supply Chain Management and Advanced Planning

Aggregation of Mixed Integer Production Models by Shadow Prices in Supply Chain Management

Christoph Schneeweiß and Erich Kleindienst

Chair of Operations Research
University of Mannheim
L 5, 6
D-68131 Mannheim, Germany

Abstract: *In supply chain management production planning is often separated into several planning levels. These levels have different degrees of detail and are usually connected by aggregation-disaggregation devices. Particularly aggregate parameters, like aggregate holding cost and capacity consumption rates, are to be determined in an optimal way. Following the aggregation levels of the traditional (MIT) hierarchical production planning approach we are analysing different aggregation devices for an aggregate linear capacity adaptation model and an adjoining detailed mixed integer production model. In particular, focusing on the aggregation of demand we are developing two aggregation procedures in using shadow prices of the inventory balance constraints. An extensive numerical investigation is comparing these new aggregation devices for mixed integer models with the more traditional approaches based on an aggregation of work content and on even simpler aggregation procedures in practice.*

Keywords: *hierarchical production planning, distributed decision making, shadow prices*

1. Introduction

Aggregation and disaggregation is one of the main concerns of production planning. This became more than obvious already in the seminal work on hierarchical production planning (HPP) in the late nineteen seventies (e.g., see [Hax/Meal 1975], [Bitran et al. 1981], [Hax/Candea 1984]). Today, the complexity of the planning task in modern supply chain management (SCM) even more requires production models to be split up at least into a medium-term and a short-term problem. These models cannot be treated independently from each other but are connected simply because the medium-term model is mainly an aggregate of the short-term detailed model.

Many attempts have been made in the nineteen eighties (e.g., see [Zipkin 1979], [Axsäter 1981], [Leisten 1998]), to analyze the aggregation-disaggregation problem. The analysis was restricted to LP models, i.e., both the aggregate and the detailed model were assumed to be linear and the aggregation was performed by an aggregation of columns and/or rows. Thus the often cumbersome solution of the detailed model could be replaced with the far simpler solution of the aggregate model.

The results particularly Zipkin and Axsäter established may essentially be summarized as follows: In case aggregation weights are chosen appropriately, Zipkin has shown that the optimal value of the objective function of the aggregate model is equal to the optimal value of the objective function of the detailed (non-aggregated) model. In general, however, feasibility of the disaggregation of the aggregate solution cannot be guaranteed, i.e., there is no guarantee for *consistency*. Axsäter formulates necessary but not sufficient conditions guaranteeing a feasible disaggregation of the aggregate optimal solution in multi-stage production planning. In particular, in case of a one-stage production planning situation, for aggregation weights not being period-dependent Axsäter can show [Axsäter 1981] that feasibility is assured. However, there is usually no guarantee for optimality.

The problems one usually encounters in practice, though, are more involved than those analyzed in the early studies. Typically, the detailed model is not linear but one has to account for setups for which the derived results are no longer applicable. Moreover, stochastics is involved and there is even information asymmetry between the detailed and the aggregate model. Finally, and this is an important observation, production planning is not really interested in aggregation-disaggregation problems but simply in aggregation-allocation problems. To be more specific: on the detailed level one is calculating the actual production plan whereas at the medium-term level capacities are determined. These capacities are then allocated to manufacture the individual products.

Confining the discussion to a detailed short-term mixed integer production planning problem and to an adjoint aggregate medium-term linear capacity planning problem, one has a setting that is typical of many practical applications. Particularly modern SCM and production planning and control (PPC) software with its medium-term and short-term level (e.g., see APO [SAP-APO 2000] or RHYTHM

(Trade Matrix) [RHYTHM 1999]) has to solve the aggregation problem. This problem, however, is not properly addressed but is left for the customer. Thus it is the customer's task, e.g., to feed the software with appropriate aggregate cost parameters and capacity consumption rates. Moreover, the classical HPP model of Hax and Meal ([Hax/Meal 1975]) does not provide a solution either, since in their basic HP model the non-realistic assumption is made that all detailed parameters are equal so that an aggregation becomes trivial and is no issue.

A particular problem occurs for the aggregation of demand. In this case it becomes obvious that the often encountered device of simply adding numbers of units usually will not work. What seems at least to be necessary is to aggregate demand according to its work content. But even this type of aggregation might be questioned.

What is, therefore, the rationale an aggregation is based on? Obviously, it seems to be reasonable to design an aggregation device such that the overall performance of the system is optimized. Thus, optimization and aggregation have to be performed simultaneously. This is obvious since one of the very reasons for an aggregation is to reduce complexity, which of course should be achieved without losing too much optimality. The aggregation design, proposed in this paper, of employing shadow prices in aggregating demand is exactly along these lines.

The proposed approach uses Zipkin's and Axsäter's results. In the case of a multi-period production planning model a criteria-oriented aggregation of a detailed model using Zipkin's LP-aggregation requires a simultaneous aggregation of columns and rows. Clearly, an aggregation of demand results in an aggregation of all inventory balance equations that belong to a particular period and product group (aggregation of rows). On the other hand, in aggregating production and inventory variables, one has the usual column aggregation.

In contrast to the continuous case, shadow prices can no longer be calculated exactly but must be approximated. As in the LP-aggregation the proposed approach uses an iterative algorithm to adapt capacity decisions and aggregation weights in order to optimize the overall performance of the system. Furthermore, Axsäter's result of a consistent disaggregation of an aggregate solution is taken into account by period-independent aggregation weights, which represents a necessary but not sufficient condition for consistency.

To analyze the aggregation problem let us rely on a comparatively simple setting to be stated in Section 2. Section 3 will then place the problem into the general frame of distributed decision making (DDM). Next, in Section 4, we present a new method which is based on aggregation weights being dependent on the shadow prices for the constraints defined by the inventory balance equations. Carrying out an extensive numerical analysis, Section 5 compares the proposed procedure with the traditional approaches. Finally, the last section summarizes the results and points to some open questions left for further research.

2. Problem statement and traditional solutions

Before analyzing the aggregation problem in more general terms, let us first define the production planning situation we are focusing on. Let us investigate the typical two-stage production planning situation in which capacities are determined on the medium-term level whereas production quantities are chosen on an adjoint short-term level. Usually the medium-term model works with parameters that are aggregates of the short-term model. This latter (detailed) model describes setups and is therefore taken to be a mixed integer model while the aggregate model is assumed to be a typical linear capacity planning model. The aggregate model works with product groups whereas the detailed one is based on individual products. Let us start with the detailed model.

2.1. Detailed production model

Consider a short-term lotsizing model with sequence-independent setup costs and setup times and let us assume the individual products to be grouped into product groups yielding the following mixed integer programming model. For each product group i an independent model can be formulated.

Let us use the following indices, parameters, and decision variables.

Indices:

j product, $j \in J^i$

t period, $t = 1, ..., T$

i product group, $i = 1, ..., n$

J^i set of all products j belonging to product group i (preassigned)

Data and parameters:

d_{jt} forecast of demand in period t of product j

a_j capacity consumption rate of product j

h_j unit holding cost of product j

$y_{j0}^{L'}$ initial stock of product j

c_j^s setup cost per setup of product j

s_j setup time per setup of product j

K_{it} capacity provided by the aggregate level for period t (see ($A7$))

Decision variables:

y_{jt} product lotsize of j in t

y^L_{jt} inventory of j in t

δ_{jt} setup indicator

For each group i $(i = 1, \ldots, n)$ one has

$$C_i = \min \left[\sum_{j \in J^i} \sum_t (h_j y^L_{jt} + c^s_j \delta_{jt}) \right] \qquad (D1)$$

s.t.

$$y^L_{jt} = y^L_{j,t-1} + y_{jt} - d_{jt} \qquad \forall j \in J^i, t \qquad (D2)$$

$$y^L_{j0} = y^{L'}_{j0} \qquad \forall j \in J^i$$

$$\sum_{j \in J^i} (a_j \cdot y_{jt} + s_j \delta_{jt}) \leq K_{it} \quad \forall t \qquad (D3)$$

$$y_{jt} \leq M \delta_{jt} \qquad \forall j \in J^i, t \qquad (D4)$$

$$y_{jt}, y^L_{jt} \geq 0 \qquad \forall j \in J^i, t \qquad (D5)$$

$$\delta_{jt} \in \{0, 1\} \qquad \forall j \in J^i, t$$

$$M := \max_{jt} y_{jt} \qquad \forall j \in J^i, t$$

The objective function $(D1)$ minimizes the detailed inventory holding and setup costs while the decision field consists of the inventory balance equations $(D2)$, and the capacity constraints $(D3)$ taking into account capacity consumption rates a_j and setup times s_j. The detailed production model allocates the medium-term capacity K_{it} to the individual products, and hence $(D3)$ is representing the so-called coupling condition [Schneeweiss 1999] which decribes the top-down influence of the medium-term model. Note that in order to guarantee feasibility within the iterations of the algorithm to be described in Section 3, the short-term detailed production model will be allowed to make use of additional capacity of group i (see Eqs. $(D1')$ and $(D3')$ below).

2.2. Aggregate production model

To determine capacities, let us take the following LP model of which the parameters are aggregates of the detailed model and the variables are representing product groups.

Aggregate decision variables:

x_{it} lotsize of product group i at t

x_{it}^L inventory of product group i at t

K_t medium-term capacity at t

K_t^+ capacity expansion at t

K_t^- capacity reduction at t

Data and parameters:

$\bar{d}_{it}$ aggregate forecast of demand of product group i in period t

$\bar{a}_i$ aggregate consumption rate of product group i

$\bar{h}_i$ aggregate unit holding cost of product group i

k unit cost of capacity

c^+ capacity extension

c^- capacity reduction

$K^{+\max}$ maximum capacity expansion per period

$K^{-\max}$ minimum capacity expansion per period

K_0' initial capacity

$$\bar{C} = \min\left[\sum_t \left(kK_t + c^+K_t^+ + c^-K_t^- + \sum_i \bar{h}_i x_{it}^L\right)\right] \quad (A1)$$

s.t.

$$K_t = K_{t-1} + K_t^+ - K_t^- \ \forall t \quad (A2)$$

$$K_t^+ \leq K^{+\max} \quad \forall t \quad (A3)$$

$$K_t^- \leq K^{-\min} \quad \forall t$$

$$K_0 = K_0' \quad (A4)$$

$$x_{it}^L = x_{i,t-1}^L + x_{it} - \bar{d}_{it} \quad \forall i,t \quad (A5)$$

$$x_{i0}^L = x_{iT}^L \quad \forall i$$

$$\sum_i \bar{a}_i x_{it} \leq K_t \quad \forall t \quad (A6)$$

$$x_{it}, x_{it}^L, K_t, K_t^+, K_t^- \geq 0 \quad \forall i,t$$

The objective function $(A1)$ minimizes aggregate inventory holding and capacity costs. The decision field consists of the capacity balance equation (A2), limitation of capacity expansion and reduction (A3), initial capacity (A4), inventory balance equation ($A5$) and the capacity constraint ($A6$).

The *instruction* (i.e., the top-down influence of the capacity model on the production model i) is given by

$$IN_i^* := K_{it} = K_t \frac{\bar{a}_i x_{it}^*}{\sum_{i'} \bar{a}_{i'} x_{i't}^*} \quad \forall i,t \tag{A7}$$

with the star denoting (here and subsequently) an optimal value. Because of a limited capacity reduction and/or possibly of a high cost of capacity extension and reduction, surplus capacity can appear. Surplus capacity is allocated among the product groups according to its proportional capacity usage. Note that in allocating capacity to product group i the aggregate consumption rate $\bar{a}_i$ is needed.

2.3. Coupling of the aggregate capacity model and detailed production model

The aggregate model and the detailed model are closely connected by a top-down and a bottom-up coupling device. The top-down coupling is simply given by the allocation of capacity as specified in the instruction ($A7$). This instruction is influencing the decision space of the detailed model $i = 1,\ldots,n$ through the capacity relation ($D3$). The bottom-up coupling is far more involved. It is achieved by an aggregation procedure. All parameters $(\bar{h}_i, \bar{a}_i)$ of the medium-term model (except k) are aggregates of the short-term parameters, and the same holds for medium-term demand $(\bar{d}_{it})$.

In aggregating the parameters, let us adopt a linear aggregation rule, i.e., for the aggregate holding cost parameters let us take

$$\bar{h}_i := \sum_{j \in J^i} g_{ij}^L h_j \qquad \forall i \tag{1}$$

and for the aggregate consumption rates

$$\bar{a}_i := \sum_{j \in J^i} g_{ij}^a \left(a_j + \frac{s_j}{\bar{y}_j}\right) =: \sum_{j \in J^i} g_{ij}^a a'_j \qquad \forall i. \tag{2}$$

The weights g_{ij}^L and g_{ij}^a actually describe the bottom-up influence and are taken to be linear functions of the detailed solutions to be defined in Eqs. (6) and (7) below. In Eq. (2), the detailed capacity consumption rate a_j is increased by a mean setup time $\frac{s_j}{\bar{y}_j}$ with

$$\bar{y}_j := \frac{\sum_t y_{jt}}{\sum_t \delta_{jt}} \qquad \forall j \tag{3}$$

describing the average lotsize of product j resulting in the modified consumption rate

$$a'_j := a_j + \frac{s_j}{\bar{y}_j} \qquad \forall j. \tag{4}$$

For the weights g^L_{ij} and g^a_{ij} and the way how *demand* is aggregated let us consider two prominent schemes:

(1) the addition of demand, the so-called '*addition approach*', and

(2) the addition of the work content of demand, the so-called '*work content approach*'.

(1) Addition approach (*AA*)

The addition approach simply aggregates demand in taking the sum of demand of all products comprising a group:

$$\bar{d}_{it} := \sum_{j \in J^i} d_{jt} \qquad \forall i,t \tag{5}$$

and for the weights let us take

$$g^L_{ij} := \frac{\sum\limits_t y^L_{jt}}{\sum\limits_{j' \in J^i} \sum\limits_t y^L_{j't}} \qquad j \in J^i \quad \forall i \quad \text{and} \tag{6}$$

$$g^a_{ij} := \frac{\sum\limits_t y_{jt}}{\sum\limits_{j' \in J^i} \sum\limits_t y_{j't}} \qquad j \in J^i \quad \forall i. \tag{7}$$

The weight g^L_{ij} describes the relative amount of stock product j is holding within the product group i. Similarly, the weight g^a_{ij} describes the percentage of the production quantity of product j within product group i. Hence, in aggregating we assume that the contribution of detailed holding cost h_j and consumption rate a_j is proportional to product $j's$ amount of inventory and production, respectively.

Our numerical analysis will study this scheme in more detail. Clearly, for non-linear (MIP) models, particularly the 'naive' addition of numbers of product units (Eq. (5))

will heavily depend on how a unit of a product is defined. To avoid this difficulty, one does often find in practice not a simple addition of units but an addition of their work content.

(2) Work content approach (*WA*)

According to Eq. (4), the work content of demand $d_{jt}(j \in J^i)$ may be approximated by $a'_j d_{jt}$ such that, for group $i, i = 1, \ldots, n$, one has the (total) work content of demand in period t

$$\bar{d}^w_{it} := \sum_{j \in J^i} a'_j d_{jt} \quad \forall i, t. \tag{8}$$

Since demand is expressed in work content, the aggregate holding cost $\bar{h}^w_i$ is adapted to cost per capacity unit. According to Zipkin's LP-Aggregation [Zipkin 1979], let us take

$$\bar{h}^w_i := \frac{\sum\limits_{j \in J^i} \sum\limits_t h_j y^L_{jt}}{\sum\limits_{j \in J^i} \sum\limits_t a'_j y^L_{jt}} \qquad \forall i \tag{9}$$

which represents the share of cumulated holding cost related to the work content of the entire amount of stock of product group i. This may likewise be expressed by

$$\bar{h}^w_i := \sum_{j \in J^i} g^{L^w}_{ij} h_j \tag{10}$$

with

$$g^{L^w}_{ij} := \frac{\sum\limits_t y^L_{jt}}{\sum\limits_{j' \in J^i} \sum\limits_t a'_{j'} y^L_{j't}} \qquad \forall j \in J^i, i. \tag{11}$$

Clearly, for the aggregate consumption rate $\bar{a}^w_i$ one has

$$\bar{a}^w_i = \frac{\sum\limits_{j \in J^i} \sum\limits_t a'_j y_{jt}}{\sum\limits_{j \in J^i} \sum\limits_t a'_j y_{jt}} = 1. \tag{12}$$

Again, this type of aggregation will be analyzed numerically in Section 5.

Before introducing an aggregation based on shadow prices, let us first discuss the aggregation-allocation problem in more general terms.

3. Aggregation as a particular DDM problem

For a deeper understanding of the aggregation-allocation problem it seems to be appropriate to discuss the problem within the framework of distributed decision making (DDM) [Schneeweiss 1999]. Indeed, the detailed and aggregate model constitute a DDM problem with the aggregate model being responsible for determining the capacity while the detailed model calculates lotsizes. The separation of the two types of decisions may be understood as a seggregation of a simultaneous model in which the capacity and the production quantities are determined simultaneously. This model may be formulated as follows:

$$TC = \min\left\{\sum_t (k \cdot K_t + c^+ K_t^+ + c^- K_t^- + \sum_j \sum_t (h_j y_{jt}^L + c_j^s \delta_{jt})\right\} \qquad (S1)$$

s.t.

$$\begin{aligned}
K_t &= K_{t-1} + K_t^+ - K_t^- && \forall t \\
K_t^+ &\leq K^{+\max} && \forall t \\
K_t^- &\leq K^{-\max} && \forall t \\
K_0 &= K_0'
\end{aligned}$$

$$y_{jt}^L = y_{j,t-1}^L + y_{jt} - d_{jt} \qquad \forall j,t \qquad (S2)$$

$$y_{j0}^L = y_{j0}^{L'} \qquad \forall j$$

$$\sum_j (a_j \cdot y_{jt} + s_j \delta_{jt}) \leq K_t \qquad \forall t \qquad (S3)$$

$$y_{jt} \leq M\delta_{jt} \qquad \forall j,t$$

$$\begin{aligned}
y_{jt}, y_{jt}^L, K_t, K_t^+, K_t^- &\geq 0 && \forall j,t \\
\delta_{jt} &\in \{0,1\} && \forall j,t \\
M &:= \max_{jt}\, y_{jt} && \forall j,t.
\end{aligned}$$

There are mainly three reasons for separating the simultaneous model into an aggregate medium-term and a detailed short-term model. First, the separation usually reduces computational complexity, secondly, the aggregate model is of conceptual importance and may be used to formulate aggregate aims and restrictions, and thirdly, the DDM model can easily be employed to accommodate informational asymmetry. As to the second reason, conceptual aspects are of predominant importance in practice. Obviously, longer-term decisions should not be influenced by any small detail of the short-term situation. Hence, it is necessary to have some reliable aggregate values on which more general considerations could be based. This is not only true for some aggregate financial indicators but often even more for properties like stability, robustness, or flexibility of a longer-term decision. Particularly, production theory (e.g., see [Fandel 1991]) with its medium-term Leontief production functions provides a prominent example for a more general, less detailed, description of production processes.

As to the third aspect mentioned above, aggregation is closely related to the information that is needed and is available at the aggregate level. For our particular production situation, generally, the capacity decision has to be made earlier, and therefore usually is made under a poorer state of information than the production decision. This latter observation goes beyond the model formulation we presented in the last section. Indeed, within a more realistic context, the detailed model should be understood as an anticipated model which describes the production situation as it appears at the time when the capacity decision has to be made. Since we are focusing on the pure aggregation problem, however, and not on arguments for performing an aggregation we do not intend to discuss this additional aspect in the present investigation (but, e.g., see [Schneeweiss 1999], Chapter 6).

Hence, we are left here with the first reason for separating the simultaneous model, i.e., the computational aspect. Indeed, in aggregating, the simultaneous model with its mixed integer variables (δ_{jt}) can be split up into n problems involving only $|J^i| \cdot T$ variables. This computational advantage may compensate the suboptimality which goes along with the separation and aggregation procedure. Suboptimality is caused by essentially three closely related effects, (1) the way how items j are grouped, (2) the way how they are aggregated, and (3) the way how the hierarchical system of the aggregate and detailed model is solved.

(1) Clustering items to groups depends on the particular production setting. Generally, the parameters associated with the individual items should not be too diverse.

(2) The aggregation of parameters and of demand has been described in the previous section and is assumed to be linear, employing weights determined by the optimal solution of the detailed models. Though these parameters are optimized in accordance with the optimization of the entire hierarchical system, they still depend on the specific (linear) aggregation rule and the whole solution procedure.

(3) The solution procedure itself might not be optimal. In principle, the detailed model (of group i) might be solved for each numerical value of the instruction, i.e., in performing a complete enumeration, for each capacity vector $\{K_{i1}, \dots, K_{iT}\}(i = 1, \dots, n)$, a detailed production model could be optimized and the result could be evaluated in terms of the aggregate model. Clearly, for higher dimensional K-vectors, this approach is computationally rather demanding. Hence, we use a search procedure which explicitly accounts for the decision space of the aggregate model. In particular, we are employing a so-called negotiation-oriented algorithm (see [Schneeweiss 1999], Chapter 3). This algorithm consists of the the following 4 steps:

(Step 1) Calculate a solution of the detailed model

(Step 2) Calculate aggregate parameters

(Step 3) Calculate a solution of the aggregate model

(Step 4) Calculate the instruction ($A4$), insert the instruction in Eq. ($D3$) of the detailed model and go to (1)

As mentioned in Section 2.1, feasibility of the detailed production model of group i within the iterations of the algorithm is not guaranteed. Hence, the detailed production model will be allowed to make use of additional (positive) capacity ΔK_{it}. Besides, the model represents a constructional hierarchy such that the same capacity cost k is applied as in the aggregate model and capacity extension and reduction is considered as well. Thus, the criterion of the detailed production model (D1) is replaced with

$$C_i = \min[\sum_{j\in J^i} \sum_t (h_j y_{jt}^L + c_j^s \delta_{jt}) + k \cdot \Delta K_{it} + c^+ \Delta K_{it}^+ + c^- \Delta K_{it}^-], \qquad (D1')$$

and the capacity constraint ($D3$) becomes

$$\sum (a_j y_{jt} + s_j \delta_{jt}) \leq K_{it} + \Delta K_{it} \qquad \forall t. \qquad (D3')$$

Furthermore, the additional capacity balance equations are added

$$\Delta K_{it} = \Delta K_{it-1} + \Delta K_{it}^+ - \Delta K_{it}^- \quad \forall t$$
$$\Delta K_{i0} = 0.$$

The capacities ΔK_{it} are considered in the capacity constraint of the aggregate model in replacing equation ($A6$) by

$$\sum_i (\bar{a}_i x_{it}) + \overline{\Delta KN}_t \leq K_t \qquad \forall t \qquad (A6')$$

with $\overline{\Delta KN}_t$ defined as

$$\overline{\Delta KN}_t = \sum_i \Delta K_{it} \qquad \forall t$$

representing the overall additional capacity of the detailed production model of all product groups in period t. Note that $\overline{\Delta KN}_t$ is a constant in ($A6'$). Within the iterations of the algorithm, $\overline{\Delta KN}_t$ is adapted by exponential smoothing in order to support the convergence of the negotiation-oriented algorithm.

Clearly, the algorithm could result in a suboptimal solution, which will be one of the questions to be investigated in the subsequent numerical analysis in Section 5. Before doing so, the next section will analyze the second reason for a possible suboptimality, i.e., the specific aggregation device, particularly regarding the aggregation of demand.

4. Aggregation of demand by shadow prices

As stated in Section 3, let us now introduce a third way of aggregating demand. This approach is a criteria-oriented aggregation taking the capacity usage and the cost situation into account. More specifically, it uses the shadow prices of the inventory balance equations of the detailed production model. Let us first, in Section 4.1, give some general comments on the aggregation of demand by shadow prices and let us then focus on two approximations of obtaining shadow prices for mixed integer programs.

4.1. Some general considerations

Aggregation of demand by shadow prices is similar to the approach of the traditional LP-aggregation (e.g., see [Zipkin 1979]). In contrast to the LP-aggregation, however, for our aggregation/allocation problem the aggregate model is not derived from a detailed model in simply aggregating variables. Indeed, both models need not and should not be of the same structure. While the aggregate model is linear, this is not the case for the detailed model.

For given shadow prices u_{jit} related to the dynamic demand constraints ($D2$), let us sketch an outline of the general idea of aggregating demand. According to [Axsäter 1986], in enabling consistency of the aggregate solution, let us work with period-independent shadow prices:

$$u_{ji} := \frac{\sum_{t=1}^{T} u_{jit}}{T} \qquad \forall j,i \tag{13}$$

such that

$$\bar{d}_{it}^{sh} = \sum_{j \in J^i} u_{ji} d_{jt} \qquad \forall i,t \tag{14}$$

with $\bar{d}_{it}^{sh}$ representing the aggregate demand expressed by shadow prices. Since demand is expressed by shadow prices, cost and production parameters must be adapted. According to Zipkin's LP-aggregation one obtains

$$\bar{a}_i := \frac{\sum_{j \in J^i} \sum_t a'_j y_{jt}}{\sum_{j \in J^i} \sum_t u_{ji} y_{jt}} \qquad \forall i, \tag{15}$$

representing the share of the cumulated capacity usage of all products belonging to the same product group related to the cumulated production measured in shadow price units. The aggregate consumption rate can also be expressed by

$$\bar{a}_i := \sum_{j \in J^i} g_{ij}^{a^{sh}} a'_j \tag{16}$$

with

$$g_{ij}^{a^{sh}} = \frac{\sum_t y_{jt}}{\sum_{j' \in J^i} \sum_t u_{j'i} y_{j't}} \qquad \forall j \in J^i, i. \tag{17}$$

Due to satisfaction of demand in the detailed model (see Eq. (D5)), the overall production quantity of a product is equal to the overall demand within the production horizon, i.e.,

$$\sum_t y_{jt} = \sum_t d_{jt} \qquad \forall j, \tag{18}$$

and hence $g_{ij}^{a^{sh}}$ may be expressed by

$$g_{ij}^{a^{sh}} = \frac{\sum_t d_{jt}}{\sum_{j' \in J^i} \sum_t u_{j'i} d_{j't}} \qquad \forall j \in J^i, i. \tag{19}$$

Similarly, aggregate holding cost $\bar{h}_i$ is calculated as

$$\bar{h}_i := \frac{\sum_{j \in J^i} \sum_t h_j y_{jt}^L}{\sum_{j \in J^i} \sum_t u_{ji} y_{jt}^L} \qquad \forall i, \tag{20}$$

which represents the share of the cumulated holding cost of all stock belonging to the same product group related to the cumulated stock of that product group expressed in shadow price units. Aggregate holding cost may again be expressed by

$$\bar{h}_i := \sum_{j \in J^i} g_{ij}^{L^{sh}} h_j \tag{21}$$

with

$$g_{ij}^{L^{sh}} = \frac{\sum_t y_{jt}^L}{\sum_{j' \in J^i} \sum_t u_{j'i} y_{j't}^L} \qquad \forall j \in J^i, i = 1, \ldots, n. \tag{22}$$

The main problem with the 'shadow price aggregation' is the determination of the dual in case of integer variables. Therefore the next section is investigating this particular problem.

4.2. Approximation of shadow prices in mixed integer programs

Shadow prices in mixed integer programs do not provide appropriate information to aggregate demand, since a marginal change of the right-hand side does not necessarily have an impact on the value of the objective function. In general, shadow prices in mixed integer programs are not easy to determine. The usual relationship between primal and dual linear programs, e.g., the complementary slackness condition, does not hold (e.g., see [Williams 1993]). Several approaches have been proposed but none of practical usefulness. For example, cutting-plane algorithms can be applied to solve mixed integer programs and to determine shadow prices. However, the shadow prices of the generated cuts cannot appropriately be interpreted [Gomory/Baumol 1960].

Therefore, let us describe two approaches to derive at least suitable approximations. The first is an approximation in using *average* setup costs and setup times, the so-called *average shadow price approach.* In the second approach we calculate an optimal solution of the detailed model (for each product group) and fix the binary variables in the mixed integer program by their optimal values. The resulting linear program is then used to calculate dual variables. This approach will be called *local shadow price approach.*

(1) Average shadow price approach (ASA)

To determine approximate shadow prices in the average approach, the mixed integer (detailed) production model is solved (possibly only heuristically) and average unit setup times and setup costs are calculated. These parameter values are then employed to linearize the mixed integer production model and shadow prices are determined. To be more specific, the approach replaces the capacity relation ($D3$) with the stationary continuous expression

$$\sum_{j \in J^i} (a_j y_{jt} + s_j \frac{y_{jt}}{\bar{y}_j}) \leq K_{it} \qquad \forall t \tag{23}$$

with $\bar{y}_j$ defined as

$$\bar{y}_j := \frac{\sum_t y^*_{jt}}{\sum_t \delta^*_{jt}} \qquad \forall j \tag{24}$$

and y^*_{jt} and δ^*_{jt} being optimal product lotsize and setup indicator of product j in period t, respectively.

In fact, using (23) is in line with ideas employed in the Hax/Meal approach (see the 'family' model in their investigation [Hax/Candea 1984]).

(2) Local shadow price approach (LSA)

In this second procedure we first solve (possibly heuristically) the mixed integer model. Then, in a second step, all binary variables are fixed to the determined optimal values ending up in a linear program, the so-called 'residual LP' (see [Appa 1997]). Finally the residual LP is solved resulting in approximate shadow prices.

Compared with the first approach, these approximate shadow prices are based on a particular *(local)* solution, while the first approach uses average parameter values

$\frac{s_j}{\bar{y}_j}$. These values may be derived from the same integer solution but, of course, (24) is not restricted to this particular integer solution but could have been obtained by a whole class of 'similar' solutions. This has the effect that different detailed solutions may result in the same average setup costs and setup times.

5. Numerical investigations

In the previous sections four different approaches of aggregating demand have been presented. The intention of the numerical investigation now is to compare these approaches, in order to clarify five questions:

(1) Which approach leads to the best results in case of low, medium and high setup costs or setup times?

(2) What is the impact of heterogeniety within a product group?

(3) What is the influence of the type of demand?

(4) What is the impact of modifying the capacity extension and reduction costs?

(5) What are the differences in computing time?

To analyze these questions, the aggregate and detailed production model have to be specified.

5.1. Specification of the model

Let us first specify the aggregate model and then the detailed one.

(1) The *aggregate* production model is taken to be a single-stage, multi-period, deterministic medium-term limited capacity adaptation model on the basis of product groups and one capacity resource. For the first three investigations, we restrict the analysis to one product group. In the last investigation we then consider two product groups consisting of two and three products, respectively. A planning horizon of 12 months in the first three investigations is assumed, whereas for the fourth investigation the horizon is randomly chosen between 9 and 12 periods. Unit capacity cost k, capacity expansion cost c^+ and reduction cost c^- as well as initial capacity K_0^I are given in table 1. All remaining data specifying criteria and decision space is determined by the aggregation procedure and defined on the detailed level.

k	c^+	c^-	K_0^I
10	4	4	20

Table 1. Capacity-related parameters

(2) The *detailed* production model is taken to be a single-stage multi-period production planning model with sequence-independend setup costs and times. The product group consists of two products. Capacity consumption rates a_j and holding costs h_j are summarized in Table 2.

Product j	1	2
a_j	0.01	2.00
h_j	2.00	0.01
h_j/a_j	200	0.005

Table 2. Capacity consumption a_j and holding cost h_j

Two different demand patterns are considered: almost linear increasing demand and almost saisonal demand. Table 3 shows the linear demand pattern 1 and Table 4 the saisonal demand pattern 2. $\bar{d}_t$ denotes aggregate demand in adding detailed demand, and $\bar{d}_t^w$ represents the aggregated demand by work content.

t	1	2	3	4	5	6	7	8	9	10	11	12
d_{1t}	20	40	60	80	100	120	140	160	180	200	220	240
d_{2t}	1	4	1	1	1	1	1	1	1	1	1	1
$\bar{d}_t$	21	44	61	81	101	121	141	161	181	201	221	241
$\bar{d}_t^w$	2.2	8.4	2.6	2.8	3.0	3.2	3.4	3.6	3.8	4.0	4.2	4.4

Table 3. Demand pattern 1

The seasonal demand is given in Table 4 representing demand patterns being shifted against each other. (Note that in order to allow the addition method to be meaningful we assume units of a comparable size.)

t	1	2	3	4	5	6	7	8	9	10	11	12
d_{1t}	20	40	60	80	100	120	140	120	100	80	60	40
d_{2t}	4	2	1	1	1	1	1	1	1	1	2	4
$\bar{d}_t$	24	42	61	81	101	121	141	121	101	81	62	44
$\bar{d}_t w$	8.2	4.4	2.6	2.8	3.0	3.2	3.4	3.2	3.0	2.8	4.6	8.4

Table 4. Demand pattern 2

In the first numerical investigation, the suitability of the four different approaches is especially investigated with respect to the impact of setups. Hence, for each demand pattern nine problem instances are defined being characterized by different setup times and setup costs. The problem instances differ in no, medium, and high setup times and costs, respectively (Table 5). Medium setup times and costs require at least three setups of a product within the planning horizon while high setup times and costs need at least two setups.

Setup Costs / **Setup Time**	**No**		**Medium**		**High**	
	0	0	1000	80	3000	160
No	0	0	0	0	0	0
	0	0	1000	80	3000	160
Medium	10	50	10	50	10	50
	0	0	1000	80	3000	160
High	40	200	40	200	40	200

Table 5. Setup costs and setup times

In the fourth investigation, parameter settings are randomly generated. All parameters are realizations of uniformly distributed random variables defined on the intervals given in Table 6. Detailed demand d_{jt} is determined as a product of saisonality factor f^{l}_{jt} multiplied by the realization of a uniform distributed random variable z_j defined in Table 6.

	Lower Limit	**Upper Limit**
Periods	9	12
Products within product group 1	2	2
Products within product group 2	3	3
Demand	30	70
Saisonality factor	0.4	5.0
Setup cost	2	20
Setup time	2	30
Consumption rate	0.01	4
Holding cost	0.01	4
Capacity cost	5	15
Capacity extension cost	2	10
Capacity reduction cost	2	10

Table 6. Generation of parameters

5.2. Results for the specified set of parameters

Let us first analyze a situation that is specified by the parameter sets defined in Tables 1 to 5. Subsequently, in Section 5.3 we then extend the analysis to the far richer set of parameters defined in Table 6.

5.2.1. The impact of setup times and setup costs

This investigation analyzes, for the specific setting of Tables 1 to 5, the different approaches in case of no, of medium, and of strong seasonality, respectively.

(1) Demand Pattern 1

Table 7 shows the numerical results of the nine problem instances in case of linearly increasing demand. Each Problem is solved in employing the four different approaches, i.e. aggregation of demand by addition (AA), by work content (WA) and, by the two approximations of shadow prices (ASA) and (LSA). As benchmark we take the overall cost of the simultaneous model in terms of overall cost defined by (TC) (see Eq. (S1)).

Setup time \ Setup cost	no		medium		high	
no	1,13	1, 08	1,04	1,03	1,02	1,03
	1,00	1,00	1,03	1,03	1,02	1,02
medium	1,73	1,31	1,12	1,09	1,07	1,06
	1,33	1,33	1,07	1,08	1,05	1,05
high	1,83	1,29	1,23	1,18	1,17	1, 15
	1,43	1,30	1,17	1,17	1,13	1,14

Legend:

AA	WA
ASA	LSA

Table 7. Cost deviation from the simultaneous model: linear increasing demand

For small and medium setup times, the aggregation of demand by the local shadow price approach is causing the smallest cost deviation. However, in case of high setup times and medium and high setup costs, it is the aggregation by work content (WA) that turns out to perform best. The aggregation of demand by addition shows almost always the greatest cost deviations from the simultaneous model.

Let us now analyze the result in more detail.

No setup costs and setup times

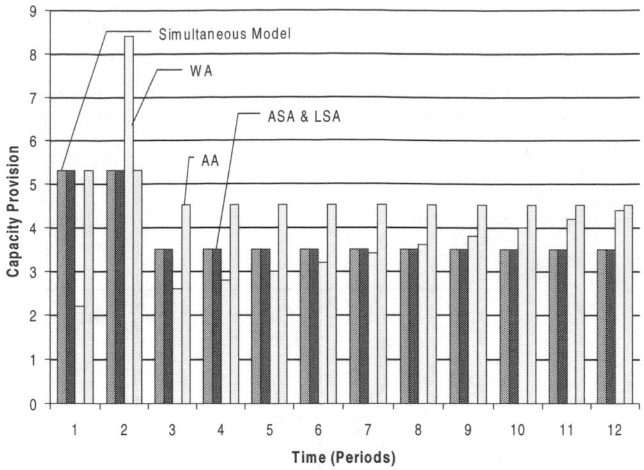

Fig. 1. Capacity provision in case of no setup costs and setup times

In case of the linear setting, Fig. 1 shows the optimal capacity provision being determined by the different approaches of aggregation of demand together with the simultaneous model. The closer the capacity decision $K^{SM} := (K_1^{SM}, ..., K_T^{SM})$ of the simultaneous model is to the capacity decision being determined by the different approaches, the smaller are capacity and holding cost incurred by the detailed model. The different approaches have to consider that the increasing demand of product 1 causes only little capacity usage and that it is preferable to produce product 2 in advance in order to satisfy the demand peak in the first period by providing additional capacities. Note that product 2 has low holding cost compared to product 1 (see Table 2).

Both shadow price approaches (ASA and LSA) lead to the same capacity provision as the optimal model. The work content approach (WA) provides capacity according to the capacity demand and does not provide additional capacity in period 1 for the production of product 2. Moreover, the addition approach provides an almost constant capacity provision, since this approach only considers the required capacity of the products within the product group by an average aggregate consumption rate. Because of the required satisfaction of demand and no setup costs and times in case of the addition approach, the aggregation weights (7) only depend on the detailed demand, i.e., (7) is to be replaced by

$$g_{ij}^a := \frac{\sum_t d_{jt}}{\sum_{j' \in J^i} \sum_t d_{j't}} \quad j \in J^i, \ \forall i.$$

In order to fulfill the increasing demand, production is shifted to earlier periods resulting in unused capacity in periods 3 to 7. Note that in this scenario almost in all cases the addition approach leads to worse results than the other approaches.

High setup costs and times

Fig. 2 shows the result in case of high setup costs and high setup times. Due to the high setup times and setup costs, the simultaneous model allocates the required capacity in period 1, 6 and 10 such that the demand is produced in these periods. Because of the linearization, all aggregation approaches provide capacity in all periods. Especially, the addition approach (AA) provides too much capacity in all periods. The shadow price approaches (ASA and LSA) yield the least cost deviation from the simultaneous model while the work content approach leads to slightly worse cost deviations.

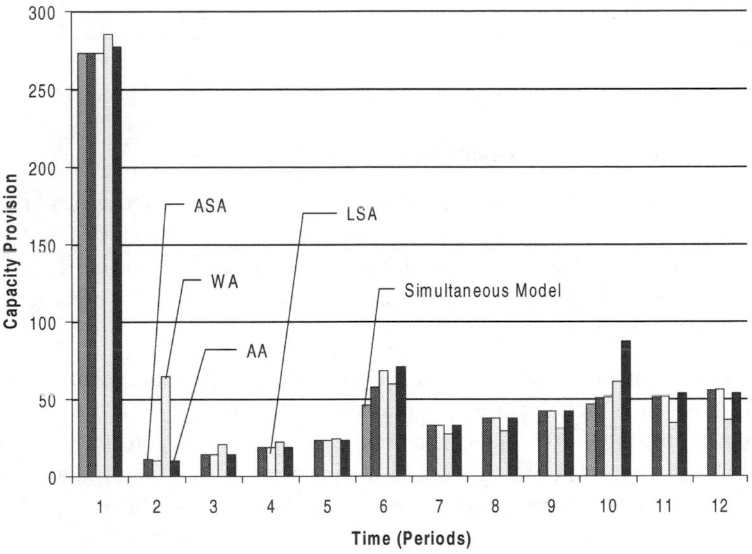

Fig. 2. Capacity provision in case of high setup costs and times

(2) Demand Pattern 2

Table 8 shows the numerical results of the 9 problems in case of seasonal demand. Note that the average shadow price approach (ASA) is suitable in almost all cases. Only in case of low setup costs and high setup times the work content approach leads to significantly better results. Again, the addition approach (AA) shows almost always the greatest cost deviations from the simultaneous model, due to the wrong calculation of the required capacity.

Setup time \ Setup cost	no		medium		high	
no	1,08	1, 16	1,09	1,09	1,07	1,06
	1,00	1,00	1,09	1,09	1,06	1,06
medium	1,79	1,54	1,15	1,15	1,10	1,10
	1,61	1,57	1,12	1,12	1,08	1,08
high	1,73	1,38	1,26	1,25	1,19	1,22
	1,33	1,36	1,20	1,19	1,16	1,16

Legend:	
AA	WA
ASA	LSA

Table 8. Deviation from the simultaneous model: demand pattern 2

5.2.2. The impact of heterogeneity within a product group

In the numerical investigation of the previous section, the characteristics of the products within the product group do vary significantly, e.g., product 1 has relative holding cost of 200, whereas product 2 has only a value of 0.005 (see Table 2). Let us therefore compare the aggregation procedures in relation to the heterogeneity of the product group.

Apart from inventory holding cost and consumption rates, all data corresponds to the specification of the model. Different parameter settings $p = 1, \ldots, 8$ are investigated: In parameter setting 1 of Table 9 inventory holding cost and consumption rates are equal to 1, i.e., relative holding costs of the products within the product group are taken to be the same. Subsequently, the relative holding cost of product 1 is continuously increased whereas the relative holding cost of product 2 is continuously decreased. Note that inventory holding costs and consumption rates of parameter setting 5 correspond to the initial parameter setting in Table 2. Besides, high setup cost and times are applied and demand has the demand pattern 1.

p	1	2	3	4	5	6	7	8
h_1	1.00	1.10	1.30	1.80	2.00	2.50	3.00	5.00
h_2	1.00	0.70	0.40	0.02	0.01	0.01	0.01	0.01
a_1	1.00	0.70	0.40	0.02	0.01	0.01	0.01	0.01
a_2	1.00	1.10	1.30	1.80	2.00	2.50	3.00	5.00
h_1/a_1	1.00	1.571	3.250	90.0	200.0	250.0	300.0	500.0
h_2/a_2	1.00	0.636	0.308	0.011	0.005	0.004	0.003	0.002

Table 9. Heterogeneity within a product group

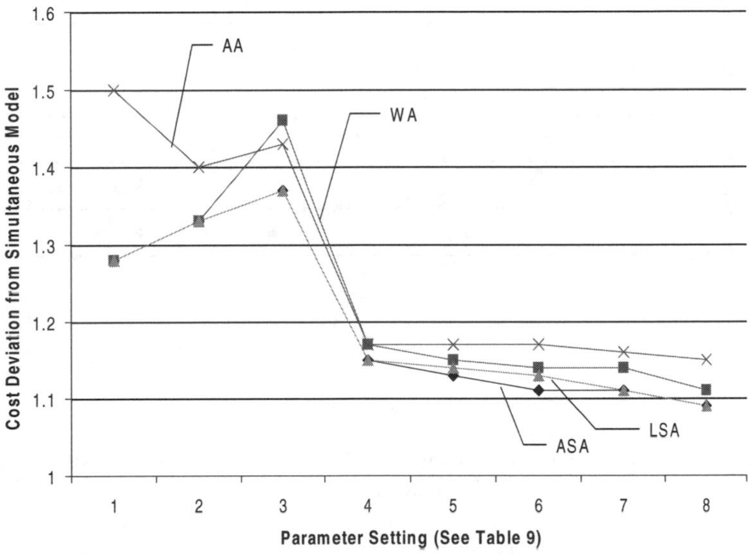

Fig. 3. Cost deviation from simultaneous model in case of heterogeneity

Fig. 3 shows the cost deviation of the different approaches from the simultaneous model. Note that because of different setup times and setup costs within the product group there is still a heterogeneity even in case of the same consumption rates and inventory holding costs (see parameter setting 1). In parameter setting 1 the addition approach performs worse than the other approaches, since this approach only considers the required capacity of the products within the product group by an average aggregate consumption rate. Increasing heterogeneity within the product group (parameter settings 2 to 8), the addition approach and the work content approach are more sensitive to an increase in heterogeneity. In the example the shadow price approaches always outperform the traditional approaches.

5.2.3. The impact of capacity extension cost and reduction cost

The aggregation approaches are influenced by the capacity extension and reduction costs. High capacity extension and reduction costs in comparison to the capacity cost lead to fewer changes of the capacity provision and to a higher level of stock. Fig. 4 shows the cost deviation of the different approaches from the simultaneous model by changing concurrently the capacity extension and reduction costs, i.e. $c = c^+ = c^-$. High setup costs and times as well as increasing demand pattern 1 are assumed.

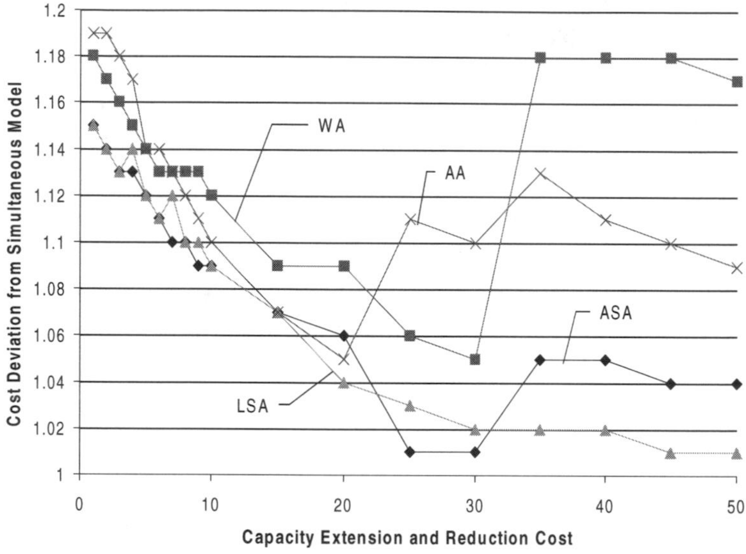

Fig. 4. Cost deviation from simultaneous model for different capacity extension and reduction costs

Generally, increasing extension and reduction costs cause lower cost deviations from the simultaneous model since capacity provision is smoothed and can therefore better be approximated by the aggregate production model. The shadow price approaches (ASA and LSA) outperform the other approaches which provide too much capacity especially in case of high extension and reduction costs resulting in higher cost.

5.3. Investigations using randomly generated parameter settings

We are now broadening the analysis in not restricting the investigation to just one specific parameter set but in considering a large number of sets being randomly generated.

In Section 3 it has been pointed out that the main reason for an aggregation is the limited computing capacity. This aspect, however, is not obvious in the previous numerical investigations. Up to now, in the considered model all products have been aggregated into one product group. The detailed production model has the same number of binary variables as the simultaneous model. It must usually be solved several times using the negotiation-oriented algorithm. Hence, there is no advantage regarding computing time. However, if the aggregate capacity planning considers several product groups, a remarkable advantage occurs: Since all products use the same capacity, aggregate capacity planning decides on the allocation of common capacity and is able to assign appropriate capacity to each product group. Thus, the detailed overall production model is separated into product groups such that the number of binary variables is significantly reduced compared to the simultaneous model.

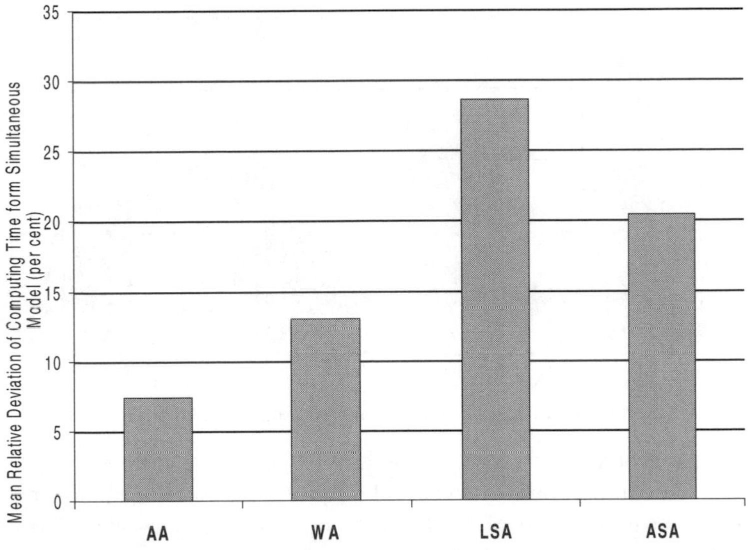

Fig. 5. Relative deviation of computing time from the simultaneous model

The subsequent investigation shows the advantage of the aggregation approaches. Similarly to the previous section, 60 test cases are randomly generated. Two product groups are considered consisting of two and three products, respectively.

Fig. 5 shows the deviation in computing time of the aggregation models as compared to the simultaneous model. For each aggregation approach the average computing time is shown. The coefficient of variation turns out to be almost identical for all four approaches.

The advantage of the aggregation approaches are obvious since these approaches need on average only 16% of the computing time of the simultaneous model. The addition approach leads to the shortest computing time of 8% of the simultaneous model. On the other hand, the average shadow price approach needs on average 19% of the computing time of the simultaneous model. This is because the shadow price approaches (ASA and LSA) need more iterations to converge. On the average, the shadow price approach requires 24.8 iterations while for the addition approach it is only 11.3. However, as shown in Fig. 6, the latter approach leads to better results than the other three approaches.

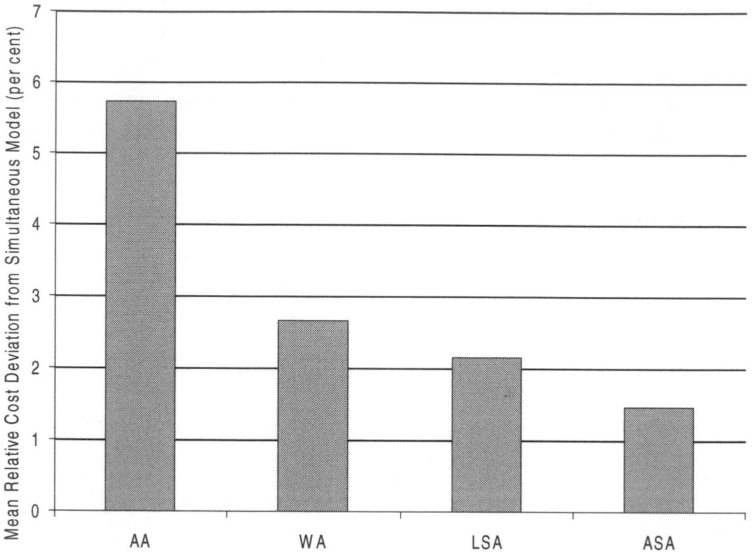

Fig. 6. Mean cost deviation from the simultaneous model

Fig. 6 gives a general impression of the advantages of the different approaches. The results are still preliminary since only a particular class of models has been analyzed and a careful statistical analysis has not yet been completed. The results, however, plainly show that the shadow price aggregation procedures are approaches that should be taken into account seriously.

6. Summary and concluding remarks

The paper analyzed different aggregation procedures for an aggregate linear capacity adaptation model and a detailed mixed integer production model. In particular, we were focusing on the open question of aggregating demand. We introduced two aggregation procedures which employ shadow prices of inventory balance equations and evalutated the performance of these new procedures with an extensive numerical investigation.

In case of a linear detailed production model, the advantage of the shadow price approach is obvious. If the composition of aggregate demand changes during the planning horizon and the products have different capacity consumption rates, the *addition approach* does not consider the changing demand of capacity. In the *work content approach*, on the other hand, this issue is taken into account by expressing demand by work content. Moreover, if aggregate demand consists of products having different relative inventory holding costs, the contribution of demand to the overall (dual) criteria is not visible any more to both the addition approach and the approach of adding the work content. Only the shadow price procedure differentiates between products having a substantial influence and those having only a minor impact on the overall performance.

If the detailed model is not linear, but accounts for setups, the main problem is the determination of appropriate approximations for the shadow prices. Two approaches are discussed in the paper: the average approach and the local approach. Generally, in addition to the capacity usage and the holding cost, the resulting shadow prices consider setup costs as well. Hence, the impact of average setup costs is considered in aggregate demand such that a better capacity adaptation decision may be expected than in the traditional approaches.

In our numerical investigation we could show that, in general, the (average) shadow price approach performed rather satisfactoy and gave superior results. As to the computing time the average approach needed about 20% of the time necessary for the simultaneous model which is about twice as much for the work content approach and three times larger as for the simple addition approach. Clearly, these results heavily depend not only on the structure of the models being investigated but also on the particular numerical values of the parameters. For models consisting of more than two product groups, the positive effects of saving computing time will increase considerably. Generally, the results show that in a specific practical setting it turns out to be highly advisable to particularly analyze the performance of the shadow price aggregation procedures.

In our investigation we mainly justified aggregation caused by the computational difficulties to solve the simultaneous model. In using aggregations, however, we had to accept several approximations. These are, first, the approximate calculation of shadow prices, secondly, the advice of taking a linear aggregation and, thirdly, the application of the possibly suboptimal negotiation-orientied algorithm. Thus focusing only on computational aspects, for particular situations, there might be approximate procedures that do not rely on aggregations. Thus, to a certain extent, our investigations are of a preliminary nature.

The full significance of our results my be seen in case of situations determined by information asymmetry between the capacity and the production model in which the aggregation model has an independent real meaning. The same holds, e.g., for performance criteria that may only be defined on aggregate variables. In these cases aggregation cannot be avoided and hence, the way to aggregate becomes of crucial importance. Investigations considering these more general settings are on the way.

References

Appa, G. 1997. The use of linear programming duality in mixed integer programming. In: IMA Journal of Mathematics Applied in Business and Industry 8, pp 225-242.

Axsäter, S. 1981. Aggregation of product data for hierarchical production planning. In: Operations Research 29, pp 744-756.

Axsäter, S. 1986. On the feasibility of aggregate production plans. In: Operations Research 34, pp 796-800.

Bitran, G., Haas, E., and Hax, A. 1981. Hierarchical production planning: A single stage system. In: Operations Research 29, pp 717-743.

Fandel, G. 1991. Theory of production and cost. Springer, Heidelberg.

Gomory, R.E., Baumol, W.J. 1960. Integer programming and pricing. In: Econometrica 28, pp 521-550.

Hax, A.C., Meal, D. 1975. Hierarchical integration of production planning and scheduling. In: Geisler, M.A. (ed.), Logistics, TIMS studies in the Management Sciences, North Holland, Amsterdam.

Hax, A.C., Candea, D. 1984. Production and Inventory Management, Prentice-Hall, Englewood Cliffs, N.J.

Leisten, R. 1998. An LP-aggregation view on aggregation in multi-level production planning. In: Annals of Operations Research 82, pp 413-434.

RHYTHM 1999. Supply Chain Management Software Package of i2, http://tradematrix.com.

SAP-APO 2000. SAP - Advanced Planner and Optimizer, http://www.sap.com.

Schneeweiss, Ch. 1999. Hierarchies in distributed decision making. Springer, Heidelberg.

Williams, H.P. 1993. Model building in mathematical programming. Wiley, Chichester.

Zipkin, P.H. 1979. Aggregation in Linear Programming. Ph. D. Thesis, Yale University, New Haven.

Customer Orientation in Advanced Planning Systems

Bernhard Fleischmann, Herbert Meyr

Department of Production and Logistics
University of Augsburg
Universitaetsstr. 16
D-86135 Augsburg, Germany

Abstract: *Customer satisfaction is a major objective of Supply Chain Management. This also applies to "Advanced Planning Systems" (APS), computerized planning systems which try to support the various planning processes to be tackled in supply chains. "Order Promising" and "Demand Fulfillment" software modules of these systems are helpful in promising short and reliable customer order delivery dates and in tracking customer orders along the whole process between order entry and order delivery.*

However, the corresponding planning tasks at and after the interface between forecast-driven and order-oriented planning have found little attention in the scientific literature up to now. Even a clear statement of the planning requirements and the definition of proper objectives are still open issues. The following paper identifies such planning tasks and shows their varying importance for different lines of business by means of the decoupling point concept. Mathematical optimization models are presented which may be helpful for both understanding the planning functions and improving the quality of customer related software modules within APS.

Keywords: *demand fulfillment, available-to-promise, advanced planning systems*

1. Introduction

Various definitions of *Supply Chain Management* (SCM) can be found in the scientific world and they sometimes differ substantially. However, most of them agree with Christopher (1992, p. 24) that "the ultimate purpose of any logistics system is to satisfy customers" and that customer satisfaction is one of the central issues of SCM. The SCM euphoria of the mid and late nineties also promoted the rise of *Advanced Planning Systems* (APS), computerized systems that try to support the planning of supply chains by means of mathematical methods of Operations Research (OR). Thus it is not surprising that APS also claim to particularly take care of customers or, more precisely, of customer orders.

APS have a common, modular structure which is shown in Fig. 1 (see Meyr et al., 2002). Usually, they consist of several software modules which try to support the various short- to long-term logistical planning tasks of supply chains, occurring within procurement, production, distribution or sales, for example. *Strategic Network Planning* modules tackle long-term strategic network design issues like determining the locations and sizes of suppliers, plants and stocking points. *Demand Planning* mainly deals with sales forecasting, but also what-if-analyses of planned promotions or the determination of safety stocks are within the domain of these modules. *Master Planning* modules coordinate the mid-term material flow of the supply chain as a whole, i.e. between suppliers, plants, distribution centers and customers, and balance working time against seasonal stocks. *Purchasing & Material Requirements Planning* should care about short-term relations with suppliers, e.g. supplier selection and ordering of material. However, these planning tasks are only seldom supported by APS. The tasks of short-term *Production Planning* and *Scheduling* are, for example, machine assignment, lot-sizing, sequencing and scheduling. Planning methods of these modules particularly have to fit the organizational needs of the production system under consideration. *Distribution* and *Transport Planning* deal with the determination of delivery areas, the deployment (see Sect. 3.3.), vehicle loading and vehicle routing. The information flow between these modules usually is coordinated by means of Hierarchical Planning (see Fleischmann et al., 2002).

Last but not least, there are normally also modules for *Demand Fulfillment* (i.e. taking care about customer orders after they enter a company's planning system) *& ATP*, which exclusively serve the purpose of customer satisfaction. These modules match the available inventory and projected supply (the so-called *available-to-promise (ATP)* quantities), which have been triggered by forecasts for potential future sales, with the arriving customer orders. For example, they check whether a customer order is technically feasible, and they promise the customer a soon and hopefully reliable delivery date for his order (*order promising*). This task of great practical importance has first been tackled by the software providers. In the early times of APS there was a sense of insecurity among academics what these modules are able to do and serve for. In the meantime, the capabilities of these modules are fairly well known and it turned out that their theoretical basis is rather poor. Demand fulfillment is a

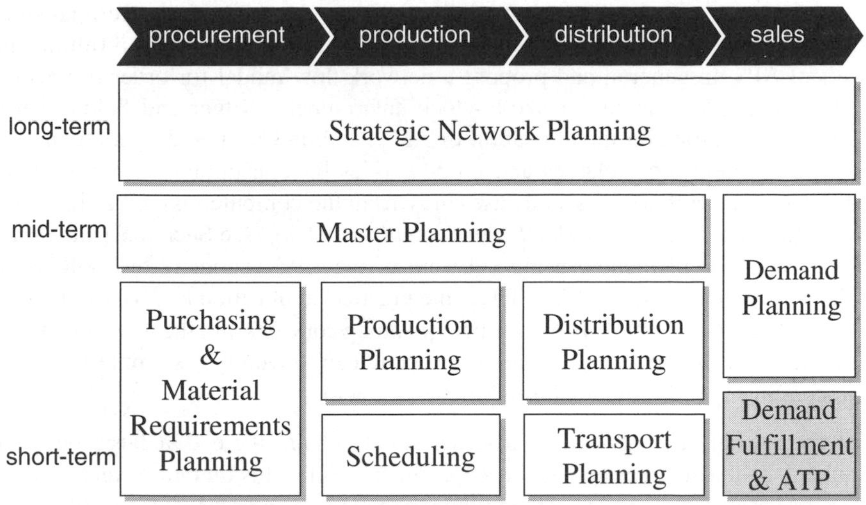

Fig. 1. Structure of Advanced Planning Systems (see Meyr et al., 2002)

topic which has largely been neglected in the scientific literature — at least, as far as OR models and methods are concerned. Since the extent, to which customer orders penetrate into a supply chain, varies for different lines of business and different types of supply chains, there is still some confusion what the planning tasks of demand fulfillment actually are. As we will see in the following, the decoupling point concept will help to answer this question.

The term "available-to-promise" is not a new term that came up together with APS. Schwendinger (1979) already showed that ATP can be used to improve customer service and discussed the relation to the master production schedule. However, demand fulfillment and order promising/ATP calculation were and are quite underrepresented in most textbooks on production and operations management. Some exceptions are, for example, Fogarty et al. (1991, p. 139 ff.), Günther and Tempelmeier (2003, Chapt. 15) and Vollmann et al. (1997, p. 214 ff.), who discuss methods and show examples for the ATP calculation and consumption (see also Sect. 3.1.). Günther and Tempelmeier (2003) also propose a model for the batch allocation of several orders to unassigned stock in a single product, make-to-stock environment (see Sections 4.1. and 4.2.). Vollmann et al. (1997, Chapt. 8) furthermore discuss the impact of different positions of the decoupling point (see Sect. 2.) on demand management, in general. Fischer (2001) comprehensively reviews ATP related work, classifies the different planning tasks concerning ATP and proposes and tests two methods for *shortage planning* (see Sect. 3.4.) on the basis of practical data from the consumer goods industry.

Most publications on ATP, however, are motivated by APS. First, handbooks and white papers of software vendors, introducing the Demand Fulfillment & ATP modules of their APS, have to be mentioned. Additionally, Knolmayer et al. (2002,

Sect. 3.1.5) present the ATP functionality of APO, the APS of the German software company SAP. Fleischmann and Meyr (2003) discuss the demand fulfillment tasks of APS, in general, and propose a network flow model for order promising and shortage planning in a make-to-stock environment. Kilger and Schneeweiss (2002b) concentrate on the allocation of ATP, resulting from an aggregate master plan, to different order classes and propose rules for consuming this "allocated" ATP. The same authors present a case study from the computer assembly industry, where (besides others) the tasks *demand-supply matching* (see Sect. 3.3.) and *order promising* are implemented using software of the APS vendor i2 technologies (Kilger and Schneeweiss, 2002a). The same practical application is also taken up by Fleischmann et al. (2002). They compare planning concepts and the role of demand fulfillment for the two supply chain types computer assembly (assemble-to-order) and consumer goods manufacturing (make-to-stock).

For the special case of a make-to-order supply chain, there is a large body of literature on due date setting and order promising. Since this literature can be easier classified using explanations of the following sections, an overview of such literature is postponed to Sect. 4.4.

The literature on demand fulfillment and ATP, as discussed above, lack a general theoretical foundation. Based on the decoupling point concept, this paper intends

- to identify and structure the various planning tasks of demand fulfillment with regard to decisions and objectives,
- to define more precisely the terms ATP and *capable-to-promise (CTP)*, which are quite often used in a vague sense by APS vendors and in the scientific literature, and
- to present linear (LP) and mixed integer programming (MIP) models that optimize the decisions within demand fulfillment and allow an easier understanding of the different planning tasks concerned.

Section 2. discusses the role of the decoupling point for demand fulfillment. To stress the differences, only the three quite opposite types of decoupling points "make-to-stock", "assemble-to-order" and "make-to-order" are compared in this paper. Section 3.1. presents two workflows illustrating the planning processes to be executed when (re-)calculating ATP/CTP and when new customer orders arrive. Sections 3.2. to 3.4. then introduce the different planning tasks of demand fulfillment, namely "order promising", "demand-supply matching" and "shortage planning", and discuss their varying relevance with respect to the three types of decoupling points. In Sect. 4., LP and MIP models for the different decoupling points are proposed.

2. Influence of decoupling points

In order to allow a proper definition of "demand fulfillment" and its various planning tasks, the concept of decoupling points — to our knowledge going back to Sharman

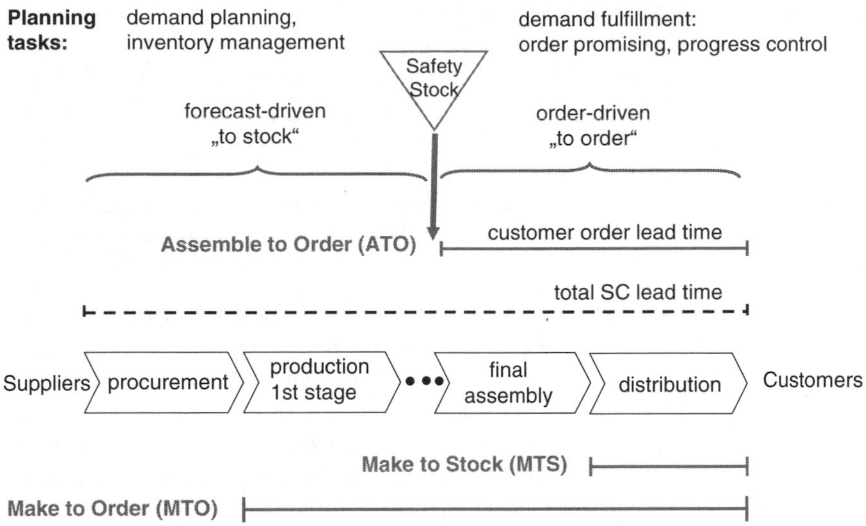

Fig. 2. MTO, ATO and MTS decoupling points

(1984) and Hoekstra and Romme (1991) — has to be introduced first. Figure 2 shows some of the logistical processes (e.g. procurement, production, distribution) that have to be tackled when managing supply chains. These processes can be subdivided into *order-driven* and *forecast-driven* ones. Order-driven processes are triggered by customer orders, i.e. they are only started if a customer order has arrived. For the forecast-driven (logistical and planning) processes, customer orders are not yet known and thus have to be anticipated by means of demand forecasts. The interface between order-driven and the forecast-driven processes is called a *decoupling point* (or *order penetration point*) of this member.

In order to hedge against forecast errors, a safety stock should be installed. Thus, a decoupling point usually also entails a stocking point. Forecast-driven processes upstream from the decoupling point push products into this stock and thus are called "to stock" processes, whereas customer orders pull products out of this stock. Thus, the order-driven processes downstream from the decoupling point are also denoted as "to order" processes.

The time between the order entry and the delivery of the products to the respective customer is called the *customer order lead time* or *service time*. It equals the duration of fulfilling all order-driven processes downstream from the decoupling point and therefore depends mainly on the position of the decoupling point, which may vary substantially for different lines of business and different types of supply chains. For example, in case of an *assemble-to-order* (ATO) decoupling point, all final products are assembled and distributed on basis of customer orders, but the component stock at the decoupling point is refilled on basis of demand forecasts. The upper part of Fig. 2 shows an example for this situation. In a *make-to-stock* (MTS) supply chain, *all products* are made to stock, so that the service time consists only of the lead time for the distribution, usually 1–3 days. In a *make-to-order* (MTO) situation, however, *all production processes* (incl. pre-assembly) are driven by orders. By refining the process model of the supply chain, further decoupling points can be defined. For example, Hoekstra and Romme (1991, p. 7) also distinguish between *purchase-and-make-to-order* decoupling points (where the service time equals the total SC lead time) and *make-and-ship-to-stock* decoupling points (where final items not only are made to stock and stored centrally, but also shipped to regional warehouses on basis of forecasts).

Both type and value of stocks vary depending on the position of the decoupling point. Whereas in MTS supply chains expensive final items have to be stored, in ATO supply chains cheaper components and in MTO supply chains just raw materials have to be held in inventory. Altogether, the position of the decoupling point has serious impacts on planning. The shorter the service time is, the more important forecast-driven planning tasks, i.e. demand planning (e.g. forecasting) and inventory management (e.g. safety stock planning), are. On the other hand, the longer the service time is, the more crucial are order-driven planning tasks — subsumed under the generic term "demand fulfillment". Here, tasks like promising reliable delivery dates to customers (order promising) or guiding and tracking orders through all order-driven processes (order management and progress control) are comprised. The aim of this paper is to better define these tasks, to show their distinct applications for different positions of decoupling points and to propose mathematical models representing these different applications.

The position of the decoupling point is sometimes pre-defined by technological restrictions and the type of business. For example, speciality machinery *can only* be made to order. However, quite often there is a choice where to locate a decoupling point and what service time to offer to a customer. However, this *strategic* planning problem is not a concern of demand fulfillment and of this paper. Note that different decoupling points can be installed for different types of final products. Furthermore, decoupling points may even vary with respect to different markets or different customer groups being addressed. Thus, it is nothing unusual, that the same product is made to order for a regional market and to stock for a foreign market. In this case, only a certain part of the overall customer orders are known at the time of production and the rest has to be forecasted. As soon as such a mixture of orders and forecasts has to be considered, the decoupling point concept seems not to be very useful any longer (Meyr, 2002). However, since this paper aims at providing general insights, the above simplification — to distinguish between *either* forecast-driven *or* order-driven processes — is not crucial. Furthermore, it is sufficient to restrict ourselves to the three "pure" decoupling points MTO, ATO and MTS introduced in Fig. 2.

A characteristic of the MTS and ATO supply chains is that the major bottleneck for the demand fulfillment are the available stocks (of finished products and components, respectively). For MTS this is even the only bottleneck, since the processes downstream from the decoupling point, i.e. just the delivery to the customers, are usually not restricted. However, in the ATO case (and for any decoupling point between the pure MTO and MTS), there may be an additional restriction by the capacity of the assembly process. But in the MTO case, the demand fulfillment is mainly restricted by the capacities of the machines and the flow times through a maybe complex multistage production system. In the vast literature on MTO order promising and due date setting (see Sect. 4.4.) usually no availability of stock is considered.

The focus of this paper is on MTS and ATO. In these cases, demand fulfillment is based on *available-to-promise (ATP) quantities*, i.e. the stocks on hand or projected stocks at the decoupling point that are not yet assigned to promised customer orders. For ATO, one has also to consider the *capable-to-promise (CTP) quantities*, i.e. the remaining capacity of the assembly lines, if this capacity is a potential bottleneck. More precise definitions and the calculation of ATP and CTP quantities are explained in the next section.

3. Planning tasks

In the Subsections 3.2. to 3.4. the different planning tasks and planning processes of demand fulfillment are discussed. Before, Section 3.1. explains some common notions and procedures, in particular the ATP/CTP calculation and two workflows where it is embedded.

3.1. Generic workflows

The left-hand side of Fig. 3 presents the *ATP/CTP recalculation workflow*, the right-hand side the *order entry workflow*.

The **ATP/CTP recalculation workflow** computes ATP and CTP quantities, that can be consumed by new (customer or production) orders arriving at the decoupling point. This workflow is used when ATP and CTP quantities are calculated for the first time or when they need to be re-calculated because the input data have been updated or unforeseen events in the supply or demand processes have occurred, e.g. delays of the projected supply or cancellations of already committed orders by the customers.

Input data for the workflow are

- already committed (promised), but not yet fulfilled orders on the demand side and
- inventory on hand and projected supply of products (for ATP) and
- projected capacity of resources (CTP)

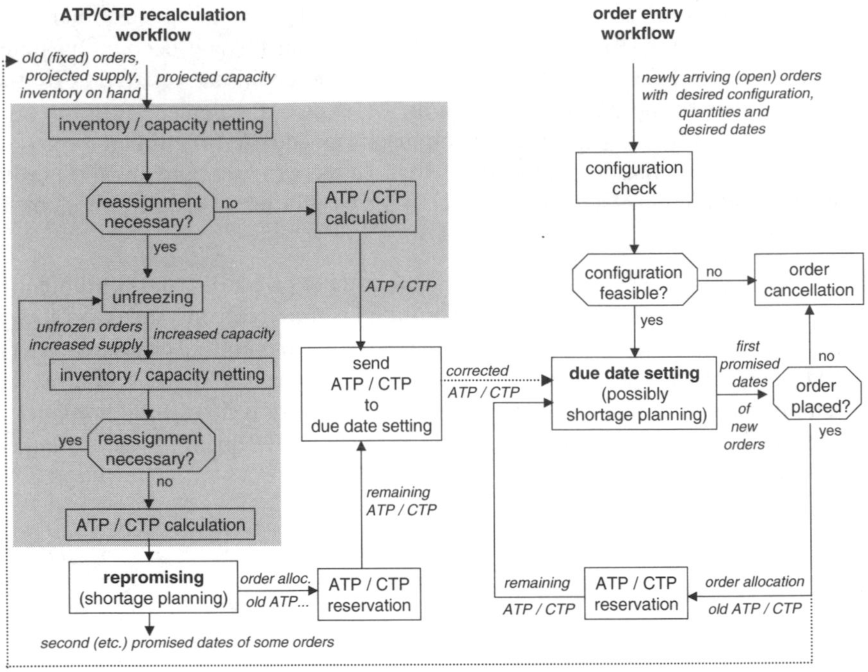

Fig. 3. ATP/CTP (re-)calculation and order entry workflows

on the supply side. The projected supply may consist of past supply orders that are still "in the pipeline" and moreover of the quantities foreseen in the master plan. An *inventory / capacity netting* procedure checks whether the overall projected supply is sufficient to satisfy all actually fixed orders on time, i.e. with respect to their already promised due dates. If this is the case, the corresponding correct ATP and CTP quantities, that remain for being consumed by newly arriving orders, can be computed in an *ATP/CTP calculation* procedure. Otherwise, the old *assignment* of the orders to the supply is not valid any longer and has to be thought over. Therefore, either some already fixed orders have to be *unfrozen* (they are allowed to get a new and thus worse due date) or supply and capacity have to be accelerated and increased, e.g. by means of negotiations with suppliers or overtime. These firefighting actions have to be repeated until projected supply and capacity are sufficient to serve the remaining, still frozen orders on time.

Subsequently, in a further *repromising* step, new (second, third etc.) promised due dates have to be determined for the unfrozen orders and the ATP/CTP quantities have to be reduced accordingly in an additional *ATP/ CTP reservation* procedure. The output of the ATP/CTP recalculation workflow are repromised due dates for some (unfrozen) orders and correct(ed) ATP/CTP quantities, that can be promised to newly arriving orders.

The updated ATP/CTP quantities are one input to the **order entry workflow**. Further input data are newly arriving orders (e.g. customer requests, orders to be released to the shop floor) with desired quantities, desired completion dates and (for customer requests) a desired configuration. This configuration has to be checked for technical feasibility first. Orders that cannot be built physically have to be cancelled. This procedure seems trivial, but the determination of such orders can be a quite complex task, for example, in a mass customization environment, where final products are configured by the customer himself choosing (from a long list) product options which do not necessarily match to each other (see ILOG, 2001).

For all the other (feasible) orders the *due date setting* subprocess tries to assign a planned execution date (e.g. for delivery or release) that is close to the desired date and feasible with respect to the currently available ATP and CTP quantities. This due date may either be a single *first promised date* for the order as a whole or several first promised dates for partial deliveries. However, in case of customers requesting for a delivery date of a potential order, this promised date might be too late from the customers point of view, so that the requested order is not finally placed, but cancelled. All other orders remain allocated. Thus, the corresponding ATP/CTP quantities are no longer available for further orders and have to be blocked in a subsequent *ATP/CTP reservation* procedure. For this, the *allocation of orders* to ATP and CTP, that was a further result of the due date setting subprocess, can again be used. Altogether, the output of the *order entry workflow* are accepted (fixed) orders with first promised dates assigned.

The subprocesses *repromising* and *due date setting* will be further discussed in Sections 3.2. to 3.4.. The computational aspects of the **netting** and **ATP / CTP calculation** processes, shown in the gray area of Fig. 3, are quite similar for the different demand fulfillment tasks and can be explained in further detail here.

First, the *inventory netting* and *ATP calculation* for a single item k are considered. The planning horizon is subdivided into time periods (typically days or weeks) $t = 1, \ldots, T$. All dates are assumed to be integers expressed in these periods. Let

I_{k0}	initial inventory of item k on hand,
S_{kt}	projected supply of k in period t (released supply orders for item k and master plan),
C_{kt}	aggregate promised customer orders for item k in t (where t is the shipping date for MTS and the assembly date for ATO),

denote the input data. The net inventory of item k can be calculated by

$$I_{kt} \quad := \quad I_{k,t-1} + S_{kt} - C_{kt} \qquad\qquad (t = 1, \ldots, T).$$

A reassignment is necessary if the *feasibility condition* $I_{kt} \geq 0 \;\forall\; t$ is violated. In this case some orders have to be unfrozen in order to decrease C_{kt} or supply has to be accelerated in order to increase S_{kt}. Otherwise, the ATP quantities can be computed according to

$$\begin{aligned} cATP_{kT} &:= I_{kT} \\ cATP_{k,t-1} &:= \min\{I_{k,t-1}; cATP_{kt}\} && (t = T, \ldots, 1) \\ ATP_{kt} &:= cATP_{kt} - cATP_{k,t-1} && (t = 1, \ldots, T), \end{aligned}$$

where ATP_{kt} denote the yet uncommitted quantities of item k that become available at period t and can be used at periods $s \geq t$ and the *cumulated* ATP quantities $cATP_{kt}$ denote the total ATP of item k that is available for commitment at period t.

In parallel, *capacity netting* and *CTP calculation* procedures are necessary if there are bottleneck resources l downstream from the decoupling point. With

K_{lt} projected capacity of resource l in period t,
p_{lk} capacity consumption of l when producing one unit of item k,

denoting the input data of the *capacity netting* procedure, the net capacity $\bar{K}_{lt}$ of resource l in period t can be calculated by subtracting the capacity consumption of the already committed orders of period t from the projected capacity of resource l within this period:

$$\bar{K}_{lt} := K_{lt} - \textstyle\sum_k p_{lk} C_{kt} \qquad \forall\, l,\, t.$$

If the corresponding *feasibility condition* $\bar{K}_{lt} \geq 0 \;\forall\, l, t$ is satisfied, the capacity CTP_{lt} of resource l, that is still available to serve new incoming orders in period t, can be *calculated* by:

$$CTP_{lt} := \bar{K}_{lt} \qquad \forall\, l, t.$$

Otherwise, a reassignment is necessary by unfreezing already fixed orders or by increasing the capacity K_{lt} of resource l in period t, e.g. by means of overtime. If there are several bottleneck capacities l downstream from the decoupling point, the resulting CTP quantity for a certain item is the minimum of the CTP_{lt} for all resources l required for that item. If these resources form a multi-stage production system, however, it is necessary to consider the lead times from stage to stage as well, as it is the case in many order promising concepts for MTO (see Sect. 4.4.). But in the following we assume, downstream from the decoupling point, either a single bottleneck capacity, as it is typical for ATO, or several capacities with negligible lead times in between, e.g. the various stations of the final assembly line of a car manufacturer.

Demand fulfillment has important **interfaces with the planning modules** for the processes upstream from the decoupling point. The projected supply S_{kt} and the projected capacity K_{lt}, which are used as input data in the above ATP/CTP calculations, are usually the result of the *Master Planning* which itself requires input from the *Demand Planning* (see Fig. 1). A reasonable Master Planning, e.g. within an APS, takes all capacity restrictions into account and thus ensures that the ATP quantities are also feasible with regard to the *upstream capacities*. However, if these capacities are not used up completely by the forecast demand and if the actual demand is higher, then the ATP quantities are smaller than possible.

The **replanning frequency** of both workflows may vary. The *order entry workflow* may be triggered by each arriving order or executed periodically. In the latter case, all orders arriving between two subsequent replannings, e.g. during a day, are gathered and processed in a batch. The *ATP/CTP recalculation workflow* also may be initiated periodically, for example every Monday, and/or by *"routine"* events (like updates of the Master Plan) or by certain *exceptional* events, e.g. the arrival of a very important order or the delay of a crucial projected supply.

3.2. Order promising

Order promising is the first task in the process chain of the fulfillment of a customer order. The result is a decision on the acceptance of the order and, if accepted, on the (first) promised due date. This decision requires the following steps, as shown in the order entry workflow in Fig. 3: If the customer can configure the ordered products, first it has to be checked whether the desired configuration is technically feasible. In the case of MTS or ATO, the major step is to check the availability of the stock of finished products or components, respectively, i.e. the *ATP check*. In the MTO case, the due dates have to be based primarily on the estimation of flow times and the present load of the machines (see e.g. Lawrence, 1995; Wein, 1991; Weng, 1999).

The objectives of order promising are:

- short service times
- reliable due dates
- a high revenue.

Unfortunately, the first two objectives are conflicting: An early promised due date shortens the service time, but is less reliable. A far postponed due date is reliable, but may imply an unacceptably long service time. However, the service time is mainly restricted by strategic and tactical settings, namely the position of the decoupling point, the quality of the forecast and the safety stock policy. Often there is also a generally announced service time, e.g.: "We fulfill all orders within two weeks". The objective of the short-term due date setting for an individual order is then to meet the general service time or the desired due date as well as possible subject to a given (high) reliability. The reliability is guaranteed, for ATO and MTS, by the ATP check and a calculation of the ATP quantities that considers all potential bottlenecks (see Section 3.1.).

Due date setting can take place either for a single order at its arrival or for a set of orders simultaneously. *Single order processing* is necessary if the customer expects an immediate response to his order, in particular in E-commerce. The second case, the *batch order processing*, occurs if new orders are only promised in intervals, e.g. once per day, and in shortage planning (see Section 3.4.).

For single order processing, the ATP quantities permit an easy determination of the due date: If a new order for the quantity q of product k with desired date d arrives, it can be promised to the earliest date t such that:

$$t \geq d \quad \text{and} \quad cATP_{kt} \geq q.$$

If t is not acceptable for the customer, measures of shortage planning (see Section 3.4.) can be taken. However, a great disadvantage of this procedure is, that in case of unsufficient availability the allocation of stock to the orders follows the first-come-first-served rule. This may contradict to the different importance of the customers and to the revenue objective. A solution from this dilemma consists in defining several customer classes and allocating all ATP quantities to these classes. Kilger and Schneeweiss (2002b) and Fischer (2001) discuss various allocation rules.

Batch order processing leaves more flexibility for due date setting. Optimization models are proposed in Section 4.

3.3. Demand-supply matching

Once orders have been promised, it is the task of the demand fulfillment to control the execution of all processes downstream from the decoupling point. Here, always many promised but incomplete orders are to be considered, where stocks and supply up to the decoupling point and the capacities downstream are given. Objectives are:

- to keep the promised due dates
- to perform the processes at the lowest cost.

In MTO, this is the major task, where usually only capacity restrictions are relevant (see e.g. Ashayeri and Selen, 2001; Özdamar and Yazgac, 1997). For ATO and MTS, this task is called *demand-supply matching* because given demand (the promised orders) has to be matched best with the given supply. For MTS, the only open process is the delivery of the orders from the stock to the customers. The *release of the delivery orders* usually takes place immediately with the order promising. The allocation of different types of stock, e.g. at different locations, to the delivery orders is called *deployment*. Optimization models are presented in Section 4.

For ATO, the assembly orders have to be released and sequenced on a short horizon. As opposed to the classical scheduling problem with due date restrictions, here also (and primarily) restrictions on the availability of various materials are to be considered which may be common for various orders. Planning models are discussed in Section 4.3.

3.4. Shortage planning

A frequent situation in ATO and MTS supply chains is that the ATP/CTP quantities are short so that adequate reactions are required. This is the task of *shortage planning*. It may occur at the order promising for new orders (see the order entry workflow in Fig. 3) or at the demand-supply matching due to unforeseen events like the delay of a material supply (see the ATP/CTP recalculation workflow in Fig. 3). The latter case concerns all promised orders sharing the short material, some of which have to be *repromised*.

For promising a single new order, most APS provide particular measures in the shortage case (see Fischer, 2001). They consist in a search for supply alternatives, e.g.

- the same product before or after the desired date
- substitute products
- the same product at other locations
- substitute products at other locations
- release of a new supply order,

which are simply checked according to given rules.

Shortage planning for promising or repromising a batch of orders has not been considered in literature, to our knowledge, and is not implemented in APS, in spite of its great practical relevance. The theory of inventory control tells us how much safety stock is necessary for fulfilling 99 % of the orders in time, but not how to select the 1 %, maybe some tens of orders per day, which are postponed or cancelled.

The objectives of this decision are

- a high customer satisfaction
- low costs of supply alternatives
- a minimal loss of margin.

Planning models are proposed in the following section.

4. Models

The models in the following section aim to demonstrate how the quite general functions *repromising* and *due date setting* shown in Fig. 3 can be mathematically represented by means of linear (and mixed integer) programming. Depending on the position of the decoupling point, on the practical application (i.e. the practical meaning of the input data and of the decision variables) and on the processing mode (batch or single order processing), the models can be used at several stages of the demand fulfillment process for all of the planning tasks *order promising*, *demand-supply matching* or *shortage planning* described above.

4.1. A basic order allocation model for MTS

First, a basic model is introduced which can be applied for each product k separately. Since only the availability of this single product is checked, it is well-suited for MTS situations with k being final items. The **indices** of the model are given as follows:

k	final item
i	open orders
$\Im_k$	set of all open orders i for final item k
T	planning horizon
$t = 1, \ldots, T$	time periods
$t = T + 1$	dummy period.

The **data** of the model are given by:

q_i	quantity of order i
d_i	desired delivery date of order i
ATP_{kt}	ATP quantity of item k in period t ($t = 1, \ldots, T$)
$ATP_{k,T+1}$	infinite dummy supply of item k
c_{it}	penalty costs for allocating one unit of order i to ATP_{kt}, possibly depending on the priority of order i, including: • costs for backlogging ($t = d_i + 1, \ldots, T$) • costs for early allocation ($t = 1, \ldots, d_i - 1$) • costs for non-delivery ($t = T + 1$).

More precisely, the desired delivery date d_i denotes the *shipping date* from the stockkeeping warehouse that guarantees the arrival at the customer at the desired date. The penalty costs c_{it} for early allocation $t < d_i$ just punish the reduced flexibility of due date setting for the orders that arrive later on. Inventory costs, however, are not a concern in demand fulfillment, since the inflow S_{kt} to the stock is the result of the prior forecast based planning and the outflow is determined by the quantity and date of the customer orders. A late delivery only occurs if there is no stock and an early delivery, if allowed, even reduces the stock.

The following **decision variables** are used:

$o_{it} \geq 0$ share of order i allocated to ATP_{kt} ($i \in \Im_k$)
$o_{i,T+1} \geq 0$ undelivered share of order i.

With this the **basic order allocation model** for final item k can be defined as follows:

$$\text{minimize} \quad \sum_{i \in \Im_k, t=1}^{T+1} c_{it} o_{it} \tag{1}$$

subject to

$$\sum_{i \in \Im_k} o_{it} \leq ATP_{kt} \qquad \forall t \tag{2}$$

$$\sum_{t=1}^{T+1} o_{it} = q_i \qquad \forall i \in \Im_k \tag{3}$$

The objective (1) is to minimize all penalty costs for not allocating to the desired delivery date. The model of each product k is of the network flow type with supply nodes (2) for each period t (with $ATP_{kt} > 0$) and demand nodes (3) for each order i. If a delivery to the customer before his desired date d_i is not allowed, the promised dates for delivering the quantities $o_{it} > 0$ have to be set to $max\{t; d_i\}$ and thus do not necessarily coincide with the dates t, the orders have been allocated to. Therefore, promised dates and order allocation dates may be two distinct results of the *due date setting* subprocess shown in Fig. 3. As the *order entry workflow* of Fig. 3 also illustrates (see the process *ATP reservation*), ATP quantities ATP_{kt} have to be reduced by the quantities o_{it} immediately after the allocation.

This type of models is typical for the *deployment* and *shortage planning* in MTS situations (see Fischer, 2001) when partial deliveries ("splitting" of orders) are allowed, e.g. when half of the order can be delivered in week 1 and the other half in week 2.

4.2. Single product extensions

In the following, some straightforward extensions of the basic model are proposed. They can still be solved for each final item k separately.

No reduction

Orders i that have to be delivered completely within the planning horizon must satisfy

$$o_{i,T+1} = 0. \tag{4}$$

No backlogging

Orders i that are not allowed to be backlogged must satisfy

$$o_{i,t} = 0 \qquad \forall t = d_i + 1, \ldots, T + 1. \tag{5}$$

Lost sales / Lost customers

Note that (4) and (5) force orders to be served *in any case*. Such a condition is only possible for a small number of very important orders or customers. For other orders, that are not allowed to be delayed, the decision to renounce them has to be included. To model such a situation, binary decision variables w_i are required, denoting whether such orders i are accepted ($w_i = 1$) or refused ($w_i = 0$).

With

$e_i =$ total revenue of order i
(or a penalty cost for loosing the corresponding customer)

the term

$$\ldots + \sum_i e_i w_i$$

has to be added to the objective function (1) and the constraints

$$o_{i,t} = 0 \qquad t = d_i + 1, \ldots, T \tag{6}$$

$$o_{i,T+1} \leq q_i \cdot (1 - w_i) \tag{7}$$

$$\sum_{t=1}^{d_i} o_{it} \leq q_i \cdot w_i \tag{8}$$

have to be introduced. Constraints (6) and (7) enforce that for $w_i = 1$ there is no delay neither cancellation. For $w_i = 0$, the complete quantity q_i is cancelled, due to (6)-(8) and (3).

Limited order splitting

Furthermore, partial deliveries and split orders may be allowed for some orders i, but only in a limited way, for example, because a customer accepts no more than two deliveries for a certain order i.

Such a situation can be modeled by introducing the data

Max^D = maximal number of (partial) deliveries per order
F_i = fixed costs for one (partial) delivery of order i

and the binary variables y_{it} $(t = d_i, \ldots, T)$ which take on the value 1 if there is a (partial) delivery of order i in period t and 0, otherwise.

Then the term

$$\ldots + \sum_{i,t=d_i}^{T} F_i y_{it}$$

has to be added to the objective function (1) and the constraints

$$o_{it} \leq q_i \cdot y_{it} \qquad t = d_i, \ldots, T \tag{9}$$

$$\sum_{t=d_i}^{T} y_{it} \leq Max^D \tag{10}$$

have to be introduced.

If split orders are not allowed, e.g. because the model is used for *order promising* and a *unique* delivery date is required, binary variables are always necessary and Max^D has to be set to 1. Relaxing the binary variables, solving the continuous problem by linear programming and promising the date of the last delivery computed $(argmax_t\{o_{it} > 0\})$ is only a heuristic way of tackling the problem because the (penalty) costs of partial deliveries instead of full deliveries have wrongly been used.

Alternative locations

The above models concentrate on a single location that offers ATP for a product k. Quite often, however, components can be sourced from different alternative locations v, then incurring additional costs c_{vi}^T per unit for the transport from source v to the destination where order i is demanded. Let the data ATP_{kvt} denote the ATP of product k which can be supplied by location v in period t.

Then the nonnegative continuous variables o_{ivt} define the share of order i which is allocated to the ATP_{kvt} of location v in period t.

To model this situation, the transport costs $c_{vi}^T o_{ivt}$ have to be added to the objective function (1) and constraints (2) have to be replaced with

$$\sum_{i \in \Im_k} o_{ivt} \leq ATP_{kvt} \qquad \forall v,\ t. \tag{11}$$

For ease of readability, transport times have been assumed to be zero. If fixed transport costs cannot be disregarded, additional binary variables have to be introduced.

4.3. Order allocation for ATO supply chains

In ATO supply chains a finished product k is assembled from several "components" j and, on the other hand, a component j may be used by several products k. In this case, multi-product, multi-component models are required. ATP quantities should now be provided on the component level.

Several order lines / pre-products

In order to model such a situation the following additional data and variables are required.

Data:

f_{ij}	amount of component j needed for order i
ATP_{jt}	unassigned supply of component j in period t $(= 1, \ldots T)$ (available to be promised)
CTP_t	unassigned capacity of a single bottleneck resource in period t $(= 1, \ldots T)$
p_i	consumption of CTP when assembling on unit of order i
c_{it}	cost of assembling one unit of order i in period t, incl. • penalty for early assembly in periods $t < d_i$ • penalty for delayed assembly in periods $t > d_i$
$\bar{c}_{jt}$	penalty for allocating ATP_{jt} unnecessarily early, decreasing in time, e.g. $\bar{c}_{jt} := (T - t)\bar{c} \; \forall \; j, \; t = 1, \ldots, T$, where $\bar{c}$ is a (small) parameter

Variables:

$o_{it} \geq 0$	share of order i assembled in period t $(t = 1, \ldots, T + 1)$
$z_{jt} \geq 0$	consumption of ATP_{jt} $(t = 1, \ldots, T + 1)$

The **ATO model** has to simultaneously consider the orders $i \in \Im_k$ for all finished products k that are related by common components j (by means of bill-of-material-coefficients $f_{ij} > 0$):

$$\text{minimize} \qquad \sum_{i,t=1}^{T+1} c_{it} o_{it} + \sum_{j,t=1}^{T} \bar{c}_{jt} z_{jt} \tag{12}$$

subject to

$$\sum_{t=1}^{T+1} o_{it} = q_i \qquad \forall i \tag{13}$$

$$\sum_{s=1}^{t} z_{js} \geq \sum_{i,s=1}^{t} f_{ij} o_{is} \qquad \forall j,\, t = 1, \ldots, T+1 \tag{14}$$

$$z_{jt} \leq ATP_{jt} \qquad \forall j,\, t = 1, \ldots, T \tag{15}$$

$$\sum_{i} p_i o_{it} \leq CTP_t \qquad t = 1, \ldots, T \tag{16}$$

The objective function (12) punishes early or late assembly of orders i and offers incentives for allocating the ATP of components j as late as possible. Equations (13) ensure that all orders i are either assembled ($o_{it} > 0, t = 1, \ldots, T$) or cancelled ($o_{i,T+1} > 0$). Because of (14) the respective components j are available in time for assembly. Constraints (15) and (16) limit the usage of ATP and CTP to the projected (and still unassigned) supply. Without loss of generality, only a single bottleneck resource (for assembly) is assumed (16). Again, delivery dates have to be derived from the assembly quantities o_{it} (see Section 4.1.).

After solving the ATO model, the ATP quantities ATP_{jt} have to be reduced by z_{jt} (see *ATP reservation* subprocess in Fig. 3) and CTP_t by $\sum_i p_i o_{it}$. If not all orders i have been accepted, the allocation of the ATP consumption z_{jt} to the respective orders i might be of interest. For this a more detailed model with variables z_{ijt} denoting the share of ATP_{jt} that has been allocated to order i ($t = 1, \ldots, T+1$) can be used where (14) and (15) are replaced by

$$\sum_{s=1}^{t} z_{ijs} \geq \sum_{s=1}^{t} f_{ij} o_{is} \qquad \forall i, j,\, t = 1, \ldots, T+1 \tag{17}$$

$$\sum_{i} z_{ijt} \leq ATP_{jt} \qquad \forall j,\, t = 1, \ldots, T. \tag{18}$$

In this case, also the costs $\bar{c}_{ijt}$ of consuming one unit of ATP_{jt} can be allocated to an order i, directly.

A single new order i can be delivered *on time* if

$$cATP_{j,d_i} \geq f_{ij} q_i \tag{19}$$

is satisfied for all components j concerned. Otherwise, the order can first be finished at the earliest assembly date t that satisfies $cATP_{jt} \geq f_{ij} q_i \; \forall j$.

Product substitution / downgrading

Furthermore, there may be several alternative bill-of-materials r for a certain order j. For example, hard-disks of several suppliers can alternatively form the same finished product k, namely a personal computer being specified by a hard-disk of a certain size, e.g. 40 Gigabyte. Also *downgrading* can be possible, i.e. a customer would also accept a higher value product instead of a lower value product if he only has to pay the price of the cheaper one. For example, it may be convenient to deliver a computer with a 60 Gigabyte hard-disk in case the originally ordered 40 Gigabyte hard-disks are out of stock because of a shortage situation.

Therefore, the following data and variables have to be introduced:

Data:

f_{ijr}	number of components j needed to assemble order i when using the r-th bill-of-material of order j

Variables:

$z_{jtr} \geq 0$	consumption of ATP_{jt} when using the r-th bill-of-material of order j

Then constraints (14) and (15) of the ATO model have to be replaced with

$$\sum_{s=1}^{t} z_{jsr} \geq \sum_{i,s=1}^{t} f_{ijr} o_{is} \qquad \forall j, r,\ t = 1, \ldots, T+1 \tag{20}$$

$$\sum_{r} z_{jtr} \leq ATP_{jt} \qquad \forall j,\ t = 1, \ldots, T. \tag{21}$$

In this case, preferences for different components j also have to be included into the penalty costs $\bar{c}_{jt}$ of the objective function (12), e.g. by setting $\bar{c}_{jt} := (T-t) \cdot W_j,\ t = 1, \ldots, T$, with W_j denoting the value of component j.

4.4. Order allocation for MTO supply chains

As pointed out in Section 2., in MTO supply chains production capacities of resources downstream from the decoupling point are usually assumed to be the only bottlenecks. In this case, for all resources l which are potential bottlenecks, the remaining capacity, *capable to* be *promised* to a certain order, has to be checked and booked.

With p_{il} denoting the capacity consumption of resource l if one unit of order i is produced, CTP_{lt} denoting the unassigned capacity of resource l in period t and the remaining data and variables as introduced in Sect. 4.1., a **basic order allocation model for MTO** can be defined as follows:

$$\text{minimize} \qquad \sum_{i,t=1}^{T+1} c_{it} o_{it} \tag{22}$$

subject to

$$\sum_i p_{il} o_{it} \leq CTP_{lt} \qquad \forall l, \; t = 1, \dots, T \tag{23}$$

$$\sum_{t=1}^{T+1} o_{it} = q_i \qquad \forall i \tag{24}$$

In contrast to the MTS and ATO models, the availability of finished products or components is not checked any longer. In other words, ATP constraints are missing. Now just the *capability* to produce a new order i is checked. The capacity constraints (16) of the ATO model have been extended by several bottleneck resources to be checked (23), in order to indicate that all production processes downstream from the decoupling point may be crucial. If the resources are not dedicated to a single finished product, the MTO model is harder to solve than the MTS model because orders $i \in \Im_k$ for *all* finished products k, which can be produced on potential bottleneck resources l, have to be considered at the same time.

However, the MTO model is just a *basic* model because it assumes that an order i consumes CTP_{lt} of all bottleneck resources l simultaneously, i.e. in the same period t. This may be realistic for flow lines with serially connected stations, where the overall bottleneck depends on the current mix of orders, e.g. in some chemical industries or in the automotive industry. For job shops with several production stages, alternative routings through the shops and significant flow times, the basic model is unsuited.

More refined models obviously depend on the characteristics of the production system under consideration. Since there is a rich literature on due date setting and order promising for MTO supply chains, we omit to present further models here and just give a brief literature overview. The literature can be divided into three broad categories.

Papers of the first one use a *stochastic model* of the production system and estimate the flow time through the system in order to promise due dates for new orders. Lawrence (1995), Moses (1999) and Wein (1991) calculate the flow times with respect to the current utilization of the production system. The first author tackles a multistage production system, whereas the latter two restrict themselves to a single station. Weng (1999) deals with due date setting *and* order acceptance in a multi-stage system with a steady state flow time, i.e. the current utilization is not taken into consideration.

The second category comprises *deterministic* approaches for *job shop scheduling*. Cheng and Gupta (1989) early presented a comprehensive survey of scheduling research concerning due date setting decisions. Later on Taylor and Plenert (1999) and Jeong et al. (2002, Sect. 4) dealt with inserting a new job into a given schedule of old jobs, whereas Li and Cheng (1999) also allow the rescheduling of the old jobs. More precisely, the latter paper analyses the computational complexity of calculating due dates for a batch of new jobs by updating the schedule of the old jobs (with due dates already assigned) on a single machine. Usually, due date setting in a deterministic job shop environment does not take into consideration the desired dates of customers.

The third category represents papers that are better suited to a rather mid-term demand-supply matching than to a short-term due date setting with online response because of the computational burden required. Ashayeri and Selen (2001) apply a MIP model to decide about the acceptance of orders in a hybrid make-to-order and make-to-stock environment. Özdamar and Yazgac (1997) also use MIP and linear programming to plan (aggregate) capacities and to determine due dates for a multi-stage production system.

5. Summary and conclusions

It has been shown that the position of the decoupling point has a significant influence on the various planning tasks of demand fulfillment. For this reason, the tasks *order promising*, *demand-supply matching* and *shortage planning* have been discussed with respect to the three decoupling points *make-to-stock* (MTS), *assemble-to-order* (ATO) and *make-to-order* (MTO). Order promising makes decisions about the acceptance of orders and sets due dates for new orders. Demand-supply matching cares about the execution of the processes downstream from the decoupling point by allocating already promised but still incomplete orders to the respective unassigned stock on hand and projected supply. Shortage planning has to decide about adequate reactions, in case (un)finished products (ATP) or production capacity (CTP) are short of, and about the subset of orders that cannot be fulfilled as desired.

Order promising is particularly relevant for ATO and MTO supply chains because of the rather long customer order lead times predominant there. The type and relevance of stocks to be considered also varies with respect to the position of the decoupling point. In MTS supply chains, the major focus is the availability (ATP) of finished products. ATO supply chains have to take care of component availability (ATP), but sometimes additionally assembly capacity (CTP) can be restrictive. In MTO supply chains, however, material availability usually needs not to be considered, but production capacities (CTP) of the many potential bottleneck resources downstream from the decoupling point have to be respected. In Sect. 3.1., workflows and algorithms for the (re-)calculation of ATP and CTP were presented. Furthermore, in Sect. 4. linear and mixed integer programming models were proposed, which match the different needs of MTS, ATO and MTO supply chains.

Customer satisfaction will remain a major concern of companies in the future. The capability to provide information about the status of customer orders is and will be an important reason for buying an APS. However, tracking and tracing of customer orders should only be a welcome side effect of an efficient demand fulfillment. When comparing the LP and MIP models of Sect. 4. with the simple rules used in APS — and in practice — now, there seems to be a substantial potential of improving supply chain performance. However, much research still has to be done to put more sophisticated OR methods for demand fulfillment into practice. Fischer (2001, Chapt. 3.4) made only a first step towards this direction.

Within this paper, from a conceptual point of view, only "pure" decoupling points have been considered, i.e. it was assumed that a certain planning activity is either *exclusively* driven by forecasts or *exclusively* driven be customer orders. However, in practice there are hybrids in between. Quite often only a share but not all of the orders are known at the time of planning, so that the missing rest has to be forecasted (Meyr, 2002). The ATP consumption rule "*to first look whether an item is available at some stocking point (= made to forecast) and, if none is found, to generate a production order for this customer order (= make to order)*" is an example, how such a hybrid situation is currently tackled in APS. This type of "forecast consumption" is mentioned in some textbooks (see e.g. Vollmann et al., 1997, p. 217 ff.), but an overall framework is missing. For example, it is still an open question how to link the ATP and forecast consumption of order promising with demand planning (forecast updating) and safety stock planning/refilling.

Further research effort has to be put on allocation mechanisms that assign the projected production quantities of an aggregate master plan to different order classes for a first-come-first-served consumption in a later online order promising process (see Sect. 3.2. and Kilger and Schneeweiss, 2002b, Sect. 9.2). Here, the revenues of different order classes have to be taken into consideration, too. The currently promoted "*profitable-to-promise*" extensions of the traditional ATP and CTP logic in APS show that there is a need for such procedures in practice. This allocation problem is closely related to "revenue (or yield) management" (see e.g. Klein, 2001), which is well-known in the service sector.

References

Ashayeri J., Selen W. (2001): Order selection optimization in hybrid make–to–order and make–to–stock markets, in: Journal of the Operational Research Society 52, pp. 1098–1106.

Cheng T., Gupta M. (1989): Survey of scheduling research involving due–date determination decisions. In: European Journal of Operational Research 38, pp. 156–166.

Christopher M. (1992): Logistics and Supply Chain Management. Pitman Publishing, London.

Fischer M. (2001): Available-to-Promise: Aufgaben und Verfahren im Rahmen des Supply Chain Management. S. Roderer Verlag, Regensburg.

Fleischmann B., Meyr H. (2003): Planning hierarchy, modeling and Advanced Planning Systems. To appear in: Graves S.C., de Kok A.G. (eds.) Supply Chain Management: Design, Coordination and Operation. Handbooks in Operations Research and Management Science, North–Holland, Amsterdam et al.

Fleischmann B., Meyr H., Wagner M. (2002): Advanced planning. In: Stadtler H., Kilger C. (eds.) Supply Chain Management and Advanced Planning. 2nd edn. Springer, Berlin et al., chapt. 4, pp. 71–95.

Fogarty D., Blackstone Jr. J., Hoffmann T. (1991): Production & Inventory Management. 2nd edn. South–Western Publishing Co., Cincinnati Ohio.

Günther H.-O., Tempelmeier H. (2003): Produktion und Logistik. 5. Aufl. Springer, Berlin et al.

Hoekstra S., Romme J. (1991, eds.): Integral Logistic Structures: Developing Customer–oriented Goods Flow. Industrial Press Inc., New York.

ILOG (2001): ILOG configurator. Technical report, ILOG Worldwide Information Center, http://www.ilog.com/products/configurator/wp_configurator.pdf (2002/10/4).

Jeong B., Sim S.-B., Jeong H.-S., Kim S.-W. (2002): An available–to–promise system for TFT LCD manufacturing in supply chain. In: Computers & Industrial Engineering 43, pp. 191–212.

Kilger C., Schneeweiss L. (2002a): Computer assembly. In: Stadtler H., Kilger C. (eds.) Supply Chain Management and Advanced Planning. 2nd edn. Springer, Berlin et al., chapt. 20, pp. 335–352.

Kilger C., Schneeweiss L. (2002b): Demand fulfilment and ATP. In: Stadtler H., Kilger C. (eds.) Supply Chain Management and Advanced Planning. 2nd edn. Springer, Berlin et al., chapt. 9, pp. 161–175.

Klein R. (2001): Revenue Management: Quantitative Methoden zur Erlösmaximierung in der Dienstleistungsproduktion. In: Betriebswirtschaftliche Forschung und Praxis 3, S. 245–259.

Knolmayer G., Mertens P., Zeier A. (2002): Supply Chain Management Based on SAP Systems. Springer, Berlin et al.

Lawrence S. (1995): Estimating flowtimes and setting due–dates in complex production systems. In: IIE Transactions 27, pp. 657–668.

Li C.-L., Cheng T. (1999): Due–date determination with resequencing. In: IIE Transactions 31, pp. 183–188.

Meyr H. (2002): Die Bedeutung von Entkopplungspunkten für das Management und die Planung von Supply Chains. Arbeitspapier, Lehrstuhl für Produktion und Logistik, Universität Augsburg, Germany.

Meyr H., Wagner M., Rohde J. (2002): Structure of Advanced Planning Systems. In: Stadtler H., Kilger C. (eds.) Supply Chain Management and Advanced Planning. 2nd edn. Springer, Berlin et al., chapt. 5, pp. 99–104.

Moses S. (1999): Due date assignment using feedback control with reinforcement learning. In: IIE Transactions 31, pp. 989–999.

Özdamar L., Yazgac T. (1997): Capacity driven due date setting in make–to–order production systems. In: International Journal of Production Economics 49, pp. 29–44.

Schwendinger J. (1979): Master Production Scheduling's Available to Promise. In: APICS Conference Proceedings, pp. 316–330.

Sharman G. (1984): The rediscovery of logistics. In: Harvard Business Review, Sept./Oct. 1984 (reprinted in: Christopher M. (1992, ed.): Logistics — Strategic Issues. Chapman & Hall, London, p. 1–16).

Taylor S., Plenert G. (1999): Finite capacity promising. In: Production and Inventory Management Journal, 3rd quarter, pp. 50–56.

Vollmann T., Berry W., Whybark D. (1997): Manufacturing Planning and Control Systems. 4th edn. Irwin (McGraw–Hill), Boston et al.

Wein L. (1991): Due–date setting and priority sequencing in a multiclass M/G/1 queue. In: Management Science 37/7, pp. 834–850.

Weng Z. (1999): Strategies for integrating lead time and customer–order decisions. In: IIE Transactions 31, pp. 161–171.

Order Picking: A Survey of Planning Problems and Methods

Gerhard Wäscher

Department of Business Economics - Management Science -
Faculty of Economic Management
Otto-von-Guericke-University of Magdeburg
Universitaetsplatz 2
D-39106 Magdeburg, Germany

Abstract: *Order picking – as a warehouse function – is often considered to be critical for the public manifestation of a supply chain. Underperformance can result both in unsatisfactory customer service and in high cost. In this paper the author will give an overview of planning problems and corresponding methods which have been suggested in the literature for the reduction of cost and the improvement of customer service in picker-to-product systems. In particular, the following central issues will be addressed: item location, order batching, and picker routing.*

Keywords: *order picking, warehouse management, location, batching, routing*

1. Introduction

Order picking is a warehouse function critical to each supply chain. Underperformance results in unsatisfactory customer service (long processing and delivery times, incorrect shipments) and high costs (labour cost, cost of additional and/or emergency shipments), both being a significant threat to the competitiveness of the total chain. Despite its criticality, order picking is not really a topic of major interest, neither in academic research nor in industrial practice. Like other warehousing operations, it appears to be one of the most frequently overlooked, underfunded, and inadequately planned corporate functions (Tompkins et al., 1996). Furthermore, managers seem to be unaware of advanced planning techniques and their potential with respect to reducing cost and improving customer service (Petersen, 1999, p. 1054).

The aim of this paper, therefore, is to review these planning techniques and to demonstrate what benefits can be expected from their use in practice. Due to limitations of space, the focus of the paper will be on conventional (manual) order picking systems, for which the main operational planning issues will be introduced, namely the assignment of items to storage locations, the transformation of customer orders into picking orders, and the routing of pickers through the warehouse. Corresponding planning techniques will be presented and discussed.

2. Order picking as a warehouse function

Order picking can be defined as the retrieval of items from their warehouse locations in order to satisfy demands from (internal or external) customers (Petersen/Schmenner, 1999, p. 481). As a warehouse function order picking arises because incoming articles are received and stored in (large-volume) unit loads while customers order small volumes (less-than-unit loads) of different articles. Typically, thousands of customer orders have to be processed in a distribution warehouse per day.

Even though there have been various attempts to automate the picking process, picker-less systems are rarely found in practice. Order picking – like many other material-handling activities – still is a repetitive, labour-intensive activity these days (Petersen, 1999, p. 1055). Order picking systems, which involve human operators can be organized in two ways, namely as a *product-to-picker system*, in which the requested products are delivered automatically to a person at an input/output (I/O) point, or as a *picker-to-product system*, in which a person (*order picker*) travels to storage locations in order to collect the required products. Product-to-picker systems have been studied extensively (Cormier/Gunn 1992), therefore the focus of this paper will be on picking systems of the second type.

Typically, when order picking is organized as a picker-to-product system, the storage area of the warehouse is divided into two parts, namely into a *reserve (storage) area*, in which full unit loads are stored (usually on pallets), and into a *forward (picking) area,* which is specifically designed to support and facilitate the picking process of small, fast moving items and is replenished from the reserve storage area (Ballou, 1967, p. 60). The picking area consists of a number of *aisles* with the different products (*items*) stored at both sides of the aisles. The operations of the order pickers may be restricted to a single aisle each (as in *person-aboard automatic storage/retrieval systems*), or they may be free to access any aisle (as in more conventional picking systems). Like it is common practice in the literature, the order picking area of a warehouse will be addressed as the "*order-picking warehouse*" below.

3. Order picking system

3.1. Basic system design and layout

In the order-picking warehouse to be considered here, the items are stored on pallets in pallet racks. Picking is carried out from the lowest level, only. The *storage locations* (*bays*) are of identical size, each can accommodate a single pallet. They are located in a number of parallel, straight (*picking*) *aisles*, which run perpendicular to the front end of the picking area. The (picking) aisles are of equal length and width (*rectangular layout*). Changing from one (picking) aisle to another is possible by means of two *cross aisles*, one at the front and one at the rear of the warehouse. Fig. 1 depicts the layout of the picking area, which is consistent with the warehouse layout literature (e.g. Bassan et al., 1980; Caron et al., 2000). More specifically, it can be characterized as a *one-block layout*. (By introduction of one or several additional cross aisles, a *multi-block layout* would be obtained.) In the literature, the layout of Fig. 1 (see next page) is often considered as the *basic layout* of an order picking area (Roodbergen/de Koster, 2001b, p. 32).

The *input/output* (*I/O*) *point* (also called *depot* or *dock*) defines a location where the order picker enters the picking area, and where she/he afterwards returns to in order to deposit the picked items. It will be assumed that the (I/O) point is located in the middle of the front end of the warehouse.

The basis of the actual picking process is provided by a set of *customer orders*, each one consisting of a number of order lines. An *order line* or *position* represents a product or item type (identified by an article number) and the corresponding quantity, which has been requested by the customer. The set of customer orders is assumed to be fixed and known in advance (*off-line problem*). Usually, the customer orders will not be processed one by one. Instead, at first, the set of customer orders is rearranged into a set of *picking orders*. A picking order may consist of a subset of the positions from a customer order (in particular, if the customer order is large), it may comprise several complete customer orders (in case of relatively small customer orders), or it may contain subsets of positions from several customer orders.

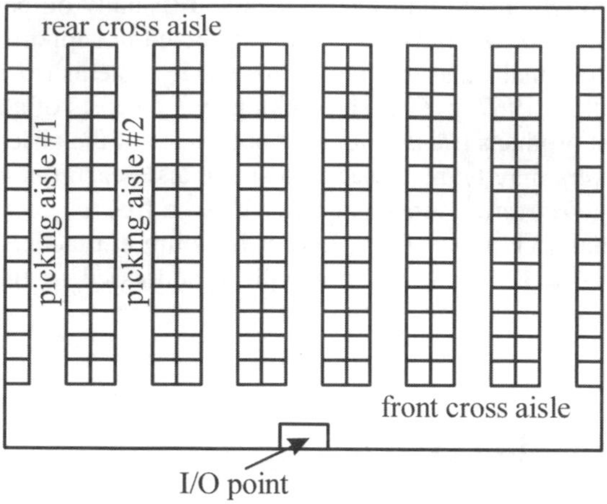

Fig. 1. Picking-area layout

The actual picking process starts when the order picker receives a *pick list* at the I/O point. Each pick list is a picking order to which information has been added about

- the locations where the items are stored, and
- the sequence according to which the locations are to be visited.

In order to pick the requested items, the order picker collects a device such as a small picking truck or a roll cage. Then she/he walks or rides to the respective storage locations (*pick location*) and retrieves the products in the necessary quantities. The items are packed on the picking device, which facilitates transportation of the picked items, but also enables her/him to collect items at several storage locations before she/he returns to the I/O point.

It is assumed that the aisles are wide enough to allow for overtaking and two-way-travel. Items can be picked from both sides of an aisle in a single move (i.e. the picker does not have to change her/his position significantly) such that the horizontal distance between the racks in an aisle can be neglected ("narrow" aisles). These characteristics define a standard order-picking warehouse to which we will refer to unless otherwise stated.

3.2. Planning issues concerning policies and operations

For this review, a given order-picking warehouse of the standard type will be assumed. Design issues, such as questions of layout optimization, will not be discussed, here. Instead, we refer to the literature (e.g. Caron et al., 2000; Roodbergen, 2001; Vaughan/Petersen, 1999). The remaining planning issues have to be addressed on two levels, on the level of policies and on the level of operations. They are related to three main complexes (Caron et al., 1998),

- the assignment of items to storage locations (*storage location*),
- the transformation of customer orders into picking orders (*order consolidation*), and
- the routing of pickers through the warehouse (*picker routing*).

In general, *policies* can be looked upon as basic principles according to which processes are organized. They define the framework for subsequent operational decisions. A *storage policy* determines how storage locations are allocated to products. In *dedicated storage* all products are stored at fixed locations. Each article can be found in the same location for a relatively long period of time. Within this framework it has to be decided where the various item types should be stored (*item location problem*). *Randomized storage* is a storage policy in which an incoming pallet is assigned to one of the currently available, empty locations. Over time, the same article will be found in different locations. In conventional order-picking systems, usually dedicated storage is preferred because the order picker will become familiar with the locations of the various item types, which – in the long run – will allow for a more efficient order picking.

The *order consolidation policy* is the principle according to which customer orders are rearranged into picking orders. In *single order picking* each customer order is directly taken as a picking order. Alternatively, when the order size is small in relation to the capacity of the transportation device, *order batching* may be applied. In this case, several customer orders are combined into a *batch*, i.e. a single picking order, which is retrieved by a single picker. The option of batching customer orders gives rise to the question of how a given set of customer orders should be combined into smaller subsets each of which representing a picking order (*order batching problem*).

A *routing policy* is a principle for the design of picking tours through the warehouse. *Individual routing* means that for each picking order it has to be decided in which sequence the various pick locations are to be visited (*picker routing problem*). In other words, within the framework of individual routing an individual, usually optimal tour has to be developed for each picking order. In practice, frequently *standardized routing* is applied. The picking tour that corresponds to a particular picking order is then developed on the basis of a simple *routing strategy*. (A brief description of such routing strategies can be found, e.g., in Petersen/Schmenner, 1999, pp. 482-487.) The most commonly-known strategies are the so-called traversal, return, largest-gap and composite strategies (see Fig. 2). They have in common that only *pick-location aisles* are visited, i.e. aisles which contain at least one pick location. The strategies will be introduced for one-block layouts only, here. As for modifications for multi-block layouts, we refer to the literature (e.g. Roodbergen, 2001, pp. 38 et sqq.)

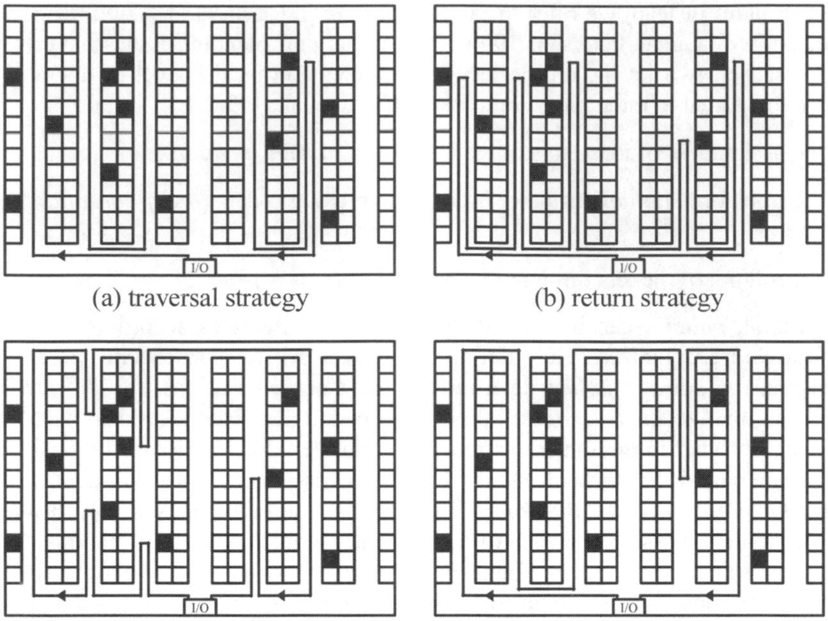

(a) traversal strategy (b) return strategy

(c) largest-gap stategy (d) composite strategy

Fig. 2. Routing strategies for a one-block layout

The black-marked bays of Fig. 2 indicate a set of *pick locations*, i.e. locations of items, which have to be picked according to a given picking order (for this particular picker routing problem see de Koster/van der Poort, 1998, p. 471). Application of the *traversal strategy* (see Fig. 2a), also called *S-shape strategy* (e.g. see Roodbergen, 2001, p. 33), generates a tour in which each pick-location aisle is traversed completely (with the exception of the last one, if an odd number of pick-location aisles has to be visited). The picker starts at the I/O point, walks/rides to the left-most pick-location aisle containing pick locations, enters it from the front and leaves it at the rear, then proceeds to the next pick-location aisle, which is traversed from the rear to the front, etc., until the last item has been picked from which location the picker returns to the I/O point.

When the *return strategy* (see Fig. 2b) is applied, the order picker enters and leaves all pick-location aisles from the same cross aisle (i.e. usually from the front cross aisle). She/he traverses each pick-location aisle up the farthest pick location and returns from there to the cross aisle.

According to the largest-gap strategy (see Fig. 2c), return trips into pick-location aisles can be performed from both the front and the rear cross aisle. At which location the picker has to turn back in a pick-location aisle is determined by the largest gap. A gap represents a separation between the locations of two adjacent items to be picked (picks) in a picking aisle, or between the location of the first pick in a picking aisle and the front cross aisle, or between the location of the last pick in a picking aisle and the rear cross aisle. The picker takes a return trip from both the front and the rear cross aisle if the largest gap is between two adjacent picks. Otherwise, a return trip from either the front or the rear cross aisle is used. In each case, the largest gap of a pick-location aisle to be visited represents the portion of the aisles that will not be traversed by the order picker (Petersen/Schmenner, 1999, pp. 485 et sqq.). The left-most aisle that has to be visited will be traversed completely in order to reach the rear cross aisle. Likewise, in order to make her/his way back to the depot, the order picker will pass through the right-most pick-location aisle to be visited completely from the rear to the front.

Thc *composite strategy* (Petersen, 1997, p. 1102; see Fig. 2d) combines elements from both traversal and return strategy. It seeks to minimize the distance between the farthest pick locations in two adjacent aisles (Petersen/Schmenner, 1999, pp. 486 et sqq.).

3.3. Planning goals

Within the framework of a given (standard) order-picking warehouse, minimization of the total time necessary to process a given set of customer orders, or, equivalently, to pick all items of a given set of customer orders (*total processing time, total picking time*) is the central goal for planning and controlling the picking processes. On one hand, a reduction of the total picking time corresponds to an increase in the speed of the picking activities, resulting in shorter delivery times. This, in turn, will improve the customer service. Likewise, on the other hand, a reduction in the total processing time leads to a smaller demand of man-power (order pickers). In the short run, labour costs related to overtime, temporary staff etc. can be reduced. In the long run, the necessary number of permanent staff may also decrease.

Improving the performance and reducing the cost of the system therefore means reducing the total picking time (Caron et al., 2000, p. 101). From this point of view it is worthwhile to analyse what the components make up for the total picking time and how these components can be influenced by the above-described decisions. The time necessary to complete picking of a customer/picking order includes (Petersen, 1999, p. 1055)

- the time needed at the I/O point for performing the necessary administrative (obtaining and studying the pick list) and set-up tasks (e.g. collecting a picking cart or vehicle),
- the time for traveling from the I/O point to the first storage location, between the storage locations, and back to the I/O point from the last storage location,
- the time needed at each storage location for identifying the storage location and the article, picking the required quantity, placing the items on the picking cart

or vehicle, sorting them if necessary, and confirming the pick on the pick list, and

- the time needed at the I/O point for performing the final administrative and other closing tasks (unloading the picking cart or vehicle, sorting the collected items, depositing the transportation device, etc.).

Most of these time elements are independent from the above-described decisions. The exception is the time the order picker spends for traveling between the storage locations and from and to the I/O point. Thus, the minimization of the *total travel time*, i.e. the time necessary to collect all items of a given set of customer orders, can serve as a goal in decisions, which have to be made on the policy and operations levels.

Furthermore, it is usually realistic to assume (Jarvis/McDowell, 1991, p. 94) that the total travel time is a monotone increasing function of the total distance the order pickers have to cover in order to collect all items of a set of customer orders (*total travel distance*). If the total travel distance is reduced, then also both the total travel time and the total picking time will decrease. Consequently, models and methods for decision problems on the policy and operations level often include minimization of the total travel distance as an auxiliary goal.

Finally, it has to be noted that – as long as the set of customer orders is fixed – it also makes sense to replace the goals introduced above by corresponding averages, i.e. to consider the minimization of the average total picking time per order, the average total travel time per order, or the average total travel distance (also: average tour length) per order instead.

4. Item location

4.1. Problem definition

The item-location problem for dedicated storage can be stated as follows:

> Given an order-picking warehouse with specified potential locations for the storage of item types and a set of customer orders each requiring to collect a specific set of items, how should the item types be assigned to the available locations such that the total length of the picking tours necessary to collect all items is minimized.

It has to be noted that the item location problem is strongly interconnected with both the order batching and the picker routing problem. In fact, only a simultaneous solution of all these problems could prepare the road to “globally” optimal solution. Again, this is not a very realistic approach. Instead, one usually ignores the order batching-problem at this stage by simply taking the customer orders as picking orders. The remaining problem, however, still is a very difficult one. If we assume for a moment that we have solved the sequencing problem for each of the picking orders beforehand, then we would know how many times we have to proceed from an item type i to an item type j, and the remaining item location problem could be modelled as a quadratic assignment problem. This optimization problem is known to be NP-hard, thus we conclude that the original item location problem is also NP-hard at least. As the size of the instances of the quadratic assignment problem, which can be solved to an optimum, is rather limited (25 item types/locations) while – in relation to this size – real-world item location-problems tend to be quite large (more than 500 item types/locations), it cannot be expected that exact solution methods are applicable to real-world problem instances. Consequently, all methods suggested for the item location problem in the literature so far are heuristics.

4.2. (Heuristic) solution approaches

Heuristic approaches to the item location problem can be distinguished into three classes of methods, turnover-based, complementarity-based, and contact-based methods.

4.2.1. Turnover-based methods

Turnover-based methods (also: *volume-based* or *frequency-based methods*) consider the demand frequencies of the item types, only. Here, the turnover or demand frequency of an item type is equal to the number of times it appears in a customer order during a specific period of time. It can be expected that the distribution of these frequency has a direct influence on the extent to which alternative storage policies affect picking times and costs (Kallina/Lynn, 1976; Malmborg, 1996). The distribution is usually represented by an ABC curve, which – in this context – can be characterized by a percentage ratio such as 20/80 which means that 20% of the item types are responsible for 80% of the demand frequencies (for details see Malmborg, 1996, pp. 365 et sqq.).

In case all item types require a single storage location each (i.e. the same amount of storage space), the item types are sorted in a non-increasing order of these frequencies, while, on the other hand, the available locations are sorted in a non-decreasing order with respect to their distances from the I/O point. Then the first item type is assigned to the first location, the second item is assigned to the second location, etc., yielding a solution in which frequently demanded items are located in close neighbourhood to the I/O point while less demanded items are located further away (for this *standard frequency-based location strategy* see Neal, 1962). It can be shown (Kallina, 1976) that this procedure provides an optimal solution for a rather restricted planning situation, namely when each picking order consists of one position each (i.e. in the case of an out-and-back system, which is more typical for a product-to-picker system). In the system considered here, an – often large

– number of items has to be collected on a tour through the warehouse. As the standard frequency-based location strategy – like the other frequency-based methods, which will be discussed below – ignores this aspect it cannot be expected that their application provides optimal (or even near-optimal) solutions for the above-stated item location problem.

Instead of considering the exact distances between the available locations and the I/O point, in the literature, at times, "*storage-allocation patterns*" are used according to which item types are assigned to locations (Petersen, 1999; Petersen/Schmenner, 1999, pp. 487 et sqq.). Such storage-allocation patterns are depicted in Fig. 3. They indicate, where high-frequency, medium-frequency, and low-frequency item types are to be stored. Jarvis and McDowell (1991) have proven that when the traversal strategy is applied for solving the routing problem, within-aisle storage provides an optimal allocation scheme for symmetric order-picking warehouses with respect to the average tour length. They have also shown, however, that this is not necessarily the case for a non-symmetric warehouse, where the I/O point is not located in the middle of the front of the warehouse. Petersen and Schmenner (1999), by means of extensive numerical experiments, have evaluated – among other policies – diagonal, within-aisle, and across-aisle storage. They found that within-aisle storage generally outperforms diagonal and across-aisle storage, providing average tour length savings of 10-20% (Petersen/Schmenner, 1999, pp. 494, 498).

An early modification of the standard frequency-based location strategy does not only take into account the demand frequencies of the item types but also their space requirements, which may be different for different item types. Heskett (1963, 1964) introduced the so-called *cube-per-order index* (COI) which is defined as the ratio of the required storage space to be allocated to an item type to its demand frequency per period (also see Ballou, 1967; Kallina/Lynn, 1976). The concept of the COI is to locate compact, high-frequency item types (low COI) close to the input-output point, and shift bulky, slow-moving items to remote storage locations. Several extensions of the COI concept have been described in the literature, in which aspects such as inventory cost (Wilson, 1977), or zoning constraints (Malmborg, 1995) have been considered. Again, results stemming from this research are of little value for the problem under discussion here, because they have been deduced under the assumption of a simple out-and-back system, too.

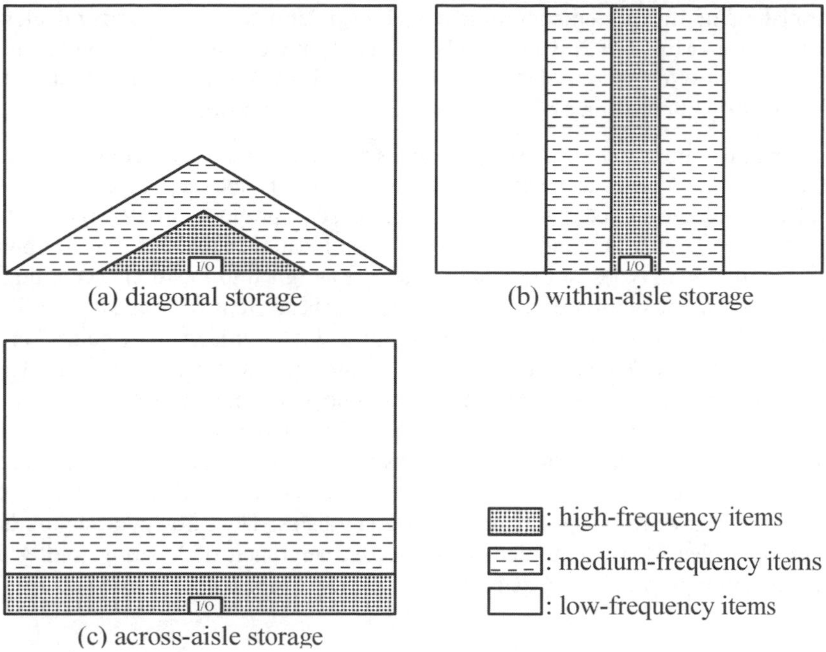

Fig. 3. Storage allocation patterns

4.2.2. Complementarity-based methods

A second class of methods tries to take into account the complementarity between items, which is documented by the fact that certain pairs of item types are demanded together more frequently and therefore appear more often together in the same customer/picking order than others. These methods, which will be called *complementarity-based* here, cluster the item types into groups according to a measure of the strength of the joint demand (complementarity) and locate the members of a cluster as close to each other as possible. Thus, two major phases can be distinguished:

- identification of clusters of item types, which are demanded together frequently (clustering problem);
- clusterwise assignment of items to locations (location-assignment *problem*).

During the first phase, it has to be determined how the complementarity between the item types should be measured, how many clusters should be formed, and, of course, which item types go into each cluster.

Rosenwein (1994) has shown that the clustering problem can be formulated as a p-median problem, which is also frequently used in general cluster analysis (for a formulation of the p-median problem and its relationship with general cluster analysis see Mulvey/Crowder, 1979). His approach is based on a non-complementarity measure ("distance") for each pair (i, j) of item types i and j. Liu (1999, p. 991), on the other hand, uses a measure of similarity.

In general, the drawback of these approaches is related to the problem of assigning the clustered item types to locations. Rosenwein (1994) does not explain how this problem should be solved. Liu (1999, pp. 997 et sqq.) proposes to identify the item type with the largest demand and assign it to a location closest to the I/O point. Then all other item types of the same cluster are assigned to locations according to the standard frequency-based location strategy. These steps are repeated until all item types have been assigned. Liu exemplifies his approach on a simple order picking system, which basically consists of one picking aisle. However, for a multi-aisle multi-block system, location assignment will have to follow one of the storage-allocation patterns (diagonal, within-aisle, and across-aisle storage) described above. Solutions obtained in this way appear not be very satisfactory, as it is very likely – especially with a small number of clusters – that item types of a single cluster have to be split between different aisles. That, however, contradicts the original idea of this complementarity-based approach of locating jointly demanded item types in close proximity.

4.2.3. Contact-based methods

Another basic drawback of the complementarity-based approach to the item location problem can be seen in the fact that, even though two item types i and j appear in the same customer order, an order picker will not necessarily proceed directly from the location of item type i to the location of item type j (or vice versa). Thus, in order to minimize the total travel distance, it would be more desirable to take into account the number of times an order picker really travels directly between the locations of two item types i and j, i.e. the number of times she/he picks either item type j directly after item type i, or item type i directly after item type j, respectively. Methods, which allocate item types to locations with respect to the number of these direct travels (*contacts*), will be called *contact-based*, here. Unfortunately, the *contact frequencies* c(i,j) between item types i and j are not known in advance but stem from the (optimal) solutions of the routing problems related to the set of customer/picking orders under consideration. The solution of the routing problems, however, is dependent on the location of the item types, which again demonstrates the strong interrelationship between item location and routing. Due to the fact that a simultaneous solution of both problems is not a realistic approach, at least not for problem instances of the size encountered in practice, contact-based solution methods alternate between the two problem types.

The method of van Oudheusden et al. (1988, pp. 279 et sqq.) can be characterized as a classic local-search method. It starts from an initial allocation of item types to storage locations, for which the distances d(i,j) between all pairs (i,j) of item types i and j are computed. Given these distances, an (optimal) solution is determined for each of the routing problems associated with the set of customer/picking orders. These solutions provide the contact frequencies c(i,j) for every item pair (i,j). The total travel distance TTD associated with the initial item allocation can be calculated as

(1) $$\mathrm{TTD} = \sum_{i \in I} \sum_{j \in I} d(i,j) \cdot c(i,j)$$

(I: index set of item types). Based on the current values of the contact frequencies c(i,j), the method tries to improve the value of (1) by means of a pairwise exchange of the locations of two item types. The improvement phase is performed in terms of a strict hill-descending procedure in which an exchange of locations is accepted only if the value of (1) is reduced. After each exchange, the distances d(i,j) are updated, while the contact frequencies c(i,j) are left unchanged for the time being. This is for the obvious reason that an update of the c(i,j)-values is a very time-consuming activity because it requires to determine all picking tours anew. The contact frequencies c(i,j) will not be updated before no further exchange of locations can be identified, which improves the value of (1). At that stage, the routing problems are resolved and the new, "real" value of TTD is computed on the basis of the new contact frequencies. The current item allocation now serves as the starting point for another execution of the improvement phase. The method terminates if the contact frequencies have been updated but no pairwise exchange of item locations can be found that would improve the current objective function value (1). The authors applied their approach to real-world data from a central warehouse of an integrated steel mill. They found that the existing, obviously not very well planned item allocation could be improved significantly and that, in connection with improved routing, savings in picker travel time of up to 83% were possible (van Oudheusden et al., 1988, pp. 281 et sqq.).

Reschke and Wäscher (2000) present three local search-methods, which are also based on the pairwise exchange of storage locations. However, their methods are different to that of van Oudheusden et al. in the sense that the exact value of the new total travel distance TTD is computed each time before the decision is made about whether to accept an exchange or not. Reschke and Wäscher demonstrate that it is not necessary to determine a new (optimal) tour for every customer/picking order at each iteration but that it is sufficient to consider only such tours, which contain exactly one of the two exchange items (Reschke/Wäscher, 2000, pp. 143 et sqq.). The first proposed method is a classic (2-opt) hill-descending method, which only accepts an exchange of locations if it improves the current solution. The remaining two methods are based on Simulated Annealing (e.g. see van Laarhoven/Aarts, 1992) and Threshold Accepting (see Dueck/Scheuer, 1990), which – at least temporarily – allow the objective function value (1) to deteriorate in order to avoid being trapped in a local minimum.

4.3. Discussion

In general, it has to be stated, that there is very little reliable information available with respect to the (relative) solution quality and computing times of the presented algorithms. According to the best of our knowledge, the numerical experiments carried out by Reschke and Wäscher (2000, pp. 144 et sqq.) are the only ones in which several methods have been directly compared to each other so far. The focus of these experiments was on contact-based methods. The authors implemented the method by van Oudheusden et al. and the three above-described local search-methods and applied them to 140 randomly generated problem instances. The problem instances were grouped into 14 problem classes characterized by parameters such as the average number of positions per customer/picking order, degree of complementarity between item types and skew of the ABC-curve of the demand frequencies. Initial solutions were provided by the standard frequency-based location strategy. The corresponding objective function values also served as benchmarks for the assessment of the solution quality.

It could be shown that all local search-methods improve the initial solutions significantly. The solution quality of Simulated Annealing and of Threshold Accepting turned out to be almost equivalent. On the average, these methods reduced the objective function value to 61-77% of the benchmark. Generally, the results indicate the existence of significant opportunities for picker-productivity improvement in practice, where items are usually assigned to storage locations by means of the standard frequency-based location strategy. On each of the problem classes, Simulated Annealing and Threshold Accepting both outperformed the classic 2-opt hill-descending method, which, on average, reduced the objective function values down to 66-77% of the benchmark. The hill-descending method, in turn, outperformed the method by van Oudheusden et al., which achieved a reduction down to 69-83% of the benchmark. For Simulated Annealing and Threshold Accepting the improvements were generally larger on problem instances with a smaller number of picks per customer/picking order, less skew of the ABC frequency curve and a smaller degree of complementarity.

On the other hand, improvements in the solution quality come at the expense of dramatically increased computing times. As could be expected with respect to the extensive computations necessary at each iteration (determination of the new optimal picking tours), the computing times per problem instance can easily amount to hours for Simulated Annealing and Threshold Accepting on a PC. However, such computing times may still be acceptable in practice, because the item-location problem is usually not a time-critical one and solved in long time intervals (once a year or once in six months) only.

5. Order batching

5.1. Problem statement

The order batching problem can be stated as follows:

> Given a set of customer orders, each consisting of a number of orderlines, a given assignment of items to storage locations in a standard order-picking warehouse and a given capacity of the picking device, how should the customer orders be grouped (batched) into picking orders such that no customer order is split between two or more picking orders and the total lengths of all picker tours necessary to collect all items is minimized.

The batching problem is also known to be NP-hard. Consequently, with respect to the size of problem instances encountered in practice, research has concentrated on methods of the heuristic type.

5.2. Solution methods

The heuristics suggested in the literature for the order batching problem can be classified into *priority rule-based algorithms, seed algorithms and savings algorithms.*

5.2.1. Priority rule-based algorithms

These algorithms assign a priority to each customer order, at first. Then, in the order given by the priorities, the customer orders are assigned one by one to batches (picking orders) in a way that the capacity constraint is not violated.

Several suggestions have been made in the literature with respect to the determination of the priorities. The most straightforward specification is the First-Come-First-Serve (FCFS) Rule. Gibson and Sharp (1992) suggested two-dimensional and four-dimensional space-filling curves to be used. These approaches map the coordinates of the locations of the items of a customer order into a (theta-) value on the unit circle. The theta-values range from 0 to 1. The larger the theta-value is, which has been assigned to a customer order, the higher is its priority.

Next-Fit (batches are completed with orders in the sequence given by the priorities; every time the addition of another customer order would violate the capacity constraint, a new batch is started), First-Fit (batches are numbered in the sequence in which they are started; the current customer order is assigned to a batch with the smallest number into which it fits), and Best-Fit (of those batches into which a customer order would fit, it is assigned to that one where it leaves the smallest remaining capacity) are specifications of the *batch selection rule*.

5.2.2. Seed algorithms

Seed Algorithms have been introduced into the literature by Elsayed (1981) and by Elsayed and Stern (1983), who considered them for automatic warehouses in the first place. A systematic study for manual warehouses is presented in de Koster et al. (1999). Seed methods generate batches sequentially, i.e. a new batch is not started before the current one has been closed. In order to form a batch, a customer order is selected as the so-called "seed" of the batch. Further, not yet assigned customer orders are added to the batch until its capacity is exhausted.

For the *seed-selection rule*, several options have been discussed in the literature (de Koster et al., 1999, p. 1483), namely – among others – the selection of a random order, an order with the largest number of positions (i.e. selection of the "largest" order), an order with the longest picking tour, an order with the most distantly-located item (i.e. the item located furthest away from the depot), an order with the largest number of aisles to be visited, an order with the largest aisle range (i.e. the largest difference between the aisle numbers of the right-most and the left-most aisle to be visited), etc. The seed-selection rule can be applied in two ways (de Koster et al., 1999, p. 1484), in a *single mode* (in which the originally selected customer order only serves as seed for the present batch) or a *cumulative mode* (in which all customer orders already assigned to the current batch make up for the seed of the batch).

The *order-congruency rule* determines which unassigned customer order should be the next one to be added to the current batch. Usually, an order is selected which "distance" to the seed of the current batch is minimal. This distance between an unassigned order and the seed can be defined in several ways, e.g. (de Koster et al., 1999, p. 1484) as

- the sum of the travel distances (measured in length or time units or in the number of aisles) between every location of a seed item and the closest location of any item in the order,
- the sum of the travel distances between every location of an item in the order and the closest location of any item in the seed,
- the number of additional aisles which have to be visited if the order would be added to the seed,
- the difference between the gravity centre of the seed and the gravity centre of the order (where the gravity centre of an order is defined as the average aisle number of the locations of the items in an order), etc.

5.2.3. Savings algorithms

Savings algorithms (de Koster et al., 1999, pp. 1485-1487; Elsayed/Unal, 1989, pp. 1099-1101) are based on the well-known Clarke-and-Wright-Algorithm for the vehicle-routing problem (Clarke/Wright, 1964). Let d(q) be the length of the picking tour for order q, d(r) the length of the respective tour for order r, and d(q∘r) the length of a single picking tour in which the items of both order q and r are collected. Thus, the savings s(q,r) of combining the two orders q and r in a single tour can be computed as s(q,r) = d(q) + d(r) - d(q∘r).

The pairs (q,r) of the customer orders are sorted in a non-ascending order. According to this order the pairs are examined. Three situations have to be considered:

- None of the orders q and r has been assigned: In this case, a new batch is opened, and q and r are assigned to it.
- One of the orders q and r has already been assigned: The other order will be assigned to the same batch if the remaining capacity is large enough. Otherwise the next order will be checked.
- Both orders q and r have already been assigned: In this case, the next pair of orders will be checked.

In the end, customer orders might be left which cannot be combined with each other, due to the limited capacity of the picking device. They are assigned to an individual batch each. Furthermore, a recalculation of the savings s(q,r) any time one or two customer orders have been assigned to a batch is likely to improve the solution quality of the algorithm.

The EQUAL-Algorithm (Elsayed/Unal, 1989, pp. 1099 et sqq.) is a savings algorithm that generates batches sequentially. The first batch is started with a pair of customer orders q and r which can be combined in a batch and for which the savings s(q,r) are maximal. These two orders are taken as an initial seed. Then an order is added to the batch, which is chosen such that the savings of combining the seed with an unassigned order is maximized and the capacity of the picking device is not violated. The old seed and the newly added customer order form the new seed. This is repeated until the capacity of the picking device does not permit to add another customer order. Then a new batch is opened and completed in the same way etc.

In the Small-Large- (SL-) Algorithm (Elsayed/Unal, 1989, p. 1100), the set of customer orders is divided into two subsets, namely into a set of large orders (containing a number of items larger than a pre-specified number) and into a set of small orders (containing the remaining orders). To the set of large orders, the EQUAL-Algorithm is applied. Next, the set of small orders is sorted in non-ascending order of their size. In this sequence, the small orders are assigned, each order to that batch where it results in the largest savings without violating the remaining capacity. For an order which cannot be assigned a new batch is opened.

5.3. Discussion

The FCFS-Heuristic cannot really be considered as a competitive method for the solution of the order batching problem. In fact, it is usually only taken as a benchmark method to which other methods are compared in terms of solution quality and computing times. Gibson and Sharp (1992) have carried out numerical experiments with priority rule-based algorithms, in which the priorities were determined by means of space-filling curves, and with a basic seed algorithm, which they introduced into the literature under the name of Sequential Minimum Distance (SMD) Batching Heuristic. They found (Gibson/Sharp, 1992, p. 67) that for warehouses where the distances between locations are measured according to an aisle metric (and not in terms of a Euclidian, Chebyshev, or rectilinear metric), the SMD Heuristic provided the best solutions.

De Koster et al. (1999) have carried out extensive numerical experiments with seed and savings algorithms. The heuristics were evaluated with respect to different parameters such as the warehouse type, the location of the depot, and the number of orders per batch. Two routing strategies, traversal and largest-gap, were investigated. The total travel time served as the overall performance measure, permitting that influencing factors such as the travel speed within aisles, the speed outside aisles, and the time to enter and leave aisles could be considered. The authors concluded (de Koster et al., 1999, pp. 1498 et sqq.) that the routing strategy should be selected first before the batching strategy is chosen. In case of a large number of items to be picked per aisle and substantial aisle-changing time, the traversal strategy is favourable, otherwise the largest-gap strategy is to be preferred. If the traversal strategy is used and the capacity of the picking vehicle is large, then seed algorithms provide the best results. On the other hand, if the largest-gap strategy is applied and the capacity of the picking vehicle is small, then savings algorithms provide superior results. In this situation, the best results were obtained by the basic algorithm, which included recalculation of the savings s(q,r). However, these results came at the expense of long computing times. It consumed about ten times the computing time of the other savings algorithms and about 100-200 times the computing time of seed algorithms.

6. Picker routing

6.1. Problem statement

The third problem to be considered here concerns the routing of the order pickers. It can be formulated as follows:

> Given an assignment of items to storage locations in a standard order-picking warehouse and a set of picking orders each requiring to pick a certain set of items, in which sequence should the locations of the items in each picking order be visited such that the length of the total travel distance is minimized.

We note that, at this stage, the picking orders are fixed. The total length of all picking tours will be minimized if each tour length is minimized individually.

Thus, for each picking order, a Traveling Salesman Problem (TSP) has to be solved to give an optimal tour between the locations of the items to be picked. The general TSP is known to be NP-hard. However, Ratliff and Rosenthal (1983) have shown that the above TSP related to order picking in a rectangular warehouse can be solved in polynomial time.

6.2. Solution methods

6.2.1. Exact (optimal) methods

In order to formulate a model of the picker routing problem, an approach outlined in de Koster/van der Poort (1998), Roodbergen (2001), and Roodbergen/de Koster (2001b) will be described. According to this approach, the picker routing problem in a standard warehouse can be modelled by means of a valued, undirected multi-graph G. Let m denote the number of locations from which items have to be picked as defined by the corresponding picking order. Furthermore, let n denote the number of picking aisles in the warehouse. Then the vertex set V of the graph G consists of m elements v_i, each one representing a pick location i (i = 1, ..., m), n elements a_j, where a_j represents the location of the front end of aisle j, n elements b_j, where b_j represents the location of the rear end of aisle j (j = 1, ..., n), and an element v_0 representing the location of the I/O point.

Any two vertices which correspond to adjacent locations in the warehouse are connected by a pair of undirected, parallel arcs. Two arcs are introduced because the path between two adjacent locations may be chosen more than once in a picking tour, while – on the other hand – in an optimal (minimum length) tour the order picker will not have to walk more than twice between any pair of locations (Ratliff/Rosenthal, 1983, p. 510). The values assigned to each arc represent the length of the path between the corresponding two locations. A multi-graph G, which has been constructed in this way to represent a routing problem in a standard warehouse, will be called an *order-picking graph* (de Koster/van der Poort, 1998, p. 471).

An order-picking tour is a cycle in G that contains each of the vertices v_i (i = 0, 1, ..., m) at least once, the length of the tour is the sum of the values of the arcs included in the cycle. A subgraph T of G that contains all vertices v_i (i = 0, 1, ..., m) of G will be called a *tour subgraph* of G if there is an order-picking tour that uses each arc in T exactly once. As an order-picking tour can be generated from a given tour subgraph by a very simple (efficient) procedure (Ratliff/Rosenthal, 1983, pp. 518 et sqq.), the problem of constructing a minimum-length picking tour in an order-picking graph of a standard order-picking warehouse is reduced to finding a minimum-length tour subgraph of the corresponding order-picking graph. Ratliff and Rosenthal (1983, pp. 513-516) present an algorithm for this problem, which is linear in the number of aisles. Therefore, their optimal algorithm is fast enough to be applied to any real-world instance of the picker-routing problem in standard warehouses.

Goetschalckx and Ratliff (1988) developed an efficient optimal algorithm for the picker-routing problem in a one-block warehouse with wide aisles, where the order picker cannot reach items on both sides without changing her/his position. Furthermore, the authors discovered that unless the pick density (i.e. the number of the locations from which items have to be picked in relation to the total number of locations) is greater than 50%, picking from both sides of the aisle in the same pass yields significantly shorter tours than picking one side first and then returning on the other side.

Based on the algorithm by Ratliff and Rosenthal, several approaches have been developed for solving picker-routing problems in other, non-standard warehouses. In de Koster/van der Poort (1998) the algorithm is modified for solving such problems in warehouses with decentralized depositing, in Roodbergen/de Koster (2001b) for problems in order-picking warehouses with a middle cross aisle. In Roodbergen/de Koster (2001a) the authors use a branch-and-bound method to obtain optimal tours for warehouses with multiple cross aisles.

6.2.2. Heuristic methods

The above-introduced routing strategies (traversal, return, largest-gap, combined) can be seen as heuristic solution methods for the picker-routing problem. Initially, research efforts concerning this type of methods concentrated on the development of approximations for the (average) tour length. Kunder and Gudehus (1975) consider the traversal and the return strategy and present formulae from which the (expected) average travel time per pick can be computed for any value of parameters such as the number of aisles, aisle length, aisle width, number of articles in the warehouse, number of pick locations, picker speed, etc. Their research is extended by Hall (1993), who considers the traversal and largest-gap strategy. His analysis shows that the largest-gap strategy is to be favoured in warehouses with narrow aisles if the number of picks is less than 3.8, otherwise the traversal strategy appears to be superior. Petersen (1997) compared – among others – traversal, return, largest-gap, and composite routing strategies by means of numerical experiments. He found that the composite and largest-gap heuristics perform best. In these three papers, however, analysis and experiments are carried out under the assumption that pick locations are independent and uniformly distributed (which does not appear to be very realistic for order-picking warehouses).

Caron et al. (1998) investigate the expected total travel distance of the traversal and the return strategy for COI-based storage. The deduced approximations are validated by means of numerical experiments. The authors find that whether the traversal or the return strategy has to be preferred is affected by the average number of picks per aisle and the skew of the ABC frequency curve in the first place while the number of aisles is a less critical parameter. The return strategy outperforms the traversal strategy only for a small number of picks per aisle (i.e. < 1) and for skewed ABC curves; otherwise the traversal strategy is superior. For a large number of picks per tour the traversal strategy outperforms the return strategy, irrespective of the skew of the ABC curve (Caron et al., 1998, p. 731).

Petersen (1999) compares several routing strategies (traversal, largest-gap, composite) in a volume-based storage environment by means of extensive numerical experiments. The performance measure is the (average) total time necessary to collect all items of a picking order and includes a time-estimate for all non travel-related activities. His findings are (Petersen, 1999, pp. 1059 et sqq.) that for within-aisle storage the composite routing strategy performs best. For small picking orders the performance of the largest-gap strategy is almost identical, but it becomes inferior for picking orders containing more than nine positions. For order sizes of more than 28 positions the largest-gap strategy even becomes inferior to the traversal strategy. For diagonal storage, both composite and largest-gap strategies perform almost equally well and outperform the traversal strategy for all order sizes considered (up to 50 positions).

6.3. Discussion

The application of a routing heuristic instead of an optimal algorithm involves accepting an inferior solution quality. De Koster and van der Poort (1998) carried out a series of numerical experiments in order to compare the performance of the traversal heuristic to that of an optimal algorithm for three different types of order-picking warehouses (narrow-aisle high-bay warehouse, shelf picking, and standard warehouse). The authors assumed randomly distributed picking locations. For the first two types they found that the traversal strategy generated solutions which were – on average – between 7.3% and 20.8% above the optimum in terms of travel time and between 2.4% and 5.8% above the optimum in terms of total picking time. The differences were more significant for the standard warehouse, in which the heuristic rated above the optimum between 26.6% and 34.2% with respect to travel time and between 11.2% and 13.9% with respect to total picking time. In Petersen's experiments (Petersen 1997) also random storage has been assumed. The heuristics, which came out best, composite and largest-gap, were found to be 9-10% over optimal on average in terms of tour length. In another series of experiments, in which frequency-based storage was assumed, Petersen and Schmenner (1999) compared the solutions of several heuristics to those obtained by an optimal algorithm. The more advanced heuristics, largest-gap, composite, and midpoint, came out, on average, 7.1%, 10.2%, and 12.0% over optimal. With 27.9% and 30.9% over optimal, the simpler return and traversal strategies performed significantly worse (Petersen/Schmenner, 1999, p. 492).

Given the fact that the Ratliff-Rosenthal-Algorithm solves the picker-routing problem in polynomial time and can be applied to any real-world problem instance, and given the inferior solution quality of heuristic routing methods, one may ask why anyone would use a heuristic method. First of all, our discussion has focussed on routing problems in standard order-picking warehouses. Real-world warehouses may have different layouts or other specific properties for which no exact algorithm has been developed so far. Secondly, the difference between a minimum-length tour and a heuristically-obtained solution may not always be really significant, because practical situations exist in which total travel time represents only a relatively small proportion of the total picking time. De Koster and van der Poort (1998, p. 478) mention that the travel time is often only about 50% of the (total) picking time. Finally, optimal tours may not always work in practice, because they can be confusing for the order picker and increase the probability of missing picks. Heuristics, on the other hand, often can be understood and remembered more easily and require less concentration when being executed. These advantages of heuristics have to be compared against the savings in travel time and travel distance from optimal routing (Petersen, 1999, p. 1054).

7. Conclusions

It should have become clear from the previous discussion that by means of advanced planning techniques, which are available today, it is possible to improve the performance of order picking operations significantly, both with respect to order processing times and picking costs. On the other hand, it is also obvious that the present knowledge is still insufficient in several areas and that additional studies are necessary to improve the state-of-the-art. This concerns the solution methods for the item-location problem, which seem to provide good-quality solution but require too much computing effort. With respect to the order-batching problem it is striking that only construction methods have been presented in the literature so far, while neither any improvement methods have been suggested nor the application of meta-heuristics has been investigated. Finally, due to the close relationship between order-batching and optimal routing, it might be worthwhile to consider a simultaneous solution approach for these two problem areas.

References

Ballou, R. H. (1967): Improving the Physical Layout of Merchandise in Warehouses. In: Journal of Marketing 31, July, pp. 60-64.

Bassan, Y., Roll, Y., Rosenblatt, M.J. (1980): Internal Layout Design of a Warehouse. In: AIIE Transactions 12, pp. 317-322.

Caron, F., Marchet, G., Perego, A. (1998): Routine Policies and COI-Based Storage Policies in Picker-to-Part Systems. In: International Journal of Production Research 36, pp. 713-732.

Caron, F., Marchet, G., Perego, A. (2000): Optimal Layout in Low-Level Picker-to-Part Systems. In: International Journal of Production Research 38, pp. 101-117.

Clarke, G., Wright, W. (1964): Scheduling of Vehicles from a Central Depot to a Number of Delivery Points. In: Operations Research 12, pp. 568-581.

Cormier, G., Gunn, E.A. (1992): A Review of Warehouse Models. In: European Journal of Operational Research 58, pp. 3-13.

Dueck, G., Scheuer, T. (1990): Threshold Accepting: A General Purpose Optimization Algorithm Appearing Superior to Simulated Annealing. In: Journal of Computational Physics 90, pp. 161-175.

Elsayed, E.A. (1981): Algorithms for Optimal Material Handling in Automatic Warehousing Systems. In: International Journal of Production Research 19, pp. 525-535.

Elsayed, E.A., Stern, R.G. (1983): Computerized Algorithms for Order Processing in Automated Warehousing Systems. In: International Journal of Production Research 21, pp. 579-586.

Elsayed, E.A., Unal, O.I. (1989): Order Batching Algorithms and Travel-Time Estimation for Automated Storage/Retrieval Systems. In: International Journal of Production Research 27, pp. 1097-1114.

Gibson, D.R., Sharp, G.P. (1992): Order Batching Procedures. In: European Journal of Operational Research 58, pp. 57-67.

Goetschalckx, M., Ratliff, H.D. (1988): Order Picking in an Aisle. In: IIE Transactions 20, No. 1, pp. 53-62.

Hall, R. H. (1993): Distance Approximations for Routing Manual Pickers in a Warehouse. In: IIE Transactions 24, No. 4 (July), pp. 76-87.

Heskett, J.L. (1963): Cube-per-Order Index – A Key to Warehouse Stock Location. In: Transportation and Distribution Management 3, April, pp. 27-31.

Heskett, J.L. (1964): Putting the Cube-per-Order Index to Work in Warehouse Layout. In: Transportation and Distribution Management 4, August, pp. 23-30.

Jarvis, J.M., McDowell, E.D. (1991): Optimal Product Layout in an Order Picking Warehouse. In: IIE Transactions 23, pp. 93-102.

Kallina, C. (1976): Optimality of the Cube-per-Order Index Rule for Stock Location in a Distribution Warehouse. Working Paper, American Can Company, March 1976.

Kallina, C., Lynn, J. (1976): Application of the Cube-per-Order Index Rule for Stock Location in a Distribution Warehouse. In: Interfaces **7**, No. 1 (November), pp. 37-46.

Koster, de M.B.M., Poort, van der E.S., Wolters, M. (1999): Efficient Orderbatching Methods in Warehouses. In: International Journal of Production Research 37, pp. 1479-1504.

Koster, de R., Poort, van der E. (1998): Routing Orderpickers in a Warehouse: A Comparison Between Optimal and Heuristic Solutions. In: IIE Transactions 30, pp. 469-480.

Kunder, R., Gudehus, T. (1975): Mittlere Wegzeiten beim eindimensionalen Kommissionieren. In: Zeitschrift für Operations Research 19, B53-B72.

Laarhoven, van P.J.M., Aarts, E.J.H. (1992): Simulated Annealing: Theory and Applications. Dordrecht et al.

Liu, C.-M. (1999): Clustering Techniques for Stock Location and Order-Picking in a Distribution Center. In: Computers & Operations Research 26, pp. 989-1002.

Malmborg, C.J. (1995): Optimiztion of Cube-per-Order Index Layouts with Zoning Constraints. In: International Journal of Production Research 33, pp. 465-482.

Malmborg, C.J. (1996): Storage Assignment Policy Tradeoffs. In: International Journal of Production Research 34, pp. 363-378.

Mulvey, J.M., Crowder, H. (1979): Cluster Analysis: An Application of Langrangean Relaxation. In: Management Science 25, pp. 329-340.

Neal, F.L. (1962): Controlling Warehouse Handling Costs by Means of Stock Location Audits. In: Transportation and Distribution Management 2, May, pp. 31-33.

Oudheusden, van D. L., Tzen, Y.-J., Ko, H.-T. (1988): Improving Storage and Order Picking in a Person-on-Board AS/R System: A Case Study. In: Engineering Costs and Production Economics 13, pp. 273-283.

Petersen II, C.G. (1997): An Evaluation of Order Picking Routing Policies. In: International Journal of Operations and Production Management 17, pp. 1098-1111.

Petersen II, C.G. (1999): The Impact of Routing and Storage Policies on Warehouse Efficiency. In: International Journal of Operations and Production Management 19, pp. 1053-1064.

Petersen II, C.G., Schmenner, R. W. (1999): An Evaluation of Routing and Volume-based Storage Policies in an Order Picking Operation. In: Decision Sciences 30, pp. 481-501.

Ratliff, H., Rosenthal, A. (1983): Orderpicking in a Rectangular Warehouse: A Solvable Case of the Traveling Salesman Problem. In: Operations Research 31, pp. 507-521.

Reschke, V., Wäscher, G. (2000): Local Search-Verfahren für die Lagerplatzvergabe in Mann-zur-Ware-Kommissioniersystemen. In: Logistik 2000plus: Herausforderungen,

Trends, Konzepte. Begleitband zur 6. Magdeburger Logistik-Tagung, Magdeburg, 16./17.11.2000 (Hrsg.: Inderfurth, K., Schenk, M., Ziems, D.). Magdeburg: Otto-von-Guericke-Universität und LOGiSCH GmbH, pp. 136-151.

Roodbergen, K.J. (2001): Layout and Routing Methods for Warehouses. Doctoral Dissertation, Erasmus Research Institute of Management (ERIM), Erasmus University, Rotterdam (ERIM Ph.D. Series Research in Management 4, TRAIL Thesis Series No. T2001/3).

Roodbergen, K.J., Koster, de R. (2001a): Routing Methods for Warehouses with Multiple Cross Aisles. In: International Journal of Production Research 39, pp. 1865-1883.

Roodbergen, K.J., Koster, de R. (2001b): Routing Order Pickers in a Warehouse with a Middle Aisle. In: European Journal of Operational Research 133, pp. 32-43.

Rosenwein, M.B. (1994): An Application of Cluster Analysis to the Problem of Locating Items within a Warehouse. In: IIE Transactions 26, No. 1, pp. 101-103.

Tompkins, J.A., White, J.A., Bozer, Y.A., Frazelle, E., Tanchoo, J.M.A., Trevino, J. (1996): Facilities Planning. 2nd ed., New York: John Wiley.

Vaughan, T. S., Petersen, C. G. (1999): The Effect of Warehouse Cross Aisles on Order Picking Efficiency. In: International Journal of Production Research 37, pp. 881-897.

Wilson, H. G. (1977): Order Quantity, Product Popularity, and the Location of Stock in a Warehouse. In: AIIE Transactions 9, pp. 230-237.

Advanced Purchasing and Order Optimization

Horst Tempelmeier, Gabriele Reith-Ahlemeier

Department of Production and Operations Management
University of Cologne
Albertus-Magnus-Platz
D-50923 Cologne, Germany

Abstract: *In this paper we consider the problem of simultaneous supplier selection and purchase order sizing for several items under dynamic demand conditions and under consideration of limited capacity. Suppliers offer any combination of all-units and/or incremental quantity discounts which may vary over time. Although the problem refers to a typical planning task of a purchasing agent, and is often solved without any algorithmic assistance, in an Advanced Planning System as well as a Business-to-Business (B2B) environment the necessity for the automatic execution of this planning task within the procurement process becomes evident. A new model formulation for this problem is presented and a simple but easily extendible heuristic procedure is developed and tested.*

Keywords: *supplier selection, dynamic order sizing, heuristic solution methods*

1. Introduction

The WEB-based automation of routine procurement processes for maintenance, repair, and operations (MRO) products aims at the realization of significant cost-savings through the streamlining of the traditionally labor-intensive and time-consuming tasks of procurement. This is particularly obvious for products with high volume and low value. However, some writers and consultants celebrating the new world of electronic business and marketplaces seem to overlook that the substitution of the human purchasing agent by a software solution does not dissolve the decision problems of supplier selection and order sizing that formerly made up part of the purchasing agent's tasks. It should be kept in mind, that the full potential for cost-reduction will only be realized, if the complete business process of purchasing can be automated, including the relevant operational purchasing decisions that may heavily influence the performance of a company's purchasing function. Advanced Planning Software vendors are now increasing their efforts for supporting Business-to-Business (B2B) procurement scenarios including planning tools either for automated application within the standard IT-based workflow or as a decision support tool made available on the desktop of the purchasing agent.

In a typical industrial purchasing environment the purchasing agent has the task of supplier selection and order sizing given several suppliers that often offer their customers lower unit prices on orders for larger quantities. In addition, base prices may vary over time due to marketing actions of the suppliers. Furthermore, order sizes may be restricted by different types of capacity constraints, such as storage constraints, material handling constraints, container sizes, or limited transportation capacities.

In this paper we present a planning model for supporting short-term supplier selection and order sizing under dynamic demand conditions and with respect to several types of constrained capacities. We develop a heuristic solution procedure that can be applied as a decision support module within an automated procurement process and which can be plugged into a standard Avanced Planning System.

2. Previous work

In the last years, an increasing amount of literature has appeared that addresses purchasing problems, including supplier selection, mainly with the focus on a long-term framework of supply chain management. See [1], [10], [16], [19], [21], [28], [29], and the references given therein. In the short-term planning environment focussing on the operational decision problems of order sizing and supplier selection that we consider, however, usually it is assumed that the set of suppliers and the purchasing conditions, including discount structures, are already in place. Benton [5] and Rubin [24] present heuristics to solve such problems, but they consider stationary demand and only all-units discount structures.

Although research on production lot sizing and purchase order sizing dates back to the beginning of the 20th century and a large number of research papers have been written, the literature on order sizing under consideration of quantity discounts comprises only a small number of publications. Among these, many papers focus on order sizing under stationary demand conditions, and therefore are not adequate for an operative planning environment, which is dominated by time-varying demands and changing prices and discount structures over time.

Recent overviews over the literature related to the order sizing decision are provided by Benton [6] and Munson and Rosenblatt [20]. Relevant work that focusses on dynamic demand conditions includes [2], [3], [4], [7], [8], [9], [11], [12], [13], [14], [15], [18], and [25]. A paper by Prentis and Khumawala [22] seems to be the only one where quantity discounts in the context of a multi-level MRP-type product structure are considered.

Most of the work that has been done so far concentrates on isolated aspects of the overall problem faced by a purchasing agent. Reducing the complexity through setting several assumptions obviously increases the probability that a specialized (exact or heuristic) and possibly elegant solution algorithm can be developed to solve the resulting model. For example, if capacity constraints are completely ignored and if only incremental quantity discounts are considered, it is possible to construct a shortest-path network where the cost associated to an arc starting in a node, which represents a specific order period, are computed based on the cheapest supplier available in that period and for the order quantity corresponding to that arc. See [30] and [26]. However, this elegant approach is not applicable if all-units discount structures are in effect, which is the case in the majority of planning situations found in industrial purchasing practice [20], and it is also not applicable if capacity constraints are relevant. Up to our knowledge, currently there is no solution approach available for the order sizing and supplier selection problem that simultaneously accounts for dynamic demands, time-varying prices and discount structures, and the different types of capacity constraints mentioned above.

3. A new model formulation

In the sequel we present a new model formulation for the problem of dynamic simultaneous supplier selection and order sizing. In particular we consider several products subject to the following assumptions:

1. Dynamic deterministic demands.
2. Zero inventory at the beginning and the end of the planning horizon.
3. Stockouts not permitted.
4. Several suppliers for each product, each supplier with
   (a) Time-varying deterministic prices dictated by time-varying (all-units or incremental) quantity discount structures with several discount levels. This includes rising or falling prices starting with a specific period as well as special prices for limited time intervals.
   (b) Supplier-specific as well as product-specific fixed ordering costs (transportation costs etc.).
   (c) Product- and supplier-specific delivery calendars; i. e. although the demand periods are days, a supplier may follow a delivery schedule including delivery only on, say, Mondays and Thursdays.
   (d) Product-specific delivery lead times.
   (e) Supplier-specific and product-specific minimum and/or maximum order sizes.
   (f) Supplier-specific capacity constraints (e. g. in transportation).
5. Holding costs depending on the purchasing price.
6. Handling and storage capacity constraints.

These problem characteristics are relevant in many industrial purchasing environments. In the sequel, the following symbols are used:

Parameters:

$a_{k\tau}^{l}$ $= \begin{cases} 1, & \text{if supplier } l \text{ can deliver item } k \text{ in period } \tau \\ 0, & \text{else} \end{cases}$

$b_{j\tau}$ Capacity of handling-resource j of the purchasing company in period τ

$b_{j\tau}^{l}$ Capacity of handling-resource j of supplier l in period τ

$c_{k\tau}^{lr}$ Average unit price in discount level r for item k and supplier l in period τ

d_{kt} Net requirements for item k in period t

$f_{k\tau}^{lr}$ Variable purchasing costs in period τ for item k and supplier l associated with the portion of the order quantity up to the lower limit of the current discount level r

$g_{k\tau}^{lr}$ Upper limit of discount level r for item k and supplier l in period τ; $g_{k\tau}^{l0} = 0$

h Holding cost percentage per period

$h_{k\tau t}^{lr}$ Inventory holding costs for the complete demand of item k in period t, if it is delivered by supplier l in period τ with discount level r; $h_{k\tau t}^{lr} = h \cdot p_{k\tau}^{lr} \cdot d_{kt} \cdot (t - \tau)$

$\mathcal{J}^{\mathcal{H}}$ Set of indices of handling-resources of the purchasing company

$\mathcal{J}^{\mathcal{L}}$ Set of indices of storage-resources of the purchasing company

$\mathcal{J}^{\mathcal{S}^l}$ Set of indices of handling-resources of supplier l

K Number of items

$\mathcal{K}^l$ Set of indices of items that can be ordered from supplier l

L Number of suppliers

$\mathcal{L}^k$ Set of indices of suppliers that can deliver item k

$p_{k\tau}^{lr}$ Unit price in discount level r for item k and supplier l in period τ

$R_{k\tau}^l$ Number of discount levels for item k and supplier l in period τ

$s_{k\tau}^l$ Fixed ordering costs for item k ordered from supplier l in period τ

S_τ^l Fixed ordering costs for supplier l in period τ

tb_{jk} Capacity absorption factor of resource j for handling item k

tb_{jk}^l Capacity absorption factor of resource j of supplier l for handling item k

tw_{jk} Capacity absorption factor of storage-resource j for holding item k

T Number of demand periods

$v_{k\tau}^{lr}$ Difference between the order quantity for item k in period τ from supplier l and the base quantity of the associated discount level r

$w_{j\vartheta}$ Capacity of storage-resource j in period ϑ

Decision variables:

α_τ^l Binary variable for selecting supplier l in period τ

$\delta_{k\tau t}^{lr}$ Proportion of demand for item k in period t, that is delivered by supplier l in period τ with discount level r

$\gamma_{k\tau}^{lr}$ Binary variable for selecting discount level r in period τ for item k supplier l

$q_{k\tau}^{lr}$ Quantity ordered from item k and supplier l in period τ with discount level r

The following mixed-integer linear optimization model (**C**apacitated **M**ulti-**S**upplier **O**rder **Q**uantity **P**roblem with Time-**V**arying **D**iscounts) captures the above-mentioned assumptions.

Model CMSOQP$_{\mathbf{VD}}$

$$\begin{aligned}\text{Minimize } Z = & \sum_{k=1}^{K} \sum_{\tau=1}^{T} \sum_{t=\tau}^{T} \sum_{l=1}^{L} \sum_{r=1}^{R_{k\tau}^l} h_{k\tau t}^{lr} \cdot \delta_{k\tau t}^{lr} \\ & + \sum_{k=1}^{K} \sum_{\tau=1}^{T} \sum_{l=1}^{L} \sum_{r=1}^{R_{k\tau}^l} \left[(s_{k\tau}^l + f_{k\tau}^{lr}) \cdot \gamma_{k\tau}^{lr} + p_{k\tau}^{lr} \cdot v_{k\tau}^{lr} \right] \\ & + \sum_{\tau=1}^{T} \sum_{l=1}^{L} S_\tau^l \cdot \alpha_\tau^l\end{aligned} \tag{1}$$

s. t.

Demand fulfillment:

$$\sum_{\tau=1}^{t}\sum_{l=1}^{L}\sum_{r=1}^{R_{k\tau}^{l}} \delta_{k\tau t}^{lr} = 1 \qquad \begin{array}{c} k = 1,2,\ldots,K \\ t = 1,2,\ldots,T \end{array} \tag{2}$$

Definition of order sizes:

$$\sum_{t=\tau}^{T} d_{kt}\cdot\delta_{k\tau t}^{lr} = q_{k\tau}^{lr} \qquad \begin{array}{c} l = 1,2,\ldots,L;\quad r = 1,2,\ldots,R_{k\tau}^{l} \\ k = 1,2,\ldots,K;\quad \tau = 1,2,\ldots,T \end{array} \tag{3}$$

Upper limit of a discount level:

$$q_{k\tau}^{lr} \le g_{k\tau}^{lr}\cdot\gamma_{k\tau}^{lr} \qquad \begin{array}{c} l = 1,2,\ldots,L;\quad r = 1,2,\ldots,R_{k\tau}^{l} \\ k = 1,2,\ldots,K;\quad \tau = 1,2,\ldots,T \end{array} \tag{4}$$

Lower limit of a discount level:

$$q_{k\tau}^{lr} \ge (g_{k\tau}^{l,r-1}+1)\cdot\gamma_{k\tau}^{lr} \qquad \begin{array}{c} l = 1,2,\ldots,L;\quad r = 1,2,\ldots,R_{k\tau}^{l} \\ k = 1,2,\ldots,K;\quad \tau = 1,2,\ldots,T \end{array} \tag{5}$$

At most one active discount level per delivery period:

$$\sum_{r=1}^{R_{k\tau}^{l}} \gamma_{k\tau}^{lr} \le a_{k\tau}^{l} \qquad \begin{array}{r} l = 1,2,\ldots,L \\ k = 1,2,\ldots,K;\quad \tau = 1,2,\ldots,T \end{array} \tag{6}$$

Define fixed ordering costs and discount level for the selected delivery period:

$$\delta_{k\tau t}^{lr} \le \gamma_{k\tau}^{lr} \qquad \begin{array}{r} l = 1,2,\ldots,L;\quad r = 1,2,\ldots,R_{k\tau}^{l};\quad k = 1,2,\ldots,K \\ \tau = 1,2,\ldots,T;\quad t = \tau,\tau+1,\ldots,T \;\mid\; d_{kt} > 0 \end{array} \tag{7}$$

Handling capacity of the purchasing company:

$$\sum_{k=1}^{K} tb_{jk}\cdot\sum_{l\in\mathcal{L}^{k}}\sum_{r=1}^{R_{k\tau}^{l}} q_{k\tau}^{lr} \le b_{j\tau} \qquad j\in\mathcal{J}^{\mathcal{H}};\quad \tau = 1,2,\ldots,T \tag{8}$$

Supplier's handling capacity:

$$\sum_{k \in \mathcal{K}^l} tb^l_{jk} \cdot \sum_{r=1}^{R^l_{k\tau}} q^{lr}_{k\tau} \leq b^l_{j\tau} \cdot \alpha^l_\tau \qquad \begin{array}{r} l = 1, 2, \ldots, L \\ j \in \mathcal{J}^{\mathcal{S}^l}; \tau = 1, 2, \ldots, T \end{array} \tag{9}$$

Minimum order size:

$$\sum_{k \in \mathcal{K}^l} \sum_{r=1}^{R^l_{k\tau}} q^{lr}_{k\tau} \geq mb^l_\tau \cdot \alpha^l_\tau \qquad l = 1, 2, \ldots, L; \quad \tau = 1, 2, \ldots, T \tag{10}$$

Storage capacity of the purchasing company:

$$\sum_{k=1}^{K} \sum_{\tau=1}^{\vartheta} \sum_{t=\vartheta+1}^{T} \sum_{l=1}^{L} \sum_{r=1}^{R^l_{k\tau}} tw_{jk} \cdot d_{kt} \cdot \delta^{lr}_{k\tau t} \leq w_{j\vartheta} \qquad \begin{array}{r} j \in \mathcal{J}^{\mathcal{L}} \\ \vartheta = 1, 2, \ldots, T \end{array} \tag{11}$$

Portion of the variable costs associated to the current discount level:

$$v^{lr}_{k\tau} = q^{lr}_{k\tau} - g^{l,r-1}_{k\tau} \cdot \gamma^{lr}_{k\tau} \qquad \begin{array}{r} l = 1, 2, \ldots, L; \quad r = 1, 2, \ldots, R^l_{k\tau} \\ k = 1, 2, \ldots, K; \quad \tau = 1, 2, \ldots, T \end{array} \tag{12}$$

Holding costs:

$$h^{lr}_{k\tau t} = h \cdot c^{lr}_{k\tau} \cdot d_{kt} \cdot (t - \tau) \qquad \begin{array}{r} l = 1, 2, \ldots, L \\ r = 1, 2, \ldots, R^l_{k\tau}; \quad k = 1, 2, \ldots, K \\ \tau = 1, 2, \ldots, T; \quad t = \tau, \tau + 1, \ldots, T \end{array} \tag{13}$$

Decision variables:

$$\gamma^{lr}_{k\tau} \in \{0, 1\} \qquad \begin{array}{r} l = 1, 2, \ldots, L; \quad r = 1, 2, \ldots, R^l_{k\tau} \\ k = 1, 2, \ldots, K; \quad \tau = 1, 2, \ldots, T \end{array} \tag{14}$$

$$\alpha^l_\tau \in \{0, 1\} \qquad l = 1, 2, \ldots, L; \quad \tau = 1, 2, \ldots, T \tag{15}$$

$$\delta^{lr}_{k\tau t} \geq 0 \qquad \begin{array}{r} l = 1, 2, \ldots, L \\ r = 1, 2, \ldots, R^l_{k\tau}; \quad k = 1, 2, \ldots, K \\ \tau = 1, 2, \ldots, T; \quad t = \tau, \tau + 1, \ldots, T \end{array} \tag{16}$$

The model formulation is based on the well-known analogy between the plant location problem and the dynamic lot sizing problem [17], [26]. The objective function (1) comprises holding costs, product-specific fixed and variable purchasing costs as well as fixed purchasing costs that occur independent from the number of items ordered from a specific supplier in a given period. Constraints (2) ensure that the complete demand for item k in period t is delivered at the latest in period t by any of the available suppliers with a specific price. Equations (3) define the order sizes. The selection of the applicable discount class is obtained through constraints (4) – (6). In addition to that, constraints (6) serve to define the supplier specific delivery calendars. Constraints (7) ensure the inclusion of fixed ordering costs in the objective function in case of delivery.

The remaining restrictions refer to the limited capacities. Constraints (8) limit the amount of incoming orders at the purchasing company's warehouse. Constraints (9) ensure that the suppliers' handling capacities are not overburdened. Constraints (10) limit the order sizes. Constraints (11) limit the amount of inventory. Maximum and minimum product-specific order sizes – which may be valid for certain periods – and even forbidden ranges of order sizes can easily be modeled with the help of dummy discount levels with associated prohibitively high prices.

Note that the items are linked through the capacity constraints as well as through the item-independent fixed ordering costs $S_\tau^l (l = 1, 2, \ldots, L; \tau = 1, 2, \ldots, T)$, that can be considered as joint setup costs.

Supplier-specific lead-times are accounted for through the setting of the $a_{k\tau}^l$-values. If supplier l has lead time z_k^l (based on the planning time 0), then we have $(a_{k\tau}^l = 0 \mid \tau < z_k^l)$.

The remaining constraints (12) and (13) are auxiliary constraints. The variable $v_{k\tau}^{lr}$, defined by (12), denotes the difference between the order quantity in period τ from supplier l and the base quantity of the associated discount level r. The coefficient $f_{k\tau}^{lr}$ denotes the variable purchasing costs associated with the portion of the order quantity up to the lower limit of the discount level r, which is relevant for the current order size. For the case of *incremental discounts* this term evaluates to

$$f_{k\tau}^{lr} = \sum_{i=1}^{r-1} \left(g_{k\tau}^{li} - g_{k\tau}^{l,i-1}\right) \cdot p_{k\tau}^{li} \tag{17}$$

In the case of *all-units discounts* we have

$$f_{k\tau}^{lr} = g_{k\tau}^{l,r-1} \cdot p_{k\tau}^{lr} \tag{18}$$

By adding the cost for the remaining quantity $v_{k\tau}^{lr} = q_{k\tau}^{lr} - g_{k\tau}^{l,r-1}$ we get the complete variable ordering costs for ordering the quantity $q_{k\tau}^{lr}$. As far as the variable ordering costs are concerned, the difference between all-units and incremental discount structures can thus be reflected through the simple preparation of the input data. Table 1 shows the differences between the $f_{k\tau}^{lr}$-values for item k with all-units and incremental discount schemes for different values of the order size q.

r	$g_{k\tau}^{lr}$	$p_{k\tau}^{lr}$	all-units	incremental
0	0	–	–	–
1	100	4.1	$f_{k\tau}^{l1}(q=50)=0$	$f_{k\tau}^{l1}(q=50)=0$
2	250	3.72	$f_{k\tau}^{l2}(q=200)=372$	$f_{k\tau}^{l2}(q=200)=410$
3	∞	3.55	$f_{k\tau}^{l3}(q=400)=887.5$	$f_{k\tau}^{l3}(q=400)=410+558=968$

Table 1. Comparison of all-units and incremental discount schemes

Model CMSOQP$_{\mathrm{VD}}$ captures planning situations where some suppliers offer all-units discounts and others use an incremental discount scheme for the same item whitin a unifying framework. It is even possible that a supplier switches from all-units to incremental discounts within the planning horizon of the model.

It is well-known that – opposite to the undiscounted and uncapacitated single-item lotsizing problem – under the condition of *all-units quantity discounts* in the optimal solution a single demand may be fullfilled by two different orders with different prices. In the presence of multiple suppliers, a period demand may even be fullfilled by different suppliers. Moreover, under capacity constraints a single period demand may be delivered from different suppliers in different periods.

The proposed model has the nice characteristic that it is much tighter than the standard "Big-M"-based lot size model formulation. In several computational tests we found that the solution time was dramatically reduced, however, not enough to find the exact solution for any problem size.

Unfortunately, as the holding cost coefficient $h_{k\tau t}^{lr}$ in the objective function (1) depends on the mean purchasing price for all units included in an order, as given by equation (19), for *incremental discounts* the objective function is *non-linear.*

$$c_{k\tau}^{lr} = \frac{f_{k\tau}^{lr} + v_{k\tau}^{lr} \cdot p_{k\tau}^{lr}}{q_{k\tau}^{lr}} \tag{19}$$

For that reason in the numerical test discussed later we approximate the average price in the case of incremental discounts by replacing the order size with the upper limit of the current discount level. Only for small problems with discrete demands it is possible to introduce as many unit-sized dummy discount levels with $g_{k\tau}^{lr} - g_{k\tau}^{l,r-1} = 1$ as there are total demands. For these problem instances it is then possible to compute the exact solution to the resulting linear MIP representation of the non-linear problem. As the number of binary variables increases dramatically as a function of the problem size, for larger problems we only can use dummy discount levels with sizes wider than a unit. As a consequence, the resulting approximate model which can be solved to optimality with a standard MIP-solver provides a heuristic solution which then has to be evaluated with the correct non-linear objective function. Only in the case of no capacity constraints and if exclusively incremental discounts are in effect, the above-mentioned shortest-path approach can be used to solve the problem exactly.

4. A new heuristic

In view of its complexity model $CMSOQP_{VD}$ can be solved exactly only for rather small problem instances. In our tests we used CPLEX 6.6 for parallel computers running on a UNIX-based host using eight parallel processors. Depending on the problem data, CPU times required for finding the exact solutions for problem instances with 3 products, 30 periods, 5 discount levels and 3 suppliers ranged between a few seconds and several hours.

Therefore, in order to solve model $CMSOQP_{VD}$ in a routine planning environment, a fast heuristic solution procedure is required. Reith-Ahlemeier [23] has developed a branch-and-bound heuristic as well as a Lagrangean relaxation-based heuristic, which both provide near-optimum solutions of model $CMSOQP_{VD}$. The latter is based on the relaxation of the constraints (2) and (8) – (11). The Lagrangean multipliers are adjusted via standard subgradient optimization techniques. The relaxed problem arising in each iteration is decomposed into several continuous and binary knapsack problems. The solutions of these subproblems provide a lower bound of the objective value of model $CMSOQP_{VD}$. In each iteration, based on the current Lagrangean multipliers a feasible solution and a corresponding upper bound is computed. Although the Lagrangean-relaxation based heuristic finds solutions which are near to optimality, the computation times required prevent its routine application within a standard purchasing process.

A building block of any Lagrangean relaxation-based heuristic is a procedure for finding an as good as possible feasible solution. For the considered model $CMSOQP_{VD}$ feasible solutions were computed with the help of a newly-developed fast and simple local search heuristic, which will be presented in the sequel. This heuristic can either be used as part of the Lagrangean-relaxation based heuristic for the computation of the upper bound of the objective value. Alternatively, in cases when the Lagrangean relaxation-based heuristic is too time-consuming for a practical application, the heuristic can also be applied on a stand-alone basis to solve model $CMSOQP_{VD}$. Mainly with this latter application in mind, the development of the heuristic was guided by several requirements that industrial users attached importance to during several discussions:

1. The heuristic must consider all aspects included in model $CMSOQP_{VD}$ (i. e. solve the *complete* problem).
2. It must be fast.
3. It must be easily extendible with respect to additional constraints without a major redesign of the complete solution procedure.
4. It must be understandable by the user.

Based on these requirements, we developed a heuristic solution method that consists basically of two main phases. In phase one (construction phase), an initial solution is constructed. In phase two (improvement phase) several local search procedures are iteratively applied to improve a given solution. Fig. 4. summarizes the overall structure of the heuristic.

Phase I: Initial solution	
	For each item, solve a single-item order sizing problem, neglecting the capacity constraints.
	If the order schedule violates any capacity constraints, construct a feasible solution by a sequence of moves with shifting, combining and splitting orders.
Phase II: Improvement steps	
	Step 1: Take measures to reduce the fixed ordering costs.
	Step 2: Take measures to reduce the variable ordering costs.
	Step 3: Take measures to reduce the holding costs.

Fig. 1. Overall structure of the heuristic

4.1. Phase I: Initial solution

The first phase of the heuristic starts with neglecting any capacity constraints. This gives rise to single-item order quantity problems, which are solved by the heuristic ISSOS-procedure proposed by Tempelmeier [27]. In a second step, each type of capacity constraint is considered in sequence. In case of a violation, several options to attain feasibility are considered. Among these, that one which is associated with the lowest total costs is realized. Basically, orders are constructed that consist of an integer number of period demands, that touch the lower limit of a discount level or that are equal to an upper bound set by a capacity constraint. While lower bounds on order sizes are observed by moving and combining orders, the capacity constraints that limit order sizes from above are taken into account through the splitting of orders. An overview over the steps performed to find an initial solution is given in Fig.4.1..

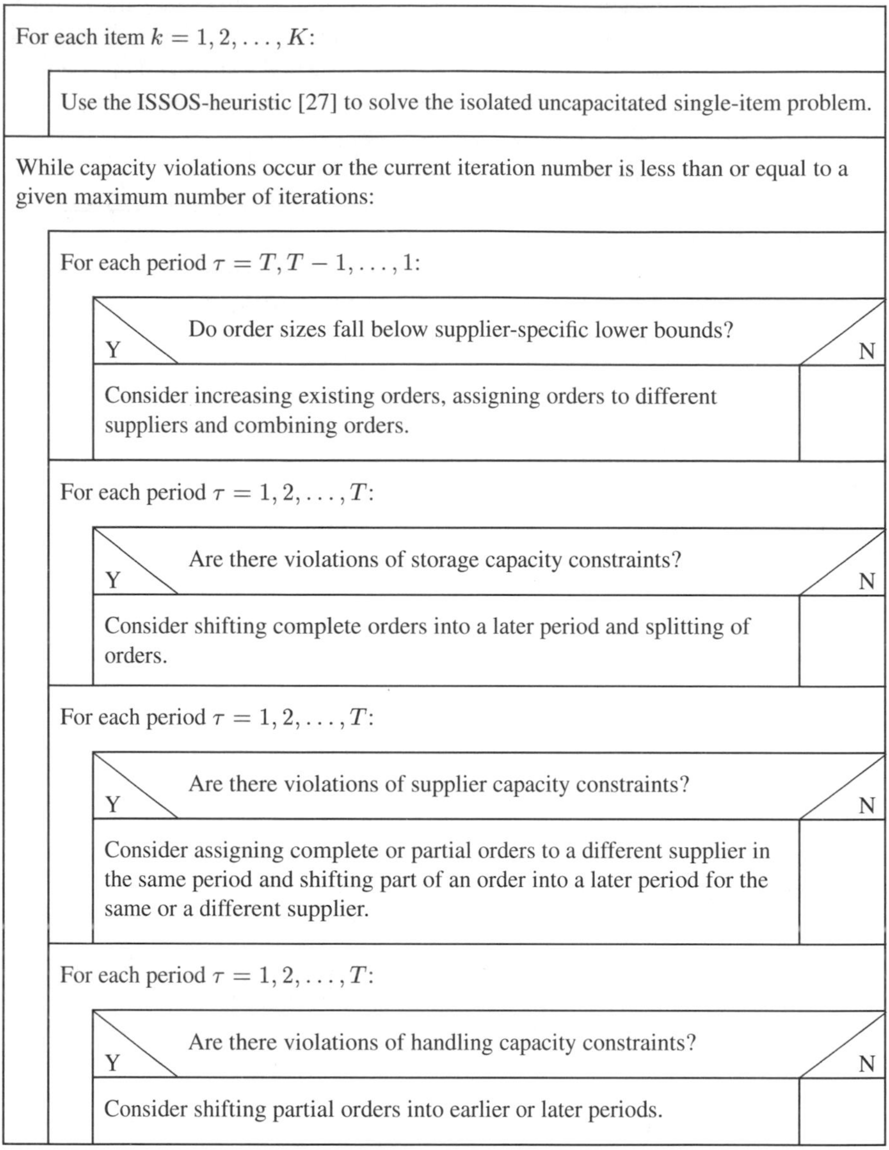

For each item $k = 1, 2, \ldots, K$:
Use the ISSOS-heuristic [27] to solve the isolated uncapacitated single-item problem.
While capacity violations occur or the current iteration number is less than or equal to a given maximum number of iterations:
For each period $\tau = T, T-1, \ldots, 1$:
Do order sizes fall below supplier-specific lower bounds?
Y
N
Consider increasing existing orders, assigning orders to different suppliers and combining orders.
For each period $\tau = 1, 2, \ldots, T$:
Are there violations of storage capacity constraints?
Y
N
Consider shifting complete orders into a later period and splitting of orders.
For each period $\tau = 1, 2, \ldots, T$:
Are there violations of supplier capacity constraints?
Y
N
Consider assigning complete or partial orders to a different supplier in the same period and shifting part of an order into a later period for the same or a different supplier.
For each period $\tau = 1, 2, \ldots, T$:
Are there violations of handling capacity constraints?
Y
N
Consider shifting partial orders into earlier or later periods.

Fig. 2. Phase I: Finding an initial solution

In each feasibility attaining step, among all options considered that one with the minimum total costs is selected. The individual steps taken to attain feasibility are performed iteratively until all constraints have been satisfied. Because of the interactions between the constraints, iterations are necessary, as it may happen, that with the elimination of one capacity violation another one is exceeded. The next iteration then will remove the new violation. The sequential structure of the procedure enables an easy integration of other capacity constraints.

4.2. Phase II: Improvement steps

In most cases the initial solution may be improved with respect to several aspects. We try to reduce each component of the objective function, i. e. fixed ordering costs, variable ordering costs, and holding costs, in turn, thereby considering solely changes of the solution that ensure feasibility of the order schedule with respect to all capacity constraints.

IMPROVEMENT STEP 1: REDUCTION OF THE FIXED ORDERING COSTS

A reduction of the fixed ordering costs is possible, if two different orders are combined to a single one. To accomplish this, three options are considered, as show in Fig. 4.2..

First, it may have happened that in phase I, caused by a supplier's capacity constraint, an order has been split into several parts that are now assigned to different suppliers. If it is possible to consolidate these orders and assign the new order to a single supplier without capacity violation, a reduction of the fixed ordering costs will result. As a by-product, if the enlarged order falls into a higher discount class, also the variable ordering costs may decline.

A second option is the combination of orders for different products in one period, that can be delivered from one supplier. In this way the fixed ordering costs are reduced, but it may happen, that the alternative supplier has higher prices, so that the variable costs may increase.

Third, for each product the consolidation of orders from different periods is considered. This is favourable, as long as the increase of holding costs is less than the decrease of fixed costs. A combination of such orders to a bigger one normally increases the holding costs. Therefore it is only realized, if the reduction of the ordering costs (including reduced variable ordering costs) exceeds this increase.

IMPROVEMENT STEP 2: REDUCTION OF THE VARIABLE ORDERING COSTS

The variable ordering costs may be reduced by increasing the order size up to a higher discount level. This effect is much more obviously in the case of all-units disounts. But also when a supplier offers incremental discounts there may be cost reductions, as higher discount-levels normally stand for lower prices. For that reason as many later orders as required to reach at least the next discount level are combined with the actually regarded order. As before, the shifting is only performed, when the total costs are reduced. See Fig. 4.2. for this improvement step.

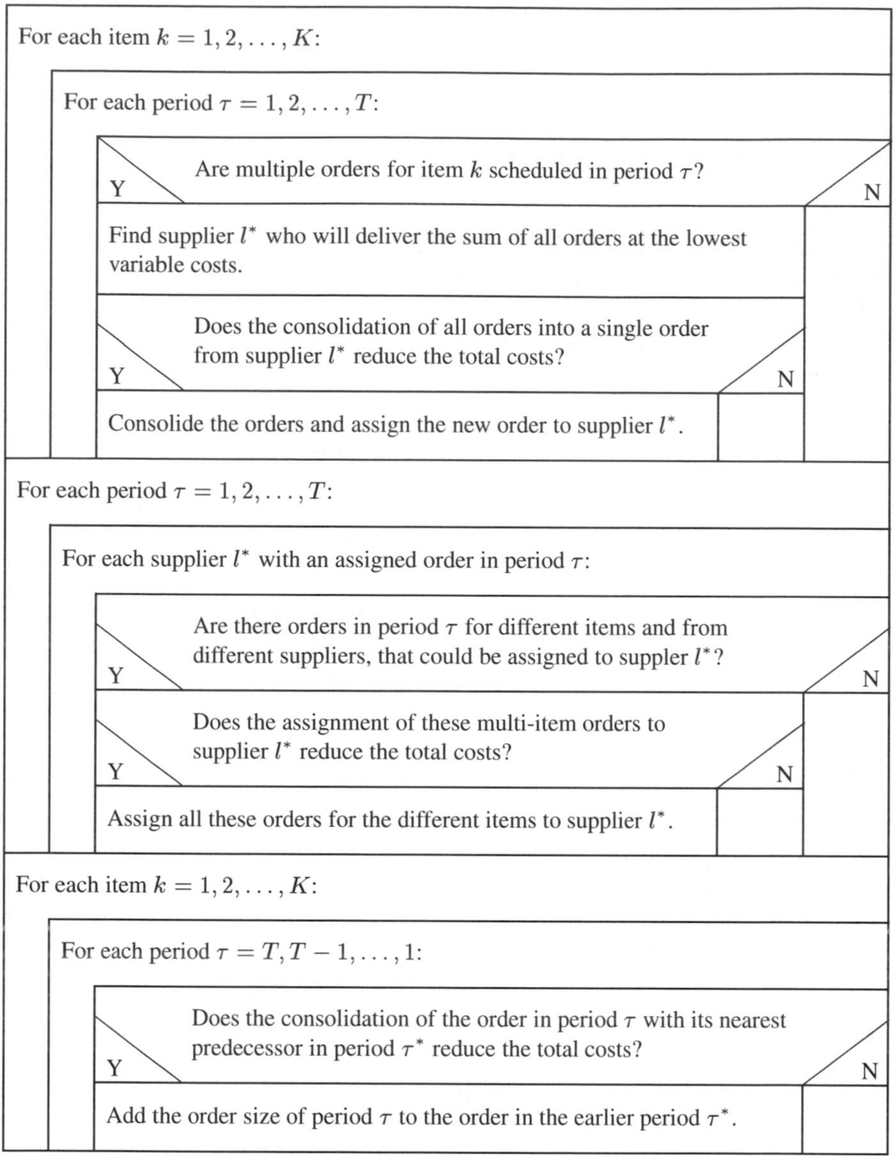

Fig. 3. Improvement step 1: Reduction of fixed costs

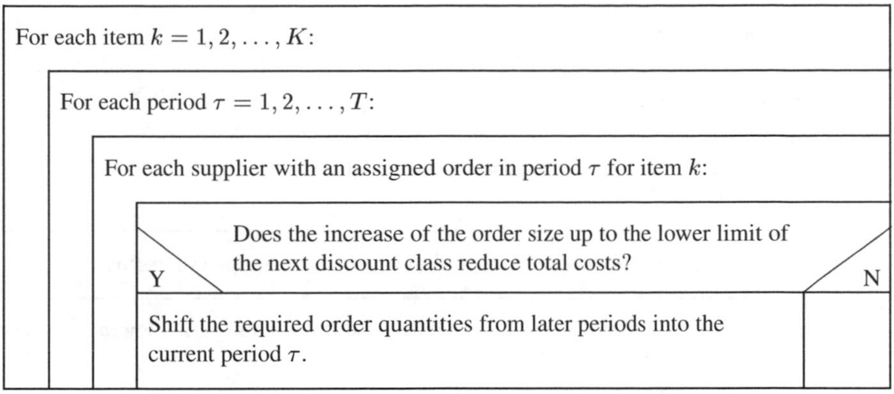

Fig. 4. Improvement step 2: Reduction of variable ordering costs

IMPROVEMENT STEP 3: REDUCTION OF THE HOLDING COSTS

While improvement steps 1 and 2 reduce the number of orders and by that counteract the tendency of phase I to create many and small orders, step 3 tries to shift only parts of existing orders. Reducing holding costs means ordering more synchronously with the demand. Therefore, two options, as shown in Fig. 4.2., are considered.

First, a portion of a given order is moved to the period of the next order. The shifted quantity depends on the demands that have to be fulfilled until the next order is placed. In contrast to placing a new order, only the sizes of existing orders are changed.

Second, the movement does not take place up to the next existing order, but to the next demand period. By that, holding costs for the relevant demand are reduced to zero. But with the new order, that is placed, additional to changed variable ordering costs, the fixed costs also have to be regarded.

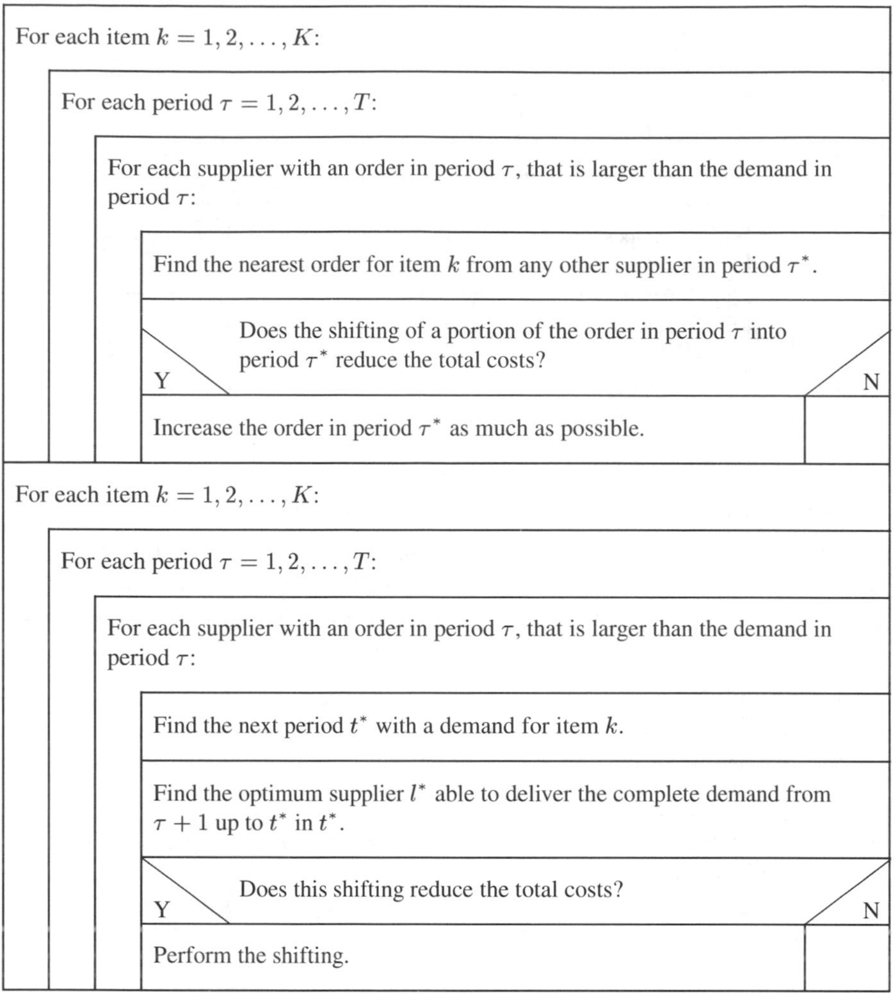

Fig. 5. Improvement step 3: Reduction of holding costs

5. Numerical results

In order to evaluate the performance of the heuristic, a numerical experiment was set up. To enable a comparison of the heuristic and the exact solution we considered a problem with T = 15 periods and K=3 products, which are available from L=3 alternative suppliers. The discount structures used by the suppliers were taken from industrial practice. For each product five demand series were generated based on a gamma-distribution with varying coefficients of variation. From the set of 125 possible combinations of the product-specific demand series we selected ten combinations (demand profiles) that are characterized in Table 5.. To examine the heuristic's behaviour under differing fixed ordering/holding-cost ratios, we used six TBO-profiles (time between orders) with different lengths of the expected order-cycle. With respect to target TBOs of approximately 3 and 6 periods, several scenarios of supplier-specific, product-specific and a combination of supplier- and product-specific fixed ordering costs were generated. Finally, we used capacity-profiles to test the quality of the heuristic under different capacity constraints.

Profile	Demand	TBO (cycle, costs)	Capacity constraints
1	constant	short, both	handling capacity
2	variable	short, product	storage capacity
3	irregular	short, supplier	supplier's capacity
4	highly irregular	long, both	minimum order size
5	sporadic	long, product	no constraint
6	constant to irregular	long, supplier	all constraints
7	irregular to sporadic	–	–
8	constant to sporadic	–	–
9	constant to sporadic	–	–
10	constant to sporadic	–	–

Table 2. Profiles

Combining these profiles resulted in 360 test-instances. With these instances the heuristic's suitability for all-units and incremental discounts was tested. To this end two problem groups were created, each comprising all the 360 instances, but differing in the discount structure.

In addition to that, for problem instances with incremental discounts we created several smaller instances using dummy discount levels which allowed the computation of the exact solution.

Problem Group	
A-A	All-units discounts
A-I	Incremental discounts
B	A-A with forbidden delivery periods
C	A-A with simple special discounts
D	A-A with complex special discounts

Table 3. Problem groups

In addition, three further problem groups were used to examine the heuristic's behaviour under the assumption of forbidden delivery periods or when special prices for limited periods are given. The latter was considered for simple as well as for complex special price structures. See Table 5. for an overview of the problem groups.

The heuristic was implemented and tested in Visual Basic 6.0 on a Pentium-based Windows 2000 personal computer with 400Mhz clock speed. For the exact solution we used ILOG CPLEX 6.6 on a UNIX-based host with eight parallel processors. While the exact solution process on the host took between a few seconds and several hours, the heuristic solution requires constantly only a few seconds. The left side of Table 5. shows the percentage deviation of the objective value found by the heuristic from the exact one aggregated by profile type. On the right the reduction of the objective value due to the improvement phase is given.

	Deviation from exact solution			Reduction through improvement		
Profile	Demand	TBO	Capacity	Demand	TBO	Capacity
1	2.40	2.11	5.08	-1.89	-0.81	-2.78
2	2.52	2.26	1.93	-1.74	-0.69	-2.20
3	2.51	2.05	1.92	-1.70	-1.42	-1.24
4	3.86	2.56	1.84	-1.72	-1.39	-1.11
5	0.91	2.75	1.80	-1.05	-1.20	-1.27
6	2.23	3.12	2.25	-1.79	-4.44	-1.35
7	4.21			-1.51		
8	2.29			-1.67		
9	1.75			-1.86		
10	2.05			-1.65		
Average	2.47			-1.66		

Table 4. Solution quality separated by profiles (in %)

Table 5 summarizes the deviations from the exact solutions for the five problem groups. For the problem group A-I with incremental discounts there is no value given, as no exact solution is available for these problem instances. The smaller instances – created especially for this group – lead to an average deviation from the exact solution of 1.18 percent.

Summarizing the numerical results, the proposed heuristic on the average provides near-optimal solutions in very short time. For the considered problem instances the largest deviation from the optimum was 13 % and only a few problem instances showed deviations of more than 5 %. Each solution is generated very quickly, taking usually less than one second.

Group	Deviation from exact solution	Reduction through improvement
A-A	2.47	-2.08
A-I	–	-0.65
B	2.66	-1.97
C	2.42	-1.94
D	2.35	-1.66
Average	2.47	-1.66

Table 5. Solution quality separated by problem groups (in %)

6. Concluding remarks

In this paper, we have developed a new model formulation and a simple and fast heuristic solution method for the dynamic order sizing and supplier selection problem under assumptions that are relevant for industrial purchasing practice. The heuristic is designed in a modular form such that further constraints – e. g. additional types of capacity constraints – just as further improvement steps can easily be included. Because of the short time to generate a solution, as shown in the above experiments, the heuristic is suitable for application as a dicesion support tool in an interactive environment. By that, it can be used in Advanced Planning Systems as well as in eBusiness.

References

1. Anupindi, R., Bassok, Y. (1999) Supply contracts with quantity commitments and stochastic demand. In: Tayur, S. (Ed.) Quantitative Models for Supply Chain Management. Kluwer, Boston, 197–232.

2. Benton, W. C. (1985) Multiple price breaks and alternative purchase lot sizing procedures in material requirements planning systems. International Journal of Production Research 23(5): 1025–1047.

3. Benton, W. C. (1986) Purchase lot sizing research for MRP systems. Operations & Productions Management 6(1): 5–14.

4. Benton, W. C., Whybark, D. C. (1982) Material Requirements Planning (MRP) and Purchase Discounts. Journal of Operations Management 2(2): 137–143.

5. Benton, W. C. (1991) Quantity discount decisions under conditions of multiple items, multiple suppliers and resource limitations. International Journal of Production Research 29(10): 1953–1961.

6. Benton, W. C., Park, S. (1996) A classification of literature on determining the lot size under quantity discounts. European Journal of Operational Research 92: 219–238.

7. Bregman, R. L. (1991) An experimental comparison of MRP purchase discount methods. Journal of the Operational Research Society 42(3): 235–245.

8. Bregman, R. L., Silver, E. A. (1993) A modification of the Silver-Meal heuristic to handle MRP purchase discount situations. Journal of the Operational Research Society 44(7): 717–723.

9. Callarman, T. E., Whybark, D. C. (1981) Determining purchase quantities for MRP requirements. Journal of Purchasing and Materials Management 17(3): 25–30.

10. Chaudhry, S. S., Forst, F. G., Zydiak, J. L. (1993) Vendor selection with price breaks. European Journal of Operational Research 70:52–66.

11. Christoph, O. B., LaForge, R. L. (1989) The performance of MRP purchase lot-size procedures under actual multiple purchase discount conditions. Decision Sciences 20: 348–358.

12. Chung, C.-S., Chiang, D. T., Lu, C.-Y. (1987) An optimal algorithm for the quantity discount problem. Journal of Operations Management 7(1, 2): 165–177.

13. Chung, C.-S., Hum, S.-H., Kirca, O. (1996) The coordinated replenishment dynamic lot-sizing problem with quantity discounts. European Journal of Operational Research 94: 122–133.

14. Chung, C.-S., Hum, S.-H., Kirca, O. (2000) An optimal procedure for the coordinated replenishment dynamic lot-sizing problem with quantity discounts. Naval Research

Logistics 47: 686–695.

15. Chyr, F., Huang, S.-T., de Lai, S. (1999) A dynamic lot-sizing modell with quantity discount. Production Planning & Control 10(1): 67–75.

16. Jayaraman, V., Srivastava, R., Benton, W. C. (1999) Supplier selection and order quantity allocation: a comprehensive model. Journal of Supply Chain Management 35(2): 50–58.

17. Krarup, J. and Bilde, O. (1977) Plant location, set covering and economic lot size: an O(nm)-algorithm for structured problems. In: Collatz, L. and Meinardus, G. (Eds.) Numerische Methoden bei Optimierungsaufgaben Band 3 — Optimierung bei graphentheoretischen und ganzzahligen Problemen. Birkhäuser, Basel, 155–180.

18. LaForge, R. L., Patterson, J. W. (1985) Adjusting the part-period algorithm for purchase quantity discounts. Production and Inventory Management Journal (1): 138–150.

19. Munson, C. L., Rosenblatt, M. J. (1997) The impact of local content rules on global sourcing decisions. Production and Operations Management 6(3): 277–290.

20. Munson, C. L., Rosenblatt, M. J. (1998) Theories and realities of quantity discounts: an exploratory study. Production and Operations Management 7(4): 352–369.

21. Munson, C. L., Rosenblatt, M. J. (2001) Coordinating a three-level supply chain with quantity discounts. IIE Transactions 33: 371–384.

22. Prentis, E. L., Khumawala, B. M. (1989) MRP lot sizing with variable production/purchasing costs: formulation and solution. International Journal of Production Research 27(6): 965–984.

23. Reith-Ahlemeier, G. (2002) Ressourcenorientierte Bestellmengenplanung und Lieferantenauswahl – Modelle und Algorithmen für Supply Chain Optimierung und E-Commerce. Books on Demand, Norderstedt. (In german.)

24. Rubin, P. A., Benton, W. C. (1993) Jointly constrained order quantities with all-units discounts. Naval Research Logistics 40: 255–278.

25. Tersine, R. J., Toelle, R. A. (1985) Lot size determination with quantity discounts. Production and Inventory Management Journal (3): 1–23.

26. Tempelmeier, H. (2002) Material-Logistik – Modelle und Algorithmen für die Produktionsplanung und -steuerung und das Supply Chain Management. 5th. Ed., Springer, Berlin. (In german.)

27. Tempelmeier, H. (2003) A simple heuristic for dynamic order sizing and supplier selection with time-varying data. Production and Operations Management, to appear.

28. Tsay, A. A., Nahmias, S., Agrawal, N. (1999) Modeling supply chain contracts: a review. In: Tayur, S. (Ed.) Quantitative Models for Supply Chain Management. Kluwer, Boston, 299–336.

29. Zeng, A. Z. (1998) Single or multiple sourcing: an integrated optimization framework for sustaining time-based competitiveness. Journal of Marketing Theory and Practice 6(4): 10–25.

30. Zipkin, P. H. (2000) Foundations of Inventory Management. McGraw-Hill, Boston.

Optimal Maintenance in the Supply Chain

Joachim Reese

Department of Production and Economic Science
Faculty of Economics and Management
University of Lueneburg
Scharnhorststr. 1
D-21332 Lueneburg, Germany

Abstract: *A supply chain can be characterized as a network of production and logistics processes with a finite number of elements usually belonging to different companies and hierarchies. Thus, SCM means a close, trustful cooperation within this network. Reliability of the network elements is one of the critical success factors for that form of cooperation. Here we consider an element of the supply chain within a JIT setting which is „technically" unreliable, e.g. due to a reduced machine productivity over time, and which therefore has to be maintained in order to fulfill the organizational issues of reliability. Traditional maintenance policies will fail due to extraordinary production and organization requirements. Though system defects are discovered immediately, because the monitoring of the production and logistics process is improved towards perfection, no other than a few defects should be repaired immediately. Any stoppage of machines during the production period would decrease the reliability of the network element. Therefore a special preventive maintenance policy is developed where the maintenance activities must not interfere with production and are shifted to the end of each production period. The problem is modelled by its cost and production functions and a control theoretic formulation is proposed to solve it.*

Keywords: *maintenance management, just-in-time, control theory*

1. Introduction

Supply chains are considered in order to coordinate production processes more efficiently. As a rule, such chains do not only support market and hierarchy mechanisms. Moreover, other lateral coordination mechanisms have been developed which have proved to be superior when adopting supply chains (Huiskonen and Pirttilä, 2002). Generally, a chain is constructed as hybrid network between independent companies. Nevertheless, it is intended that the companies involved in such a network work together permanently. Due to uncertainties, they do not cooperate on the basis of a classical but a relational contract. There has been done a lot of research in recent years with regard to supply chain management, i.e. optimizing the coordination processes between the members of the supply chain (cf. e.g. Stadtler and Kilger 2000 and the other contributions in this book for an overview). Though multiple management methods have been proposed, e.g. operational research techniques (cf. e.g. Maloni and Benton, 1999, Korpela et al., 2002) and MRP (cf. e.g. Dolgui and Ould-Louly, 2002), there is meanwhile some theoretical (e.g. Zimmer, 2002) and empirical evidence (Balmana and Balmès, 2000; Gallois et al., 2000; Werner, 2000; Wildemann, 2000) that synchronization of production as well as the adoption of the pull principle might be critical success factors for many supply chains. JIT production and logistic procedures are established in a large number of cases. In another respect, research progress is not as promising: The internal preconditions within a single chain member's competency area, i.e. whether the design and control of the production components are suited to support supply chain management in a JIT setting, have not been in the same focus of research activities, especially as concerns the reliability of the components (but see e.g. Lulu and Black 1987, Wu et al. 1992, Abdulnour et al. 1995, Paknejad et al. 1995).

A JIT system supposed to realize supply chain management is extraordinarily sensitive toward any unreliability of the elements of the chain. A defect of a machine or another productive component beyond a narrow range, i.e. that exceeds a given rate of deterioration of the production rate, causes a system break-down due to the non-availability of systematic storage quantities of the goods produced.

In the case of JIT production, the traditional maintenance policies will usually fail because of the unique system requirements, especially the lack of any redundancy. It is true that system defects are discovered immediately, because the monitoring of the production process is improved toward perfection, but necessary maintenance activities should be shifted to the end of the production period as far as possible. Production must go on until day's work is done. As any stoppage of machines would be the worst case in a JIT production system, prevention plays the most important role in the optimal maintenance policy (Wu et al., 1992; Abdulnour et al., 1995). Similar to the repair problem, preventive maintenance should never interfere with production (Cadley et al., 1989, p. 95).

As compared with buffered production, a suboptimal state of the JIT production system has direct consequences. Production time is enlarged in each period by an overtime period that can be calculated from the production losses in the regular time period. Additional cost arises which must be taken into account when determining the optimal interval. Due to the fact that this interval shrinks as against traditional production systems, maintenance efforts are distributed among more periods.

In this paper, we consider a single-stage JIT system with given order arrivals of the same type and one unreliable machine. The degree of unreliability is expressed by a decrease of the production rate that is constant in every period, but decreases from period to period if there is no maintenance at the periods' end. The relevant cost is cost of maintenance as well as regular and overtime production cost. In section 2 the production system is modeled, and the cost and the production functions are discussed. Section 3 offers a control theoretic formulation of the problem. An iterative method of determining the optimal control of the maintenance policy is presented in section 4. Section 5 extends the problem toward a stochastic demand process. In section 6 we show how the maintenance policy and KANBAN control of the JIT system depend on each other. Further extensions are pointed out in section 7.

2. Production and maintenance function

We consider a single-stage JIT system, where a single item is produced in given lots. The arrival rate of orders from a customer in the supply chain is given by λ^0, the standard production rate is μ^0. The finished products are delivered to a distribution stock from which they are pulled by the customer or the distribution agent, respectively. The arrival rate at the distribution stock λ^1 equals μ^0. Furthermore, if there exists KANBAN control for the demand rate μ^1 of the finished products it can be stated: $\mu^1 = \lambda^0$. This simple production system is visualized in Fig. 1.

We now assume that the production system is unreliable. The standard production rate μ^0 will therefore decrease over of time if there is no maintenance performed. This can be expressed by a general production rate $\mu(t)$, $\frac{d\mu(t)}{dt} < 0,\ t \geq 0$. The planning horizon is denoted as Z. It can be subdivided into periods of production and periods of maintenance. Whenever the system is unproductive, it can be maintained. This is a straight consequence from the JIT philosophy that the utilization of the system is maximized. Let $p(t)$ denote a binary variable which describes the productivity in the production period t. If $p(t)=1$, the system is productive in t. Else it is maintained $(p(t)=0)$ in order to increase the production rate again and to re-establish the state μ^0, respectively. The maintenance periods can be analogously described by $m(t) \in \{0,1\}$. Obviously, the total production time is then given as

$$P_\tau = \int_0^\tau p(t)dt\,. \tag{2.1}$$

The maintenance time is

$$M_\tau = \int_0^\tau m(t)dt\,. \tag{2.2}$$

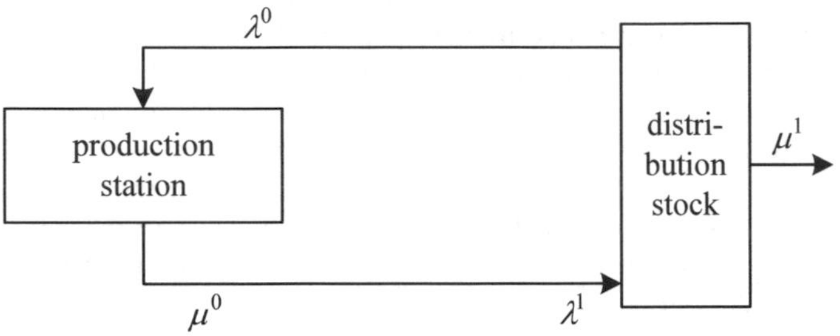

λ^0, λ^1: arrival rates

μ^0, μ^1 : service rates

Fig. 1. Production system

The system behavior is thus modeled by a sequence of production and maintenance periods (cf. Fig. 2). Every production period $p_i = [t_{i-1}, \underline{t}_i)$ is followed by a maintenance period $m_i = [\underline{t}_i, t_i)$ and vice versa. The periodical switches are calculated as follows:

$$\underline{t}_i = \arg\min_{t \geq t_{i-1}} \left[m(t)=1 \right],\ i = 1,\ldots,\mathrm{T} \tag{2.3a}$$

$$\bar{t}_i = \arg\min_{t \geq \underline{t}_i} \left[p(t)=1 \right],\ i = 1,\ldots,\mathrm{T}\text{-}1 \tag{2.3b}$$

$$\bar{t}_0 = 0 \tag{2.3c}$$

$$\bar{t}_T = Z\,. \tag{2.3d}$$

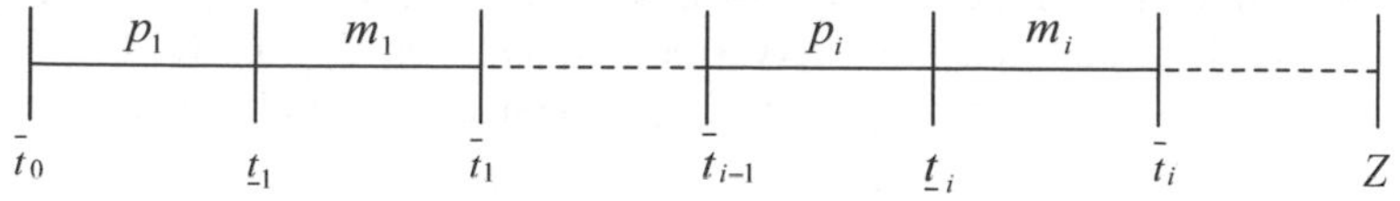

Fig. 2. Sequence of production and maintenance periods

The relevant cost of the JIT system may be easily derived from the maintenance periods and the production function. Let c_1 denote the cost of maintenance per time unit and c_2 the overtime production cost per unit. Overtime production is necessary in two cases: On the one hand, fluctuations of the demand rate cannot be denied, so that overtime is inevitable whenever $\lambda^0 > \mu^0$ holds in any period. On the other hand, the production capacity is adjusted to the standard production rate. With every system unreliability, the production schedule cannot be met in the regular production period. So we have a partial cost function with costs depending on the maintenance efforts :

$$\tilde{C} = c_1 \sum_i \int_{\underline{t}_i}^{\bar{t}_i} d\tau + c_2 \sum_i \int_{\bar{t}_{i-1}}^{\underline{t}_i} \left[\mu^0 - \mu\left(\tau - \bar{t}_{i-1}\right)\right] d\tau \,. \tag{2.4}$$

The first term of (2.4) explains the cost which arises due to maintenance activities. The second term shows the additional production cost of that quantity which has to be realized in the overtime periods due to a decreasing productivity. It is evident that the more the maintenance periods are extended the less overtime production occurs because of $\mu\left(\tau - \bar{t}_{i-1}\right)$ better approximates μ^0. In (2.4) it is furthermore assumed that every maintenance activity re-establishes the original state of the production system with $\mu = \mu^0$. As compared with the system of buffered production, it is obvious that there is no inventory cost in the cost function, but every lack of maintenance immediately causes additional production cost.

3. A control theoretic model

In order to solve the described problem, we first of all give a discrete control theoretic formulation. Let 1,...,T denote discrete time periods. Every period consists of a regular production interval (with c_3 unit cost of regular production), an overtime production interval (with c_2 unit cost of overtime production) and a maintenance interval (with c_1 cost per time unit). It is assumed that $c_2 > c_3$. We further assume that the state of the system is well-known and constant within each period. Therefore, the regular production quantity of period t is given by the state variable T_t;

the quantity requested in period t by the customers is denoted by Σ_t. The quantity to be produced in the overtime interval consequently is $\lambda_t - \mu_t$ if $\lambda_t > \mu_t$. The control variable is the time u_t spent for maintenance in period t. These basic assumptions are summarized in Fig. 3.

regular production interval	overtime production interval	maintenance interval	
c_3	c_2	c_1	(unit cost)
1	$\frac{\max\left[\lambda_t - \mu_t, 0\right]}{\mu_t}$	u_t	(total length of a period t)

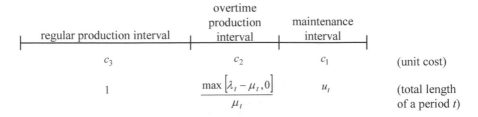

Fig. 3. Basic assumptions

The cost function now reads

$$C = \sum_{t=1}^{T} F\left[\mu_t, u_t, t\right]$$
$$= c_3 \sum_{t=1}^{T} \min\left[\mu_t, \lambda_t\right] + c_2 \sum_{t=1}^{T} \max\left[\lambda_t - \mu_t, 0\right] + c_1 \sum_{t=1}^{T} u_t . \tag{3.1}$$

Here, it is taken into account that in single periods a non-optimal utilization of the system capacity may occur. The state equation here describes the change of the production rate $\Delta\mu_t$ between two periods (cf. Kamien and Schwartz 1981, p. 111, for a general interpretation). It is formulated as follows:

$$\Delta\mu_t = -d_t + f(\mu_t) . \tag{3.2}$$

$\Delta\mu_t$ depends on the degree of obsolescence in the course of time d_t and the amount of maintenance that was done at the end of the preceding period. f can be interpreted as the function of labor productivity when maintaining the system (see also Thompson 1968). We note that

$$\Delta\mu_t = \mu_{t+1} - \mu_t , \qquad t = 1, \ldots, T \tag{3.3}$$

and $\mu_1 = \mu_{T+1} = \mu^0$. According to given time restrictions we further assume that u_t cannot exceed an upper bound $\bar{u}$.

The Hamiltonian (cf. Sethi and Thompson 1981, pp. 221; Kamien and Schwartz 1981, pp. 186; Feichtinger and Hartl 1986, pp. 283) for this control problem now is

$$H_t = F(\mu_t, u_t, t) + \gamma_{t+1}\left[-d_t + f(u_t)\right]. \tag{3.4}$$

Applying the maximum principle of optimal control theory (Sethi and Thompson 1981, pp. 235; Feichtinger 1982; Weiser 1990, pp. 72; Geisel 2000, pp. 104) , the necessary conditions for an optimal time path are:

$$\frac{\delta H_t}{\delta u_t} = c_1 + \gamma_{t+1}\frac{\delta f}{\delta u_t} = 0 \tag{3.5}$$

$$-\frac{\delta H_t}{\delta \mu_t} = \left\{\begin{array}{ll} -(c_3 - c_2) & \text{if } \mu_t < \lambda_t \\ 0 & \text{else} \end{array}\right\} = \Delta\gamma_t \tag{3.6}$$

with $\Delta\gamma_t = \gamma_{t+1} - \gamma_t$ *and* $\gamma_T = 0.$

$$\Delta\mu_t = -d_t + f(u_t)\,. \tag{3.7}$$

From the necessary conditions we receive the following general results. The adjoint variables can be specified as

$$\gamma_t = i_t\ (c_3 - c_2)\,, \tag{3.8}$$

where i_t denotes the number of periods $\tau \in [t, T-1]$ with $\mu_\tau < \lambda_\tau$, i.e. where the demand is not met in the regular production period. For the state variables, it can be easily verified that

$$\mu_t = \mu^0 - t\,d_t + \sum_{\tau=1}^{t} f(u_t)\,. \tag{3.9}$$

Considering the optimality condition for the control variables

$$\frac{\delta f}{\delta u_t} = -c_1/\gamma_{t+1}\,, \tag{3.10}$$

the state variables can be calculated. From the optimality conditions of the control variables we can see that the optimal maintenance policy first of all depends on the labour productivity of each hour spent for maintenance. In case of a constant labour productivity, the optimal control policy is bang-bang. u_t equals either 0 or $\bar{u}$. Interior solutions are only found if the labor productivity increases or decreases over time.

4. An iterative solution of the optimal control problem

Solving the control problem explicitly is complicated by the problem's discontinuity. Here we suggest an iterative method that starts with an estimation of the number of periods with an excess demand. Let j denote the corresponding step of the iterative procedure. Then, an initialization may be as follows ($j = 0$):

$$i_t^{\,0} = (T - t)/2 \tag{4.1}$$

That means, if there is no other information, we assume that in every second period the market demand will not be met by the corresponding production rate in the regular production period. In case of evidence any other starting solution may be preferred, of course. Now we receive preliminary solutions for the adjoint variables $\gamma_t^{\,0}$, the control variables $u_t^{\,0}$, and the state variables $\mu_t^{\,0}$ by applying the necessary conditions of the optimal control problem. A subsequent comparison between $\mu_t^{\,0}$ and the given demand values λ_t improves the approximation for i_t. These values are denoted by $i_t^{\,1}$. Accordingly, $\gamma_t^{\,1}$, $u_t^{\,1}$, and $\mu_t^{\,1}$ are calculated. The procedure continues step by step as long as there is any change in the calculation of $i_t^{\,j}$. The final solution is realized, when

$$i_t^{\,j+1} = i_t^{\,j} \;\; \forall \; t=1,\ldots,T\,. \tag{4.2}$$

A convergency proof is given in Noeske and Reese (2003).

A numerical example shall demonstrate how the method works. Consider a simple state equation

$$\Delta \mu_t = -225 + f(u_t) \tag{4.3}$$

with a maintenance function

$$f(u_t) = u_t^{\,2}\;,\; u_t \leq 15\,. \tag{4.4}$$

By (4.3) and (4.4) we describe a linear obsolescence of the machine over time and an extremely high productivity of maintenance efforts. The costs of maintenance and production are assumed as $c_1 = 1.200$, $c_2 = 60$, and $c_3 = 30$. At given deterministic demand rates λ_t (cf. Table 1) and a standard production rate $\mu^0 = 2.000$ the optimal path of control over $T = 6$ periods is summarized in Table 1. After two steps we find the final solution which shows increasing maintenance effort over time. While maintenance does not seem so important in the first two periods, a maximum maintenance is optimal in the periods 3 to 6. As compared with the first iterative step, maintenance activities in the final solution are shifted to the future. Different demand rates may possibly delay or accelerate this tendency, but they can never stop it.

t	1	2	3	4	5	6
λ_t	2.000	1.800	1.600	1.700	1.600	1.900
i_t^0	5/2	2	3/2	1	1/2	0
u_t^0	8	10	40/3	15	15	15
μ_t^0	1.839	1.714	1.667	1.667	1.667	1.667
i_t^1	3	2	1	1	0	0
u_t^1	20/3	10	15	15	15	15
μ_t^1	1.819	1.694	1.694	1.694	1.694	1.694
i_t^2	3	2	1	1	0	0
u_t^2	20/3	10	15	15	15	15
μ_t	1.819	1.694	1.694	1.694	1.694	1.694

Table 1. Numerical example of the iterative solution technique

5. Stochastic demand process

In practice, the demand process is not deterministic but stochastic. There will be a certain information about the demands which can be expressed by a probability distribution. Here we assume a *M/D/1* system with a deterministic production process, but randomly distributed demands. Let Λ denote the stochastic variable of the demand process and $G(\cdot)$ the corresponding distribution function. Furthermore, we introduce $\Im_t$ as a stochastic variable which denotes the number of periods with

$$\mu_\tau < \Lambda_\tau,\ \tau \in [t, T-1]. \tag{5.1}$$

We can now describe the probability that this number of periods is equal to i_t by

$$g(i_t) = p(\Im_t = 1) = p(\Im_{t+1} = i)\ G(\mu_t) + p(\Im_{t+1} = i-1)\ [1 - G(\mu_t)] \tag{5.2}$$

with $p(\Im_t = 0) = 1$. By continuous substitution we obtain:

$$g(i_t) = \sum_{\{t_1,\ldots,t_i\} \subseteq \{t,\ldots,T-1\}} \prod_{\tau \in \{t_1,\ldots,t_i\}} [1 - G(\mu_t)] \prod_{\tau \notin \{t_1,\ldots,t_i\}\, \tau \in \{t,\ldots,T-1\}} G(\mu_t) \qquad (5.3)$$

The iterative solution method can be adopted to the stochastic system behavior as follows:

1. Take any starting solution $\mu_1{}^0,\ldots, \mu_T{}^0$ and $g^0(i_t)$ as granted. Start with $j = 1$.
2. Calculate $g^j(i_t)$ for all i_t, $t = 1,\ldots,T$ at the actual production rates.
3. Compare the distribution $g^j(i_t)$ with the distribution $g^{j-1}(i_t)$. If "equivalence" is given for all i_t stop the procedure. The final solution is given by the last calculation of control and state variables. Otherwise, continue with step 4.
4. Calculate the distribution $\Gamma(\cdot)$ of the conjoint variables γ_t, $U(\cdot)$ of the maintenance times u_t and $M(\cdot)$ of the production rates μ_t.
5. Calculate the expected values $E(\mu_t)$ of the production rates and continue with step 2 for $j := j+1$.

It is obvious that beside the production rates, the maintenance efforts have to be calculated as expected values, too.

6. KANBAN control

JIT systems are often combined with a KANBAN control mechanism. There are K KANBANs in the system which define production orders as well as the amount of the distribution stock. The initial state of the system is visualized in Fig. 4. While in a pure JIT system with no KANBAN control the system's feasibility is defined by the identity of demand and production in each period, the corresponding feasibility conditions in a KANBAN controlled JIT system depend on the number of KANBANs K. First of all, in a reliable system the feasibility is only guaranteed if

$$\int_0^t \mu^0 \, d\tau + K \geq \int_0^t \lambda(\tau)\, d\tau \quad \text{for all } t \leq T. \qquad (6.1)$$

For the unreliable system, as it was generally described in section 2, the feasibility conditions have to be modified toward

$$\sum_{i=1}^{I} \int_{\bar{t}_{i-1}}^{t_i} \left[\mu^0 - \mu(\tau - \bar{t}_{i-})\right] d\tau + K \geq \int_0^{t_i} \lambda(t)\, d\tau \quad \text{for } I = 1,\ldots,T. \qquad (6.2)$$

Consequently, there arises additional inventory cost that depends on the number of KANBANs. Preventive maintenance has to be especially taken into consideration, whenever the feasibility conditions are guaranteed only by an increased K.

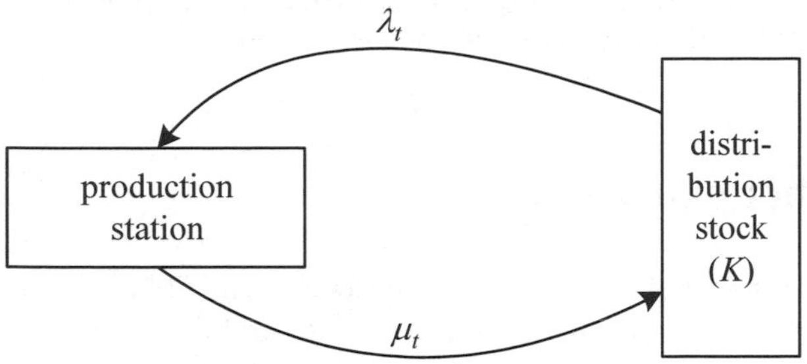

Fig. 4. Initial state of the system

Let us consider a $M/M/1$ JIT system with KANBAN control. While the demand process is given exogenously, the parameters of the production process are controlled by the maintenance activities. If one neglects the transportation time between the production site and the distribution stock, the reorder cycle of one production unit is defined as the sum of the waiting time $\frac{\rho}{[\mu(1-\rho)]}$ and the production time $\frac{1}{\mu}$, i.e. the reorder cycle is given as $\frac{1}{[\mu(1-\rho)]}$. Here, ρ denotes the degree of service, so that $\rho = \frac{\lambda}{\mu}$ holds (cf. for these results also Hillier and Lieberman, 1974). If no shortages are permitted, the number of KANBANs can be derived as the demand during the reorder cycle, also including a safety factor s:

$$K = \frac{1}{[\mu(1-\rho)]}\lambda(1+s) = \frac{\rho(1+s)}{(1-\rho)}. \tag{6.3}$$

We conclude that every maintenance reduces ρ and therefore allows a reduction of the number of KANBANs. The question arises to what extent such a decrease is economical because the cost of maintenance may overcompensate the inventory cost.

In a $M/M/1$ JIT system the average amount of inventory is $K - \frac{\rho(1-\rho^K)}{(1-\rho)}$ (cf. Buzacott and Shantikumar, 1993, p. 105). If c_4 denotes the unit cost of inventory, the total inventory cost is given as

$$C_I = c_4 \left[K - \frac{\rho(1-\rho^K)}{(1-\rho)} \right]. \tag{6.4}$$

This function is strictly increasing with *K*. Regarding the control problem in section 3, the cost function has to be reformulated accordingly.

7. Further extensions

When considering unreliable production systems, the kind of unreliability is manifold. In all preceding sections, we assumed a general description of unreliability, so that there can exist infinite different states which alter continuously. The discussion of the optimal maintenance in JIT systems can be specified by selecting concrete reliability formulations. Exemplarily, here we pick up one elementary definition from literature and discuss the consequences for a JIT system.

In many practical situations, system reliability is given over N periods. After that, the system switches from the standard state (μ^0) to a suboptimal state (μ^1) (cf. Hsu and Tapiero, 1992). If the binary maintenance variables are denoted by $m_t \in \{0, 1\}$, this generally means

$$\mu_t = \left[\max_{n=1,\dots,N} m_{t-n} \right] \mu^0 + \left[1 - \max_{n=1,\dots,N} m_{t-n} \right] \mu^1, m \in \{0,1\}. \tag{6.5}$$

Obviously, the state equation is as follows:

$$\Delta \mu_t = \begin{cases} \mu^1 - \mu^0 & \text{if } m_{t-N} = 1,\ m_\tau = 0 \qquad \text{for all } t-N < \tau < t \\ \mu^0 - \mu^1 & \text{if } m_t = 1,\ m_\tau = 0 \qquad \text{for all } t-N \le \tau < t \\ 0 & \text{else} \end{cases} \tag{6.6}$$

Maintenance may be interpreted as an activity to bring the JIT system back to the original standard state. There is no discussion about the degree of maintenance, i.e. the time spent for maintenance, but only if such activities should be done now or later. Assuming a general deterioration of the system's performance with a factor $\alpha < 1$, where the system is not maintained at the end of the period, the production rate of the next period is

$$\mu_{t+1} = (1-m_t)\, \alpha \mu_t + m_t \mu^0,\ m_t \in \{0,1\}. \tag{6.7}$$

From this it follows immediately that

$$\Delta \mu_t = [(1-m_t)\, \alpha - 1]\ \mu_t + m_t \mu^0. \tag{6.8}$$

With (6.8) instead of (3.2) the control theoretic problem in section 3 has to be reformulated again.

8. Conclusions

The efficiency of a complex supply network between independent firms are based on a close cooperation of all partners. As the network usually concentrates on value added activities, inventories of finished or semi-finished goods have to be avoided to a great extent. Therefore, special maintenance periods for maintaining the machines have to be arranged at the end of each production period in addition to those periods which are well-known from the literature as overtime production periods. In this paper, we show that there is a trade-off between maintenance and overtime production due to decreasing machine productivity. If the members of the supply network refuse that kind of (costly) flexibility – which is of course expensive - there arise unreliable partnerships because products cannot be completely made to order. One major consequence is the bullwhip effect (cf. the contribution of Takahashi and Myreshka in this volume). On the other hand, considering permanent maintenance intervals allows a further reduction of flexibility costs as compared with the mere installation of overtime production periods.

The model described here applies dynamic optimization in general and control theory in particular which has proved to be efficient in the field of maintenance management (Feichtinger and Hartl 1986, pp. 283). The control theoretic model offers clear insights in the progress of a multi-period production process and its cost effects with special respect to the trade-off between cost of overtime production and cost of maintenance. Furthermore, it is explained how this model can be extended toward other pull systems which are discussed in the literature as e.g. KANBAN systems and other JIT systems.

References

Abdulnour, G., Dudek, R.A., Smith, M.L. (1995): Effect of maintenance policies on the just-in-time production system. In: International Journal of Production Research 33, pp. 565-583.

Balmana, G., Balmès, R. (2000): Monitoring flows: theory and application. In: Supply Chain Forum 1, pp. 30-39.

Buzacott, J., Shantikumar, J.G. (1993): Stochastic models of manufacturing sys-tems. Prentive-Hall, Englewood Cliffs.

Cadley, J.A., Heintz H.E., Vogrich L. (1989), Insights from simulating JIT manu-facturing. In: Interfaces 19, pp. 88-97.

Dolgui, A., Ould-Louly, M.-A. (2002): A model for supply planning under lead time uncertainty. In: International Journal of Production Economics 78, pp. 145-152.

Feichtinger, G. (1982): Anwendungen des Maximumprinzips im Operations Research. In: Operations Research Spektrum 4, pp. 171-190, 195-212.

Feichtinger, G., Hartl, R.F. (1986): Optimale Kontrolle ökonomischer Prozesse. De Gruyter, Berlin and New York.

Gallois, P.-M., Devulder, Ch., Ferreira, S.L. (2000): Global synchronous manufacturing and logistics optimization: a success story. In: Supply Chain Forum 1, pp. 56-69.

Geisel, R. (2000): Strategien einer einsatzsynchronen Beschaffung. Deutscher Universitäts-Verlag, Wiesbaden.

Hillier, F.S., Lieberman, G.J. (1974): Operations research, 2nd ed., Holden-Day, San Francisco.

Hsu, L.-F., Tapiero, C.S. (1992): Integration of process monitoring, quality control and maintenance in an M|G|1 with queue-like production system. In: International Journal of Production Research 30, pp. 2363-2379.

Huiskonen, J., Pirttilä, T. (2002): Lateral coordination in a logistics outsourcing partnership. In: International Journal of Production Economics 78, pp. 177-182.

Kamien, M.I., Schwartz, N.L. (1981): Dynamic optimization. North-Holland, New York et al.

Korpela, J., Kyläheiko, K., Lehmusvaara, A., Tuominen, M. (2002): An analytic approach to production capacity allocation and supply chain design. In: International Journal of Production Economics 78, pp. 187-195.

Lulu, M., Black, J.T. (1987): Effect of process unreliability on integrated manufacturing/production systems. In: Journal of Manufacturing Systems 6, pp. 15-22.

Maloni, M.J., Benton, W.C. (1997): Supply chain partnerships: opportunities for operations research. In: European Journal of Operational Research 101, pp. 419-429.

Noeske, M., Reese, J. (2003): Optimale Instandhaltung in JIT-Prozessen. Arbeitsbericht no. 286, Lüneburg.

Paknejad, M.J., Nasri, F., Affisco, J.F. (1995): Defective units in a continuous review (s,Q) system. In: International Journal of Production Research 33, pp. 2767-2777.

Sethi, S.P., Thompson, G.L. (1981): Optimal control theory. Martinus Nijhoff Publishing, Boston et al.

Stadtler, H., Kilger, C. (2000): Supply chain management and advanced planning: concepts, models, software and case studies. Springer, Berlin et al.

Thompson, G.L. (1968): Optimal maintenance policy and sale date of a machine. In: Management Science 14, pp. 543-550.

Weiser, Ch. (1990): Simultane Optimierung von Preis- und Investitionsstrategien. Ein diskreter kontrolltheoretischer Ansatz. Deutscher Universitäts-Verlag, Wiesbaden.

Werner, H. (2000): Supply Chain Management. Gabler, Wiesbaden.

Wildemann, H. (2000): Supply Chain Management. Transfer-Centrum Verlag, Munich.

Wu, B., Seddon, J.J.M., Currie, W.L. (1992): Computer-aided dynamic preventive maintenance within the manufacturing environment. In: International Journal of Production Research 30, pp. 2683-2696.

Zimmer, K. (2002): Supply chain coordination with uncertain just-in-time delivery. In: International Journal of Production Economics 77, pp. 1-15.

Hybrid Flow Shop Scheduling with Batching Requirements

Stefan Voß, Andreas Witt

Department of Business Science
University of Hamburg
Von-Melle-Park 5
D-20146 Hamburg, Germany

Gesellschaft für Informationssysteme mbH
Eisenhuettenstr. 99
D-38239 Salzgitter, Germany

Abstract: *This paper deals with a real-world scheduling problem in the steel industry in which the resources form a hybrid flow shop consisting of 16 production stages. Furthermore, sequence-dependent setup states have to be considered at two production stages leading to a batching problem. The objective is to minimize the weighted tardiness. As problem instances consist of about 30,000 jobs an exact calculation of a schedule is not practicable. Instead, a heuristic solution procedure using dispatching rules is applied. In order to form batches the employed rules are modified accordingly.*

Keywords: *hybrid flow shop, flexible flow shop, batching, dispatching rules, weighted tardiness*

1. Introduction

Due to intense performance improvements of information technology in the last decade quantitative models have become applicable to large size real-world scheduling problems. Particularly in supply chain management the partner-companies are in the need of an extensive tuning of their activities. Apart from a fast data transmission this also presumes a high actuality and correctness of planning results. The use of quantitative models and procedures lays the foundations for this purpose what was recognized by software vendors and led to the development of corresponding planning systems (for example the APO – advanced planner and optimizer – of the SAP AG). In supply chain management many problems still need a careful consideration regarding solution procedures to support respective systems (as their planning functionality is still in its infancy at places).

In this paper a real-world problem of a German steel manufacturer is presented. The overall objective is to have up-to-date schedules for the resources permanently available in order to produce with low costs and to be able to quote delivery dates for new customer orders. This is an important requirement due to the strong integration of the supply chains with other companies. While the overall objective needs to be operationalized it is an important issue to differentiate various objectives and to evaluate their consequences for the steel manufacturer. Therefore, in this paper we aim at a concise discussion of the problem and some options for defining an objective function (e.g., based on tardiness values). Once an objective is defined algorithms for solving the problem need to be developed and tested on real-world instances.

At first we give a general problem description in Section 2. Section 3 contains a brief review of objectives pursued in the scheduling literature and an introduction into batching approaches of machine scheduling as this is an essential feature of our problem. Since we have to handle large size problem instances an exact algorithm to calculate a schedule does not seem to be applicable. Instead we describe dispatching rules that are able to form batches in Section 4 and present results in Section 5.

2. Problem description

For steel companies production is often arranged in a way commonly known as a flow shop (see, e.g., Tang et al., 2000, and Tang et al., 2001, for a survey on related problems in steel production). Here we consider the specific case of a German steel manufacturer. The production of the steel company is basically structured as a flow shop with S = 16 stages. That is, the stages s = 1, …, S are traversed by all jobs i = 1, …, I in the same sequence. The features of the products are defined by the customers leading to a large number of product variants. It is not possible to produce standard products to stock as this would lead to unacceptable high inventories. Instead the production of a certain product variant is only initiated when a customer places an appropriate order (make-to-order). According to the functioning in ERP-systems (enterprise resource planning systems) production jobs are created for every position in a customer order and for every stage in the flow shop. Thus the usual notion "activity" or "operation" of machine scheduling corresponds with the expression "job" in our case whereas the usual notion "job" of machine scheduling corresponds with the expression "customer order". Furthermore, the jobs of different orders may be connected by precedence relations if, e.g., a job supplies several succeeding jobs that likewise supply different orders. All jobs and orders connected this way form a network and thus a problem treated in project management. All single projects together represent a multiple project scheduling problem.

Additionally to the general precedence relations there are more deviations from classical flow shop problems mostly treated in the scheduling literature that we have to take into account and that make the problem more complex and thus more difficult to solve. Three of the stages are formed by parallel machines what is commonly denoted as a "hybrid flow shop" (Gupta, 1988, or Voß, 1993) or a "flexible flow shop" (Wittrock, 1988). Therefore, we differentiate stages $s = 1, \ldots, S$ and machines or resources $r = 1, \ldots, R$, respectively. The parallel machines are uniform, i.e., they run with different speeds. For equal speeds we would use the expression "identical parallel machines". Some of the jobs may be handled by each of the parallel machines, others may be assigned to certain machines due to technological restrictions. The machines that execute the processing at the production stages are indicated by the index r. For the production of an end product it is not necessary that each stage is traversed. Single stages may be skipped, i.e., the processing time at these stages is equal to zero and the completion may be reached at a stage $s < S$. In total there are about 90 different routings in our case on which the products can traverse the flexible flow shop. The routing defines which production stages must be traversed to manufacture a certain product. It is predetermined which routing is assigned to a sub-project depending on the product variant. At all stages breakdowns may occur due to maintenance activities or holidays. Thus the capacities of the stages are variable over time. Conventionally, every machine can process at most one job at a time. At two stages there are waiting times after the completion of a job because the metal is heated and has to cool down after the processing.

At two stages each consisting of one machine we have to consider three sequence-dependent setup states $a = 1, \ldots, A_r$ with $A_r = 3$ which are defined as follows: The metal runs through a bath of zinc by which it is coated at these stages. The states 1 and 3 indicated by a low and a high lead concentration in the zinc bath are supposed to be preserved for a certain period since it is expensive to arrange them. The present estimation of the planning department for this period amounts to about two weeks because there is no exact accounting data available. State 3 cannot be arranged directly after state 1. Thus the states are sequence-dependent. Between the setup states 1 and 3 the transition state 2 with a variable concentration of lead is traversed that may be shorter than two weeks since it is a transition state. Lead must be permanently added to the bath if the concentration has to be kept constant. If a lower (higher) concentration is to be realized the quantity of added lead must be decreased (increased) and state 2 is traversed this way. Metal that goes through the bath while state 2 is being traversed receives an undefined lead coat because the concentration is variable. A changeover from one state to another takes place without a breakdown of the machine. This means that the processing of jobs may continue during a changeover what is typical for steel or chemical industries when concentrations are changed. A setup duration is relevant for the transition state 2 because this state has a minimal duration no matter if jobs are processed or not. This setup duration is the minimal time that is needed to traverse the transition state.

To arrange state 1 or 3 is only reasonable if there are enough jobs available that have to be processed with the according setup state (lead concentration, respectively). Thus we are confronted with a batching problem at these two stages because jobs have to be collected in order to fill a period of time that is long enough to justify the high setup costs. According to the classification of Jordan, 1996, the batching is preemptive with item or job availability. This means that each job in a batch becomes available at its completion time and idle times (preemptions) between jobs do not cause new setups. It is predetermined which setup state is required by a job.

Concerning the jobs there are further exceptions that we have to observe: Every product item is assigned to a certain job and can be identified at any time as required by an efficient quality management. One job may include several physical pieces of one product variant. Therefore, the quantity of a job is measured in tons. The processing time of one job is calculated by the time per ton of the concerning stage times the quantity of the job. Predecessors or successors of a job are always assigned to another stage. The reasons for these general precedence constraints are as follows: First we have a make-to-order system what causes difficulties in case of quality problems and waste. As stated above it is not possible to keep stocks to compensate product failures at every stage. This would lead to unacceptable high inventories. All pieces that wait for processing in front of a production stage are assigned to other jobs and must not be reassigned. Instead the compensation of wasteful goods is realized by subsequently producing new parts for the job for which waste occurred. This implies that we have to start the production of new parts at the beginning of the line up to the stage where the waste turned up. If we let a job wait until the compensation pieces arrive this job may have two predecessors. Of course we could avoid this by producing two separate quantities and making two deliveries to the customer but we want to have one single delivery at the end of the line. Second it may happen that a part belonging to a certain job is cut into several parts that go into different succeeding jobs. Thus one job can supply several successor jobs. If combinations of these cases occur, complex job networks arise.

It is allowed that a job passes other jobs due to a higher priority. Different priorities are expressed by job weights. Furthermore, each job has a latest start time that can be recursively calculated starting with the due date of the concerning customer order and should be respected. However, as the production system is highly congested we cannot complete all jobs (starting at their latest start time) without violating the due dates. If a job is already late at the beginning of the planning horizon the latest start time depends on the critical path of the relevant sub-project. The critical path defines the duration for the earliest completion of a sub-project.

The requirement of the company is to be able to generate new schedules as often as necessary in order to take into account quickly all events within the production system and to be able to quote realistic due dates for new orders. Thus we have a rolling planning horizon and we must schedule all the jobs and not only a part of the jobs what would make the problem easier. Beside time-oriented, precedence- and capacity-related restrictions also technological requirements have to be considered. For example, at the rolling machines the width of the processed sheet metal has to be varied systematically because otherwise the rolls are damaged. With respect to a good transparency and comprehensibility it does not seem to be advisable to expand a planning model so wide that technological restrictions are simultaneously considered with all other restrictions. It appears to be more suggestive to execute a more general scheduling level that transfers a set of jobs for a certain period (e.g. one day) and a certain stage to a more detailed planning level that re-sequences the jobs of the set within this period considering the technological requirements of the concerned stage. It has to be ensured that the chosen period is not too short since otherwise there might be too few jobs to generate a technologically feasible sequence. In order to avoid violating precedence relations between jobs of different shop-stages by this re-sequencing we have either to establish waiting times so that successors are scheduled after the chosen period or we have to transfer respective information to the detailed planning system. In this paper we regard the more general scheduling that neglects technological restrictions including setup times.

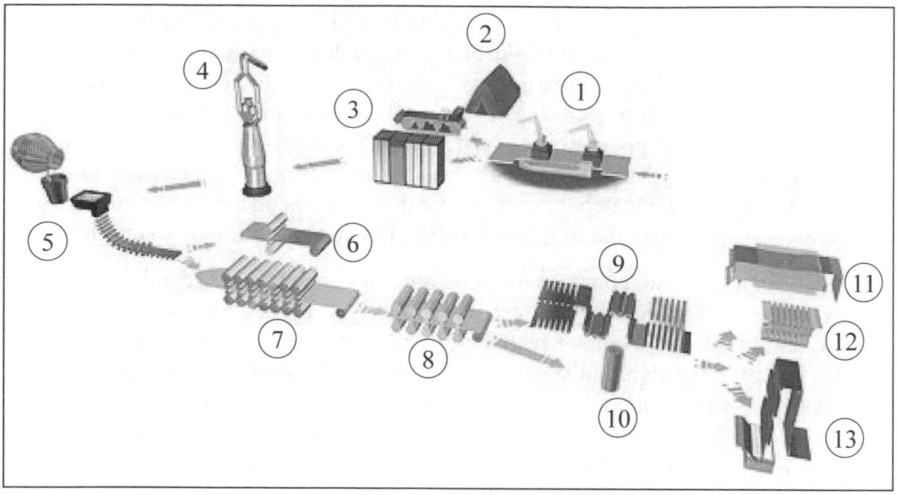

Fig. 1. Intra-organizational supply chain

The intra-organizational supply chain of the problem described above is illustrated in Figure 1. At first raw ore and coal are delivered at a harbor or by train. In the powder metal facility (2) the so-called "sinter" – the transformed ore for the furnace (4) – is produced. The coke is produced in the coking plant (3). Both the coke and the sinter are transferred to the furnace (4) where the steel is extracted. In the continuous caster (5) slabs are casted. The slabs are rolled to sheet metal in the hot rolling mill (7, 6). Another rolling process can be undertaken within the cold rolling mill (8). Due to the fact that the structure of the metal is worsened by the cold rolling process the mechanical features of the material are improved by a heating process (9, 10). In a coating facility (11) the metal can be coated whereas it can be zinced in the zincing facilities (12, 13).

3. Batching and machine scheduling: A short overview

Let C_i represent the completion time of a job i measured from a defined starting time t_0 of the planning horizon. Then we can formulate the time oriented objectives MIN ΣC_i or MIN $\Sigma w_i C_i$ with w_i representing the weight of a job and therefore the importance of the concerned customer. By including a release time r_i of a job the flow time $F_i = C_i - r_i$ can be defined. The release time equals the completion time of the last predecessor if no waiting times exist. The flow time reflects the span of time from the availability of a job until its completion. The objective MIN ($C_{max} = \max \{C_i \mid i = 1, ..., I\}$) referred to as the minimization of the makespan is often regarded as a compromise between capacity related and flow time oriented objectives because of the assumption that it will also lead to short flow times. For this reason the makespan objective became one of the most often pursued objectives in the scheduling literature.

We define the lateness of a job i as $L_i = C_i - dd_i$ with dd_i denoting the due date of job i. A positive L_i represents lateness and a negative L_i earliness. If we allow L_i to become positive and negative it means that jobs are rewarded for being early and punished for being tardy. In many cases only late jobs with positive values for L_i are considered which leads to the so-called tardiness problem where we want to minimize the sum of all $T_i = \max\{0, L_i\}$, thus MIN ΣT_i, MIN $\Sigma w_i T_i$ respectively. It reflects situations in which costs are associated with lateness but no benefits with earliness.

Due to the fact that the steel producer considered in this paper wants to realize a high capacity utilization on the one hand and to respect due dates on the other hand we are confronted with a multiple objective problem. An appropriate way to consider two (or more) objectives is to weight the expressions by two different parameters λ and $(1 - \lambda)$ with $\lambda \in [0,1]$. The parameter λ has to be determined by a decision maker (see van Wassenhove and Gelders, 1980). This way we could state our objective as follows: MIN $(\lambda C_{max} + (1 - \lambda) \Sigma w_i T_i)$. However, here we shall be concerned with the tardiness objective and set $\lambda = 0$ since we view the problem considered in this paper from a supply chain management perspective.

If changeover activities between the processing of jobs are necessary it is often cheaper or faster to partition the jobs into families if possible and to process batches consisting of jobs of the same family because there is no need for setups during the handling of one batch. Setups have only to be made between batches of different families. Jobs with the same characteristics belong to the same family. Large batches imply few setups and thus low setup costs but may come along with delays for jobs of other families. Therefore, an important objective is to find the optimal batch sizes that limit the number of setups on the one hand and the delay of jobs on the other hand. This definition of batching includes setup costs and/or times that arise between the change of batches or families, respectively, and may be sequence-dependent. The jobs of a batch can become available after processing in two different ways: either together with all other jobs of the same batch at the same time after the last job was completed or one after another at different times. The first case is often denoted as batch availability and the second as job availability (see Potts and Kovalyov, 2000, and Jordan, 1996). In both cases jobs are processed sequentially. Another difference occurs if batching machines are used that process several jobs simultaneously. For a review of recent results in this area see Potts and Kovalyov, 2000.

More general problems, e.g. project scheduling problems, in combination with batching approaches can be found in the context of process-oriented production problems. There exists an extensive literature about this kind of batching problems (see, e.g., Schwindt and Trautmann, 2000). However, the definition of batches in this area is completely different from the definition given above (see Voß and Witt, 2002a): In batching problems within process industries a batch is a combination of a task (physical or chemical transformation process, e.g. heating or filtration) and a production quantity. The production of a batch is referred to as an operation or activity. In this context batching implies a discontinuous production mode with respect to the material flow. Usually the problem of batching in process industries is to explode primary demands into batches as a first step and to schedule the resulting operations afterwards. Thc batch sizes are often predetermined by technology, regulations or an output of a higher planning level. For approaches that additionally include the problem of determining batch sizes we refer to Blömer, 1999. The second step of scheduling the batches can be realized with approaches from project scheduling.

Due to the differences we will restrict our examinations to batching problems as defined by Potts and Kovalyov, 2000, and Jordan, 1996, that focus on "discrete" production problems where the objects to be scheduled are discrete items (products or jobs). Consequently, we exclude process-oriented approaches because the problem described in Section 2 represents a batching problem with job availability where the batch sizes are not predetermined and do not consist of one product quantity but of several jobs. As can be deduced from the review of Potts and Kovalyov, 2000, recent approaches of batching and scheduling do not consider project scheduling problems. The most general problems treated are job shop and open shop problems.

4. Heuristic solution with dispatching rules

In spite of its practical relevance there has been only little research on a heuristic solution of the project scheduling problem with a weighted tardiness objective. Patterson, 1976, examines the effects of problem structure on heuristic performance using a weighted delay objective. Kurtulus and Davis, 1982, survey heuristics to minimize the sum of project delays. This is extended by Kurtulus and Narula, 1985, and Kurtulus, 1985 to the weighted delay objective for multiple projects. Kim and Schniederjans, 1989, develop an expert system for project scheduling with multiple objectives including due date satisfaction. Deckro et al., 1991, present a heuristic procedure based on Lagrangean relaxation whereas Kim and Leachman, 1993, use lateness costs for a heuristic solution. One of the most extensive surveys of dispatching rules for the resource-constrained project scheduling problem to minimize the weighted tardiness can be found in Lawrence and Morton, 1993. Leon and Balakrishnan, 1995, investigate local search strategies. Birge and Maddox, 1995, describe methods to calculate bounds on expected project tardiness. Özdamar et al., 1998, examine different dispatching rules for the tardiness and the net present value objective embedded in a multi-pass heuristic.

Due to the fact that we want to schedule very large problem instances consisting of several thousand jobs a scheduling with dispatching rules appears to be promising. For resource-constrained project scheduling problems (RCPSP) there exist two different schemes to generate schedules with dispatching rules: so-called serial and parallel generation schemes. A serial generation scheme runs through I iterations. In each iteration a set of so far scheduled jobs and a set of eligible jobs *EI* are determined. *EI* consists of jobs whose predecessors are already scheduled. From this set one job is selected, e.g., by means of a dispatching rule, and is scheduled as early as possible without violating precedence or resource restrictions. A parallel generation scheme calculates in every iteration a decision point t which is the earliest completion time among the jobs that are in process in the previous iteration. The set of eligible jobs consists of jobs that could be started at the current decision point without violating precedence or resource restrictions. From this set one or several jobs are selected and scheduled at t. For a more detailed description of schedule generation schemes see, e.g., Hartmann, 1999.

A solution procedure for our problem can slightly differ from these generation schemes since we have a flow shop and consequently a sequence of the resources. That is, we can schedule the jobs stage-wise beginning at the first stage of the flow shop. All jobs belonging to the same stage are scheduled before the jobs of the next stage are scheduled. Every time a job is scheduled its successors receive a release time r_i which is the completion time of the currently considered job plus a possible waiting time. Since a job may only have successors at a following stage precedence constraints cannot be violated this way. Consequently, we have also a (stage-wise) decision point t and a set of eligible jobs that contains the jobs that are assigned to the stage currently under consideration and whose release time is not greater than the current decision point.

Dispatching rules for the RCPSP can be classified in different ways. Drexl and Kolisch, 1993, distinguish rules according to the features static/dynamic, local/global and according to the used data. Static rules are independent of the current decision point or current schedule and calculate always the same priority value for a job while dynamic rules calculate different values depending on the current time or the current state of the system to be planned. An example for a static rule is a rule that selects always the job with the shortest processing time. So-called "slack" based rules are examples of dynamic rules if the slack is permanently updated during the solution procedure. Then the slack is the difference of the latest start time of a job and the current decision point t in a parallel generation scheme.

Lawrence, 1984, groups dispatching rules according to the used data into activity based rules, network based rules, CPM (Critical Path Method) based rules and resource based rules. There has been extensive research on dispatching rules for the RCPSP with the makespan objective (see, e.g., Alvarez-Valdes and Tamarit, 1989, Boctor, 1990, Davis and Patterson, 1975, Cooper, 1976, Kolisch, 1995, or Kolisch, 1996). We will restrict our examinations to rules that performed best in former studies and offer a fast generation of schedules because we want to solve large instances. We will focus on the objective "weighted tardiness" since we regard this to be most important for the supply chain management of the considered steel manufacturer. As mentioned above Lawrence and Morton, 1993, review and examine several rules for the multiple project scheduling problem to minimize the weighted tardiness. In a benchmark examination executed to be able to evaluate new rules the following three rules that select always the job with the greatest value perform best:

- Weighted Earliest Due Date: $\text{WEDD} = w_i / \min\{dd_o \mid o \in O_i\} - t_0)$
- Weighted Latest Finish Time: $\text{WLFT} = w_i / (LS_i + d_i - t_0)$
- Weighted Minimum Slack: $\text{WMINSLK} = w_i / (LS_i - t_0)$

where O_i is the set of all downstream orders that are supplied by job i. For the WLFT and the WMINSLK rules we calculate earliest and latest start times ES_i and LS_i for every job based on the relevant critical path or due date.

$$ES_i = \begin{cases} 0 & \text{if } P_i = \{0\} \\ \max\{(ES_h + d_h) \mid h \in P_i\} & \text{otherwise} \end{cases}$$

$$LS_i = \begin{cases} \max\{\min\{dd_o \mid o \in O_i\}, \min\{CP_o \mid o \in O_i\}\} - d_i & \text{if } i \in P_{I+1} \\ \min\{(LS_k - d_i) \mid k \in S_i\} & \text{otherwise} \end{cases}$$

where CP_o is the smallest critical path of all downstream orders $o \in O_i$ and P_i (S_i) denotes the set of all predecessors (successors) of job i That is, we pursue the strategy to supply an order as early as possible if the due date is already exceeded because the critical path defines a sequence of jobs that have to be processed without any delay in order to supply the customer as early as possible. This way of calculating earliest and latest start times is very similar to the calculation in usual multiple project problems (see, e.g., Lawrence and Morton, 1993). Actually, every sub-network of jobs that supply certain orders at the end represents one project. In multiple project problems there is usually one due date for every sub-project. Our problem is slightly different because there may be more than one order and consequently more than one due date at the end of a sub-project. Therefore, we choose the earliest due date or critical path, respectively. The earliest and latest finish times are calculated as: $EF_i = ES_i + d_i$ and $LF_i = LS_i + d_i$.

We modify the WEDD rule as follows since we have to allow the orders to be beyond their due date at t_0 what would otherwise result in a negative denominator:

- $\text{WEDD} = w_i / (\max\{\min\{dd_o \mid o \in O_i\}, \min\{CP_o \mid o \in O_i\}\} - t_0)$

Additionally, Lawrence and Morton, 1993, examine another rule called R&M heuristic according to Rachamadugu and Morton, 1982:

- $RM_i = \dfrac{w_i}{\pi_i} \cdot \exp\left(\dfrac{-\max(LS_i - t,\ 0)}{k_1 \cdot \bar{d}}\right)$

where $\bar{d}$ is the average duration of all jobs processed at the same stage, k_1 is an empirically determined "look-ahead" parameter and π_i is a process time related cost of job i. Preliminary studies revealed that the parameter k_1 has a negligible influence. For this reason we set k_1 equal to one. According to Rachamadugu, 1987, this rule can be used to find an optimal sequence of jobs for a single machine weighted tardiness problem. The costs π_i can be defined locally or globally. A local definition implies that only the cost of the currently considered job is relevant whereas a global definition aggregates current and downstream costs of the sub-project the job belongs to. Thus the local and global calculations of process time related job costs can be defined as follows:

- Local process time costing: $\pi_i = d_i$
- Global process time costing: $\pi_i = \sum_{j \in U_i} d_j$

where U_i is the set of unfinished downstream jobs succeeding job i (including i).

So far we presented only rules that do not take into account parallel machines and the batching requirement. In case of several parallel resources the duration d_i is calculated by the help of the equation $d_i = q_i \cdot p_s$ with $p_r = p_s \cdot v_r$ ($r \in R_s$) where v_r is a speed-factor, p_s a stage-dependent processing time and R_s the set of parallel resources assigned to stage s. In order to include stages with $|R_s|$ parallel resources into the R&M rule we calculate an "effective number of resources" v_s' for the relevant stages and multiply the priority value RM_i with it (see Morton and Pentico, 1993). Then v_s' equals 1 if there is only one resource at stage s. All other rules remain unchanged. The selected job is always assigned to the resource that becomes free next. However, to form batches the dispatching rules must be modified more extensively. An applicable way to include setup times into the R&M rule is described by Pinedo, 1995, that can be easily adapted to setup costs. The R&M rule is extended by another exponential term:

- $$RM_i = \frac{w_i \cdot v_s'}{\pi_i} \cdot \exp\left(\frac{-\max(LS_i - t,\ 0)}{\bar{d}}\right) \cdot \exp(-sc_i)$$

where sc_i represent the setup costs that are caused if job i is selected. If a resource does not require batching the third term is always one because the setup costs are always zero. We modify the WEDD-, WLFT- and MINSLK-rules in the following ways to include setup costs:

$$\text{WEDD} = \begin{cases} w_i / (\max\{\min\{dd_o \mid o \in O_i\}, \min\{CP_o \mid o \in O_i\}\} - t_0) & \text{if } sc_i = 0 \\ w_i / ((\max\{\min\{dd_o \mid o \in O_i\}, \min\{CP_o \mid o \in O_i\}\} - t_0) \cdot sc_i) & \text{if } sc_i > 0 \end{cases}$$

$$\text{WLFT} = \begin{cases} w_i / (LS_i + d_i - t_0) & \text{if } sc_i = 0 \\ w_i / ((LS_i + d_i - t_0) \cdot sc_i) & \text{if } sc_i > 0 \end{cases}$$

$$\text{WMINSLK} = \begin{cases} w_i / (LS_i - t_0) & \text{if } sc_i = 0 \\ w_i / ((LS_i - t_0) \cdot sc_i) & \text{if } sc_i > 0 \end{cases}$$

The objective is not to calculate exact setup costs. Instead we want to create batches with the help of setup costs or setup weights. Table 1 shows the dispatching rules that we will use to solve the problem described in Section 2.

Recently, Schocke, 2000, applied another dispatching rule based on a smallest regret principle (originally presented in Drexl and Grünewald, 1993) to a hybrid flow shop problem and obtained good results. However, due to the fact that he examined much smaller problem instances and did not consider general precedence relations among the jobs his way to generate schedules was not surveyed within this study. Furthermore, preliminary calculations revealed that the forming of batches does not work as satisfyingly as with the rules described above.

R&M with process time costing	Local
	Global
WEDD	Global
WLFT	Local
WMINSLK	Local

Table 1. Dispatching rules

5. Computational results for real-world problem instances

The dispatching rules were tested for two different problem structures. The first problem neither consisted of parallel resources at certain stages of the flow shop nor of resources with setup states. This was done to be able to compare the solutions with the results of another algorithm already implemented at the steel producer. This algorithm did not take into account parallel resources or setup activities when this study was made. Because this algorithm was part of a standard software package the functionality was not known and therefore cannot be described here. Furthermore, this algorithm filled only a two week horizon at the first stage and scheduled only succeeding jobs at the following stages or jobs whose predecessors at stage one were already completed before t_0. The scheduling with dispatching rules was executed, analogously. Twenty instances were collected over a period of three months each consisting of about 30,000 jobs. The results shown in Table 2 are average objective values relative to the solutions generated by the local R&M-rule that were set to 100%. Thus, e.g., the solutions generated by the global R&M rule were about 13.6% above the objective value of the local R&M-rule on the average. The calculation time for the solution of one instance on a 450-Mhz-PC amounted to about 30 minutes. This time includes the reading of five files containing the relevant data, the creation of the project network along with a topological ordering, the scheduling itself and some evaluation routines such as the calculation of the tardiness, the flow times, the waiting times and the capacity utilization.

The local R&M-rule outperformed the other rules in all 20 cases. The better result of the local R&M-rule compared with the global variant does not concur with the results of Lawrence and Morton, 1993, where the global rule provides the best results. First we must point out that we surveyed a very special problem structure that is – contrary to the instances used by Lawrence and Morton, 1993 – not representative for project problems in general. Therefore, it does not seem to be surprising that one rule outperformed all other rules. To be able to explain the superiority of the local R&M-rule over the global rule we examined our instances and the way how the rules selected the jobs in more detail and found that the local rule preferred jobs with short processing times whereas the global rule tended to prefer jobs with longer processing times, a fact that is surprising at first view. But beyond that we discovered that sub-projects with high quantities and thus long processing times consisted of few jobs and had short routings whereas sub-projects with low quantities and thus short processing times consisted of more jobs and had longer routings. Due to the fact that the global rule sums up the processing times of downstream jobs of the same project it preferred jobs that had few downstream jobs. But these were the sub-projects with higher quantities and thus longer processing times. Obviously sub-projects, respectively orders, with long routings contained low quantities (short processing times) and sub-projects with short routings contained higher quantities. This conclusion was confirmed by the steel producer and explained as follows: Products with long routings visit more resources and are consequently more special than products with short routings. The number of possible varieties increases with the length of the routing. Consequently, products with long routings cannot be collected to high quantities because they do not occur as often as other products.

	R&M local	R&M global	WLFT	WEDD	WMINSLK	Exist. Alg.
Average weighted tardiness	100.0	113.6	128.7	125.1	131.7	120.7
Average capacity usage (%)	92.4	82.3	92.0	90.5	92.4	80.0

Table 2. Results for a flow shop

The second problem structure took into account parallel resources and resources with setup states. However, due to the fact that neither criteria which sub-project required which setup state at the relevant resources nor different processing times of uniform parallel resources were available, these parameters had to be chosen arbitrarily. It was assumed that every job assigned to a stage with parallel resources could be processed by each of the resources and that the resources were identical instead of uniform because the real processing times in the steel plant did not differ very much. In case of, e.g., two parallel resources the processing times were set half the processing time given by the case without parallel resources. Therefore, a stage with parallel resources was not able to process the jobs faster compared with the plain flow shop. The required setup states were determined randomly. As can be derived from Table 3 the local R&M-rule performed best again. Also the number of changeovers in relation to the average tardiness seems to be the best with the local R&M-rule.

The cost rates for changeovers at the stages 13 and 14 were kept constant for all rules and instances and were chosen arbitrarily in a way that the length of the batches resulted in about two weeks no matter which rule was used. At the end of the planning horizon the problem turned up that there was very often only one eligible job so that it was difficult to form batches if the next eligible job required a different setup state. As a result we observed changeovers after every job without any batching. In order to avoid this it was examined in case of a necessary changeover which setup state was required by the jobs arriving and therefore becoming eligible shortly after the current decision point t. In case of another job requiring the present setup state a short idle time was accepted and a changeover avoided this way.

	R&M local	R&M global	WLFT	WEDD	WMINSLK
Average weighted tardiness	100.0	113.6	109.6	107.1	115.4
Average capacity usage (%)	88.7	79.7	90.6	89.1	92.3
Average number of changeovers	24.4	28.5	23.8	31	23.9

Table 3. Results for a hybrid flow shop with batching

6. Conclusions

In this paper we have presented a real-world scheduling problem in the steel industry. Due to the fact that there are general precedence relations among the jobs it is reasonable to relate it to the resource constrained project scheduling problem although the resources are structured as a hybrid flow shop. The discussion in Section 3 reflects the diversity of possible objectives and their practical relevance.

Since problem instances considered in this paper consist of about 30,000 production jobs forming several thousand projects it is not possible to apply an exact algorithm to generate schedules daily in a rolling planning horizon. A fast heuristic solution procedure based on different dispatching rules that are capable to realize low tardiness and to form batches was developed. The way to establish batches by dispatching rules seems to be a new enhancement for the scheduling of resource-constrained projects. However, other requirements had to be left to future issues, namely the detailed connection of the procedure with a rolling planning horizon along with the embedding into a hierarchical planning approach and the control of inventory levels at the single stages. Some experiments regarding limited intermediate storage and a procedure to control work-in-process can be found in Voß and Witt, 2002b. Besides, the development of an efficient improvement procedure for problem instances consisting of 30,000 jobs is another challenge.

References

Alvarez-Valdes, R., Tamarit, J.M. (1989): Heuristic algorithms for resource-constrained project scheduling: A review and empirical analysis. In: Slowinski R., Weglarz J. (eds.) Advances in Project Scheduling. Elsevier, Amsterdam, pp. 113-134.

Birge, J.R., Maddox, M.J. (1995): Bounds on expected project tardiness: in: Operations Research 43, pp. 838-850.

Boctor, F.F. (1990): Some efficient multi-heuristic procedures for resource-constrained project scheduling. In: European Journal of Operational Research 49, pp. 3-13.

Blömer, F. (1999): Produktionsplanung und -steuerung in der chemischen Industrie – Ressourceneinsatzplanung von Batchprozessen auf Mehrzweckanlagen. Gabler, Wiesbaden.

Cooper, D.F. (1976): Heuristics for scheduling resource-constrained projects: An experimental investigation. In: Management Science 22, pp. 1186-1194.

Davis, E.W., Patterson, J.H. (1975): A comparison of heuristic and optimal solutions in resource-constrained project scheduling. In: Management Science 21, pp. 944-955.

Deckro, R.F., Winkovsky, E.P., Hebert J.E., Gagnon R. (1991): A decomposition approach to multi-project-scheduling. In: European Journal of Operational Research 51, pp. 110 -118.

Drexl, A., Grünewald, J. (1993): Nonpreemptive multi-mode resource-constrained project scheduling. In: IIE Transactions 25/5, pp. 74-81.

Drexl, A., Kolisch, R. (1993): Produktionsplanung und -steuerung bei Einzel- und Kleinserienfertigung. In: Wirtschaftswissenschaftliches Studium 22/2, S. 60-66.

Gupta, J.N.D. (1988): Two-stage, hybrid flow shop scheduling problem. In: Journal of the Operational Research Society 39, pp. 359-364.

Jordan, C. (1996): Batching and scheduling, Models and methods for several problem classes. Lecture Notes in Economics and Mathematical Systems, Vol. 437, Springer, Berlin.

Hartmann, S. (1999): Project scheduling under limited resources: Models, methods and applications. Lecture Notes in Economics and Mathematical Systems, Vol. 478, Springer, Berlin.

Kim, S.Y., Leachman, R.C. (1993): Multi-project scheduling with explicit lateness costs. In: IIE Transactions 25/2, pp. 34-44.

Kim, S.O., Schniederjans, M.J. (1989): Heuristic framework for the resource-constrained multi-project scheduling problem. In: Computers & Operations Research 16, pp. 541-556.

Kolisch, R. (1995): Project scheduling under resource constraints: Efficient heuristics for several problem classes. Physica, Heidelberg.

Kolisch, R. (1996): Efficient priority rules for the resource-constrained project scheduling problem. In: Journal of Operations Management 14, pp. 179-192.

Kurtulus, I.S. (1985): Multiproject scheduling: Analysis of scheduling strategies under unequal delay penalties. In: Journal of Operations Management 5, pp. 291-307.

Kurtulus, I.S., Davis, E.W. (1982): Multi-project scheduling: Categorization of heuristic rules performance. In: Management Science 28, pp. 161-172.

Kurtulus, I.S., Narula S.C. (1985): Multi-project scheduling: Analysis of project performance. In: IIE Transactions 17/2, pp. 58-65.

Lawrence, S.R. (1984): An experimental investigation of heuristic scheduling techniques. Graduate School of Industrial Administration, Carnegie-Mellon University, Pittsburgh.

Lawrence, S.R., Morton, T.E. (1993): Resource-constrained multi-project scheduling with tardy costs: Comparing myopic, bottleneck, and resource pricing heuristics. In: European Journal of Operational Research 64, pp. 168-187.

Leon, V.J., Balakrishnan, R. (1995): Strength and adaptability of problem-space based neighborhoods for resource-constrained scheduling. In: OR Spektrum 17, pp. 173-182.

Morton, T.E., Pentico, D.W. (1993): Heuristic Scheduling Systems. Wiley, New York.

Özdamar, L., Ulusoy, G., Bayyigit, M. (1998): A heuristic treatment of tardiness and net present value criteria in resource constrained project scheduling. In: International Journal of Physical Distribution & Logistics Management 28, pp. 805-824.

Patterson, J.H. (1976): Project scheduling: The effects of problem structure on heuristic performance, in: Naval Research Logistics Quarterly 23, pp. 95-123.

Pinedo, M. (1995): Scheduling: Theory, algorithms and systems. Prentice Hall, Englewood Cliffs.

Potts, C.N., Kovalyov, M.Y. (2000): Scheduling with batching: A review. In: European Journal of Operational Research 120, pp. 228-249.

Rachamadugu, R.M.V (1987): A note on the weighted tardiness problem. In: Operations Research 35, pp. 450-452.

Rachamadugu, R.M.V., Morton, T.E. (1982): Myopic heuristics for the single machine weighted tardiness problem. Working Paper No. 28-81-82, Graduate School of Industrial Administration, Carnegie Mellon University, Pittsburgh.

Schwindt, C., Trautmann, N. (2000): Batch scheduling in process industries: An application of resource-constrained project scheduling. In: OR Spektrum 22, pp. 501-524.

Schocke, K.-O. (2000): Maschinenbelegungsplanung mehrstufiger Fließfertigungen: Vom Modell zum Leitstand. Gabler, Wiesbaden.

Tang, L., Liu, J., Rong, A., Yang, Z. (2000): A multiple travelling salesman problem model for hot rolling scheduling in Shanghai Baoshan Iron & Steel Complex. In: European Journal of Operational Research 124, pp. 267-282.

Tang, L., Liu, J., Rong, A., Yang, Z. (2001): A review of planning and scheduling systems and methods for integrated steel production. In: European Journal of Operational Research 133, pp. 1-20.

Voß, S. (1993): The two-stage hybrid-flowshop scheduling problem with sequence-dependent setup times. In: Fandel, G., Gulledge, T., Jones, A. (eds.) Operations Research in Production Planning and Control. Springer, Berlin, pp. 336-352.

Voß, S., Witt, A. (2002a): Batching in der Produktionsplanung – Projektplanung mit reihenfolgeabhängigen Rüstkosten. Working Paper, Technische Universität Braunschweig.

Voß, S., Witt, A. (2002b): Heuristic flow shop scheduling with limited intermediate storage. Working Paper, Technische Universität Braunschweig.

Wassenhove, van L.N., Gelders, L.F. (1980): Solving a bicriterion scheduling problem. In: European Journal of Operational Research 4, pp. 42-48.

Wittrock, R. (1988): An adaptable scheduling algorithm for flexible flow lines. In: Operations Research 36, pp. 445-453.

Information System for Supporting Supply Chain Management

Richard Lackes

Department of Business Informatics
Faculty of Economics
University of Dortmund
Vogelpothsweg 87
D-44227 Dortmund, Germany

Abstract: *To the analysis of the weak points of an uncoordinated procedure in the customer-supplier-relationship potentials for a supply chain management are outlined. Propositions for the conversion of the supply chain management and its boundaries are analyzed crucially. An information system put down onto the importance of the supply chain management is designed and tested for practical implementation. A supply chain oriented production planning and control system coordinates under resort on the available decentralised PPC-system's of the enterprises in the supply chain their dispositions. The architecture, necessary for that, the needed data and the functionality are introduced and discussed.*

Keywords: *supply chain architecture, supply chain management, supply chain production planning and control, logistic concepts, information preview, data relevance of decisions, planning horizon, coordination measurements, master plan, restrictions of supply chain management*

1. Introduction

In recent years there has been increasing discussion of innovative logistic conceptions as applied to supply chain management (SCM). SCM concerns itself with the construction and the use of multilevel logistics chains by which different independent enterprises are connected with one another. The links are evolved through the material flow which is determined by supply relationships in a work sharing economic system. Inverse to the material flow an appropriate information flow can be identified which is used for documentation, release and control of the movement of the material.

Practice and experience demonstrated a need for SCM (Handfield, Nichols, 1999, pp. 1 et sqq.). An integrating view throughout the entire logistics chain "from your supplier's supplier to your customer's customer" (Supply-Chain Council, 2002, p. 3) would present an enhanced potential for rationalization (Cooper, Ellram, 1993, p. 15 et sqq.; Cooper, Lambert, Pagh 1997; Zäpfel, Wasner, 1999). The whole process would benefit from greater flexibility and reduction of inefficiencies as there would be greater coordination by the participating enterprises in the value chain (Corsten, Gössinger, 2001, p. 83.). The reasons for the improvement as a result of the coordination of the decision makers in a supply chain are as follows (Wildemann, 2000, pp. 49-86):

- Decrease of the production and transactions costs.
- Reduction of delivery times.
- Improvement in quality.
- Increase of flexibility.

The realization of this potential for rationalization implies that the decision making processes of the different participants in a supply chain are in harmony with one another so that an optimum for the whole chain will be achieved. This could mean that the profits or costs of individual companies would suffer if the practices were uncoordinated (Gericke, et al., 1999, pp. 13-16).

In accordance with the SCOR-model, which was propagated by the Supply-Chain Council, the SCM embraces a strategic and long-term operational scope of duties in which strategies and capacities and their allocation in the supply chain are defined. As one is here concerned with decisions which are usually very seldom altered and a business information system is mainly suitable for short term operational tasks the main emphasis will be focused on the operational area. Neither the locations nor the capacities in a supply chain can be altered therefore one is mainly concerned with the use of the capacities.

2. Individual inspection of enterprises: depiction and analysis

Before one considers the different forms and potentials of a SCM one must critically analyse the "classical" individual functional mode of a customer-supplier relationship. A comprehension of the problems provides a good starting point for an improved SCM.

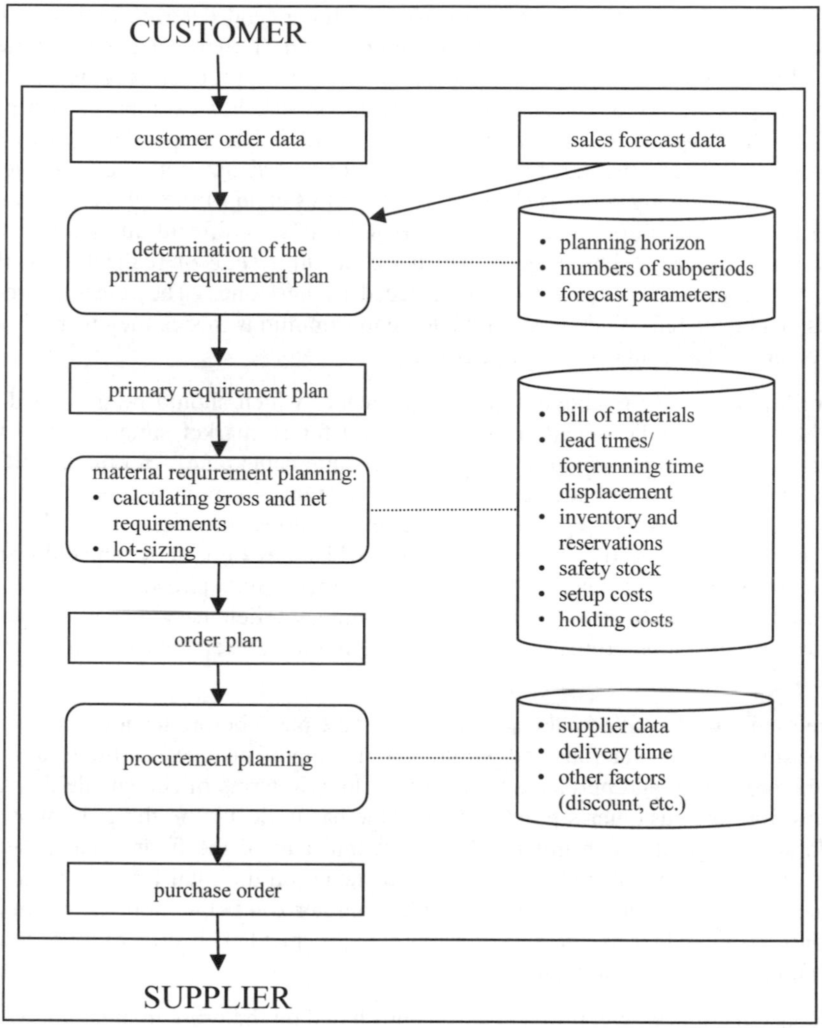

Fig. 1. Overview of the material requirement planning

An enterprise receives from its sales sector concrete customer orders, which among other things specifies the product which is to be delivered, the quantity, and an exact delivery date (see Fig. 1). When one has assembled the customers' orders one can develop a primary requirements plan (Lackes, 1998, p. 293 et sqq.; Fandel, François, Gubitz, 1997, p. 128 et sqq.). This plan documents the planning of the outlet quantity for the market of the final products which are to be made available with reference to the whole planning horizon; this is divided into subperiods. This primary requirement plan is the starting point for the material requirement planning (Lackes, 1998, p. 293 et sqq.; Fandel, François, Gubitz, 1997, p. 158 et sqq.). This process calculates the parts requirements – taking into account the available inventory and the necessary lead times, and determines production orders and procuring orders. In a planning horizon of T time periods a T dimensional primary requirement vector for every marketable product becomes a T dimensional order vector for all considered components. For external parts a purchase order is issued if a favourable quantity of orders has been calculated within the delivery-time in the purchase order vector. In accordance with the principle of a revolving planning process (Kurbel, 1998, p. 188 et sqq.) the whole procedure will be again run through at regular intervals or if a significant alteration in the environment occurs. The projects which are not in a state of realization at this point in time will be discarded and replaced by new ones. The released orders must not be altered. When these prove to be too ambitious in size they increase the inventory and of course the storage costs.

A critical point of the above described procedure which should be improved by SCM is the potential deviation from the valid future market situation from the market situation represented in the primary requirements plan. An effective SCM should provide – with better and earlier information – a more precise picture of sales developments. Divergences from the actual market sales figures and those of the planning stage lead to inventory of parts which have not yet been sold or not completely processed and to deficiencies of stock. Both phenomena cause increased costs. Safety stock is installed for eventual deficiencies in the inventory. Thus costs resulting from the uncertainty of future market trends will be minimised.

One cannot wait until actual customer orders take place before deciding about the acquisition of raw materials and production of components because the lead times in the production and purchase are relatively long in terms of acceptable delivery times from the customer's point of view. One has to decide on the present available knowledge although this can be a poor indicator of the future market situation. The necessary planning horizon is dependant on the total lead time and the typical range of orders. The longer the planning horizon is the more uncertain becomes, in general terms, the data of primary requirement. This effect will be intensified in dynamically changing markets.

The fact that it is essential to make decisions based on the present situation, which is not necessarily an indication of the future market situation, is one of the essential cost drivers in the field of operational materials management. It is exactly this aspect which a SCM should tackle. In reverse an (operative) SCM which is directed to an improved coordination of enterprises in a material flow chain where the customer demand throughout the whole period of the planning horizon can be exactly predicted is totally unnecessary. Such an "ideal" situation exists for enterprises where for the whole planning horizon a previously determined sales programme can be realised. This situation holds when the manufacturing process bases only on received customer orders or when there exists a long waiting queue of customer orders (e.g. because the product – as it happened in the automobile industry – is in such demand that one can afford to have to sustain a "bottleneck"). In practice however this seldom happens.

The entire necessary planning horizon is one which enables to take all decisions up to a revision based on deterministic data (Lackes, 1994, p. 410 et sqq.).

The situation in an enterprise in a logistics chain which does not have a coordinated SCM can be summarised as follows:

(C1) Each enterprise resp. each decision maker in the logistics chain orientates himself exclusively around his own individual economic aims and ignores the changes which may occur in other enterprises as a result of his actions. Therefore the cost reducing lot-sizing of the required quantity could imply increasing costs for the supplier as a result of capacity problems. These could be higher than the savings due to the lot-sizing.

(C2) The decisions pertaining to the management of the material and immaterial objects of the enterprise (e.g. semi-finished goods and current bills) are based on a business information system which provides relevant methods and data.

(C3) Each individual enterprise owns a separate business information system which reports on its view on the environment and its internal state of affairs. Alterations in conditions happen as a result of (perceived) events in the environment and its own internal business.

(C4) External events are for example incoming or cancelled customer orders, materials already delivered, reports of cancelled deliveries etc. Internal events are responses from daily practice for example the completion of a production order or the breakage of a machine, outcome of plans (e.g. purchase order for a raw material).

(C5) The data stored in an information system may not represent the real state of affairs. This can be due to unknown or known inconsistencies or unavoidable uncertainties.

(C6) Each enterprise uses its own methods and algorithms (to realise its methods) to make decisions. The results of these decisions could cause alterations in reality and in the information system.

(C7) Each enterprise decides for itself according to its own criteria and objectives when and which information it provides to the business partners. The data could be deliberately false for example because for some products only a limited quota is delivered and the personal position is enhanced by exaggerating the quantity which has been ordered.

The SCM aims at the use of rationalization potential in the logistics chain in that:

- It reduces thc uncertainty in the relevant data, or at least the resulting costs of this uncertainty (risk reduction) and/or
- decisions between the enterprises in a logistics chain are coordinated in a better way (coordination improvement) and/or
- the total costs of the participating enterprises are intended to be optimized (cost improvement).

In order to realize a SCM in a logistics chain modifications are possible in the business information systems concerning the data, in the decision making process of each participating enterprise (on a methodical level or a normative level) as well as in the data interchange and communications behaviour between them. Furthermore one would have to discuss the necessity of taking compensatory measures or incentives in order to achieve an adequate allocation of cost saving measures among all the participants.

The following alternatives to implement a SCM are discussed further down:

- Providing additional information on the part of the customer namely:
  a) primary requirement data
  b) inventory data
  c) purchase planning data
- Coordination by the use of a central information system and a common consistent decision making.

At this stage, another quite promising alternative should not be discussed, namely the coordination by creating solid and stable basic conditions and by using steady decision and communication strategies as they are pursued for example in just-in-time concepts (Lackes, 1994; Fandel, François, 1989).

3. Risk reducing supply chain management by providing additional customer data

3.1. Conveyance of the customers' primary requirements data

Many recent publications emphasize that it is important to the suppliers to receive information at an early stage about the situation and development of their customers' market (Zäpfel, Wasner, 1999). That is because then early adaptations can be made and shortage and too high inventories would be avoided.

In general it is not sensible to provide only the basic customer order data to the supplier because the primary requirement amounts are relevant for their planning and necessary supply practices. Even assuming that the current customer order data would not be at the disposal of the supplier but at least the data pertaining to the primary requirements plan would be known, the relevance of this additional information is restricted. One cannot accurately even forecast a correct trend because during the process of materials requirement planning data are modified because of stock inventories, lot-sizing and temporal displacements.

It has to be asked under which conditions the availability of the primary requirements plan can lead to an improvement of the supplier's materials disposition. This can only be the case when

1. the security level of the primary requirements information is relatively high,
2. the planning horizon, the primary requirements is based on, is long enough,
3. the total production coefficient of the parts to be supplied with regard to the final products of the customer is known. This coefficient depends on the parts structure and the technological methods in use. Extra amounts for quality faults and their variances are main reasons for uncertainties.
4. The entire lead time and its variance is known because it determines the time-lag between the occurrence of a demand and the instruction to provide the material, as it is meaningful for the supplier,
5. the inventories and the planned safety stocks are known, because demand will be buffered, or in case of a drop in the safety stock additional demand will be induced,
6. the methods of the lot-sizing and the cost factors relevant for the lot-sizing are known because these will determine the real operations and the temporal requirements structure of the components,
7. the supplier's external parts quota is known and is not changed when generating new purchase orders (e.g. in the context of a price competition).

These are extensive restrictions so that this alternative is only of practical relevance in companies which can forecast their outlet quantities, have a very low vertical range of manufacture, seldom or never size lots and only contract a small number of regular suppliers with medium-ranged constant quota. Moreover the supplier's planning horizon must also be able to be provided with enough information. If the planning horizon of a supplier is for example twelve months then giving him a two month detailed primary requirements plan will be of little use to him.

Enterprises which most qualify for these arrangements are those whose suppliers are themselves wholesalers who insist on short delivery times by their own suppliers and therefore can work with short planning horizons. The effect of rationalization is suddenly interrupted as soon as a supplier with high lead times and therefore inevitably long planning horizons appears in the material flow.

The above mentioned restrictions do not apply to most enterprises, especially not in industry, so that the importance of this additional knowledge about their customers is quite low. Therefore an effective SCM is not realisable. Customers should also not underestimate that the revelation of their own outlet forecasts is a very sensitive area. Stock market prices, creditworthiness assessments and the position of price bargaining (not only with the suppliers and customers of the supply chain!) could be influenced, so that the willingness to provide correct data ought not to be a prerequisite.

3.2. Conveyance of the customer's inventory

A further suggestion for realising SCM demands – in addition to the outlet data – the transparency of the inventories of the customers (Zäpfel, Wasner, 1999). It allows estimating how much the notified sales figures really do lead to orders for the suppliers or only in fact cutback the inventory of the customers. Generally the restrictions here are the same as outlined above. The fifth requirement above is merely revoked so that the buffer function of stocks is rather more predictable. On the whole this is not a recommendable and efficient procedure for most companies to install a SCM.

3.3. Conveyance of the customer's forecast data

The installation of a preview information system can greatly increase the potential for rationalisation (Lee, Padmanabhan, Whang, 1997, p. 550.). The supplier knows not only the present purchase orders but is also informed about the planned order quantities in the near future.

In principal this implies the provision of information from the results of the material disposition of the customer for supplied products. These can be used for the determination of the primary requirements plan of the customer. As a result of the preview provided by the customer some of the forecasts can be left out or the quality of the forecasting can be improved. Structural breaks in the demand can be recognized early. Adjustments can therefore be more quickly and cheaply achieved. A condition for this is however that the customer at an early stage divides his planned order quantity among the relevant suppliers. It can be recommended to use fixed quotas for all the suppliers in a supply chain.

The economic value of this additional information depends on:

- the preview range, in particular in relation to the relevant planning horizon of the supplier,
- the binding of the preview data and the ensuing risk reduction in the primary requirements data;

- the difference between the conventionally ascertained primary requirements quantity (e.g. by a forecast procedure) and that as a result of the preview conveyed by the primary requirements quantity. In particular in case of structural breaks conventional forecast procedures would fail and indeed finally lead to substantially expensive miscalculations.
- The level of the shortage and holding cost figures.

The safety stock is among other things derived from the parameters as described above. If the security profit by the preview is considerable one will on the long run need less safety stock and decrease corresponding holding costs.

An especially critical factor is the reliability of the preview information. If this is totally without obligation then the risk reduction is only limited. If it has a measure of certainty, the benefit of the supplier is increased; the flexibility and the scope in disposition of the customer suffer. Preview systems have already been successfully applied in the automobile subcontractor industry. There a balance in interests between supplier and customer was found so that the certainty grade of the forecast data was differentiated in accordance with their temporal distance. Therefore among other things a production release time span (e.g. four weeks) and a material release time span (e.g. three months) were defined. For the required quantity of parts inside the material release time span it is assured that in any case – also when the products are not purchased – the material prices will be paid. The same applies to production prices inside the production release time span. Furthermore variations as defined by specified ranges of time are permissible e.g. +/-10% for the preview data of the first month. If the customer does not keep within the agreed bandwidths penalties have to be paid. Although the control of the adherence to these ranges can be very complex due to the revolving planning and the market position of the participating enterprises can be very divergent the disciplinary effect of such a preview system can be quite considerable. Preview systems have proved to be a good instrument of the SCM because, where they can be implemented, they provide a suitable solution of the binding problems.

3.4. Necessary planning horizon for relevant data and restrictions of supply chain management

The entire necessary planning horizon is one which enables to take all decisions up to a revision based on deterministic data (Lackes, 1994, p. 410 et sqq.). The following example with three products shows the data relevance of decisions for the material requirement planning which was planned for a certain planning horizon.

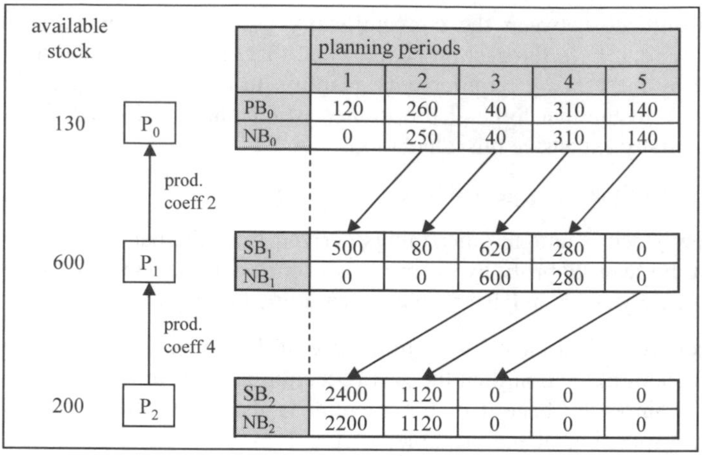

Fig. 2. Example

The basis is the data about the primary requirement demonstrating the future sales market. The primary demand vector PB_0 = (120; 260; 40; 310; 140) for the final product P_0 covers a planning horizon of five periods. Under consideration of the available stock (130) the net demand NB_0 results. Without a lot-sizing the vectors for net demand and order are identical. In order to be able to provide the planned amounts of final products in time, ingoing components need an earlier deadline due to the lead time of the production process. The period between the date of completion of a product and the latest possible date of provision for the component is called forerunning time displacement. It is mainly determined by the lead time of the part to be produced. The forerunning time displacement in our example shall be one (between P_0 and P_1) resp. two periods (between P_1 and P_2). Due to the forerunning time displacement a vector of secondary requirement SB_1 = (500; 80; 620; 280; 0) results considering in addition the production coefficient of two. The same proceeding leads to a vector of net requirement NB_2 = (2200; 1120; 0; 0; 0) for product P_2. The decision to be taken today to obtain product P_2 (e.g. to order 2200 items) is based on this data. As you can see easily from the example, decision relevant data comes from the value of the primary requirement of 310 planned for period four.

This simple example already shows that even the sales concepts influencing today's dispositions have to go further into the future the longer the complete lead time of the products is. It goes without saying that greater vertical range of manufacture also correlate with relatively long (total) lead times. Furthermore, the lot-sizing influences the required planning horizon. The order range expressed in the batches is an additional factor extending the necessary planning horizon. In the example above, take for the product P_1 a lot-size in period three and four, and you get a net demand vector NB_1 = (0; 0; 880; 0; 0) which would then lead to NB_2 = (3320; 0; 0; 0; 0) for product P_2. In that case, today's order of 3320 results from the value of the primary requirement of 310 and 140 planned for period four and five.

Therefore, large order ranges (large batches) and long lead times prolong extensively the necessary planning horizon. Relatively large batches are always required if the relation between setup costs and stock costs is high. The longer the necessary planning horizon for the sales planning is the more difficult it is to get valid data as the data for the planning becomes less reliable. In that case, today's disposition may be based on qualitatively bad data, especially on lower disposition levels (i.e. purchasing).[1]

If already a single enterprise has difficulties to scheme out the planning horizon with valid data, this will be even more critical within supply chains as the relevant planning horizon reaches much further into the future. It is mainly determined by the lead time of the entire material flow of the supply chain. The fundamental starting data for the whole supply chain are the data of primary requirements of the supply chain's head, i.e. of those enterprises at the end of the chain of the material flow. They must be able to provide sufficient valid data for the whole planning horizon relevant for the entire supply chain. In my opinion, this is a fundamental restriction to the success of a multi-level supply chain. Only as many enterprises may be integrated into the supply chain as it is possible at the highest level – the intersection to scope of distribution – to obtain enough valid data for the relevant planning horizon.

Vice versa this means that an effective SCM requires for the whole supply chain

- a reduction of the lead time,
- a reduction of setup costs so that smaller batches become profitable and
- an improvement of the sales planning quality for the enterprises at the end of the supply chain and therefore higher reliability of the data for the relevant planning horizon.

Reductions of the lead time are particularly to be achieved by cutting down waiting periods. The processing times are technologically variable only in strict limits. The reduction of the setup time correlates directly with the reduction of the setup costs and the smaller batches. While waiting periods are in most cases periods arising from bottleneck situations at certain workstations. They are reducible (within limits) by improved internal logistics and capacity extensions.

---

[1] One has to concern that short planning horizons (e.g. it is difficult to predict sufficient valid sales market data) lead to the wrong interpretation of zero requirements by using this proceeding (Lackes, R., 1994, p. 414)!

4. Supply chain oriented production planning system

The following shall demonstrate the realisation of an SCM by providing a central information system for the purpose of coordinating the enterprises involved in the supply chain. First of all, a formal architecture model is designed and we shall focus afterwards on the manner of action of a central supply chain production planning system (SC-PPS). The requirements for the needed data and the data interchange will be discussed.

4.1. Supply chain architecture

Formalising the supply chain architecture with regard to the production management interrelations it requires more than just examinations on enterprise level. Furthermore, contemplations of the parts levels are needed as they provide a much more differentiated knowledge. For example, cycles in the supply chain would develop on the enterprise level if a delivering company obtained goods – directly or indirectly – via other companies from the company supplied. No cycles on the product level would arise if a completely different product range was affected.

An enterprise E_n (n=1,...,N) can be defined – from the perspective of their produced parts – as 5-tuple $E_n = (P_n, TS_n, t_{Dn}, w_n, v_n)$ with

- the set of the parts $P_n = \{P_{n1}, P_{n2}, ..., P_{nM_n}\}$, $M_n \geq 1$;
- the parts structure illustrated in a gozintograph $TS_n \subseteq P_n \times P_n$, whereas $(x,y) \in TS_n$ shall mean that part x goes directly into part y;
- the lead time $t_{Dn} : P_n \rightarrow \Re_0^+$;
- the production coefficient $w_n : TS_n \rightarrow \Re^+$;
- the forerunning time displacement $v_n : TS_n \rightarrow \Re_0^+$.

A gozintograph is – for a parts manufacturer typical for the industry – a quasi-hierarchy and therefore does not possess any cycles in the flow of material (Fandel, François, Gubitz., 1997, p. 164 et sqq.). This shall be assumed below. Thus, a disposition level $DS : P_n \rightarrow N_0$ can clearly be calculated recursively.

$$DS(P_{nm}) = \begin{cases} 0 & \text{if } P_{nm} \text{ is a final product, i.e. } \nexists\,(P_{nm}, P_{n\tilde{m}}) \in TS_n \\ 1 + \max\{DS(P_{n\tilde{m}}) \mid (P_{nm}, P_{n\tilde{m}}) \in TS_n\} & \text{else} \end{cases}$$
$$\text{for any } \tilde{m} \in \{1,...,M_n\}$$

The set of final products $EP_n \subseteq P_n$ covers all parts P_{nm} with $DS(P_{nm}) = 0$.
The set of external parts $FP_n \subseteq P_n$ covers all parts P_{nm} implying:

$$\nexists\,(P_{n\tilde{m}}, P_{nm}) \in TS_n \text{ for any } \tilde{m} \in \{1,...,M_n\}$$

The set of final and external parts does not necessarily need to be disjunct like in e.g. commercial enterprises.

The supply relation between the enterprises is constituted by the delivery of the materials which are final products for the supplying enterprise and external parts for the enterprise supplied.

$$SUP \subseteq \bigcup_{n=1}^{N} EP_n \times \bigcup_{n=1}^{N} FP_{\tilde{n}}$$

$$\text{where } \left(P_{nm}, P_{\tilde{n}\tilde{m}}\right) \in SUP, \quad P_{nm} \in P_n \text{ and } P_{\tilde{n}\tilde{m}} \in P_{\tilde{n}}$$
$$\text{with } n, \tilde{n} \in \{1,\ldots, N\}, n \neq \tilde{n};\; m \in \{1,\ldots, M_n\},\; \tilde{m} \in \{1,\ldots, M_{\tilde{n}}\}$$

4.2. Supply chain production planning system (SC-PPS)

Let us follow the basic idea that decisions should be oriented at the overall optimum within the supply chain (regardless of the effects on the enterprises involved). It is therefore advisable for those enterprises to improve the coordination by combining the individual decentralised PPC-systems into one central supply chain PPC-system. The reliable philosophy of gradual planning (Fandel, 1991, p. 8) may be kept. A pre-requisite for a SC-PPS would be a central high-level gozintograph reflecting the constructive composition of all parts among the entire logistics chain. The intersections between the enterprises are the respective external parts of the enterprise supplied and the final products of the supplying enterprises. Fig. 3 illustrates a corresponding example.

Formally, an SC-gozintograph SC-GOZ = (P; K; sc-w; sc-v) is obtained for the combination of all company-own gozintographs whereas

- P the total set of all parts $P = \bigcup_{n=1}^{N} P_n$,
- K the relation of the material flow $K = \bigcup_{n=1}^{N} TS_n \cup SUP$,
- sc-w the production coefficient $sc - w : K \rightarrow \Re^{+}$ with

$$sc\text{-}w(k) = \begin{cases} \alpha(k) & \text{if } k \in SUP \\ w(k) & \text{if } k \notin SUP \end{cases}$$

where

$\alpha : SUP \rightarrow \left]0,1\right]$ is the share of a bought-in part on the total required quantity of the customer;

$\alpha\left(P_{nm}, P_{\tilde{n}\tilde{m}}\right) = 1$, if E_n is sole supplier to enterprise $E_{\tilde{n}}$ with regard to product $P_{\tilde{n}\tilde{m}}$.

– sc-v shows the forerunning time displacement $sc-v: K \rightarrow \Re_0^+$ with

$$sc-v(k)=\begin{cases} v_n(k) & \text{if } k \notin SUP \\ t_{Tr}(k) & \text{if } k=(P_{nm}, P_{\tilde{n}\tilde{m}}) \in SUP \text{ and} \\ & t_{Tr} = \text{time to deliver product } P_{nm} \\ & \text{to customer } E_{\tilde{n}} \ (n, \tilde{n} \in \{1,\ldots,N\}) \end{cases}$$

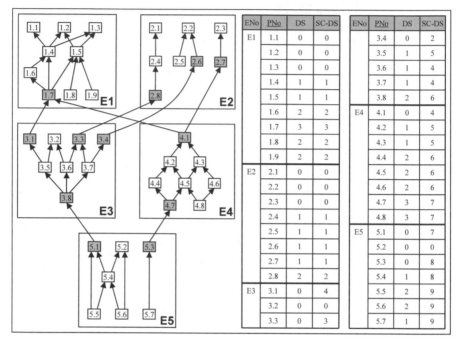

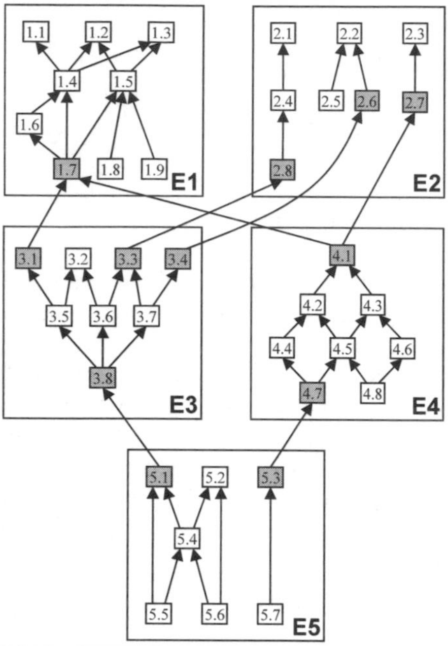

ENo	PNo	DS	SC-DS
E1	1.1	0	0
	1.2	0	0
	1.3	0	0
	1.4	1	1
	1.5	1	1
	1.6	2	2
	1.7	3	3
	1.8	2	2
	1.9	2	2
E2	2.1	0	0
	2.2	0	0
	2.3	0	0
	2.4	1	1
	2.5	1	1
	2.6	1	1
	2.7	1	1
	2.8	2	2
E3	3.1	0	4
	3.2	0	0
	3.3	0	3

ENo	PNo	DS	SC-DS
	3.4	0	2
	3.5	1	5
	3.6	1	4
	3.7	1	4
	3.8	2	6
E4	4.1	0	4
	4.2	1	5
	4.3	1	5
	4.4	2	6
	4.5	2	6
	4.6	2	6
	4.7	3	7
	4.8	3	7
E5	5.1	0	7
	5.2	0	0
	5.3	0	8
	5.4	1	8
	5.5	2	9
	5.6	2	9
	5.7	1	9

Fig. 3. Supply chain gozintograph

The set of nodes of the SC-gozintograph is gained from the total set of nodes of all individual gozintographs representing the respective parts. Therefore, the intersection parts are multiply represented in different nodes. The connections of the material flow combine the individual gozintographs by their material supply relationship.

At the intersections between the enterprises linked together in the supply chain new production coefficients have to be generated. They correspond to the share of the quantity of an order of the product in question which belongs to the supplier looked at.

If there are further suppliers outside the supply chain, the sum of those "production coefficients" does not have to add up to 1. A dynamically changing "production coefficient" illustrating the respective order strategy is certainly also possible.

It is not a question of a technically determined but a economically determined factor.

The forerunning time displacement sc-v at the newly created intersection edges corresponds to the concerned product's transportation time between supplier and customer. In a decentralised PPC-system the agreed delivery time is used for a definite order on the part of the customer. However, in this case the time of the order is not relevant. Instead, it is the time when the finished product must be available at the latest. Therefore, the forerunning time displacement can only be the transportation time.

Cycle structures in gozintographs, as they can appear for example in the process industry (Scheer, 1998, p. 130 et sqq.), always constitute a special case which should be dealt with separately in the material requirement planning. Therefore, we want to concentrate below on non-cycle structures of the material flow typical for the industry so that even the SC-gozintograph is quasi-hierarchical in the supply chain. The SC-disposition levels being used as criteria for the sequence of the material requirement planning in a SC-PPS are calculated as follows:[2]

$$\mathrm{SC\text{-}DS}(P_{nm}) = \begin{cases} 0 & \text{if } P_{nm} \in EP_n \text{ and } \nexists \, (P_{nm}, P_{\tilde{n}\tilde{m}}) \in SUP \\ 1 + \max\left\{\mathrm{SC\text{-}DS}(P_{\tilde{n}\tilde{m}}) \mid (P_{nm}, P_{\tilde{n}\tilde{m}}) \in K\right\} & \text{else} \end{cases}$$
$$\text{for any } \tilde{n} \in \{1,\dots,N\};\ \tilde{m} \in \{1,\dots,M_{\tilde{n}}\}$$

According to the sequence dictated by the SC-DS, the material requirements calculation starting at level zero would, therefore, be carried out at the final products of the entire supply chain. The necessary data is to be found for the most parts in decentralised information systems and only for intersection products in the central information system. The algorithm for the material requirements calculation with a gross-net calculation and lot-sizing is only affected by modifications in the following aspects:

(1) Primary requirement planning
(2) Treating of the intersection products
(3) Different lengths of sub periods in the period break-down
(4) Relevant planning horizon

(1) Primary requirement planning: Starting point of the material requirements calculation is the data of the primary requirement plan which is set up for the marketable products. When considered individually, these are the final products and the marketable semi finished products of the individual enterprises. This means slight modifications for the SC-PPS of a supply chain. Final products of the supply chain are only those products P_{nm} with SC-DS(P_{nm})=0; $n \in \{1,\dots,N\}$; $m \in \{1,\dots,M_n\}$. These are the final products which are at the very end of the material flow of a

[2] We furthermore assume that no connected component exists in the SC-gozintograph which nodes belong exclusively to a specific enterprise. These were not relevant for the SCM and could be treat independent from that.

supply chain. Their customers for this product are therefore not administered within the supply chain. The originally final products of supply chain enterprises being delivered to other members of the supply chain fail, in the view of the supply chain, to be final products. They are "internal" nodes of the SC-gozintograph and no longer need a primary requirement plan. If all customers are members of the supply chain, the secondary requirement resulting from the supply of the customer replaces the original decentralised planned primary requirement for these products. Is there additionally a customer demand for this product outside the supply chain, it corresponds to the character of a marketable semi finished product in the view of the individual enterprise. In that case, external sales for these products must be planned separately as individual primary requirement. A similar phenomenon in the opposite direction can be found in the parts not entirely to be obtained from suppliers within the supply chain. They are therefore, from the view of the supply chain, internal parts as well as bought-in parts. This must be considered separately for the lot-sizing within the material requirements disposition.

(2) Treatment of intersection parts: If the material requirements disposition for part $P_{nm} \in FP_n$ obtained from at least one supplier of the supply chain (i.e. $(P_{\tilde{n}\tilde{m}}, P_{nm}) \in SUP$ for at least one part $P_{\tilde{n}\tilde{m}} \in EP_{\tilde{n}}$), is carried out, the hereby implied demand for requirements explosion is to be calculated after the lot-sizing for all bought-in parts) concerned. For this, it is necessary to go back to the forerunning time displacement sc-v($P_{\tilde{n}\tilde{m}}, P_{nm}$) and the production coefficient sc-w($P_{\tilde{n}\tilde{m}}, P_{nm}$) which can be found in the SC-PPS. Furthermore, it is to consider that parts of the order may come to a supplier external to the supply chain. In this case, a respective plan of procurement orders must be made out. Only the supply within the supply chain is treated like a production order in SC-PPS. If the algorithm meets a part $P_{\tilde{n}\tilde{m}} \in EP_{\tilde{n}}$ which is to be delivered to at least one customer of the supply chain (i.e. $(P_{\tilde{n}\tilde{m}}, P_{nm}) \in SUP$ for at least one part $P_{nm} \in FP_n$), the secondary requirement resulting from the supply chain needs to be determined. This can be done with a period suitable summation of all demands of requirements explosion already calculated from customers. In addition, it needs to be considered for those parts that an individual primary requirement can be included into the planning if there are also customers outside the supply chain.

(3) Different lengths of sub periods of the period break-down: Although it would be certainly most convenient for a SC-PPS to insist on that all companies involved should use the same unit of period break-down, one will mostly meet, for autonomy reasons, differently structured unit of sub periods. Therefore, a transformation of the customer's planning data must be made according to his unit of period break-down into the unit of period break-down of the supplier at transitions between the enterprises linked directly within the material flow of the supply chain. If the supplier's screening is finer, the highest flexibility is secured by assigning the amounts to the last sub period which is still completely in the sub period of the period break-down of the customer. If the screening is rather rough, we have an aggregation.

(4) Relevant planning horizon: One very critical point is the fact that the relevant planning horizon – on same conditions – will be much larger in a supply chain than in an individual single scan as it is inter alia the lead time of the complete material flow in the supply chain that needs to be considered. There will be enterprises in the supply chain that have had more valid forecasted sales than they needed for their individually relevant planning horizon but abstained to integrate the data into the primary requirement plan for cost reasons. For those, the demand for a longer planning horizon will not be critical. It will be harder for the companies with a more dynamic market as this represents more difficulties for estimations over a longer period. Depending on the decrease of the reliability of the forecasted sales with a growing planning horizon, the dispositions' quality in the supply chain and therefore the convenience of an SCM will decrease as well. Here, we find the restrictions of a SCM.

Apart from the facts concerning the elementary functioning of SC-PPS, many more features may be discussed. In particular the question if one should waive the lot-sizing for intersection parts on the part of the customer in order to avoid a double lot-sizing (namely a second time at the supplier's) and to allow the supplier a more flexible room for manoeuvre (greater degree of freedom for scheduling and capacity requirements planning, less bottlenecks, lower adjustment costs if capacity problems arise). However, this could be a disadvantage for the customer as one may differ from his minimal cost purchasing batch. A compromise could be to provide both the information – with and without lot-sizing.

4.3. Information technological realisation of a SC-PPS

It needs to be taken into account, for the information technological realisation of a SC-PPS, that a completely centralised solution in the form of a global information system for all companies of the supply chain is not eligible. Not only cost reasons but also the following facts are against it:

- In most parts, there are already working decentralised information systems in place which are adjusted to individual needs.
- The production planning and control are embedded into more extensive ERP-systems performing further functions.
- Apart from business partner within the supply chain external customers and suppliers have to be considered as well.
- Enterprises may be integrated into several different supply chains and
- such an extensive abandoning of autonomy cannot be expected.

For the above mentioned reasons, the SC-PPS needs to be constructed as a mainly virtual information system laying down the basic conditions and the rules for the process and supporting the necessary data interchange between the parties involved in the supply chain. The question is if a direct immediate interchange of the data about requirements and planned orders between customer and supplier is preferred or rather an indirect one via a central section which could also take on functions like aggregation and converting.

Depending on the outcome of this question, relevant data should be administered centrally but separately to the intersection products (e.g. for identification of corresponding part numbers, production coefficients, forerunning time displacement, SC-disposition level, perhaps even of inventory etc.). Alternatively, the data may – after a single calculation or classification – be integrated into decentralised information systems (e.g. the SC-disposition level). Additional service functions are imaginable to be organised centrally like for example converting the different measurements of products (e.g. customer one: pallets, customer two: kilogramme, supplier: per item) and assigning different planning period break-down or collecting controlling data relevant for the whole supply chain. These centrally collected and analysed controlling data may help not only to identify weak points (the knowledge of these can be used for a reengineering of the supply chain) but also success and cost relevant factors serving as a basis for allocating savings achieved through SCM to the involved. But altogether the SC-PPS will use the functionalities and data of the decentralised PPC-systems.

It would be ideal for the master plan of the supply chain if the material requirement planning was carried out synchronically. However, a standardised clocking of the planning moves may often be impossible to realise due to individual internal specifications. Therefore, both alternatives – synchronous and asynchronous processing of SC-PPS – are to be demonstrated.

A synchronous sequence enclosing the whole supply chain – not embedded into a central SC-PPS for the program-based material requirements calculation but using the functionalities of the decentralised PPC-systems – needs definitions of product oriented planning sections (PS) for the enterprises joined in the supply chain. A planning section covers all parts within an enterprise being linked direct or indirect to each other by (internal) connections of the material flow. An enterprise may have several planning section. If the planning sections are arranged in the correct order, one obtains a planning system which is altogether consistent in itself.

Let $E_1, E_2, ..., E_N$ be the enterprises in the supply chain, whereas $E_n=(P_n, TS_n, t_{Dn}, w_n, v_n)$ with the final products EP_n as earlier defined $(n=1,...,N)$. Definition for SC-gozintograph as above.

Every enterprise E_n has the planning sections $B_{n1}, B_{n2}, ..., B_{nR_n}$ $(R_n \geq 1)$ $(n = 1,...,N)$ with

$$B_{nr} \subseteq P_n \qquad (r = 1,...,R)$$

$$B_{nr} \cap B_{n\tilde{r}} = \varnothing \qquad (r, \tilde{r} = 1,..,R), r \neq \tilde{r}$$

$$\bigcup_{r=1}^{R} B_{nr} = P_n$$

Obviously every planning section contains at least one final product of the enterprise concerned (see Fig. 4).

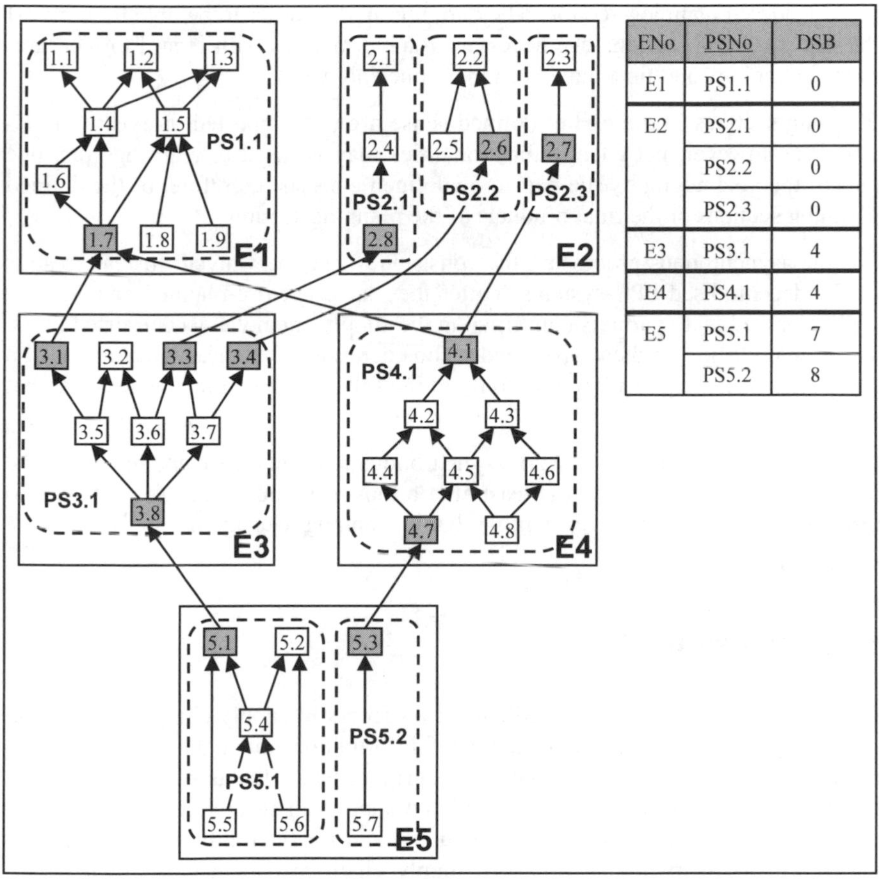

ENo	PSNo	DSB
E1	PS1.1	0
E2	PS2.1	0
	PS2.2	0
	PS2.3	0
E3	PS3.1	4
E4	PS4.1	4
E5	PS5.1	7
	PS5.2	8

Fig. 4. Planning sections at the example of Fig. 3

The disposition levels for the planning sections DSB_{nr} result from the maximum SC-disposition level of their final products, i.e.

$$DSB_{nr} = \text{Max}\{SC - DS(P_{nm}) | P_{nm} \in EP_n, P_{nm} \in B_{nr} (r = 1,..., R_n)\} \qquad (n = 1,..., N)$$

After all enterprises of the supply chain having determined their primary requirements for the planning horizon relevant to the supply chain the decentralised PPC-systems are called to carry out the material requirement planning. In order to have all data necessary for planning available at all times, the call is made in the sequence given by the disposition level of the planning sections DSB_{nr} (ascending, starting at level zero). This means that the first planning sections are those including the final products of the complete supply chain. Apart from the enterprise internal results of the material requirement planning, data also relevant for other areas of the SC-PPS are determined e.g. net demands planned for the complete planning horizon or planned procurement orders of the intersection parts within the considered planning section. They are required in order to be able to work off the next planning section. The necessary transformations with regard to measurement technology and time have been mentioned above.

Planning sections in the earlier defined sense are not supported in existing PPC-systems. However, net change functionalities may be used to rearrange just one part of the gozintograph. The part to be defined consists, therefore, of the defined planning sections or the final products of the planning section.

For the asynchronous processing the consistency may be waived. Instead, results of the decentralised PPC-systems – after they have been re-planned or revised – will be passed on to partners concerned in the supply chain via decentralised users. Those may decide on themselves under consideration of this new information if a revision is necessary or if they use only in the following planning cycle the at that stage latest data.

One compromise could be to work asynchronous in normal case and to choose the more costly synchronous way at least after a longer period of time (e.g. every two months) in order to obtain constantly reliable planning data again.

5. Conclusion

Information is the essential ingredient for a successful supply chain management. Especially the availability and quality of information about the product's sales market at the end of the supply chain is a critical factor for its success and determines the size and the effectiveness of the supply chain architecture. Measurements and investments for higher data quality and for flexibility against data variances are necessary for an effective supply chain management. A concept for realising supply chain management in the operative planning phase is the supply chain production planning system (SC-PPS) as described above. It combines existing ERP-systems of decentralized enterprises in a supply chain with a central coordination system.

References

Cooper, J., Ellram, L.M. (1993): Characteristics of Supply Chain Management and the Implications for Purchasing and Logistics Strategy. In: The International Journal of Logistics Management, Vol. 4, No. 2, pp. 13-24.

Cooper, M.C., Lambert, D.M., Pagh J.D. (1997): Supply Chain Management: More Than a New Name for Logistics. In: The International Journal of Logistics Management, Vol. 8, No. 1, pp. 1-14.

Corsten, H., Gössinger, R. (2001): Einführung in das Supply Chain Management. Oldenbourg, München, Wien.

Fandel, G. (1991): A Theoretical Basis for the Rational Formation of Production Planning and Control (PPC) Systems. In: Fandel, G., Zäpfel, G. (eds.): Modern Production Concepts – Theory and Applications. Springer, Berlin et al., pp. 3-17.

Fandel, G., François, P. (1989): Just-in-Time-Produktion und -Beschaffung – Funktionsweise, Einsatzvoraussetzungen und Grenzen. In: Zeitschrift für Betriebswirtschaftslehre, No. 59, pp. 531-544.

Fandel, G., François, P., Gubitz, K.-M. (1997): PPS- und integrierte betriebliche Softwaresysteme: Grundlagen – Methoden – Marktanalyse, 2nd edn. Springer, Berlin et al.

Gericke, J. et al. (1999): Anforderungen an das Controlling von Supply Chains. In: Logistik Spektrum, Vol. 11, No. 2, pp. 13-16.

Handfield, R.B., Nichols, E.L. (1999): Introduction to Supply Chain Management. Prentice Hall, Upper Saddle River NJ et al.

Kurbel, K. (1998): Produktionsplanung und -steuerung – methodische Grundlagen von PPS-Systemen und Erweiterungen, 2nd edn. Oldenbourg, München, Wien.

Lackes, R. (1994): Just-in-time Produktion: Systemarchitektur – wissenbasierte Planungsunterstützung – Informationssysteme. Gabler, Wiesbaden.

Lackes, R. (1998): Kapazitätsoreintierte Produktionsplanung und -steuerung. In: Corsten, H., Gössinger, R. (eds.): Dezentrale Produktionsplanungs- und steuerungssysteme: eine Einführung in zehn Lektionen. Kohlhammer, Stuttgart et al., pp. 289-316.

Lee, H.L., Padmanabhan, V., Whang, S. (1997): Information Distortion in a Supply Chain: The Bullwhip Effect. In: Management Science, Vol. 43, No. 4, p. 550. pp. 546-558

Supply-Chain Council (2002): Supply-Chain Operations Reference-model – Overview of SCOR Version 5.0.Supply-Chain Council, Inc., Pittsburgh PA.

Scheer, A.-W. (1998): Wirtschaftsinformatik – Referenzmodelle für industrielle Geschäftsprozesse, 2nd edn. Springer, Berlin et al.

Wildemann, H. (2000): Von Just-In-Time zu Supply Chain Management. In: Wildemann, H.: Supply Chain Management. Transfer-Centrum-Verlag, München, pp. 49-86.

Zäpfel, G., Wasner, M. (1999): Der Peitschenschlageffekt der Logistikkette und Möglichkeiten der Überwindung chaotischen Verhaltens. In: Logistik-Management, No. 4, pp. 297-309.